DATE DUE

American Pop

American Pop

c.1

Popular Culture Decade by Decade

VOLUME 2
1930–1959

Edited by Bob Batchelor

GREENWOOD PRESS
Westport, Connecticut • London

Library of Congress Cataloging-in-Publication Data

American pop : popular culture decade by decade / Bob Batchelor, set editor.
      p. cm.
   Includes bibliographical references and index.
   ISBN 978–0–313–34410–7 (set : alk. paper)—ISBN 978–0–313–36412–9 (v. 1 : alk. paper)—
ISBN 978–0–313–36414–3 (v. 2 : alk. paper)—ISBN 978–0–313–36416–7 (v. 3 : alk. paper)—
ISBN 978–0–313–36418–1 (v. 4 : alk. paper)   1. Popular culture—United States.
2. United States—Civilization.   3. National characteristics, American.   I. Batchelor, Bob.
   E169.1.A4475   2009
   973—dc22   2008036699

British Library Cataloguing in Publication Data is available.

Library of Congress Catalog Card Number: 2008036699
ISBN: 978–0–313–34410–7 (set)
      978–0–313–36412–9 (vol 1)
      978–0–313–36414–3 (vol 2)
      978–0–313–36416–7 (vol 3)
      978–0–313–36418–1 (vol 4)

First published in 2009

Greenwood Press, 88 Post Road West, Westport, CT 06881
An imprint of Greenwood Publishing Group, Inc.
www.greenwood.com

Printed in the United States of America

The paper used in this book complies with the
Permanent Paper Standard issued by the National
Information Standards Organization (Z39.48–1984).

10 9 8 7 6 5 4 3 2 1

The publisher has done its best to make sure the instructions and/or recipes in this book are correct.
However, users should apply judgment and experience when preparing recipes, especially parents
and teachers working with young people. The publisher accepts no responsibility for the outcome
of any recipe included in this volume.

Contents

1940s

1950s

Foreword: Popular Culture's Roots Run Deep

Ray B. Browne

Ray and Pat Browne Popular Culture Library
Bowling Green State University, Bowling Green, Ohio

Although *American Pop* focuses on popular culture as it developed in the twentieth century, it is critical that readers understand that most of these topics did not spring to life without roots running deep into the nation's past. In today's fast-paced, computer-dominated society, it is easy to forget history and innovation because so much of American idealism is based on looking toward the bright future. We are a nation obsessed with the idea that better days are on the horizon.

What one discovers when examining the development of culture over the course of the twentieth century is that each innovation builds off a predecessor. America has always had a popular culture, although what that means might change with each new technological breakthrough, national craze, or demographic shift. And, while defining culture is not an easy task, it can be seen as a kind of living entity. Similar to a growing garden, culture is the gatherings of community beliefs and behaviors, which depends on its roots for sustenance. As the plants grow both individually and collectively, they develop and influence the surrounding societies.

People in Colonial America, for example, had their cultural roots deeply implanted from the cultures of the lands from which they emigrated, but every people or group of individuals must harmonize the old with the new in order to justify one's culture. The unifying themes that emerged from the development of a new national culture enabled people to make sense of the world and their relationship to it. American colonists, therefore, adjusted to the old-world cultures of the people who were already settling the nation, while at the same time creating a new popular culture based on their lives as members of the new country.

The harmonization of the new with the old might be called *folk-pop* or *pop-folk* because the result led to a new everyday culture. This evolution is a neverending process in which the new is blended with the old and a new is born. Human nature demands cultural and individual cooperation for safety and advancement, which it achieves in various ways. Inventions and discoveries, for example, are not as helpful in shaping cultures as are innovation and dissemination of those inventions and discoveries. Culture must speak to its constituencies in their vernacular before it can be understood and fully appreciated. Cultures both lead and follow cultural politics, policies, and social movements.

The fields of entertainment from which the colonists could draw were rich: traveling acrobats, jugglers, circuses of various kinds, animal shows, "magic lantern" shows, group or individual singers, Black "Olios" (one-act specialities), drinking houses, card games, and other group activities.

In the conventional forms of culture development certain figures stand tall. Benjamin Franklin, after his move to Philadelphia, contributed in various ways through his writings in *Poor Richard's Almanac* (1732–1757) and others. He stated that his highest admiration was for "the people of this province…chiefly industrious farmers, artificers [skilled craftsmen] or men in trade [who] are fond of freedom." Inventor of the lightning rod and the Franklin Stove, and many more technological and cultural innovations, no one did more to advance popular culture in these early days than Franklin. In the twenty-first century, one finds similar figures who are much revered for their ability to create. Steve Jobs, Apple founder and executive, is a modern day Franklin in many respects, inventing products that transform popular culture, while at the same time, cementing his place in that history.

Less comprehensive but far more inflammatory were the political contributions of Thomas Paine (1737–1809). On January 10, 1776, he published *Common Sense* and sold it for a few cents so that everybody could own a copy. In a few months no fewer than 500,000 copies had been sold. Another of his great contributions was *The American Crisis,* which opens with the fiery words, "These are the times that try men's souls." Paine intuited and valued the power of the popular culture and wrote his works as if by a common citizen for other common citizens. Today's Thomas Paines may be the countless citizen journalists, primarily Internet-based, blogging, posting, and carrying out the kind of agenda Paine advocated. The writer turned to pamphlets as a method of keeping down price, just as today's bloggers use inexpensive tools to reach audiences nationwide.

Another powerful voice in popular culture was Harriet Beecher Stowe. Through *Uncle Tom's Cabin* (1852) Stowe alerted the public to the evils of slavery (with the help of the Almighty, in her words). After the enormous success of the work, the author claimed that God had dictated the book, with her merely writing down His words. Regardless of these claims, for the next 50 years the work was performed on stages worldwide more frequently than any other play in English (with the possible exception of Shakespeare's collected works).

A little more than a century later, racism still plagued the nation, but instead of being represented by a novel, two charismatic leaders took center stage. Dr. Martin Luther King Jr. and Malcolm X stood at opposite poles in the fight for equality, King preaching nonviolence, while Malcolm advocated "by any means necessary." As powerful as these leaders were, however, they became icons after their assassinations. As a result, their images transcend who they were as leaders, attaining a kind of immortality as popular culture figures.

Colonists loved professional plays. The first such presentation in America was "Ye Beare and Ye Cubbin Accomac County" staged in Virginia in 1665. The first theater in the Colonies was built in Williamsburg, Virginia, sometime between 1716 and 1718.

Romeo and Juliet may have been presented in New York City in 1730 and *Richard III* in 1750, in addition to Williamsburg a year later. In 1752 the Charleston, South Carolina, theater presented 58 different offerings, including Shakespeare. Fourteen of Shakespeare's plays were staged 150 times in pre-Revolutionary Virginia, and from the 1850s to the Civil War Shakespeare was performed in all the major cities and several small ones.

For the second half of the nineteenth century one of the distributors of popular culture was widespread black-faced minstrelsy—thousands of such dramatics were presented on stage by whites with faces blackened by charcoal. No one can identify exactly when and why the first Negro minstrel show became so popular. Some authorities suggest that African Americans seem to be natural-born entertainers. Others are firm in their belief that the minstrel show flourished because blacks saw it as a means of social equality with whites who otherwise held them in slavery.

Minstrelsy was in its heyday from 1830 to 1870. So-called songsters, cheap songbooks running from 20 to some 50 pages and selling for 10–50 cents, were the main distributors of minstrel pieces, as well as songs from other sources. During the popularity of the minstrel show there were more than 100 shows running and some 2,000 songsters distributing at least 20,000 songs. Not all minstrel shows were black-on-white. Some were black-on-black, after black actors realized that white shows were exploiting them and they could in fact create their own shows. Minstrel shows were later eclipsed by vaudeville.

From these beginnings, one can trace the origins of Tin Pan Alley, which helped launch ragtime and jazz. In addition, the songsters and minstrel shows initiated a kind of crossover success that became the gold standard in the music business. "Crossing over," or scoring hit records in different genres, would come to define many of the industry's biggest stars from Elvis Presley and Johnny Cash to Chuck Berry and Little Richard.

The most enduring form of popular culture is the printed page, even though some observers feel that books, magazines, and newspapers are doomed in the Internet age. Books in particular, though, carry a special place in peoples' hearts, not only as tools for learning but as objects of affection. Many readers simply like to hold a book in their hands and feel the pages glide through their fingers. Even the most ardent techie does not get the same emotional lift from reading text on a screen, whether a laptop or hand-held device.

The most influential literary form breaching the gap between the nineteenth and twentieth centuries has been the detective story. This form of literature has from its beginning satisfied deep interests of large groups. From the earliest times, people have wanted answers to the mysteries of life that keeps us continually looking back at history. Our fascination with the archaeological and anthropological past, for example, leads many to believe in monsters such as Big-Foot (Sasquatch) and the Loch Ness Monster. Many small towns and local villages have similar folktales of creatures frequenting dark mountains, forests, and deep lakes. Today, this love affair with fear and the unknown drives much of the current film and television industries. From the low budget sensation *The Blair Witch Project* to big budget movies filled with blood and gore, people thrive on their imaginations resulting from a collective indoctrination to fear.

These prehistoric beings supposedly living among us also help keep alive the mysteries and manifestations of the past, delivering some kind of answer in the form of explanations and comforting conclusions. Histories and mysteries need what scholar Russel Nye called a "hook" to keep readers on the edge of their curiosity. But mysteries search more deeply into human existence and help explain us to ourselves. Einstein was certainly right when he said, "The most beautiful thing we can experience is the mysterious. It is the source of all true art and science." The enticement of the mysterious is a never fading light in the darkness of life's many anxieties.

Literary interest in horror developed in Europe in Mary Shelley's *Frankenstein* (1818) and pushed ahead vigorously in the *Memoirs* of Francois Eugene Vidocq, a reformed French thief who joined the police force and electrified Europe with publication of his underground activities in 1829. Edgar Allan Poe (1809–1849) caught the imagination of Americans beginning with *Murders in the Rue Morgue* (1841). Film scholars see Poe's writing inspiring the American film noir movement in the 1940s, 1950s, and 1960s.

The coals ignited by the interest in mystery and drama glowed especially in the publication of the adventures of Sherlock Holmes and Dr. Watson in 1887. Many Americans tried their pens at the art. Mark Twain published several works in the type, for instance, but found little success. But the door into the riches of mysteries had been opened to authors and readers of the twenty-first century. Mystery, having metamorphosed through the broadened titles of "Crime Fiction" and lately "Novels of Suspense," is the most popular form of fiction today, and is being used by historians for the true human emotions and actions contained in them. Historians a century or more from now may find themselves doing the same with the novels of Stephen King or James Patterson, novelists who sell millions of books, yet are taken less seriously by the cultural elite because they do so well.

One of the results of popular culture's interest in the make-believe and distortion of the minstrel show was the literary hoax, which flourished in such works as Poe's "Balloon Hoax," published in the *New York Sun* on April 13, 1844, an account of eight men crossing the Atlantic in a large balloon held up by coal gas. Others include Mark Twain's "The Petrified Man" (one of several by him), in which a character is discovered with his thumb on his nose in the timeless insulting gesture—the credulous public does not recognize the joke.

Other real-life hoaxes cropped up on every street corner. P. T. Barnum (1810–1891), famous for working under the philosophy that there's a sucker born every minute, opened his American Museum of Freaks in New York City, exhibiting all kinds of freaks and captivating the public especially with his Cardiff Giant, a plaster duplicate of the discovery on a farm outside Cardiff, New York. It was 10 feet long and weighed 3,000 pounds and had been proven a hoax, but still fascinated the public. The hoax, literary or physical, fed the American dreams of freedom and expansion and was an example of the American dream of personal fulfillment.

Another stalk growing from the same root included the works of the so-called Southwest humorists, who carried on in their stories and language the literature of the hoax. David Ross Locke (Petroleum V. Nasby), Henry Wheeler Show (Josh Billings), and George Washington and his Sut Lovingood stories created exaggerated physical and linguistic caricatures of their fellow citizens in a world they expected and hoped would be recognized as hoaxes. Instead of laughable hoaxes, however, they created a world of reality that is carried over in American popular culture today. The stereotype of the illiterate Southerner has a central role in the twenty-first century, particularly in television sit-coms and movies. The standup routines of Jeff Foxworthy and Larry the Cable Guy are built around the premise of the South being strangely (although often lovingly) different than the rest of the nation.

Another popular form of literature developed out of the idea of the hoax—graphic caricature and literature. Although the caricature had been common from the earliest days of America, the so-called common caricature known as the comic strip narrative, developed by the Swiss cartoonist Rodolphe Topfer in 1846, was probably introduced into America in the *San Francisco Examiner* on February 16, 1896, as "The Yellow Kid." Since then most newspapers have run their series of comic pages in the United States and abroad—especially in Japan, where they are read by all members of a family under the name *anime*. They are likewise pervasive in American (and world) culture, especially in animation, movies, and advertising, particularly when used to pitch products to children and young people.

Because of our growing knowledge of and interest in archaeology and anthropology, our interest in the 6,000 or so languages spoken worldwide, and the suspicion that humanity may be doomed to future space travel and colonization, more works are developing in comics and movies of the extreme past and the imaginative future. Such comic strips and books, now called graphic novels, to a certain extent feed on the hoax works of the nineteenth century and intellectually are not rocket science, as we freely admit.

Many of the ideas and artwork in today's comic books are useful in understanding modern popular culture and its influence. For example, graphic novels have been published for both political parties in the 2008 presidential campaigns. Furthermore, many of the ideas and artwork are highly suggestive to the genuine rocket scientist, and the art work is highly prized for its newness of ideas and execution of detail by comic book aficionados. One original picture of Mickey Mouse, for example, recently sold for $700,000. Many comic book fans live in a world of their own making, but to a certain extent in America's broad, rich, and complicated popular culture, each area is something of an island of culture all its own, justifying its existence.

Just as English poet William Wordsworth said that the child is father to the man, so a culture in one form and one power or another is always a product and variant of its predecessors. It grows and alters or breaks down the restrictions of its sometimes elite, sometimes popular predecessors as the force of the new development becomes overwhelming and suggestive. Sometimes the popular culture grows and sometimes fades, but, although it may diminish in use and memory, it seldom disappears. Popular culture is like animated wall murals and graffiti that permanently etches a record of the lifeblood of a culture of the moment.

The cornucopia of twentieth-century present and developing American popular culture has resulted from the free flow of opportunity provided by its predecessors. So it was up to the last century. The garden of popular culture seemed to the culture traditionalist a patch of weeds overwhelming the flowers. But a new culture in the process of finding and developing itself was not crowded. The new cultures were driven by the changing dynamic of a new people in a new land with opportunities for all men and women to live by and in the cultures they both desired and found satisfactory. Suggestions and opportunities will continue to be found and developed.

The power of the twentieth century continues to develop in the twenty-first as the richest and most energetic culture so far produced continues to flourish—sometimes to the bewilderment and consternation of the citizenry, but always irresistibly, Americans and non-Americans—as long as human nature insists that it wants or needs something new, improved, or just different and finds it in America. Popular culture is the voice of a worldwide, but especially American, growing insistence on democracy in all aspects of life, and the voices of the people—especially in America—will continue to flourish, be creative, and heard.

From the beginning, American popular culture, given a virgin land in which to grow, has developed fully and rapidly. Its influence has been especially forceful domestically and globally in the twentieth century as a result of its growth in the preceding century in the arts and extended cultures. American popular culture impacts the cultures of the world everyday, creating and resolving tensions that are labeled "Created and Made in America." In the popular cultural world in all its manifestations the most influential label on world life at the present is and in the future will be "Lived in America."

Preface

American Pop: Popular Culture Decade by Decade provides a survey of popular culture across America from 1900 to the present and presents the heart and soul of America, acting as a unifying bridge across time and bringing together generations of diverse backgrounds. Whether looking at the bright lights of the Jazz Age in the 1920s, the rock 'n' roll and lifestyle revolutions of the 1960s and 1970s, or the thriving social networking Web sites of today, each period in America's cultural history develops its own unique take on the qualities that define our lives. *American Pop* is a four-volume set that examines the trends and events across decades and eras by shedding light on the experiences of Americans young and old, rich and poor, along with the influences of arts, entertainment, sports, and other cultural forces.

Based partly on Greenwood's "American Popular Culture through History" series, this four-volume set is designed to give students and general readers a broad and interdisciplinary overview of the numerous aspects of popular culture. Each of the topical chapters stands alone as a testament to the individual decade, yet taken together, they offer an integrated history and allow readers to make connections among each of the decades. Of course, this organization also encourages readers to compare the sometimes striking differences among decades.

WHAT'S INCLUDED IN *AMERICAN POP*

The volumes in this set cover the following chronological periods.

- Volume 1, 1900–1929
- Volume 2, 1930–1959
- Volume 3, 1960–1989
- Volume 4, 1990–Present

Each volume, in turn, covers the popular culture of the decades through chapters focused on specific areas of popular culture, including:

An Overview of the Decade	Fashion
Advertising	Food
Architecture	Music
Books, Newspapers, Magazines, and Comics	Sports and Leisure
	Travel
Entertainment	Visual Arts

In addition, each group of chapters is preceded by a timeline of events for the decade, which gives extra oversight and context to the study of the period.

Sidebars and Other Features

Within many of the chapters, the text is supplemented by sidebars that feature the significant, fascinating, troubling, or just plain weird people, trends, books, movies, radio and television programs, advertisements, places, and events of the decade. In addition sidebars provide lists of new words and phrases for the decade; new foods introduced during the decade; and "How Others See Us," information on how people outside of the United States adopted, reacted to, or disdained American popular culture. The chapters are enhanced with photos and illustrations from the period. Each volume closes with a Resource Guide, providing selected books, articles, Web sites, and videos for further research.

The appendices feature "The Cost of Products"—which spans from 1900 to the present and shows the prices of selected items from food to clothing to furniture—and a list of potential classroom resources of activities and assignments for teachers to use in a school setting. A carefully selected general bibliography for the set, covering popular culture resources of a general or sizeable nature, rounds out the final volume. A comprehensive index offers access to the entire set.

ACKNOWLEDGMENTS

American Pop is an audacious project that pulls together more than one million words about popular culture in the twentieth and twenty-first centuries. A series like this one owes a large debt to many wonderful authors, researchers, writers, and editors. First and foremost, my deepest gratitude goes out to Ray B. Browne, the series editor of the original "American Popular Culture through History" books. Like so many other popular culture scholars over the past several decades, I owe Ray more than I could ever hope to repay.

I would also like to thank all of the authors who poured their collective hearts into the series: David Blanke, Kathleen Drowne, Patrick Huber, William H. Young, Nancy K. Young, Robert Sickels, Edward J. Rielly, Kelly Boyer Sagert, Scott Stoddart, and Marc Oxoby. Their work provides the backbone of this collection. Several excellent writers contributed to the more than 300 sidebars that appear throughout this set: Mary Kay Linge, Ken Zachmann, Martha Whitt, Micah L. Issitt, Josef Benson, Cindy Williams, Joy Austin, Angelica Benjamin, Peter Lazazzaro, Jillian Mann, Vanessa Martinez, Jessica Schultz, Jessica Seriano, and Brie Tomaszewski.

Not even Superman could edit a collection like *American Pop* without a superstar team of editors. I have been lucky to benefit from the wisdom and leadership skills of

Kristi Ward and Anne Thompson throughout the project. *American Pop* would not exist without their enthusiasm, hard work, and dedication. Thanks also to Cindy Williams for her original editing of the project. She is wonderful.

My great honor in editing *American Pop* has been picking up where Ray left off. I have had the pleasure of writing three books in the series, so all told, I have spent more than five years of my life with this series. My sincere thanks go to my parents, Jon and Linda Bowen, and my brother Bill Coyle for their support. As always, my wife, Kathy, has lived this collection with me. I appreciate her sense of humor, sound advice, and thoughtfulness. My whole heart belongs to our daughter Kassie. Her smile, hugs, and kisses were always awesome diversions from writing and editing.

Bob Batchelor
University of South Florida
Tampa, Florida

Introduction

How does one encapsulate the Great Depression, World War II, and the early Cold War and at the same time do justice to three of the primary events in American history? The challenge is uncovering a method that simultaneously captures the era's broadness and also keeps it manageable. One solution is to look at the time period thematically. Breaking popular culture into broad categories enables an integrated perspective to bubble to the surface, yet still allows the nuances of each individual event to shine through.

By examining popular culture within the following categories—leaders, money, innovation, and culture—an overview of the 1930–1959 period will emerge that discusses the major issues driving everyday America during that time. A historical perspective makes it much easier to recognize forces driving change in popular culture, which may or may not have been discernable at the time. Few people, for example, could have fully understood how the financial mechanisms put in place after the collapse of Wall Street would unfold, or foresee how the technological innovations associated with America's war effort would transform consumerism in the postwar world.

Popular culture is about context. It may be difficult, if not impossible, to statistically measure the impact of Franklin D. Roosevelt (FDR) on the cultural development of the 1930s and 1940s, but understanding his leadership does provide the framework for grasping the broader meaning of culture during his tenure as an iconic political leader. Even more difficult is placing Elvis Presley into context over the course of a long career as a popular culture figure.

The ability to examine the actions of the government or a particular leader or group of leaders is arguably the most positive aspect of popular culture. Rooted in free speech, the rise of mass media enabled Americans to criticize their leaders and institutions, thus opening new opportunities for collective education and information.

As millions of Americans interacted with mass media, whether watching the same Hollywood movies or listening to Roosevelt's radio addresses during World Ward II, a common language developed that created lines of communication between disparate groups. The downside of this unintended focus on mass communications, some argued, was that a growing fascination with pop culture actually diverted attention from important challenges the nation faced, ultimately serving as a kind of placebo. Therefore, popular culture enabled people to feel good about the world around them without really forcing them to directly confront critical issues.

LEADERS

Franklin D. Roosevelt is the dominant political and cultural figure of the 1930s and 1940s. The Roosevelt administration received criticism, however, even as it fought to alleviate the problems plaguing the economy during the Great Depression. In 1933 and 1934, unions organized around the country to fight for better wages, working conditions, and hours. On Labor Day in 1934, more than 300,000 textile workers from New England to the southern states staged a strike that became the most violent in American history. In Fall River, Massachusetts, approximately 10,000 protestors surrounded a mill, trapping the strikebreakers inside. Riots broke out across New England, and at many sites corporate guards, special deputies, and the police fought with strikers and their supporters. As the violence increased, the National Guard was mobilized in every New England state except New Hampshire and Vermont. President Roosevelt had to intervene personally to end the confrontation between owners and workers.

Roosevelt took office in the midst of a banking crisis, but with a deft touch and a supportive Congress, he got the Emergency Banking Act passed in 1933, which allayed depositors' fears and gave banks a shot of confidence. Next, Roosevelt used a series of fireside chats to calm the nation, and he created programs that put people back to work and gave them hope for the future.

The Roosevelt administration heard the pleas of those who wanted to work but could not find jobs. Roosevelt championed the Civil Works Administration in 1933 and within two weeks 800,000 people were put to work. Several months later, more than four million people were working in the program, which focused on the construction of roads, bridges, schools, playgrounds, and hospitals. Roosevelt and his aides realized that hunger was not negotiable and that putting people to work would relieve some of the doldrums the nation confronted.

In early 1933 the Civilian Conservation Corps (CCC) began operations with an initial enrollment of 250,000 at a cost of $500 million. The next summer, Roosevelt enlarged the group to 350,000, then to 500,000 in 1935. CCC "soil soldiers" built roads, installed telephone lines, planted trees, and worked for several federal agencies. Although the CCC was a nationwide effort, it helped ease the plight of northeastern urban centers by relocating young unemployed men out of the cities.

Later, Roosevelt pushed through the Emergency Relief Appropriation of 1935, which enabled him to create the Works Progress Administration (WPA). Although the WPA cost more than making direct payments to the poor, the program helped lift people's spirits, in the northeast and elsewhere, making them feel worthy of having a job.

By pushing the boundaries of the federal government into areas it had traditionally resisted, FDR changed the way people viewed the institution. Roosevelt's moves personalized the government. He convinced people that the government could help them and should be involved in areas that were previously off limits.

Roosevelt expanded the government's power, as well as the president's role as national leader, to exert influence on the corporate sector and in people's private lives. He achieved these measures because the nation so desperately wanted out of the Great Depression. Roosevelt's initiatives, although seemingly haphazard at the time, were acts of mercy. In return, the public accepted the government intervention and turned the president into a national hero.

MONEY

In 1931 nearly 200,000 New Yorkers were evicted from their apartments for failure to pay rent. Many who were not evicted sold off their valuables so they could pay, or they moved from apartment to apartment. If furniture had been purchased on credit, owners simply left it behind when they could no longer make payments. In Philadelphia 1,300 evictions occurred per month during the year following the Wall Street crash.

Given its place at the heart of the American economic system, the northeast suffered mightily during the Great Depression. New York City reigned as the capital of global finance. The American people looked to Wall Street financiers to bail them out, as did the entire world, which hoped that an economic recovery would begin in New York City.

Prior to the crash, the *New York Times* and the *Wall Street Journal* had trumpeted the success of the market and kept tabs on the stock market's movers and shakers. Despite the widespread panic gripping the nation after the collapse, newspapers across the region were filled with reassuring stories about the long-term viability of the market system.

Psychologically, money was at the center of American culture in the 1920s. Brokers and investment bankers were society's new superheroes. Markets fluctuations, hot stocks, and trading exploits became juicy gossip items during this era. The growing consumer culture required money. The impulse to live it up necessitated an ever-growing cash flow. Many relied on stocks and a line of credit to finance their new lifestyles. The "get rich quick" mentality lured people into the market.

Men in conservative dark suits swarmed up and down Wall Street, streaming in and out of the buildings that line the financial epicenter of the American economy. Looking west toward Trinity Church, the scene was awash in a sea of fashionable hats—most men sporting the tan, round-brimmed ones popular at the time.

Wall Street represented a new religion in the United States. Its priests were the men who ran Wall Street's successful brokerages and investment banks. These men formed a sort of exclusive gentleman's club, each belonging to the same clubs, vacationing together, and mainly living on the Upper East Side of Manhattan. The ultimate club was the New York Stock Exchange, with a mere 1,100 seats. The only way in was to purchase an existing seat from one of the members or investment banks that owned the seat.

While Wall Street's leaders breezed through an insulated world high above the trading floor, an entirely different kind of trader fueled the stock overspeculation that would lead to the crash. Many traders only cared about stock fluctuation, borrowing enough money to buy and sell, then quickly moving the stock to make money on the difference. Timing, not knowledge, mattered most. By the summer of 1929, stock market value hit $67 billion, up from $27 billion two years earlier.

The economic freefall that took place in and after October 1929 decimated the American economy. Within three years, 75 percent of the value of all securities—a whopping $90 billion—disappeared. The year after the crash, more than 26,000 businesses went bankrupt, surpassed in 1931 by more than 28,000 failures. In December 1930 the Bank of the United States went bankrupt, wiping out approximately 400,000 depositors.

As debilitating as the stock market crash was to the nation's economy, the crushing blow came from the way it demoralized the American people. The collapse shocked everyone and shook people's faith in the national economic system. Businessmen and corporations reacted by making drastic cuts, while anxious consumers virtually stopped spending beyond bare necessities. Millions of workers lost their jobs as businesses desperately cut their operations to the bare essentials. Construction in New York City, for example, came to a near halt as 64 percent of construction workers were laid off soon after the stock market collapsed. Unemployment in 1929 was slightly over three percent, but by 1932 the figure had reached 24 percent. Millions more were involuntarily working in part-time positions.

The psychological toll unemployment took on the American people caused high levels of stress and anxiety. While some took to the streets to sell whatever they could gather, others turned to crime in an effort to find food. In Pittsburgh a man stole a loaf of bread to feed his children, and then later hanged himself in shame. In New York City, hundreds of thousands of unemployed or underemployed workers turned to soup kitchens. By October 1933, New York City counted 1.25 million people on relief. Even more telling is that another one million were eligible for relief but did not accept it. Six thousand New Yorkers tried to make money selling apples on the streets. But by the end of 1931, most street vendors were gone. Grocery store sales dropped by 50 percent during the Depression. Many urban dwellers scoured garbage cans and dumps looking for food. Studies estimated that 65 percent of the African American children in Harlem were plagued by malnutrition during this time.

Countless people in New York City were forced to live on the streets or in shantytowns located along the banks of the East River and the Hudson River. These clusters of makeshift abodes were dubbed *Hoovervilles*—a backhanded tribute to President Herbert Hoover. The city's largest camp was in Central Park. Ironically, the Central Park shantytown became a tourist attraction and featured daily performances by an unemployed tightrope walker and other out-of-work artists.

Even the rich were not immune to the harsh realities of the Great Depression. By the early 1930s, the situation was so glum that it became fashionable among the wealthy to brag about how much they had lost in the crash. Even professions one would think were insulated from economic hardship were affected. In Brooklyn, one-third of all doctors were forced out of business.

When people learned of the role business leaders had played in the stock market crash, they changed their formerly favorable opinions to outright scorn. The Wall Street collapse proved that these exalted financial leaders did not know what they were talking in the years leading up to that fateful October as they continually hyped the market. Remarkably, in the days immediately after the collapse, the nation's business leaders (from Sears, AT&T, and General Motors, among others) issued cheery reports about swelling sales and stability in an attempt to bolster public confidence.

The Depression in the northeast was not confined to the region's urban centers. Farming—work still performed by one-fourth of the U.S. population—had been depressed for nearly a decade. Farmers suffered as exports, crop prices, and land values all dropped. The Great Depression hit farmers and rural areas in the Midwest and west much harder than the northeast because those areas depended much more on farming as part of the regional economy. In addition, many of the farmers who left their land during the crisis headed west to find a better life in California's agricultural regions and urban centers.

The bleak economic conditions in the northeast led to direct confrontation between those who were suffering and various authorities. The Communist and Socialist parties, for instance, agitated unemployed workers to rise up against those controlling the economy. While party bosses, like the communist leader William Z. Foster, dreamed of the end of the capitalist system, hungry and fearful workers demanded food, jobs, and some form of meaningful relief. In early 1930, communist activists staged rallies against unemployment that drew protestors in New York, Washington, D.C., Boston, and many other cities. At some sites, demonstrators fought with police, who used force against the agitators, including tear gas in the nation's capital. New York police used nightsticks to break up a crowd of 35,000 who had turned out in Union Square to hear Foster speak.

INNOVATION

Innovation is usually associated with machinery, manufacturing, and assembly. In the 1950s, however, innovation took hold in the food industry, serving as a vital weapon in the Cold War battle with the Soviet Union. Although it is difficult to imagine in the twenty-first century, the way Americans manufactured, sold, and prepared food transformed the very notion of food from simple nourishment into a symbol of national might. The supermarket, of all places, helped America prove its global power.

When Queen Elizabeth II visited the United States in 1957, her trip included a stop at a typical supermarket. Two years later, Soviet leader Nikita Khrushchev toured America. He formally requested that he be given the chance to meet John Wayne and visit Disneyland (denied over security concerns), but it was an impromptu trip to a California supermarket that befuddled him. Khrushchev did not need an interpreter to understand how American abundance dwarfed the meager foodstuffs available in the Soviet Union. Furthermore, he could not have predicted how the economic showdown between the two nations would eventually topple the Berlin Wall more than four decades later, essentially ending the Cold War.

The idea of abundance powered the United States during the post–World War II era and into the early Cold War. Simultaneously, the mass communications industries of public relations, marketing, and advertising became better at spreading the message of American affluence domestically and globally.

For example, General Dwight Eisenhower employed the ad agency Batten, Darton, Durstine, and Osborne (BBD&O) when he ran for the presidency in 1952. The firm mapped out a strategy that emphasized Eisenhower's image as a commander and wise father figure, without engaging in a deep discussion of the issues. As a result, he won in a landslide over his Democratic challenger, Adlai Stevenson, whose issues-based candidacy earned him the reputation as an "egghead" among voters.

Looking at advertisements for common consumer goods in the 1950s, one would assume that the typical American lived in some suburban utopia of sparkling cleanliness, wide smiles, and overwhelming satisfaction. At home, the race for new, better, and improved products led to neighbors fighting to keep up with one another. Overseas, war-torn Europe rode American purse strings in its rebuilding effort, linking the United States and the Continent for the next 50 years. In the Soviet Union, however, the communist system could not offer the same kind of idyllic vision. The race between the U.S. and U.S.S.R. boiled down to one of abundance, guaranteeing that the United States would ultimately win the Cold War, if the war remained cold.

CULTURE

Unintended consequences often sprout up at odd places. For example, if it were not for the need to ration paper in the 1940s, the publishing industry may never have figured out the desire for mass-market paperbacks. At the same time, if American GIs during World War II did not have so much free time on their hands on bases at home and abroad, then they might not have turned to reading to fill idle hours. Luckily, however, these sparks came together to ignite the creation of cheap paperbacks. As a result, hundreds of millions of books went into print that otherwise may have been lost to history's dustbin.

One could argue that the creation of tens or hundreds of millions of cheap paperbacks did unimaginable damage to the environment or that they may still be rotting away in landfills, but mass production enabled many outstanding works to stay in print. *The Great Gatsby,* for one, may have been virtually lost if not for mass-market paperbacks, even though F. Scott Fitzgerald, who died in December 1940, would not personally reap any of the financial rewards from the reprints. Ernest Hemingway, although hardly in need of additional publicity in the 1940s and 1950s, still benefited from a new generation of readers introduced to his work.

Perhaps for the first time in American history, publishers had to devise new ways to get books into the hands of literature-starved readers. The postal system had the capacity to handle a book order business, so publishers set up book clubs that mailed books to readers based on their specific interests. Soon, more than a million books a month were sold through the dozens of book clubs across America.

Mass-market paperbacks were also sent to soldiers fighting during World War II, spawning a love for reading that then, in turn, swelled book club memberships after soldiers returned from the war. Reading for pleasure probably reached its all-time pinnacle in the mid-1940s.

In the 1950s, the love of reading left over from the war, combined with America's obsession with self-education, led to the Great Books Program, an intensive reading course through 54-volumes from across history. Devised by University of Chicago President Robert Maynard Hutchins and professor Mortimer J. Adler, the set promised to teach the reader everything that the "well-read" person should know, from Aristotle and Plato to Milton and Shakespeare. The affluence of the 1950s, however, enabled middle-class purchasers to buy the series in fancy, leather-bound editions. Series marketers understood that consumers wanted something elegant to display in their home libraries.

The prewar 1930s and the postwar 1950s present a study in stark contrasts. People in the 1930s battled the twin evils of financial misery and global anxiety represented by the Great Depression and military turmoil in Europe. As unrest overseas laid the groundwork for war, Americans turned to President Franklin D. Roosevelt for relief from the economic chaos at home.

The 1950s, on the other hand, symbolized a new beginning for the United States. The launch of the "American century" delivered unprecedented prosperity for much of the nation. Driven by innovation and new technologies, the subsequent abundance of consumer goods transformed life. The cause of national anxiety changed dramatically in the two eras, from real war in Europe to Cold War across the globe, primarily fought in the minds of politicians and diplomats in Washington, D.C., and Moscow.

Standing between these contrasting times is the 1940s—filled with World War II and the immediate slide into the Cold War. The Great Depression and the war fundamentally altered American society. The national popular culture structure responded to the twin crises on a number of fronts, from use as a weapon to increase nationalistic feelings or to prop people back up when their darkest days still seemed ahead of them. Hollywood, for example, responded to World War II by producing films that emphasized America's heroism and patriotism. The film industry also kept citizens informed by creating a variety of newsreels, documentaries, and special reports about the day's issues.

The fascination with movies carried over from the 1940s to the 1950s. When soldiers returned from the war, they had money to spend. The booming economy and college aid programs gave them new opportunities to either work at high-paying jobs or go back to school for little or no money. In 1946 more than 100 million people went to the movies each week, about two-thirds of the total population.

Certainly, the nostalgic feelings later generations held regarding the 1950s glossed over a darker, troubling time, fueled by rapid cultural changes and emotions still fresh from World War II. For those willing to view the postwar world as a new beginning, however, the future looked dazzling.

1930s

Timeline

of Popular Culture Events, 1930s

1930

May 27: The Chrysler Building opens in New York City; it is briefly the world's tallest skyscraper.

November 17: Bobby Jones wins the Grand Slam of golf and announces his retirement.

U.S. population stands at approximately 123 million. Unemployment is about 4.5 million, almost 9 percent of the total workforce, for the year.

Men selling apples at a nickel apiece begin to appear on street corners.

Miniature golf becomes a fad, and dance marathons regain popularity.

Commercial air travel between New York and Los Angeles is initiated in October. United Airlines hires the first stewardesses.

Grant Wood's *American Gothic* is unveiled at the Art Institute of Chicago in the fall.

The impact of the movies is felt in fashion: the cool, sophisticated looks of Greta Garbo, Joan Crawford, Jean Harlow, and Marlene Dietrich gain popularity.

Little Caesar, a gangster epic starring Edward G. Robinson, opens, and *Anna Christie* allows audiences to hear Greta Garbo talk.

1931

May 1: The Empire State Building opens in New York City; it is the world's tallest skyscraper.

October: Chester Gould's *Dick Tracy* makes its debut in newspaper comic strips.

Unemployment swells to 16 percent; 8 million are out of work. For the first time ever in America, more people are leaving the country than are entering it.

Babe Ruth and Lou Gehrig hit 46 home runs apiece for the New York Yankees.

Birds Eye frozen vegetables appear, along with Hostess Twinkies and Snickers candy bars.

"Life is Just a Bowl of Cherries," recorded by Rudy Vallee, reflects American disdain for the Depression, Bing Crosby's rendition of "Where the Blue of the Night Meets the Gold of the Day" establishes his fame as a crooner, and Kate Smith's "When the Moon Comes Over the Mountain" sells so well she is named America's "Songbird of the South."

Pearl Buck's *The Good Earth* dominates the best-seller lists.

Two new afternoon radio serials, based on popular comic strips, come on the air: *Buck Rogers* and *Little Orphan Annie.*

The movie *Dracula* reflects the growing popularity of horror films and makes Bela Lugosi a star. It is followed by *Frankenstein,* which establishes the fame of Boris Karloff.

1932

February: The first Winter Olympics are held at Lake Placid, New York, sparking an interest in skiing.

March: The infant son of Charles and Anne Lindbergh is kidnapped, setting off sensational press coverage. His body is found in May.

Unemployment reaches almost 24 percent; 14 million are without jobs. Wages are 60 percent less than in 1929. Franklin D. Roosevelt promises a "new deal" at the Democratic convention in June; he defeats incumbent Herbert Hoover for the presidency in the November elections.

Despite the Depression, Radio City Music Hall, part of the unfinished Rockefeller Center, opens in New York City at Christmastime.

The song "Brother, Can You Spare a Dime?" sums up the disillusionment that accompanies the worsening Depression.

The Jack Benny Program and *The Fred Allen Show* premiere on network radio.

The first Big Little Book comes out; it features *Dick Tracy.*

Shirley Temple makes her film debut at three years old.

Walt Disney receives a special Academy Award for his creation of Mickey Mouse.

1933

February: Congress votes to repeal Prohibition. By early December, enough states approve the measure, and the Twenty-first Amendment (Repeal) is passed.

March: Franklin D. Roosevelt assumes the presidency. He faces 25 percent unemployment, with 15 million workers affected. Family income has dropped almost 40 percent since the onset of the Depression.

March: President Roosevelt begins his *Fireside Chats* on radio, drawing record audiences.

May: The Century of Progress Exposition opens in Chicago; architecturally, it features a mix of Modernism and traditional revival styles.

Erle Stanley Gardner writes his first Perry Mason mystery, *The Case of the Velvet Claws.*

Bridge becomes the most popular card game; the sales of expert Ely Culbertson's *Contract Bridge Blue Book,* first published in 1931, soar.

"Who's Afraid of the Big Bad Wolf?" a song from Walt Disney's cartoon *The Three Little Pigs,* expresses the hope following Roosevelt's inauguration.

42nd Street and *Gold Diggers of 1933* are the definitive Depression musicals; *King Kong* and *The Invisible Man* demonstrate how movie special effects can create great entertainment.

The first All-Star baseball game is played; the American League wins.

1934

May 28: The Dionne quintuplets are born in Ontario; the event attracts unprecedented press coverage and public interest.

September 18: Bruno Hauptmann is arrested for kidnapping Charles Lindbergh's infant son.

December: Benny Goodman's *Let's Dance* show brings big-band swing to radio nightly.

Unemployment drops slightly to about 22 percent; 11 million are out of work.

The National Recovery Administration's emblem, a blue eagle, and the slogan "We Do Our Part" are seen in factories, stores, and shops everywhere.

John Dillinger, "Baby Face" Nelson, "Pretty Boy" Floyd, and Bonnie and Clyde are shot and killed by law officers, effectively ending the reign of colorful gangsters.

Frank Capra's *It Happened One Night,* one of the Depression era's "screwball comedies," sweeps the Academy Awards.

Hervey Allen's *Anthony Adverse* leads the best-seller lists for fiction.

The Chrysler Airflow, the first mass-produced car to incorporate streamlined design, is introduced.

1935

January 1: The trial of Bruno Hauptmann begins for the kidnapping and murder of the Lindbergh baby. He is convicted of all charges by mid-February.

April: *Your Hit Parade* begins on NBC radio, tracking the most popular records of the week, and a new comedy series, *Fibber McGee and Molly,* also debuts on the network.

May 24: the first major league baseball game played under lights occurs in Cincinnati.

Unemployment dips to about 21 percent; 10 million are out of work. One out of four households receives some kind of relief.

George Gershwin's folk opera *Porgy and Bess* opens on Broadway in October.

Bingo is allowed in movie theaters and becomes a craze, as do chain letters.

The board game Monopoly becomes an overnight sensation.

The Marx Brothers challenge high culture in *A Night at the Opera.*

Cole Porter's "Begin the Beguine," as recorded by Artie Shaw, is a big hit.

1936

April 3: Bruno Hauptmann is executed for kidnapping and killing the infant son of Charles Lindbergh, ending one of the most sensational investigations and trials in U.S. history.

August: The Summer Olympics are held in Berlin; Jesse Owens humiliates Hitler and the Nazis, along with their racist theories, by winning four gold medals in track events.

December 11: The abdication of King Edward VIII of England for "the woman I love," Wallis Warfield Simpson, becomes the biggest news story.

Girl Scouts inaugurate annual cookie sales.

Unemployment drops to 17 percent—about 8 million workers. In November, President Roosevelt defeats challenger Alf Landon,

523 electoral votes to 8, losing only Vermont and Maine.

The Douglas DC-3 begins production in June. The airplane quickly sets the standards for luxury and safety in air travel.

Famed director Cecil B. DeMille begins hosting *Lux Radio Theater* in June; it becomes a major dramatic show, with scripts based on popular movies of the time.

Margaret Mitchell's *Gone with the Wind* sells over a million copies by December and eclipses all competition.

Dancer Fred Astaire finds himself a major singing star with four hits: "Let's Face the Music and Dance," "Let Yourself Go," "The Way You Look Tonight," and "Pick Yourself Up." The songs all come from his movies with Ginger Rogers.

Over 5,000 artists paint thousands of murals in post offices, train stations, courthouses, and other buildings across the country as part of the Federal Arts Program.

1937

March: Teenagers jitterbug in the aisles of New York's Paramount Theater to the swing of Benny Goodman.

May 9: *The Chase and Sanborn Hour* introduces ventriloquist Edgar Bergen and Charlie McCarthy on NBC radio.

July 2: Aviatrix Amelia Earhart disappears over the Pacific Ocean.

Unemployment drops to 14 percent; 7 million workers are without jobs. Toward the end of the year, the stock market again declines, and the nation moves toward a recession.

The German dirigible *Hindenburg* crashes at Lakehurst, New Jersey, on May 6; the disaster is reported live on radio.

Beginning in December, Arturo Toscanini and the NBC Symphony Orchestra bring classical music to a large radio audience.

Howard Johnson begins franchising restaurants, opening the market to chain eateries and fast food.

Gone with the Wind continues to outsell all other books.

Walt Disney's *Snow White and the Seven Dwarfs,* all-color and all-animated, opens.

1938

January 16: The growing popularity of jazz and swing gives rise to a concert by Benny Goodman's band in New York's Carnegie Hall.

June: An issue of *Action Comics* features the adventures of a brand-new character, Superman.

June 22: Joe Louis knocks out Max Schmeling to retain his heavyweight crown and avenge an earlier loss to the German boxer.

With a recession, unemployment jumps to 19 percent, or 9 million jobless. Defense spending increases, however, and the country begins to pull out of its decline.

The Fair Labor Standards Act is passed, outlawing most labor for children aged 15 and under.

Howard Hughes flies around the world in 3 days, 19 hours, and 14 minutes in July. "Wrong Way" Corrigan flies to Dublin instead of California (as he planned) that same month.

Orson Welles, as a Halloween prank, frightens many Americans with his radio adaptation of H. G. Wells's *War of the Worlds.*

Dale Carnegie's *How to Win Friends and Influence People* enters its second year as a leader among nonfiction books.

The Andy Hardy films begin, with Mickey Rooney in the title role.

Singer Frank Sinatra makes his radio debut on small stations in the New York area.

1939

March: Swallowing goldfish becomes a campus fad.

April 9: Singer Marian Anderson draws 75,000 to an open-air concert in Washington, D.C., after being barred from Constitution Hall by the Daughters of the American Revolution.

April 30: The New York World's Fair opens, despite depressing international news. Germany is excluded. The extravaganza is billed as "The World of Tomorrow." The opening ceremonies are televised, and TV monitors are a big hit at the fairgrounds.

September 1: Germany invades Poland; World War II begins.

December 15: After a year of promotion, the film version of *Gone with the Wind* opens overshadowing all other movie events.

U.S. population at the end of the decade stands at approximately 130 million; it has grown about 7 percent during the decade, well below past averages. Unemployment dips to 17 percent, or 8 million jobless.

Nylon stockings go on sale in the face of a silk shortage.

The Glenn Miller Orchestra has hits with "Little Brown Jug," "Sunrise Serenade," and "In the Mood."

Reporter Edward R. Murrow broadcasts nightly from London for CBS; more and more airtime is devoted to war news.

Overview

of the 1930s

Dust Bowl Era
Great Depression

NICKNAMES OF THE DECADE

The study of the 1930s actually begins on Thursday, October 24, 1929. That autumn day the stock market collapsed and signaled the onset of the Great Depression. The grim years that ensued shaped the 1930s, including its popular culture.

Similarly, the decade symbolically ended on September 1, 1939, when Germany invaded Poland. Hitler's Nazi army smashed through Poland, ending the false peace of the late 1930s and effectively starting World War II.

Prior to the opening of the New York's World Fair in 1939, officials buried a time capsule. The capsule, a tube sponsored by Westinghouse, stood 8 feet long, 8 inches in diameter, and weighed 800 pounds. The capsule was sunk 50 feet into the earth. Detailed instructions on locating it, along with an inventory of its holdings, were left with 3,650 libraries and museums around the world in the hopes that 5,000 years hence (the year 6939), someone would find it.

The time capsule's contents are fascinating: seeds, coins and paper money, a can opener, a safety pin, swatches of cloth and plastics, a cement sample, a microfilm essay about life on earth in the 1930s running some 10 million words long and featuring over 1,000 pictures, a sound newsreel, and other artifacts. Popular culture items also filled the capsule: a Mickey Mouse cup, playing cards and a set of bridge rules, some

rhinestone jewelry from Woolworth's, a reproduction of Grant Wood's painting *American Gothic,* the sheet music for "Flat Foot Floogie," a copy of *Gone with the Wind,* and several popular newspapers and magazines. Topping the list is the 1938–1939 Sears, Roebuck catalog, a hefty opus that will fill any gaps about American consumer culture for future civilizations that might unearth the capsule.[1]

FRANKLIN D. ROOSEVELT

Franklin Delano Roosevelt (1882–1945) overshadowed the decade. He swept into national prominence in 1932, first at the Democratic national convention, promising a New Deal for Americans weary of the Depression, and then soundly defeated Herbert Hoover for the presidency. Roosevelt's unending stream of ideas and suggestions set him in opposition to Hoover, who seemed to lack fresh solutions for the growing economic crisis.

Roosevelt had his Hundred Days (his first 100 days in office, when much significant legislation was passed) and his Brain Trust (the group of prominent leaders who advised Roosevelt on important economic issues, including Columbia University professors Raymond Moley, Adolph Berle, and Rexford Tugwell, among others); he had Eleanor, one of the best-known First Ladies in history; he had his dapper cigarette holder; and he even had Fala, his Scottish terrier. Roosevelt mastered the news media more than any president before him. Hoover stood stiff and uncomfortable before microphones and cameras; Roosevelt reveled in the attention. His celebrity equaled the era's movie and radio stars. His *Fireside Chats* on national radio drew larger audiences than the top-rated network shows. Roosevelt did not just make news. He *was* news.

On February 15, 1933, a disgruntled anarchist, Giuseppe Zangara attempted to assassinate Roosevelt. Zangara, who said in his defense only that "I hate all presidents" and "too many people are starving to death," fired six shots at Roosevelt in Miami. Although the then-president-elect emerged unhurt, two bullets struck Chicago's mayor, Anton Cermak, who died from his wounds several weeks later.

Just as it had been when Leon Czolgosz assassinated President William McKinley in 1901, public outrage demanded swift justice. Zangara was indicted the day of the attack and pleaded guilty. The state of Florida electrocuted him on March 20, just five weeks after the crime. Americans devoured radio and newspaper accounts throughout February and March. The ensuing media circus enabled people to momentarily forget the Depression.

Buoyed by an outpouring of sympathy along with his electoral mandate, President Roosevelt enjoyed a turbulent first term. He was re-elected in 1936 by an overwhelming majority. Despite his energy, Roosevelt could not seem to cure the nation's economic ills. Severe labor disorder (marked by sit-down strikes) and the growth of unions marked his second term. A 1937 Gallup Poll showed 70 percent of Americans favored the existence of unions, but most opposed the sit-down tactics. FDR's popularity declined as labor disputes grew uglier and especially as the economic challenges went unmet.

Nevertheless, Roosevelt remained a figure of endless media coverage and public interest. Despite his political setbacks in the later 1930s, the threat of war convinced a majority of Americans to return him to office for an unprecedented third term in 1940.

TIME MAN OF THE YEAR
1930 Mohandas Karamchand Gandhi (pacifist organizer for democracy, India)
1931 Pierre Laval (premier of France)
1932 Franklin Delano Roosevelt (32nd president of the United States)
1933 Hugh Samuel Johnson (presidential advisor, head of National Recovery Administration)
1934 Franklin Delano Roosevelt
1935 Haile Selassie (king of Ethiopia)
1936 Mrs. Wallis Warfield Simpson (married the former king of England)
1937 Generalissimo and Madame Chiang Kai-Shek (leaders of China)
1938 Adolf Hitler (chancellor of Germany)
1939 Joseph Stalin (leader of the Soviet Union)

THE GREAT DEPRESSION

The Great Depression defined American life for a generation. Perhaps only the Civil War applied greater stress and touched proportionally more people. National income fell by 50 percent. Economic challenges led to rising divorce and separation rates. Couples postponed marriage; 290,000 fewer people got married in 1932 than in 1920. Those who did marry frequently continued living at home or doubled up with friends. Fewer children were being born, and the size of the typical American family shrank to the smallest of any decade. The birthrate fell below the replacement level for the first time ever, and a more liberal attitude toward birth control developed.[2]

By 1932, one out of every five American workers was unemployed. Others were underemployed, having to adjust to reduced hours. The shame of unemployment drove many from their spouses, and child neglect became a problem, leading to a lack of supervision, disease, and malnutrition. For older children, there was a silver lining: they stayed in school longer, continuing their educations instead of hunting for nonexistent jobs. Others opted to hit the road. Thousands of young

A family from the 1930s in their living room. Prints & Photographs Division, Library of Congress.

people wandered the country hoping for the best in the midst of hard times.

As the Depression worsened in the early 1930s, the volume of manufactured goods dropped sharply, as did national payrolls. Companies responded by laying off workers, slashing dividends, reducing inventories, cutting wages, forgoing improvements, and reducing production. In 1930 2,600 businesses folded, 28,000 in 1931, and almost 32,000 in 1932. Unemployment skyrocketed from 429,000 in 1929 to 15 million in 1933.

Construction of new housing dropped 95 percent between 1928 and 1933. Home repairs dropped by 90 percent and housing prices declined, wiping out holdings and equity. The middle class was hit particularly hard; while those who were poor usually rented their homes, the middle class had its first experience with poverty, struggling to purchase or hold on to their own homes. By 1933, half of all home mortgages stood technically in default.[3]

People borrowed on their tangible and intangible assets, including life insurance, mortgages,

and household possessions, but often these were not enough. Without the means to pay rent or maintain mortgages, more and more citizens lost their homes. Evictions grew ominously in the early years of the decade. By 1931, some 15,000 people became homeless in New York City alone. The city lacked resources to house them, so they wandered the streets in search of shelter.[4]

Popular culture, however, offered an escape from unpleasant realities. At the same time, it reinforced family intimacy. Parents and children bonded in the living room listening to the radio. Books, newspapers, and magazines, along with movies, were also enormously popular. Movies grew in importance, perhaps surpassing radio, which had been the primary form of mass media. An average of 60 to 75 million people went to the movies each week, more than 60 percent of the total population.

RURAL HARDSHIPS

Throughout the Depression, American agriculture had the most difficulty among all the industrial sectors. Small, traditional family-owned farms faced the greatest threat. Agricultural income dropped 50 percent, resulting in farms being abandoned or lost to banks. In 1932, over 200,000 farms, homes, and businesses were foreclosed. In order to stave off disaster, people left their own properties and turned to sharecropping and tenant farming. As banks and other lenders attempted to take over farms in default, "penny auctions" erupted. Buyers would get a farm's goods for pennies, return them to the owner, and turn the cash over to the bank as payment for the mortgage. The foreclosures continued almost unabated into the mid-1930s.

To add to farmers' woes, severe droughts led to the Dust Bowl, a time when rural land in the Great Plains dried up and turned into a fine dust. "Black rollers" were moving clouds of precious topsoil, dislodged from the earth, billowing across the countryside like a thunderstorm. Sometimes they were accompanied by a few drops of "black rain," water mixed with the dust that left a smear of mud wherever it landed. Occasionally, the storms lasted several days, the blowing soil piling up in drifts against buildings and along fences. The sandy dust, from several inches to more than a foot, obliterated highways.

URBAN HARDSHIPS

People in cities faced the crisis in a more visible way. A word from the nineteenth century re-entered the national vocabulary: breadline. Unable to afford food, many city dwellers waited in a breadline. Run primarily by charitable organizations, soup kitchens attracted long lines of hungry people. Although there are virtually no verified cases of starvation during the Depression, many individuals and families went to bed hungry each night.

One famous image of the Depression is a person standing on a street corner selling apples for a nickel apiece. This image evolved through a mixture of good corporate marketing and public desperation. In 1929 and 1930, the Pacific Northwest had an apple surplus. The International Apple Shippers' Association persuaded thousands of individuals to each buy a carton of 72 Northwest apples for $1.75. The association convinced these would-be entrepreneurs that, after expenses, they could make $1.85 a day by hawking apples on a busy corner. The slogan "Buy an apple a day and ease the Depression away!" turned into a scheme that had thousands of takers in most larger American cities.[5]

Despite the elevation of the nickel apple into a symbol for the Depression, most of the jobless found more profitable pursuits. By 1932 thousands of novice bootblacks were trying their hand at the shoe shine business. Others took up door-to-door sales, making the Fuller Brush Company one of the most profitable firms of the decade. Some passed out handbills or placed ads on car windshields. Still others attempted mining—coal, gold, silver—whatever the earth would give up. The goal was self-reliance, to avoid going on the dole. In the 1930s, the thought of accepting public relief still bore a stigma, a carryover from earlier years.

EMPLOYMENT AND THE ECONOMY

By 1932, 40 million Americans, urban and rural, knew poverty to some degree. Necessity required husbands to allow their spouses to work, suppressing old prejudices about working women. As the number of factory and other male-dominated jobs decreased, more men joined the ranks of the unemployed. Often, the only jobs available were clerical and domestic ones, occupations traditionally held by women. A shift in employment patterns occurred, with the percentage of men in the workforce declining as the number of women taking jobs increased. But there was a price to pay: all social ills, from juvenile delinquency to divorce, were laid at the feet of working mothers. Furthermore, 75 percent of women believed that if the husband had a paying position, the wife should not work, thereby freeing up jobs for men.[6]

Race also factored in employment status. The existing inequities between blacks and whites worsened during the Depression. Skilled black workers' wages fell much faster than those of white employees. The National Recovery Administration (NRA) was a government agency established to provide aid to the needy, but its rules contained a grandfather clause that allowed wage discrepancies based on past money earned. For many blacks, NRA meant "Negro Run Around" and "Negroes Rarely Allowed." Black sharecroppers and tenant farmers in the South received some 70 percent less in relief payments than white farmers, a situation that often forced them off the land entirely.[7]

With worsening conditions, the cost of living dropped, but that did not help the millions who had less to spend. The consumer price index, if measured as 100 in 1929, had declined to 80.8 in 1932. The nickel itself took on a certain significance. Five cents in the pocket meant a person was not totally down and out. In 1936, three times more nickels and dimes were minted than in 1934.

Although Americans had long paid cash for virtually everything except housing, the Depression brought about some subtle changes. People did not default on most loans; banks might go under, but individuals were usually reliable about repaying debt. As a result, automobile financing actually grew during the 1930s, and department stores and other retail establishments likewise extended credit throughout this turbulent decade.

Worry and uncertainty marked the closing years of the 1930s. Between 1933 and 1939, at least 10 percent of the workforce remained jobless. For naysayers who opposed government

Black sharecroppers did not receive as much aid as white workers. This family worked on the Pettway Plantation in Gee's Bend, Alabama, 1939. Prints & Photographs Division, Library of Congress.

involvement in employment because they considered it meddling, the word "boondoggle" entered the language. Originally intended to mean "simple craftwork-like woven belts," it came to signify any silly, useless project, and it usually implied the government had a hand in it. For the unemployed, however, the jobs provided by the NRA and the Works Progress Administration (WPA), along with all their associated agencies, were real lifesavers, not expensive make-work. The NRA Blue Eagle ("We Do Our Part") was an icon of the times, proudly displayed in commercial establishments everywhere. Whether it was pouring concrete in a large city or building a highway through mountainous terrain, 20 percent of the total workforce labored in some capacity in these organizations' programs.[8]

American Heritage Interest

In the 1930s one of the missions of the WPA was to provide jobs related to culture and history. The Library of Congress went in search of the roots of early American music, compiling a series of records that helped preserve a rapidly disappearing art. In addition, the WPA organized and published both *The Index of American Design,* a compendium of national arts and skills, and *The Historical American Buildings Survey,* a vast collection of measured drawings of virtually every important architectural site in the nation. Along with this official search for the American past came a substantial growth of interest in the nation's heritage. For example, square dancing flourished, and traditional country music began to be heard on the radio.

The National Youth Association (NYA) was a New Deal Program, part of the WPA, which trained unemployed, out-of-school youth, and provided work-study training for students from high through graduate school. Here young women are in classes at Camp Roosevelt, in Ocala, Florida, probably 1938. Prints & Photographs Division, Library of Congress.

Toward the end of the 1930s, in a gesture that probably said as much about the ailing economy as did anything else, President Roosevelt moved the commemoration of Thanksgiving from the last Thursday in November to the fourth Thursday in the month. This official shift had nothing to do with patriotism or reverence for the nation's founding. FDR did it to extend the Christmas shopping season.

MAJOR NEWS STORIES

The Lindbergh Kidnapping

Amid the economic woes, the public found escape in the problems of others. A prime example was the March 1, 1932, kidnapping of the infant son of Charles and Anne Lindbergh, considered the "Crime of the Century." Still a hero to Americans because of his solo flight across the Atlantic in 1927,

Lindbergh had retreated with his wife to rural New Jersey to escape the endless publicity surrounding the "Lone Eagle." Unfortunately, the kidnapping made the Lindberghs the most visible parents in the nation, and they would remain that way for several years as the press shadowed their every move.

The Lindbergh case had all the makings of a movie or radio drama: handsome, famous parents; a heinous crime; and an equally fascinating cast of secondary players. On May 12, 1932, the infant's body was located, but a suspect was not arrested until 1934. After a series of cruel hoaxes, officials charged Bruno Hauptmann with the kidnapping. In January 1935, almost three years after the crime, a trial commenced in the rural town of Flemington, New Jersey. An army of reporters descended on the village to record the proceedings. The public stayed glued to its radios for the latest reports; newspapers issued extra editions chronicling the courtroom scenes. The Depression, the

In 1934, on a tiny farm near Callander, Ontario, Elzipe Dionne gave birth to five girls—Annette, Cécile, Emilie, Marie, and Yvonne—in a span of 30 minutes, a rare medical occurrence. Immediately dubbed "the quints" by both the press and their huge, adoring public, people inundated the family with gifts. Thousands of Americans made the drive to the little Canadian village. Some 3,000 visitors a day descended on the town, where the fortunate got a glimpse of the quints on display in the public nursery. For almost a decade, their every activity was reported, gifts streamed in unabated, and the Dionne family struggled with celebrity. The little girls were made to endorse products of every description, their faces peering out from advertisements and billboards. Despite an almost sideshow-like atmosphere surrounding the humble Dionne home, all five girls survived and grew into normal, healthy children.

New Deal, and even Roosevelt were put aside for six weeks as evidence was presented. In the end, officials convicted and then executed Hauptmann. The nation, temporarily sated, reverted to more mundane interests.

Edward VIII and Mrs. Simpson

The abdication and subsequent marriage of King Edward VIII of England proved to be another popular distraction from the economic problems. When the handsome bachelor king renounced the throne in December 1936, the world gasped. His reason was simple: he wished to marry Wallis Warfield Simpson, an American divorcée, a move that Parliament would not allow. Thus, for "the woman I love," King Edward gave up his crown.

Mrs. Simpson and the king had already been the subject of gossip, but no one suspected he would abdicate. The American press relentlessly covered the couple in its quest for stories about "Wally and the Prince." The whole affair did much to usher in the use of telephoto lenses, as eager photographers tried to get a shot of the two aboard the royal yacht.

To ensure that a maximum number of people heard his proclamation, Edward used a radio hookup in Windsor Castle. He understood the

Amelia Earhart at 31, when she first became famous (1928). Prints & Photographs Division, Library of Congress.

immediacy of radio, and the live broadcast connected him to his subjects, along with millions of fascinated Americans. In many ways, the king's words had an impact similar to the *Fireside Chats* that had been so carefully scripted and delivered by President Roosevelt. The two leaders were discovering the power of electronic media.

From Edward's December abdication until his June 1937 marriage to Mrs. Simpson, the press was persistent and its readers insatiable. Following the marriage, the couple continued to be hounded by reporters and photographers. Although the furor eventually died down, the Duke and Duchess of Windsor, as the couple then became, continued to be forever dogged by the endless publicity generated by their fairy-tale romance.

The Disappearance of Amelia Earhart

Amelia Earhart (1897–1937) was a young woman flyer who, in 1928, had become famous as the first woman to fly the Atlantic, but as a passenger. In 1932 she made her own solo flight across the Atlantic, flying from Newfoundland to Northern Ireland. She was married to a well-to-do publisher, George Putnam, who helped publicize her flights, and Earhart was active in giving speeches that promoted flying.

In May 1937 she and her navigator, Frederick J. Noonan, began an intended 27,000-mile journey that followed the Equator, but somewhere over the central Pacific Ocean, her plane disappeared.

Earhart's lost flight was chronicled in news stories that rivaled the emotion of any event of the decade. Extensive searches were immediately instituted, but no traces of the ill-fated plane could be found. The disappearance of Amelia Earhart has entered American popular folklore; movies have been produced, books have been written, new searches have been attempted, and conspiracy theories advanced, but she remains missing, a tantalizing, unsolved mystery of the 1930s.

Advertising

of the 1930s

The 1920s—the Jazz Age, the Roaring Twenties—were years of advertising excess. The decade even adopted a word to describe its approach to selling: "ballyhoo." This nineteenth-century term means to exaggerate blatantly, to win attention in any way possible. By 1929, advertising revenues peaked at $3.4 billion, a new record.

It seemed that the most challenging task facing advertisers was showing the public new and different ways to spend money. Ads showed how goods and services would enhance one's social status, deliver benefits, and bring pleasure. With disposable cash, consumers faced an endless array of choices. For the most part, the public accepted uncritically all the ballyhoo; the economy was strong and the government benign, reluctant to intervene.

With the Great Crash of 1929, everything changed significantly. Should advertisements reflect the realities of the crisis, or should they ignore the economic collapse? Businesses quickly felt the economic pressures and cut ad budgets. After a decade of almost uninterrupted growth, advertising agencies slashed salaries and eliminated jobs. Ads were done as cheaply as possible. The public faced a steadily shrinking number of print ads, although radio promotions increased.

The changes, however, were not seen only in business and advertising. Unemployment soared everywhere. With less money to spend, distrust of advertising grew. People grew suspicious, especially of extravagant claims. Their fears were fueled by books like *100,000,000 Guinea Pigs* (1933), *Skin Deep* (1934), *Eat, Drink and Be Wary* (1935), *The Popular Practice of Fraud* (1935), *Partners in Plunder* (1935), and the magazine *Ballyhoo* (1931–1939). *Ballyhoo* refused all paid ads; instead, it ran trenchant parodies of the real thing.

Organizations like Consumers Union and Consumers Research enjoyed rapid growth and prosperity throughout the 1930s. Their success reflected public discontent with inflated claims and shoddy products. Government, slow to exert any pressures on advertising during the 1920s, responded with the Pure Food, Drug, and Cosmetic Act of 1938. The Federal Trade Commission and the Securities and Exchange Commission, along with the U.S. Post Office and the Internal Revenue Service, began to increase their supervisory and regulatory controls over advertising.[1]

EFFECTS OF THE DEPRESSION

Advertisers took note and toned down the clamor and hoopla used to hype products in the early part of the decade. Yet, advertising in the Depression seldom reflected the nation's problems. Despair and social upheaval were rarely even hinted at in print or on the radio. Occasionally, an ad or commercial suggested the need for a good appearance in order to gain or hold a job, or it urged forbearance toward those less successful. More frequently, advertisements showed the consumer in his or her preferred environment—the man in his office, the woman in her home—and in the presence of the product.

Despite its refusal to acknowledge the crisis directly, advertising did change. More direct ads replaced the hazy view of an optimistic future with a more hard-edged depiction of the present—a present without the Depression, however. Advertisers faced the paradoxical situation of both reassuring the consumer that prosperity was right around the corner while simultaneously urging hard work and sacrifice in order to weather the economic storm of tough times.

Thus, many, if not most, of Depression-era messages remained cheery, with automobiles, soft drinks, cigarettes, and foodstuffs dominating. Advertisers were delighted by a new subculture of teenagers. They targeted school supplies and clothing directly at teens, not their parents. The makers of products once aimed at housewives changed their entire advertising strategies. Fleischmann's Yeast was not just for baking anymore; now, it promised to clear pimply complexions. Planter's Peanuts were no longer a light snack; if a teen offered friends some Planters, that gesture guaranteed popularity. Advertising found a new audience.

The rise of self-service supermarkets and large department stores in which clerks were scarce caused consumers to receive less direct advice about what to buy. Instead, they had to rely increasingly on advertising to make their decisions about quality and value. Advertising therefore became both educator and adviser.

To accommodate this change, ads focused less on the consumer and more on the product. The message meant to bolster confidence about price and value, and to reassure a clientele that felt uncertain about the rapid changes in society and technology.

An unspoken aura of guilt hung over Depression-era ad copy. If consumers did not possess or employ a specific product, it was implied that they would pay a terrible price. Letting insurance

This poster for five and dime stores, where many items were priced at 5 or 10 cents, was created by the Federal Arts Project, which provided work to illustrators in the 1930s. Prints & Photographs Division, Library of Congress.

policies lapse would force children to drop out of school and go to work; reluctance to buy a new appliance would lead to social ostracism; failure to practice good hygiene would create a bad first impression; sobbing women and stern-faced men provided true confessions of what happened when they neglected to buy certain products or perform particular acts. At the same time, most ads simply promised a better life and better days ahead.

In the meantime, ad revenues plunged to a low of $1.3 billion in 1933, about a third of what they had been three years earlier. The nature of the advertisements themselves changed. Some agency art directors felt that too much detail in an ad was distracting; simplicity developed into the key to communicating a message. Wordy parables and long testimonials were eliminated. Lengthy statements about the product or service were couched in terms of how the product or service benefited the consumer. For the duration of the Depression, no matter the product, advertisers stressed durability and dependability. Automobile manufacturers mentioned price openly, since the economy concerned financially strapped consumers. Jingles disappeared from magazines, although they had a firm hold on radio. As the economy improved after 1933, scattered images of gracious living reappeared, but copy remained appreciably shorter.

ADVERTISING TRENDS

Not everyone subscribed to simplification in advertisements. Many agencies and clients continued to favor loud, cluttered messages. The graceful Art Deco typefaces of the 1920s were replaced by a plain block style that resembled newspaper headlines. Many print ads of the 1930s used bold type, harsh black-and-white photographs, and

Despite the Depression and the fact that few could buy a new car, this highly streamlined design is eye-catching both for the advertising and for the car featured in this 1936 V-8 Ford Coupe ad. Prints & Photographs Division, Library of Congress.

CELEBRITY ENDORSEMENTS IN THE 1930s

Celebrity endorsements are partnerships between companies and corporations, in which celebrities loan their image and/or testimonial to the company's advertisements in return for compensation. Most early celebrity endorsements featured athletes, such as Olympic swimmer Johnny Weissmuller, whose image appeared on the cover of the breakfast cereal Wheaties. This tradition continued into the twentieth and twenty-first centuries, with celebrities like Olympic gymnast Mary Lou Retton and basketball star Michael Jordan following Weissmuller's example. Celebrity endorsements proved enormously successful, and companies soon began forming long-term advertising agreements with high profile stars.

Film stars like Charlie Chaplin and Shirley Temple, among the best known personalities of their era, endorsed hundreds of products during their careers. These partnerships eventually led to "celebrity branding," wherein celebrities and manufacturers partnered to create products branded with the celebrity's name. Shirley Temple was one of the first celebrities with a host of products bearing her name, including brand toys and children's clothing. In the twentieth and twenty-first centuries, celebrity branding became far more common, as entrepreneurial celebrities, like singer and actress Jennifer Lopez, began taking on roles in designing products released under their names.

a terse, direct prose style that dropped subtlety for the hard sell. More and more ads promoted contests and giveaways, further cluttering the ad space. Much of this emphasis on promotions came from the success of radio. In all, it was a nervous, tense display, perhaps echoing the tenor of the times. As the decade progressed, agencies continued to cut costs, with lush illustrations and imaginative graphics usually among the victims.[2]

At the same time, innovative ideas in technology, design, and architecture worked into the world of style. Elements of contemporary art, such as expressionism, cubism, abstraction, and

BURMA-SHAVE

One of the few bright spots in the 1930s was outdoor advertising. The 1920s are often referred to as the Golden Age of Billboards, but the 1930s continued that exuberance. In 1932, about 320 advertising firms used outdoor ads on a nationwide basis; by 1939, over 500 companies used billboards. Outdoor advertising traditionally aimed at a broad middle- and lower-middle-class audience. It was direct and realistic, and it had to convey its entire message quickly. Whereas magazines were turning increasingly to photography to display products, billboards and posters clung to the traditional painted and airbrushed illustration. In addition, the use of gentle, unsatiric humor in outdoor signs expanded throughout the 1930s.

One of the most unusual ad campaigns in the long history of American outdoor advertising was that launched by Burma-Shave in 1925. Burma-Shave (technically the Burma-Vita Company) was a struggling firm attempting to market men's brushless shaving cream. They had tried giving out sample jars, but this approach was unsuccessful. Then, using pieces of scrap wood, the Minnesota-based company erected small roadside signs that gave a serial message. As cars raced by, the drivers could read them in order. Soon the signs were being professionally manufactured; the messages consisted of simple, lighthearted poems, a sign for each line. By the 1930s, little red Burma-Shave signs could be found alongside virtually every highway in the country. The campaign kicked into high gear and a national reach, with yearly contests urging consumers to send in verses they had written. And write them they did. In 1931, motorists would have read, "Half a pound / for half a buck / come on shavers / you're in luck / Burma-Shave." Or, in 1934, they would have read, "He had the ring / he had the flat / but she felt his chin / and that was that / Burma-Shave."

So it went throughout the decade. Some 200 new verses were written and posted by 1940, and the campaign continued unabated until 1963 with hundreds of additional poems. In 1938, over 7,000 sets of verse stood by the highway, which translated into more than 40,000 individual signs. Throughout the decade, and with the emergence of a true national campaign, Burma-Shave saw its fortunes rise sharply. The end of signs by the road in 1963 signified the loss of a part of Americana known to everyone who traveled by car in those days.

Source: For the story of Burma-Shave and many examples of their ads, see Frank Rowsome Jr., *The Verse by the Side of the Road: The Story of Burma-Shave Signs and Jingles* (Lexington, MA: The Stephen Greene Press, 1965).

impressionism, surfaced with some regularity on the ad pages of mass-circulation magazines. These ads kept words to a minimum, thus allowing pictures to carry the message. Ads evoked emotions through color choices and broke down shapes to their basic components. Technology was suggested by a deliberately distorted arrangements of motifs, while delicate illustrations conveyed a sense of the seasons. It was one more way of suggesting the new and the novel in a visual manner. This use of the techniques of modern art was, however, in the minority, and stands as a reaction to the highly realistic illustrations of the 1910s and 1920s. Streamlining—a new style of design most often used for vehicles, including automobiles, trains, and airplanes—gave a new, rounded, flowing look to design and was found in some advertising of the 1930s.

Market researchers like George Gallup and A. C. Nielsen (of the Gallup Poll and Nielsen Ratings, respectively) discovered that the majority of Depression-era audiences wanted clear and simple ads. As a result, the use of comic strip characters and cartoon drawings emerged. Speech balloons, a device taken from comics, were used freely. Ads used photographs, instead of drawings, to add authenticity and impact. Illustrators, working in oil and watercolor, were in less demand as art and design became secondary to the print message.[3]

As photography became more prominent in ads, many looked on it as more real than a painted illustration. The rise of consumerism and the desire for greater truth in advertising also gave photography a strong boost. The fact that photographs could be retouched, manipulated, and distorted seemed not to matter.

Men and Women in Ads of the 1930s

The message given in an overwhelming majority of magazine ads from the decade is that men are producers and women consumers. Naturally, most commercial messages were directed at women, an approach that resulted in rampant stereotyping of both sexes. The consumer, when depicted in ads, was typically a woman—a sophisticated, modern woman who made most of the purchasing choices for her family. A man's home may have been his castle, but a woman managed it. In the world portrayed by advertisers, men held down jobs and women did the shopping.

Print ads almost always depicted an urban or suburban scene. While skyscrapers represented the office environment, large factories represented the manufacturing world, and home was an apartment, a house on a city street, or a cozy dwelling in the suburbs.

RADIO ADVERTISING

People might quote ad copy they saw in a magazine, but it was much more likely they could repeat the jingles and slogans they heard on the radio. People sincerely believed that widely promoted products were somehow superior to less ballyhooed ones. Although radio advertising began in 1922, it did not truly hit its stride until the next decade. With the incredible growth of broadcasting, radio commercials helped bring

---

ADVERTISING SLOGANS OF THE 1930s

"Drink a bite to eat at 10, 2 and 4 o'clock,"
  Dr Pepper, 1926

"M'm! M'm! Good!" Campbell's Soup, 1931*

"The breakfast of champions," Wheaties, 1933*

"When you care enough to send the very best,"
  Hallmark Cards, 1934*

"Snap! Crackle! Pop!" Kellogg's Rice Krispies,
  1930s*

---

*Among Advertising Age's "The Advertising Century: Top 100 Advertising Campaigns," http://adage.com/century/campaigns.html.

---

about greater homogeneity in national patterns of taste and consumption.

One of the most popular formats for a broadcast ad was the singing commercial. The ad would begin with an incidental opening (humorously known as the "cowcatcher"), move to the actual commercial message, and close with a final plug (called the "hitchhiker"). As stations played these ditties throughout the day, listeners, like it or not, soon knew them by heart.[4]

By advertising nationwide on network radio, manufacturers were able to establish unparalleled brand loyalty. For example, by sponsoring *The Chase and Sanborn Hour* (1929–1948), a little-known coffee rose to become a national leader in sales. Miracle Whip salad dressing was introduced in 1933; its manufacturer, Kraft Foods, promoted it in both major magazine campaigns and on the radio. *The Kraft Music Hall* (1934–1949) was hosted by the popular Bing Crosby for most of its years on the air. Within a decade, Kraft's Miracle Whip attained half the market for sandwich spreads.

In the late afternoons, children everywhere stopped what they were doing to listen to *Jack Armstrong, the All-American Boy*. From 1933 until 1951, Jack and his pals urged kids to "Just buy Wheaties / The best breakfast food in the land!" As a result, General Mills rose to become a leading cereal manufacturer. Pepsodent toothpaste likewise found a vast audience with its sponsorship of the enormously popular *Amos 'n Andy* from 1929 until 1939. Just before dropping *Amos 'n Andy,* the company started to underwrite *The Pepsodent Show Starring Bob Hope,* a relationship that lasted until the dawn of television. With two of the biggest programs on radio, Pepsodent stood as a major force in the competitive dental hygiene industry. Similar stories could be told about Jell-O, Lucky Strike cigarettes, Ovaltine, Pepsi-Cola, and a host of other products that came to be identified—and purchased—as a result of their association with network broadcasting.

As the 1930s progressed, radio commercials grew more blatant. The entire emphasis was on encouraging the listener to buy. Repetition,

BETTY CROCKER

Betty Crocker was invented in 1921 by the Washburn-Crosby Company (which later became General Mills) as the company symbol. She appeared as a nutrition expert in various kinds of print media. Her name was derived from the last name of a former company director, William G. Crocker, and "Betty," a popular first name of the time. Though she emerged in the 1920s, it was in the 1930s that she became most influential. General Mills found Betty Crocker did best on radio, so she soon had a regular radio show that, not incidentally, touted company products. The producers aimed the show at housewives, with Crocker paying a friendly visit to each listener's home and proffering advice on better homemaking. Listeners wrote letters to Crocker that "she" (an anonymous woman reading from a script in the studio) responded to on air. Other sponsors followed suit, and radio advisers became all the rage. These imaginary personalities were the symbolic representatives of large corporations.

Betty Crocker was finally given a face in 1936. Motherly, her hair streaked with a touch of gray, she was emblematic of good American cooking. Her countenance has continued to look out at consumers ever since; some eight makeovers later—sometimes younger, sometimes just a bit older—Betty Crocker still epitomizes motherhood and apple pie, especially if that pie is baked with Gold Medal Flour, a long-time staple in the General Mills pantry.

In the end, the popular Betty Crocker radio show addressed aspects of the Depression. It played on the air five times a week, and the sponsor, General Mills, saw to it that two of each week's broadcasts included menus and recipes oriented toward families on relief. It was a small gesture of recognition, but it nonetheless acknowledged that not everyone was participating in the American Dream of work and prosperity.

For more information see Charles Goodrum and Helen Dalrymple, *Advertising in America: The First 200 Years* (New York: Harry N. Abrams, Inc., 1990), 38–40.

music, and sound effects left little doubt about any brand name. Those attempting to assess the decade through commercial radio broadcasting would not realize that there was a major economic Depression affecting the country. But radio, after all, provided escapism, and that is the way the growing audience wanted it. What helped was that the announcer spoke directly to the listener, which fostered the illusion of intimacy. The listener got to know the announcer, a fact that broadcasters used to their advantage. Don Wilson (*The Jack Benny Program* and Lucky Strike cigarettes), Harlow Wilcox (*Fibber McGee and Molly* and Johnson's Wax), Harry Von Zell (*Eddie Cantor* and Pabst Blue Ribbon Beer), Ed Herlihy (*Kraft Music Hall* and Kraft foods), Westbrook Van Voorhis (*The March of Time* and *Time* magazine), and dozens of others emerged as celebrities, often becoming significant parts of shows, as well as spokesmen for the sponsors' products.

A sure way to enhance sales of new products was to have a memorable label or trademark. For instance, in 1921 the giant food processor General Mills created a corporate symbol and spokesperson in Betty Crocker. In 1936, the Minnesota Valley Canning Company went to a large New York advertising firm for advice on lagging sales. Out of that meeting came the Jolly Green Giant, another enduring icon in the annals of American marketing. Consumers liked the smiling giant (the fact that he was green never seemed to bother anyone) holding up equally huge corn and peas, and sales surged. Perhaps his sheer size suggested health and vitality—and he possessed echoes of the beloved Paul Bunyan, another wholly invented figure.

RACIST ADVERTISING

A number of American products, especially foods, have long used African Americans as part of their labeling: Cream of Wheat (hot cereal), Aunt Jemima (instant pancake mix), and Uncle Ben (rice products) are probably the best known. The racial stereotyping is obvious, right down to the demeaning use of "uncle" and "aunt." This carries over directly from the days of slavery and "Uncle Tom" and "Uncle Remus," drawing uncomfortable connections between race and servitude. For example, Rastus, the beaming chef on the Cream of Wheat label, creates an image of master and servant. Throughout the 1930s, print ads showed him serving white children steaming bowls of their favorite hot cereal. To be sure, images like these supported much of the racial stereotyping so rampant in the United States during the first half of the twentieth century.

Worse than the silent countenance of Rastus, however, was the written speech attributed to Aunt Jemima. In the November 1939 issue of *Good Housekeeping,* she said, "Don't you fret, Honey! Jus' feastify dem wif my pancakes!" And that same month, in the *Saturday Evening Post* she implored the reader to "Thrill yo' appetite wif' my down South treat!" The ads' hackneyed dialect thereby perpetuated the destructive image of the African American who spoke a minstrel-show form of English. Such egregious stereotyping was common in large-circulation, middle-class magazines during the 1930s, sometimes lasting until the 1950s.

Even products like chewing gum were sometimes advertised in demeaning ways. In a 1933 cartoon ad, Beech-Nut gum showed white adventurers (adult male, adolescent boy, and girl) getting captured by buffoonish black cannibals in what was supposed to be Africa. Only by dint of Beech-Nut gum and some silly magic tricks—the latter available for free, for only five outside wrappers—did they gain their freedom. The trio became honored tribal magicians in the process. This image of white superiority over bloodthirsty but ultimately childlike tribesmen is a sad commentary on the state of racial awareness and sensitivity in 1930s advertising.[5]

From these degrading advertisements it was a small step to the stereotyped antics of Eddie Anderson as "Rochester" on Jack Benny's radio show and the steady stream of dialect jokes on the tremendously popular *Amos 'n Andy.* This media cross-reinforcement of deeply ingrained cultural racism continued well beyond the thirties.

ADVERTISING AND SMOKING

Smoking was heavily advertised during the Depression years. Ads for Camel cigarettes touted the pleasures of smoking for women. As a rule, the person pictured with a cigarette was an attractive socialite; if upper-class women could openly smoke, then why not all women? For men and women alike, cigarettes signified urbanity and sophistication. They required little time and they were convenient. In fact, cigarettes were *streamlined*—they fit the imagery of the time. Other ads continued with a more traditional approach: men enjoying a male prerogative, often by themselves or in the company of other men.

In 1937, a national survey found that 95 percent of men smoked openly on the street, but only 28 percent thought women should have the same privilege. Those interviewed could find some support for their attitudes. Throughout the 1930s, most religious magazines continued to rail against women smoking at all. Tobacco use nevertheless continued its climb among both men and women throughout the decade. One example of the power of advertising, 66 percent of all men under 40 smoked during the 1930s, and 26 percent of women under 40 enjoyed cigarettes. More revealing, however, is another set of figures: 40 percent of men *over* 40 smoked, but only 9 percent of women *over* 40 smoked. Obviously, smoking was a generational custom, one that was promoted to the fashionable young and was fueled by the ceaseless ad campaigns that urged increased tobacco consumption.[6]

As the propriety of women's smoking grew, cigarette manufacturers faced the challenge of appealing to everyone. Should ads target both men and women, or should they create separate campaigns for each sex? For instance, the Marlboro brand was advertised from 1924 to 1954 as a sophisticated woman's cigarette. During the 1930s, Marlboros had an "ivory tip" and a red "beauty tip"; the latter was pushed because it showed no lipstick smears. In addition, Marlboros were touted as being "mild as May," hardly a slogan to appeal to a male audience. This approach had little effect on sales, and

Marlboros languished in the lower ranks of popularity until they became a "man's cigarette" in 1954. Conversely, Lucky Strikes claimed that they could help one avoid overeating: "When tempted, reach for a Lucky instead!" Even more feminized was the slogan "Reach for a Lucky instead of a sweet!" This ploy apparently worked; Lucky Strike was one of the leading brands of the decade. Another successful campaign was that mounted by Chesterfields. The company ran illustrations of women happily staring at men smoking and saying, "Blow Some My Way." This imaginative piece of prose first appeared in 1926 and was revived in 1931. With the growing proportion of younger women taking up smoking in the 1930s, these advertisements had obviously struck a chord.

Architecture

of the 1930s

The architectural and design word of the 1930s was Modernism, expressed as either Art Deco or Streamline Moderne. The style included items as diverse as buildings, automobiles, radio cabinets, fabric patterns, and kitchen china. In the turmoil of the 1930s, people viewed conventional art as stagnant. They embraced Modernism as the new symbol of the age.

ART DECO, STREAMLINING, AND MODERNITY

The chief characteristic of most modern design during the 1930s is the lack of ornament. Lines—both straight and curving, but always uncluttered—dominate. In many ways, the architects and designers of the period rebelled against the ornamentation of the Victorian and Edwardian eras, when applied decoration went to excess. This rebellion included many of the characteristic motifs of Art Deco, a modern style that had grown out of *L'Exposition Internationale des Arts Decoratifs et Industriels Modernes,* a lavish 1925 exhibition held in Paris. American architects and designers embraced much of Art Deco—the chevrons and jagged lightning bolts, the setback skyscrapers with their fantastical upper stories, and the extensive use of glass, mirrors, and plastics. But as the 1930s progressed, "Streamline Moderne" emerged and these flourishes were dismissed as mere indulgences. The streamline aesthetic was just that: smooth surfaces devoid of any adornments. The ovoid, or teardrop, shape was the essence of streamlining. It signified the age of the smooth-running, efficient machine.

Art Deco and the Streamline movements shared an affinity for geometric form, but generally the geometry in Streamline Moderne stood more abstract and less representational than Art Deco. Art Deco was essentially a substitution of machinelike decoration for more traditional motifs, evoking the spirit of mass production (stamping it out) and repetition (the assembly line).

Both Art Deco and Streamline Moderne style moved from high art into the everyday world of commercialism. With sales dwindling because of the depressed economy, manufacturers turned to industrial designers to sell more products. They fashioned "objects of desire," not necessarily essential things.

For instance, mass-produced streamlined salt and pepper shakers, finished in shiny chrome or stainless steel, paid homage to the silversmith. At the same time, they acknowledged the popularization of that tradition by their numbers and resultant low price. Architects and designers frequently rejected one-of-a-kind crafts and specialized works of art, and aimed at larger markets. The thirties

Art Deco at Chicago's Century of Progress. The 1933 exposition featured many buildings executed in the still-popular Art Deco tradition, as shown in this poster. Prints & Photographs Division, Library of Congress.

therefore witnessed the acceptance of the machine itself as art. The use of such mass-produced items in a traditional, or non-modern, house (Queen Anne, Colonial, Georgian, etc.) cut across all lines of tradition and class.

THE SKYSCRAPER

During the period 1929–1931, New Yorkers gawked while several Modernistic skyscrapers raced to completion, often at the rate of more than a story a day. Collectively, they would epitomize the last of the Roaring Twenties and, at the same time, the onset of a new decade.

Leading the contest was the Chrysler Building (1930; William Van Alen), a magnificent Art Deco tower clad in stainless steel and decorated with details symbolizing the giant automotive manufacturer. A few blocks away stood the emerging skeleton of the Empire State Building (1931; Shreve, Lamb & Harmon) with its sleek, vertical Art Deco styling. The two battled over the claim of being the "world's tallest building." The stately Woolworth Building, farther downtown, had held that distinction since 1913.

The Chrysler Building opened its doors first, but its 77 stories and 1,046-foot height were temporary titleholders. In 1931, the Empire State Building, at 102 stories and 1,250 feet, took the skyscraper honors that it would retain for the next 42 years. To accomplish this feat, it boasted a mooring mast for dirigibles. No lighter-than-air craft ever docked there, but the towering mast was altered and became the city's primary television antenna in 1951.[1]

Ironically, the completion of these two towers coincided with the onset of the Great Depression. They both opened to empty offices and "space available" signs, and wags pronounced the Empire State Building the "Empty State Building." Iconic as they are today, both buildings are relics, Art Deco masterpieces erected in a period that was in the process of rejecting that very style. The Crash hit the architectural and building professions hard: between 1929 and 1933, employment in the building trades fell 63 percent. In New York City alone, 85 percent of all architects were unemployed. Major construction initiatives like these two structures virtually disappeared in the economic woes of the Depression.[2]

THE INTERNATIONAL STYLE

For larger commercial and public buildings, it had only been a few years since the Neoclassical Revival was the rage in the United States. Architect John Russell Pope was commissioned to design the Jefferson Memorial in 1934 and the National Gallery of Art in 1937 in Washington, D.C., and

Empire State Building, 1931. Prints & Photographs Division, Library of Congress.

The steady emigration of architects from troubled Europe helped introduce fresh, modern tenets, and their American counterparts realized they would have to adapt to a new, more austere, linear approach to design. The Modernism of the 1930s was a marriage of art and industrial design. In 1932, historian Henry-Russell Hitchcock and architect Philip Johnson mounted an important show at New York's Museum of Modern Art called Modern Architecture. The exhibition displayed the work of several contemporary architects, most of them European, and identified their work as the International Style. The exhibit later traveled for almost two years and visited many American cities. Hitchcock and Johnson also wrote *The International Style: Architecture Since 1922* (1932), a seminal book that introduced many to these new design trends.

For the general public, the International Style could be summarized as austere, rectilinear buildings with wide expanses of plain walls, usually finished in white. The structures themselves were often done in concrete, with the upper stories sometimes cantilevered out over the basic foundations. Doors and windows lacked trim, and the effect was one of smoothness, a rejection of the traditional textures of stone, brick, and wood. Hitchcock and Johnson, in both their exhibition and book, argued that a building should be "honest"; it should be a reflection of itself and its underlying construction. It should not be disguised to fit an arbitrary style. By repudiating most decorative elements, the International Style opened the way for the unadorned glass-and-steel skyscrapers that would characterize much of American commercial architecture for the remainder of the twentieth century. The hubcaps and hood ornaments of the Art Deco Chrysler Building, beloved by generations of onlookers, were declared passé even as the building opened its doors.

One of the first major structures to reflect the new style was the Philadelphia Savings Fund Society (PSFS) building, erected in 1932 in the heart of downtown Philadelphia. Its lower portion, with stainless steel cladding and rounded corners, is clearly inspired by European Modernism. Jointly designed by the American George Howe and the Swiss émigré William Lescaze, the PSFS building shed existing traditions and boldly proclaimed

most people found his traditional, classical designs appropriate. At the same time, the effects of both industrialization and politics challenged the insularity of architecture across the country.

itself in the International Style. Not everyone embraced the International Style. Art Deco still had some important adherents who particularly admired its use of freely applied ornamentation. In addition, the world of industrial design was opening up new vistas with flowing, streamlined shapes that were being called "Moderne." Thus the stark austerity of the International Style had limited appeal.

The Depression and World War II slowed the skyscraper revolution, but the daring buildings erected during the 1930s probably had more impact on how Americans perceived Modernism than any paintings or sculptures created at the same time.[3]

FRANK LLOYD WRIGHT

During all this tumult, Frank Lloyd Wright (1867–1959), who continued as the dean of American architects, was uncharacteristically quiet. In the public's eye, his career had floundered somewhat during the later 1920s, and he had been relegated to "grand old man" status. He was 65 when the PSFS building went up in 1932, and no one expected any new statements to be coming from him. True to form, he surprised everyone.

Between 1935 and 1937, Wright designed one of the finest, most distinctive homes ever built in the United States. In a daring series of cantilevered reinforced concrete slabs projecting through and over a mountain creek in the forested mountains east of Pittsburgh, Wright took the "less is more" credo of the Internationalists and erected the Kaufmann House at Bear Run, Pennsylvania, more popularly known as "Fallingwater." Although Wright was unusually outspoken in his criticism of the European Modernists and their effects on design during the twenties and thirties, Fallingwater is in many respects a tip of the hat to their influence. He had the gray concrete painted white, the favorite hue of the day for modern houses. Further, he employed contemporary technology as easily as any Modernist architect, and he eschewed applied decoration. But Wright married Fallingwater to its precipitous terrain; in much architecture of the 1930s, the natural environment was ignored, even leveled. For too many, the machine—technology—overcame nature; for

Fallingwater, 1939. This photo was taken as part of the Library of Congress's Historic American Building Survey (HABS) documentation project, which began in 1933 as a cooperative venture among the National Parks Service, Library of Congress, and private sector to document significant American buildings. Prints & Photographs Division, Library of Congress.

Wright, ever the iconoclast and lover of the natural world, the site was one with the house. He neither altered nor ignored anything.

Fallingwater, a building that demonstrates the potential of modern architecture, has become one of Wright's best-known and best-loved works. It is not cold and academic, as are too many modern efforts. Although it can be seen as a linked series of abstract forms, the effect it has on viewers is one of warmth and human scale.

Back in the limelight with Fallingwater, Wright moved on to other achievements during the period. In the Johnson Wax offices (1936–1939) in Racine, Wisconsin, he based his design on the latest trends in streamlining and made them the focus of his plan. Borrowing from the popular industrial designers of the day, Wright created tubular metal furniture on the main floor that echoed the circles of light and concrete directly above the heads of the workers. Instead of being threatening, the design was bright and airy, creating a most pleasant working environment. For the modern world, Wright attempted to equate the workplace with a spiritual experience, just as the cathedral did in the past.

Responding to a 1938 challenge from *Life* magazine to design a small, inexpensive residence, Wright closed out the decade working on his concept of the Usonian house. The word "Usonian" was his creation, taking the abbreviation of "*United States*" and indicating a kind of broad agrarianism for urban people. Like his earlier Prairie Houses, these buildings were rectilinear in design. All unnecessary elements were eliminated through technological innovation and standardized materials. Although only a few were built, the Usonian homes presaged the enormously popular ranch houses of the 1950s. (See Architecture of the 1950s.) It could fairly be said that one of Wright's major accomplishments was not imitating the Modernists, but taking their concepts and motifs and making them uniquely his own.

MASS HOUSING

The need for shelter among average people may have been low on the professional agenda, but housing was an important component of New Deal policies. As a result, the Roosevelt administration focused on planning the financial aspects of housing rather than the architectural ones.

New Deal planners envisioned a series of subsistence homesteads and greenbelt towns in an effort to provide better housing for people of moderate means. They also worked to create, through the Public Works Administration (PWA), over 40 housing projects for low income families. Idealistic in intent, but flawed in execution, this last effort unfortunately made the term "projects" a charged one, usually negative. Architecturally, none of these worthy attempts displayed much distinction, and the profession itself tended to ignore them.

Little truly Modernist housing was erected during the Depression years, and most of that went unseen by the general public. The 1933 Chicago World's Fair, or "Century of Progress," did display two futuristic homes designed by George Fred Keck. His House of Tomorrow and Crystal House elicited some public enthusiasm, but it was mainly limited to the exposition. His designs demonstrated the potential of mass-producing homes just like any other machine-made product, but neither consumers nor the housing industry seemed particularly interested in exploring the subject. Where their residences were concerned, Americans continued to prefer traditional design and construction.

The lack of innovation was only part of a larger problem. In the early 1930s, housing starts declined by 90 percent, which translates nationally to 937,000 new units in 1925 and only 84,000 in 1933. The residential landscape therefore consisted of older homes, not new ones. In addition, in 1933 over 1.5 million homes were in default or in the process of foreclosure.[4]

Most middle-class Americans continued living in traditional houses throughout the decade. The money they invested in their dwellings was at some risk, but the Federal Home Loan Bank Act of 1932 stabilized many of the tottering savings and loan associations that held mortgages. Two years later, the Federal Housing Act gave active support to the housing industry. It issued 20-year mortgages with low down payments. Chronic unemployment and decreased wages, however, made it impossible for many to build or buy. A housing shortage grew throughout the depression. By the end of the decade, only 41 percent of Americans owned their homes.[5]

Some good things did emerge from the depressed building market. In an attempt to keep construction prices low, manufacturers came up with products like prefabricated door and window units, exterior-grade (i.e., weather-resistant) plywood, improved drywall, and better glues and caulking. Wall paneling was also introduced, and Knotty Pine became a best seller for those who could afford it and wanted a Colonial look in their decor.

PERIOD REVIVALS

In 1931, the American Institute of Interior Decorators (now the American Society of Interior

Decorators) was formed, reflecting the growing interest in applied design. But this group, and others like it, was also concerned with historical accuracy in the many revival movements gaining interest in the country. Colonial Williamsburg opened to the public in 1932, providing added impetus for the group's aim of accurate preservation. Specialty magazines with titles like *The Decorator's Digest* (1932) and *The Interior Decorator* (1934) found a ready audience. A small fad for the authentic "early American" look ensued; an open fireplace, a replica spinning wheel, and the cobbler's bench as coffee table became the style.

The number of professional interior decorators swelled in the United States during the 1920s and 1930s. Many were women, often from upper-class backgrounds. Mainstream women's magazines, such as *House & Garden* and *Better Homes and Gardens,* featured their work and ideas. Large, influential department stores like Wanamaker's, Marshall Field, Macy's, Lord & Taylor, and B. Altman included the latest in interior decorating trends in their furniture and accessory displays.

The movement toward a simpler, more secure, past remained in vogue throughout the thirties. It dominated American domestic architecture, and the resultant styles were called "period revivals." By and large, the favorites were Colonial, Tudor, and Spanish Revival. Quaintness and eclecticism were important, regardless of the actual style.

Antiquing became a major pursuit, and Sunday drives were often dedicated to finding bits of Americana in out-of-the-way places. Factory reproductions of old things—spinning wheels, deacon's benches, high-boys, wagon wheels, and such—sold well, particularly if they were done in Colonial Maple, genuine or not.

GAS STATIONS

The period revival trend even influenced common businesses such as gas stations. The favorite design for a new station during much of the 1920s and 1930s was a modification of a standard house or cottage plan, with a canopy extending out over the pump(s). Two oil companies, Pure and Phillips, introduced imitations of traditional, steeply pitched English cottages for their stations during the 1920s. By the early 1930s, almost 7,000 of these period structures were sprinkled throughout the mainland, largely in the Midwest. Their success led to Colonial, Georgian, Mission, and even Asian-style stations. The thirties also witnessed a proliferation of vernacular structures—lighthouses, giant oilcans, ice-bergs, tepees, coffeepots, windmills—that competed for highway attention.

Texaco hired Walter Dorwin Teague, a respected modern designer, to create a generic station in 1937. The result was the classic International version, complete with white-porcelained enamel steel tiles. In a similar vein, several other designers worked with the lowly gas station during the Depression. Raymond Loewy produced plans for both Shell and Union Oil prototypes, as did Norman Bel Geddes for Mobilgas. Although all the designs were quite modern, none of them survived beyond the drawing board.[6]

FAIRS AND EXPOSITIONS

The changes in architecture in the 1930s were displayed at the two World's Fairs during the decade: the Chicago World's Fair (1933–1934) and the New York World's Fair (1939–1940). These expositions presented markedly different architectural forms.

Although mired in the depression, Chicago responded to hosting the fair. The Windy City was the "City of the Big Shoulders…Building, breaking, rebuilding," so said poet Carl Sandburg, and thus the city fathers planned for the "Century of Progress." Across 400 acres of marshes along Lake Michigan arose a fantasy metropolis not unlike Hollywood's Emerald City in the *Wizard of Oz* (1939). The exposition served as a testament to Art Deco in American architectural design. Its theme was "Advancement through Technology," personifying optimism in the face of economic challenges.

Chicago's exposition opened in May 1933. Originally planned for only one year, officials held the fair over for a second record-breaking season, finally closing in late summer 1934. Unlike most ventures of this kind, it made a profit. It was the largest show of its kind up until then, and it served as the perfect antidote to the dreariness of the Depression. More than 20 million people flocked to the fair.

Architecture

Poster for the 1933–1934 Chicago World's Fair, showing the fairgrounds with the Chicago skyline. Prints & Photographs Division, Library of Congress.

The Trylon and Perisphere, the official symbols of the 1939 New York World's Fair, in an exciting poster depicting the sleek, streamlined celebration of modernity. Prints & Photographs Division, Library of Congress.

The towering Hall of Science reinforced the idea that here, truly, was the future. Its working models of new technological devices were fascinating, and an aerial tour via the Sky Ride, a 1930s version of the monorail, took the daring above the fairgrounds.

Special trains were run to Chicago from across the continent. Eventually, the sleek cars and engines of the Union Pacific's City of Salina and the Burlington Line's Pioneer Zephyr became parts of the displays. The Pioneer Zephyr established a speed record, reaching Chicago from Denver—a distance of just over 1,000 miles—in 13 hours, traveling at 77.6 mph.[7]

The New York World's Fair was the spectacle of the decade from its Spring 1939 opening until its Autumn 1940 closing. Not even the German invasion of Poland in September 1939 forced it

closed. Located on over 1,200 reclaimed acres, the entire extravaganza was laid out in "zones," an idea much in vogue at the time. The Long Island Rail Road delivered fairgoers to an ultramodern terminal where Greyhound buses, designed by the renowned Raymond Loewy, ferried around the fair's over 65 miles of paved streets and footpaths. Cool, white fluorescent tubes bathed the event in light, the first large-scale public demonstration of that form of lighting.

The most distinguished designers and architects of the era worked at the fair, underwritten by the nation's corporate might. In many ways, the New York World's Fair symbolized the marriage between industry and the arts. An official stated goal of the extravaganza sought to bring together architecture and commerce, to show that modernity, industrial design, and popular culture could coexist. As a result, virtually nothing escaped commercialization. Over 25,000 different items bore the official imprint of the fair, ranging from Heinz pickles to a pin proclaiming "Time for Saraka," a popular laxative. There was even an official song of the fair, "Dawn of a New Day," penned by George and Ira Gershwin and recorded by several leading bands.

In many ways the fair celebrated the American automobile. General Motors, Ford, and Chrysler had enormous exhibits. "Futurama," General Motors' vast network of miniature buildings, highways, and motor vehicles, enthralled over 10 million visitors, and proved to be the most popular attraction. Created by architect Albert Kahn and designer Norman Bel Geddes, Futurama displayed a technological landscape circa 1960, including 500,000 model buildings and 50,000 cars, some 10,000 of which actually moved. The automobile dominated GM's utopia, a rather accurate prognostication.

Automotive culture served as the fair's major element, with streamlining as its primary motif.

The Golden Gate Bridge under construction. Prints & Photographs Division, Library of Congress.

It represented leaving the roughhewn past behind for a sleek, smooth future. Streamlining thus became an economic metaphor. A sticky economy gave way to a frictionless one; urbanity replaced rusticity. With the aid of consumer engineering,

GOLDEN GATE BRIDGE

The Golden Gate Bridge spans 1.2 miles over the San Francisco Bay, stretching from San Francisco to Marin County, California. At the time of its construction, the Golden Gate was the longest suspension bridge in existence and one of the largest engineering feats in history. The idea to span the bay was first suggested in the nineteenth century, when the only method of crossing was by ferry. It wasn't until the 1920s, however, that San Francisco City Engineer Michael M. O'Shaughnessy launched the idea in motion, inviting some of the era's leading engineers to submit proposals for a bridge. The contract was won by engineer Joseph Strauss, who believed that the bridge could be built for an estimated $25 million.

Construction began on January 5, 1933, and consisted of a long-term project to excavate more than 3.25 million cubic feet of dirt to make space for anchorages. Construction on the central portions of the bridge was dangerous and difficult, and 11 workers were killed in construction accidents. In June 1936, the engineering team decided to add the most extensive safety feature in the history of bridge building—a giant net slung under the construction site at a cost of over $130,000. Nineteen workers fell from the bridge scaffolding and were saved by the net, becoming members of the informal group known as the Halfway to Hell Club. The bridge was completed in 1937, at more than $1 million under the original budget. The city opened the bridge to the public on May 27, 1937, and more than 18,000 people gathered to be the first to cross the bridge in their own unique ways, including roller skates, backwards, and on stilts. After a week of celebration called the "Golden Gate Bridge Fiesta," the bridge was opened to automobile traffic. In 1994, the American Society of Civil Engineers named the Golden Gate Bridge one of the Seven Wonders of the Modern World.

people flocked to carefully designed products that symbolized the end of drudgery. Citizens faced a materialistic future filled with new appliances and the blessings of industry.

Overlooking the fair were the Trylon and Perisphere, the official symbols of the event. The name Trylon, a 728-foot needle-like pyramid, was derived from a *tri*angle and a p*ylon*. The Perisphere beside the Trylon was a 180-foot-diameter hollow sphere. Inside was "Democracity," a vast model of the utopian city of tomorrow. Conceived and designed by Henry Dreyfuss, "Democracity" gave visitors a glimpse of an ordered, prosperous future with its workers marching with automaton-like precision.

DESIGN

The 1920s and the 1930s presented a problem for American design, both interior and architectural. The bold ideas of Art Deco were fresh and new in the 1920s, but in the 1930s they were beginning to seem passé. How an item looked was as important as how well it functioned: enter industrial design. The smooth, machine-like Streamline Moderne was supplanting Art Deco, and the flood of European designers and architects to the United States in the years preceding World War II meant the International Style was also gaining new adherents. In this way the Depression decade proved itself a time of change in the decorative arts, a period when a number of products were destined to become icons in American consumer culture.

Norman Bel Geddes

Norman Bel Geddes (1893–1958) first made a name for himself in stage design, and although he would design television studios in the 1950s, in the thirties he moved from the theater to commercial and industrial art. In 1932, Bel Geddes published *Horizons,* a visionary book in which he applied streamlining to transportation, housing, and everyday products and prophesied that streamlined shapes would eventually be applied to radios, furniture, cars, and other everyday objects, thereby changing the way the average person viewed the material world. Bel Geddes's drawings

revealed ships with torpedo shapes and airplanes that resembled flying wings with teardrop pontoons. These ideas were echoed in Chrysler's 1934 Airflow, an automobile ahead of its time. Taken together, *Horizons,* the Airflow, and Bel Geddes's designs with Albert Kahn at the Futurama exhibits at the New York World's Fair in 1939 made Bel Geddes the popular spokesman for the future.

The Chrysler Airflow

Thanks to an almost unlimited advertising budget, wide brand recognition, a far-flung chain of dealerships, and—most importantly—a relatively low sticker price, the Chrysler Airflow line generated a lot of interest. The Airflow's headlights appeared to blend in smoothly with the flow of the chassis. A roundly sloping hood and a swept-back windshield, along with some chrome detailing, completed the emphasis on streamlined design. Beneath the sheet metal, however, was merely a 1934 Chrysler, a rather staid automobile that had undergone few real changes. By no stretch of the imagination, then, could the Airflows be considered great commercial successes. After an initial flurry of interest and sales, the public looked elsewhere. Chrysler was nonetheless preparing consumers for the direction automotive design would take for the remainder of the decade.

Indeed, the Airflow brought about a new approach to automotive marketing. Instead of being perceived as utilitarian vehicles, American cars increasingly became design statements, rather than being perceived as strictly utilitarian. This change in conceptual thinking was not limited to expensive brands, or to small manufacturers offering only two or three custom models; it permeated the industry, and Detroit was frequently the leader, not the follower.

Since streamlining was the vogue in design during the 1930s, it was only natural that the automobile industry would become part of this movement. Art Deco, so important in the twenties and early thirties, was not well suited to industrial design, especially transportation. Its emphasis on angularity and verticality was ideal for architecture but worked poorly when translated to airplanes, trains, ocean liners, and cars. Thus the gradual shift to Streamline Moderne and its stress on the imagery of speed played well with automobile manufacturers. A sleek, forward-looking car suggested much more to a receptive public than a traditional boxy auto ever could.

Unfortunately, the recession that struck the country in 1937 doomed the pioneering Airflow. With sales lagging, Chrysler faced financial difficulties and withdrew its precedent-setting cars in 1937, to focus on more traditional models. Ironically, the last years of the decade saw many other auto manufacturers incorporate streamline qualities into their products, so the demise of the Airflows did not belittle their ultimate impact. New design treatments became the rule throughout the industry. Streamlined buses, trucks, and automobiles were becoming commonplace by the late 1930s, and they underwent subtle changes with each model year.

The innovative designers behind the Airflow brought acceptance of the concept of "planned obsolescence." In each successive model of a product, improvements were loudly proclaimed. Although such changes usually signified little more than cosmetic additions, the growing consumer market responded by eagerly buying the newest models, convinced that this year's model was somehow better than last year's. More often than not, the changes consisted of altering the exterior housing of the interior workings, a strategy that continues to the present day.

Henry Dreyfuss

One of Norman Bel Geddes's students in stage design was Henry Dreyfuss (1904–1972). Like his mentor, Dreyfuss worked with a number of theatrical productions until 1935, when he went to work for AT&T and created the cradle telephone of 1937. It stands as one of his most memorable and widely used creations. The basic black dial model remained the standard until 1950, when it was replaced by yet another Dreyfuss design.

His crowning achievement, however, was the 20th Century Limited, the great streamlined train of 1938. So thorough was Dreyfuss, he even designed the tableware and matchbook covers used in the passenger cars. The train's

CEDRIC GIBBONS

In Hollywood, Cedric Gibbons (1893–1960) of Metro-Goldwyn-Mayer was one of the great proponents of Modernist design. He created luxurious sets that incorporated all the motifs of both Art Deco and the Moderne movement: shiny floors, tubular chrome furniture, mirrors, and polished black surfaces. He was certainly one of the most visible designers, since millions saw his sets on the screen in movie after movie. Gibbons was also responsible for one of the most enduring icons of Hollywood: the famous Academy Award statuette, the Oscar.

RUSSEL WRIGHT

Ohio-born Russel Wright (1904–1976) was more an artist-craftsman than a designer. With no relation to architect Frank Lloyd Wright both genetically and aesthetically, he gravitated toward the commonplace, particularly household objects. Although he was less interested in industrial design than some of his contemporaries, he was a pioneer in bringing stylish plastic and aluminum serving accessories into the American kitchen, recognizing as he did an evolving servantless society and designing objects to accompany such informality. His creations were meant to go directly from the stove to the table.

A versatile man, Wright was happy creating anything from flatware to furniture. In the latter area, he is also credited with inventing the sectional sofa. His 1935 Modern Living line became quite popular, especially in blonde woods. The manufacturer linked Wright's name to the furniture in advertisements, making him well known to the public during the 1930s. He followed the Modern Living pieces with his American Modern Dinnerware, a line of ceramics that came in a variety of stylish colors, such as Seafoam Blue, Granite Grey, Chartreuse Curry, and Bean Brown, and that could be mixed or matched, another first. American Modern was introduced at the New York World's Fair.

For more information see C. Ray Smith, *Interior Design in 20th-Century America: A History* (New York: Harper and Row, 1987), 124, 224–227.

sleek, torpedo shape suggested to any and all that here was a *fast* train. Gone were the protruding stack, the ungainly cowcatcher, and all the other accoutrements usually associated with a steam locomotive. Even the coal tender immediately behind the engine was encased in a smooth metal skin.[8]

Not to be outdone, the Pennsylvania Railroad contracted the equally esteemed Raymond Loewy to design an all-new Broadway Limited. He undertook the project with zest, creating a streamlined vision of chrome, plastics, Formica, and coordinated colors. The Pullman Company, famous for generations of railroad cars, built both trains, and mainstream magazines devoted pages and pictures to each. These trains represented an engineered future of speed and luxury, not one of delays and canceled runs.

Books

Newspapers, Magazines, and Comics of the 1930s

Throughout the decade, unemployment would not go away. For many leisure time was a burden because it emphasized their loss of work. For others leisure time meant the freedom to read. Indeed, the print media enjoyed large audiences throughout the 1930s: publishers put out books in great quantities, new magazines appeared, and newspaper readership remained strong.

BOOKS

Best Sellers

In the 1930s, best-seller status meant that a book sold over 1 million copies, usually within a year. Many succeeded, despite the economic downturn. In those days, virtually all books were available only in hardbound editions. Cheaper paperback reprints did not become a major force in American publishing until 1939 with the founding of Pocket Books. (See Books, Newspapers, Magazines, and Comics of the 1940s.)

An overriding theme of escapism ran through many of the popular books of the decade. Almost half the best-selling novels of the period 1930–1939 were detective stories. Works with exotic locales and historical settings were also strong contenders, with about a quarter of the best sellers fitting into that broad category. Erskine Caldwell

(1903–1987), a writer of earthy tales about the South, carved out a particular genre for himself with three big sellers (*Tobacco Road,* 1932; *God's Little Acre,* 1933; and *Journeyman,* 1935), but he pales in comparison to a certain pair of detective novelists, Ellery Queen and Erle Stanley Gardner.

Ellery Queen was actually the pen name of two cousins, Frederic Dannay (1905–1982) and Manfred B. Lee (1905–1971). They began their joint career in the 1920s and wrote best sellers in the 1930s and 1940s with titles like *The Dutch Shoe Mystery* (1931), *The Egyptian Cross Mystery* (1932), and *The Chinese Orange Mystery* (1934). Their stories were tales of detection, with little violence beyond the mandatory murder that sets the case in motion.

Even more impressive was the accomplishment of Erle Stanley Gardner (1889–1970). Gardner, who wrote over 80 mysteries, created the character of Perry Mason, a resourceful lawyer/ detective who never lost a case, no matter the odds. The first Perry Mason book, *The Case of the Velvet Claws,* appeared in 1933, launching the author's career. In the 1930s alone, he wrote 24 detective novels under his own name, and one under the pseudonym A. A. Fair. In sheer sales, Gardner stood as the best-selling writer of the period. Perry Mason became a character known to virtually everyone, whether through the novels themselves or through six feature films: *The Case of the Howling Dog* (1934), *The Case of the Curious Bride* (1935), *The Case of the Lucky Legs* (1935), *The Case of the Velvet Claws* (1936), *The Case of the Black Cat* (1936), and *The Case of the Stuttering Bishop* (1937).[1]

Not everything written in the 1930s dealt with detectives. Four of the decade's top-selling novels focused on history and a sense of place and continuity. In each the land provides roots and belonging. *God's Little Acre* (Erskine Caldwell, 1933), *Gone with the Wind* (Margaret Mitchell, 1936), *The Good Earth* (Pearl S. Buck, 1931), and *The Grapes of Wrath* (John Steinbeck, 1939) told huge audiences that it was of utmost importance to establish a connection to the land. Being out of touch with one's heritage caused destruction.

Nobody told that story better than Margaret Mitchell (1900–1949). A reporter for the *Atlanta Journal,* Mitchell began *Gone with the Wind* in 1926, ostensibly for her own amusement. The story of Scarlett O'Hara, Rhett Butler, and Tara (Scarlett's family home) grew to become part of the national memory. A tale of how people beset with calamity overcame disaster, the story fit the Depression era. The closing words of the novel, spoken by the Scarlett, seemed to many a prescription for all the problems of the time: "I'll think of it all tomorrow.... After all, tomorrow is another day."[2]

By the end of the decade, the book had numerous reprintings, was available in a variety of translations, and continued to sell briskly. In 1939, three years after the book's initial publication, the movie version electrified audiences, becoming one of the greatest films Hollywood ever turned out, while remaining a faithful adaptation of the novel.

Other writers also successfully tackled historical events in fiction. Writers like Pearl S. Buck (*The Good Earth,* 1931), Charles Nordhoff and James Norman Hall (*Mutiny on the Bounty,* 1932), and Hervey Allen (*Anthony Adverse,* 1933) achieved success in this area. Walter D. Edmonds (*Drums Along the Mohawk,* 1936) and Kenneth Roberts (*Northwest Passage,* 1937) continued with romantic narratives about the American past, a topic that grew in popularity throughout the troubled

Margaret Mitchell holding her book *Gone With the Wind,* 1938. Prints & Photographs Division, Library of Congress.

decade. Hollywood made big-budget movies of all these novels, capitalizing on their fame at the time.

Some writers attempted to speak more directly about the Depression. James T. Farrell (1904–1979) took a decidedly anti-capitalist view in his naturalistic *Studs Lonigan* trilogy (1932–1935). John Dos Passos (1896–1970) wrote from an openly Marxist point of view in his trilogy *USA* (1930–1936). Their work has come down to the present as significant contributions to American literature, but they were hardly best sellers. John Steinbeck (1902–1968) trod proletarian ground in *In Dubious Battle* (1936), and then returned to some of those themes in 1939 with his hugely

NOTABLE BOOKS

The Secret of the Old Clock (the first Nancy Drew book), Carolyn Keene (1930)

The Good Earth, Pearl S. Buck (1931)

Little House in the Big Woods, Laura Ingalls Wilder (1932)

Mutiny on the Bounty, Charles Nordhoff and James Norman Hall (1932)

Tobacco Road, Erskine Caldwell (1932)

The Case of the Velvet Claws, Erle Stanley Gardner (1933)

The Thin Man, Dashiell Hammett (1933)

Goodbye, Mr. Chips, James Hilton (1934)

Murder on the Orient Express, Agatha Christie (1934)

How to Win Friends and Influence People, Dale Carnegie (1936)

Gone with the Wind, Margaret Mitchell (1936)

Of Mice and Men, John Steinbeck (1937)

The Hobbit, J.R.R. Tolkien (1937)

Grapes of Wrath, John Steinbeck (1939)

successful *The Grapes of Wrath.* In fact, *The Grapes of Wrath* is one of the few books critical of the American political and economic system ever to achieve widespread popular success.

Nonfiction

In nonfiction, relatively few books written about the Depression, the New Deal, or the impending war sold well. Self-help, biographies, memoirs, travel books, and cookbooks seemed to rule the day.

In 1936 Dale Carnegie (1888–1955) brought out *How to Win Friends and Influence People,* a book that outlined easy steps for achieving the title's promise. *Reader's Digest* condensed his work that same year. With this tie-in, the book remained in print throughout most of the remainder of the century, achieving sales in excess of 10 million copies.

Book Clubs

For fiction and nonfiction alike, there were book clubs, led by the Book-of-the-Month Club (organized in 1926) and the Literary Guild (founded in 1927), both of which flourished during the 1930s. With large membership lists, these organizations caused many books that otherwise might have languished to achieve best-seller status. Both clubs were attacked by literary snobs for lowering tastes and moving toward homogenization in literature. "Standardization" became a negative rallying cry for those opposed to any broadening of the readership base. Standardization or not, the huge print runs for book-club editions could be more than 75,000 copies for titles by the most popular authors. They may have played to a mass audience, but the clubs were often the difference between success and disappointment for writers.

Federal Writers Project

Many writers found the Depression difficult. Fortunately, the government organized the Federal Writers Project (FWP) in 1935 as a method of providing meaningful work for otherwise unemployed authors. During its peak year, 1936, the FWP employed some 6,500 writers. They ranged from second-string reporters to prominent, published authors down on their luck. In fact, only about 10 percent qualified as working professionals when they were enlisted in the program.

From the beginning, Henry Alsberg, who oversaw the program, decreed that fiction was to be avoided. It was simply too open to criticism and misinterpretation to be underwritten by the government. Taking the safe road, the group began the task of creating a series of guidebooks to the nation, an effort that culminated with the *American Guide* series, a set of 53 volumes that described all the states and regions of the country.

The *American Guides* provided exhaustive coverage. From folklore to ecology, the guides gave polished commentaries on the true state of the union during the late 1930s. Since most of the writers remained anonymous, appropriate credit for well-crafted writing could not be assigned accurately, but the consistent quality of the undertaking demonstrated that professionals were doing the work. By salvaging crumbling documents and locating long-lost records, the project helped preserve elements of American history that might otherwise have been lost.[3]

MAGAZINES

General Magazines

There were over 3,000 periodicals during the 1930s, but fewer than 100 titles reached a large, diverse audience. Instead, most targeted small, selected audiences. When the decade began, national magazine circulation stood at approximately 80 million; by 1940, it was close to 100 million. People continued to read and subscribe to magazines despite the crisis.

Ironically, although most mass market periodicals survived the economic turmoil, a few have since fallen by the wayside. In general, popular or

Cosmopolitan, promising both glamour and a short story by Ernest Hemingway. Prints & Photographs Division, Library of Congress.

mass magazines depended on continuing reader loyalty and advertising revenues for survival. During the 1930s, the *Saturday Evening Post* (founded 1821; ceased weekly publication 1969), *Ladies' Home Journal* (1883), *Good Housekeeping* (1885), *Cosmopolitan* (1886), *Collier's* (1888; ceased publication 1957), *Vogue* (1892), *House Beautiful* (1896), *Redbook* (1902), *Better Homes and Gardens* (1922), *Reader's Digest* (1922), and *Time* (1923) were among the survivors, enjoying both numerous readers and substantial advertising volume.

On the other hand, some notable American magazines disappeared. Sentiment could not keep them afloat. Thus *Scribner's* (later called *The Century*; 1870–1930), *The Smart Set* (1900–1930), *Vanity Fair* (1913–1936), *Literary Digest* (1890–1938), and the oldest of them all, *The North American Review* (1815–1939), were among the many journals that saw their last issues during the 1930s.

Many new titles came into being during these turbulent years. Such well-known periodicals as *Advertising Age* (1930), *Fortune* (1930), *Broadcasting* (1931), *Family Circle* (1932), *Esquire* (1933), *Newsweek* (1933), *U.S. News & World Report* (1933), *Bride's Magazine* (free handout prior to becoming a full-fledged periodical in 1934), *Mademoiselle* (1935), *Yankee* (1935), *Consumer Reports* (1936), *Life* (1936; ceased weekly publication 1972), *Look* (1937–1971), *Popular Photography* (1937), *Woman's Day* (1937, which began

NEW MAGAZINES

Advertising Age, 1930

Fortune, 1930

Family Circle, 1932

Esquire, 1933

Newsweek, 1933

U.S. News & World Report, 1933

Bride's Magazine, 1934

Mademoiselle, 1935

Consumer Reports, 1936

Life, 1936

Woman's Day, 1937

as *A&P Menu Sheet*), *U.S. Camera* (1938), and *Glamour* (1939) were founded at this time. All survived the decade.

Saturday Evening Post

The giant among popular American magazines of the 1930s was the *Saturday Evening Post*. In each issue, this large-format weekly offered a mix of fact and fiction, lots of photographs and illustrations, many features, often a cover by the renowned artist Norman Rockwell, and pages of advertising (more in good economic times, fewer in bad)—the lifeblood of the magazine. The *Saturday Evening Post* ran over 200 short stories a year; unlike today, many magazines ran stories during the period, and the industry as a whole published some 1,000 fiction pieces annually.

George Horace Lorimer (1867–1937) served as the magazine's editor for many years. He had joined the *Post* in 1898, became acting editor in 1899, and assumed full command shortly thereafter. By the Great Crash of 1929, the *Saturday Evening Post* was the unchallenged carrier of an American vision of opportunity and prosperity. The stock market debacle did little to change that view—at least from the *Post's* perspective. Lorimer and his associates worked hard at presenting an endless, uplifting variety of historical romances, sports yarns, westerns, and urban tales with businessman heroes, along with nonfiction success stories that would have made Horatio Alger proud.

The magazine's huge subscription list suggests that many readers wanted a continuation of that success-oriented vision; in 1929 the *Post* sold nearly 3 million copies a week, a figure that dropped only slightly during the next decade, making it the undisputed leader of American magazines. Lorimer was steadfastly opposed to President Roosevelt and his policies, but that opposition had little impact on subscribers, who voted for Roosevelt and the New Deal.[4]

Advertisers eyed the subscription numbers and saw a true mass audience. Since the magazine had national distribution, it served as a marketplace for products available everywhere. The *Post* pioneered the standardization of consumer wants, and most of its ad copy reflected this unification of the buying public. Even in the depths of the Depression, nationally known products were displayed in the pages of the *Saturday Evening Post.*

Reader's Digest

Reader's Digest also flourished during the 1930s. Founded in 1922 by DeWitt and Lila Wallace (1889–1981 and 1889–1984 respectively), the familiar, purse-sized anthology of condensed articles circulated about 250,000 copies a month in 1930. By the end of the decade, the figure swelled to 4 million. Such extraordinary success grew out of the content of the monthly: like the *Saturday Evening Post,* the *Digest* celebrated the American way of life, a robustly conservative and insular view that argued for hard work, family, and common sense.

People liked the *Digest's* message; that the magazine boiled books and articles down to their basic content added to its appeal. Plus, the *Digest* titillated its readers with slightly suggestive jokes and articles that included sex. Never off-color, the *Reader's Digest* nonetheless kept the subject of sex before its growing audience, and no one seemed offended.

In order to find articles appropriate to the magazine's ideology, editors at the *Digest* culled a rather narrow range of publications. Not surprisingly, the *Saturday Evening Post* was one of them, as were such lesser-known (but equally conservative) journals as the *North American Review, McClure's,* and *Forum.* Often, the articles excerpted for publication in the *Digest* were "plants": pieces placed by the editors in other publications for later inclusion in the *Digest.* In this way, the *Reader's Digest* fostered the illusion that it was being selective, choosing only the best from a range of magazines.

In 1931, the *Digest* introduced unsigned, original articles in its contents, which became so successful that signed authorship took over by 1933. During the mid-1930s, half the magazine consisted of such materials. Even though these commissioned pieces tended to reinforce the philosophy of the Wallaces, the public received them enthusiastically. The chatty, upbeat writing, along with the jokes, features ("My Most Unforgettable Character," "Life in These United States," and others), and tidbits of folk wisdom kept attracting more readers. Despite its success, the *Digest* remained a bare-bones magazine. Simple line illustrations did not appear until 1939. The magazine did not introduce advertising until 1955. Prior to that, the *Digest* had relied on subscriptions and newsstand sales alone, believing that advertisements might compromise the content of the magazine and its relationship with both readers and contributors.[5]

Life and Look

A major figure in American journalistic history is Henry R. Luce (1898–1967). In 1923 he created *Time* magazine, the first modern newsweekly. In 1930, he brought forth *Fortune,* a thick, slick periodical devoted to business. It was a spin-off of *Time's* "Business" section, and despite the gloomy state of the economy, it quickly reached a large, enthusiastic audience.

One of Luce's proudest accomplishments came in 1936 with the beginning of *Life* magazine. The title comes from an older *Life,* a humor magazine founded in 1883. It had fallen on hard times in the 1930s and was put up for sale. Luce happened to be toying with the name *Look,* but a bargain price for the humor magazine changed his mind. He bought the struggling *Life* to acquire the name for his own publication, a journal that would prove to be a bold new venture into photojournalism.

On November 23, 1936, the slim first issue of *Life* magazine appeared on newsstands. It cost a dime and offered more photographs than text. The premier issue was an instant hit, selling out wherever it was available. Within four months, it was selling over a million copies a week on newsstands, making it one of the most successful magazine start-ups ever. In fact, the immediate success of *Life* almost did it in. Luce actually lost $6 million with those first issues. He had estimated the new magazine would sell 250,000 copies per week in its first months; since ad rates were based on the lower circulation, Luce had to make up the per-copy costs out of his own corporate pockets.

The success of *Life* did not go unnoticed. In 1933 Gardner Cowles Jr., a friend of Luce's, began syndicating the popular picture section of his

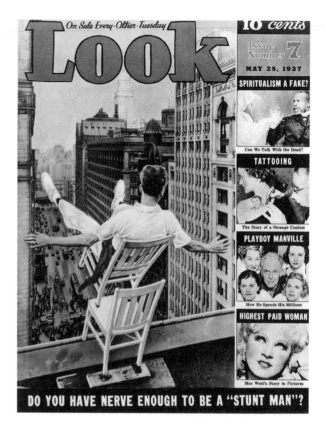

Look magazine cover illustration showing daredevil balanced on chairs on the edge of a building, plus plenty of entertaining extra features, 1937. Prints & Photographs Division, Library of Congress.

family's newspaper, the *Des Moines Register and Tribune,* to 26 different papers. That move did not satisfy demand, so he decided to launch his own photojournalism magazine in 1937. He borrowed some start-up money from Luce, and the title he chose was *Look,* the same one his friend had toyed with earlier.

Until its demise in 1971 (it was briefly resurrected in the mid-1970s, but was finally laid to rest in 1979), *Look* survived in the shadow of *Life. Look* was seen by many as a cheap imitation, a magazine that focused on personalities and glamour. *Life,* on the other hand, was perceived by many as going after the meatier, more important stories. The distinctions between the two publications might be a bit exaggerated, but they nevertheless persisted throughout the life of both magazines.[6]

Life began with an emphasis on celebrity, and the magazine regularly ran glossy photo essays on the doings of the upper classes. In addition, gore and grisliness got plenty of space, along with humorous pictures of cute animals and children. *Life* might be perceived as serious and thought-provoking, but it was also capable of playing to the lowest common denominator. Neither advertisers nor readers seemed to object to the mix, however; its circulation continued to rise throughout the decade, and when the clouds of World War II began to build in Asia and Europe, it was *Life* staffers, cameras in hand, who recorded the descent into conflict.

Liberty

Bernarr Macfadden (1868–1955) a colorful, self-proclaimed "physical culturist," had burst upon the magazine scene in 1899 with the wildly successful *Physical Culture,* a journal promising long life and good health through diet and exercise. In 1919 Macfadden introduced *True Story,* the first of an extensive line of confessional magazines he would publish. It, too, did extremely well, and in 1931 he purchased a struggling weekly called *Liberty.*

Liberty had first appeared on newsstands in 1924, the shared child of the *Chicago Tribune* and the *New York Daily News.* The magazine featured some of the tabloid sensationalism of the *Daily News,* but it never developed a solid advertising base. It consistently lost money—even as it built circulation—and was finally sold to Macfadden.[7]

Throughout the 1930s, only three weekly general-interest magazines could boast a steady circulation of over 1 million or more: *Saturday Evening Post, Collier's* (a weekly very much in the *Post* mold), and *Liberty.* All three paid little heed to the Depression, filling their pages with fiction, a few facts, and lots of entertainment that provided an uplift in troubled times. Yet, even with that impressive circulation, *Liberty* lacked significant advertising and was in financial difficulty.

Liberty was different from most other general magazines. It featured a "Reading Time" block which guaranteed that a particular piece would take no more than "9 minutes, 40 seconds" (or whatever figures were provided) to read. The articles tended toward the tawdry and sensational, with breathless prose on Al Capone, Huey Long, and other questionable celebrities. Macfadden

TARGETED ADVERTISING BEGINS

Under Macfadden's guidance, *Liberty* continued to gain readers, but it suffered from the reputation of being directed at the working class, not the more affluent middle class. Many advertisers spent their ad dollars on other publications. For instance, the new *Esquire* (introduced in 1933) was one of the first American magazines to employ target marketing. It identified its audience, and then sold potential advertisers on readership profiles created for just this purpose. *Fortune* (1930) did likewise, becoming one of the most advertising-heavy monthly magazines in the country. *Time* followed suit, especially in light of the challenges laid down by two 1933 upstarts, *Newsweek* and *U.S. News & World Report.* Finally, *Life*'s immediate acceptance by middle-class readers convinced advertisers that this was the place to be; by 1939 it charged more for ad space than any of its competitors, and would-be advertisers lined up to place their copy.

In reality, advertising expenditures in magazines rose very little in the 1930s—from $150 million in 1931 to $156 million in 1940—but advertisers grew much more selective about where they placed their dollars. It was the beginning of the end for the old-fashioned general magazine. Even with his marketing genius, Macfadden could not attract substantially increased advertising, and so *Liberty* struggled until it died quietly in 1951. With its demise, the nation lost one of the most popular magazines of the 1930s.

did, however, use *Liberty* as his personal soapbox to urge the re-election of Roosevelt in 1936, a stand that placed him and his magazine poles apart from the more conservative *Saturday Evening Post* and *Reader's Digest.*

It was not with *Liberty,* however, that Macfadden marked his place in American publishing history. It was with the confessional magazine that he created. The success of his *True Story* helped Macfadden spawn *True Detective Mysteries, True Experiences, True Ghost Stories, True Lovers, True Romances,* and *Master Detective,* along with *Click, Hollywood, Modern Marriage, Modern Screen,*

Motion Picture, Movie Classic, Photoplay, Screenland, Screen Romances, and *Silver Screen.* In 1933, he even brought out *Babies, Just Babies,* a short-lived journal that boasted Eleanor Roosevelt as one of its editors.

As if the many magazines were not enough, Macfadden also owned ten newspapers. In 1935 the monthly circulation of all Macfadden publications totaled over 7 million copies.

Confessional magazines reached their peak in the 1930s. Their appeal was pure escapism, and a "their problems are worse than mine" attitude struck a resonant chord with Depression-era readers. For instance, a popular 1932 film, *I Am a Fugitive from a Chain Gang,* first appeared as a feature in *True Detective Mysteries* in 1931. The public response to this article was such that Hollywood quickly bought the rights and rushed the movie into production.

PULP MAGAZINES

Close cousins to the confessional journals were the pulp magazines, so called because they were usually printed on thick, cheap pulpwood paper. Pulps were somewhat akin to comic strips in their simplicity. They had been around since the nineteenth century and the heyday of the dime novel. With best sellers drawing large audiences and comic strips a daily reading experience for millions, the pulps occupied a middle ground between the two. In content they stood closer to short stories than they did to the much more visual comic strips of the day. But their content—action, adventure, detectives, cowboys, romance, love, and sex—was more often in the spirit of an adventure comic strip than of the subtleties in a novel. They almost always featured a lurid cover, a tradition that the comic books of the late 1930s enthusiastically adopted.

No matter how the pulps were classified, millions of them sold each month. They were shunned by critics and librarians, but their fans didn't care. Pulps such as *Argosy Weekly, The Bat, Black Mask Magazine, Nick Carter, The Spider,* or *Thrilling Detective* were the perfect distraction for people with time on their hands and a desire to escape from the harsh realities around them.[8]

These magazines also brought about a surge of interest in science fiction and fantasy. Magazines like *Amazing Stories, Astounding Stories,* and *Wonder Stories* collectively sold more than 1.5 million issues a year at the height of their popularity in the mid-1930s. These futuristic compilations effectively recorded the aspirations of the present, both visually and in their texts.

For the writers involved with the pulp industry, it was not an easy way to get rich. Major periodicals like *Redbook* and the *Saturday Evening Post* often paid over $1000 for a piece by a well-known

WORDS AND PHRASES

accessorize	nutburger
bagel	okey-dokey
bazillion	payola
bazooka	phoney baloney
blabbermouth	photojournalist
black market	pizzazz
burp	rat race
cheesy	re-run
cliff-hanger	scaredy-cat
corny	schmaltzy
dognapping	schmooze
expressway	slap-happy
fave	snazzy
flopperoo	storm-trooper
gotcha	stripper
guesstimate	supermarket
hep-cat	switcheroo
hooha	toots
little league	video
marvy	V.I.P.
mook	wacky
moolah	walkathon
moxie	widget
multicultural	zesty
nickel-and-dime	

author. Virtually all the major popular writers of the decade eventually wrote for magazine publication. Some, like Rex Beach, Corey Ford, MacKinlay Kantor, Kathleen Norris, Mary Roberts Rinehart, Damon Runyon, Raphael Sabatini, and P. G. Wodehouse, made their real incomes from magazines, not from books. But for the pulps, the going rate was a strict, quantitative one: three or four cents a word. A 3000-word story might fetch $120, and rarely did writers retain rights to their work. But such hard-nosed economics was in keeping with the genre, from the cheap printing and paper to the garish illustrations and melodramatic stories.

In cities, newsboys, often very young, were essential sales representatives for newspapers. Prints & Photographs Division, Library of Congress.

NEWSPAPERS

Background

The newspaper business changed significantly during the Depression. The flush times of the 1920s had led American newspapers to believe that readership and advertising volume would continue to rise each year. In reality, American newspapers had been in decline throughout the first third of the twentieth century, going from 2,200 separate dailies in 1900 to 1,942 dailies in 1930, and culminating with 1,888 dailies at the end of the decade. Most of this loss took place because of a movement toward consolidation.[9]

During the first third of the twentieth century, papers tended to be more general and less partisan in their content, resulting in larger cities having too many overlapping newspapers. Businesses preferred one or two dominant papers in which to advertise, rather than a cluster of overlapping ones that individually reached fewer people. Newspaper publishers began to combine morning and evening editions into a single issue, a procedure that allowed for changing editions and more efficient use of their facilities. Finally, as manufacturing and delivery costs rose markedly, borderline operations were eliminated or consolidated.

Chain Ownership

Coupled with consolidation was chain ownership of several papers. Chain ownership reduced materials and labor costs, and meant shared staff and facilities. In 1900, eight chains controlled 27 papers; by the mid-1930s, over sixty chains controlled over 328 papers, accounting for 40 percent of total newspaper circulation. Most of these linked papers were larger urban ones, as Scripps-Howard, Gannett, Hearst, and Cox moved into chain ownership. The days of the independent daily, bravely charting its own course, were numbered.

Between 1930 and 1940, almost half of the independent papers in the country either went out of business or became parts of chains. Rural and small-town weeklies stopped trying to compete with their city counterparts and began to focus almost exclusively on local events. In the meantime, competition continued to decline. In 1930, eight major cities of over 100,000 people had only one paper; by 1940, the number had swelled to 25. Even New York City felt the change; early in the century, it had boasted some 20 dailies. It began the 1930s with nine daily papers, but by 1940 the number was reduced to seven.

Newspaper Decline

As the country fell more deeply into the Depression, advertising space plummeted. In 1929, newspapers displayed a record-setting $860 million in advertising. By 1933, that figure had shrunk to $470 million. A slow comeback began in the mid-1930s, but the recession of 1938 stalled it. By 1939, advertising expenditures of $552 million had risen only to 1920 levels. As is usually the case, smaller papers suffered the most from the decline.

Radio probably did more damage to the newspaper business and readership than did the Depression. Newspapers might be the average American's first choice for news, but radios were becoming omnipresent, a ready source for late-breaking stories. Also, radio took an increasing portion of ad revenue, gave instantaneous news updates, provided live sporting events, consistently entertained—and it came into homes for free. Radio's popularity zoomed upward during the 1930s, going from 14 million home receivers in 1930 to over 44 million by 1940. In fact, one way many newspapers stayed profitable was to acquire radio stations. Publishers saw radio as a surefire moneymaker and invested in stations accordingly. In 1930, newspaper interests owned about 90 stations; by 1940, 250 stations were affiliated with newspaper publishing companies.

Newspapers became more visual in an attempt to attract readers and advertisers. Wirephotos (photographs electronically carried by wire directly to a newspaper office) were introduced in the early 1920s. The photographer's life, as well as that of the subjects, became easier when electric flashbulbs replaced the annoying and dangerous explosive-powder lights in 1931. The Associated Press initiated a wirephoto service in 1935, allowing subscribers fast access to photographs of news events. Competing news syndicates quickly followed suit. By 1938, about a third of a big metropolitan daily's content consisted of pictures. By 1939, color telephotos were a reality, and were almost immediately incorporated into the Sunday magazine sections of many papers.

Syndication

Recognizing the success of *Time, Life,* and other newsmagazines, newspapers increasingly compartmentalized their stories in the 1930s, and, despite drops in their revenue, most big-city papers expanded their operations. With the furor

in Washington about Roosevelt and the New Deal, newspaper bureaus in the nation's capital experienced rapid growth. The president inaugurated regular press conferences, as well as his successful *Fireside Chats* on radio. As war in Europe became more and more likely, overseas coverage saw a similar expansion.

Given the excitement in Washington and foreign countries, smaller papers were at a disadvantage. They could ill afford to staff bureaus in cities far from their home base. Thus, news syndicates like the Associated Press (AP) and United Press (UP) experienced tremendous growth. They could provide the reporters and the stories—for a fee, of course—that an individual newspaper could not hope to provide. Although both the AP and the UP go back to the late nineteenth century, it was in the 1930s that they came into their own. As news became less regional and more national and international, only the far-flung syndicates could file regular stories for their growing lists of subscribers.

With widespread syndication came a degree of standardization. The syndicated features found in one paper might just as easily be found in another. This standardization occurred not just with news stories; the comics, the horoscopes, the bridge columns, the latest Hollywood gossip, the box scores, the advice columnists, the financial pages—all graced the paper because they were syndicated. In fact, comics gained the enviable reputation of being the single most popular feature in American dailies throughout the 1930s.

Columnists

The success of syndicated materials led to syndicated columnists, who spurned objectivity in favor of lively, colorful, opinionated styles. Their pieces usually appeared on the editorial page. In the early 1930s, most of them tended to be anti-New Deal, but they had little effect on legislation or voters. As proof of this, in 1932, 60 percent of American daily newspapers opposed Roosevelt, yet he won by a landslide. In 1936, 63 percent opposed his candidacy, but again he won overwhelmingly. By 1940, 75 percent of the dailies voiced opposition, and yet again was the president re-elected.

Not all syndicated columnists wrote political pieces for the editorial page. Many commented on the passing scene. One of the most widely syndicated writers in the 1930s was O. O. McIntyre, whose column was titled "New York Day by Day." His unpretentious columns seemed to appeal most to those outside big cities, although the title might suggest otherwise.

Some columnists relied on gossip and watching celebrities. Chief among them was Walter Winchell (1897–1972), whose "On Broadway" was carried by over 1,000 papers, most of them a considerable distance from New York City. His "Winchellisms" occasionally entered the language briefly, such as "middle-aisle," a verb form that meant to wed. "Renovate," on the other hand, signified a divorce (from Reno, Nevada, where divorce was easily accomplished). Winchell also had a long-running radio news show that began with a staccato telegraph sound, and then "Good evening, Mr. and Mrs. North America and all the ships at sea … let's go to press! FLASH!" The 15-minute show ran from 1930 until 1949 as *The Jergens Journal*. It was consistently one of the nation's top-rated radio programs. Capitalizing on Winchell's fame, the Metro-Goldwyn-Mayer film studio released *Broadway Melody of 1936*. In this movie, radio star Jack Benny plays a Winchell-like columnist hungry for a story.

Close on Winchell's heels, at least in 1930s popularity, were Hedda Hopper (1890–1966) and Louella Parsons (1881–1972). Both women wrote widely syndicated newspaper columns that focused almost exclusively on Hollywood and the stars. Their success helped spawn a number of movie magazines, ranging from the purely gossipy *Screen Romances* to the slightly serious *Silver Screen*. Parsons parlayed her fame and influence into a popular radio show, *Hollywood Hotel* (1934–1938), which she hosted. Hopper followed with *The Hedda Hopper Show* (1939–1951), a 15-minute mix of chatter and celebrities.

Other columnists mixed gossip and political rumors, such as Drew Pearson (1897–1969) and Robert S. Allen with their "Washington Merry-Go-Round." This widely circulated column grew out of a book by the same name that they anonymously published in 1932. The success of the book, a collection of articles rejected by their respective newspapers, led to their syndication by United Features, and even some radio time. From 1935 to 1940 they were on the Mutual Network with their investigative reports.[10]

Warm, humorous writers also enjoyed wide syndication. For example, Eleanor Roosevelt, the First Lady, had a long-running column entitled "My Day." It began in 1935 and chronicled her thoughts and activities for many readers. The folksy Will Rogers (1879–1935), the "Cowboy Philosopher," wrote a daily paragraph on some current topic. Similarly, poet Edgar Guest (1881–1959) began contributing verse to his syndicate at the turn of the century. Over the next sixty years, he composed over 11,000 poems. By the 1930s, he was appearing in hundreds of papers. The poetry, usually lightly humorous and sentimental ("It takes a heap o'livin' in a house t'make it home") became beloved by several generations of newspaper readers.

Finally, among all the syndicated writers were those who monitored the nation's manners and mores. Emily Post (1872–1960) provided the last word on etiquette; her 1930s column was syndicated in over 200 papers and she even had a radio show that premiered in 1931. Dorothy Dix (Elizabeth M. Gilmer [1870–1951]) and Beatrice Fairfax (Marie Manning [1873–1945]) wrote advice-to-the-lovelorn columns. Dix was the highest-paid woman columnist of the 1930s, and Fairfax was memorialized in song. In 1930, George and Ira Gershwin penned "But Not for Me." In this number, lyricist Ira Gershwin has the words, "Beatrice Fairfax, don't you dare," probably the only mention of a columnist in the annals of American popular music. All three women became unofficial arbiters of taste and behavior, their words anxiously read by millions who wanted to know about proper dining and dating.

Reporting

The surprising success of so many columnists led to a rise in interpretive stories by regular (i.e., non-syndicated) reporters in the 1930s. In traditional newsgathering, the four *w*'s were predominant: Who? What? When? Where? The 1930s, however, found a fifth *w*, often a significant part of the story: Why? Certainly the era was one of confusion, and it reassured people to have events explained in easily understood terms. As a result, reporters delved more and more into the details behind a story, interpreting the facts as they were presented. It may have challenged traditional tenets about objectivity, but it became part of American journalism.[11]

For the average reader, however, the popular image of the newspaper reporter was not molded by adherence to journalistic standards or by writing ability. Throughout the decade, Hollywood released a string of movies about newspapers and reporters. These films created the stereotype of the fast-talking, wisecracking reporter who always gets the story. Starting in 1931 with *The Front Page,* a film version of the Ben Hecht-Charles MacArthur play of the same name, the image of the busy newsroom, the harried editor, the race to make a deadline, and the constant chatter of all involved became the standard. *Platinum Blonde* (1931) featured Jean Harlow in a comedic romance with an ambitious reporter.

COMICS AND CARTOONS

In the 1930s, rare was the American newspaper that did not have at least a full page of comics: *Blondie, Dick Tracy, Flash Gordon, The Gumps, Krazy Kat, Mary Worth,* and others. Today, the 1930s are seen as a high point for cartoon art, and many of the artists of the period have enjoyed museum retrospectives of their work. During the 1930s, however, the comics were usually viewed as little more than daily doses of humor and adventure, a mindless respite from the grim realities of the time.

Little Orphan Annie

Little Orphan Annie enjoyed widespread popularity almost from its debut in 1924. Harold Gray lacked any outstanding artistic skills, but he excelled at spinning a good yarn. Annie was an orphan inexplicably adopted by Daddy Warbucks, although the plucky redhead spent little time with her guardian. As a rule, she was on the road with her faithful dog, Sandy, getting involved with some of the most complex plotting ever to appear in comics. The speech balloons above each character were filled to capacity.

During the 1930s, *Annie's* mix of ultraconservative capitalism and strong nationalism appealed to many. Gray had little patience with things like child labor laws, poverty, or welfare, so Annie always picked up odd jobs, no matter how menial. A strong person (i.e., a good person) found work; those who did not were bums. Those who lived "on the dole" were beneath contempt. With high unemployment and a worsening depression, such messages might have seemed out of step with the times, but they didn't seem to bother faithful readers. As the threat of war grew in the latter part of the decade, Gray went after foreigners with an enthusiastic nativism.

Annie was a rarity: she was a female with no particular super powers, but she was tough and her adventures charmed children and adolescents. Her popularity resulted in two feature movies, *Little Orphan Annie* in 1932, and a follow-up in 1939. The National Broadcasting Company introduced a long-running radio serial in 1931. Sponsored by Ovaltine, a popular chocolate powder that was mixed with milk, the serial soon offered premiums to listeners. Toys and novelties featuring both Annie and Sandy, alongside wristwatches, pop-up books, and cheap jewelry, were popular throughout the 1930s available from catalogs and dime stores.

Dick Tracy

In a somewhat similar manner, Chester Gould was responding to the headlines and sensationalism that accompanied crime and lawlessness during the period. Because of Prohibition, bootlegging was rampant, and various gangs and factions were at war with each other over the lucrative trade. In the early 1930s, the law seemed powerless against figures like Al Capone and John Dillinger, and Hollywood responded with a deluge of gangster films. The comic pages, however, had seen little of criminals. Thus, *Dick* (from American slang, meaning a detective) *Tracy* (a pun on "trace," to locate or apprehend) broke new ground and quickly won a sizable audience.

The world of *Dick Tracy* was both visually and morally a world of black and white. Gould was

"Little Orphan Annie" was popular from the time it debuted in 1925. In this 13-frame comic strip, Little Orphan Annie falls asleep while reading an adventure book about prehistoric times; it shows her adventures when transported through a dream to the era of cave dwellers and dinosaurs, 1925. Prints & Photographs Division, Library of Congress.

a mediocre artist, but he made the most of his limited talents. Stark silhouettes, speeding cars, the precise rendering of guns and other mechanical objects, along with some of the most bizarre villains ever drawn, were his trademarks. The law was always right, and if Tracy had to shoot a bad guy, that was the price for a life of crime. If he accomplished this task with a machine gun and mowed down a whole group of thugs in one bullet-filled pass, so much the better. Death was a regular feature of the strip, but it was so staged and apparently painless that few complained.

Tracy's popularity soon carried over into all kinds of Dick Tracy toy guns, games, badges, and the like. The detective appeared in four movie serials between 1937 and 1941. There was also a radio serial in the late afternoon (1935–1948).

Blondie

Not all strips espoused a right-wing point of view. To be sure, most were apolitical. A case in point was *Blondie,* a family strip that premiered in 1930. The creation of Murat "Chic" Young, the strip began with the whimsical adventures of a flapper named Blondie, who wowed the boys and had not a care in the world. Her primary beau was Dagwood Bumstead, an earnest college student and heir to millions, who won her hand in marriage. But then the Depression worsened.

The story of a "dumb blonde" about to become very rich probably had limited appeal to an audience facing economic crisis, so Young changed the strip: Dagwood was disinherited, Blondie went from flapper to middle-class housewife, the couple lived in a typical small house, and the focus shifted subtly from Blondie to Dagwood.

Dagwood emerged as a well-meaning bumbler who needed the common sense of Blondie to muddle through, although he occasionally enjoyed small victories. His inimitable Dagwood Sandwich, a tasty concoction made from everything in the refrigerator and pantry has become a classic bit of Americana.

A portrait of normalcy in chaotic times, the strip quickly became a favorite. Movie rights were assigned, and Penny Singleton and Arthur Lake achieved minor stardom as the leads in 28 *Blondie* features that ran from 1938 to 1950.

Toys, games, and novelties appeared, and by the end of the decade a radio comedy had been produced, starring Penny Singleton.

Science Fiction

Science fiction came to the comics in 1929 with *Buck Rogers* (Phil Nowlan [1888–1940] and Dick Calkins [1895–1962]). Because it was new and different, the series enjoyed a certain following, but the images of scientific invention came across as crude and dated even by the standards of the early 1930s. In 1934, however, Alex Raymond's (1909–1956) stylish *Flash Gordon* made its newspaper debut. Here was Streamline Moderne in all its glory. Sleek rocket ships cruised to gleaming, Modernist cities. No doubt the way generations of Americans would imagine the future was influenced by this beautifully crafted strip.

Hillbilly Funnies

Hillbilly funnies also prospered during the decade. Al Capp created *Li'l Abner* in 1934. In the strip, he has Sadie Hawkins Day, a day when girls can ask boys to dances and other social affairs. This invention was soon celebrated by high schools and colleges around the country, and it served as an acknowledgment of the growing importance of teenage culture. At about the same time, Billy DeBeck (1890–1942) introduced a character named Snuffy Smith in his popular *Barney Google* strip. Although the humor in both strips could be biting, it was seldom cruel. The two series about Appalachia, rustic mountain culture, and abject poverty found audiences during the Great Depression, and each contributed to the folklore surrounding the region.

Animal Strips

During the 1930s, a favorite in the anthropomorphic animal genre was *Felix the Cat* (1923–1967). Created by Pat Sullivan in 1917 as an animated cartoon, and debuting as a comic strip in 1923, the feisty Felix was a perfect character for the Depression. He was a survivor; nothing could overcome his spirit, and he battled poverty, hunger, loneliness, and technology with equal aplomb. His ingenuity and endless good spirits made for great daily reading. The strip was taken over by Otto Messmer in the early thirties, but if anything, the series became even more lyrical and aesthetically satisfying with the change of stewardship. *Felix the Cat* continued as one of the leading newspaper comics of the decade, one of those strips that reacted to the uncertainties of the Depression with humorous scorn.

Big Little Books

A form of comic art that also appeared in the 1930s was the comic book, which had a popular antecedent in the so-called Pop-Up Books, introduced in 1932 by Blue Ribbon Books. This form consisted of small booklets that featured characters that popped up from the pages when the book was laid flat. The publishers used the heroes of the daily strips to capitalize on the popularity of newspaper comics.

The interest shown in these early Pop-Up Books immediately led to other innovations, particularly the Big Little Books. The first offering was issued in 1932 and involved the adventures of Dick Tracy. The product of the Whitman Publishing Company, the book measured 3⅝ inches wide, 4½ inches tall, and 1½ inches thick, and had cardboard covers and contained 350 pages. The left-hand page contained text, and the right-hand page featured a single frame from the comic strip. With the exception of the garishly colored

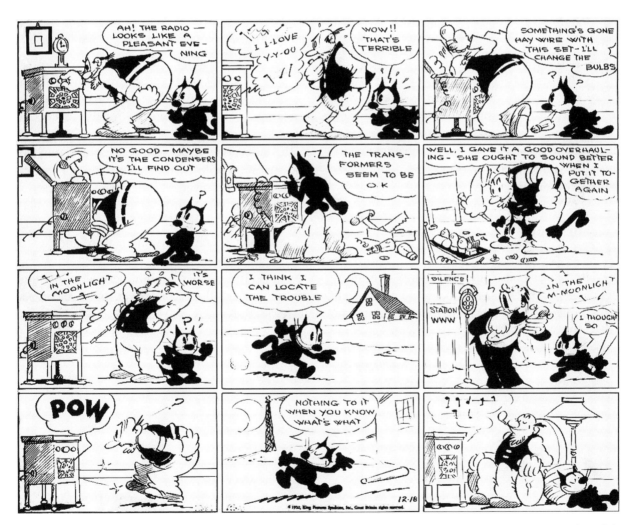

"Felix the Cat." In this episode, Felix deals with a music problem in his customary no-nonsense, cheerful, although somewhat violent, manner. Prints & Photographs Division, Library of Congress.

covers, all was in black and white. The book cost a dime and set the standards that most succeeding volumes followed.

The Big Little Books were an immediate hit. Eventually, Whitman Company issued over 400 separate titles, and other publishers quickly followed suit. Dell Publishing (Fast Action Books), Fawcett Publications (Dime Action Books), and Saalfield Publishing Company (Little Big Books) were among the industry leaders. So fierce was the competition that Whitman changed the line's name to Better Little Books and Big Big Books in 1938, an attempt to differentiate themselves from the competition. Print runs for most titles averaged 250,000 to 350,000 copies.

Initially, the majority of the Big Little Books were reprints of leading newspaper strips like *Dick Tracy, Flash Gordon, Buck Rogers, Little Orphan Annie, Tarzan,* or various Disney characters. Soon, however, they came to include illustrated novels, such as *Moby Dick, Treasure Island, A Midsummer Night's Dream,* and many others, including radio favorites such as *The Lone Ranger, The Green Hornet,* and *Jack Armstrong.* Even movie stars like Shirley Temple, Jackie Cooper, Jane Withers, Will Rogers, and Tom Mix had their own Big Little Books stories. Children and adolescents soon were building libraries of these popular, inexpensive volumes.

Comic Books

The success of newspaper comic strips and the Big Little Books hastened the birth of the modern comic book. Unsuccessful attempts had been made in the 1920s to reprint newspaper comics in some sort of booklet form. Finally, with *Funnies on Parade,* a 1933 giveaway that featured several popular cartoon characters, the concept started to catch on. This one-shot publication led to other collections of reprints, but they now cost 10 cents, the amount that all comics eventually charged throughout the 1930s. The following year saw the publication of *Famous Funnies,* the periodical generally accepted as the first modern comic book.

After the success of *Famous Funnies,* competing publishers began to enter the new comic book market. In 1935, Dell issued *Popular Comics,* another reprint series. At this time, the standard format of 64 pages per issue was established. By 1938, titles like *The Funnies, The Comics, Super Comics, King Comics,* and *Tip Top Comics* had joined the fray, and they increasingly featured all-new material. Reprints became a thing of the past.

Superman made his debut in 1938, the creation of writer Jerry Siegel (1914–1996) and artist Joe Shuster (1914–1992), in *Action Comics.* Although the industry had been turning more and more toward original (instead of reprint) action adventures, no one was prepared for the success of Superman.

In 1939, a new *Superman* comic was launched and was soon selling over one million copies per issue. In a clever reversal, a newspaper strip based on the comic book came out later that same year, and a radio show arrived close behind. Almost immediately, other publishers readied their own superheroes. Batman was introduced in 1939, and in no time at all one superhero after another graced the brightly colored covers of comic books at newsstands across the land.

Books

Entertainment

In the 1930s movie attendance and radio listenership were calculated in the tens of millions, whereas the figures for other performing arts were, at best, in the thousands. Television came about so late in the decade that people had little time to experience it.

MOVIES

Despite the economic depression and widespread unemployment, Americans still flocked to the movies. The addition of sound improved the experience, and by the early 1930s, virtually all theaters were wired for this latest technological innovation. Movies seemed a good antidote to the woes outside the theater's doors, and the few films that acknowledged the depression seldom fared well at the box office.

At the beginning of the decade, admission prices tended to range from about 25 cents to 50 cents—more for newer, highly publicized films with big-name stars at the grand movie palaces. As economic conditions worsened, attendance dropped. Initially, theater owners cut prices—by 1933 neighborhood theaters often charged only a dime and the bigger palaces maybe a quarter.

Eventually, most theaters switched to a new format: the double feature—two complete movies. One was usually a "quality picture" with

recognizable stars and more costly production values, such as special effects, location shooting, top screenwriters, a lush musical score, and heavier advertising. The second feature, however, was a "B" movie. It was short, maybe just over an hour, and inexpensively produced—a canned score, repetitive plots, crude effects, and few, if any, big stars. (This double-feature format lasted into the 1960s for movie theaters, although drive-in movies often continued showing two movies long after that.)

Patrons also got a cartoon, a newsreel, maybe a short humorous piece or a documentary, and, occasionally, an episode of a weekly serial. Many theaters added a "dish night," when cheap crockery was given away to lucky ticketholders. Other popular gimmicks included "bank night" and Bingo, both of which allowed a fortunate few in the audience to leave with some extra cash. Two-for-one passes were offered on certain days or at designated hours. Many theaters also added so-called iced air, touting the fact that it was "70 degrees cool inside."

Despite these efforts, by 1933 one-third of all American movie theaters had been forced to close. And yet, in 1934 the film business, alongside the economy, began to show signs of revival. Some of the changes remained in place; the double feature became a part of the American audience's

Entertainment

TOP ACTORS

Fred Astaire, 1899–1987

Gene Autry, 1907–1998

James Cagney, 1899–1986

Claudette Colbert, 1903–1996

Gary Cooper, 1901–1961

Joan Crawford, 1908–1977

Bette Davis, 1908–1989

W. C. Fields, 1880–1946

Errol Flynn, 1909–1959

Henry Fonda, 1905–1982

Clark Gable, 1901–1960

Greta Garbo, 1905–1990

Cary Grant, 1904–1986

Jean Harlow, 1911–1937

Katharine Hepburn, 1907–2003

Myrna Loy, 1905–1993

The Marx Brothers (Chico Marx, 1887–1961; Harpo Marx, 1888–1964; Groucho Marx, 1890–1977)

Ginger Rogers, 1911–1995

Will Rogers, 1879–1935

James Stewart, 1908–1997

Shirley Temple, 1928–

Spencer Tracy, 1900–1967

John Wayne, 1907–1979

Mae West, 1893–1980

NOTABLE MOVIES

Excluding Best Picture winners.

City Lights (1931)

Dracula (1931)

Frankenstein (1931)

42nd Street (1933)

King Kong (1933)

Little Women (1933)

The Thin Man (1934)

The Gold Diggers of 1935 (1935)

A Night at the Opera (1935)

Mr. Deeds Goes to Town (1936)

My Man Godfrey (1936)

Modern Times (1936)

Snow White and the Seven Dwarfs (1937)

Boys Town (1938)

The Wizard of Oz (1939)

Stagecoach (1939)

Mr. Smith Goes to Washington (1939)

expectations, and the iced air stayed on. In addition, although many theaters were shuttered in 1933, over 75 million people continued to go to the movies every week. By the end of the decade, movie attendance had climbed back up to around 100 million a week.

The studio system, well established by the 1920s, became more and more a partnership between business and craft. The business sector provided cash, especially in the difficult early years of the Depression, and those already in motion pictures supplied the expertise. This partnership kept Metro-Goldwyn-Mayer, Universal, Warner Brothers, Columbia Pictures, Paramount, United Artists, and all the other studios solvent and functioning, although it resulted in more attention being paid to making profits than to creating art.

Technical Changes

Sound pictures had become commonplace by the late 1920s. The approximately 19,000 movie houses around the country quickly accommodated this momentous event. The studios also complied: "100 percent talking" had become the norm for Hollywood productions by 1930.

The industry also experimented with color during the 1930s. For instance, *Paramount on Parade* (1930) featured several dance numbers in an early two-color Technicolor process, but the resultant hues were far from true. Not until 1935 and *Becky Sharp* was a satisfactory three-color process made available for feature films.

ACADEMY AWARD WINNERS

Year of release, not year of award.

1930 Movie: *All Quiet on the Western Front*
Director: Lewis Milestone, *All Quiet on the Western Front*
Actor: George Arliss, *Disraeli*
Actress: Norma Shearer, *The Divorcee*

1931 Movie: *Cimarron*
Director: Norman Taurog, *Skippy*
Actor: Lionel Barrymore, *A Free Soul*
Actress: Marie Dressler, *Min and Bill*

1932 Movie: *Grand Hotel*
Director: Frank Borzage, *Bad Girl*
Actor: Wallace Beery, *The Champ*; Fredric March, *Dr. Jekyll and Mr. Hyde*
Actress: Helen Hayes, *The Sin of Madelon Claudet*

1933 Movie: *Cavalcade*
Director: Frank Lloyd, *Cavalcade*
Actor: Charles Laughton, *The Private Life of Henry VIII*
Actress: Katharine Hepburn, *Morning Glory*

1934 Movie: *It Happened One Night*
Director: Frank Capra, *It Happened One Night*
Actor: Clark Gable, *It Happened One Night*

Actress: Claudette Colbert, *It Happened One Night*

1935 Movie: *Mutiny on the Bounty*
Director: John Ford, *The Informer*
Actor: Victor McLaglen, *The Informer*
Actress: Bette Davis, *Dangerous*

1936 Movie: *The Great Ziegfeld*
Director: Frank Capra, *Mr. Deeds Goes to Town*
Actor: Paul Muni, *The Story of Louis Pasteur*
Actress: Luise Rainer, *The Great Ziegfeld*

1937 Movie: *The Life of Emile Zola*
Director: Leo McCarey, *The Awful Truth*
Actor: Spencer Tracy, *Captains Courageous*
Actress: Luise Rainer, *The Good Earth*

1938 Movie: *You Can't Take It with You*
Director: Frank Capra, *You Can't Take It with You*
Actor: Spencer Tracy, *Boys Town*
Actress: Bette Davis, *Jezebel*

1939 Movie: *Gone with the Wind*
Director: Victor Fleming, *Gone with the Wind*
Actor: Robert Donat, *Goodbye, Mr. Chips*
Actress: Vivien Leigh, *Gone with the Wind*

Entertainment

Technicolor was expensive, so the majority of movies continued to be shot in dependable, economical black and white. Over the decade, inferior imitations of Technicolor abounded; some used sepia tones; others employed processes that washed out any vibrant hues and resulted in a diluted image. It took a long time for color of any kind to establish dominance; not until the late 1960s did the balance shift to color films.

Gangster Films

One of the first movie crazes of the 1930s was gangster films. Most followed a predictable pattern: a small-time mobster (juvenile delinquent, sociopath, thief, etc.) rises in his "profession." He enjoys wealth and power, often for much of the movie, but then he must pay. Usually his downfall is abrupt, whereas his success has been lengthy and celebrated. In the eyes of many, the gangster remained a glamorous figure. During a time of economic and social disorder, life on the wrong side of the law had its appeal. Films like *Little Caesar* (1930), *Public Enemy* (1931) with James Cagney, and *Scarface* (1932) gave the public a distorted view of the American myth of success. In these films, education is a waste of time for the man of action. Those with formal learning are portrayed as weak and powerless.

I Am a Fugitive from a Chain Gang (1932) was not a typical gangster movie. Directed by Mervyn LeRoy, it portrays the true story of a man caught in an unjust prison system. The main character is a victim of the cruelties of the Southern chain gangs. He escapes and moves back into legitimate society, where he achieves success. He is found out and returned to prison. *I Am a Fugitive from a Chain Gang* provides no easy solutions in its dark closing frames. Many in the audience could see certain parallels in their lives: as individuals up against seemingly uncaring, insurmountable forces.

Criminals, with such romanticized names as "Legs" Diamond, "Baby Face" Nelson, "Machine Gun" Kelly, "Pretty Boy" Floyd, "Ma" Barker, and Bonnie and Clyde, captured the nation's imagination. With law enforcement often seen as inept and corrupt, the success of these real and on-screen outlaws fed into a national resentment toward authority and its failures. Small wonder, then, that crime films found a receptive audience.

MOVIE CENSORSHIP IN THE 1930s

Much was made of gangster films, so much so that the movie industry considered self-censorship—or face the probability that outsiders would take on the job. In 1933, a group of Catholic bishops established the Legion of Decency to cleanse films of elements they thought harmful to the public, especially youth. They threatened boycotts of both studios and individual movies if they did not meet and maintain certain standards. In response, in 1934 Hollywood created the Production Code Administration, colloquially known as "The Breen Office" for its leader, Joseph I. Breen. It was designed to supplant the industry association that attempted to monitor content, the Motion Picture Producers and Distributors of America, or "Hays Office," led by Will Hays. The Breen Office was responsible for enforcing "The Code," a lengthy, detailed listing of what should be avoided in American movies: no swearing, no sex, no drugs, no explicit violence, no nudity, and so forth. The code had evolved since its initial appearance in 1922, but it had not been strictly enforced. Breen, caving in to a lot of outside pressure, particularly from the Legion of Decency, began to apply the code restrictions without appeal. Producers and directors had to cease making their gangster sagas, at least in the manner of the early thirties.

The Police and G-Men

Although gangster and crime films were popular, a renewed respect for law and order began to manifest itself in films of the mid-1930s, perhaps reflecting a public desire for authority figures. The new heroes were the once-maligned federal law enforcement officers, or G-men, as they were popularly called (for "government men"). Villains remained plentiful in these movies, but they were hissed at, not admired. Oily lawyers, crooked politicians, dealers, and manipulators were convenient targets, and federal agents, along with honest public servants and brash reporters, rooted them out and exposed their malfeasance. *G-Men* (1935) features former bad guy Jimmy Cagney in the FBI, and *Bullets or Ballots* (1936) has Edward G. Robinson as a lawman who goes undercover, thus allowing him to be both hero and gangster in the same film.

On a different note, Warner Oland began a popular series of films as Charlie Chan, the fictional Chinese detective of many Earl Derr Biggers potboilers. Between 1931 and his death in 1938, Oland made sixteen Charlie Chan films; Sidney Toler took over the role in 1938 and churned out twenty-two more before his demise in 1947. These cheaply made whodunits delighted audiences throughout the thirties, and fans apparently did not care that the Swedish-born Oland portrayed an Asian character. These movies helped reinforce the Code edicts against crime and corruption. Not only that, they supplied a healthy dose of thrills, and the box office receipts were substantial. (Widely considered racist in later years because they reinforced stereotypes about Chinese Americans being odd, exotic, and speaking poor English, and because both actors who portrayed Chan were not Chinese, the movies nonetheless enjoyed an afterlife even beyond the 1940s as the movies were re-run on television.)

Westerns

No genre of film better exemplifies good triumphing over evil than the western. To be sure, there was no shortage of cowboy movies during the 1930s.

Most westerns from the era are extremely low-budget productions, shot on the back lots of small Hollywood studios. Formula writers like Zane Grey provided endless plots for these quintessential "B" pictures. Grey alone contributed *The Border Legion* (1930), *Fighting Caravans* (1931, with a young Gary Cooper), *Riders of the Purple Sage* (1931), and *Robber's Roost* (1932). Actors including Hoot Gibson, Buck Jones, Tim McCoy, Tex Ritter, Bob Steele, Ken Maynard, and William Boyd (better known as Hopalong Cassidy) dutifully mounted their steeds and rode into the sunset in one picture or serial after another.

The mythic qualities of the western—wide-open spaces, rugged independence, clear-cut moral decisions—have appealed to audiences since the beginnings of the film industry. John Ford's epic *Stagecoach* (1939) is considered a model for bringing most of the symbolic connotations together. *Stagecoach,* however, was not a shot-on-the-cheap production; it starred John Wayne, Claire Trevor, and Thomas Mitchell, and was photographed in Monument Valley, Arizona. It was a breakthrough film for Wayne, putting him in the select company of actors like Gary Cooper (*The Plainsman,* 1936), Henry Fonda (*The Trail of the Lonesome Pine,* 1936), Tyrone Power (*Jesse James,* 1939), and Errol Flynn (*Dodge City,* 1939).

Most of the 1930s "B" westerns have been forgotten, but the values they represented live on in the American psyche. A few performers—Tom Mix (with over 400 low-budget westerns in a career that spanned almost 30 years), Gene Autry, and Roy Rogers—rose to a kind of quasi-star status in the industry. Mix was the real thing, a former marshal and a marvelous rider, thanks in part to his wonder horse Tony, whereas Autry and Rogers were the Singing Cowboys, vocalizing and strumming their guitars, often while astride their own prize horses, Champion and Trigger. The violence was low and the humor was corny, but for several generations of moviegoers, Mix, Autry, and Rogers epitomized the straight-talkin', sharp-shootin' cowboy.

Musicals

Musicals were not much in favor at the box office until 1933 when an almost bankrupt Warner Brothers released *42nd Street.*[1] Labeled a "back-stage musical" because it supposedly gave the audience an insider's view of the doings of the cast, it helped create the myth of the gutsy chorus girl. In the plot, Ruby Keeler takes over at the last minute for the ailing star. Featuring a memorable score by Harry Warren and Al Dubin, *42nd Street* signaled the rebirth of the musical, and it allowed for social commentary not often found in popular films. Some 25 percent of the labor force was unemployed in 1933, probably the bleakest year of the Depression. The worsening crisis had shaken the country's faith in hard work and deferred gratification. *42nd Street* affirmed the mythology of labor and its resultant rewards: dancing your heart out brought about good things.

Flush with success, Warner Brothers released *Gold Diggers of 1933,* reinforcing this very point. Ginger Rogers sings "We're in the Money," but ends on a somewhat somber note. Joan Blondell, usually a wisecracking comedian, sings "Remember My Forgotten Man," a haunting number which features images of hollow-faced men, mostly forgotten veterans, marching in hopeless circles.

The studio completed its 1933 trilogy of musicals with *Footlight Parade.* Jimmy Cagney starred as a hardworking producer who was broke, but not down and out.

Numerous other singers and dancers rose to brief or continuing movie fame during the Depression years. Bing Crosby, a star of radio and recordings, churned out numerous mediocre films that capitalized on his easygoing crooning style. The pictures did reasonably well, and demonstrated how radio, recording, and film can interconnect.

Busby Berkeley

The movies *42nd Street, Gold Diggers of 1933,* and *Footlight Parade* boasted remarkable choreography by Busby Berkeley, who created a bold and imaginative visual style. Berkeley had come to Hollywood from Broadway, and he created amazing film sequences using masses of dancers. With military precision, the performers blossomed into lush flowers, became complex geometric forms, shrank and expanded—all in time to a jazzy musical score. The "Berkeley top shot," an overhead camera that looked directly down on the dancers, allowed all the surreal shapes and patterns to evolve. Berkeley's dancers were clearly members of the chorus, sweating and straining for minimal pay, not elitist members of a ballet troupe. The working-class plots addressed the very real issues of unemployment and getting by as best as one could.

Berkeley's sets were also significant. The Depression musicals allowed Art Deco or, as it later came to be known in the 1930s, Streamline Moderne, to dominate the background throughout both the dance numbers and the narrative. (See Architecture of the 1930s.) These were hard, shiny, glossy sets, stripped down to basic black and white with chromium accents.

Fred Astaire and Ginger Rogers

As the Depression wore down, the slick imagery of Fred Astaire (1899–1987) and Ginger Rogers (1911–1995) began to replace the earnestness and the sense of responsibility in the movie musicals of the early 1930s. Fred and Ginger's dancing was carefree and fun, not regimented and geometric. The grace, flawless timing, and pure sense of style of Fred and Ginger made them stars overnight, beginning with *Flying Down to Rio* (1933). Astaire did his own choreography, and he brought a level of sophistication to the movies never before seen. The duo starred in eight more films during the thirties, including *The Gay Divorcee* (1934), *Top Hat* (1935), *Swing Time* (1936), *Shall We Dance?* (1937), and *The Story of Vernon and Irene Castle* (1939).

Motion picture poster for *Swing Time* shows Fred Astaire and Ginger Rogers dancing; in background, a nightclub scene, 1936. Prints & Photographs Division, Library of Congress.

The two danced in Hollywood's interpretation of the big-city nightclub, their stark modernity and polished surfaces effectively displaying Astaire's tuxedos and Rogers's gowns. These sequences satisfied an audience hungry for images of good fortune, and not necessarily the plucky chorus-girl-makes-good films shown earlier. Because of the popular success of the Astaire-Rogers films, screen musicals achieved a remarkable urbanity in the later years of the decade.[2]

W. C. Fields and Mae West

Comedians W. C. Fields (1880–1946) and Mae West (1893–1980) brought both physical humor and a way with words to the movies of the 1930s. Both had come from theatrical backgrounds, and Fields had enjoyed some success in silent films. Fields appeared in a number of classic short features, among them *The Dentist* (1932) and *Tillie and Gus* (1933). In *The Old-Fashioned Way* (1934), Fields hit his stride as a movie comedian. He played a cheat, a fraud, and various other irreverent roles. With his film persona well established, Fields followed with a succession of popular comedies such as *It's a Gift* (1934) and *You Can't Cheat an Honest Man* (1939).

Mae West, on the other hand, had made her reputation on stage as the queen of suggestiveness. With looks, double entendres, and a sinuous walk, she was considered "too hot" for movies in the 1920s. As receipts dropped during the Depression, the studios welcomed West to the film capital. In her debut picture, *Night After Night* (1932), she infatuates the usually unflappable George Raft with her sex appeal. The new Hollywood Code had not yet come into effect, and West took advantage of the fact. Innuendos fly and her notoriety became immediate. Quickly following up on her fame, West wrote and starred in *She Done Him Wrong* (1933), a re-creation of her stage role as Diamond Lil. This risqué comedy, which also featured Cary Grant, helped push him to the public's attention while further burnishing Mae West's colorful image. Several more adult comedies followed, although nervous censors at the new Breen Office tried—not always successfully—to make her tone down some of the more outrageous dialogue and situations. Her success

Mae West. Prints & Photographs Division, Library of Congress.

was such that in 1936 she reported an income of $480,833, making her one of the highest-paid individuals in the nation, regardless of profession.

The Marx Brothers

Throughout the 1930s a madcap trio of brothers undermined just about every convention they encountered. They were the Marx Brothers—Groucho, the brains and wiseacre of the trio; Chico, the piano-playing caricature of an Italian immigrant; and Harpo, the lecherous yet harmless mime. In reality, there were five Marx brothers. Gummo, the middle son, left the group early, preferring the private sector to the uncertainties

Entertainment

to Washington (1939; Capra) demonstrated how American beliefs could be sustained. The themes of these warm, optimistic films range from a once-wealthy man reduced to being a butler, and teaching his rich employers that money cannot buy happiness (*My Man Godfrey*), to that of a multi-millionaire who wants to give his fortune away to needy people (*Mr. Deeds Goes to Town*).

Fantasy and Horror

Fantasy and horror presented another cinematic way of escaping the harsh realities of the Depression. In 1931, Universal Studios released director Tod Browning's *Dracula*. Dark and shadowy, it introduced American moviegoers to a new type of picture. Bela Lugosi, an unknown Hungarian actor with a bizarre accent, played the evil Count, a role that catapulted him to instant fame. A colorful advertising campaign—"This ruthless, strange, exciting drama of the 'undead,'" cried the theater placards—simply furthered public curiosity.

Universal had an even bigger hit later that year with *Frankenstein*. This venerable Mary Shelley tale of science run amok had been brought to the movies several times before. Director James Whale cast Boris Karloff, a veteran English actor, as the vilified monster. It was a brilliant move; overnight Karloff became the definitive Frankenstein—or, more properly—Frankensteinian monster. (The doctor's name has become, incorrectly, the name of the monster; Karloff's character lacks a name.)

Setting the film in a bleak, fantastic land not unlike the Transylvania of *Dracula*, Whale builds suspense, refusing to let the audience see what Dr. Frankenstein has wrought, until suddenly he reveals the creature. And what the audience sees is the lumbering gait, the wires and pins, the deep-set eyes, and the strained, pathetic attempt to speak—coupled with the realization that "It's alive!"—to quote a famous line from one of the movie's many sequels.

Soon Dracula and Frankenstein were joined by *The Mummy* (1932, Boris Karloff); *The White Zombie* (1932, Bela Lugosi); *The Ghoul* (1934, Boris Karloff); *The Black Cat* (1934, Bela Lugosi and Boris Karloff together); *The Bride of Frankenstein* (1935, James Whale once more

directing, and Karloff reprising his character); *Dracula's Daughter* (1936, Lugosi doing likewise); and countless other monsters and mutants.

Special effects contributed to the success of these movies, but characterization and the establishment of mood and setting were also important. The makeup for the creature in *Frankenstein* was important, but the plot focused on Dr. Frankenstein and his creation.

In the fantasy films released during the early 1930s, the grotesqueries were often more important than the stories unfolding on screen. For example, *King Kong*'s (1933) story of a mythic "king of the apes" has remained a popular favorite. The scene atop the Empire State Building in which Kong, larger than life, grasps a tiny Fay Wray with his furry paw is memorable because of the technical wizardry of the sequence. Acting and character are virtually absent; any emotions stirred by the episode are due to editing, miniatures, and other devices. Audiences at the time did not know that Kong was a composite of models, both full-scale (the massive head, in particular) and miniature (most of the action scenes).

The overwhelming success of the film led RKO to rush out *Son of Kong* later that same year. The mystery and grandeur were gone, however, and the movie languished at the box office.

Teen Films

In the 1930s Hollywood discovered that teenagers could be a marketable commodity. In 1937, MGM began to release the Andy Hardy movies. *A Family Affair* (1937) was a lighthearted look at small-town America. Mickey Rooney stars as Andy, a typical American teen, and Lionel Barrymore as Judge Hardy, his father, a fountain of sage advice. The studio quickly followed with *You're Only Young Once, Judge Hardy's Children, Love Finds Andy Hardy,* and *Out West with the Hardys,* all released in 1938. In *You're Only Young Once,* veteran actor Lewis Stone replaces Barrymore, a role he repeated for the next 14 Andy Hardy stories. The series relentlessly reinforced a mythic American way of life, and ignored any unsettling contemporary events. Audiences flocked to these simplistic movies that sugarcoated both past and present.

Mickey Rooney, by virtue of his role as Andy Hardy, came to symbolize the American male teenager, or at least the way millions of anxious parents and politicians wanted to perceive him. Judy Garland, another stock player from the MGM studios, emerged as the model teenage girl. The two were teamed up numerous times in subsequent years. Garland went on to portray Dorothy in the *Wizard of Oz* (1939).

Child Actors

Not all of Hollywood's focus was on teenagers, however. Child actors, or those under ten years of age, have always been a part of movies, but they inevitably grew up. Despite the Depression, dancing schools flourished as kids tried to master tap and ballroom dancing. By the mid-1930s, the studios faced a glut of unemployed child actors, a situation that mirrored the real world.

A truly precocious little girl named Shirley Temple (1928–) was the most popular movie star of the era. Between 1934 and 1939, she took top billing in thirteen films. After a few unremarkable one- and two-reelers made at age five, she stole the show in *Stand Up and Cheer* (1934). In quick succession, she was cast in *Little Miss Marker* (1934) and *Now and Forever* (1934). Her career took off. Within two years, her fan mail topped 60,000 letters a month.[4]

While the child actress was busily churning out films, a huge Shirley Temple industry kicked into high gear, mass-producing records, books, playthings, and clothes popularized in her movies. In 1933 alone, merchandisers sold 1.5 million Shirley dolls. Just like Barbie dolls today, the Shirley dolls could be had in many varieties and prices. Even the boxes they came in were considered valuable.

Soon Temple's income from endorsing these items exceeded anything the studio paid her. It was said she was photographed more than President Roosevelt; she appeared on the cover of *Time* magazine (the youngest subject ever); and she was the top Hollywood box-office attraction from 1935 to 1938.

The persona Shirley Temple created in her films was perfect for the Depression years. A combination of self-reliance and innocence, she

HOW OTHERS SEE US

Shirley Temple (1928–)

Shirley Temple skyrocketed to fame in 1934, when the six-year-old starred in four blockbuster films and established herself as the best-known and most popular child star in Hollywood history. Within months, movies featuring her blond ringlets and dimpled smile were being exported to foreign markets.

In Britain, the press gushed, and a mute 12-year-old gained the power to speak, such was her excitement on seeing the Temple film *Bright Eyes* (1934). In Paraguay, a government official bemoaned his daughters' insistence on acquiring all the Shirley Temple dolls, dresses, and paraphernalia they could find.

Nowhere was Temple more popular than in Germany. Despite being banned in Berlin for its supposedly excessive gangsterism and gunplay, her film *Baby Take a Bow* (1934) packed moviegoers into theaters in both its English- and German-language versions.

Temple's popularity in this part of the world had a dark underside. It was widely understood at the time that her appeal to German audiences stemmed from those trademark reddish-blond ringlets and that rosy pink skin. She was the very model of Aryan perfection then being promoted by Germany's Nazi government. Press accounts noted that the success of *Bright Eyes* in German cinemas in the spring of 1935 helped in her "conquest" of the Fatherland.

If Temple was aware of this use of her image, she kept it to herself. Much later, when she was appointed U.S. ambassador to Czechoslovakia in 1989, a Czech official approached her at an event and pulled a card from his wallet. "I thought it would be his Communist Party card, but it was the Shirley Temple Fan Club," Ambassador Shirley Temple Black told a reporter. Many Czechs "seemed to feel I was a returning relative."

guided adults through a threatening world while simultaneously needing their love and wisdom. Her character worked hard, was honest and fair in all her dealings, radiated wholesomeness,

Shirley Temple in *Poor Little Rich Girl* (1936). Courtesy of Photofest.

and—most important—was capable of righting a world gone askew.

Newsreels and World Events

At the end of the decade, the nation went from the economic woes of the Depression to the realization that the United States would soon be involved in a conflict. Hollywood was of two minds about the impending crisis. The majority of commercial films portrayed an innocent world where no mention was made of current events, while a tiny minority did just that.

The March of Time, a monthly newsreel series, premiered in 1934. Underwritten by the publishing house of *Time, Life,* and *Fortune* magazines, these fifteen-minute documentaries discussed contemporary issues in frank, unequivocal language and images. Almost from its inception,

The March of Time dealt with fascism, neutrality, isolationism, and especially Nazism and the rise of Adolf Hitler. But these quarter-hour newsreels were just a small part of the larger theatrical bill.

United Artists released *Blockade* in 1938. Marketed as a drama about espionage, it is set in the Spanish Civil War. Starring Henry Fonda and Madeleine Carroll, *Blockade* quietly sided with the Spanish government through the respected presence of Fonda and took a small stand against the rising forces of fascism. Warner Brothers brought out *Confessions of a Nazi Spy* early in 1939. This film, through its title, reflected the popular consensus of whom everyone knew the enemy would be, prompting a protest from the German government. Warner Brothers cast their veteran star Edward G. Robinson as a G-man ferreting out a vast Nazi conspiracy within America's borders.[5]

The German invasion of Poland in September 1939 shook Americans and the film industry out of their complacency, yet both patrons and studios continued to prefer that their entertainment be nontopical. Not until Pearl Harbor in December 1941 did Hollywood awaken to events of the time. Then war movies started to pour out.

The Wizard of Oz and *Gone with the Wind*

In 1939 Metro-Goldwyn-Mayer released two of the greatest pictures of the 1930s: *The Wizard of Oz* and *Gone with the Wind.*

The Wizard of Oz has enchanted generations of children and adults with its combination of the real and the fantastic. It made a star of Judy Garland, and the memorable Harold Arlen-E. Y. Harburg score won two Academy Awards. The ingenious mix of Technicolor and sepia—particularly at the opening of the story—illustrated new uses for color processing, but the success of *The Wizard of Oz* depended on the perfect meshing of story, stars, music, and technology. Director Victor Fleming would never again achieve the sustained level of imagination he briefly enjoyed on that film, although he would share in the overall direction of *Gone with the Wind.*

Loosely based on the book by L. Frank Baum, *The Wizard of Oz* contained some elements of the prairie populism that often cropped up in the

book, and aside from a few glimpses of honorable poverty (Uncle Henry and Auntie Em's farm, for instance), it avoided anything topical. True, the "real" world of Kansas was presented in sepia, whereas the "dream" world of Oz was presented in Technicolor. It is doubtful, however, that the producers were attempting to make subtle references to the 1930s or agrarianism. The one exception might have been the wondrous Edwin B. Willis sets. They were pure Streamline Moderne, with the towers of the Emerald City evoking an optimistic view of the future. In fact, the New York World's Fair (1939–1940) was running at the same time as the movie, and the resemblances between "The World of Tomorrow" and the Emerald City were probably not entirely coincidental. The escapism of *The Wizard of Oz* likely stemmed both from events of the 1930s and the growing threat of world war, but Dorothy was levelheaded, and she finally returned to Kansas and good Midwestern sensibility.

Entertainment

In a similar vein, *Gone with the Wind* cloaked itself in a romantic story while resisting any contemporary references. Based on Margaret Mitchell's blockbuster 1936 best seller of the same name, *Gone with the Wind* enjoyed some of the best pre-release press of any movie before or since. A nationwide, two-and-a-half-year contest was conducted to select who would play Scarlett; Clark Gable had the role of Rhett secured. The part of Scarlett O'Hara finally went to a talented 25-year-old English actress, Vivien Leigh. Fan magazines reported on anything even remotely associated with the project, and MGM replicated the portico of Tara, Scarlett's family home, for a gala opening night at Loew's Grand Theater in Atlanta. All the hoopla paid off: *Gone with the Wind* was an immediate, enduring hit.

The movie did not come about easily. Although very much the project of producer David O. Selznick, it required a director. George Cukor started as director, but after nine weeks of shooting he was replaced by Victor Fleming. Not even Fleming, fresh from his success with *The Wizard of Oz,* could handle such a mammoth production;

Clark Gable as Rhett Butler in *Gone with the Wind*. Prints & Photographs Division, Library of Congress.

he collapsed on the set, and Sam Wood finally finished it. A number of screenwriters wrote and rewrote the script, cameramen came and went. No one seemed absolutely sure who should get credit for what, although the Academy nonetheless awarded the Best Director prize to Fleming, along with seven additional Oscars to others connected with the production.

Gone with the Wind wrapped up the 1930s in grand style. An expensive exercise in historical escapism, it tapped into the country's continuing fascination with its own past. Perhaps the story's recurring theme of overcoming adversity, of moving from victim to survivor, was about as timely as *Gone with the Wind* ever got. But for sheer entertainment—the real reason people attend the movies—it stood as the champion of the decade.

RADIO

Radio prospered in the 1930s. At the beginning of the 1930s, slightly over 600 AM (amplitude modulation) stations were on the air, broadcasting to some 12 million receiving sets. By 1940, the figures had grown to over 800 stations and 51 million sets.

Many of the larger, floor-model receivers could serve as fine pieces of furniture with exotic veneers; a top-of-the-line radio could cost hundreds of dollars. Since American family life in the evenings revolved around the radio, this investment was seldom begrudged. Manufacturers pitched their products as much for their elegance as for their electronic excellence.

As it insinuated itself into Americans' everyday lives, radio assumed a unique importance: it provided up-to-the-minute news, weather, and sports; it entertained with music, drama and comedy; and it educated with self-help and instructional shows. Radio leveled regional and social differences by its very ubiquity.

For most Americans, radio was considered a necessity. Even in the worst of the Depression, very few people defaulted on their radio payments. Advertisers quickly grasped the importance of radio and put their dollars into commercials: ad spending went from slightly over $3 million in 1932 to well over $100 million by 1940.

RADIO DEBUTS OF THE 1930s

The George Burns and Gracie Allen Show (1931): comedy sketches and musical numbers starring the married comic duo.

The Breakfast Club (1933): morning variety show featuring talk, music, and topical comedy—the first successful morning program in this now-ubiquitous format.

Lux Radio Theater (1934): dramatic anthology series that adapted Broadway plays and Hollywood films into one-hour broadcasts, often voiced by the original stars.

Fibber McGee and Molly (1935): situation comedy about the foibles and schemes of a small-town man and his patient wife (played by Jim and Marian Jordan), along with their friends, neighbors, and visitors.

Your Hit Parade (1935): weekly presentation of the nation's most popular songs, based on sales, airplay, and jukebox selections.

The Edgar Bergen and Charlie McCarthy Show (1937): comedy-variety show featuring ventriloquist Edgar Bergen and his dummies, including Charlie McCarthy and Mortimer Snerd.

The Guiding Light (1937): dramatic serial that would become American television's longest-running daytime soap opera.

The Shadow (1937): mystery series famous for its sinister opening line: "Who knows what evil lurks in the hearts of men? The Shadow knows."

Network broadcasting, began in the 1920s, saw rapid growth in the 1930s: the National Broadcasting Company (NBC), with two networks, the Blue and the Red; the Columbia Broadcasting System (CBS); and the Mutual Broadcasting System (MBS), founded in 1934. This growth meant the demise of much local, or independent, programming. As the networks grew, costs rose and famous entertainers were signed to binding contracts. Small stations quickly affiliated with the networks, which had greater resources for developing new shows. In the meantime, countless orchestras, combos, comedians, and other local talent lost jobs as their stations affiliated with the networks.

By 1931, most radio stations were essentially carriers of network programming. In turn, advertising agencies began to develop their own ideas and formats. The agency-run radio department emerged as one of the most important divisions at broadcast studios. Although the networks were still given the right to approve programming, the big sponsors had grown so powerful that such approval was more a formality than a privilege. In addition, syndicates began to prepackage all manner of shows for both networks and independent stations. These productions were particularly attractive to smaller stations that could not afford to put together anything on their own that approached the syndicates' caliber of work.

Comedy and Variety Shows on the Radio

American radio introduced hundreds of personalities who became household names. Some of these entertainers moved directly to radio from vaudeville, while others mixed film and radio careers.

One example is Rudy Vallee (1901–1986), a modestly talented crooner who achieved great fame and popularity during the 1930s. Vallee left Yale University in 1928 to form a band, The Connecticut Yankees, with himself as vocalist. Several of his club appearances were carried live on radio, introducing listeners to his signature singing style—a weak voice projected by a megaphone. By staying very close to the sensitive radio microphone, he could achieve the same amplification effect.

Vallee made his series radio debut in *The Fleischmann Hour* at the end of the 1920s, opening each segment with his familiar "Heigh-ho, everybody!" This NBC show quickly became a network hit and set a standard for much subsequent musical variety programming. In 1936, the show became *The Royal Gelatin Hour,* and continued into 1939. The series came about because of Vallee's popularity, but it was underwritten by corporate interests, in this case yeast and gelatin manufacturers. Vallee was nominally in charge, but his sponsors, along with their advertising agencies, had control of all content.

Vallee's guests were usually fellow performers, although the show broke new ground showcasing dramatic readings by stage and film actors. These passages were written for radio and not the theater, suggesting the growing importance of the medium.

Amos 'n Andy

Freeman Gosden (1899–1982) and Charles Correll (1890–1972), better known as *Amos 'n Andy,* starred in what was probably the most popular radio show of all time.

Amos 'n Andy started out as *Sam 'n' Henry* in 1926 in Chicago. The station unwisely gave up the show, and Gosden and Correll changed the name to *Amos 'n Andy* to avoid any copyright battles. In 1929, NBC picked up their contract, giving the show national exposure. It was an immediate hit, and its popularity continued throughout the 1930s. *Amos 'n Andy* was so popular that theaters would stop their movies and pipe in the nightly broadcasts, rather than lose potential audiences to home radios.

During its thirty-odd years on the air, *Amos 'n Andy* attracted some of the largest repeat audiences in the history of radio. The show ran fifteen minutes a day, five days a week, and was usually broadcast in the early evening. Gosden (Amos) and Correll (Andy) were two white male performers of many voices; their characters were blacks, and included both men and women. The series was, in some ways, a radio version of the old-time minstrel show: white performers in blackface doing caricatures of African Americans. In fact, the two actors frequently posed in full makeup for publicity shots, and no attempt was made to hide their identities. Their scripts were written in a stereotypical Negro dialect—and delivered exactly as written. Phrases like "Hello dere, Sapphire," and "Holy mackerel, Andy!" became part of national speech, and listeners exchanged summaries of the previous night's episode, usually delivering them in some approximation of the characters' patois.

What should have been an issue of racial stereotyping seldom entered discussions of *Amos 'n Andy.* One reason was that racial insensitivity was much more overt. Movies caricatured African

Americans; recordings featuring black artists were sold as "race records"; and other radio shows had characters just as stereotypical. The NAACP voiced criticisms of the series, but to little avail. In the meantime, the show continued to attract a true mass audience that cut across the lines of race, age, and gender.

A better explanation would be that the shows were genuinely funny. Characters were likable, the plots told tight stories, and there was no meanness or violence. In 1930, at the height of their popularity, Gosden and Correll made a movie that did not do well; perhaps hearing the show—as opposed to seeing it—tempered the obvious stereotyping.

Entertainment

Other Radio Comedians

The networks, along with larger independent stations, searched for other comedians. In 1932 CBS gave George Burns and Gracie Allen, a real-life married couple, shared billing with the Guy Lombardo orchestra on *The Robert Burns Panatela Show* (named for a brand of cigars). A mix of music and comedy, the show attracted a strong following, and it was soon renamed *The Burns and Allen Show.*

Shows like *Amos 'n Andy* and *Burns and Allen* demonstrated a new approach to comedy. The routines were clever and quick, relying on verbal humor instead of visual antics. Familiar, evolving characters were created. Audiences had expectations about how Amos, Andy, George, and Gracie would act in given situations. Instead of isolated skits or one-liners with no reference to the deliverer, radio comedy moved more and more in the direction of humor that relied on audience identification of the comedian.

When they were in vaudeville, George Burns was the funny man, and Gracie Allen fed him lines. But the couple discovered that when the roles were reversed, the laughs increased. Thus Burns became the bemused husband of the implacably daffy Gracie. He may have seemed the straight man, but he frequently got to deliver the rejoinders, not just the setups. A brilliant comedian in her own right, Gracie had to remain in character throughout the show. Listeners looked forward to her non sequiturs and her scatterbrained ideas.

"WHO WAS THAT MASKED MAN? IT'S THE LONE RANGER!"

An exciting afternoon of radio was capped by the half-hour *The Lone Ranger,* a show that usually came on just before Mom summoned everyone to dinner. Adapted from a series of books by Fran Striker, *Lone Ranger* was not just a radio program; the masked hero also appeared in a movie serial, Big Little Books, comic books, and a newspaper comic strip during the 1930s. Kids everywhere knew about the Lone Ranger, his wonder horse Silver, and his faithful Indian sidekick Tonto, who in each episode uttered his mysterious "kemo sabe" (no exact translation exists, because it was made up). The show's stirring theme music was lifted from the overture to Rossini's opera *William Tell,* making it possibly the best-known classical composition of the day. *The Lone Ranger* later became an equally popular early television show for children, airing from 1949 through 1957.

Week after week, this domestic narrative played out and the team proved ideal for the natural intimacy that defines radio.

Similarly, former vaudevillian Jack Benny developed his own memorable character. *The Jack Benny Show* (NBC, 1932–1955) quickly became a listener favorite. Jack Benny himself, miser, would-be violinist, and a perpetually youthful thirty-nine, was the main character, but he had an outstanding cast of regulars—announcer Don Wilson, bandleader Phil Harris, impressionist Mel Blanc, and Eddie Anderson as the put-upon Rochester, Benny's faithful servant. Each of them had an identity that was sustained in every broadcast, creating familiarity and continuity.

Soap Operas

Soap operas—so called because most of them were sponsored by soap companies and dealt with emotional stories and characters—became an important part of the typical radio day on 1930s radio. The first soap operas began in the late 1920s, and they were usually broadcast daily on weekday mornings and early afternoons, the

Entertainment

assumption being that housewives would tune in for their favorite fifteen-minute dramas. It was further assumed that men would not listen, so the soaps became a small but significant area of network radio created by and for women, an unusual situation in what was essentially a male-dominated medium.

Some of the more popular 1930s soap operas, some of which endured through to the 1950s, included:

- *Backstage Wife* (1935–1959, NBC)
- *Just Plain Bill* (1932–1955, CBS)
- *Lorenzo Jones* (1937–1955, NBC)
- *Ma Perkins* (1933–1960, NBC and CBS—this show was on both networks simultaneously for a while)
- *One Man's Family* (1932–1959, NBC—an evening show)
- *Our Gal Sunday* (1937–1959, CBS)
- *Pepper Young's Family* (1936–1959, NBC)
- *The Romance of Helen Trent* (1933–1960, CBS)
- *Stella Dallas* (1937–1955, NBC)
- *When a Girl Marries* (1939–1957, CBS)

A few radio soap operas even made the transition to television. Seldom were big-name actors involved; the soap opera world was a tight one, and players would rush from stage to stage, studio to studio, in order to perform their roles in multiple dramas.

For listeners, the daily serials dished up a bit of escapism. They featured molasses-like pacing and their simple plotting and black-and-white characters required minimal attentiveness. Often set in rural locales, the stories took simple folk and cast them in dramatic situations. Moralistic and conservative, the soap operas served as a kind of guidepost in the 1930s.

Radio Drama

Many serious dramatic series were created during the decade, among them *Lux Radio Theatre* (Lux was a popular beauty soap). Hosted from 1936 until 1945 by celebrated Hollywood director Cecil B. DeMille, *Lux Radio Theatre* presented one-hour adaptations of leading motion pictures, often using the same stars who had appeared in the movie. The series illustrated the close connections between film and radio, and publicized motion pictures on a top-ranked radio show.

Another acclaimed dramatic series in the 1930s was *First Nighter* (1929–1953). Supposedly broadcast from "The Little Theater Off Times Square," this show actually originated in Chicago and, later, Hollywood. Each episode had Mr. First Nighter being shown to his seat by an usher. Over the years, various actors took a seat on the aisle; it was their job to introduce an hour-long radio version of a stage production or—more likely—an original radio drama. The shows were of uneven quality, but captured a good audience share. *First Nighter* introduced more Americans to the stage, or at least the radio version of a play, than had ever actually attended a theatrical production.

News and Information

Although entertainment shows occupied much of the broadcast day, radio was becoming the primary carrier of news and information. As the Great Depression deepened in the early thirties, President-elect Franklin D. Roosevelt began using radio as a weapon against discontent. In March 1933, just days after taking office, Roosevelt initiated a remarkable series of broadcasts to the American people called *Fireside Chats.*

Originating directly from the White House, these informal conversations were aimed at putting the public more at ease about the ongoing crisis. During the next several years, the president would conduct over forty such chats, beginning each with a reassuring, "My dear friends." He chose his words carefully, using a simple vocabulary without condescending to his audience. As a result, he built a sense of intimacy between his listeners and himself. Critics charged him with unfairly utilizing the airwaves for political purposes, but the president remained undeterred. It is estimated that upwards of a quarter of the nation tuned into the *Fireside Chats,* or some 30 million listeners. Never before had such a vast audience simultaneously shared in a public speech, making Franklin D. Roosevelt the nation's first media-savvy president.[6]

At the same time, a number of radio news reporters rose to prominence. Newscasters (the relatively new designation that replaced "reporters") like Elmer Davis, Gabriel Heatter, H. V. Kaltenborn, Raymond Gram Swing, Lowell Thomas, and Walter Winchell were on the air, redefining the traditional image of a reporter. Instead of a straight, objective reading of events, they brought a personal style to their scripts, often adding interpretive commentary to ongoing stories.

With war imminent, people relied on their radios for late-breaking bulletins about the deteriorating international situation. In any discussion of that period, the name of Edward R. Murrow emerges ahead of those of his contemporaries. A member of the CBS news team, Murrow brought an unequalled sincerity and gravity to his reports; he was a calming voice in the face of disaster. (See Entertainment of the 1940s.)

Father Coughlin

Father Charles E. Coughlin (1891–1979), a priest at the Shrine of the Little Flower in Royal Oak, Michigan, illustrates how radio can be abused while staying within the narrow confines of the law. Beginning in 1930, Father Coughlin initiated a series of political radio sermons. His message was simple: a cabal of international bankers, consisting of Jewish financiers, Wall Street brokers, and Communist sympathizers (and later sympathizers of the New Deal), threatened the very foundations of democracy, and only a turn to Italian-style fascism would save the Republic. He mixed invective with a mellow delivery that often lulled listeners to accept his true message. In the depths of the Depression, Father Coughlin held sway over an audience estimated at upwards of 40 million listeners, more than Roosevelt usually got for his *Fireside Chats*. They inundated his church with at least 80,000 letters a week, most containing a contribution. In no time, the Shrine of the Little Flower was taking in $5 million a year.[7]

The Columbia Broadcasting System, his parent network, became troubled when Coughlin refused them access to his scripts prior to delivery; they canceled his contract in 1933. Undeterred, Coughlin organized an independent network financed by listener contributions. He, and several other disaffected politicians, created the Union Party in 1936. His new party did poorly, and stations began to leave the organization. The Catholic

Church took a stand against his extreme political positions, and by the end of the decade he was unable to afford either a network or radio time.

The War of the Worlds

On Halloween 1938, another radio innovator demonstrated ways that the strengths of radio might be misused, albeit innocently. That evening, Orson Welles broadcast a dramatization of H. G. Wells's novel *The War of the Worlds* as part of his series *Mercury Theatre on the Air.*

Despite repeated statements throughout the broadcast that the show was a dramatization, many in the audience became convinced it was real. Welles had cleverly camouflaged his warnings so that many missed them. For much of the hour, the inattentive worried that Martian invaders were roaming the swamps of New Jersey. It was a perfect demonstration of the imaginative power of radio, along with the potential for mass hysteria brought about by slick production methods.

Since the government controlled the airways, *The War of the Worlds* raised the issue of responsibility. If a gullible public was fooled by a radio show, whose responsibility was it to ensure that the public was not fooled again? Because of the furor the broadcast evoked, the Federal Communications Commission came down heavily against productions that might frighten or dupe the public. It was an acknowledgment that radio was a medium of unquestioned power, one that needed rules so that power could not be abused.[8]

TELEVISION

Throughout the 1930s, engineers labored to make television a reality for Americans. Everyone knew that the technical problems associated with the medium would be ironed out; it was just a question of when. Leading the attack was David Sarnoff and his team at the labs of the Radio Corporation of America. As a vice president of the RCA colossus in the 1920s, Sarnoff had established the first radio network, the National Broadcasting Company. He popularized the word "television," seeing in it the potential to meld sound and image, and to transmit the result over great distances.

The 1929 stock market crash and the continuing popularity of radio—along with the huge profits radio generated—dissuaded most sustained efforts at any commercial exploitation of television. Nonetheless, the experiments continued: in 1930, NBC was granted permission to operate W2XBS (the predecessor of today's WNBC) in New York City; the following year found CBS operating W2XAB (today's WCBS), also out of New York. The rivals used movie theaters and popular radio and vaudeville personalities as hosts to promote their new technologies. Only a few thousand receivers existed, however, and most of them were in metropolitan New York.

In the summer of 1936, NBC television went on the air. It was a limited affair—space atop the Empire State Building, a handful of bulky receiving sets, and an invitation-only group of about 200 people. David Sarnoff appeared on screen, as did some radio personalities, a few models and other entertainers. Despite the limited facilities, the people present sensed the importance of this event.

Expanding the boundaries of television, NBC telecast a variety show from the stage of the newly built Radio City Music Hall, and its mobile units covered several baseball games and other sporting events in the New York area. RCA continued its experimental broadcasts, and crews televised the annual Macy's Thanksgiving Parade for the first time in 1939.

Prior to the Macy's parade, RCA went public at the New York World's Fair in June 1939, introducing television to a mass audience. Throughout each day, RCA featured continuous telecasting by its affiliate, NBC, using banks of receivers where people could watch the proceedings. RCA even had sets for sale, at prices ranging from $199.50 (roughly $2,500 in today's dollars) to $600 ($7,500).

President Roosevelt attended the dedication of the RCA Pavilion, and he appeared on television, the first head of state ever seen on the new medium. A short time later, the king and queen of England also appeared. Exhibits sponsored by Ford, Westinghouse, and General Electric also featured TV. By the end of 1939, it became clear that television would be the next major entertainment medium. Only the onset of World War II prevented its immediate, widespread adoption.[9]

THEATER

In the 1930s, few people attended theatrical productions. Theater was primarily an urban entertainment, and tickets were expensive—several dollars—versus a dime or quarter for a movie ticket.

The advent of sound in the movies further reduced theater attendance. In addition, since a successful play was usually adapted to film, moviegoers might get to see some of the original cast in the motion-picture version. Thus, one very popular art form brought a less popular one to a mass audience through a media crossover. The film version could differ markedly from the stage original, but millions of people could see the movie of the play.

Musicals

Many plays did experience commercial success in the 1930s. Certainly, almost anything that Richard Rodgers and Lorenz Hart, Cole Porter, or George and Ira Gershwin penned stood a good chance of being big box office. These men were composers and lyricists, and their forte was the Broadway musical. Usually musicals were bright and breezy, with a fair number of hummable tunes. Anything that took minds off unemployment and discouraging economic news was favored over something that reinforced glum feelings.

Rodgers and Hart were among the most prolific composers in the 1930s. Songs like "Ten Cents a Dance" (*Simple Simon*, 1930), "Little Girl Blue" (*Jumbo*, 1935), and "My Funny Valentine" (*Babes in Arms*, 1937) set a new standard for the musical theater. Thanks to recordings, radio, and the movies, their music achieved two distinctions: much of it became popular in its own time, and—more importantly—many of their songs have become known to generations of music lovers.

Cole Porter contributed some of the more adult and sophisticated lyrics of the period, such as "Love for Sale" (1930). Like Rodgers and Hart, Porter's view of the world had little to do with the economic crisis or the New Deal, although they did not escape passing mention in his remarkable catalog of songs. Thanks again to movies, radio, and recordings, he became widely known, and his

Entertainment

out to people who normally were not involved in theatrical activities.

DANCE

In the 1930s, few Americans were even aware of the movements in modern dance. With the Depression and declining audiences, dance companies found themselves facing dire times. A few pioneers—Martha Graham, Hanya Holm, Doris Humphrey, Charles Weidman, Ruth Page—worked tirelessly in the 1930s, but with little or no acclaim.

The popular art of dancing still managed to flourish, however. Broadway musicals, in particular, redefined stage choreography, and Hollywood's "All Talking! All Singing! All Dancing!" extravaganzas presented dancers as they had never been seen before. The movie camera discovered new angles, new shots, and new methods of presenting action. Ruby Keeler did not just tap dance; now she had dozens—or hundreds—of others exactly synchronized with her, thanks to choreographer Busby Berkeley's gift for positioning and moving dancers in front of the all-seeing camera. Performers like Ann Miller (*New Faces of 1937,* her debut; many others), Buddy Ebsen (*Broadway Melody of 1936;* many others) and Ray Bolger (*The Great Ziegfeld,* 1936; many others) rose from obscurity to major dancing roles in dozens of Hollywood musicals.

For millions of moviegoers, this *was* dancing. Nothing esoteric here. Fifty chorus girls, for instance, pranced on the wings of an airplane in *Flying Down to Rio* (1933), epitomizing film musicals. Fred Astaire and Ginger Rogers brought debonair ballroom dancing to new heights, and choreographers presented their numbers in new and offbeat ways. As far as the musicals of stage and screen were concerned, dancing was in fine health.

Meanwhile, the American people were dancing as never before. The jitterbug, the Lindy, the Camel Walk, the Shorty George, the Suzie-Q, the Sabu, the Toddle, even the old Lambeth Walk—along with waltzes, fox-trots, congas, sambas, and rumbas—brought millions onto the floor. In the 1930s, swing was king. The big bands played everywhere, and what they played was dance music. Halls, open-air pavilions, and clubs open to dancing flourished.

The 1920s had loosened the strictures against public dancing, especially popular dances like the Charleston. By the 1930s, only a few religious groups and some straitlaced communities still had rules regarding dancing. It was cheap entertainment, and at just the right time. Radio had come into its own, including more music shows on its schedules. The sales of recordings—dance recordings—skyrocketed, and radio and the movies mirrored this interest.[12]

Fashion

of the 1930s

In order to talk about the fashions of the 1930s, it is necessary to know what came before. The stylish woman of 1900–1920 wore clothes draped over her body in a voluminous manner suggestive of Art Nouveau design. At the same time, she remained very much a part of the Victorian era, with layers and layers of material.

With the onset of the Roaring Twenties, radical changes occurred for those at the forefront of style. The Art Deco woman's clothes made her appear boyish; instead of the flowing lines of a few years earlier, the look became angular and sinewy. Revolutionary changes occurred during the 1920s: skirts went up—often to the knee—and multiple layers of clothing were shed for what seemed to many to be a shocking brevity of attire.

WOMEN'S FASHIONS

The stock market crash of 1929 destroyed much of the youthful exuberance of the decade, signaling a time to grow up and act like an adult. The most noticeable change in dress emerged with the rediscovery of curves. The waist and bust, both seemingly lost in the 1920s became objects of attention. The improvements in undergarments emphasized the feminine bosom. Waists were cinched by belts. In addition, the back—once hidden, now often revealed—became a focal point.

The knees, however, disappeared as skirts got progressively longer, before creeping back up near the end of the decade.

Youthful slimness remained the ideal—to be both curvaceous and slender simultaneously. In addition, the clingy clothes of the fashionable demanded that no unwanted lumps or bulges disturb the smooth lines of fabric. The popularity of various diets during the decade testifies to the need to be slender. The hunger women faced during the depression seldom entered the picture.

Women in the 1930s, especially younger women, looked to the movies, the big department stores, mail-order catalogs, and magazines to learn current styles. The important thing was that Sears & Roebuck (or Ward's, or Macy's, or the local department store) had items in stock that resembled what Joan Crawford wore on film or what *Vogue* insisted represented the season. Paris continued as the fashion capital of the world until after World War II, but what Paris designers dictated and what the women of America wore did not necessarily match, especially during the Depression. (See Fashion of the 1940s.)

For most American women, ready-to-wear ruled the day. Mass production and availability in stores nationwide only increased popularity. The idea of custom-tailored, one-of-a-kind outfits was foreign to the vast majority of shoppers.

The development of assembly-line technology for the clothing industry allowed the greatest range of styles and prices ever seen. If a dress was on sale, so much the better. American fashion, by and large, was very democratic in its appeal.

In order to hold down costs, some manufacturers offered garments that could be finished at home. A woman would pick out a dress by traditional size, knowing that all the difficult sewing had been completed. Collars, cuffs, and other finish work on shoulders and sleeves were done by professional tailors; the buyer simply stitched up the seams and hem.[1]

Creating or updating one's own wardrobe became popular. McCall's and Butterick published numerous clothes patterns, while piece-goods shops offered a wide variety of fabrics and materials. Big merchandisers like Sears, Roebuck encouraged the trend by featuring sewing, knitting, and crocheting supplies in their stores and catalogs.

As the decade progressed, the popularity of printed fabrics grew significantly. These quickly replaced the costly embroidery of the past, and they had another practical side: spots or stains were less likely to show up on prints than on solids, keeping cleaning costs to a minimum. The simple print dress, manufactured from synthetic materials like rayon and cut to fit average figures, came to be an overwhelming favorite of women during the 1930s. Sears, Roebuck probably carried the use of prints to its extreme in the early 1930s with its "Hooverettes," simple wraparound dresses that tied at the side and could fit anyone. They were reversible, so when one side got soiled, the whole dress could be turned inside out to expose clean material. First called "Sears-ettes," they came to be humorously associated with President Hoover and the nation's economic woes. They sold at an attractive Depression price: two for 98 cents.[2]

Motion pictures and fan magazines set fashion trends. The images projected on the silver screen were reinforced by photo spreads in the hugely popular movie magazines available. Audiences could copy Hollywood fashions and hairstyles. Newsstand fan magazines like *Hollywood, Modern Screen, Movie Mirror, Photoplay, Screenland,* and *Silver Screen* included extensive layouts on what stars wore at any given time or in a particular film. In earlier times, actors were responsible for their own clothes, but by the 1930s the leading performers were outfitted by the studios both on and off the screen. The major studios also staffed their own fashion designers, who prepared the costumes for upcoming features. Retailers studied what the designers created. Soon after a film's release, copies of the fashions appeared on retail racks. As a result, women were no longer imitating high society styles; they were mimicking what they saw in the movies.[3]

Often the stars—Loretta Young, Fay Wray, Claudette Colbert, and little Shirley Temple—modeled fashions in the larger catalogs, making the Hollywood–consumer connection even stronger. The star's signature might even be stitched into the label. The studios also featured their own stars whenever they could, whether it was Jean Harlow on a Columbia Pictures set in a clinging gown that left little to the imagination, or Katharine Hepburn in slacks and a shirt, riding a bicycle at Warner Brothers. Blue jeans began to appear in westerns, and actresses like Barbara Stanwyck were photographed wearing denim. Never before had popular media so influenced the fashion choices of a generation of consumers.[4]

The rebellion against the insouciant twenties began at the feet and worked its way upward. By the depths of the Depression, the hemline descended to midcalf or lower. At the same time, more and more material was being cut on the bias, which meant the fabric hugged the figure, displaying the natural lines of the wearer, and giving a fluid drape to the article of clothing. In response to hard economic times, manufacturers used cheaper materials. For example, cotton replaced silk and rayon replaced linen. An inexpensive way to dress up a dated outfit was to add bold, unusual buttons.

Belts, along with fitted skirts, brought back feminine waists and hips. The brassiere became an important part of a woman's overall wardrobe. Led by companies like Maidenform and Warners, the constricting bandeaux of the 1920s gave way in the 1930s to bras that actually came in sizes. This innovation greatly improved both the fit and the comfort of the wearer, as well as enhanced her figure. Another improvement came with the

The very well-dressed U.S. Olympics Women's Swimming Team as they sailed July 15, 1936, on the *Manhattan* for Berlin and the Olympic Games. Their outfits show the trends of the decade: smaller hats and more defined and belted waistlines. AP Photo.

development of Lastex by the United States Rubber Company in 1931. This fiber could be woven with just about any fabric, providing both strength and stretch. Thus were the heavy girdles of the past replaced by lighter, better-fitting models.

In another concession to the Depression, women could buy cheap undergarments devoid of lace or trim. Needlework magazines provided handy transfers and instructions so the consumer could embroider her undergarments. Silk lingerie became available only to the well-off; Dupont's rayon emerged as the fabric of choice for everyone else. Nylon stockings, long promised and thought to be indestructible, finally made their appearance in 1939 and were a huge success. Until then, women wore silk or rayon hose and cotton weaves.

Women's shoulders were enhanced as the padded look grew in popularity. At the same time, sleeves became puffier, creating a new silhouette

FASHION TRENDS OF THE 1930s

The 1930s were a time of conservative fashion as many turned to practical and affordable clothing. Sportswear became briefer and less constricting.

Women: Trousers rise in popularity; smaller hats are in style, but all adorned with feathers in the early years of the decade; pillbox hats and snoods (1935) for long hair; natural waistlines are belted and more defined; hemlines drop; tanned skin becomes stylish; makeup is more natural looking, but eyebrows are plucked into thin high curves (1932–1936); bias cut dresses are popular; shorts for sportswear make an entrance; puffy sleeves are in vogue; skirts become shorter at end of decade; patterned housedresses are worn for everyday wear.

Men: Suits are less formal, less baggy; the one-piece swimsuit is prevalent by end of the decade.

Young girls: Simple dresses and playsuits are most popular; by adolescence, teenagers are wearing adult clothing.

Young boys: Scaled down men's suits with shorts and sailor suits are worn for dress-up occasions; older boys wear knickers; by teen years, they trade knickers for long pants.

for the upper body that diminished the waist. The total look emphasized slender yet natural lines, rising to an obvious bust and squared-off shoulders. Topping it all off was a hat, an essential item for the well-dressed woman.

Smaller hats replaced the helmet-like cloche of the 1920s, frequently perched at a jaunty angle. These smaller hats came in many styles. The so-called Empress Eugenie, a soft felt hat often with a feather for decoration, gained distinction when Greta Garbo wore one in the movie *Romance* (1930). Another favorite was the pillbox, flat-topped and round of design, which also gained impetus from Garbo in *As You Desire Me* (1932). Variants on Tyrolean models that resembled men's fedoras, tams, turbans, babushkas, berets, and sailor hats were also popular, since fashion demanded that women cover their heads.

In 1933, the composer Irving Berlin wrote the music and lyrics for a song titled "Easter Parade," which appeared in his topical Broadway musical *As Thousands Cheer*. It begins with a reference to an Easter bonnet, a clear reference to the importance hats continued to play in a woman's wardrobe. The hats might not have been bonnets anymore, but they were still worn.

SPORTSWEAR

At the same time that suits and dresses became more formal, sports attire did the opposite. Many women, for example, no longer wore heavy stockings while playing tennis. They played bare-legged in skirts and wore socks, thereby shedding corsets, garters, hose, and other unneeded garments. By 1933, conservative shorts or culottes might occasionally be seen on the courts. Women began wearing slacks for golf, bicycling, and other sports. Sometimes these slack outfits were called "pajamas" because of their loose fit, but they were definitely sportswear, not pajamas. By the middle of the decade, many younger women were being seen in public clad in shorts instead of slacks.[5]

In a similar way, the bathing suit became much more form-fitting and streamlined. Prior to the 1930s, most women's bathing costumes were made of dark, heavy wool, hardly conducive to sunning or swimming. In the early 1930s, designers used new, lighter materials. Two-piece suits became popular by mid-decade as a result. Lastex, with its ability to stretch, became not just the miracle fabric of girdles and other undergarments, but of the swimsuit industry. Women who took swimming seriously wore rubber bathing caps that covered most or all of their hair. These came in a variety of colors and could be coordinated with bathing suits.

One of the side effects of the enthusiasm for outdoor activities was that women acquired suntans. Prior to the mid-1920s, a proper woman avoided the sun. A tan was a cultural taboo; only the poorest working farmer's wife had a sunburned neck and arms, whereas a society lady carried a parasol, wore a wide-brimmed hat or bonnet, and kept her pale skin unblemished. All that changed in the 1930s. Women and men from high society reveled in deep tans acquired on

In this unusual group, we see half a century of women's bathing suits, shown at the Quota Club convention, 1931. The women second from the left and second from the right are wearing the most modern suits for the early 1930s. Prints & Photographs Division, Library of Congress.

luxury vacations, and the working class soaked up the sun's rays to replicate the look. The stigma disappeared.

COSMETICS AND ACCESSORIES

Following the lead of numerous stars, powder, rouge, and mascara received widespread use and acceptance. Women started putting on dark nail polish, matching it to a lipstick. Names like Max Factor, Elizabeth Arden, Revlon, and Maybelline could be found in even the most humble medicine chest. Women plucked out natural eyebrows and then penciled in sharply arched ones. Fan magazines frequently published features showing a popular actress in the process of applying her makeup and giving advice about techniques.

Not many women could afford expensive jewelry, so costume jewelry became fashionable. Hatpins and clips were an essential part of a basic wardrobe, along with a variety of earrings. Bangle bracelets were also in vogue. Much of the period's costume jewelry featured Art Deco motifs. The zigzags, chevrons, and other geometric shapes that characterize Art Deco architecture were reproduced in enameled pieces, as well as in stamped metal and molded plastic. The closing years of the decade, however, witnessed a return to traditional jewelry, especially Victorian designs.

One breed of dog was immortalized in innumerable pieces of costume adornment: the terrier. President Roosevelt had Fala, his adored Scottish terrier, while William Powell and Myrna Loy had Asta, a wirehaired fox terrier and irrepressible pooch. It stole many a scene in the *Thin Man* movies of the time. (See Entertainment of the 1930s.) The public loved both pets. Pins, brooches, and other baubles poured into department and jewelry stores and made terriers the dog of choice for millions.

HAIR FASHIONS

The short hair and casual bobs of the 1920s were followed by longer tresses. Marcelled waves and permanents grew in popularity with improved electric curling irons and permanent-wave machines that allowed curls to stay in place for extended periods of time. The sculpted look firmly took hold and, despite the Depression, beauty shops prospered with the new hairstyles.

In the early 1930s, Jean Harlow, "the Blonde Bombshell," introduced platinum blonde hair.

Jean Harlow in the 1930s, "the Blonde Bombshell," introduced platinum blonde hair. The color promptly caught the public fancy, in large part because of the success of Harlow's movies and the enthusiasm of her fans. AP Photo.

The color promptly caught the public fancy, in large part because of the success of Harlow's movies and the enthusiasm of her fans. Not everyone could be a platinum bombshell, but dyes, henna rinses, and bleaches were in vogue as women tried to improve on nature.

John Breck, a New England manufacturer of shampoos, had a stroke of marketing genius in the early thirties. Until then, all commercial shampoos came in only one variety, which washed most normal hair. In 1933, Breck began to package his product in three types: dry, normal, and oily. Soon, Breck's Shampoo was available nationally, and for decades his three varieties dominated the market.[6]

Although the electric hair dryer had been around since the 1920s, during the 1930s refinements such as variable temperature settings and multiple speeds made them a quantum leap ahead of towels and the primitive electric models of a few years earlier.

MEN'S FASHIONS

As always, any fashion shifts for men were more evolutionary than revolutionary. The lounge suit, less formal than the traditional business suit, made its appearance. Single-breasted jackets became just as acceptable as the more traditional double-breasted models. The seersucker suit allowed men something lighter than wool and gabardines, and the so-called Palm Beach cotton and mohair suits were big sellers.

Padded shoulders signaled perhaps the biggest style change in men's clothing. Much like women's fashions, the waist was taken in, and the shoulders became broader as the decade passed. The wide trouser from the 1920s remained, although at first somewhat slimmed down from its earlier widths. By the mid-thirties, however, young men's styles displayed high, exaggerated waistbands and a return to extremely wide cuffed bottoms (twenty-two inches was thought stylish). After about 1935, pants were slimmer and straighter again. Older and more conservative males tended to avoid these trends. The zipper fly, a standard on most men's pants by mid-decade, replaced old-fashioned buttons. With that exception, for the average man a suit purchased in 1939 closely resembled one bought in 1930.

Men's bathing apparel was as conservative as their business suits. In the early 1930s, dark, heavy, knit wool trunks and matching sleeveless knit shirts were pretty much the rule at public beaches. Then, a few daring men at New York beaches started going topless. This controversial new custom immediately caught on with young men around the nation. Sears, Roebuck sold topless trunks by 1934. Two-piece male bathing attire fought against this trend for the remainder of the decade, but the one-piece suit and bare chest were the clear victors.[7]

Johnny Weissmuller, the Olympic swimming champion and later the star of a number of *Tarzan* films, modeled swimsuits for BVD. By 1939 he was featured in ads wearing a one-piece top-

Sports figures Johnny Weissmuller (swimming champion who went on to become Tarzan in films), right, and boxer Jack Dempsey in bathing suits typical of the early 1930s. Dark, heavy, knit wool trunks and similar sleeveless tops were the rule for men, 1930. Prints & Photographs Division, Library of Congress.

less suit that contained Lastex for a smoother, better fit. His trunks still had the white belt that had been a part of men's bathing attire since the 1920s, but they were essentially an abridged version of the past. Even more daring was the loincloth he sported in *Tarzan, the Ape Man* (1932).

Lastex, so important to both women's undergarments and men's swimsuits, also helped modify male fashions in another way. Since the elasticized sock was reinforced with Lastexmen, men no longer needed to use garters to hold up their socks.

Men's underwear also changed. Jockey introduced its now-famous brief in 1934. Until that time, underclothing for men tended to be bulky and generally uncomfortable. Long johns and union suits (i.e., long underwear that covered arms, legs, and torso) were still worn by old-fashioned males, and even scratchy wool undergarments had their adherents. The acceptance of the soft cotton Jockey briefs demonstrated a final rejection of all the clothing restrictions placed on men by the repressive Victorian era.

In the wildly successful movie *It Happened One Night* (1934), Clark Gable removes his outer shirt and reveals he is not wearing an undershirt. Popular mythology has it that the sales of undershirts plummeted after the film's release, although any hard figures to support this are nonexistent. In the same movie, Claudette Colbert dons Gable's pajama top because she has no sleepwear with her. As a result, it is said, millions of women demanded man-styled pajamas of their own. These two stories, embedded as they are in American popular culture, illustrate how people were influenced by what they saw on the screen. (See Entertainment of the 1930s.)

In footwear, the Bass Shoe Company began to produce its famous Bass Weejuns (the odd name comes from the final two syllables of "Norwegian," the shoes' place of ancestry) in 1936. Comfortable, slip-on moccasins, Weejuns became an instant hit among men, particularly college students. They epitomized a more casual mode of dress and helped popularize the term "loafer" for footwear. A custom among many men who wore loafers was to insert a shiny penny in the piece of leather that went across the instep, giving birth to the "penny loafer."[8]

PERSONAL GROOMING

Although their clothing styles may not have changed radically during the decade, some men's personal grooming habits underwent a shift. Most important was the introduction of dry shaving, which replaced the use of a razor and soap. The Schick Corporation introduced the first electric razor in 1931, after much experimentation in its development of a small electric motor. It was an instant success. By the end of the decade, the numerous companies in the electric shaver business were selling 1.5 million models a year. The shavers were not cheap—anywhere from $15 to $25 each—but the high cost did not adversely affect sales.

Fashion

ANTIPERSPIRANT

Antiperspirants are drugs that reduce moisture produced by glands under the skin's surface. Most modern antiperspirants are combined with deodorants, which use perfumes and bactericidal agents to reduce the odor of bodily secretions. While deodorants are classified as cosmetics, antiperspirants are classified as drugs by the Food and Drug Administration because they alter the physiology of the body. Though the exact mechanism underlying the function of antiperspirants is poorly understood, it is believed that chemicals in the substances temporarily seal pores in the skin, thereby preventing the secretion of moisture. The first deodorant on record, known as "Mum," was introduced in the late nineteenth century, but it wasn't until 1935 that the first antiperspirant, known as "Arrid," sold in the United States. Within the next decade, companies like Arrid began blending antiperspirant and deodorants to create all-purpose grooming aids to prevent both odor and moisture. Over time, competition within the industry increased and led to the invention of new antiperspirant and deodorant products, including the "roll-on" deodorant of the late 1940s and the aerosol sprays of the 1950s. The invention of the antiperspirant was an important step in the history of cosmetics and deodorants, and antiperspirants remain cornerstones of the personal grooming industry today.

Electric shaving became so popular that hotels, ocean liners, trains, and passenger airplanes had to provide outlets in the bathroom. By the end of the decade, electric shavers were being manufactured for women, gaining quick acceptance.

Until the 1930s, antiperspirants and deodorants were marketed almost exclusively for women. It was not considered manly to use such products. But that all changed when advertisers, rather timidly at first, began to target men. Lifebuoy Soap's introduction of the term "B.O." (for "body odor," which was typically spoken with a foghorn-like voice in radio commercials) made a previously unspoken topic shed some of its taboo status.

Most American men still combed their hair in the pompadour style, using hair creams or greases to achieve the slicked down look. Once again, the movies had a significant impact on appearance. As more and more Hollywood actors appeared with their hair untreated and tousled by the breeze, the pomade look gave way. By the end of the decade, many men relied on nothing more than a comb and plain water.

The vast majority of males still wore hats and caps, but these were less formal than in the past. Among the most popular styles were soft felt snap-brims and Panamas, the latter a lightweight, unlined woven hat that was a favorite in warm weather.

CHILDREN'S FASHIONS

The vagaries of fashion did not omit children, especially little girls. During the 1930s, two influences determined the directions their styles took: first, the outfits worn by Princesses Elizabeth and Margaret, two popular members of the English royal family; and second, anything worn by the child star Shirley Temple. These were the days when girls dressed as children, not miniaturized adults. Saque dresses (simple dresses worn with bloomers beneath), pinafores, sunsuits, and playsuits ruled. Cheap to buy and to make, these styles dominated the thirties.

Little boys, on the other hand, wore scaled-down versions of men's suits, and these with shorts rather than pants. Sailor suits were another favorite, complete with scarves, insignia, and bell-bottoms. For boys ages eight to around twelve, knickers (pants that ended just below the knee and tucked into high argyle socks) continued to be popular. Like men, most boys owned several hats, including the traditional white canvas sailor's cap. Another big seller was the aviator's helmet, a strapped leather item that covered the head, including the ears, with cheap goggles attached. Charles Lindbergh wore one when he flew across the Atlantic, and popular pilots like Wiley Post and Roscoe Turner sported them. (See Travel of the 1930s.)

By adolescence, both girls and boys progressed to adult clothing. Boys shed their shorts for "longies" (long pants), and girls wore more conventional dresses. As teenagers, they were of course exposed to most clothing fads. The severity of the Depression, however, kept many teens from indulging. Most crazes were brief and of little long-term impact.

Food

of the 1930s

In his second inaugural address on January 20, 1937, President Franklin D. Roosevelt said, "I see one-third of the nation ill-housed, ill-clad, ill-nourished," but a trip to a new supermarket would never have revealed such despair. The food sections of the leading magazines and newspapers seldom acknowledged economic realities. Only on occasion did features run regarding cost-saving meals. The government did provide information on cheap, nutritious foods and how to substitute them for high-priced varieties, but the program lacked influence.

Local, state, and federal agencies reported malnutrition among the unemployed. The few cases of actual starvation were limited to large cities or chronically poor groups, such as Appalachian miners. The presence of bread lines testified to the hunger experienced by some. But, although hunger existed, food companies continued to advertise their regular products.

The Great Depression brought about massive governmental transformations, employment patterns went through significant alterations, and dreams of financial security were shattered, but the average American noticed only slight changes in his or her accustomed diet.

During the 1930s, nutritionists—both real and self-proclaimed—stressed the importance of vitamins in a person's diet. As a result, many people

took vitamin supplements. Food processors began adding vitamins to their products and boasted how they were "vitamin enriched."[1]

Fashion also entered the nutritional picture. Although the reed-thin flapper of the 1920s was no longer stylish, slimness—especially for women—continued to be the standard for attractiveness. As a result, a wave of diets appeared in the popular press. In an ironic turnabout, some Americans rummaged through garbage for edible scraps, while others tried to limit their intake of food to be thin, thus achieving a fashionable look.

Meanwhile, the production of foodstuffs moved from small producers to large corporations. National brands like Post, Heinz, Kellogg, and Campbell's spent huge amounts on mass media advertising campaigns to keep their products in front of the consumer.

The American Diet

The emphasis on promoting widely known brands and foods led to a general acceptance of an "American diet." Exotic, regional, and ethnic foods fell by the wayside, replaced by a national menu. About the only exception to this shift was Italian cooking, which gained a tenuous foothold in a nation rapidly simplifying its tastes in food. Dishes like spaghetti and meatballs cooked

FOOD HIGHLIGHTS OF THE 1930s

1930 The Continental Baking Company changes the course of commercial bread products forever when it introduces loaves cut into slices.

1930 The Birds Eye label appears with the official introduction of commercially packaged frozen, or "frosted," food. It was named for scientist Clarence Birdseye, who perfected a method of flash-freezing perishables and lent his name (as two separate words) to the new brand of frozen food.

1931 "Pure food" zealot Alfred W. McCann, who throughout the late 1920s had somewhat successfully crusaded against the dangers of "acidosis" (the notion that eating foods in wrong proportions causes "acid" foods to overwhelm alkaline foods, in turn causing dreadful diseases) delivers an impassioned radio address on the subject, only to collapse and die from a heart attack at age 52.

1931 Hostess Twinkies make their first appearance. Easy to put into a lunch pail or pick up on the run, Twinkies are an immediate hit both with those who eat them and, more specifically, with housewives who find relief from one more baking chore.

1931 Mars, Inc., introduces its Snickers candy bar, and Welch's pushes its Sugar Daddy caramel-flavored sucker.

1931 General Mills executive Carl Smith gets the idea for premixed biscuit batter from a chef on board a train. By 1931 Bisquick premixed biscuit mix appears on grocers' shelves, alongside a promotional giveaway, a baking pan.

1932 Fritos Corn Chips are sold in 5¢ bags.

1932 General Foods acquires the rights to sell a German product, Sanka decaffeinated coffee.

1932 Three candy bars are introduced: 3 Musketeers, Heath Bars, and Pay Day.

1933 Kraft Caramels are introduced.

1934 Nabisco's Ritz Crackers appear on the market, using a name derived from the fashionable Ritz Hotel in Paris, connecting crackers with elegance and prestige.

1936 Cartoonist Chic Young invents the "Dagwood sandwich" in his comic strip *Blondie*. It consists of tongue, onion, mustard, sardine, beans, and horseradish, but by 1944, the concoction towers with so many ingredients that Dagwood devises a dowel made from a frankfurter to hold it together.

1936 Mars Bars and 5th Avenue candy bars appear.

1937 Kraft Foods unveils Kraft Dinner in a package that promises a macaroni and cheese "Meal for 4 in 9 minutes."

1937 Ragú spaghetti sauce also creates, within minutes, a traditional hot meal for the table, and cleanup is minimized. Sales soar, and the old idea of laboring over a hot stove takes another blow.

1937 Using a recipe from a chef in New Orleans, Vernon Rudolph starts selling Krispy Kreme doughnuts from a shop in Old Salem in Winston-Salem, North Carolina.

1937 Hormel introduces Spam.

1937 General Mills conducts a contest to name the country's most popular baseball announcer for its radio broadcasts sponsored by the Wheaties cereal brand. The top prize is a trip to California and a screen test, and the winner is Ronald "Dutch" Reagan.

1938 Nestlé's Crunch and Hershey's Krackel candy bars are welcomed by the snack-eating public.

Food

in a mild tomato sauce continued to enjoy wide popularity.[2]

Culinary standards dropped some: canned peas may not have been as tasty as fresh ones, but they (and other canned vegetables) were more convenient, possibly cheaper, and had a more consistent, if diluted, quality. In fact, people generally accepted the dilution of quality. Any revolution that did occur happened in the arena of efficiency and economy.

Pockets of distinctive foods held on, despite the relentless popularization of the all-American menu. County fairs, regional festivals, and church bazaars still served the distinctive foods of ethnic groups and specific locales. In the South, pork barbeque continued to be a community favorite, whereas in the West it was beef. Scandinavian dishes were devoured in the north central states, Mexican dishes persisted in the Southwest, and New Englanders still enjoyed boiled dinners.

By the beginning of the 1930s, Americans were reasonably educated about what and what not to consume, so the decade witnessed few changes in dietary habits. Changes took place in technologies for preserving and preparing food and how companies distributed and marketed foodstuffs.

Traditional Grocery Stores

The early 1930s saw a nationwide system of small grocery stores serving both urban neighborhoods and rural areas. In the cities, housewives walked to the friendly grocer to pick up the day's essentials. Except for people who lived in the country or far-flung suburbs, the idea of getting into an automobile and driving to buy groceries would have been unthinkable. In many cases, separate trips to a butcher, a bakery, and maybe a produce dealer took place, since most grocery stores of the era mainly carried staples, such as canned goods and prepackaged products. The full-service supermarket only emerged in the 1930s.

In urban areas, workers delivered dairy products directly to the customer's residence. The milkman made his rounds before dawn, leaving milk, eggs, and butter according to the wishes of the homemaker. Empty bottles, always returnable, were put out on the stoop (an all-purpose term

meaning the front door, the back porch, a side entrance, or wherever it was agreed such items would be placed) with notes for the next delivery. Often these items rested in a milk box, a small, insulated container which held several quart bottles, along with a few other items. In more remote rural areas, enterprising village grocers sent huckster wagons out into the countryside. The word "huckster" did not have the negative connotations of cheap salesmanship that it possesses today; in earlier years, it signified a dealer of varied small items. Typically, these wagons contained canned goods and prepared foods, which could be traded for fresh dairy products, eggs, meats, and poultry. Pushcarts were a common urban feature in the 1930s, displaying an array of fresh fruits and vegetables. Grocery outlets out in the country mostly remained small, mom-and-pop enterprises with a decidedly local clientele.[3]

Chain Stores & Supermarkets

Some little stores were part of larger chains, including A&P (The Great Atlantic and Pacific Tea Company), IGA (Independent Grocers' Alliance), Grand Union, and several others, which laid the groundwork for today's one-stop shopping. Piggly Wiggly, a chain based in the Memphis, Tennessee, area boasted self-service as early as 1916, but the idea caught on slowly. Even in 1930, most chain outlets were still neighborhood groceries. These stores often lacked self-service, seldom had meat counters, instead carrying canned meats rather than fresh cuts, and featured few fruits and vegetables. Their connection to a larger chain entitled them to feature the company's label on various goods and perhaps allowed them to charge a slightly lower price on those products.

The first supermarket pioneers appeared in the thirties. In 1930, the King Kullen Market opened in Jamaica, New York. Called the "World's Greatest Price Wrecker," it was possibly the first real supermarket in the United States. By 1931, the Safeway chain closed many of its small stores and converted them into larger operations. The following year, the Big Bear Super Market opened in Elizabeth, New Jersey, advertising cut-rate prices. In 1933 a Cincinnati-based Albers group dubbed itself Albers Super Mkts., Inc., the first corporate use of the term "supermarket." That same year, the Kroger chain opened a freestanding store in Indianapolis that boasted a surrounding parking lot, which represented the gradual ending of "walking to the store."[4]

By contemporary standards, these early supermarkets hardly qualified as "super." They had crowded, narrow aisles, and their inventory would look absolutely puny compared to the enormous stock carried by a modern market. Housewives used cloth bags, paper sacks, cardboard boxes, or baskets to carry their purchases. The wheeled shopping cart came into existence in 1937.

The phenomenon of the supermarket was based primarily on low prices, not convenience. In fact, many shoppers called them "cheapies." The first tended to be bare-bones operations, often located in abandoned warehouses, with unfinished wooden shelves and tables holding merchandise. Although the small grocery stores against which they competed were seldom much better aesthetically, their cozier neighborhood ambience perhaps made them seem more pleasant.

Early supermarkets did, however, offer lower prices. Buying in bulk and selling in quantity attracted customers, particularly during the depression. A media-driven campaign to create the image of the thrifty housewife, a woman skilled in shopping and economical food preparation changed attitudes about buying patterns. Lower prices encouraged consumers to save money at every turn. The picture of the smart shopper emerged as a dominant motif during the Depression.[5]

Self-Service

Perhaps the most significant shopping innovation of the 1930s was self-service. Until then, most stores, with the exception of the Piggly Wiggly markets (Kroger offered some self-service innovations in several of its early stores), consisted of shelves along the walls holding the goods, and a counter strategically placed, which blocked the customer from reaching the groceries. Instead, the grocer took the shopper's order, and assistants gathered the desired items and placed them on the counter. Next, they were bagged, the bill totaled, money changed hands or credit was arranged (if a customer was known, weekly or monthly tallies were commonplace), and this completed the transaction. There were few opportunities to read labels, compare packaging, or do all the other little things that self-service enabled.

The shift to self-service forced grocers to cut back on some services, such as home delivery. The delivery boy did not disappear entirely, however. A special bicycle, called a "cycle truck," with a small front wheel allowed an oversized wire basket capable of holding several bulging sacks of purchases to be attached ahead of the handlebars. A common sight in American cities throughout the first half of the century, these trucks carried mail, ferried parts within a large factory, and did general hauling. During the 1930s, such bicycles emphasized the familiarity between grocer and consumer.

The practice of phoning in an order to a favorite grocer also began to decline. The size and anonymity of larger stores precluded this kind of close relationship, just as most of them refused to grant credit to shoppers. The custom of holding or reserving special items for special customers also grew less common.

On the positive side, a bigger store meant a larger inventory. Instead of one brand of canned peas, a supermarket might feature two or three. The careful shopper could save a few precious cents by comparison buying. Consumers free to wander the aisles might become aware of new products or new brands. The big food manufacturers were supportive of self-service, and they worked hard to gain prominent placement in the new stores. And, if they were willing to admit it, many old-time grocers also welcomed the idea. Self-service reduced their labor costs, which in turn increased profitability. By 1937, supermarkets accounted for about one-third of the grocery business.

New Products

In 1939, A&P introduced the self-service meat department. It had its own line of prepackaged meats, allowing the customer to choose cuts and sizes without a clerk.

Until the late 1930s, perhaps a few boxes of frozen vegetables might be seen inside a large, glass-fronted freezer cabinet. The shopper had no access, so an assistant on the other side retrieved whatever choices the buyer made. Most boxes bore the red, white, and blue Birds Eye label. The official introduction of commercially packaged frozen, or "frosted," food took place in 1930, thanks to the efforts of Clarence Birdseye, the scientist who perfected a method of flash-freezing perishables and lent his name (as two separate words) to the industry leader.

Actually, frozen foods were not new; since early in the century growers had packed berries and fruits in a mix of ice and salt for wholesale distribution later. Birds Eye, on the other hand, solved the dual problem of freezing small quantities of produce quickly in order to preserve texture and flavor and putting it up in consumer-sized packages. Birds Eye developed a modern, less expensive, freezer case around 1934 and leased it to grocers for next to nothing. Soon, both grocers and consumers overcame their reluctance, and frozen food became a standard item in stores. Birds Eye also helped its cause by printing and distributing small, pamphlet-like cookbooks (e.g., *20 Minute Meals,* 1932).

Candy

Because sugar was inexpensive during the 1930s, it became a cooking staple in the home. Manufacturers also used sugar freely in many commercial products. In fact, people consumed more sugar per capita during the Depression than ever before or since.

The cheap cost of sugar allowed candy manufacturers to keep prices low. The strong sales that candy bars maintained in the face of an economic depression convinced manufacturers to bring out new, sweet concoctions. In 1931, Mars, Inc., introduced its Snickers bar, Hostess brought out Twinkies, and Welch's pushed its Sugar Daddy sucker. A year later, Mars promoted the 3 Musketeers, a blend of one part chocolate nougat, one part vanilla, and one part strawberry. The toffee-flavored Heath Bar came along in 1932, as did Pay Day. Kraft Caramels debuted the next year; Mars Bars and 5th Avenue came out in 1936. An Amos 'n Andy candy bar even appeared, based on the popular radio series of the same name. When the

popularity of the show waned during the 1940s, the bar disappeared.[6]

Food Preparation

During the 1930s, food trends focused on products that involved little or no tedious preparation. For many reasons, the live-in cook had become a thing of the past by the 1920s.

Technology altered the traditional rhythms of American life. Companies introduced new appliances, but women still faced chores that in earlier times a maid would have done. Middle-class American women discovered that expectations about what they should do were being raised, not lowered, despite the innovations. They were supposed to be volunteers, join clubs, participate in leisure activities, have hours and energy remaining for their children, and spend more time with their husbands.

As a result, the ritual of dining went through significant change. Meals became simpler, with fewer courses, featured less complex menus, which meant fewer dishes to clean. When Campbell's figured out in the 1890s how to condense soup (eliminating the water, the consumer would replace it when preparing the soup), it hit upon what would be the major trend in processed food thereafter: package the product in the simplest way possible and keep any preparation to a minimum. The big food processors and manufacturers enthusiastically participated in this conversion. For them, it meant the opportunity to introduce new products that could be advertised offering "speed," "simplicity," and "efficiency."

A good example is Bisquick, which made its first appearance in grocery stores in 1931. It promised to lighten the housewife's workload, and it did. A mix of flour and baking soda, Bisquick enabled baking (especially "quick biscuits") in one easy step. Although it was a boon to cooks, it added to the woes of bakeries. Already reeling from the Depression, one-third of all American baking establishments went out of business between 1930 and 1933. Sales of baked goods plummeted, and millions of households turned to home baking as a means of cutting costs. Of course, much of this drop was accounted for by fewer sales of commercial desserts: pies, cakes, and fancy pastries were among the first things to be cut from tight budgets.

Another example is Spam. Introduced by Hormel in early 1937, Spam was truly unique. It came in a small, rectangular can that could be opened by a key that unrolled a metal strip. The vacuum sealed container let out a little whoosh of air when a person turned the key. The strip came off, a knife was run around the insides, loosing the spiced, processed meat from the can, and Spam was ready to serve. Spam required no heating, although it could be fried, broiled, or chopped up and served with other dishes; indeed, its uses were only limited by one's imagination. Best of all, Spam was inexpensive. Spam entered the national diet almost from the moment it appeared and typified the urge for effortless cooking.

Ragú spaghetti sauce (1937) and Kraft macaroni and cheese dinners (also 1937) illustrate the quest for kitchen simplicity. Neither product required much preparation other than serving; culinary purists might have grimaced at the thought, but the average housewife obviously felt otherwise. Within minutes, a traditional hot meal could be put on the table, and cleanup was minimum. Sales soared, and the old idea of laboring over a hot stove took another blow.

Fritos Corn Chips (1932), Nabisco's Ritz Crackers (1934), and Lay's Potato Chips (1939) provided easy snacks and additions to meals. A popular recipe in the 1930s was to take some crackers, butter them, and toast them in the oven. A variation had the consumer dipping the cracker in water and then heating it so it would puff up. These new approaches to an old commodity were promptly embraced by the public, with Ritz Crackers rivaling Spam for the varied ways they could be fixed and served.

Not all the pre-prepared, precooked food of the 1930s went solely to adults. The Fremont Canning Company, based in Michigan, began experimenting with strained foods in the late 1920s. During the 1930s, Fremont was recognized for its Gerber Baby Foods, and they dominated a relatively new niche in groceries. Until that time, food for infants was a specialty product, usually found in drugstores. Gerber, however, marketed its jars of strained foods to the public as an everyday item in grocery stores, and succeeded beyond anyone's expectations. On all their jars was a drawing of a cute baby, done by artist Dorothy Hope Smith in 1928. It became their trademark and contributed mightily to their success. By the early 1930s the Gerber sketch had become America's best-known baby. Within a few years, the product line had undergone expansion, and American mothers considered the new baby foods an essential part of any grocery list.[7]

Refrigeration

For much of the decade, most average Americans still owned iceboxes. Usually built with a wooden exterior that enclosed some form of insulated interior, iceboxes ranged from a basic one-compartment unit to more sophisticated models with several doors and different interior arrangements. No matter how fancy, the icebox required a block (or blocks) of ice as a refrigerant. The degree of insulation reflected the quality of the box, but inevitably the ice would melt and have to be replaced. That meant the iceman would have to stop by, usually via horse-drawn wagon, although trucks began to appear more and more by the late 1930s. He carried large blocks of ice. He chipped off a chunk that fit neatly into the home icebox.

By modern standards, iceboxes were messy and inefficient, with limited storage capacities. The ice melted rather rapidly, and despite drains and other devices, the housewife always had to contend with diminishing cold, along with drips and puddles. Finally, iceboxes did not hold much food, given their refrigerating limitations. This disadvantage necessitated frequent visits to the market to restock perishables.

In 1925, the General Electric Company (GE) introduced what came to be called the Monitor Top refrigerator. The compressor motor was housed in a cylinder (the "monitor") atop the actual refrigerator. By 1929, GE sold some 50,000 of these, and the modern kitchen was becoming a reality. Despite the Depression, the company's sales passed 1 million units in 1931 and continued to climb.

With the success of its refrigerator assured, and with profits rolling in, General Electric had the lion's share of the market. The Monitor Top cost an expensive $525 in the 1920s, but it came down to a more reasonable $290 ($3,500 in today's dollars) in the early 1930s. In an effort to keep sales strong in a depressed economy, GE convinced Hollywood to produce a one-hour documentary called *Three Women* (1935). Starring, among others, the gossip columnist Hedda Hopper and the cowboy actor Johnny Mack Brown, it celebrated the "complete electric kitchen."[8]

In 1935 Sears, Roebuck hired noted designer Raymond Loewy to create a streamlined refrigerator for their Coldspot brand. This particular unit, far more contemporary than the pedestrian Monitor Top, later became a design classic. At the same time, rivals Kelvinator and Frigidaire sold large numbers of their own models. By 1941, more than 3 million electric refrigerators could be found in American kitchens.

The Depression-era electric refrigerator was an improvement, but it did have limitations. The freezer space was a minuscule interior box with a couple of small trays of ice cubes—a big advance over chipping off pieces of ice from a block—and the unit had a shallow meat tray directly underneath. Frost collected throughout the freezing compartment of the refrigerator, forcing the owner to defrost it periodically by removing everything from the interior of the unit and getting rid of the accumulated ice and frost.

With the advent of frozen foods, the tiny box inside the refrigerator was not nearly large enough. Most frozen foods and ice cream had to be consumed when purchased, and meat could not be bought in any quantity. Manufacturers addressed this issue, and by the end of the 1930s the latest models had considerably larger freezing compartments. Both the food companies and the appliance makers published pamphlets that showed the housewife how to use the new devices, and gave hints and recipes that aided in the actual cooking processes. For example, GE had *The Silent Hostess Treasure Book* (1930), Westinghouse printed *The Refrigerator Book* (1933), *Famous Dishes from Every State* came from Frigidaire in 1936.[9]

In 1930, the Proctor Company (later Proctor-Silex) brought out a pop-up toaster that improved on previous designs, leading to many new toasters, sandwich grills, waffle irons, and similar appliances during the decade. In keeping with the Streamline Moderne vogue, many of these models were sleek, rounded, and chromed. They could be brought directly to the table, instead of being kept in the kitchen. The housewife could then join her family, in keeping with the attitude that a woman's place extended beyond the confines of the kitchen.

A popular pastime in the 1930s was inviting friends or neighbors over for an informal supper. Often these gatherings were potluck, with each guest providing a dish. With everyone contributing, individual expenses were minimal. Since informality ruled, cooking at the table—using, for example, an electric grill or an electric waffle iron—proved sociable. No one thought it improper to prepare food so publicly with shiny new appliances. In 1930, the Sunbeam Corporation introduced its Mixmaster, destined to become a staple in American kitchens. Priced inexpensively, it allowed the cook to stir, cream, fold, and blend. It also further simplified cooking. Despite the Depression, the Mixmaster sold briskly, and

1930s-era refrigerator. This model has no freezer, an innovation that began to be introduced later in the decade. Prints & Photographs Division, Library of Congress.

Food

diner, and appealed to both women and families. Many historic buildings or quaint refurbished houses had tearooms, thus reinforcing their safe image and attracting patrons in search of a picturesque setting.

With fewer people eating out during the 1930s, many tearooms failed. In addition, the attempts by tearoom owners to make the surroundings charming and cozy failed to appeal to men. Supporters of the overall tearoom concept—no alcohol, an emphasis on salads and other wholesome food—suggested that perhaps a new name was in order if such places expected to stay in business. What emerged in the later 1930s was the term "motor inn," which suggested a rural, folksy setting, but also suggested the more masculine automobile in its nuances. This new connotation led to the increasing acceptance of the family-oriented restaurant, making it a permanent part of the highway landscape.

DRINK

Alcoholic Beverages

From 1920 until 1933, the Eighteenth Amendment, or Volstead Act, prohibited the sale or purchase of alcoholic beverages. Prohibition took a heavy toll on brewers, distillers, and places that served alcohol. The Twenty-first Amendment, or Repeal, was passed in 1933, and people were again free to enjoy alcoholic beverages, restaurants could serve them, and stores could sell bottled alcoholic beverages.

During the years of Prohibition, restaurateurs watched profits shrink, often to the point of bankruptcy. Alcoholic drinks historically served as moneymakers in the restaurant trade; when alcohol could no longer be served legally, business suffered unless drinks were served illegally—as they were in many restaurants. Prohibition resulted in the rise of the speakeasies, establishments where one knocked, gave a password, and then entered a secret world of glitter, fun, and drinks. The illegality of liquor made it expensive; smugglers, bootleggers, and occasional gangsters had to be paid off, often along with cooperative police officers. Being able to drink was a mark of conspicuous consumption and rebellion;

it meant a person had the cash indulge a habit not sanctioned by ment. It allowed people to thumb authority.[12]

The gangster films of Edward (e.g., *Little Caesar*, 1930) and James *Public Enemy*, 1931) chronicled the of the late 1920s and early 1930s. Im guys and loose women, along with and freely flowing liquor, influence tudes toward law and order. It beca laugh at any drinking restrictions; place for others, not for a smart gi woman. One particularly strong i time was of men and women drinki change from earlier years when drin marily a male prerogative.

The sophisticated dramas and con era showed similar views of public sumption. In her first talking movi *Christie*, 1930), Greta Garbo whisp with ginger ale," and audiences lo Harlow, clad in a slinky gown, sipp in *Platinum Blonde* (1931). Evider able people consumed alcohol and cret of it.

One product that survived Pro "near beer." The Volstead Act define erages as anything containing more cent alcohol. A concoction that had since the early 1900s, near beer wa alcohol. Supplying yeast and malt for tion of this beverage helped many b in business. A variation on near be dle beer," regular near beer spiked Needless to say, this latter variant wa its consumption flourished both in speakeasies.

Because of alcohol's high cost dur tion, most drinkers tended to be mi above; the old imagery of alcohol be of the poor and downtrodden no true. Thus, when Repeal came along of consumers was in place. Repeal br base, but drinking in the 1930s lost stigma it had held prior to Prohibitic

During Prohibition, Americans c cohol that was inferior or adulterate

Sunbeam came out with a whole line of accessories, from juice extractors to choppers and shredders. With its success, the word "Mixmaster" entered the language to denote any home mixer.

In the early years of the century, the Hamilton Beach Company had designed a high-speed electric mixer for restaurant and drugstore soda fountains. They, along with their competitors, improved on the simple gadget. The Waring Blendor—always spelled with an *o*—capitalized on the popularity of bandleader Fred Waring. In reality, he did not invent it; he just lent his name and financial support to it. Company officials introduced Maestro Waring to the device in 1936, and he saw it as a way to make frothy, iced drinks, principally daiquiris, which he favored. The machine's inventor had been pushing it for milkshakes, but with Waring's backing, the Blendor quickly became identified as a bar accessory.[10]

EATING OUT

During the Depression, the majority of people ate most of their meals at home, with the one possible exception being lunch. Nevertheless, many individuals frequented commercial establishments, such as those who chose not to cook, or those who were on the road and unable to do so.[11]

Diners

In urban areas diners were a familiar sight, an outgrowth of the old-fashioned food stand and lunch wagon. Diners, however, evolved into distinctive architectural entities. Once a place for workingmen to grab a bite near a factory, later models were shiny, streamlined eateries that catered to anyone wanting a meal: rich or poor, blue-collar or professional.

Diners were always cheap, a step up from a hot dog stand, but a step or two removed from "real" restaurants. They usually stayed open twenty-four hours, seven days a week. Their menus were endless, and they served breakfast all day long. By the end of the decade, thousands of diners dotted the downtowns and roadsides of American cities. Numerous companies mass produced stainless steel structures that resembled a railroad dining

car. They could be trucked to a site, and erected in a matter of hours. The resultant design—a long, narrow room with a shiny, plastic-topped counter running its length, complete with chrome stools and booths upholstered in plastic—became part of the American scene.

Restaurants

By the end of the 1920s, some 2,400 chain restaurants existed in the United States; despite the Depression, the number grew to about 3,000 by 1939. Most eating establishments, however, were still individually owned and operated. Howard Johnson's, usually associated with multiple flavors of ice cream, pioneered the concept of franchising. Instead of owning his restaurants outright, Johnson sold the privilege of running them to agents or franchisees. These investors replicated the firm's distinctive Colonial building with the bright orange roof and cupola; they used the same menu, offered the same twenty-odd ice cream flavors, and took a percentage of the profits. Ultimate control, however, remained with Howard Johnson, the owner. By 1940, Johnson had more than 125 sites, with only one-third of them owned directly by the company. The rest were franchised.

The success of urban chain restaurants led to imitation. Names like Toddle House, Krystal, and White Castle became familiar sights on busy street corners throughout the country. As a rule, they catered to busy working people during the day and to individuals and small groups at night. On the other hand, restaurants like A&W Root Beer and Hot Shoppes (started in 1927 by the Marriott Hotel family) aimed more for the suburban market, particularly people with cars. These roadside stands were not drive-ins, which, although initiated in the 1930s, did not flourish until after World War II. The stands usually located their operations in less densely populated suburban neighborhoods, often adjacent to the popular auto camps and tourist cabins outside city centers. These locations made them attractive to family-oriented customers, especially travelers. By employing standardized designs, building materials, and menus, the chains were the precursors of the fast-food restaurants of today. Their standardization kept costs down and made them

Food

Kewpee Hotels "Hamburgs" restaurant, a good example of a streamlined diner, ca. 19[...] Division, Library of Congress.

attractive eating places for millions of Americans looking for quick, cheap food.

One entrepreneur who closely observed the growth of both chain and independent dining was Duncan Hines. Over the years, he compiled a list of his likes and dislikes in American restaurants. In lieu of Christmas cards, he shared this list with friends. Finally, in 1936 he published it as *Adventures in Good Eating*. The book went through innumerable editions and sold 450,000 copies by the end of the decade.

In his book, Hines stressed cleanliness, neatness, decor (too much decoration probably hid dirt, in his estimation), good coffee, and the serving of hearty portions of solid American food (meat and potatoes), and maybe an occasional

seafood item. Hines did a[...] home economists, and t[...] to nationalize the Americ[...] road. Many a restaurate[...] sign that read "Recommer[...] by the entrance.

Tearooms

When people wanted t[...] and wanted a place mor[...] they chose tearooms. Tea[...] ity by capitalizing on the[...] timate restaurant that se[...] than tea or coffee. They s[...] saloons, were less bright[...]

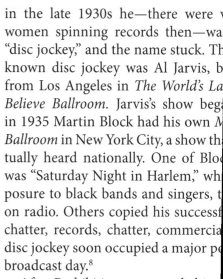

in the late 1930s he—there were [...] women spinning records then—wa[...] "disc jockey," and the name stuck. Th[...] known disc jockey was Al Jarvis, b[...] from Los Angeles in *The World's La[...] Believe Ballroom.* Jarvis's show beg[...] in 1935 Martin Block had his own *M[...] Ballroom* in New York City, a show tha[...] tually heard nationally. One of Blo[...] was "Saturday Night in Harlem," wh[...] posure to black bands and singers, t[...] on radio. Others copied his successf[...] chatter, records, chatter, commercia[...] disc jockey soon occupied a major p[...] broadcast day.[8]

After Prohibition was repealed in [...] could legally consume alcohol again.[...] strongly embraced by the music busin[...] els. The reopening of lounges, bars, ar[...] meant they had to have live or rec[...] The jukebox became a standard fixt[...] establishments, its neon and flashing [...] as a kind of summation of 1930s des[...] skyscraper in miniature. More impo[...] a moneymaker. By 1939, over 225,0[...] could be found across the nation, an[...] almost half of all records sold. Their p[...]

In 1932, Duke Ellington penned a little ditty called "It Don't Mean a Thing (If It Ain't Got That Swing)." Hardly his greatest composition, its title nevertheless sums up the music scene for much of the 1930s. Swing was king, and all other music had to follow in its footsteps. In no period, before or since, has one musical form so captured the popular fancy. The 1920s has been labeled the Jazz Age, more for its association with gangsters, drinking, sex, and general disregard for gentility than for the music itself. The 1930s, on the other hand, may properly be labeled the Swing Age.

Perhaps the best way to describe the swing phenomenon is to say that it involved a contagious rhythmic feeling, a desire to snap the fingers, tap the toes, and get up and dance. That definition, of course, focuses on the physical side of swing. Historically, swing referred to the emergence of innumerable large bands during the 1930s that performed primarily for dancers, which is not to say that swing was limited to orchestras. To be sure, sextets, quartets, trios, and singers all "swung."

The swing of the 1930s grew out of jazz, and yet those who embraced swing were not all necessarily familiar with jazz. Swing was part of a much larger cultural, historical, and musical movement that swept aside virtually everything before it.

The Crash [...] Two-thirds [...] were out of [...] problem was [...] for struggling [...] producers to [...]

BLACK MU[...]

A number [...] ing the 1920[...] new directic [...] thought an i[...] bands, and t[...] A few comp[...] did issue wh[...] were recordi[...] by black perf[...] ers. It was [...] when sales v[...] of white liste[...] in this music [...]

The dawn [...] ence already [...] both black an[...] musicians kr[...] heard on rec[...] outlets obse[...] radio station[...]

Sports

and Leisure of the 1930s

The onset of the Great Depression presented Americans with a paradoxical situation: increasing layoffs and swelling unemployment gave millions increased leisure time, but such leisure was, in effect, imposed idleness. The challenge became how to fill empty hours with meaningful activities at a minimal cost.

SPORTS

The spectacular rise of radio in the 1930s meant that athletics could be brought into the home. The sports broadcaster, or "sportscaster," took on an important role at stations and networks. The 1930s also saw the mixing of entertainment and business with sports. Colleges and universities, realizing that they could make money from athletics, hired sports information directors who promoted whatever sport was being played. This professionalization of athletics meant that winning became all-important. With only a few exceptions, the gentleman amateur became a relic of the past, replaced by the player who earned a paycheck.

Television, still in its developmental stage, was not a factor in these shifts, but change was in the air. In 1939 the first telecast of a major league baseball game was broadcast—the Brooklyn Dodgers against the Cincinnati Reds. It was also the first year of a televised game between Columbia University and Princeton University.

Baseball

Attendance plummeted at professional baseball games throughout the decade and would not recover until after 1945. One reason was that people could no longer afford to attend ball games. That was just one cause, however. For traditionalists, baseball was a "daylight game," and 3 P.M. was the proper starting time. Since the owners didn't want to spend money on lighting, they opposed night games. In 1935, the Cincinnati Reds, despite objections, installed lights so they could play night games, and their attendance soared. Other teams either quickly followed suit or planned for the change (though Wrigley Field, home of the Chicago Cubs, did not install lights until 1988). In another move to boost attendance, 1933 saw the first major-league All-Star Game take to the field. The game took place in conjunction with Chicago's Century of Progress Exposition, but it quickly became an annual event.[1]

The biggest star in the major leagues at the beginning of the decade was Babe Ruth. Others—Lou Gehrig, Dizzy Dean, Joe DiMaggio—attracted fans, but none was as towering as Ruth. In 1930, he made $80,000 as a Yankee—more than any

An NBC television crew broadcasts baseball on TV for the first time during a game between Columbia University and Princeton at New York's Baker Field in 1939. Two mobile vans sent the television signal to the transmitter at the Empire State Building for broadcasts to homes equipped with television. AP Photo.

other player, and more than President Hoover. Ruth quipped, "I had a better year." For the fans, he was the Sultan of Swat, and the Great Bambino. But Ruth also epitomized something else: in many ways he was the product of publicity, a figure created by mass media and zealous press agents.

Traditionally, newspapers or specialized publications covered baseball. *The Sporting News,* founded in 1886, was the premier sports magazine of the 1930s. By the Depression, the *News* devoted most of its reporting to baseball and enjoyed a high level of respect among fans. Newspapers emulated *The Sporting News,* thereby popularizing complete box scores, endless statistics, and in-depth articles about players that have since characterized baseball reporting. Newspapers' best sportswriters accompanied the home team when it played away games. Reporters like Daniel M. Daniel, Marshall Hunt, Red Smith, Paul Gallico, Ring Lardner, and Grantland Rice became celebrated in their own right as they followed the game.

Radio proved to be an effective way to relate the events of a game as it unfolded. At first, the owners and leagues opposed broadcasting games, arguing that it would keep away the crowds. Newspapers and *The Sporting News* also derided the practice. In a makeshift agreement, two stations per community were typically allowed to broadcast games, but by 1938, 260 stations were carrying baseball.

Much radio baseball in the 1930s only seemed live. The broadcast was a recreated narrative done in a studio, not at the ballpark. Because of technical limitations, the sportscaster frequently was isolated behind a microphone in a studio, relying on telephones to bring him details of the unfolding contest. His real job entailed filling empty airtime, creating the illusion of constant action. Chatter was his skill, and millions faithfully listened to descriptions of a runner sliding home or a "long, pop fly to center field…" and so on for nine innings.

By the early 1930s, sports ranked second only to music in terms of airtime. A new generation

WORLD SERIES

1930 Philadelphia Athletics (AL), 4 games; St. Louis Cardinals (NL), 2 games

1931 St. Louis Cardinals (NL), 4 games; Philadelphia Athletics (AL), 3 games

1932 New York Yankees (AL), 4 games; Chicago Cubs (NL), 0 games

1933 New York Giants (NL), 4 games; Washington Senators (AL), 1 game

1934 St. Louis Cardinals (NL), 4 games; Detroit Tigers (AL), 3 games

1935 Detroit Tigers (AL), 4 games; Chicago Cubs (NL), 2 games

1936 New York Yankees (AL), 4 games; New York Giants (NL), 2 games

1937 New York Yankees (AL), 4 games; New York Giants (NL), 1 game

1938 New York Yankees (AL), 4 games; Chicago Cubs (NL), 0 games

1939 New York Yankees (AL), 4 games; Cincinnati Reds (NL), 0 games

of electronic reporters—Tom Manning, Jack Graney, Bill Dyer, Ted Husing, Arch McDonald, Fred Hoey, and Harry Caray—became household names as they broadcast the play-by-play over the family radio. A young man named Ronald "Dutch" Reagan did Chicago Cubs games for an Iowa station. He later became an actor, and finally the fortieth president of the United States.[2]

Together, the sportswriters and sportscasters created images of athletes that often exceeded their actual feats, giving rise to the sports celebrity and sports hero. The rigorous training and endless practice were forgotten, replaced by images of instant success and adulation for the lucky few.

Softball

Softball originated in 1887 as a form of indoor baseball suited for play in gymnasiums and other indoor facilities. It was not until 1926, however, that the game got its present name and began working toward standardized rules. With the onset of the Depression, softball bloomed, as factories and offices, schools, churches, unions, and even neighborhoods put players on the field.

The Chicago World's Fair of 1933 sponsored a softball tournament with designated slow- and fast-pitch categories. These events garnered considerable publicity, and it is estimated that over a million Americans played softball in some capacity by 1936. Both the CBS and NBC radio networks covered national championships, and the number of players kept growing. By the end of the decade, five million Americans participated, and almost a quarter of them were women. Millions more attended the games, and attempts were made to create professional softball teams.[3]

As part of the national recovery effort, the government built thousands of parks and recreational areas around the country; many were constructed with the official dimensions of a softball diamond clearly in mind. The National Youth Administration (NYA) built fields on private property, allowing churches and fraternal organizations to have proper playing areas. The Federal Rural Electrification Program introduced night lighting to hundreds of such fields long before the major baseball leagues enjoyed night play. So widespread was softball that many sporting equipment manufacturers saw an upturn in business despite the economic hard times. President Roosevelt himself sponsored a team, the White House Purgers. In many ways, softball became the true national pastime—open to anyone, regardless of social or economic status.

Football

In contrast to today, football was not well publicized during the 1930s. Professional games were virtually invisible, played before small crowds on open fields or in small stadiums. College football had a bigger following. Colleges and universities worked hard at stirring popular interest in the game. In 1935, the Orange Bowl was created, followed the next year by the Sun Bowl, and in 1937 by the Sugar Bowl and the Cotton Bowl.

Schools also instituted rule changes that quickened the play of football and cut down on injuries. In 1932, officials introduced a clause into collegiate rules that made the ball dead when any part of the player (except feet and hands) touched the ground. Padding became a requirement, and in 1939 helmets were mandated for collegiate players. The size of the ball was reduced so it was easier to grasp, which led to more passing and a more visual game.

Basketball

Like football, basketball was primarily a collegiate sport. For professional basketball, there were two groups, the American Basketball League (ABL), established in 1933, and the National Basketball League (NBL), created in 1937. The two leagues merged to form the National Basketball Association (NBA) in 1949. Despite attempts at organization, American basketball during the 1930s consisted largely of individual teams and colleges. Few stars emerged, and the sport struggled to survive.

At the beginning of the decade, basketball was a slow, low-scoring sport. Final scores of 18–14 or 21–15 were not uncommon. Defense ruled the game. In an attempt to speed up play, the leagues adopted the ten-second rule in 1932, requiring a team to shoot the ball within ten seconds. After each score, officials returned the ball to center court, where the players reassembled for a new tip-off. Officials abolished the rule in the 1937–1938 season, another effort to make the game fan-friendly. Madison Square Garden in New York City hosted the first big college tournament in 1934. In 1938 the tournament became the National Invitational Tournament (NIT).

Hank Luisetti of Stanford University was probably the first real basketball star. He scored 1,500 points between 1936 and 1939. Luisetti perfected the one-handed jump shot. Until then, virtually all shots were two-handed. His popularity earned him top billing in a 1938 movie called *Campus Confessions*. Despite its lurid title, it was billed as a "peppy college romance [with] a real basketball game!"

Elite Sports: Horse Racing, Tennis, and Golf

Horse racing, tennis, and golf have traditionally been viewed as the pursuits of the wealthy.

Yet, for brief periods during the Depression, each emerged as front-page news.

In racing, a horse named Gallant Fox captivated millions. The steed galloped to victories in the Preakness, the Belmont Stakes, and the Kentucky Derby during the 1930 season, winning the Triple Crown, racing's highest honor. Gallant Fox's son, Omaha, repeated the feat in 1935, and War Admiral managed it yet again in 1937, thus maintaining a high level of interest in horse racing throughout the decade. Seabiscuit was a small and crooked-gaited horse beloved by the public because he won race after race in 1937. He went on to a thrilling match race against the Triple Crown winner Admiral in 1938, which Seabiscuit won.

Although tennis was perceived as an activity for a wealthy, leisured class, it was estimated that some 11 million Americans played the game during the 1930s. In those days, professional players were virtually invisible. They played at private clubs and were ineligible for the major tournaments. In 1931 "Big Bill" Tilden, the leading player of the late 1920s, gave up his amateur standing and turned professional. His departure relegated tennis to the back pages of the sports section. In 1938, interest in tennis revived when Don Budge achieved the Grand Slam of tennis, winning the Australian, French, English (Wimbledon), and the U.S. Open tournaments, all amateur events. The first player ever to do so, Budge received a flurry of publicity. For a few fleeting moments, tennis reappeared on the front pages, but Budge turned pro shortly thereafter and, like Tilden, disappeared.

Golf did not come into its own until after the late 1940s, but a young amateur from Georgia named Bobby Jones captured the public imagination in the 1930s. Unlike tennis, both professionals and amateurs golfers played in open tournaments. Jones achieved what many in golf believed unattainable: golf's version of the Grand Slam. In 1930, he won the British Amateur and the British Open. When he returned to America, he received a ticker-tape parade in New York City. But that was just the start. He followed those victories by winning both the U.S. Open and the U.S. Amateur championships, giving him all four major championships.

To most fans, Bobby Jones symbolized the little guy beating the pros, and he became golf's first real superstar. He soon retired from the game, but remained in the limelight throughout the decade. Jones capitalized on his popularity with a number of endorsements and used the media to stay involved. He had a weekly radio show that recreated highlights of his illustrious career, made several golf instruction films for Warner Brothers, lent his name to Spalding for a new line of clubs, and played an important role in designing and setting up a new course in Augusta, Georgia, the course that later became home to the Master's Golf Tournament.

The Depression did have a positive effect on everyday golfers. As memberships fell off in once-exclusive country clubs and private courses, the directors opened them to public play. In addition, many municipal courses were built during the Depression years, doubling the number from a decade earlier.

Boxing

During the 1930s professional boxing made headlines almost constantly. The sport's most important title, the heavyweight crown, rested uneasily on a series of heads from 1930 until 1937. The rotation began in 1930, when German boxer Max Schmeling gained the heavyweight title by defeating the reigning champion, American Jack Sharkey. Schmeling lost to Sharkey in a 15-round rematch in 1932. Next, Primo Carnera of Italy knocked out Sharkey for the title in 1933. Carnera then got kayoed by Max Baer in 1934. In the next shuffle, Jim Braddock defeated Baer the following year. More important, perhaps, was a 1936 nontitle bout involving former champion Schmeling and a rising young African American boxer named Joe Louis. Schmeling floored Louis and seemed poised to regain the title; however, Schmeling was denied the bout, and Louis instead faced Braddock. In 1937, Louis won the fight and officials proclaimed this American the world's heavyweight champion.

Joe Louis reigned, undefeated, from 1937 until his retirement in 1949. He defended his title 25 times and stood as an immensely popular champion. But of all his victories, none was sweeter than his defeating Schmeling in a much-ballyhooed 1938 championship fight, a match that established the power of radio. More than half the radio owners in the United States—over 22 million people—listened in as Louis pummeled his opponent. For both fighters, tremendous national pride was at stake. Schmeling's handlers talked of him as the "hope of the Aryan race," and the Nazi propaganda machine spewed out reams of racist hatred in the days before the fight. The quiet Louis, "the Brown Bomber," typified much that was good about America in an era of segregation in most sports, and hopes ran high. Once in the ring, Schmeling was down and out in the first round, and Americans breathed a collective sigh of relief. Louis's decisive victory salvaged American honor and silenced many racists and Nazi sympathizers.

Although few Americans ever attended a prizefight, public interest skyrocketed and popular culture reflected this enthusiasm. Hollywood found staging and filming a match easy to do, and made numerous fight movies. In 1931, Wallace Beery and Jackie Cooper filmed the justly famous *The Champ*. James Cagney continued his action films with 1932's *Winner Take All*. An emerging Spencer Tracy had a bit part in *Society Girl* (1932). *Police Call* (1933) was actually a "B" boxing epic, as were *Kelly the Second* (1936) and *The Kid Comes Back* (1937). Better by far was *Cain and Mabel* (1936), a big-budget pugilistic comedy with Clark Gable and Marion Davies. Ham Fisher's popular comic strip character Joe Palooka was featured in *For the Love of Pete* (1936) and *Taking the Count* (1937). Two boxing features with primarily black casts were *Spirit of Youth* (1937; starring Joe Louis as himself) and *Keep Punching* (1939; featuring light heavyweight Henry Armstrong). *They Made Me a Criminal* (1939; with John Garfield) and a screen adaptation of Clifford Odets's *Golden Boy* (1939; featuring William Holden in a star-making role) took a more serious look at the fight business.

OLYMPICS

By the summer of 1936, when the Olympics were held in Berlin, Adolf Hitler had risen to become the leader of Germany. He decided to make the Olympics a showplace for his National

Sports

Jesse Owens at the start of record breaking 200-meter race at the 1936 Olympic Games in Berlin. Prints & Photographs Division, Library of Congress.

Socialist, or Nazi, party and its ideologies. Americans were vaguely aware of Nazism and its racist politics, but the truth became more widely known during the Summer Games. Hitler banned all German Jews from participating, a move that led to unsuccessful calls for other nations to boycott the games. In fact, two American Jewish athletes were prevented by their coach, not German authorities, from running in the 400-meter relay in order to avoid controversy.

During the games, Jesse Owens, a black track star from Ohio State University, distinguished himself and brought honor to the United States by winning four gold medals: the 100- and 200-meter dashes, the broad jump, and as a member of the 400-meter relay team mentioned above. Owens's victories challenged the Nazi view of

Aryan superiority. Although it is believed that Hitler refused to award Owens his medal, Hitler was actually prevented by the Olympic Committee from presenting any further medals after the first day.[4] Nonetheless publicity about Hitler's beliefs about Aryan superiority awakened many Americans to the true nature of Nazi-run Germany.

LEISURE PASTIMES IN THE 1930s

During the early days of the economic crisis, the average workweek declined from 48 to 40 hours. In addition, the National Recovery Administration (NRA) instituted work codes and fair practices that further reduced hours on the job, especially overtime. By 1935, two-thirds of the American employees covered by these codes worked fewer than 40 hours a week.

People sought activities to fill their increased free time. Cities and towns, along with schools and local businesses, sponsored various hobby clubs, and local YMCAs and YWCAs became important resources. Despite these efforts, a marked rise in sedentary, solitary behaviors occurred during the grimmest days of the Depression.

Endurance Contests and Other Fads

Despite the dour atmosphere surrounding the Depression, the era still saw as much silly behavior as any period in American history. As a rule, fads were cheap and time consuming, public and escapist, and they attracted both adults and children. Sometimes the subject was food, whereby people consumed prodigious quantities of virtually anything edible. Spectators and participants flocked to pie-eating and egg-eating contests, along with clam-shucking, gum-chewing, hotdog-munching, and coffee-drinking challenges.

Many fads focused on endurance. For instance, tree sitters climbed to the highest branches of a tree or to the top of a pole and then attempted to remain aloft for weeks on end. Generally, some convenient means of collecting money was available on the ground, although most sitters went to their perches only after arranging a fee. Once up in the air, sitters whiled away weeks or even months, depending on the deals they had made.[5]

These feats inspired other endurance contests: six-day bicycle races, 4,000-mile roller derbies, and seesaw-riding contests. There were talking marathons, walking marathons, non-stop piano playing, and kiss-a-thons. Six-day bike races took place on makeshift wooden tracks. Two-person teams, usually a man and a woman, circled the track for six entire days, taking turns and fighting exhaustion. Movie stars, especially women, were seen on bicycles in publicity shots. Sales of women's bikes soared. Joe E. Brown, a rubber-faced comedian, hopped on the cycling craze with *6 Day Bike Rider* (1934), an innocuous little movie that emphasized the popularity of the fad.

Likewise, roller-skating briefly became the rage. It was cheap entertainment; abandoned warehouses and other indoor spaces became skating rinks. The Roller Derby was modeled after the six-day bicycle races. A co-ed team skated around a track for 4,000 miles. The event began in the early afternoon and continued until about midnight, assuring the maximum number of paying spectators. For 35 days the teams skated, interspersing regular skating with "jams" and "sprints." A jam involved getting a number of racers simultaneously on the track, thus assuring collisions and general mayhem. A sprint involved skating fast for a brief period of time.

Dance marathons originated in the 1920s and had seemingly run their course by 1930. But in the early days of the Depression, people rediscovered the dance marathon. The rules were simple: a couple had to dance, or at least keep moving, for an hour. They then got 15 minutes off, and then it was back on the floor for another hour. If one fell asleep while on the floor, the other was responsible for keeping him or her upright and mobile. The two could make $20 to $30 a week just holding each other up and shuffling their feet; plus, they got eight free meals a day. Dancing all day and long into the night consumed an enormous number of calories, so the meals were rich and filling.

June Hovick, later a Hollywood star under the name June Havoc, achieved the dance marathon record in 1934: 3,600 hours, equal to about five months, of continuous dancing. Hovick and Elmer Dupree, her partner, shared a prize of $40. In 1938, Horace McCoy wrote a best seller about

The exhaustion is clearly evident for this couple at a marathon dance contest. These contests provided a way for teams to make a few dollars and get some free meals. Prints & Photographs Division, Library of Congress.

the craze titled *They Shoot Horses, Don't They?* (which was made into a movie in 1970). The title says it all: dance marathons were not fun. Entrants suffered mightily for the meager prizes and free food.

Chain Letters and Jokes

In the spring of 1935, a new fad swept the country: the chain letter. Chain letters (today's chain e-mail) have continued, although none ever equaled the frenzy generated by its first appearance. A person received a letter with five or six names and addresses listed at the bottom. The recipient crossed out the first name and wrote his or her name at the bottom of the list. But there was a catch: the recipient had to send a dime to the person whose name was scratched out. Also, he had to send copies of the letter to five additional

Sports

people. In five progressions, assuming the chain remained unbroken, the sender's name reached the top, and in theory at least, he made a small fortune in dimes. In practice, however, seldom did the chain remain intact and even less frequently did anyone make any money. The fad began in Denver, swamping the local post offices; even the White House received letters. After about three months of virtual hysteria, the atmosphere calmed, and by July the fad had passed.

President Herbert Hoover, the nation's much-maligned leader at the start of the Depression, found his surname the butt of many a neologism. "Hoovercart" and "Hooverwagon" rodeos first appeared in North Carolina in 1933 and soon spread across the country. The events consisted of mules pulling the back halves of Model T Fords over an obstacle course. If the contraption fell apart, so much the better. Wasn't the economy doing the same thing?

The rodeos were just one way of ridiculing the president. People called any makeshift collection of tents, cardboard boxes, tarpaper shacks, and the like that sufficed as housing for the homeless and unemployed a "Hooverville." Most large cities had Hoovervilles, which were usually located close to the railroad tracks.

In a similar vein, "Hoover blankets" were the accumulated newspapers under which the jobless and homeless slept. "Hoover flags" referred to empty pockets. When people turned their pockets inside out to show they were broke, the white linings somewhat resembled flags. The euphemism "Hoover hogs" referred to rabbits consumed for food. Rundown shoes, usually with visible holes in the soles, became "Hoover shoes," and "Hoover leather" meant the cardboard used to resole them. Not all associations were totally negative, however. A "Hoovercrat" was someone who still had faith in the beleaguered president, although that usage was probably damning with faint praise.

Jokes could also make fun of the times. In the 1930s, this meant the rise of the "knock-knock" jokes, which reached their first peak in 1936. There was even a minor hit by the Vincent Lopez Orchestra titled "The Knock-Knock Song." In the course of the melody, the band members cried out, "Knock, knock!" A vocalist would respond

with "Who's there?" And this cued yet another corny punchline, but listeners loved it.

GAMES

Games of Chance

In the midst of an economic depression anything that promised easy money drew an audience. A 1939 poll found that one-third of the population admitted to occasionally betting a nickel or so on a game of chance.[6]

A company picnic might stage contests with small cash prizes. Churches got into the act by staging bingo in their parish halls. Slot machines, pinball machines, and punchboards were among the devices favored by Americans to win money effortlessly.

By the mid-1930s, thousands of sanctioned Bingo parties were held almost every night of the week across the country. Some considered it a form of legalized gambling, and opponents conducted sporadic efforts to ban the games, but public support won out, much to the relief of small churches and fraternal lodges.[7]

Another idea that blossomed in the 1930s was the punchboard, a small block of cardboard containing 1,000 holes. Each hole had a slip of paper, or ticket, inserted in it. Only one of the tickets won. For a nickel, a person could punch out a ticket and see if it was the lucky one. If so, the lucky winner received $2.50. Obviously, with 1,000 holes, a nickel each hole, and only one $2.50 winner, punchboards were enormously profitable ($1,000 \times .05 = \$50.00$ per board) to the house, not to those who gambled on them. By 1939, it was estimated that some 15,000 punchboards were being manufactured daily.

"Poor Man's Billiards" was the popular name given bagatelle, a simple game that involved a board with holes at one end. In the early years of the twentieth century, all that bagatelle required was a cue and small ball. Places that had the game usually charged five cents for ten shots. If the player managed to sink all or most of the shots, prizes were given. Bagatelle quickly grew in complexity during the 1920s and 1930s. At first, pins were arranged so as to block direct shots to a hole, and these obstacles brought about a shift

Sports

in the name to pin games. Finally, the cue stick was eliminated, and pin games evolved into pinball. The first pin machine, called the "Whoopie Game," came out in 1930. The shooter had to employ a mechanical plunger to propel the ball through an increasingly complex course. As before, high scores received prizes. Establishments with pinball successfully evaded the gambling laws for many years by claiming they were games of skill, not games of chance. By 1933, 62 different pinball games were available, and some 250,000 of them were sold annually.

Table Games

Ping-Pong became a minor fad in the 1920s when Parker Brothers trademarked their sets using as their own a name that had existed since the game began in the 1880s. Ping-Pong supposedly suggested the sound of the ball hitting the paddle, which enthusiasts preferred over table tennis. In 1931, the American Ping-Pong Association was formed and sponsored tournaments where only Parker Brothers equipment could be used. To compete, the New York Table Tennis Association formed, with no royalties to Parker Brothers. The two organizations eventually merged as the U.S. Table Tennis Association, and players competed internationally. The 1930s saw some five million tennis tables in private homes.[8]

Pick-Up Sticks was introduced in 1936. The game was based on Jack Straws, an earlier American version, and Marokko, a Hungarian import. In its original form, the jackstraw, a strip of wood

A game of bridge in Oklahoma in the 1930s. Contract bridge was immensely popular, complete with best-selling books and avidly followed tournaments. Prints & Photographs Division, Library of Congress.

with a hooked end, was used to dislodge specific numbered sticks. In less than a year, the new version sold three million sets.

Contract Bridge became the rage for any adult in the 1930s. Ely Culbertson, a master at traditional bridge, popularized this form of the card game. In contract bridge, partners collaborated by "bidding" their hands, an attempt to inform one another of the value of individual cards. The winning team established a "contract" of how many tricks it anticipated taking.

Despite the complexities of contract bridge, tournaments were soon arranged. Elaborate scoring rules, complete with extra points and penalties, were worked out and made part of the game. The more arcane the rules and scoring, the better people seemed to like it. Even in the worst of the Depression, the sales of playing cards rose. By 1931, over 500,000 people had signed up to take bridge lessons at YMCAs, parks, and other places that offered them. Experts estimated that 20 million people played the game.

Bridge tournaments were often broadcast, hand-by-hand, over the radio, as experts explained rules and strategies, along with the actual play, to eager listeners. Culbertson found himself on the best-seller lists with a series of how-to books. His first two were initially published in 1930 and sold steadily for years. One even had annual updates. He also ran a daily column in hundreds of newspapers showing how to play sample hands.

Board games also increased in popularity during the thirties. Monopoly, the undisputed champion, made its national debut in 1935. Its origins probably date back to 1904 and The Landlord's Game, a little-known diversion that used real estate transactions as part of its strategy. Almost 30 years later, Charles Darrow borrowed from both The Landlord's Game and another real estate contest called the Atlantic City Game, which helps explain the Atlantic City addresses on the properties in Monopoly. Darrow copyrighted his game in 1933 and sold several thousand home-made versions through the mail before attempting to get game manufacturer Parker Brothers to market his creation.

Parker Brothers ignored him. Darrow privately printed some sets and in 1934 got Wanamaker's Department Store in Philadelphia and F.A.O.

Schwarz in New York to stock them. They were immediately successful. Parker Brothers took another look, and Darrow and Parker Brothers finally reached an agreement in 1935, after which Monopoly grew to be the most successful board game in history. Some believe that the capitalistic focus of the game and the chance for great wealth made Monopoly a favorite during the Depression, but Monopoly's continuing popularity in the strong economic times of today suggest that it is popular simply because it is a good game.[9]

TOYS

During the Depression toy sales plummeted, and many companies went out of business. But, as factories closed down or slowed production, the survivors had first choice of materials. As a result, overall quality of American-made toys rose.

An example is the American Flyer wagon. In 1923, the Liberty Coaster Company was founded in Chicago. By using the metal-stamping technology of the automobile industry, the firm could mass-produce sturdy wagons in great numbers. With an eye to marketing and current fads, the company changed its name to Radio Steel and Manufacturing in 1930 and produced 1,500 distinctive red Radio Flyer wagons a day. The firm mounted a mammoth display at Chicago's Century of Progress exposition featuring "Coaster Boy" astride his Radio Flyer. It stood over four stories tall, and alerted crowds to the popular product.

Toward the middle of the 1930s, Radio Steel brought out wagons based on the great streamlined locomotives then setting speed records and the Chrysler Airflow, the nation's first mass-market streamlined car, yet sales continued to be dominated by the trusty red wagon with the wooden sides.

A flood of cheap, often shoddy toys from foreign manufacturers also came on the market. Many were made of celluloid, a highly flammable substance best known as the primary component of older motion picture film and shirt collars. Since it could be molded into virtually any shape, manufacturers used celluloid for inexpensive toys—baby rattles, ping-pong balls, and figurines. Japan became the world's leading exporter

Sports

of celluloid products during the 1920s and 1930s, endlessly replicating much of American popular culture. Comic-strip characters, sports heroes, movie stars, and other celebrities poured forth in figurine or doll form, some done skillfully and accurately, while others were simply crude caricatures. Consumers associated these cheap toys with low quality, and "Made in Japan" grew into a term of scorn for many Americans. Scorn notwithstanding, sales remained strong throughout the Depression.

A more important fad originated in the Far East: the yo-yo, a simple amusement with a long history that peaked in the Depression. In 1928, Filipino American Pedro Flores began manufacturing the spinning wooden disks. Because yo-yos have a heritage in the Philippines—the name derived from the Filipino word for "spring"—skilled Filipinos were hired to go to schools and other places children might hang out to demonstrate the new models and the latest tricks. Yo-yo companies used this marketing ploy successfully, and the yo-yo caught on. Celebrities were seen with them, Bing Crosby crooned about them, and millions bought them.

A cartoon character added greatly to the health of the toy industry in the 1930s. Mickey Mouse, the animated creation of the Walt Disney Studios,

An early model of the Viewmaster. © Adams Picture Library t/a apl / Alamy.

THE VIEW-MASTER

At the 1939 World's Fair in New York, photographer William Gruber of Portland, Oregon, debuted a new invention that eventually became one of the most popular toys in American history. Gruber's invention, ultimately called the "View-Master," was a simple machine that used stereoscopic photographs to create a three-dimensional slide show. The idea of stereoscopic photography was not new in Gruber's time, with stereoscopes for viewing images available in the nineteenth century, and was already a popular novelty item in many stores. Gruber used the same technology but mounted pairs of photographs on a spinning disk, a reel, to allow the user to cycle through sets of images. Over the course of a year, more than 1,000 stores began carrying View-Masters. Gruber thought of his invention as simply a novelty, but the unique product had a much larger impact than he had predicted. During the 1940s, the U.S. military used View-Masters for training, distributing thousands of the them through recruitment and training locations across the nation. Early View-Master reels featured pictures of popular tourist locations like Niagara Falls and the Grand Canyon. Later, the entertainment industry obtained the rights to produce reels with scenes based on film and television characters. After the technology was co-opted by the entertainment industry, marketers began to realize the potential of the View-Master as a child's toy. Gruber's design was remarkably enduring and remained largely unchanged from 1939 through to the twenty-first century.

first appeared on film in 1928's *Steamboat Willie*. Over 15 different Mickey Mouse toys came out in 1931 alone. The studio's cartoons of the 1930s captured a huge audience, but the paraphernalia associated with the entire Disney menagerie—from watches, costume jewelry, and clocks to clothing, soap, and dolls—developed into an industry of its own.

For example, the Lionel Corporation, best known for its detailed model trains, produced a Mickey and Minnie Mouse handcar in 1934,

Sports

a time when the company's sales slowed. The Disney-inspired novelty item did extremely well and helped keep the train maker in business.

Cheap, mass-produced miniature tin and lead soldiers enjoyed substantial sales. Most were crude and not terribly realistic, but that did not seem to deter boys intent on staging backyard battles. Perhaps it was the threat of a new world war that spurred the popularity of infantrymen, tanks, cannons, and other martial miniatures.

Most families could not afford store-bought toys during the Depression, hence the popularity of handmade games and toys in the 1930s. Rubber-band "guns" were perfect for shooting desperadoes. The "pistol" was a piece of scrap wood, its "ammunition" consisting of bands taken from old inner tubes. Music could be made with whistles crafted from willow or cane. Modern communication could be accomplished with two empty cans and a long piece of string. For millions of kids during the Depression years, homemade stilts, kites, slingshots, and other makeshift substitutes rivaled any commercial versions.[10]

HOBBIES

With high unemployment and reduced working hours, hobbies of every description boomed during the Depression. Some were enriching, others were merely ways to pass the time. Listening to the radio, going to the movies, and window shopping may not have been traditional hobbies, but they helped fill the void for Americans short on cash and long on time.

More rewarding pursuits also flourished, and the hobby industry expanded while other businesses closed. In addition, municipalities sponsored hobby clubs, how-to classes, and the like. New job skills, like woodworking and auto mechanics, could be learned in a relaxed, no-risk atmosphere, and leisure developed into a kind of substitute work. Commentators and politicians made a concerted effort to define the hobbyist as someone who actively participated in an avocation and, in so doing, learned from it and remained productive.[11]

For example, many city dwellers took up gardening, which helped them save on food bills and engage in healthy work. Most cities had community plots, with neighbors dividing up both chores and space. Garden clubs, once the domains of well-to-do ladies of leisure, welcomed a much more diverse membership, and the exchange of gardening lore became their primary focus.

Hobbies magazine debuted in 1931, followed by hobby columns in many newspapers and magazines. The radio show *Hobby Lobby* was broadcast to more than 150 stations in the mid-1930s. The show made listeners aware of new activities, particularly those that helped others in some way. Special interest clubs of every sort strove to get their ideas on the show, and the voluntarism espoused by *Hobby Lobby* led to the formation of still more clubs.

Despite all the emphasis on being productive and learning new skills, many of the most popular hobbies of the 1930s achieved neither. For example, proponents of hobbies as a form of work argued for cutting the intricate pieces of a jigsaw

Franklin D. Roosevelt examining his postage stamp collection, 1936. Prints & Photographs Division, Library of Congress.

Sports

puzzle by hand and then selling the finished product. Most people, however, preferred simply to assemble the puzzle. Either way, jigsaw puzzles were one of the most popular time killers of the Depression. At first, they tended to be intricately cut from wood and rather expensive, so their market was limited. But 1934 saw the introduction of die-cut cardboard puzzles. These were so cheap they could be given away as premiums. Jigsaw puzzles were available everywhere, from newsstands to book stores and from upscale department stores to Woolworth's.

At the beginning of 1932, over 2 million puzzles were sold weekly. Stores featured "puzzles of the week" and "weekly jigs." In the early 1930s, jigsaw puzzles sold at a rate of about 10 million a week. Stores rented puzzles, and puzzle club members swapped favorites with friends. The craze cooled down upon the inauguration of Franklin Roosevelt, although sales remained high throughout the decade.

Stamp collecting really gained publicity during the 1930s. President Roosevelt was an ardent collector, and his enthusiasm led others to the hobby. In addition, the decade saw countless new American commemorative stamps printed, which further sparked public interest. Of course, it did not hurt that Roosevelt's postmaster general was James A. Farley, a close friend who supported his boss's passion by constantly ordering new issues. The president himself designed a number of commemorative stamps and was probably the envy of collectors around the nation.[12]

Commemorative stamps honored everything under the sun, from current and historic events (Olympics, 1932), holidays (Arbor Day, 1932; Mother's Day, 1934), famous people (Admiral Richard E. Byrd, 1933) to national parks (1934). By and large, the U.S. stamps of the 1930s were especially handsome, produced from exquisitely detailed engravings. The sales of albums and related paraphernalia reflected the ever-increasing popularity of the hobby. Schools and churches encouraged philately, and there was even a radio program for collectors.

Woodworking, ceramics, model airplanes, collectibles, coins, railroad layouts, watercolors and oils, hiking and camping, photography—the list of hobbies pursued during the 1930s is endless. Their most important contribution during the Depression years was a capacity to impart a sense of self-worth to the hobbyist. Jobs may have been scarce, but working hard at a hobby fulfilled the need for self-esteem, that what a person was doing had value, and the hobby itself took attention away from the economic difficulties of the day.

Sports

Travel

of the 1930s

The worst days of the Depression saw large numbers of the unemployed just drifting. They moved from town to town, always with the faint hope that the next stop would mean a job. While this aimless search hardly qualified as travel, it nevertheless illustrated the American penchant for moving on and finding something better. In 1932, about a million people roamed the rails and highways of the country, victims of an economy in which they played little part.

The terrible Dust Bowl of the 1930s also put thousands on the road. The Dust Bowl referred to the location (the Southern Plain states of Oklahoma, Kansas, Texas, New Mexico, Nevada, and Arkansas) and the period, 1931 to 1939, when drought combined with bad farming methods and poverty to decimate farming in the area. John Steinbeck's *The Grapes of Wrath* (1939), an American literary classic, chronicles the exodus of Oklahoma farmers from their devastated land and their journey to California in hopes of a new beginning. Here was travel of a totally different kind, with images of "Okies," their jalopies and wagons piled high with meager possessions, wandering the highways of a nation that seemed to be turning its back on them. In many ways, these people were refugees in their own country.

Many other Americans, however, traveled for recreation. These better-off people had the desire—and the means—to enjoy touring, be it by car, train, plane, or ocean liner.

AUTOMOBILE TRAVEL

Americans continued to buy new cars even during the worst years of the Depression, although they actually bought more used cars than new ones throughout 1934 and 1935. Half of American families owned their own vehicles, although most bought the cheapest car they could. By 1935, 95 percent of all the automobiles sold cost under $750 (about $9,300 in contemporary dollars). Gasoline was one of the few commodities to enjoy steady sales throughout the Depression years. In fact, in a survey conducted during the 1930s, keeping one's car ranked ahead of home ownership or having a telephone, electric lighting, or even a bathtub.[1] Cars of the era began to be designed in a streamlined style around 1934, popularized by the Chrysler Airflow, with flowing lines and rounded edges.

Starting in the 1920s, and growing steadily in the 1930s, American families embraced the Sunday drive. Most travelers accepted the dirt, gravel, ruts, rocks, and holes as part of the driving experience. There was no need to rush, because implicit in the Sunday drive was a lack of a set destination; the family was just out for a drive.

STREAMLINING

In the 1930s, America's leading automobile manufacturers like Ford, Chrysler, and Cadillac, released cars that took design cues from the pages of science fiction. This design trend was called "streamlining," and it developed from the science of aerodynamics. Norman Bel Geddes (1893–1958) was one of its chief and most innovative designers. The basic idea was to use rounded shapes that tapered along their length to reduce drag and enhance the passage of air around the vehicle. Combining a desire to build faster cars with futuristic designs, similar to artists' renderings of space craft and jets, the streamlined car was born, and the design trend dominated the industry for over a decade. Streamlining wasn't used only for cars; it was also integrated into the design of car trailers, trains, and boats, as well as for buildings, in industrial design, and in such kitchen appliances as refrigerators, electric mixers, and blenders. Acknowledging the link to the aircraft industry, some designers also outfitted their vehicles with design elements borrowed from aircrafts. The streamlining trend was symbolic of the newest advances in science, and by 1939, the word "streamlined" had been co-opted in popular culture to mean "efficient," "modern," and "advanced." While the popularity of streamlining eventually declined, the science of aerodynamics remained of prime interest to the vehicle industry, and over the ensuing decades designers continued to use streamlining to enhance speed and acceleration, while much of the futuristic detailing was replaced by more modest designs.

The beautiful 1937 Chrysler Airflow four-door sedan in the showroom of the Chrysler Building, New York City, 1937. Prints & Photographs Division, Library of Congress.

Taking a Sunday drive—or any drive—was challenging: automatic transmissions were rare in lower-priced models, air conditioning was all but unobtainable, and even the best tires tended to be unreliable. No well-equipped driver set forth without a spare or two, as well as a complete kit for repairing and/or changing tires. Gas tanks were small, and gasoline mileage was poor: the average vehicle had a cruising range of about 50 miles. If those limitations were not enough, money was scarce, so the 1930s witnessed a high proportion of creaky, dilapidated automobiles laboring down the nation's roads.

Those roads were mostly unpaved. Many city streets were paved, but that paving could consist of bricks, cobblestones, and other rough surfaces. And once a driver reached the outskirts of town, conditions changed abruptly. No interstate highways yet existed; four-lane "superhighways" weren't even considered by highway departments until 1938. In all, the country had about 500,000 miles of two-lane highways during the 1930s, and only about 70 percent of these miles were paved.[2]

As the decade wore on, more and more roads were built, and many existing ones were surfaced. Some of the credit for this goes to the Civilian Conservation Corps (CCC), the Works Progress Administration (WPA), and other federally funded New Deal groups that changed the landscape of the nation. The WPA alone was responsible for over half a million miles of such construction.

Amenities such as service stations, rest rooms, lodging, and restaurants tended to be few and far between. As traffic increased, however, strip development along the highway followed. Gas stations, eateries, cabins, and souvenir shops multiplied. Astute travelers quickly mastered interpreting the signs along the road, not just what they said—"gas," "food," "lodging"—but also what they signified. Coca-Cola, Sealy mattresses, Howard Johnson's foods, and Texaco gasoline were comforting reminders of American efficiency and know-how, and the highway served as a popular promenade to display and advertise them.

By the end of the decade, commercial strips had become part of the roadside landscape. In addition, small shopping centers had begun to appear, usually close to a busy highway and with easy access. These forerunners of the malls of the postwar years were simple affairs, usually an L-shaped cluster of stores and a large paved parking area.

In 1935, the city fathers of Oklahoma City used traffic woes as a way to raise income. The parking meter, or Park-O-Meter, came into being. Initially, they cost $58 apiece and paid for themselves in short order. After that, the income went to the municipality. Other cities soon adopted the device, and the parking meter became a part of the American scene.

A popular comic strip of the era was Frank King's *Gasoline Alley*. The title refers to a narrow lane that bisected many residential blocks of the time. People built their garages so they would face this alley and not the street; the front-facing driveway was still relatively unknown. The gentle, good-natured strip often focused on the activities of the alley: cars, their repairs, their performance, and general automotive lore. Readership of the strip stood in the millions.

Frank Capra's comedy *It Happened One Night* (1934) offers endless examples of the trials and tribulations of road travel in 1930s America. The two stars, Clark Gable and Claudette Colbert, hitchhike, and ride in buses and taxis and, at times, in decrepit automobiles. Closed gas stations, run-down auto camps (a cross between a motel and a roadside cabin), and mechanical breakdowns compound their woes. Presumably, everything depicted in the movie had at one time

or another happened to members of the audience, and so a close sense of identification between fiction and reality was quickly established. (See Entertainment of the 1930s.)

LODGING

For those driving long distances, lodging could prove challenging. As a rule, traditional hotels were located in towns and cities, generally close to the railroad station. These were often ornate structures occupying prime business land, and their expensive construction costs were reflected in room rates and restaurant charges. Since their primary clientele had been males who traveled alone on business, rooms tended to be small and unadorned, and most hotels did almost nothing to cater to families. Their restaurants exuded a masculine air, with a smoky bar or lounge as important as tables for diners.

The advent of the automobile, however, changed who traveled and the way they did it. Auto camps began to spring up throughout the country. Typically, they offered a gas pump, a small convenience store with some cheap souvenirs and a few groceries, and a choice between a single-room cabin and a place for erecting a tent. The more luxurious provided a bare-bones recreation hall, café, and covered camping facilities.[3]

Competition among roadside auto camps forced them to improve their offerings. They began providing raised platforms that kept the tent floor dry during rain. Ramshackle cabins were replaced by more orderly rows of reasonably well-constructed cottages. By the mid-1930s, *Popular Mechanics,* a magazine with a large following among do-it-yourselfers, ran articles explaining how to build tourist cabins that would attract business. Folksy names like "Para Dice," "Dew Drop Inn," and "Tumble Inn" added to the appeal of these tourist stops. It was apparent that the family was welcome.

The auto camps and freestanding cabins continued to evolve. Connecting roofs, or carports, between buildings linked the cottages and protected parked vehicles. This innovation led to the creation and construction of the auto court or, as it came to be known, the motel (motor + hotel). It first appeared in California.

Motels appealed to families. They were cheap, and no porters, bell captains, or other personnel stood around expecting a tip. Bags could be transported from auto to room quickly, with no embarrassing parade through a lobby, so there was no need for expensive luggage. Both check-in and checkout were speedy, and parking convenience was assured. Most motels at first tended to be only one story in height, eliminating the chore of lugging bags up flights of stairs. The room itself frequently had a window or two that provided some ventilation; it also had a screen door, and gave a sense of openness. Hotel rooms, on the other hand were frequently up several flights of narrow stairs, and might have only one small window that looked out on an airshaft.

By the mid-1930s, a swimming pool, perhaps some playground equipment—all visible from the highway—became standard fixtures for motels wanting to catch motorists' attention, especially those traveling with children. It did not matter whether the pool was actually used; it, along with the clustered beach chairs and umbrellas, suggested a level of quality higher than competitors who did not offer such amenities.

Some operators formed chains with such names as Alamo Plaza, United Motor Courts, Deluxe Motor Courts, and TraveLodge. The number of courts and motels went from slightly over 3,000 at the end of the 1920s to well over 13,000 in 1939. At the same time, hotels reported sharp drops in occupancy rates. It was estimated that about 85 percent of all vacationers traveled by car during the period. Tourist facilities of all kinds quadrupled between 1927 and 1935, going from about 5,000 establishments to some 20,000.[4]

Despite the rapid growth of the motel business, some doubt lingered about this economical form of lodging in the minds of many Americans. Motels allowed people to travel almost anonymously. Presumably, not everyone stopping at a motel had honorable intentions. In a lurid article written for the popular *American Magazine* at the end of the decade, F.B.I. Director J. Edgar Hoover proclaimed motels, tourist cabins, and anything in between to be immoral and leading to corruption. Hoover's words carried considerable weight, even if much of the message consisted of sensationalism.

TRAILERS

Not everyone, however, needed a motel. Home craftsmen had been fashioning vehicles to tow behind their automobiles for some years, and so the concept was neither new nor foreign to consumers. In the 1920s and 1930s, the trunk on the average automobile was small by today's standards. Seats did not recline, and interior space was cramped.

At the end of the 1920s, handyman Arthur Sherman built himself a box on wheels. He fashioned his creation out of Masonite, a cheap hardboard. Acquaintances admired his work, so he had carpenters assemble several more, and sold them. Then a few more, and a few more after that, until, in 1936, he had 1,100 people working for him, putting together his trademark covered wagons at the rate of 1,000 a month.

The Sherman covered wagon was simplicity itself. At just under $400, it was fairly affordable, easy to maintain, and could be readily imitated. By 1936 at least 700 commercial builders were assembling trailers of one form or another.

The manufacturers began to make their vehicles larger, adding more and more amenities like complete kitchenettes, chemical toilets, self-contained water supplies, and increased storage. By 1935, thousands of families were packing up and moving to trailer camps across the nation. Florida led the rankings, with over 17,000 camps available, most of which could accommodate about 100 trailers each. California boasted some 6,000 camps. Every state in the union had facilities; North Dakota, at the bottom of the list, had more than 100. These nomads had discovered that living in a trailer was generally cheaper than residing in a conventional home, plus they found themselves among like-minded individuals.[5]

In the midst of this boom, Wally Byam formed the Airstream Trailer Company. His product was constructed entirely of aluminum, instead of the usual hardboard and wood framing then in vogue, and his creation was ultra-streamlined, resembling an airplane or a spaceship more than a conventional trailer. Byam saw his product as a recreational camper, not as a home on wheels. His Airstream Trailer would eventually become one

Travel

Trailers on the move in Florida in 1939. The popularity of trailers lasted until the end of the decade and the onset of World War II. Prints & Photographs Division, Library of Congress.

of the most popular and enduring travel trailers of all time.

Widely read magazines, such as *Harper's, Life, Popular Mechanics,* the *Saturday Evening Post,* and *Time,* chronicled the phenomenon, but the bottom fell out of the trailer market in the recession of 1938. Before it collapsed, however, popular culture picked up on its success. *Ella Cinders,* a nationally syndicated newspaper comic strip, had a long-running episode that dealt with the subject, and several radio soap operas had their heroines living the trailer life. Montgomery Ward, the huge merchandiser, added a furnished trailer to its catalog. There was even the "Roosevelt caravan," a string of fifty trailers pulled by new cars promoting Franklin Roosevelt and his programs as part of the 1936 presidential campaign.

PUBLIC TRANSPORTATION

The automobile was not the only way to get to a destination; mass transit was a major force in the country's urban centers. For example, the adventuresome could go from Boston to New York City by bus and trolley. The journey first involved obtaining a "wayfinder," a detailed listing of regional routes and schedules. Once aboard, there were numerous stops in New England towns and the expenditure of twenty-plus hours to do it. But the final fare, at about a nickel each stop, was approximately $2.40. By using a combination of buses, trolleys, and electric interurban rail transit, even a trip to New York City from Chicago was possible.[6]

Because of the slow improvement of state and federal roads, bus usage grew rapidly. In 1930, 20 percent of all intercity travel was by bus, and that figure continued to increase during the Depression years. Greyhound Bus Lines had coast-to-coast routes in the thirties, and their success led a number of smaller companies to form National Trailways in 1936. The additional lines meant that the United States had an effective intercity and cross-country bus system in place by 1935.

Around 1935, the Greyhound Corporation began running full-page, four-color advertisements in the *Saturday Evening Post* extolling the pleasures of a long-distance trip via a Greyhound. The illustrations showed buses that were progressively more streamlined over time. Although the ads depicted happy families getting on board, most bus passengers were commercial travelers such as salesmen, going from town to town to conduct business. The average American family travelled by car. Nevertheless, the impact of increased bus use was felt by the nation's railroads; they saw both the number of passengers and revenues decline.

Where buses could offer distinctive service was in the area of tours. These were extremely lucrative, and Greyhound in particular offered tour packages around the country. Tours usually included round-trip transportation, hotel accommodations, and visits to selected sites. Niagara Falls, the national parks, big cities, and scenic vistas were popular destinations. Greyhound's organized tours were so successful that the company created its own travel agencies; they did well throughout the Depression era.[7]

The aforementioned *It Happened One Night* employs a Greyhound bus as part of its story. Likewise, other films used "the Hound" as a basis for their plotting. *Fugitive Lovers* (1934), a comedy starring Robert Montgomery, was a big box-office draw. Montgomery embarks on a picturesque cross-country bus tour with—among others—the Three Stooges as company. The movie marked an early outing for the zany trio, but the fabulous scenery and the comforts of the bus may have been the most lasting impressions audiences carried away from the film.

Most cities boasted at least a couple of taxi companies, although the economic downturn hit cabs hard and many firms went under. During the grimmest years of the crisis, a typical taxi charge might total twenty cents for a one-mile ride, about half of the fare just a few years earlier. The survivors, however, profited in the later 1930s and became a familiar part of the urban scene.

TRAIN TRAVEL

The railroads were slow in adapting to the modern needs of actual or potential passengers. Air travel was still in its relative infancy, the bus and coach lines appeared to offer little real competition, and auto travel, though growing rapidly, did not figure into their calculations.

The 1930s witnessed a profound shift in public opinion about travel. The automobile could take people anywhere. Buses, too, had become more popular; 1935 witnessed a first: more people rode buses than trains. Despite the shifting demographics, trains still offered a variety of choices to the consumer. The country was crisscrossed with railroad tracks, and dozens of companies vied for passengers. Very few towns were not served by a railroad. Great terminals in the nation's cities welcomed passengers into a temple-like atmosphere, a world of bustling African American porters, clouds of steam, and boards with endless lists of arrivals and departures.

The railroads' miscalculations were based on a history of success. Much of the National Park system in the West had grown because of the impact of passenger rail service. For instance, Yellowstone Park, isolated from any major highways, welcomed 45,000 rail visitors in 1915; only 7,500 came by automobile. By 1930, with an improved road system, a paltry 27,000 took the train to the park; 195,000 drove their cars. For the American traveler, momentous change had occurred, but the still prosperous railroad companies ignored the message.[8]

In spectacular magazine and poster advertisements, the railroads continued to present the romance of steam engines and gorgeous vistas. The enticements of the ads may have convinced some families to visit Glacier or Yosemite, but they had no interest in taking a train to do it.

It would be unfair to say that the railroads ignored passenger service. During the 1930s, every

Travel

day, at every hour, passenger trains were pulling out of and into stations across the nation. Some of the trains were quite miserable, with old, dilapidated cars, poor service, and erratic schedules. Some were merely adequate; others were quite good, with dining cars, bar cars, sleepers, and compartments, ranging from staterooms to an efficiency module called a "roomette," a self-contained unit that was introduced on selected trains in 1937.[9]

Several of the major American railroads spent prodigious amounts to create and maintain a few luxury trains. They realized that people with money were abandoning traditional train transportation for airlines and highway travel to travel first class. In addition, railroads cut fares to lure more passengers, and they offered coach travelers amenities such as lounge cars equipped with radios, a tacit admission of the role radio was coming to play in Americans' lives. The Baltimore & Ohio Railroad air-conditioned its all-parlor train, the New York to Washington Columbian, in 1931. This move was an industry first; by 1936 almost 6,000 passenger cars enjoyed this feature.

The change that most people noticed, however, was the move to streamlining. The sleek, forward-looking engines of the Grand Central Railroad, the Pennsylvania, the Burlington, the Santa Fe, the Southern Pacific, and the Union Pacific have come to be associated with the 1930s and the 1940s. Names like the Super Chief, the California Zephyr, the Hiawatha, the Broadway Limited, the Twentieth Century, and the Mercury can still conjure up pictures of beautiful people in elegant clothes, sipping cocktails while the sun dips behind snow-capped mountains. These diesel-powered locomotives may not have been much faster than their more traditional steam counterparts, but they *looked* faster, and they also looked modern and fashionable.[10]

Hollywood has always liked trains. The camera can remain focused on a limited set, and the passing scenery is just background. A film like 1934's very successful *Twentieth Century* was a case in point: adapted from the stage, the story unfolds during the railroad trip itself. During the course of the film, glamorous actors like Carole Lombard and John Barrymore move from modern compartments to a sleek cocktail lounge. Always in the background is the motif of motion,

Advertisement for Southern Pacific Railway, showing the new streamlined train, the interior of a dining car, and a map of the four routes of Southern Pacific, 1937. Prints & Photographs Division, Library of Congress.

of movement—from one affair to another or from one place to another. *The Silver Streak* (1934; not to be confused with the 1976 comedy *Silver Streak*), set in the West, gives a tightly controlled picture of railroads and speed. A train must race against time in order to save lives. The image of the engine cutting a swath of smoke and steam in the vastness of the desert is well done.

AIR TRAVEL

Perhaps nothing captured the American travel imagination like the magnificent zeppelins, or dirigibles, which traversed the skies during the early 1930s. Named for Count Ferdinand von Zeppelin (1838–1917), a German scientist and engineer instrumental in the development of lighter-than-air craft, the great airships were poised to become a significant force in aviation.[11]

Hollywood brought out several movies that featured zeppelins. Howard Hughes directed *Hell's Angels* (1930), a special-effects-filled picture that featured dogfights around a German zeppelin in World War I. Another aerial epic was *Dirigible* (1931).

The U.S. Navy saw dirigibles as an effective extension of the fleet. In the midst of the Depression, the admirals persuaded Congress to approve the construction of the *Akron* (1931) and the *Macon* (1933). The *Akron* generated a lot of good publicity for the navy, flying around the country and engaging in maneuvers. It carried four small biplanes on its huge frame, releasing them while airborne and then recapturing them while still aloft. In 1933 the *Akron* went down in a storm with the loss of 73 lives, the worst air disaster until that time. The *Macon* likewise plunged into the ocean in 1935. With these two failures, the U.S. government effectively retired from any further airship development until World War II.

At the same time, the privately owned Goodyear Tire and Rubber Company, long active in dirigible research, continued work with non-rigid airships, or blimps. By the outbreak of World War II in 1941, Goodyear blimps had transported several hundred thousand passengers and carried countless advertising messages on their exteriors.

Despite the setbacks suffered by the U.S. Navy, Germany strove to perfect these unwieldy craft and was the nation most advanced in overall airship utilization. The pride of their fleet was the *Graf Zeppelin,* a mammoth 775-foot dirigible that circumnavigated the globe, including stops at Lakehurst, New Jersey, and Los Angeles. As a result of these exploits, the United States in 1930 issued a set of three commemorative airmail stamps, each depicting the *Graf Zeppelin* in flight. Now extremely rare and valuable, the stamps were in denominations of 65¢, $1.30, and $2.60. Three years later, to celebrate Chicago's Century of Progress Exposition, another stamp was printed, this one showing the *Graf Zeppelin* heading for the towers of Chicago. It came in a fifty-cent denomination and is equally sought after by philatelists.

The *Graf Zeppelin's* sister ship, the *Hindenburg,* was built in 1936; it was the most luxurious

dirigible in the skies, and great hopes were held out for it to make such air travel commonplace between America and Europe. The *Hindenburg* flew without incident from Germany to Lakehurst and back in May 1936, accomplishing the journey in the record time of just under 65 hours. As a result, public interest in airships was at an all-time high, and it appeared that regular transatlantic dirigible travel was now a reality. Nine more flights ensued, usually with several celebrities on board. The passengers raved about the smooth, quiet ride.[12]

In May 1937, as always, a crowd turned out at Lakehurst for the *Hindenburg's* arrival; among them was Herb Morrison, a reporter for NBC Radio News. As it approached the mooring mast, something went terribly wrong and the airship burst into flames. Morrison, microphone in hand, managed to report the disaster live over the airwaves. As he watched and reported—"Oh, the humanity!" he cried—38 people died in the flaming wreckage. Theories for the cause include lightning igniting the hydrogen gas that powered the *Hindenburg* or an electric spark (possibly caused by lightning) setting fire to its outer skin covering. After the disaster, no one wanted anything to do with airships. The tragedy, however, did little to diminish the public's fascination with daredevil airplane stunts and feats, such as wing walkers, aerial acrobatics, races, and mock combat.

Charles Lindbergh (1902–1974), who had thrilled the country with his solo flight to Paris in 1927, took to the air again during the 1930s. He and his wife, Anne Morrow Lindbergh, envisioned great growth in commercial aviation and worked to create a North Atlantic route for future airliners. Following these journeys she wrote a pair of best sellers—*North to the Orient* (1935) and *Listen! The Wind* (1938)—about their adventures.

With each passing year in the decade, airplanes were flying higher, faster, and longer. In 1931, the American aviator Wiley Post (1898–1935) kept listeners glued to their radios or readers eagerly awaiting the latest newspaper edition that chronicled his latest exploit. That year, Post raced around the world in his *Winnie Mae,* a single-engine, high-wing monoplane with detachable landing gear that gave it greater speed and distance. Post

Travel

telegraphed accounts of his journey to a news syndicate which released them to a waiting public. Even with all the ballyhoo, he accomplished something significant: he and his navigator had circled the globe in 8 days, 15 hours, and 51 minutes, a new record. Post—dashing in a black eye patch and leather gear—took off again in 1933, but this time he was alone. He and the *Winnie Mae* beat their own record by over 21 hours, making him both the fastest and the first to do it solo. Distances were shrinking, and the public avidly followed each new accomplishment.[13]

The annual National Air Races involved two events that gripped public attention, the Thompson Trophy and the Bendix Trophy races. The first was a closed-course race where small planes buzzed around a set pattern that used tall pylons as markers. The closer and faster a pilot could shave a pylon, the better the elapsed time. The Thomson Trophy races were dangerous, and a number of daring fliers crashed and died.

The Bendix Trophy was based on time and distance, usually a coast-to-coast flight. Initiated in 1931, this race drew the top aviators of the day. Jimmy Doolittle of the Army Air Corps, Howard Hughes, Frank "Meteor Man" Hawks, and Roscoe Turner were some of the pilots who combined distance with speed and endurance. In fact, Hughes carried these goals far beyond the original boundaries of the event. A movie director, inventor, and millionaire, he climbed into his self-designed *Hughes Special* in 1935 and reached the almost unbelievable airspeed of 325 miles per hour. Two years later he sped across the country in under eight hours, and in 1938 he circled the globe in three days, nineteen hours, and fourteen minutes, more than halving Wiley Post's 1933 record.

The public also followed a young aviatrix—as women pilots were then called—named Amelia Earhart. In 1928, she had earned fame as the first woman to fly the Atlantic, but as a passenger. Earhart quickly became something of a celebrity. In 1932, at the age of 35, she made her own solo flight across the Atlantic, again the first woman to do so. She flew from Hawaii to California in 1935, quickly following that exploit with yet another solo flight from Mexico City to New Jersey. She was the first flier, male or female, to accomplish either of these feats. She announced plans for a round-the-world flight in 1937. Somewhere over the vast reaches of the Pacific, her plane disappeared, and the plane, Earhart, and her navigator Frederick J. Noonan, have never been found.

The daring of these pilots spread to the newspaper comics. Adventure series like *Ace Drummond* (1935–1940) competed for space on the crowded funny pages. Purportedly drawn by Captain Eddie Rickenbacker, a renowned World War I flying ace, the strip was really the work of Clayton Knight. It included a small panel entitled *Hall of Fame of the Air,* where the exploits of real fliers were celebrated. Frank Miller's *Barney Baxter in the Air* (1935–1950), aimed at the youth market, involved an adolescent boy in all sorts of aerial adventures. With the approach of World War II, Barney pushes hard for military preparedness, making his strip one of the first major series to suggest that war was inevitable and the nation needed to be ready for it.

Probably the most popular of all the flying strips was *Smilin' Jack* (1933–1973), a mix of humor, romance, and adventure. The creation of Zack Mosley, the series reminded readers of Wiley Post and even Amelia Earhart, since women fliers appeared in the stories. Awkwardly drawn, the strip enthralled its readers with its meticulous attention to mechanical detail. The romance may have come directly from radio soap operas, but the airplanes came from the headlines.[14]

By the mid-1930s, altitudes above several thousand feet, speeds over 125 miles per hour, and distances exceeding a thousand miles were made commonplace by technological advances. To lure first-time travelers, as well as more seasoned fliers, aeronautical designers worked diligently to make the aircraft of the 1930s suggest speed and efficiency. As a result, sleek, streamlined forms began to characterize commercial aircraft—shapes that have continued to dominate flight to the present.[15]

No airplane of the period better summarizes the changeover than the Douglas DC-3. These craft, designed in 1933 as the DC-1 and first manufactured as the DC-2, carried their passengers in relative comfort during the day. However, the airlines also wanted to offer customers berths for long-distance night flying. In 1936 Douglas introduced

Travel

the DC-3, a larger version of the DC-2. By day it seated 21 persons; at night it offered berths for 14 in its "skysleeper" or Douglas Sleeper Transport. The DC-3 was fast—it could cruise at almost 200 mph, an astonishing speed for any commercial plane at the time—and it was fabulously reliable. Over 11,000 DC-3s were built, making it the most successful and most profitable airplane of all time. In 1939, the DC-3 carried some three-quarters of all air passengers in the United States.

The 1930s saw the theatrical release of over 25 commercial films that were aviation-oriented. The decade opened with two World War I dramas, director Howard Hughes's *Hell's Angels* (1930) and Howard Hawks's *The Dawn Patrol* (1930). These movies indicated the direction the majority of future aviation pictures would take: war stories with lots of combat footage.

Mostly forgotten potboilers, aviation movies did provide an exciting moment or two of flying during the early days of the Depression. But a pair of exceptions also came along: *King Kong* (1933) and *Flying Down to Rio* (1933). *King Kong* was not an aviation film; it was a classic mix of horror and fantasy. The final sequence, however, with the giant ape perched atop the newly built Empire State Building, brushing off attacking army biplanes as if they were annoying gnats, is an iconic cinematic moment. (See Entertainment of the 1930s.)

Flying Down to Rio likewise was not specifically an aviation movie, but it contained one of the great film flight sequences. In this musical, technology is a vehicle for showcasing the talents of dancers Fred Astaire and Ginger Rogers. But even Astaire and Rogers take a backseat to a bevy of chorus girls as they kick up their heels in unison while standing on the wings of a large airplane, flying down to the famous Brazilian city. A triumph of special effects, the scene makes absolutely no social or technological comments; rather it displays the wonder and fun only movies can provide.

The films of remainder of the decade returned to more traditional aerial imagery. As the war clouds over Asia and Europe darkened perceptibly, the American screen often emphasized thoughts of preparedness.

Test Pilot (1938) portrays a flier (Clark Gable) and a mechanic (Spencer Tracy) who put

experimental aircraft through their paces. The story includes footage about testing the military's then-new B-17 bomber and the importance attached to military superiority. By the late 1930s, any thoughts of neutrality were in the process of being conveniently forgotten by Hollywood, and the content of many action films reflected this loss of innocence.

SEA TRAVEL

Ocean travel, though the privilege of only a few, was played up in the popular press and became a subject of note during the Depression years. Most of the great liners sailed under the flags of foreign nations. Flying the tricolor of the French Line were the *Île de France* and the *Normandie,* the latter perhaps the quintessential ocean liner of the 1930s. Arriving in New York Harbor in 1935 on its maiden voyage, the *Normandie* carried almost 2,000 passengers in unsurpassed comfort.[16]

The English, once the rulers of the sea, were not to be outdone by the French. They were represented by several liners, but the *Queen Mary* served as the flagship of Cunard Lines for much of the decade. The *Queen Mary* was built in 1934 and made a triumphant New York arrival in May 1936. Like the *Normandie,* the *Queen Mary* epitomized luxurious travel. Americans were fascinated by these grand ships. Despite the absence of liners under the American flag, most of the passengers—perhaps 75 percent of the total—crossing the Atlantic were from the United States.

Using the most stylish graphics of the period, the various lines painted a picture of modern luxury at sea. The placement of the ads in magazines, newspapers, travel agencies, posters, and billboards guaranteed that millions would see the alluring vision of a lifestyle associated with the very rich.

As filmmakers became enamored of the ocean liner, a remarkable string of comedies, mysteries, and musicals came out that were set, either in whole or in part, on sleek, polished liners. First came *Transatlantic* (1931), a minor film that was, nevertheless, a pioneer. It presented Art Deco as a style of contrasting blacks, whites, and geometric forms. These decorative motifs went on to influence imitators and convinced movie patrons that life on the high seas was very good indeed.

Travel

In 1934, *Chained* brought together Clark Gable and Joan Crawford for some shipboard romance. The ship, of course, presented a backdrop consisting of the most fashionable design trends. *A Night at the Opera* (1935), featuring the Marx Brothers, has many hilarious scenes on an ocean liner, including the classic stateroom scene where a preposterous number of people, including stowaways emerging from a trunk, end up in the same tiny room.

Follow the Fleet (1936) has the unparalleled dance team of Fred Astaire and Ginger Rogers cavorting against a Moderne backdrop of ships and sailors. The following year, RKO Pictures had the duo at it again with *Shall We Dance* (1937). As always, the plot was secondary to the dancing. The story, however, does get Astaire and Rogers aboard a white, streamlined liner that echoes the ads of the major steamship companies. Both films reinforce what was already fact; art now was imitating the commonplace.

Possibly the epitome of all the liner-associated pictures is *The Big Broadcast of 1938* (1938). The movie had plenty of stars—W. C. Fields, Bob Hope, Dorothy Lamour, Martha Raye—but it also boasted a streamlined ship created by Norman Bel Geddes, one of the premier theatrical and industrial designers of the day. In a climactic race against another liner, the film's S.S. *Gigantic* resembled nothing so much as a waterborne spaceship. Here were the Buck Rogers/Flash Gordon comic strip motifs carried over into 1938 and pointed toward the optimistic world of tomorrow that would shortly be celebrated in the New York World's Fair.

Visual Arts

of the 1930s

In the eyes of most Americans, the artistic movements of the 1910s and 1920s were confusing and unintelligible. Modern art was characterized as decadent, the work of foreigners, and resistance to it was seen as proper and patriotic. A few museums presented shows that introduced new currents of visual expression, but for the most part exhibitions presented the tried and true, using representational art—still lifes, landscapes, portraits—as their foundation.

Even with the insularity of American taste, a few significant works achieved both critical and public acclaim, and Modernism crept into popular works, albeit slowly and circuitously. Tradition, in the form of representational art, continued its hold on the popular audience. That many of the traditionalists often employed Modernist motifs and techniques in their work was overlooked at the time, and only in retrospect is this aspect of their achievements acknowledged.

PAINTING AND ALLIED ARTS

Few serious artists prospered during the Depression years. Their works were seen, if at all, by a limited, elitist audience, and the larger mass audience remained ignorant of changes occurring in American art at the time. Both collectors and museums lacked the funds for purchases, and many

galleries closed. Not until the federal government took the unprecedented step of subsidizing the arts did the future brighten for talented painters and other artists.

Regionalism

If any one school of painting rose to national prominence, it was Regionalism. The artists considered Regionalists employed themes of national identity, using the land as a carrier of meaning. Instead of Paris and sidewalk cafés, the Regionalists might paint an American diner and fill it with typical small-town citizens. Regionalism celebrated a nostalgia for the past, especially the rural past that was fast disappearing with technology and urban growth. In addition, the Regionalists made no attempt to debunk American institutions and values, as did so many artists in previous decades; they preferred to mythologize American history, elevating the commonplace and giving it heroic status.

The two regionalists who attracted the most attention, both critical and popular, during the period were Grant Wood (1891–1942) and Thomas Hart Benton (1889–1975).[1] Wood was the better known, primarily on the basis of one painting, *American Gothic,* a work he first exhibited at the Art Institute of Chicago in 1930.

This simple portrait of two people drew instant acclaim. Crowds lined up to view the work, and the Art Institute promptly purchased it for their permanent collection, paying the sum of $300. Since then, Wood's picture has become instantly recognizable to millions, both in its original form and as the object of parody. Countless advertisers have employed the image, usually humorously, as the backdrop for every conceivable product, relying on the audience's familiarity with the painting to assist in presenting their message.

None of Wood's many other notable paintings ever approached *American Gothic* in popularity. He had struck a resonant chord with virtually all Americans, and he capitalized on it. Publicity photographs showed Wood attired in overalls, a folksy Iowan who represented the Heartland. He spoke obliquely about his work, changing stories about *American Gothic* to please his public.

American Gothic may be the best-known painting of the 1930s, but the self-appointed spokesperson for the Regionalists was Missouri-born Thomas Hart Benton. He demanded a manly, representational art, free of the false affectations of Modernism and European influences. In December 1934, *Time* magazine chose Benton for its cover in a wide-ranging feature on contemporary American art. Benton took this opportunity to lambaste much of the current artistic community, and claimed that Regionalism superseded any Modernist movements.

Despite his tendency to pontificate and exaggerate, Benton did have considerable popular appeal. He helped to reinvigorate the art of mural painting, contributing a number of outstanding large works that attracted wide audiences. He freely used allegory, along with the folktales and legends of heartland America, as his text.

Sunday Morning by Thomas Hart Benton. Prints & Photographs Division, Library of Congress.

Writhing, elongated figures, with all their serpentine contours, became his trademark, and he formularized it into compositions, all the time saying that his work was a repudiation of Modernism. Benton was the most colorful of the Regionalists, and he helped to make many people aware of his approach to art.

Urban Realism

The Regionalists weathered the Depression, but the impending war soon overshadowed their efforts. Meanwhile, many other artists were striving for recognition, and most could be grouped as urban and social realists. The unemployment and despair seen in many American towns and cities during the Depression brought about a new wave of interest in the urban scene. Many artists, like Edward Hopper (1882–1967) and Charles Sheeler (1883–1965), depicted the American city as cheerless, a drab, ugly place. Whereas earlier interpreters had painted the city as a lively scene, many of the urban painters of the 1930s, particularly Hopper and Sheeler, sucked the life out of it. In their work, the city tended to be eerily quiet, permeated by an overriding feeling of loneliness, as if people could not connect with each other. There was a sense of detachment—often the viewer was placed at a distance from the subject.[2]

Hopper's cityscapes were painted in such a way that the urban hustle and bustle was absent, as if a kind of inertia had stifled all activity. Sheeler's unsullied factory landscapes, on the other hand, depicted the power of industrial America, but no workers ran the machines he so lovingly detailed. With great factories standing idle in the Depression, Sheeler's paintings provided mute comment on the unrealized power of American industry. Both artists had their followers, and today they are certainly significant American painters, but their fame was limited to museums and galleries.

An altogether different view of the city was provided by Reginald Marsh (1898–1954). For him, a city street was a raucous, honky-tonk place, full of the gritty details of life. It may not have been pretty, but it was alive, and he plunged the viewer into the midst of noisy chaos, a place of bustling visual turbulence. Edward Hopper's city scenes made the onlooker ponder, but Marsh's were more celebratory—that was the way the city was, and there was no need to be moralistic about it.

Thanks to several mural commissions and his own vibrant paintings, Reginald Marsh achieved a modest popular success. Although he enjoyed satirizing the rich in many of his works, his poor and downtrodden exhibited a sense that they were comfortable and belonged in this environment. Marsh reflected the growing urbanism of the United States, and his candor in depicting the inherent life of a large American city (almost always New York) appealed to a broad cross section of the population.[3]

Federal Art Project

In 1933, the administration of President Roosevelt created the Public Works of Art Project, a six-month program designed to employ 3,750 artists and aid in the creation of over 15,000 works, including 700 public murals. Run by the Treasury Department, it was judged a success, and a much more ambitious program for all artistic endeavors grew out of it.[4]

The newly created Works Progress Administration (WPA) was given the mandate to create meaningful jobs for thousands of unemployed citizens, so it formed a number of alphabet agencies, such as the Federal Art Project (FAP). The FAP became a beacon of hope for unemployed artists and art teachers, just as similar agencies came to the aid of theater, music, and literature. In each instance, many individuals who otherwise would have been unemployed found rewarding projects within their areas of expertise. At no other time has the government offered such largesse to the arts.

The FAP peaked in 1936, when 6,000 artists and artisans were on its rolls. The program survived until 1942, making it one of the longest-running federal projects of that type. In all, the FAP spent over $35 million, dispensing assistance to about 12,000 artists. Its output was significant: over 4,500 murals, 19,000 sculptures, and more than 450,000 paintings and prints are attributed to this one agency. The FAP did have one stipulation: works had to depict American themes, either from the present or from history. Artists looked to the national past for orientation and direction, and this approach helped lead to the fascination with

EXHIBITION
ILLINOIS
FEDERAL ART PROJECT
WORKS PROGRESS ADMINISTRATION
•
FEB 16-MAR 12
FEDERAL ART GALLERY
225 W 57 St NYC
10-5 WEEKDAYS 12-5·30 SATURDAY
1-5 SUNDAY 7·30-11 PM WEDNESDAY

Poster for Federal Art Project exhibition of art from the Illinois Federal Art Project at the Federal Art Gallery, in New York City. Created between 1936 and 1938. Prints & Photographs Division, Library of Congress.

anything and everything considered early American, which boomed throughout the decade.

Many of the FAP murals depicted cowboys, farmers, aviators, laborers, mail carriers (a disproportionate number of the murals were done in post offices), and folk heroes. For the most part it was a sanitized view of early America, essentially presenting white male Americans happily working in a chosen land.[5]

Photography

At the same time that the WPA was collecting documentation about America's past through art, photographers were going into cities and out to the countryside to capture American life on film. Their work was called "social documentary"

HISPANIC AMERICAN AND AFRICAN AMERICAN ART OF THE 1930s

While the melting pot culture of the United States allows for innovative combinations of cultural traditions, racial tension and, at times, overt racism have made it difficult for minority artists to break into the professional art scene. Early Hispanic American and African American artists often produced work that directly imitated popular white artists. This changed significantly during the 1930s, when both Hispanic American and African American artists began exploring art that tapped into their own cultural traditions. African American artists found a patron in the Works Progress Administration, a federal agency that funded a number of depression-era artists. Some works depicted scenes of African American urban and rural life, often calling attention to race relations, discrimination, and other social issues. While Hispanic artists of the era had a more difficult time finding funding opportunities, there was a movement in the Southwest among artists who took their inspiration from the mural painters of Mexico, like Jose Clemente Orzoco. Hispanic painters created murals in cities in New York, Arizona, and New Mexico, murals that celebrated Hispanic culture and traditions. While intolerance and racism certainly hindered the progress of minority artists, the 1930s proved that pride in one's ethnic heritage could inspire creative evolution, which would in turn inspire generations of artists to push the limits of creative innovation.

and "photojournalism," and their photographs of coal miners, sharecroppers, child laborers, immigrants, and the destitute constituted a new level of social awareness. Photographers like Margaret Bourke-White (1906–1971), Walker Evans (1903–1975), Lewis Hine (1874–1940), Dorothea Lange (1895–1965), Carl Mydans (1907–2004), Arthur Rothstein (1915–1985), and Paul Strand (1890–1976) gained fame with their hard-hitting black-and-white studies.

Bourke-White's *You Have Seen Their Faces* (1937; written with Erskine Caldwell) stirred emotions with its portraits of American farm families

One of Walker Evans's justly famous photographs, taken in 1937, when he was working with the Resettlement Administration: "Negroes in the lineup for food at mealtime in the camp for flood refugees, Forrest City, Arkansas. 1937." Prints & Photographs Division, Library of Congress.

facing bad economic times; Rothstein's *The Depression Years* (1978) provided a photographic overview of the country during the crisis and contained a mix of urban and rural images. Evans joined forces with the writer and critic James Agee to produce *Let Us Now Praise Famous Men* (1939; revised 1941). The two focused on farm families, especially sharecroppers, and their double plight: the Dust Bowl and the economic chaos of the period. The book's combination of lyrical text and searing photographs showed just how unequal the ordinary, daily lives of people could be. Collectively, these books helped establish photojournalism as a legitimate literary form.[6]

When *Life* magazine came into being in 1936, its success was due in part to the growing public interest in photojournalism. Eastman-Kodak, the huge film and camera manufacturer, sensed they were losing a large part of the lucrative home camera market because of a flood of cheap competitors' models. In response, they brought out the Baby Brownie in 1934, a simple point-and-shoot camera that used easily available roll film. Naturally, they recommended Kodak film. The Brownie sold for an affordable $1.00; plus it took bigger pictures than most others. Despite the Depression, the Brownie swept the nation, eclipsing its competition.

Other popular developments in amateur photography included Kodak's inexpensive movie camera, the 8mm Cine-Kodak Eight, introduced in 1932. In 1935, RCA pioneered in sound photography by unveiling the Sound-on-Film movie camera, making sound home movies possible for the first time.

Sculpture

A less popular visual art was sculpture. The average citizen equated sculpture with large, public statues of long-dead historical figures that could be seen outside courthouses and in parks. Unless one lived in New York or Chicago and had access to the leading museums, modern sculpture was unseen and therefore had no popular impact.

Not so the work of Gutzon Borglum (1867–1941). The public readily accepted his creations as great sculpture. Throughout the 1930s, under the watchful eye of photographers and journalists, Borglum worked away at Mount Rushmore, a mountain located in the Black Hills of South Dakota. First with dynamite and then with pneumatic drills and 400 assistants, he roughed out the faces of four presidents—George Washington, Thomas Jefferson, Abraham Lincoln, and Theodore Roosevelt. Hitched up to a precarious system of scaffolding that allowed him to swing across the face of the mountain, he blasted away at the busts, generating not only sculpture but also lots of publicity. Critics assailed the project as

the worst kind of tasteless exhibitionism, but the public loved it. Mount Rushmore became a National Memorial, and millions have journeyed to South Dakota to see the huge likenesses of past U.S. presidents.[7]

Paul Manship (1885–1966) also exemplified American taste in sculpture for the decade. His smooth, stylized works appealed to many, and his monumental figure of Prometheus above Rockefeller Center's skating rink has charmed generations. Although the piece is quite traditional, it seemed to sum up the average American's view of what public sculpture should be: large and easily identifiable.

ILLUSTRATION

Although Americans may not have been aware of the work being done by sculptors, they didn't lack exposure to significant paintings and drawings. Continuing a trend begun in the nineteenth century, American illustrators were creating art for magazines, books, posters, and advertising. These commercial artists churned out thousands of pictures that ranged from the amateurish to works that could stand beside anything produced by serious artists. The 1930s was a rich decade for American illustration, although many of its skilled practitioners have been forgotten or remain anonymous.

N. C. Wyeth

During the 1930s, the dean of American illustrators was Newell Convers Wyeth (1882–1945). A prolific artist, Wyeth did over 3,000 magazine illustrations, beginning with a cover for the *Saturday Evening Post* in 1903. He also created murals, paintings, and advertisements.

Ladies' Home Journal, Woman's Day, Good Housekeeping, McCall's, and *Redbook* were among the magazines that used his work, and such diverse companies as International Harvester, the American Tobacco Company (Lucky Strikes), General Electric, and Coca-Cola were among his commercial associations. Even with all these commissions, he still created murals for banks, schools, hotels, and other institutions, the majority featuring episodes from American history.

Gutzon Borglum and superintendent inspecting work on the face (nose) of George Washington, Mt. Rushmore, South Dakota, 1932. Prints & Photographs Division, Library of Congress.

Financially secure, he enjoyed the luxury of painting for its own sake. In an acknowledgment of his renown and popularity, most of this mature work was purchased by museums, galleries, and individuals.[8]

Norman Rockwell

No American illustrator has enjoyed greater popularity than Norman Rockwell (1894–1978). A superb technician and stylist, Rockwell was also endowed with a storyteller's imagination. Most of his thousands of pictures were essentially narratives; they revealed a bit of story that viewers found easy to follow. His greatest successes could be viewed on the covers of the *Saturday Evening Post*, the primary carrier of his work. In all, Norman Rockwell executed 322 cover illustrations for this immensely popular magazine, a span that began in 1916, when he was only 22, and continued until 1963. Because of the magazine's large circulation, each cover was seen, on average, by four million people, giving him the largest audience ever enjoyed by an artist before or since.[9]

In reality, Norman Rockwell was a classical painter, working in the established European tradition of bourgeois storytelling. More so than N. C. Wyeth, Rockwell focused on the passing American scene. He painted small towns and their citizens, but Rockwell could hardly be considered a Regionalist. He focused on the ordinary and the familiar, and cast them in a warm, often humorous, glow. The viewer could identify with a Rockwell narrative and make sense of the story. Because of this approach, and his technical skills, he set the standards for American illustration from the 1920s through the 1950s.

The Depression never occurred in a Rockwell painting. He wisely sensed that most Americans preferred not to be reminded of the economic collapse, particularly on the covers of their favorite magazines or in the illustrations that accompanied stories or advertisements. Instead, Rockwell reassured the country that the nation's values were sound, that social and political rituals had meaning, and that the family and the individual would ultimately triumph. All the same, he suggested that a little stubbornness, a little laughter, and maybe even a bit of mischief would lighten everyone's spirits.

With the onset of the 1930s, Rockwell's *Post* covers shifted slightly from his earlier ones. He executed 67 covers during the decade, with a marked decline in the presence of children. Adults became his focus, perhaps in recognition that this was a more serious—more adult—period in the nation's history. He also allowed some contemporary celebrities into his creations: the rugged actor Gary Cooper graced a 1930 cover, allowing himself to be daintily made up by a studio employee; Jean Harlow, the reigning "Blonde Bombshell," wowed a group of gaga-eyed reporters in 1936; and two coeds swooned over a photograph of leading man Robert Taylor in 1938. In addition, Rockwell displayed a growing appreciation for fashion trends. The slim but curvaceous look favored by stylish women was duly depicted. His men, however, remained attired in shapeless suits that could come from almost any decade, a wry comment on the lack of distinctive style for most American men of the period.

Although Norman Rockwell will always be associated with the *Saturday Evening Post*, he, like N. C. Wyeth, contributed illustrations to many other magazines at the same time. His work appeared in *Boys' Life, Judge, Ladies' Home Journal, Leslie's, Liberty, Literary Digest, Popular Science*, and *Woman's Home Companion*. He devoted much energy to the Boy Scouts, illustrating their guidebooks and doing an annual calendar for them from 1925 to 1975.

By the 1930s, Rockwell's fame was assured, and advertising representatives flocked to his Vermont studio in an attempt to get him to draw or paint something extolling their products. As a result, a steady stream of illustrations poured forth lauding Fisk Tires, Overland automobiles, Edison Mazda (now General Electric), Sun-Maid Raisins, Jell-O, Coca-Cola, Orange Crush, the Red Cross—over 150 companies and organizations in all. His carefully lettered signature always appears in his work, even the most mundane advertisements. In this way, the name Rockwell soon became familiar to millions. It was a simple tactic, but it helped sustain his growing fame and popularity. Plus, his signature suggested an unspoken endorsement of the product.

Arts

Haddon Sundblom

Another illustrator needs to be mentioned, simply because one of his creations has been so completely accepted by the public. Haddon Sundblom (1899–1976) is responsible for the Santa Claus who now dominates Yuletide imagery. The artist did advertising for the Coca-Cola Company, including creating a yearly Christmas painting featuring Santa holding a Coke. Beginning in 1931, and continuing for the next thirty years, Sundblom painted Jolly Old Saint Nick enjoying "The Pause That Refreshes." Soon, every illustrator in the country was imitating the Sundblom model—rotund, ruddy complexion, big smile, twinkling eyes, and all the rest. Prior

to 1931, Santa Claus tended to be more of an elfin figure, at times almost a gnome. In addition, earlier Santas were not always so merry; they could be rather frightening or mischievous. N. C. Wyeth did several interpretations of Santa Claus, but the man behind the beard seemed almost sinister in comparison to Sundblum's merry figure. Norman Rockwell wisely adopted this generic version of Santa in the 1930s, divorcing himself from some of his own Saint Nicks of earlier years.[10]

Young boy surprising Santa Claus as he takes bottle of Coca-Cola from the refrigerator. Prints & Photographs Division, Library of Congress.

ENDNOTES FOR THE 1930s

OVERVIEW OF THE 1930s

1. Two books that cover the New York World's Fair and its time capsule in considerable detail are David Gelernter, *1939: The Lost World of the Fair* (New York: Avon Books, 1995), 269–70, 353; and Alice G. Marquis, *Hopes and Ashes: The Birth of Modern Times, 1929–1939* (New York: The Free Press, 1986).
2. Elliott West, *Growing Up in Twentieth-Century America: A History and Reference Guide* (Westport, CT: Greenwood Press, 1996), 81–169.
3. Kennth T. Jackson, *The Crabgrass Frontier* (New York: Oxford University Press, 1985), 193.
4. T. H. Watkins, *The Hungry Years: America in an Age of Crisis, 1929–1939* (New York: Henry Holt, 1999), 60.
5. Maurice Horn, ed., *100 Years of American Newspaper Comics* (New York: Gramercy Books, 1996), 197–98.
6. Winona Morgan, *The Family Meets the Depression* (Minneapolis: University of Minnesota Press, 1939), 16–19.
7. Robert S. McElvaine, *The Great Depression: America, 1929–1941* (New York: Times Books, 1961), 189–90.
8. Agnes Rogers, *I Remember Distinctly: A Family Album of the American People in the Years of Peace, 1918 to Pearl Harbor* (New York: Harper & Brothers, 1947), 154.

ADVERTISING OF THE 1930s

1. West, *Growing Up in Twentieth-Century America,* 81–169.
2. Errol Lincoln Uys, *Riding the Rails: Teenagers on the Move During the Depression* (New York: TV Books, 1999), 13–22.
3. Thomas Hine, *The Rise and Fall of the American Teenager* (New York: Avon Books [Bard], 1999), 206–7.
4. Grace Palladino, *Teenagers: An American History* (New York: Basic Books, 1996), 5, 17–25.
5. Steven M. Gelber, "A Job You Can't Lose: Work and Hobbies in the Great Depression," *Journal of Social History* 24 (1991): 747–49.

6. For more on attitudes about smoking see Michael Schudson, *Advertising, the Uneasy Persuasion: Its Dubious Impact on American Society* (New York: Basic Books, 1984); and Jane Webb Smith, *Smoke Signals: Cigarettes, Advertising, and the American Way of Life* (Chapel Hill: University of North Carolina Press, 1990).

ARCHITECTURE OF THE 1930s

1. Thomas Walton, "The Sky Was No Limit," *Portfolio* 1 (April–May 1979): 82–89.

2. David P. Handlin, *American Architecture* (New York: Thames and Hudson, 1985), 197ff.

3. William Peirce Randel, *The Evolution of American Taste* (New York: Crown Publishers, 1978), 183–85.

4. Clifford Edward Clark Jr., *The American Home: 1800–1960* (Chapel Hill: University of North Carolina Press, 1986), 193–95.

5. Much more detailed information about the housing crisis can be found in chapters 6 and 7 of David M. Kennedy, *Freedom from Fear: The American People in Depression and War, 1929–1945* (New York: Oxford University Press, 1999), 160–217.

6. John A. Jakle and Keith A Sculle, *The Gas Station in America* (Baltimore: Johns Hopkins University Press, 1994), 144–50.

7. Carl ton Jackson, *Hounds of the Road: A History of the Greyhound Bus Company* (Bowling Green, OH: Popular Press, 1984), 46–47.

8. Michael Horsham, *'20s and '30s Style* (Secaucus, NJ: Chartwell Books, 1989), 24–31.

BOOKS, NEWSPAPERS, MAGAZINES, AND COMICS OF THE 1930s

1. A good introduction to the mystery genre is Julian Symons, *Bloody Murder: From the Detective Story to the Crime Novel* (New York: Penguin Books, 1972).

2. Margaret Mitchell, *Gone with the Wind* (Garden City, NY: Garden City Books, 1936), 689.

3. Two works that give a good overview of the FWP are Jerre Mangione, *The Dream and the Deal: The Federal Writers' Project, 1935–1943* (Boston: Little, Brown, 1972); and Monty Noam Penkower, *The Federal Writers' Project: A Study in Government Patronage and the Arts* (Urbana: University of Illinois Press, 1977).

4. Jan Cohn, *Creating America: George Horace Lorimer and the* Saturday Evening Post (Pittsburgh, PA: University of Pittsburgh Press, 1989), 218–67.

5. John Heidenry, *Theirs Was the Kingdom: Lila and DeWitt Wallace and the Story of the* Reader's Digest (New York: W.W. Norton, 1993), 59–149.

6. Loudon Wainwright, *The Great American Magazine: An Inside History of* Life (New York: Alfred A. Knopf, 1986), 69–120.

7. John Tebbel and Mary Ellen Zuckerman, *The Magazine in America: 1741–1990* (New York: Oxford University Press, 1991), 193–94.

8. Frank Gruber provides an inside look at this side of magazine publishing in *The Pulp Jungle* (Los Angeles: Sherbourne Press, 1967).

9. A standard history of American newspapers is Frank Luther Mott, *American Journalism: A History, 1690–1960* (New York: Macmillan, 1962).

10. Details about all of the columnists cited can be found in John Dunning, *On the Air: The Encyclopedia of Old-Time Radio* (New York: Oxford University Press, 1998).

11. Edwin Emery, *The Press and America: An Interpretative History of Journalism* (Englewood Cliffs, NJ: Prentice-Hall, 1962), 621–50.

ENTERTAINMENT OF THE 1930s

1. Both Jerome Delamater, *Dance in the Hollywood Musical* (Ann Arbor, MI: UMI Research Press, 1981), and John Springer, *All Talking! All Singing! All Dancing!* (Secaucus, NJ: Citadel Press, 1966), cover the musical well.

2. Arlene Croce, *The Fred Astaire and Ginger Rogers Book* (New York: Outer-bridge & Lazard, 1972).

3. For more on the films of the Marx Brothers, see Richard J. Anobile, ed., *Why a Duck?* (New York: Darien House, 1971).

4. The phenomenon of youthful performers is treated in Norman J. Zierold, *The Child Stars* (New York: Coward-McCann, 1965).

5. A good overview of 1930s movies is given in John Baxter, *Hollywood in the Thirties* (New York: A.S. Barnes, 1968).

6. Arthur P. Molella and Elsa M. Bruton, *FDR, The Intimate Presidency: Franklin Delano Roosevelt, Communication, and the Mass Media in the 1930s* (Washington, DC: National Museum of American History, 1982), 46–53.

7. T. H. Watkins, *The Hungry Years: America in an Age of Crisis, 1929–1939* (New York: Henry Holt and Company, 1999), 254.

8. John Dunning, *Tune in Yesterday: The Ultimate Encyclopedia of Old-Time Radio, 1925–1976* (Englewood Cliffs, NJ: Prentice-Hall, 1976), 448–55.

9. A good introduction to television's early years is Erik Barnouw, *Tube of Plenty: The Evolution of American Television* (New York: Oxford University Press, 1982), 1–96.

10. For major plays of the period, see Gerald Bordman, *American Theatre: A Chronicle of Comedy & Drama, 1930–1969* (New York: Oxford University Press, 1996).

11. See Jane Dehart Mathews, *The Federal Theatre, 1935–1939: Plays, Relief, and Politics* (Princeton, NJ: Princeton University Press, 1967), and R. C. Reynolds, *Stage Left: The Development of the American Social Drama in the Thirties* (Troy, NY: Whitston, 1986), for more on the FTP and related subjects.

12. Marshall Stearns and Jean Stearns discuss the popularization of dance in *Jazz Dance: The Story of American Vernacular Dance* (New York: Schirmer Books, 1968).

FASHION OF THE 1930s

1. Ellie Laubner, *Collectible Fashions of the Turbulent Thirties* (Atglen, PA: Schiffer Publishing, 2000), 7.
2. Stella Blum, ed., *Everyday Fashions of the Thirties: As Pictured in Sears Catalogs* (New York: Dover Publications, 1986), 69.
3. For an overview of how the movie magazines influenced fashion, see Martin Levin, ed., *Hollywood and the Great Fan Magazines* (New York: Arbor House, 1970).
4. Kate Mulvey and Melissa Richards, *Decades of Beauty: The Changing Image of Women, 1890s–1990s* (New York: Checkmark Books, 1998), 82–97.
5. Laubner, *Collectible Fashions of the Turbulent Thirties*, 39–82.
6. Charles Panati, *Extraordinary Origins of Everyday Things* (New York: Harper & Row, 1987), 220.
7. Blum, *Everyday Fashions of the Thirties*, 66, 110, 129.
8. Panati, *Extraordinary Origins of Everyday Things*, 298.

FOOD OF THE 1930s

1. Dixon Wecter, *The Age of the Great Depression, 1929–1941* (Chicago: Quadrangle Books, 1948), 282–83.
2. An excellent introduction to the Americanization of the nation's eating habits is Harvey Levenstein's two-volume study, *Revolution at the Table: The Transformation of the American Diet* (New York: Oxford University Press, 1988) and *Paradox of Plenty: A Social History of Eating in Modern America* (New York: Oxford University Press, 1993).
3. Richard J. Hooker, *Food and Drink in America: A History* (Indianapolis, IN: Bobbs-Merrill, 1981), 306.
4. Chester H. Liebs, *Main Street to Miracle Mile: American Roadside Architecture* (Baltimore: Johns Hopkins University Press, 1985), 124–25.
5. Sherrie A. Innes, *Dinner Roles: American Women and Culinary Culture* (Iowa City: University of Iowa Press, 2001), 110–15.
6. Various candy bars are discussed in Ray Broekel, *The Great American Candy Bar Book* (Boston: Houghton Mifflin, 1982).
7. David Powers Cleary, *Great American Brands* (New York: Fairchild Publications, 1981), 112–19.
8. Ruth Schwartz Cowan, *More Work for Mother* (New York: Basic Books, 1983), 133–39.
9. Many of the pamphlets distributed to homemakers are found throughout Bunny Crumpacker, *The Old-Time Brand-Name Cookbook* (New York: Smithmark, 1998).
10. Charles Panati, *Extraordinary Origins of Everyday Things* (New York: Harper & Row, 1987), 111–13.

11. A valuable study of American restaurants is Richard Pillsbury, *From Boarding House to Bistro: The American Restaurant Then and Now* (Boston: Unwin Hyman, 1990).
12. American drinking habits and cultural responses to them are covered in Andrew Barr, *Drink: A Social History of America* (New York: Carroll & Graf, 1999).
13. For more on the Pepsi-Cola and Coca-Cola competition, see Bob Stoddard, *Pepsi-Cola: 100 Years* (Los Angeles: General Publishing Group, 1997), and Pat Watters, *Coca-Cola: An Illustrated History* (Garden City, NY: Doubleday, 1978).
14. Stephen N. Tchudi, in *Soda Poppery: The History of Soft Drinks in America* (New York: Scribner's, 1986), describes a number of popular American soft drinks.

MUSIC OF THE 1930s

1. Russell Sanjek, *Pennies from Heaven: The American Popular Music Business in the Twentieth Century* (New York: Da Capo Press, 1988), 184ff.
2. Joseph Csida and June Bundy Csida, *American Entertainment: A Unique History of Popular Show Business* (New York: Watson-Guptill, 1978), 230–31.
3. Geoffrey C. Ward and Ken Burns, *Jazz: A History of America's Music* (New York: Alfred A. Knopf, 2000), 246.
4. David Ewen, *All the Years of American Popular Music* (Englewood Cliffs, NJ: Prentice-Hall, 1977), 413, 422.
5. Ian Whitcomb, *After the Ball: Pop Music from Rag to Rock* (Baltimore: Penguin Books, 1972), 149.
6. A good survey of the songwriter's art is Alec Wilder, *American Popular Song: The Great Innovators, 1900–1950* (New York: Oxford University Press, 1972).
7. Cabell Phillips, *The* New York Times *Chronicle of American Life: From the Crash to the Blitz: 1929–1939* (New York: Macmillan, 1969), 411–12.
8. Lewis A. Erenberg, *Swingin' the Dream: Big Band Jazz and the Rebirth of American Culture* (Chicago: University of Chicago Press, 1998), 41–43.

SPORTS AND LEISURE OF THE 1930s

1. Edward White, *Creating the National Pastime: Baseball Transforms Itself, 1903–1955* (Princeton, NJ: Princeton University Press, 1996), 118–23, 164–89.
2. Benjamin G. Rader, *American Sports: From the Age of Folk Games to the Age of Spectators* (Englewood Cliffs, NJ: Prentice-Hall, 1983), 196–215.
3. Paul Dickson, *The Worth Book of Softball: A Celebration of America's True National Pastime* (New York: Facts on File, 1994), 60–82.
4. Rick Shenkman, "Adolf Hitler, Jesse Owens and the Olympics Myth of 1936." George Mason University's HNN (History News Network), http://hnn.us/articles/571.html.
5. For a broad overview of many different American fads, see Andrew Marum and Frank Parise, *Follies and*

Foibles: A View of 20th Century Fads (New York: Facts on File, 1984); Charles Panati, Panati's Parade of Fads, Follies, and Manias (New York: HarperCollins, 1991); and Paul Sann, Fads, Follies and Delusions of the American People (New York: Crown Publishers, 1967).

6. Foster Rhea Dulles, A History of Recreation: America Learns to Play (Englewood Cliffs, NJ: Prentice-Hall, 1965), 378.

7. Marvin Kaye, A Toy Is Born (New York: Stein and Day, 1973), 51–59.

8. Frank W. Hoffmann and William G. Bailey, Sports and Recreation Fads (New York: Haworth Press, 1991), 289–91.

9. Frank W. Hoffmann and William G. Bailey, Sports and Recreation Fads (New York: Haworth Press, 1991), 237–39.

10. John O'Dell, The Great American Depression Book of Fun (New York: Harper & Row, 1981), 2, 36–105.

11. Steven M. Gelber, "A Job You Can't Lose: Work and Hobbies in the Great Depression," Journal of Social History 24 (1991): 741–42, 754.

12. Arthur P. Molella and Elsa M. Bruton, FDR, the Intimate Presidency: Franklin Delano Roosevelt, Communication, and the Mass Media in the 1930s (Washington, DC: National Museum of American History, 1982), 62.

TRAVEL OF THE 1930s

1. For statistics on automobiles during the 1930s, see Automobile Manufacturers Association, Automobiles of America (Detroit, MI: Wayne State University Press, 1968); for information about car ownership, see Robert Lynd and Helen Lynd, Middletown in Transition: A Study in Cultural Conflicts (New York: Harcourt Brace, 1937).

2. Stephen W. Sears, The American Heritage History of the Automobile in America (New York: Simon and Schuster, 1977), 185–229.

3. Two good surveys of highway lodging are John A. Jakle, Keith A. Sculle, and Jefferson S. Rogers, The Motel in America (Baltimore: Johns Hopkins University Press, 1996), and John Margolies, Home Away from Home: Motels in America (Boston: Little, Brown, 1995).

4. Warren James Belasco, Americans on the Road: From Autocamp to Motel, 1910–1945 (Cambridge, MA: MIT Press, 1979), 143–44.

5. Two studies that provide detail on this aspect of travel are Donald Olen Cow Gill, Mobile Homes: A Study of Trailer Life (Washington, DC: American Council on Public Affairs, 1941); and David A. Thornburg, Galloping Bungalows: The Rise and Demise of the American House Trailer (Hamden, CT: Archon Books, 1991).

6. John Anderson Miller, Fares, Please! A Popular History of Trolleys, Horse-Cars, Street-Cars, Buses, Elevateds,

and Subways (New York: Dover Publications, 1960), 109–17.

7. Carlton Jackson, Hounds of the Road: A History of the Greyhound Bus Company (Bowling Green, OH: Popular Press, 1984), offers a detailed history of the company.

8. Alfred Runte, Trains of Discovery: Western Railroads and the National Parks (Niwot, CO: Roberts Rinehart, 1990), 57.

9. John H. White Jr., The American Railroad Passenger Car (Baltimore: Johns Hopkins University Press, 1978), 275–85.

10. Carlton Jackson, Hounds of the Road: A History of the Greyhound Bus Company (Bowling Green, OH: Popular Press, 1984), offers a detailed history of the company.

11. An introduction to this kind of air travel is Lennart Ege, Balloons and Airships (New York: Macmillan, 1974).

12. John Toland, The Great Dirigibles: Their Triumphs and Disasters (New York: Dover Publications, 1972), 309–39.

13. Introductions to the many daredevils of the era are given in American Heritage, eds., The American Heritage History of Flight (New York: Simon and Schuster, 1962).

14. Maurice Horn, ed., The World Encyclopedia of Comics (New York: Chelsea House, 1976), 624–25.

15. For more on the airplanes of the 1930s see The American Heritage History of Flight.

16. Melvin Maddocks chronicles this area of maritime history in The Great Liners (Alexandria, VA: Time-Life Books, 1978).

VISUAL ARTS OF THE 1930s

1. Benton's work can be found in Matthew Baigell, Thomas Hart Benton (New York: Harry N. Abrams, 1975); for Wood, see James Dennis, Grant Wood: A Study in American Art and Culture (Columbia: University of Missouri Press, 1986).

2. Hopper's work can be found in Lloyd Goodrich, Edward Hopper (New York: Harry N. Abrams, 1971); for Sheeler, see Martin Friedman, Charles Sheeler (New York: Watson-Guptill, 1975).

3. Marsh's work can be found in Lloyd Goodrich, Reginald Marsh (New York: Harry N. Abrams, 1972).

4. Richard D. McKinzie, The New Deal for Artists (Princeton, NJ: Princeton University Press, 1973), 8–12.

5. The popularity of murals is discussed in Karal Ann Marling, Wall-to-Wall America: A Cultural History of Post Office Murals in the Great Depression (Minneapolis: University of Minnesota Press, 1982).

6. William Stott, Documentary Expression and Thirties America (New York: Oxford University Press, 1973), 216–24, 261–314.

7. Ernie Pyle, "The Sculptor of Mount Rushmore," in Ernie's America: The Best of Ernie Pyle's 1930s Travel

Dispatches, ed. David Nichols (New York: Random House, 1989), 100–102.

8. Wyeth's work can be found in Douglas Allen and Douglas Allen Jr., *N.C. Wyeth: The Collected Paintings, Illustrations and Murals* (New York: Crown Publishers, 1972).

9. Rockwell's work can be found in Thomas S. Buechner, *Norman Rockwell: Artist and Illustrator* (New York: Harry N. Abrams, 1970); and Maureen Hart Hennessey and Anne Knutson, *Norman Rockwell: Pictures for the American People* (New York: Harry N. Abrams, 1999).

10. Arpi Ermoyan, *Famous American Illustrators* (New York: Society of Illustrators, 1997), 142–43.

1940s

Timeline

of Popular Culture Events, 1940s

1940

October 1: The Pennsylvania Turnpike officially opens.

December 8: The Chicago Bears beat the Washington Redskins 73–0 in the NFL championship game, the first professional football game broadcast nationally on radio.

December 21: Novelist F. Scott Fitzgerald dies of a heart attack.

Baldwin Hills Village construction begins in Los Angeles, California (finished in 1941).

The Lanham Act, which dedicates $150 million to the creation of housing for war workers, is passed into law.

Rockefeller Center opens in New York City.

The first Dairy Queen opens in Joliet, Illinois.

The first McDonald's drive-in restaurant opens in San Bernardino, California.

William Faulkner's *The Hamlet,* Ernest Hemingway's *For Whom the Bell Tolls,* Richard Wright's *Native Son,* and Carson McCullers' *The Heart is a Lonely Hunter* are published.

John Ford's movie adaptation of *The Grapes of Wrath* is released.

Jukeboxes appear everywhere, including stores, bars, and gas stations. A nickel buys 1 song, or 16 for 50 cents.

Eighty million people per week attend the movies.

Bugs Bunny debuts in the Warner Brothers cartoon *O'Hare.*

The Road to Singapore, starring Bob Hope, Bing Crosby, and Dorothy Lamour, is the top box office hit of the year, grossing $1.6 million.

1941

December 7: Japan attacks Pearl Harbor, Hawaii.

M&M's, Cheerios, aerosol cans, and La Choy Canned Chinese Food are introduced.

Work begins on the Pentagon in Arlington, Virginia (finished in 1943).

From May 15 to July 17, the New York Yankees' Joe DiMaggio hits safely in a record 56 straight games.

The Boston Red Sox's Ted Williams hits .406, becoming the last man of the modern era to bat over .400 for an entire season.

Quonset huts are invented at the Quonset Point Naval Station on Rhode Island.

Eudora Welty's *A Curtain of Green,* Walker Evans and James Agee's *Let Us Now Praise Famous Men,* and John Crowe Ransom's *The New Criticism* are published.

Orson Welles's *Citizen Kane* is released.

Howard Hawks's *Sergeant York,* starring Gary Cooper, is the top box office hit of the year, grossing $4 million.

The phrases "Kilroy was here" and "Rosie the Riveter" first appear.

"Uncle Sam Wants You" posters appear everywhere.

Mount Rushmore is completed.

At a folk music festival in Seattle, the term "hootenanny" is coined.

President Roosevelt approves the Manhattan Project, a secret program aiming to harness nuclear power for military purposes.

President Roosevelt issues Executive Order 8802, which bans racial discrimination in hiring practices for any work resulting from government defense practices.

1942

January: The government institutes food rationing, which would evolve into the rationing of anything deemed "essential" to the war effort, such as meat, coffee, gasoline, and rubber.

February 19: President Roosevelt issues Executive Order 9066, which calls for the "evacuation" of all enemy aliens. The order is only applied to Japanese Americans on the West Coast, and 110,000 of them are put into 10 internment camps in seven western states.

February 22: The U.S. government orders production of all civilian autos halted.

March and April: On the West Coast, Japanese and Japanese Americans are rounded up and placed in internment camps.

The U.S. Government War Production Board enacts Regulation L-85, which regulates all aspects of clothing production and inhibits the use of natural fibers.

President Roosevelt creates the Office of War Information and the War Advertising Council.

William Faulkner's *Go Down Moses and Other Stories* is published.

Janette Lowrey's *The Poky Little Puppy,* which goes on to become one of the best-selling children's hardcover books of all time, is published.

Dannon Yogurt and Kellogg's Raisin Bran are introduced.

Michael Curtiz's *Casablanca* is released.

William Wyler's *Mrs. Miniver,* starring Greer Garson, is the top box office hit of the year, grossing $6 million.

Irving Berlin's *This Is the Army* debuts on Broadway.

Bing Crosby sings "White Christmas" in the film *Holiday Inn.*

Norman Rockwell's "Four Freedoms" paintings—*Freedom of Speech, Freedom of Worship, Freedom from Want,* and *Freedom from Fear*—are published in the *Saturday Evening Post* and used by the U.S. government to help sell war bonds.

1943

April 30, 1943: The term "pin-up girl" originates in *Yank,* an armed forces newspaper.

September 20: The War Department lifts its ban on the publication of pictures of dead American soldiers. *Life* magazine subsequently publishes a full-page photo of three dead American soldiers who were killed on Buna Beach in New Guinea.

The USDA establishes Recommended Daily Allowances for dietary guidelines.

Rodgers and Hammerstein's *Oklahoma!* and Bernstein, Comden, and Green's *On the Town* debut.

The Zoot Suit Riots take place in Los Angeles in June.

Carson McCullers's short story "The Ballad of the Sad Café" is published.

The Jefferson Memorial in Washington, D.C., is completed.

For Whom the Bell Tolls, starring Ingrid Bergman and Gary Cooper, is the top box office hit of the year, grossing $11 million.

1944

Leo McCarey's *Going My Way,* starring Bing Crosby, is the top box office hit of the year, grossing $6.5 million.

Work begins on the Equitable Life Assurance Building in Portland, Oregon, designed by Pietro Belluschi (finished in 1947).

The Federal-Aid Interstate and Defense Highway Act is passed, creating the National System of Interstate Highways.

Appalachian Spring, composed by Aaron Copland and choreographed and starring Martha Graham, debuts.

Frank Sinatra's concert appearances at the Paramount Theater in New York City cause bedlam.

Leonard Bernstein composes the *Jeremiah Symphony.*

Seventeen magazine debuts.

The Supreme Court upholds the legality of Japanese internment.

1945

January 20: President Roosevelt's executive order interning Japanese Americans is lifted.

April 12: President Roosevelt dies of a cerebral hemorrhage while vacationing in Warm Springs, Georgia. Vice President Harry S. Truman becomes president.

April 29: Adolf Hitler commits suicide in his bunker.

May 7: *Life* magazine publishes a six-page photo spread entitled "Atrocities," which features horrific, graphic images from German concentration camps.

May 8, V-E Day: The German Army surrenders unconditionally, and victory in Europe is secured.

June: The United Nations Charter is signed.

August 6: America drops an atom bomb on Hiroshima, Japan.

August 9: America drops a second atom bomb on Nagasaki, Japan.

September 2, V-J Day: Japan's surrender to the Allies is signed aboard the U.S.S. *Missouri* in Tokyo Bay. The ceremony is broadcast via radio nationwide.

November: The Slinky is first sold in Philadelphia for $1.00 each.

Rodgers and Hammerstein's *Carousel* and Tennessee Williams's *The Glass Menagerie* debut on Broadway.

Karl Shapiro's *V-Letter and Other Poems,* Weegee's *Naked City,* and Randall Jarrell's "The Death of the Ball Turret Gunner" are published.

Of the 54 million total casualties of World War II, 405,399 are American.

Thrill of a Romance, starring Esther Williams, is the top box office hit of the year, grossing $4.5 million.

1946

Berlin and Fields's *Annie Get Your Gun* debuts.

Tupperware is introduced.

William Wyler's *The Best Years of Our Lives* and Howard Hawks's *The Big Sleep* are released.

Carson McCullers's *The Member of the Wedding,* Robert Penn Warren's *All the King's Men,* William Carlos Williams's *Paterson: Book I,* Weegee's *Weegee's People,* Dr. Benjamin Spock's *Common Sense Book of Baby and Child Care,* and *The Portable Faulkner* (edited by Malcom Cowley) are published.

Minute Maid Frozen Orange Juice, Maxwell House Instant Coffee, Ragu Spaghetti Sauce, Tide, and French's Instant Mashed Potatoes are introduced.

The first homes are sold in Levittown, New York.

The first televised soap opera (*Faraway Hill,* DuMont Network) debuts.

The term "Iron Curtain" is first used in a speech by Winston Churchill.

The Atomic Energy Commission is established.

The National School Lunch Act is passed to help raise the dietary standards of children, especially those from economically disadvantaged families.

The U.S. government lifts restrictions on rationed items.

The New Yorker publishes John Hersey's "Hiroshima" in August. The article later becomes a book.

Leo McCarey's *The Bells of St. Mary's,* the sequel to *Going My Way,* starring Bing Crosby, is the top box office hit of the year, grossing $8 million.

1947

June 21: CBS unveils the 33 1/3 rpm record.

December 27: *The Howdy Doody Show* debuts on NBC.

Jackie Robinson debuts with the Brooklyn Dodgers, breaking baseball's color line.

The U.S. government lifts wartime price controls.

Research begins for Seattle's Northgate Regional Shopping Center (finished in 1951).

Work begins on the United Nations Secretariat in New York City (finished in 1950).

Reynolds Wrap Aluminum Foil, Elmer's Glue, Redi Whip, and Ajax are introduced.

B. F. Goodrich introduces tubeless tires.

The term "Cold War" is first used.

The wartime draft ends.

President Truman becomes the first president to address the nation on television.

Tennessee Williams's *A Streetcar Named Desire* debuts on Broadway.

The Central Intelligence Agency is created.

The seven-game Dodgers v. Yankees World Series is the first to be televised.

William Wyler's *The Best Years of Our Lives,* starring Fredric March and Myrna Loy and released in late 1946, is the top box office hit of the year, grossing $11.5 million.

1948

June 8: *Milton Berle's Texaco Star Theater* debuts.

The Supreme Court rules that religious training in public schools is unconstitutional.

Howard Hawks's *Red River* is released.

The first Baskin-Robbins ice cream store opens.

The Road to Rio, fifth in the "Road to…" series of films, starring Bob Hope, Bing Crosby, and Dorothy Lamour, is the top box office hit of the year, grossing $4.5 million.

Cheetos, Nestlé's Quik, and V8 Juice are introduced.

Faulkner's *Intruder in the Dust* is published.

Albert Kinsey's *Sexual Behavior in the Human Male* is published.

Norman Mailer's *The Naked and the Dead* is published.

The transistor is invented.

President Truman desegregates the army.

1949

August 29: American intelligence confirms the detonation of the first Soviet atomic explosion. The Cold War immediately heightens as America loses what President Truman calls its "hammer on those boys."

General Mills and Pillsbury begin selling instant cake mix.

KitchenAid introduces consumer electric dishwashers.

Eudora Welty's *The Golden Apples* and Gwendolyn Brooks's *Annie Allen* are published.

Arthur Miller's *Death of a Salesman* and Rodgers and Hammerstein's *South Pacific* debut.

Gene Autry records "Rudolph the Red-Nosed Reindeer."

Silly Putty, Legos, Scrabble, Candyland, and Clue all debut.

These Are My Children, the first daytime TV soap opera, debuts on NBC.

The Goldbergs, the first TV sitcom, debuts on CBS.

The North Atlantic Treaty, which establishes NATO, is signed in April.

Jolson Sings Again is the top box office hit of the year, grossing $5.5 million.

Overview

of the 1940s

Birth of the Baby Boom

NICKNAME OF THE DECADE

Life during wartime didn't become a reality for most Americans until December 7, 1941, when the Japanese unleashed a surprise attack on the American fleet stationed at Pearl Harbor, Hawaii. Once America itself was attacked, World War II was a necessary war in the eyes of an overwhelming number of Americans, both for humanitarian reasons and for the very survival of the country.[1] While there were pockets of resistance to America's involvement in the war, in its drive to win the war the nation was more unified than ever before. To discuss that era as a period in which the right and wrong courses of action were readily identifiable belies the complexity of America in the 1940s. Clearly, it was a time of hope and joy for some, but for others it was also a time characterized by fear, prejudice, and uncertainty.

POLITICS AND POPULAR CULTURE DURING WORLD WAR II

From Isolationism to World War II

On September 1, 1939, German leader Adolf Hitler's forces overran Poland. On September 3, Britain declared war on Germany, a declaration France soon echoed. World War II was on, and in America fears over involvement in yet another world war began to grow. Those who understood

that America would eventually become involved understood not only the moral imperative of American participation, but also the reality that isolationism no longer worked in a world in which countries were becoming increasingly interdependent. But the isolationists didn't want to see a repeat of World War I, which they saw as a situation in which thousands of Americans went off to die in a foreign battle that wasn't America's problem.

Several factors played a role in the popular and political currency of isolationism. In 1940, 55 percent of Americans—70 million people—lived in towns with fewer than 10,000 residents. While that population composition would change dramatically in the 1940s, in 1940 rural dwellers were much less likely than their urban cosmopolitan counterparts to see the need to participate in a war. The desire for military participation was also split along class and ethnic lines. Typically, people in the higher income brackets were more in favor of intervention, with favor for such action declining concurrently with where one fit in economically. It's not shocking that among the poorest Americans (i.e., those most likely to actually have to fight on the front lines) isolationism was a popular notion. Ethnically, there was a mix of feelings. Many of the millions of European Americans who had come to America in the preceding years had done so precisely to avoid the kind of conflicts that had plagued Europe for centuries. However, many European Americans still had allegiance to their ancestral nations and couldn't stand the thought of their former homelands, where millions of relatives still lived, being overrun by Nazis.[2]

DEPICTION OF THE ENEMY DURING WORLD WAR II: GERMANS

The fear and paranoia that gripped the United States during World War II fueled the development of a variety of anti-German propaganda, from short films and radio advertisements to posters and billboards. The image of Adolf Hitler was a popular theme, and Hitler came to symbolize the German enemy as a whole. In many posters and billboards all Germans, including women and children, were depicted with Hitler's face and/or infamous mustache. The strategy of the campaign was to convince the public that a German invasion was impending in an effort to stimulate interest in military service and civilian participation. Pamphlets, radio programs, and films described how German children were taught from a young age to accept the doctrines of the Nazi movement and to place a reduced value on human life, making them more efficient soldiers. Pro-military advertisements often used words like "vicious," "barbaric," and "savage" to describe the German war effort and the Nazi state of mind. The anti-German propaganda campaign was among the most successful in American history, and the view of Germany and the German people espoused in propaganda was mirrored in the ideas and attitudes of the general public.

President Roosevelt, an incredibly astute politician, knew early on that America would have to get involved in World War II. After the Polish invasion of 1939, Germany continued to invade countries across Europe, including the Soviet Union on June 22, 1941. In September 1940, Congress passed the Selective Training and Service Act and instituted the draft. In October, FDR

publicly promised the nation that "[y]our boys are not going to be sent into any foreign wars." When asked if that would hold true if America was attacked, Roosevelt tellingly noted that in such an occurrence the war would no longer be foreign.[3]

Britain was the one major European country that had not yet fallen to the Nazis, in part because of the geographical advantage of its being an island, but the nation had no more money with which to buy American goods. All throughout 1940 and 1941 Americans listened raptly to CBS radio reporter Edward R. Murrow's crackly, live broadcasts from London, which brought to life the dire situation of Londoners experiencing nightly air attacks from the Germans.[4] Murrow's broadcasts led to an enormous outpouring of sympathy for the plight of the British. The dire straights of England's financial situation ultimately led to House Resolution 1776—better known as the Lend-Lease Act—passed by Congress in 1941. The idea was that America would lend war goods such as airplanes and foodstuff to the British, who after the war would give back the equipment not destroyed and eventually repay America in kind for the products it consumed, although no schedule for repayment was laid out.[5] Although scholars debate whether the plan really worked all that well—German submarines routinely sank British (and a few American) freighters—it still signaled America's increasing commitment to helping the Allies defeat the Axis powers, initially comprised of Germany and Italy.

In the early dawn hours of December 7, 1941, Japan launched a surprise attack on the American fleet stationed at Pearl Harbor in Hawaii. America was decidedly unprepared for an attack; in addition to the many destroyed ships, 2,390 Americans lost their lives, the largest number from a single enemy attack on American soil since the Revolutionary War, and a number that would not be surpassed until the attack on the twin towers of the World Trade Center on September 11, 2001. On December 8, FDR spoke before a joint session of Congress, declaring December 7, 1941, "a day that will live in infamy." The same day, both houses of Congress declared war on Japan. On December 11, Germany and Italy declared war on the United States, which responded with its own declaration of war against Germany and Italy. The unthinkable exception Roosevelt had earlier cited as the one situation in which he would send Americans to war—an attack on American soil—had happened. The nation was galvanized and united in its desire to respond to the attack on Pearl Harbor; the isolationist movement was over. World War II was considered by most Americans to be a just cause, a war necessary for moral, political, and strategic reasons. After Pearl Harbor there was scarcely any domestic opposition—political, ethnic, or religious—to U.S. involvement.[6]

Although his popularity was slowly beginning to wane, in 1944 FDR was elected president for an unprecedented fourth time, beating New York Governor Thomas Dewey with 53.4 percent of the popular vote.

Roosevelt had seen the country through its darkest depths, from the Great Depression to the hard-fought struggles of World War II. The effort took its toll. On April 12, 1945, President Roosevelt died of a cerebral hemorrhage while vacationing in Warm Springs, Georgia. FDR was a towering figure in popular culture, maybe the most accomplished president in history and

TIME MAN OF THE YEAR

1940 Winston Churchill (British prime minister)

1941 Franklin Delano Roosevelt (32nd president of the United States)

1942 Joseph Stalin (Soviet dictator)

1943 General George C. Marshall (chief of staff of U.S. Army)

1944 General Dwight D. Eisenhower (commander of Allied forces)

1945 Harry S. Truman (33rd president of the United States)

1946 James F. Byrnes (secretary of state)

1947 George C. Marshall (secretary of state)

1948 Harry S. Truman (33rd president of the United States)

1949 Man of the Half-Century, Winston Churchill (British prime minister)

certainly the longest serving. With his 31 "Fireside Chats" over the years—popular radio broadcasts listened to by upwards of 70 percent of Americans—and his steady leadership through years of divisive crises, Roosevelt had become an American father figure, a seemingly irreplaceable part of the landscape of everyday American life. When radio announcer Arthur Godfrey described FDR's funeral procession to the grieving nation over the radio, his voice wavered and choked up repeatedly. His tears were shared by the nation.

From World War to Cold War

Vice President Harry S. Truman, who was not yet well-known nationally, stepped into an extraordinarily difficult situation in replacing FDR as president; though the tide of the war in Europe had irrevocably turned and Allied victory was imminent, the situation in Asia was still uncertain. Truman had to decide how to use the atomic bomb, how to keep the Allies in unison, and how to follow through on Roosevelt's now shaky domestic policy.

Of the many programs started by FDR, none would have more resounding consequences on everyday American life than the ultra top-secret

Franklin D. Roosevelt, during one of his "Fireside chats" in 1937. These broadcasts, prepared for the listening American public, ran from 1933 to 1944. Prints & Photographs Division, Library of Congress.

Manhattan Project, which was centered primarily in Los Alamos, New Mexico, a government-created "secret city." The primary goal of the $2 billion-plus project was to develop a nuclear bomb before Germany did. In July 1945, just a few months after Roosevelt's death, the first nuclear blast and opening salvo of what would become the Cold War, was detonated in Alamogordo, New Mexico. Like Roosevelt, Truman saw the bomb as both a military and a diplomatic weapon. The bomb allowed Truman to break off negotiations with Russia, although it was a joint declaration of the Big Three—Britain, Russia, and the United States—that warned Japan to surrender unconditionally or face utter devastation. Japan refused the ultimatum of the Big Three and vowed to continue fighting.[7]

Scientists from the University of Chicago urged the president to drop the bomb on an uninhabited part of Japan first, as a threat, but Truman sided with his Scientific Advisory Panel, which posited that if the bomb was to be used at all, it "should be used for maximum military effect."[8] Truman, ostensibly in the interest of saving American lives, decided to drop the bomb on a Japanese city. On August 6, 1945, the first bomb was dropped on Hiroshima, killing an estimated 80,000 people immediately. Three days later, on August 9, 1945, a second bomb was dropped on Nagasaki, killing 40,000 more people. Many more would die of wounds and sickness in the coming weeks, months, and years. A week after the Nagasaki bombing, British Prime Minister Winston Churchill said simply, "America stands at this moment at the summit of the world."[9] The Atomic Age had begun. Japan officially surrendered on September 2, 1945—Victory over Japan, known as V-J Day. The bomb had ended World War II, and President Truman never publicly expressed regret for his decision to drop nuclear bombs on Japan. The term "Cold War," coined by journalist Walter Lippmann in a 1947 critique of U.S. foreign policy toward Russia, refers to a war that is not "hot," or characterized by violent physical confrontations.[10]

The Cold War between America and Russia has its seeds in World War II, but it was a series of events that took place in the immediate postwar era that led to the ongoing nature of the Cold War,

which is generally thought to have lasted until 1991. In order to stop the Russians from spreading communism—the United States adopted the Marshall Plan, which Secretary of State George C. Marshall proposed in 1947. Marshall's plan was simple: Pledge billions in aid to rebuild war-torn Europe and Japan, and when America is done, it will have contained communism in Europe and earned eternally loyal and thankful democratic allies. At home the Marshall Plan helped spur the postwar economic boom that was the largest and most sustained the country had ever seen up to that time. Naturally, Russia concurrently embarked on its own plans to gain allies and spread communism around the world; and the Cold War was beginning to come into full swing.

Fear of communism infiltrating American society was pronounced in the late 1940s, and the Republican Party, out of power for nearly 20 years, took a tough stand against communists. In the midterm elections of 1946, the Republicans won back both houses of Congress and hopes were high that a Republican would defeat Truman

Hiroshima bomb explosion, 1945. Prints & Photographs Division, Library of Congress.

in 1948. Once again, the Republicans nominated New York Governor Thomas Dewey for the presidency. Republicans accused Truman of being a Roosevelt lackey who would extend New Deal policies. On the eve of the 1948 presidential election, it looked as though he would lose to Dewey. Newspapers around the country declared Dewey the winner and ran headlines saying as much. Truman won in a squeaker, resulting in one of the most famous photos from the annals of 1940s popular culture: Truman holding up the front page of the *Chicago Daily Tribune* with a headline that reads, "DEWEY DEFEATS TRUMAN." While Truman was never as popular as his predecessor, he was not without his homespun charm, and his straightforward approach to his job—as exemplified by his oft-quoted phrases "the buck stops here" and "if you can't stand the heat, get out of the kitchen"—did win him the admiration of many Americans.

Despite Dewey's loss, the country continued to move toward the conservative conformity that would characterize the nuclear family era of the Eisenhower-led 1950s. In 1947 the Central Intelligence Agency was created to gather foreign counterintelligence and protect American interests abroad. At home, Truman launched the Loyalty-Security Program, which screened prospective government employees to ensure they weren't communists or some other sort of threat to the American way of life. Concurrently, FBI boss J. Edgar Hoover testified before the House Un-American Activities Committee (HUAC), claiming that Truman's program wasn't going far enough to root out subversive elements in society. Hoover proposed that the FBI, in conjunction with HUAC, should undertake a program to expose disloyal Americans. Over the next several years, and often with the help of confidential information supplied by Hoover's FBI, HUAC would drag suspected communists to testify before it. Often people who had done nothing more than be a member of the Communist Party were jailed or subpoenaed. HUAC would force people to testify with the promise of no repercussions, provided they were willing to name the names of other communists they knew. The most famous HUAC hearings had to do with the so-called Hollywood Ten. In 1947, ten Hollywood figures, who

either belonged or had previously belonged to the Communist Party of the United States of America (CPUSA), were directed to testify before HUAC. Not one of the Ten named names, and they were all found guilty of contempt of Congress for refusing to do so. They included the following, who were primarily screenwriters: Alvah Bessie, Herbert Biberman (director and writer), Lester Cole, Edward Dmytryk (director), Ring Lardner Jr., John Howard Lawson, Albert Maltz, Samuel Ornitz, Adrian Scott (producer and writer), and Dalton Trumbo. All were sentenced to a year in jail, although Dmytryk later retestified in 1951 and implicated some others, and as result was removed from a blacklist that denied anyone on it employment in the entertainment industry.

RACE AND GENDER

Wartime propaganda portrayed an image of a totally united America in which all had an equal part in joining together to defeat the Axis powers, which wasn't exactly true, especially for women and members of ethnic minorities. As war broke out, German and Italian Americans were initially thought to be suspect, with noncitizen Italian Americans being designated by the president as "enemy aliens." But Italians and Germans were relatively old immigrant populations—as well as European—and they had generally already dispersed and assimilated into all walks of society. For the most part, their wartime experience was much smoother than that of African Americans, Latinos, and especially Japanese Americans. Still, the needs of war in some instances created new opportunities for traditionally marginalized populations in America. Not long after war was declared, employers turned to people they normally shunned, especially women and African Americans.

Latinos benefited during wartime as well. Many Latino agricultural workers went to the cities to find work. While they were often discriminated against, they still found jobs. For example, in 1941 not a single Mexican American worked in Los Angeles shipyards, whereas by 1944 approximately 17,000 were employed in these shipyards. In addition to the 350,000 Mexican Americans drafted into the military, Latinos also filled the gaps in agricultural work created by Anglos who joined the military or who took better manufacturing jobs. In 1942 the U.S. government cut a deal with Mexico, and during the war several hundred thousand *braceros* were allowed to come to the United States and work in the field.[11]

Native Americans, who in 1940 weren't even franchised with the right to vote in New Mexico and Arizona, still served the country admirably, with 25,000 serving in the armed forces. Navajo military men are credited as having made a particularly beneficial contribution by becoming military "code-talkers," speaking their native language over the radios during military actions. America's enemies never did break the Navajo code. But while blacks and other minorities made strides, Japanese Americans were rounded up by the thousands and put into internment camps for the duration

Corporal Henry Bahe Jr., left, and Pvt. First Class George H. Kirk, Navajo code talkers serving with a Marine Signal Unit, operate a portable radio set in a jungle clearing, close behind the front lines on the island of Bougainville in New Guinea (present-day Papua New Guinea), in this December, 1943, U.S. Marine Corps photo. AP Photo/USMC via National Archives.

of the war. While there was notable progress made against discrimination based on race and gender in the 1940s, at the start of the 1950s want ads that specified race and gender preferences were still common and raised few eyebrows.

African Americans

Cumulatively, over 27 million civilians moved someplace new during the war, a disproportionately high number of which were African American.[12] Whites tended to move from the Northeast and Midwest to the Southwest and the West Coast. Conversely, blacks moved from the South to the Northeast and the Midwest to pursue the seemingly endless number of war-related jobs in the urban cities. Furthermore, the nature of agriculture in America changed forever during the war. Fully 6 million people left farms during the war, but because of better technologies and farming approaches, agricultural output increased by 25 percent.[13] The age of small family farms was essentially over; in their place were the giant agribusinesses that continue to produce the bulk of food today.

Cities boomed, as did suburbs, which sprang up around cities so that workers could commute into the cities to work during the day, and then return to the more peaceful suburbs at night. But the newly migrated African Americans typically didn't live in the suburbs. They often lived in bad conditions in overly populated sections of big cities, such as in Chicago, where 300,000 blacks lived on the South Side, an area thought to have a human capacity of just over 200,000.[14] Their increasing presence in various cities caused racial tensions to soar, as whites, who in most instances were given every priority over blacks, nevertheless felt the pressure of increased competition for jobs and housing. More than 200 recorded race riots occurred in the 1940s.

High black unemployment contributed to the black migration to urban centers to look for jobs. In the cities, blacks who secured work often found themselves in menial, unskilled jobs, a situation that became increasingly hard to take when it was obvious just by looking around that better employment opportunities were expanding rapidly for white men meeting the need for workers in the build-up toward war.

In early 1941, A. Philip Randolph, president of the Brotherhood of Sleeping Car Porters, became angry at the lack of opportunities for African Americans in an economy that should have been booming for *everyone* who wanted to work, regardless of color. Randolph planned a massive march on Washington for the late spring. Roosevelt's administration feared that the planned march would upset the perceived feeling of national unity. Roosevelt struck a deal: Randolph cancelled the march when Roosevelt issued Executive Order 8802, which banned racial discrimination in hiring practices in any work resulting from government defense contracts. The Fair Employment Practices Commission (FEPC) was established to oversee contactors and their hiring practices. Despite many whites resisting change, by mid-1943 employers had been forced to hire blacks, women, and other minorities out of necessity: Contractors simply couldn't meet demand without hiring from groups traditionally discriminated against. Although management and white-collar jobs were primarily reserved for white men, by 1943 the number of both skilled and unskilled black workers had doubled and nearly two-thirds of the one million blacks who took war-related jobs were women.[15]

Militarily, at the start of the war blacks weren't allowed in the Air Force or the Marines at all, and they could only join the Navy as part of the "messman's branch," which meant they worked in the kitchen. Both the Army and the American Red Cross separated donated blood by race.

Many notable and powerful leaders in the administration, including Secretary of War Henry Stimson and General George C. Marshall, didn't believe the armed services could or should be integrated. Roosevelt said, "The integrity of our nation and our war aims is at stake in our attitude toward minority groups at home." Still, he was in no hurry to change the norm. The irony was obvious and painful for African Americans; where was the logic in fighting against a totalitarian, anti-Semitic Germany for a country that barely paid even lip service to pressing issues of inequality within its own borders?[16]

Black leaders saw and recognized the obstacles facing them, but they also saw the war as an opportunity. Most believed in the morality of the war and that it was important that African Americans contribute to the cause, but they felt that their willingness to fight for the cause could and should draw attention to their own plight as a people who were discriminated against. In non-wartime, it's hard to say if blacks could have persuaded leaders to let them serve, but the overwhelming needs of the military branches for more soldiers resulted in a policy change: Blacks were made eligible for service in the Navy and the Marine Corps and the Army began accepting more blacks than it previously had. The number of blacks in the military jumped from under 100,000 in 1941 to almost 470,000 in 1942, although blacks in all branches of the military remained segregated throughout the war. The American armed forces didn't fully integrate until Truman ordered it in 1948.

Despite the notable and visible progress that African Americans made over the course of the 1940s, there remained much room for improvement in race relations in the country, particularly in the area of equal civil rights for blacks and other ethnic minorities.

Japanese Americans

The most visible case of institutionalized racial discrimination in America in the 1940s was the government's unconscionable treatment of Japanese Americas. In 1941, Japanese Americans made up approximately one-tenth of one percent of the total population, with only 127,000 living in the United States.[17] Japanese had long been discriminated against on the West Coast for their willingness to take low-paying jobs, which whites felt drove down their own wages, when in actuality, the Japanese took low-paying jobs because that's all they could get. Regardless, racial tensions festered on the West Coast. When the Japanese attacked Pearl Harbor in December 1941, long-simmering racial tensions boiled over. Rumors swirled about Japanese saboteurs having infiltrated American society on the West Coast. Japanese were singled out by government policies, and on the streets other Asian groups (Chinese, Koreans, etc.) were often mistakenly targeted for being Japanese as well. Despite the fact that not one Japanese American was ever found to have been a saboteur, public and political pressures mounted, and in February 1942, Roosevelt issued Executive Order 9066, which called for the evacuation of all enemy aliens, although the order was only applied to Japanese Americans on the West Coast. Initially, relocation to other parts of the country was tried, but the Japanese were unwelcome everywhere. The newly created War Relocation Authority (WRA) then changed course and, with the full support of Congress and the executive branch of government, put 110,000 Japanese Americans into 10 camps, called "internment camps," in 7 western states. Of those interred, 80,000 were U.S.-born citizens. The Japanese were unjustifiably placed in horrible places located in barren, arid areas and fenced in entirely by barbed wire. They lived in one-room barracks that were shared by either families, regardless of size, or groups of unrelated singles. The barracks were furnished only with cots, blankets, and a single light bulb. Bathrooms and dining rooms were shared communal facilities. Over the years the WRA slowly released upwards of 35,000 people from the camps and relocated them elsewhere, but that still left a huge amount of people unjustly interred. Ansel Adams (1902–1984), one of America's most well-known photographers, documented the Manzanar War Relocation Center in Northern California in 1943. In 1965, he gave the pictures to the U.S. Library of Congress. He hoped to show how Japanese Americans "suffering under a great injustice, and loss of property, businesses and professions, had overcome the sense of defeat and despair by building for themselves a vital community in an arid (but magnificent) environment."[18]

In 1944, several legal challenges to internment camps made their way to the U.S. Supreme Court, which upheld their legality in all cases.[19]

In their enforced absence, the property of Japanese Americans was sold at public auction. Cumulatively, Japanese Americans would lose

Entrance to Manzanar Relocation Center. Photograph by Ansel Adams, 1943. Prints & Photographs Division, Library of Congress.

Students sitting in a classroom laboratory. Manzanar Relocation Center, California. Photograph by Ansel Adams. Prints & Photographs Division, Library of Congress.

in excess of $400 million through forced property sales. While some Japanese were allowed to leave the camps and relocate to other parts of the country, most of the internees weren't allowed to leave until January 20, 1945, when Roosevelt's executive order was lifted. Even in the face of such discrimination, a number of Japanese Americans served in the armed forces in World War II, during which they proved themselves valorous, courageous, and loyal.

Women

Much has been made of the role of women workers—Rosie the Riveters (see Advertising of the 1940s)—during World War II. While women were essential in the war effort, two-thirds of adult women remained full-time homemakers during the war. By 1944, when the number of female employees in war-related jobs peaked, the percentage of women in the workplace had increased 24 percent since the start of the war, and women comprised 36 percent of all civilian workers.[20] During the war years, for the first time in American history married women workers outnumbered single women workers. While white women were definitely favored, the need for workers was such that employment for women from virtually all ethnicities jumped during the war.[21] Women worked in factories and in construction, as miners, welders, and riveters, and for radio stations and newspapers. Hundreds of thousands of women served in women's divisions of all branches of the military. In 1942 the government created the Women's Army Corps (WACS), the U.S. Coast Guard Women's Reserve (SPARS, which derived from the Coast Guard motto "Semper Paratus—Always Ready") and the

Women Accepted for Volunteer Emergency Services (WAVES) programs. Women did everything but fight in combat (some women held other noncombat jobs on or near the front lines) and were allowed to hold regular ranks.[22]

Women, like other minorities, were typically denied management positions and often were required to do the most menial and tedious tasks. Women (and other minorities), as decreed by the National War Labor Board in 1942, were by law supposed to get equal pay for doing equal work to that of their white male counterparts. Records show they did not; in 1943, for example, men averaged $62.95 per week and 3.5 more hours a week than women, who averaged just $44.91 per week.[23] With more women working and men at war, kids at home had more unsupervised free time, resulting in an increase in the nation's juvenile delinquency rate during the war. In fact, juvenile delinquency was the most publicized crime problem of the 1940s. Some critics have credited the rise of delinquency with being a major factor in the importance placed on family and traditional gender roles in postwar America. Women made great gains in the workplace during the war, but the gains were only temporary; for the most part, women went back home after the war, with many of their jobs being taken by returning veterans. Women's place in the work force dropped back down to prewar levels, despite surveys taken between 1943 and 1945 showing that from 61 percent to 85 percent wanted to stay employed after the war.[24]

THE BABY BOOM AND HOME LIFE

In the early years of the war, men literally began to disappear from American streets, called to military duty in far-off lands. But many men left a parting gift; marriage rates jumped by 50 percent in the early 1940s and so too did the birth rate. The baby boom is often said to have begun in 1945, when soldiers returned home from the war to relative prosperity and began having families with their wives. While that did happen, birthrates increased well before 1945, as evidenced by the rise in birthrates in the early 1940s, the "goodbye babies" who were part of what's been called the "baby boomlet." From 1940 to 1945 the nation's

population grew by 6.5 million.[25] And for every spouse left behind at home, the U.S. government would send a monthly check of $50. This was a welcome amount, especially for a small number of women—called "Allotment Annies"—who took advantage of the system and married as many men as they could in the hopes of collecting $50 checks repeatedly or $10,000 if her husband were killed in action. Just as marriage and birthrates increased, so, too, did divorce rates, as some women, left alone at home by a man they barely knew, decided against waiting for their husbands' return.

After the war, men came home ready to assume their traditional roles as heads of families. They took advantage of the newly established G. I. Bill, which would pay for soldiers' college educations and also give them low interest rates on home mortgage loans. In 1940, 109,000 men and 77,000 women received bachelor's degrees; by 1950 the numbers had jumped to 328,000 men and 103,000 women.[26] While white males gained the most from the G. I. Bill, fully 50 percent of all people who served in the armed forces had received some sort of education benefit by the time the bill ended in 1956.[27] Men who had been at war wanted to start their lives, and they didn't wait. They came home and quickly got married. In 1946, the marriage rate was 16.4 per 1,000, 25 percent higher than it had been in 1942.[28] Also in 1946, a new record high of 3.4 million babies were born, 26 percent more than in 1945. The baby boomlet that had begun a few years earlier had blossomed into the baby boom. The idea of the man off at work while his wife stayed at home caring for two or three-plus kids became a much pursued norm; the year 1957 saw 4.3 million children born—still the largest annual number in American history—making it the peak year of the baby boom. By the tail end of the baby boom in 1964, 40 percent of all Americans had been born since 1946, and this group still makes up the largest single portion of the American population.[29]

Child-oriented industries sprang up around things such as educational toys, diapers, and baby food. Dr. Benjamin Spock's 1946 book, *Common Sense Book of Baby and Child Care,* the must-read child-rearing handbook for parents of the boomers, became one of the best-selling books in history.[30] The so-called nuclear family—a father, a mother, and children—became the idealized and preferred social unit of the Cold War era and beyond.

In the 1940s, teenagers frequently hung out at drugstore lunch counters where they could get sodas, sweets, and sandwiches. By the late 1940s, in conjunction with their increased access to automobiles, they also frequented drive-in restaurants and drive-in movie theaters, which boomed with the rise of the car culture in the aftermath of the war.

Still, while the prosperity many American families experienced in the late 1940s and early 1950s was real, as early as 1948 there were signs that the strict heterosexual relationship characterized by marital fidelity, though the preferred model for all Americans, was problematic to emulate.

In 1948, Indiana University Professor Albert Kinsey, an entomologist by training, released his landmark 804-page book, *Sexual Behavior in the Human Male,* often referred to as the "Kinsey Report." The Kinsey Report challenged the reality of what was thought to be normal sexual behavior. Based on his research, Kinsey found that 85 percent of white males had premarital intercourse and 55 percent had extramarital intercourse; 69 percent of white men had experience with a prostitute; 92 percent of all men masturbated; 37 percent of all men had reached orgasm at some point in their life with another man. Kinsey's report was inflammatory and controversial, although he viewed himself as a scientist who was simply reporting the facts and offered no moral judgments to accompany his findings. Kinsey's book, scientific in nature and definitely not easy

Soda fountain in Rushing's drugstore in San Augustine, Texas, on a Saturday afternoon, April 1943. Prints & Photographs Division, Library of Congress.

reading, was a success, selling 200,000 copies in its first two months of release alone. Most of his findings were relatively tame, but those weren't the things people focused on. Over time his findings were challenged as having resulted from too limited a cross section of respondents to be very accurate. In hindsight, however, it becomes clear that the exact accuracy of his findings isn't nearly as important as the fact that the proscribed ideal of a house in the suburbs with a spouse, car, lawn, kids, and a dog wasn't for everyone.

THE TRIUMPH OF THE ASCENDING MIDDLE CLASS

The war effort had unexpected long-term effects on the shape of the postwar American work force. Americans who had previously worked for themselves, for small businesses, or as farmers, abandoned those jobs for war industry-related work, which paid well and gave one the sense of contributing to the war effort. Simultaneously, government contracts went to the companies that could produce the most products in the least amount of time. Hence, the 10 biggest companies in the country ended up with more than 30 percent of the government war contracts. After the war there were a number of strikes as workers wanted to maintain the relatively good pay and conditions of the war era. Personal income tax had grown immensely during the war, as the government scrambled to pay for the process. In 1940, of the 15 million who filed tax returns, almost half didn't make enough to be taxed. In 1942, Congress passed the revenue tax law, making most salaries taxable. The next year paycheck withholding was introduced. Accordingly, in 1945, 50 million people filed, with over 42 million owing the government. Cumulatively, taxes paid for almost half the cost of the war, with loans and bond sales paying for the rest.[31] In the immediate aftermath of the war, all kinds of products remained hard to get while factories retooled for peacetime production and the black market continued to thrive. With literally millions of veterans returning home and needing work and housing, people were afraid

America was going to reenter a depression. Now that the war was over, how could everyone possibly find work? But people's fears were allayed by 1948. Personal wealth accumulated but not spent during the heady financial years of the early 1940s, combined with the government's decision to help rebuild a devastated Europe through the Marshall Plan (which cost about 5–10 percent of the federal budget during the plan's four years) and ease the domestic income tax, spurred a massive era of consumption, which in turn led to a strong economy, plentiful with jobs.[32] Americans wanted cars, houses, TVs, you name it, and they were willing to spend money to get it. For many Americans, disposable income was a simple fact of life, and as industries returned to producing things for personal consumption, the economy boomed and unemployment remained relatively low. This led to the rise of the American middle class as the predominant slice of the American populace.

By the end of the decade, America was the most dominant and prosperous nation on earth. The country was committed to spreading democracy elsewhere around the world. In addition, America led the world in production and consumption. In postwar Asia, 400 million people dealt with starvation; stateside, Americans wondered what to do with food surpluses, and obesity was beginning to be recognized as a growing health problem. The gross national product had risen from $97 billion in 1940—roughly the same as in 1929 when the stock market crash occurred—to $210 billion in 1945. The industries that in other countries were devastated by the war (aviation, chemical engineering, electronics, steel, etc.) were booming in the states. America had the world's largest standing army and the atom bomb.[33] Not surprisingly, America became a great imperial power, and it would only become more dominant in the intervening 40-plus years of the Cold War.

Despite postwar prosperity, 30 percent of all Americans remained poor by the standards of the time; 80 percent of all homes were heated by coal or wood; 33 percent of homes had no running water, and 40 percent lacked flush toilets.

Advertising

of the 1940s

In the 1940s, the typical advertising format for radio and the nascent TV industry was one of single sponsorship for single shows. When America entered the war in 1941, advertising changed in that rather than promoting corporate products virtually all advertising, in one way or another, publicized the U.S. war effort.

SELLING THE AMERICAN WAY

The Office of War Information

In June 1942, President Roosevelt created the Office of War Information (OWI), headed by former CBS news analyst Elmer Davis. The OWI's primary purpose was to put all the government information and press services under singular leadership. The OWI did play a role in advertising America's war effort, but to many the office's responsibilities seemed to be too vast and nebulously defined. By 1943 the OWI had lost congressional support and was hence disbanded, with most of its primary responsibilities taken over by the newly formed War Advertising Council.

The War Advertising Council

Just as it had done during World War I, the advertising industry offered its services to help the war effort. In World War II, however, there was disagreement on how it should do so. Some felt that the government should pay for its advertising, whereas others in advertising did not want to essentially work for the government. In 1942 the War Advertising Council was officially created to resolve these conflicts and to coordinate the advertising industry's war effort.

Perhaps the biggest initial difficulty was that the Treasury Department felt that advertising shouldn't continue, for, in its eyes, it wasn't an essential industry. Furthermore, there was a dearth of commercial products because just about everything was being funneled to the war. Because of these shortages, President Roosevelt suggested that since there wasn't the same need to advertise, perhaps advertising costs should no longer be a tax-deductible business expense. Companies balked, because for most buying advertising, regardless of its effectiveness, was better than the alternative: paying taxes.

Madison Avenue, with the help of the War Advertising Council, convinced the Treasury Department that it should be allowed to continue advertising in what were vaguely described as "reasonable" amounts. These new ads typically included references to a product's role in helping in the war effort, no matter how dubious that claim may have been. In exchange for allowing advertising dollars to continue as a tax deduction, the industry ended up contributing approximately a billion dollar's worth of free ad space and time to the war effort. By 1943 the War Advertising Council had adopted the slogan, "A War Message in Every Ad." The council was encouraging civilians to do all kinds of things: buying war bonds, getting fingerprinted, working hard to ensure maximum production, enlisting in the armed services, galvanizing women to join the work force, and organizing campaigns for military recruitment and the salvage of fat.[1]

The industry's willingness to help the government war effort was rewarded by their being allowed to continue advertising non-government-related companies, industries, and products. In contrast to World War I, in which the advertising

War Identification Bureau poster, an ad that helped the war effort, 1940 or 1941. Prints & Photographs Division, Library of Congress.

industry lost money, during World War II advertising expenditures went from $2.2 billion in 1941 to $2.9 billion in 1945 and to $5.7 billion by 1950. The Advertising Council still exists as the Ad Council, although it's not nearly as unifying a force in the industry as it was in the 1940s.

Rosie the Riveter

The term "Rosie the Riveter" was supposedly the nickname given to Rosina Bonavita, who worked at the Convair Corporation's airplane production facilities in San Diego, California. The phrase, which quickly entered the popular lexicon in 1941, referred to newly hired women who were doing hard work on the production lines that had previously been reserved exclusively for men. The Convair Corporation was an early leader in hiring women, but the trend rapidly became national as working men became an increasingly scarce resource. The traditional prewar mentality that a woman's place was in the home gave way to the reality that women could perform factory jobs just as well as men and that it was essential to the war effort that they join the workforce. Advertisers of all kinds— from the OWI and War Advertising Council to innumerable private companies—capitalized on the phrase "Rosie the Riveter," which became a universal term that applied to all women working for the war effort.

Of the many images used to encourage women to join the workforce during World War II, the image of women in factories predominated. Perhaps the most famous Rosie was J. Howard Miller's 1942 poster, which he based on Rose Monroe, who worked in the Willow Run Aircraft Plant in Ypsilanti, Michigan (Monroe herself would later be included in a promotional film for war bonds). The poster featured a woman shown from the side to the waist up. She was wearing blue overalls and a red bandanna and was flexing her right bicep. The caption read, "We Can Do It!" Miller's Rosie helped introduce the accessories of war work— items such as tools, uniforms, and lunch pails—to the image of the feminine ideal that would emerge during the war years. Another famous Rosie was Norman Rockwell's May 29, 1943, *Saturday Evening Post* cover. Rockwell's Rosie was positioned in a pose Michelangelo had used for his Sistine

The famous 1942 poster by J. Howard Miller, which exhorted women and all Americans to do their best for the country. Prints & Photographs Division, Library of Congress.

Chapel frescoes, but this Rosie was dressed in coveralls. She was eating a ham sandwich and had a rivet gun across her lap and a halo around her head. Rosie was even popularized in song by the Kay Kyser Band's hit recording, "Rosie the Riveter."[2]

Rosie the Riveter remains a lasting and powerful symbol of American women working on production lines to help make the supplies the Allies needed to win World War II. At the conclusion of the war, women were expected to return to the home—which some women did—but World War II was the start of women joining the workforce en masse.

INSTITUTIONAL ADVERTISING

Throughout the war, companies made films of varying lengths that celebrated America's war effort, particularly concentrating on the ways their products and workers contributed to making the overall effort better. For example, U.S. Steel's *To Each Other* (1943) told the tale of the company's immense wartime production output. Similarly, General Motors made *Close Harmony* (1942), which was set in a barbershop and featured a customer answering the barber's and other customers' questions about the conversion of American factories from peacetime producers to wartime providers. Labor unions also made films that celebrated the role of the worker in a company's output and featured titles such as *United Action Means Victory* (1940). During the war, the United Auto Workers-Congress of Industrial Organizations (UAW-CIO) film department was the largest of any in the country, with some 450 prints from a variety of different sources, including the U.S. Army and Navy and the OWI. Once the war ended and advertising became more segmented, executives of companies that had used institutional advertising realized that their wartime films kept product awareness high and made the transition back to peacetime selling easier.

CORPORATE SPONSORSHIP

Early television advertising followed the model of radio in that shows were sponsored by single corporate entities. However, the influence of TV in the 1940s paled in comparison to that of radio. The preferred format for corporations to sponsor was highbrow concert music such as classical music or opera. By the 1944–1945 season, 20 out of 22 concert programs had major corporations as their sponsors. But corporations also sponsored dramatic anthologies. Perhaps the most famous examples of companies identified with dramatic radio anthologies was DuPont's *Cavalcade of America* and U.S. Steel's *Theatre Guild on the Air*. DuPont's initial sponsorship of *Cavalcade* in the mid-1930s came at a time when few companies engaged in continuous institutional advertising and the value of radio for advertisers had yet to be fully realized.

Produced in conjunction with New York's Theatre Guild, *Theatre Guild on the Air* featured radio adaptations of plays that had nothing to do with U.S. Steel, its corporate sponsor. For the most part, the Theatre Guild retained artistic control over the choice of works, but the two intermissions were filled by corporate "messages," read by actual U.S. Steel corporate officers.

It was an unusual marriage of artists and corporate types, but for the most part it worked. In the early 1950s, both *Cavalcade of America* and *Theatre Guild on the Air* made the leap from radio to TV, which many other radio shows would eventually do as well. (See Entertainment of the 1940s.)

THE "COMMON MAN"

During World War II companies aligned themselves with everyday people, G. I. Joes, John Smiths ("the average family man"), assembly line workers, and other folksy types. U.S. Steel claimed that it was the ordinary citizen whose "labor and living have established what we know as the 'American Way.'" Standard Oil ads talked about "Private Bill Jones, and the rest of us." Republic Steel ran ads featuring a G. I. named "Leatherneck Joe...Mechanic," sitting on a log looking out at readers. The copy was supposedly his words, which encouraged Americans at home to "keep America American." Some companies, including DuPont, GM, and General Electric, made films that celebrated the contributions of the ultimate American everyman: farmers.[3] Furthermore, companies that had previously relied on predominantly white work forces had begun to appeal in their advertising to a workforce that was becoming increasingly diverse, although ostensibly still pluralistic in its patriotic belief in the war effort.

Advocacy Advertising

On occasion, a company advertises to deflect attention from complaints about a particular product. An influential early example of this kind of advertising occurred in the New Haven Railroad's 1942 advertisement entitled, "The Kid in Upper 4." The primary function of the New Haven Railroad was to bring commuters into New York. Its service was frequently lacking, but was even worse during the war, as it had to yield its lines to trains carrying war-essential freight and personnel. Nelson Metcalf Jr., wrote the soon to be infamous copy with the intent to "make *everybody* who read it *feel ashamed* to complain about train service."[4]

The ad featured a young man lying in an upper berth staring wistfully upwards. But this was no ordinary kid. He was going off to the war overseas tomorrow and thinking about all that he'd leave behind: "hamburgers and pop...a dog named Shucks...[and] the mother who knit the socks he'll wear soon." The gist for consumers was "don't complain because our service is lousy; it's only lousy because we need to first accommodate the Kid in Upper 4 and others like him." The success of this ad was phenomenal. It first ran in the *New York Herald Tribune* in November 1942, and ran continuously until the end of the war. The Kid in Upper 4 became an iconic figure. He was used to sell U.S. war bonds and to raise money for the Red Cross, and he appeared in an MGM short, a song, and a variety of national magazines, including *Time, Life,* and *Newsweek.* In the end he proved to be a lasting example of the effective results possible with advocacy advertising.[5]

De Beers

In 1939, the first incarnation of the modern De Beers diamond ads appeared. By the end of the 1940s, De Beers' campaign had become a landmark in American advertising. Its campaign slogans and the direction of its advertising have changed little since their inception, making the campaign one of the most successful in history. By the early 1940s, the De Beers Consolidated Mines Limited cartel was facing trouble. Prior to the Depression, people held on to diamonds as an investment, but when the financial crisis hit, people tried to sell them. Diamonds flooded the market.[6]

The question for diamond companies was simple: How can we make diamonds a product consumers keep? In 1938, De Beers approached the advertising firm of N. W. Ayer and Son, Inc., to devise a new campaign. Two things had to happen. Diamonds had to be thought of as a commodity to be bought but not sold, and the aftermarket for diamond sales had to be destroyed. De Beers controlled over 90 percent of the diamond market, so meetings were conducted in South Africa or London, as American law prohibited monopolies from having offices in the United States. Furthermore, De Beers itself couldn't be directly sold to end users. Instead, the campaign had to speak about diamonds in general, and purchases had to occur from sellers who sold items with De Beers diamonds for consumer resale.

Ayer came up with a brilliant campaign based on its research that the postwar generation didn't even associate diamonds with romantic love, and young men were confused about how much to spend. For its copy and illustrations, Ayer chose the works of artists such as Matisse and Picasso, accompanied with poetry pertaining to the symbolism of the diamond as a token of love. The kicker was the 1947 catchphrase—"A Diamond Is Forever"—which effectively dictated that a diamond was more than a rock: It was an heirloom that must be kept in the family. Also included was the famous rhetorical question, "Is two months' salary too much for a diamond engagement ring?"[7] De Beers had made essential in the American mind a product that had no real value, and it institutionalized the idea of a diamond as the proper stone for declaring one's eternal love for another. The ads proved amazingly successful, as evidenced by both catchphrases still being used today.

COCA-COLA

Coca-Cola was wildly successful before World War II, but the war years radically transformed it, changing it from a nationally dominant to an internationally dominant product. Strangely, the advertising that helped Coca-Cola was the U.S. military. Military leaders wanted soldiers to drink "soft" drinks instead of liquor or beer. To help accommodate this policy, as well as increase the presence of Coke abroad, Coke headman Robert Woodruff instituted a policy to make Coke available to all military personnel for only a nickel, no matter where they were stationed. Coke was quickly in high demand, and in 1943 Eisenhower urged the installation of 10 new bottling plants in different places so that soldiers would have Coke no matter where they were stationed. Bottling plants followed the military and by V-J Day there were 64 plants operating worldwide.[8] During the war Coke became associated in the eyes of much of the world with America itself. After the war, the taste for Coca-Cola grew so large that Coke became the most widely distributed mass-produced product in America.

FUTURISM ON MAIN STREET

Another advertising trend during the 1940s was the move during the war toward futurism— the celebration of life-changing technologies that would make lives easier in the future. Since people were rationing many items, they dreamed of how things might be after the war. Companies promised that their wartime research would have big payoffs in the lives of postwar consumers. Some industries, such as the plastics industry and the automobile industry, fought against futuristic advertising because they knew full well that they'd have a big job ahead of them just returning to peacetime production, let alone revolutionizing their product lines.

Futurism in advertising was common in the 1940s. The legacy of the 1939–1940 New York World's Fair depiction of the future of city planning was seen in many advertisements. The new products could be radically different, so long as they fit in comfortably within the American image of small-town Main Street, U.S.A. Companies incorporated images of Main Street in their

---

ADVERTISING SLOGANS OF THE 1940s

"Better things for better living [through chemistry]," DuPont, 1939

"A diamond is forever," De Beers, 1948*

"I'm Chiquita Banana, and I've come to say..." Chiquita, 1944

"Pepsi-Cola hits the spot," Pepsi-Cola, 1940s*

"There's a Ford in your future," Ford Motor Company, 1943

"Remember, only you can prevent forest fires," USDA Forest Service, 1947; Smokey [the] Bear, 1945*

"You don't have to be Jewish to love Levy's real Jewish Rye," Levy's bread, 1949*

---

*Among Advertising Age's "The Advertising Century: Top 100 Advertising Campaigns," http://adage.com/century/campaigns.html.

campaigns to remind Americans just what it was they were fighting for.

Of course, the advertised future never came, at least not all at once, as it was promised. Furthermore, most of the innumerable small towns that had flourished as plant towns during the war never reverted to their prewar size. No plant town could reflect advertisements' depiction of small town America. The politics of such places tended to favor the companies rather than the "little people," and their increased populations brought with them all the problems associated with larger towns.

HOLLYWOOD AND THE SELLING OF THE WAR EFFORT

On December 18, 1941, just 10 days after America officially entered the war, President Roosevelt appointed Lowell Mellett as Coordinator of Government Films, thus recognizing Hollywood's role in supporting the war effort. In 1942, Mellett's office became the Bureau of Motion Pictures (BMP). Until 1943 the BMP acted as the main liaison between Washington and Hollywood.

While convincing war movies were made during World War II, most weren't as realistic or graphic as some directors and screenwriters would have liked. Likewise, newsreels, though prevalent, weren't particularly graphic when showing the war's frontlines. The watering down of war reporting and war films was primarily the result of a stricter than normal Production Code, Hollywood studio head censorship, and greater government intervention, largely by the OWI and the War Department. Because they feared too much reality might demoralize people on the home front, what was shown on movie screens of devastation occurring overseas was neither shown in full nor depicted realistically. In movies this was achieved by fabricating scenarios to show American actions abroad in the best possible light, while in newsreels events deemed likely to disturb were simply omitted.

Nevertheless, the government recognized the power of movies as a mass medium. Industry estimates during the war years put the number of people seeing a movie at 85–90 million per week or over *half* of America's entire population. The program usually consisted of the feature "A" film and shorts such as a "B" featurettes, newsreels, cartoons, and previews of coming attractions.

Movies were so popular that in 1944, Department of Commerce estimated that eighty cents of every dollar spent on "spectator amusement" (which included sports and theatre) was spent on motion pictures.[9] The government recognized Hollywood's reach and called on the industry to help it get out a wide variety of messages to the American people, both at home and abroad. In exchange for the studios' help, the government agreed to drop its anti-trust suits against the industry during the course of the war. (See Entertainment of the 1940s.)

Approximately 7,000 studio employees—around one-third of their total workforce—joined the military during World War II. Most movie stars in the military became figureheads, paraded around in front of the troops to boost morale, although some, such as Jimmy Stewart and Clark Gable, actually saw combat. Stars that didn't join the military directly still did their part to entertain the troops and help in the general war effort. For example, Veronica Lake, famous for her long blonde hair, cut her hair after the War Production Board declared long hair a hazard for women working in plants with heavy machinery (the fear was that their hair might get caught in the machinery). Likewise, stars of all kinds attended bond rallies to help sell war bonds for the United States. But most of the industry people who joined were the techies—soundmen, set-builders, lighting people, cameramen, and the like. Rather than going off to fight, however, they found themselves making movies, albeit of a very different kind.

The military had its own filmmaking branches, such as the Navy Photographic Unit and the Army Signal Corps, but their work wasn't as good as Hollywood's was. The studio techies enlisted by the various branches of the military helped bring a new quality to military training films, making films like *Safeguarding Military Secrets* (1942) and *Enemy Bacteria* (1942), a little more palatable. Several major Hollywood directors played a part in the military's use of films as well. For example, the most influential and widely seen of the government orientation movies were the seven films that comprised director Frank Capra's *Why We Fight* series (1942–1945), while John Ford's widely seen *Sex Hygiene* (1941) made clear to soldiers, in graphic fashion, the necessity to avoid sexual relations that could result in the contraction of syphilis.

Animation also played a key role in garnering support for the American war effort, with Bugs Bunny singing "Any Bonds Today?" and Donald Duck throwing tomatoes straight into Hitler's face in Disney's *Der Fuehrer's Face* (1942). In fact, Disney was the one Hollywood studio that was declared a "key war production plant," with 94 percent of its work being war related; it specialized in animated instructional films for military personnel.[10] Likewise, Tex Avery's unit at Warner Bros. got into the act with "Private Snafu." The Mel Blanc-voiced Snafu, which stands for "Situation Normal, All Fouled [or Fucked] Up," was the mascot of the biweekly featurette, the *Army-Navy Screen Magazine*. Because the *Army-Navy Screen Magazine* was distributed directly to soldiers, it wasn't subject to the same kind of censorship as a film released to the general public would have been, so it was much more bawdy, which resulted in all kinds of racy cautionary tales happening to Snafu.[11]

Along with their effectiveness at conveying crucial messages to soldiers, movies still retained their effectiveness as tools for entertainment. Movies were so popular with soldiers that by 1945, Army Overseas Motion Picture Service estimates put the number of nightly picture shows in just Europe and the Mediterranean at 2,400. When they weren't engaged in the work of war, movies relieved soldiers' boredom. Civilians were also targeted with a barrage of wartime films. Perhaps the most prevalent were the so-called victory films. Victory films were generally less than 20 minutes long and their primary purpose was to engage Americans in the war effort. Films like "*Frying Pan to Firing Line* (1942) and *Let's Share and Play Square* (1943) promoted conservation and salvage efforts, while *Winning Your Wings* (1942) was a 10-minute recruiting short for the Army Air Force that featured Lt. Jimmy Stewart. Shorts could be made relatively cheaply and distributed comparatively quickly, so the OWI relied on them heavily throughout the war to encourage Americans to participate in the war effort.

While the *Army-Navy Screen Magazine* and victory films didn't resemble typical advertising, the government was, in effect, selling ideas to its soldiers and to the civilian public.

SINGLE-PRODUCT ADVERTISING CAMPAIGNS

During the war, companies still advertised individual products, although their selling was tied into the war effort as often as possible. For example, Parker Pen ads read, "Parker red, white, and blue—the pencil for all Americans. Show your colors with this pencil," and Big Ben Clocks' motto was, "Victory won't wait for the nation that's late." Dutch Masters claimed its cigars were "An American Privilege," and Tussy Cosmetics

This *New Yorker* magazine cover from 1949 shows how television was beginning to intrude into family life. A family is at Thanksgiving dinner and the father is carving turkey, but all are intently watching football on television. Cover by Alajolov, 1949. Prints & Photographs Division, Library of Congress.

introduced "Fighting Red—new brave lipstick color by Tussy."[12] It wasn't until the late 1940s that American advertising and consumer culture reassumed a more recognizable form—ads for the products themselves. After the end of various rationing programs and the return to normal manufacturing, consumer culture in America experienced a boom the likes of which it had never seen before. The advertising campaigns for many newly available products were so successful—such as DuPont nylons—that they caused riots in the streets when they weren't available in adequate supply.

One of the more memorable ad campaigns was the 1944 advertising campaign for Chiquita Bananas. The United Fruit Company wanted a way to market imported South American bananas. The company's advertising firm devised a campaign that featured a beautiful woman of indeterminate ethnic descent, who in her attire suspiciously resembled rising star Carmen Miranda. (See Entertainment of the 1940s.) "Miss Chiquita" shook and shimmied as she sang an infectiously catchy tune that began, "I'm Chiquita banana and I've come to say…" and went on to detail how to eat, store, and cook the then exotic fruit. The advertis-ing campaign was hugely successful and bananas would go on to become one of the world's most eaten fruits.[13]

Television began to take off in the late 1940s. Advertisers did their best to market their TVs as an essential household item, such as DuMont claiming its sets were "Today's Most Welcome Gift," or GE advertising that its line "Beats Everything in Sight."[14] Most screens were small, 10 or 12 inches, but the whole unit was huge, as they often had record players, AM/FM radio sets, and record storage all in the same unit. TVs were built into cabinets that looked like furniture and advertisements of the day often discussed the dimensions and visual appeal of the cabinet just as much—or more than—the actual screen. A 1948 ad for a Farnsworth TV, for example, didn't even mention screen size: "This graceful television cabinet has been beautifully expressed in rich, lustrous mahogany. Embodying authentic eighteenth-century English design principles, its compact size and simple lines permit its use with any home decorating motif, modern or traditional."[15] Americans bought the message: in 1946, less than 10,000 TVs were sold; in 1950, the number of sets sold skyrocketed to 5 million.

Architecture

of the 1940s

As America moved increasingly toward wartime preparations, the country finally came out of the Depression. Because of this shift, the number of production jobs in urban areas skyrocketed, and the need for convenient housing for the workers became immediate. Over the course of the decade, several new housing options would become available for working Americans; the first notably different option was Baldwin Hills Village (now called Village Green) in Los Angeles, California (1940–1941).

In the 1920s, a consortium of socially conscious architects and planners, the Regional Planning Association of America (RPAA), realized America was becoming increasingly modernized and urban. They believed that nature could and should still play a role in American cities, and they sponsored a series of high-profile housing projects that were notable for attempting to integrate nature into traditionally urban locales. The last of their sponsored constructions was Baldwin Hills Village, an 80-acre development on the fringes of developed Los Angeles. A similar project was developed, called Harbor Hills, in San Pedro, California, a suburb of Los Angeles, built for workers in the defense industry. Reginald Johnson, the chief architect for Baldwin Hills Village, was also among those architects

collaborating on Harbor Hills, a 300-unit development finished in 1941.[1]

The planners of the RPAA were fully aware that Los Angeles was an automobile-dependent city but, believing that the home should be a refuge from the pressures of modern life, they devised a way to minimize the impact of cars on the home lives of the Village's residents. In the center of Baldwin Hills Village was the large Village Green, the equivalent of an open park space, which had, extending from its outer edges, long strips of green space called garden courts. On the outside edges of the garden courts were two-story row houses, which contemporary Americans would immediately recognize as typical apartment buildings. The fronts of the apartments faced in toward the green space, while the backs faced what were called garage courts (essentially parking lots). The goal was that while at home people would forget about their cars and enjoy the green spaces in which their homes were set.[2]

The designers were confident that the communal green spaces would be heavily used and would create a strong sense of community among residents. Instead, the adults generally chose to remain in their own small, individually segregated ground-floor patio areas. Furthermore, children frequently played close to home rather than in

Detail of curved interior sidewalk and open space at Harbor Hills, 1941, in the Los Angeles area, which, like Baldwin Hills, was designed to offer apartment housing but with lots of green space for residents to enjoy. Prints & Photographs Division, Library of Congress.

the central Village Green.[3] While the intentions of the RPAA weren't exactly realized in Baldwin Hills Village, its design has long since become a standard in American apartment complexes.

The federal government was keenly aware of the need for more housing for newly arriving workers in military-related industries and passed the Lanham Act of 1940, which initially committed $150 million to the creation of housing for war workers. William Wurster, a San Francisco Bay Area builder was commissioned to plan 1,677 homes for Carquinez Heights near the naval shipyards in Vallejo, California. To speed up the process, Wurster incorporated flat roofs into his homes, which allowed the ceilings and the floors to be built in the same way. Furthermore, he arranged the houses in long rows, so as to make room for

much smaller yards, the logic being that workers needed in the war effort wouldn't be spending time taking care of their yards.[4] Similarly styled developments sprang up all over America.

PREFAB HOUSING AND QUONSET HUTS

The ability to quickly make cheap but usable housing had long been a dream among American homebuilders. While prefabricated mail-order houses, farm, and commercial structures were being sold as early as the turn of the nineteenth century, prefab homes were best suited for rapidly growing areas or start-up industries. In the early 1940s, America's military was experiencing unprecedented growth; it needed buildings

Model of Wingfoot prefabricated home manufactured by Goodyear in front of a Goodyear service station, Washington, D.C., 1946. Prints & Photographs Division, Library of Congress.

in which it could house soldiers and equipment both at home and abroad.

In 1941, at the Quonset Point Naval Station in Rhode Island, the Navy's construction arm—the Seabees—created a prefabricated building that became known as the Quonset hut. With its easily assembled skeletal structure of preformed wooden ribs and exterior of corrugated steel sheets and interiors of pressed wood, the Quonset hut proved invaluable. By 1946, over 160,000 Quonset huts had been built, most of them in Europe.[5] After the war, many were brought back to America, where they served a variety of purposes, from agricultural buildings, to commercial use, and even cheap housing.

LEVITTOWN AND THE COMING OF THE SUBURBS

When the war ended in 1945, white veterans returned home to find the country waiting for them with open arms. To alleviate the possibility of servicemen living in the bleak financial conditions that characterized the 1930s, the government instituted the G. I. Bill of Rights. The G. I. Bill offered "qualified" veterans job training, money for schooling, and money to buy their own homes. While this was a wonderful opportunity for white soldiers, many minority veterans were excluded from the process due to both long-standing societal racial discrimination and institutionalized discrimination by the Federal Housing Administration (FHA), which offered builders low-cost loans while at the same time tacitly encouraging them to include restrictive racial covenants into the deeds of their properties.[6]

Aerial view of a housing development in Levittown, New York. Prints & Photographs Division, Library of Congress.

Into this milieu of unparalleled opportunity and incredible demand came William J. Levitt and his brother Alfred, who in 1946 embarked on a housing project that would change the face of the American home forever. The brothers purchased 1,500 acres of potato fields in Nassau County, Long Island, on which they intended to build small, single-family homes.[7] Coinciding with the Levitts's purchase was America's returning to a relative state of normalcy for the first time since the stock market crash began the Depression in 1929. The G. I. Bill and other government programs designed to prevent the social discord many felt might accompany the end of the war worked beyond anyone's wildest dreams, resulting in unprecedented levels of financial growth and prosperity that would last into the early 1970s. The newfound prosperity, coupled with a severe housing shortage, led to a glut of people wanting to buy homes.

Heavily influenced by the ideas of prefabrication and mass production that had so long tantalized homebuilders, the Levitts hit on the right idea at the right time. Unlike more traditional houses, Levitt homes had no basements. Instead, they rested on simple concrete slab foundations that allowed work crews to simply build up from them in an assembly line manner, complete with prefabricated parts. At the height of their productivity, workers were completing around 30 homes a day. The houses, all two-bedroom, one-bath affairs, looked more like boxes than homes and were separated only by their color, but their basic design was highly effective. The kitchens had large picture windows facing out to the front, while the rest of the rooms faced the backyard, thus ensuring more privacy than city-living, working-class folks had ever known before. Furthermore, the homes came with stoves, refrigerators, washers and (later in the 1950s, TVs), high-tech items previously reserved for America's upper classes. Not surprisingly, people flocked to Levittown, which grew in

The Farm Security Administration—Office of War Information took this picture in 1941 of "an apartment building in the Negro section" of Chicago, Illinois, 1941. Prints & Photographs Division, Library of Congress.

population from 450 in 1946 to more than 60,000 by the late 1950s.[8]

Levittown was in some ways less ethnically exclusive than its prewar predecessors were, but only as concerned whites. Prior to the war it was not at all uncommon for existing outlying areas to exclude Jews and Catholics from owning homes outside of the inner cities. But Levitt, himself Jewish, saw no reason to limit Jewish and Catholic vets from owning homes in his project.[9] However, with encouragement from the FHA in the form of loan preferences, Levitt routinely excluded African Americans, Puerto Ricans, and other ethic minorities from owning his homes by including in his deeds a covenant that forbade their sale to minorities. Furthermore, if a resident in the future decided to sell his home to a member of a minority group, he could legally be sued by his neighbors. Although the Supreme Court ruled against the constitutionality of such stipulations in 1948, the issue was fought in the courts for years, and wasn't permanently outlawed until the Fair Housing Act of 1968.[10] While Levittown itself was the product of a simple and affordable architectural design, its reverberations in American culture were immense, resulting in a kind of unintended but profoundly wide-reaching shift in the architecture of American culture. Whereas the majority of Americans lived in cities prior to World War II, after the war white Americans, in a phenomenon that would come to be known as "white flight," flocked to the suburbs that sprang up around every major city in America after the initial success of Levittown.

The need for the building of new roads and other infrastructures had disastrous repercussions for the minorities who, in part because of racial discrimination, were left behind in the cities. Long-standing urban apartments and housing areas were razed to make room for the roadway arteries needed to get suburban workers in and out of the cities; displaced residents were then moved into overcrowded and underfunded government housing projects that were miserable places to live. While American cities before the war weren't characterized by high-quality living conditions, in the postwar years they became downright wretched for the urban poor. Although there are a variety of factors involved in the continued decline of living conditions in American inner cities, some of them can be traced back to the startling success of the Levitts's simply designed but highly functional homes.

THE BEGINNING OF THE SHOPPING CENTER

Traditionally, urban shopping centers consisted of rows of shops on city streets. The consumer could use public transportation and walk from store to store. But the skyrocketing use of automobiles complicated the matter. People drove into the city to shop, but eventually ended up fighting for parking spaces or parking inconveniently far away.

In 1947, John Graham and Company began doing research for the Northgate Regional Shopping Center (1947–1951). They discovered that the proximity of smaller retailers to the bigger businesses played a role in how many consumers patronized the smaller businesses. They conceived of a shopping complex in which large stores would act as anchors on either end of a row of smaller specialty stores. But the problem remained: How do you make a consumer downtown accessible by cars but not inundated by them? Their solution was simply elegant and highly effective. Just as the Baldwin Hills Village developers had turned the apartments of the Village inward, with cars on the outside, so too did the creators of Northgate invert their replication of a downtown shopping center.[11]

Northgate was a gigantic sprawling complex with large anchor stores on either end of the double-rowed complex, as well as in the middle. Smaller shops were strung between them. The storefronts faced inward rather than out, thus the "street" going down the center of the development was internal, open only to pedestrian traffic. The outside of Northgate, with its seemingly endless expanse of parking lot, was ugly. But the inside, with no cars, the convenience of many stores in one area, no problems with Seattle's notoriously wet weather, and the freedom to walk leisurely was a consumer's, and a retailer's, dream. Northgate's success quickly spawned countless imitators.

ARCHITECTURAL INNOVATIONS

Several singular architectural innovations of the 1940s would prove to be influential. Two of the more notable innovations were Eleanor Raymond's Dover, Massachusetts, sun-heated house (1948) and Philip Johnson's New Canaan, Connecticut, glass house (1949).

Eleanor Raymond sought to make use of newly emerging technologies in her postwar home designs. One home in particular, designed for her patron, Amelia Peabody, came to be known as the "sunheated house." The south side of the upper story appeared to be made entirely of windows. However, the "windows" are actually solar collectors designed to gather heat. Although the system as designed didn't really work and was eventually replaced by a more traditional heating system, the early solar experiments and technologies would help lead to further innovations in solar technology in the ensuing decades.[12]

Perhaps the most famous home constructed in the 1940s was architect Philip Johnson's glass house. Johnson first gained recognition as an architectural critic and became director of the architecture department at the Museum of Modern Art in New York City. He and the architectural historian Henry-Russell Hitchcock produced an exhibition catalog titled *The International Style*. Typical International Style buildings were made of reinforced concrete with white walls, flat roofs, and large windows. The exteriors looked modern and clean.[13] Johnson became an architect in the early 1940s. One of his first important designs was the glass house in New Canaan, Connecticut, which he used for a time as his primary residence. Johnson based his design on the ideas of Ludwig Mies van der Rohe, a leader of the International Style. As such, the home is essentially a large all-glass rectangle, notable for its walls, which are made entirely out of glass.

LUDWIG MIES VAN DER ROHE

The German-born Mies was not formally trained as an architect, but he was nevertheless drawn to the field early. In the early 1920s he designed two plans for skyscrapers that appeared as though they were encased in glass, but they were never built. Seeking to escape Nazi oppression, Mies emigrated to the United States, where in 1938 he became the director of architecture at Chicago's Armour Institute, which in 1940 was renamed the Illinois Institute of Technology (IIT).

Mies was asked to design a new campus for the school, a project that took 15 years to complete. The cumulative project is often considered to be the first modern academic complex in America. Mies espoused an architectural philosophy he called *beinahe nichts,* "almost nothing."[14] Mies applied this motto to his vision of the IIT campus, which is notable for its asymmetrical shapes and lack of individuality among the buildings. Mies believed that modern academia would be fluid in its change and that to make distinctly different buildings designed for particular uses would limit the campus's flexibility. Instead, he strove to design a kind of essential architectural form that could be adapted for a variety of changing purposes, hence IIT's chapel didn't look much different from its classroom buildings. While the IIT campus was influential, it was the realization of Mies's vision of the skyscraper that would prove his greatest contribution to American architecture.

In 1947, the Museum of Modern Art in New York City held a well-received retrospective of Mies's work, resulting in Mies receiving major commercial commissions. Among his most important designs of the 1940s was the pair of 26-story apartment towers at 860–880 Lake Shore Drive in Chicago. Mies's 1920s vision of shining skyscrapers of glass and steel came to fruition in the Lake Shore Apartments (1948–1951). With the Lake Shore Apartments, Mies hit on a relatively simple new idea that changed skyscraper technology dramatically. Rather than putting the skeletal structure of the buildings on the inside, Mies had steel I-beams welded to the exterior of the buildings' structural columns. The I-beams broke up the tediousness of the smooth glass surfaces while also heightening the structures' sense of verticality.[15] As a result of the success of the IIT and the Lake Shore Apartments, Mies became the leader of what came to be known as the "Chicago school" of architecture, which was basically a version of the International Style.

THE EQUITABLE LIFE ASSURANCE BUILDING AND THE UNITED NATIONS SECRETARIAT

By the mid-to-late 1940s, Mies's influence was beginning to be evident in the designs of other architects. Pietro Belluschi's Equitable Life Assurance Building in Portland, Oregon (1944–1947) didn't go as far as the Lake Shore Apartments in placing its skeletal structure on the building's exterior; its windows were slightly inset. Another notable example of Mies's architectural influence could be seen in the United Nations Secretariat (1947–1950), which was designed by an international consortium of architects. While its windowed exterior conceals its skeletal structure, the comparatively smaller size of its windows makes it visually appear to be almost a kind of grid.

Mies's work in the 1940s influenced the building of urban skyscrapers in the ensuing decades. While some people felt that he had violated his own "almost nothing" philosophy in that the I- beams he incorporated into his buildings' exteriors worked as a kind of ornamentation, his landmark designs of the 1940s spawned a whole new school of architecture, which came to be known as the "Miesian Style." Miesian-inspired buildings sprang up everywhere after the 1940s, causing some to see buildings adhering to his influence as evidence of a Second International Style.

THE PENTAGON

By early 1941, it had become clear that America would eventually enter World War II. Such an undertaking required a central point from which to coordinate the dispatching of American troops at home and abroad. In order to house the varied offices of the War Department under one roof, in September 1941, U.S. Army engineers began building the Pentagon on the west bank of the Potomac River in Arlington, Virginia, just across from Washington, D.C. Upon its completion in January 1943, the Pentagon immediately became one of

Aerial view of the Pentagon, Arlington, Virginia, ca. 1947. Prints & Photographs Division, Library of Congress.

the world's largest office buildings, with more than 3.7 million square feet of office and other space, housing over 20,000 people working for the Departments of the Army, Navy, and Air Force, and the Office of the Secretary of Defense.[16]

The Pentagon was constructed in the shape of a pentagon, or five-sided figure; the 5 concentric rings are connected by 10 spoke-like corridors. The outer wall of the structure measures about one mile around and is surrounded by over 60 acres of parking lot. In addition, the Pentagon has one of the world's largest private telephone systems, with around 100,000 miles of cable handling more than 200,000 calls a day.

The building also has many shops, restaurants, and cafeterias, as well as a radio and television station, a bank, dispensary, post office, and heliport.[17]

The Pentagon is one of America's most enduring buildings, but it is just as important for what "the Pentagon" has come to mean in American popular culture. In films, literature, and the popular press, when people refer to "the Pentagon," they don't necessarily mean the building itself. Instead, the word is also a symbol of a vast, infrastructure of America's military-industrial might.

Books

Newspapers, Magazines, and Comics of the 1940s

In the early 1940s, paper rationing lead publishers to find a way to publish books that didn't use as much paper as hardcover books, which typically had thick, high-quality paper. For the first time, publishers began printing mass-market paperbacks. These books were made with thin, comparatively low-quality paper (and were much cheaper to produce than hardcovers), which meant that more books could be printed in spite of rationing. Publishers began establishing book clubs to distribute their books and feed the public's growing appetite for reading. For a monthly fee, club members would be sent a "publisher's choice" and also have the option to buy other books in a publisher's catalog at a discount. At their height in the1940s, American book clubs had over three million members who bought over one million books a month.[1] Reading was especially popular among soldiers, who often had a lot of down time on their hands. Throughout the early 1940s "victory book rallies" were held to solicit book donations for soldiers. At one two-week-long New York City Public Library Drive, over 600,000 books were donated.[2] Many soldiers developed a lifelong reading habit, and upon their return they helped to swell the membership numbers of various book clubs. With the rise of television in the 1950s, the book club craze declined from its late-1940s peak. Books became more diverse and varied in tone, subject, and style. Continuing a rise in popularity that began in the 1930s, hard-boiled detective fiction novels appeared frequently on various best-seller lists. Some of the more notable works in this vein included Raymond Chandler's continuing series of Philip Marlowe novels, *Farewell, My Lovely* (1940), *The High Window* (1942), *The Lady in the Lake* (1943), and *The Little Sister* (1949); James M. Cain's pulp classic *Mildred Pierce* (1941), and the introduction of Mickey Spillane's Mike Hammer in *I, the Jury* (1947). In addition to capturing the imaginations of American readers, throughout the decade many of these books would become source material for the series of films that have collectively come to be known as film noir. (See Entertainment of the 1940s.)

NONFICTION

During the 1940s, nonfiction books dealing with war, such Marion Hargrove's *See Here, Private Hargrove* (1942), Joseph E. Davies *Mission to Moscow* (1943), W. L. White's *They Were Expendable* (1943), Richard Tregaskis's *Guadalcanal Diary* (1948), and Major Alexander O. de Seversky's *Victory Through Air Power* (1942), were best sellers, as were books by major figures of the war era, including General George C. Marshall's *General Marshall's Report* (1945), Dwight D. Eisenhower's *Crusade in*

The Darryl F. Zanuck movie production of *The Grapes of Wrath* by John Steinbeck with Henry Fonda, Jane Darwell, and John Carradine, 1940. Courtesy of Photofest.

BOOKS TO MOVIES

In the 1940s, Hollywood repeatedly turned to popular novels for source material; this was not new, as some of the biggest box office films in history, such as *Gone with the Wind* (1939) and *The Wizard of Oz* (1939), had been adapted from novels. But during the 1940s Hollywood began adapting novels into films more quickly than in the past, so it wasn't uncommon for a book to be a popular novelistic success one year and a box office smash the next, as was the case with John Steinbeck's *Grapes of Wrath,* which was published to critical and popular acclaim in 1939, and in 1940 made into one of the most enduring films of the decade by John Ford, who won a Best Director Oscar for his work. Making movies from best-selling books helped to ensure a built-in audience that would want to see a particular film, and it would also spur book sales. Some of the many other best-selling novels of the decade that were also made into popular films included Richard Llewellyn's *How Green Was My Valley* (1941), Joseph O. Kesselring's *Arsenic and Old Lace* (1944), Jan Struther's *Mrs. Miniver* (1942), Betty Smith's *A Tree Grows in Brooklyn* (1945), Laura Z. Hobson's *Gentleman's Agreement* (1947), and Robert Penn Warren's *All the King's Men* (1949).

BOOK CENSORSHIP

Book censorship occurred in some parts of the country in the 1940s. For some authors, the notoriety could lift a title to the top of best-seller lists, which happened with Kathleen Winsor's *Forever Amber* (1944). The novel chronicles the life of Amber St. Clare, a pregnant, abandoned, and destitute London 16-year-old who eventually manages to become the mistress of King Charles II. The novel was bawdy for its time and was immediately banned in Boston for being obscene. Thsis piqued interest elsewhere, and the book sold like hotcakes; audiences were enthralled by the historical story that featured all kinds of people, from prostitutes and bandits to royalty, as well as exciting fictionalized accounts of historical occurrences such as the Great Plague and the Fire of London. When in 1947 the state of Massachusetts ruled that *Forever Amber* was not obscene, the ruling was anticlimactic, as the book had already become the best-selling novel of the decade and a blueprint for historical romances.

Europe (1948), and Winston Churchill's *Blood, Sweat, and Tears* (1941). But of all the war writers, among the most widely read stateside was Ernie Pyle, a nationally syndicated newspaper columnist for the *Washington Daily News*. Pyle was embedded with soldiers and recounted firsthand for the American people several of the major occurrences of World War II, including the D-Day invasion of Normandy in France. On April 18, 1945, he was killed by Japanese machine-gun fire on a small island near Okinawa. A posthumous collection of his works, *Last Chapter* (1946), joined his previous collections, *Brave Men* (1945) and *Here Is Your War* (1943), as a longtime best seller.

By the late 1940s, best-selling nonfiction lists became quite varied, including books on topics such as cooking and the card game Canasta, which spawned at least three best sellers in the late 1940s. Two books that proved immensely timely and popular were Dr. Benjamin Spock's *Common Sense Book of Baby and Child* (1946) and A. C. Kinsey's revolutionary *Sexual Behavior in the Human Male* (1948). As the baby boom was in full swing in the late 1940s, Dr. Spock's book became the child-rearing bible and a best seller for decades after. Another book that made a large and permanent impact was Kinsey's *Sexual Behavior in the Human Male*. Kinsey's text was dry and scientific, but it contained shocking statistics, such as his finding that 37 percent of all men had reached orgasm at some point in their life with another man.[3] Kinsey's report was controversial and some of his research methods were suspect, but the more prurient factoids stirred the curiosity of American readers, and his book became an incredibly unlikely best seller, selling 200,000 copies in its first two months of release alone, and ultimately led to a 1953 sequel, *Sexual Behavior in the Human Female,* which also became a best seller. (See Overview of the 1940s chapter.)

Because of the rise of mass-market paperbacks and book clubs in the 1940s, critically acclaimed books that in the past would have been well received by academics and students of literature found new and wider audiences. Book clubs began featuring literary titles such as John Steinbeck's *The Grapes of Wrath* (1939), Ernest Hemingway's *For Whom the Bell Tolls* (1940); *The Moon Is Down* (1942), and *Cannery Row* (1945); Betty Smith's *A Tree Grows in Brooklyn* (1943); Richard Wright's *Black Boy* (1945); and Robert Penn Warren's *All the King's Men* (1946).

1940: A YEAR OF TRANSITION

The advent of the 1940s ushered in an age of greater conservatism in American fiction; literary fiction just prior to 1940 had been characterized by a strong vein of protest, which perhaps culminated with the publication of John Steinbeck's *The Grapes of Wrath* in 1939. With World War II looming, authors were acutely aware of the danger of being labeled as communists. As a result, writers previously considered to be on the fringes began to gain critical recognition.

While fiction had previously been the bastion of WASP, primarily male writers, a diverse group of authors began to gain literary headway, including a number of important Southern, Jewish, and African American authors. In many ways,

1940 was a transitional year in American fiction. Of the many "between the wars writers" who have since been critically admired, no American author has been more lauded than William Faulkner, F. Scott Fitzgerald, and Ernest Hemingway. In 1940 both Faulkner and Hemingway published what are widely considered their final novelistic masterpieces, *The Hamlet* and *For Whom the Bell Tolls*, respectively. On December 21, 1940, Fitzgerald died of a massive heart attack in Hollywood, California, and his final, unfinished novel, *The Last Tycoon*, was published posthumously in 1941.

Faulkner's first book of the 1940s was *The Hamlet* (1940), which was followed shortly thereafter by *Go Down Moses and Other Stories* (1942), a masterful collection of short stories featuring "The Bear," perhaps Faulkner's most lauded short work. Next was the anti-racist *Intruder in the Dust* (1948), a popular success that also played a large part in his winning the 1949 Nobel Prize in Literature. Although the critical and popular recognition of Faulkner's genius was belated, it benefited other Southern writers. Because of Faulkner's growing fame and the emergence of writers such as Eudora Welty, Katherine Anne Porter, Lillian Smith, Carson McCullers, and William Alexander Percy in the 1940s, Southern literature became for the first time its own area of study.

Hemingway's reputation also escalated in the 1940s, but Hemingway's rise was perhaps due to his personality as much as to his writing. While *For Whom the Bell Tolls*, published in 1940 was an amazing text about an American who enlists in the Spanish Civil War, Hemingway's output went into steep decline after its publication. He spent the war years partly in Europe as a fiercely anti-Nazi correspondent and partly at his home in Cuba, where he patrolled the coast in his fishing boat looking for German submarines. He didn't publish another novel until 1950, *Across the River and into the Trees*. *The Old Man and the Sea* (1952), the last novel published in his lifetime, won a Pulitzer Prize in 1953 and played a role in his 1954 Nobel Prize in Literature. After *For Whom the Bell Tolls* in 1940, however, Hemingway's work never again approached the level of success of such novels as *The Sun Also Rises* (1926) and *A Farewell to Arms* (1929).

NOTABLE BOOKS

The Heart Is a Lonely Hunter, Carson McCullers (1940)

Native Son, Richard Wright (1940)

How Green Was My Valley, Richard Llewellyn (1940)

For Whom the Bell Tolls, Ernest Hemingway (1940)

Curious George, H. A. Rey and Margret Rey (1941)

The Robe, Lloyd C. Douglas (1942)

They Were Expendable, W. L. White (1942)

The Fountainhead, Ayn Rand (1943)

The Little Prince, Antoine de Saint-Exupery (1943)

A Tree Grows in Brooklyn, Betty Smith (1943)

Brideshead Revisted, Evelyn Waugh (1945)

Cannery Row, John Steinbeck (1945)

Stuart Little, E. B. White (1945)

All the King's Men, Robert Penn Warren (1946)

Common Sense Book of Baby and Child Care, Dr. Benjamin Spock (1946)

I, the Jury, Mickey Spillane (1947)

Tales of the South Pacific, James Michener (1947)

The Naked and the Dead, Norman Mailer (1948)

1984, George Orwell (1949)

FICTION: REGIONAL WRITERS

The year 1940 also saw the publication of two books that signaled coming changes in the American literary landscape, Carson McCullers's *The Heart Is a Lonely Hunter* and Richard Wright's *Native Son*. McCullers's work, alongside overdue recognition of Faulkner's genius, helped to legitimize the idea of Southern literature as the product of a unique place. The success of Southern writers led to increased attention for regional writers—writers whose work was shaped by the geographic area in which they lived. Likewise, Wright's novels paved the way for other African Americans to gain an audience with the reading public and began a move toward recognizing that much of African American literature was the product of a singular ethnic experience.

Carson McCullers (1917–1967) was among the most prolific American authors of the 1940s. She heightened the recognition of Southern literature and paved the way for other women writers, perhaps most notably Flannery O'Connor. In 1940, at age 23, McCullers published her first novel, *The Heart Is a Lonely Hunter.* Set in a small Southern town, *Hunter* tells the story of Mick Kelly, a strange young girl who looks for beauty against a background of loneliness, violence, and depravity. The book was a critical and popular success. In 1941 she published her second novel, *Reflections in a Golden Eye,* a book chronicling the lives of the inhabitants of a Southern army post. While it was critically fairly well-received, its grim depiction of humanity—including birth defects, a myriad of sexual escapades, horse torture, murder, and self-mutilation—turned off many readers. Despite this, in 1942 she proved that she was equally adept at writing short stories, as evidenced by "A Tree, A Rock, A Cloud," which was selected for inclusion in the 1942 edition of the annual O. Henry Memorial Prize Stories anthology. These were followed by a number of novels, short stories, essays, and plays.

While McCullers's works were deeply influenced by her experiences as a Southerner, Richard Wright (1908–1960) created a literary world out of his experiences as an African American. His novel, *Native Son* (1940), was about Bigger Thomas, a young African American man who responds to a violent world with violence, killing a white woman. It was among the first best-selling books by an African American writer. Whereas black authors had tried not to alienate white audiences, Wright forced readers to see the world through Bigger's eyes. Furthermore, in the 1930s, Wright was involved with the Communist Party, having worked as a reporter for the *Daily Worker;* accordingly, *Native Son* was characterized by a strong undercurrent of social protest, making the book's popular success all the more amazing.

By 1944, Wright formally broke with the Communist Party. Wright then turned to more autobiographical musings, which led to the publication of *Black Boy* in 1945. This book was a success with both the public and the critics, and served as an inspiration and a model for the work of James Baldwin and Ralph Ellison in the 1950s and 1960s. While Wright continued to publish

Portrait of Richard Wright, 1943, by Gordon Parks. Parks was a photographer then for the Farm Security Administration–Office of War Information Photograph Collection. Prints & Photographs Division, Library of Congress.

after the 1940s, his work during this decade was his most important; *Native Son* and *Black Boy* were the first of their kind and made it clear for future black writers that they could write for themselves and about themselves without fear of how white America might perceive their work.

While short-story writers as diverse as Katherine Anne Porter, William Faulkner, and John Cheever enjoyed success in the 1940s, perhaps the most successful short-story writer of this period was the Mississippi writer Eudora Welty (1909–2001). Her first short-story collection, *A Curtain of Green,* was published in 1941 and is still considered to contain some of the most interesting stories she ever wrote, including "The Petrified Man" and "Why I Live at the P.O." After publishing her first novel, *The Robber Bridegroom* (1942), Welty then published another collection of short stories, *The Wide Net,* in 1943. In 1942 and 1943, she won the O. Henry Memorial Prize for the best American short story, for "The Wide Net" and "Livvie is Back" respectively, the first of a lifetime of awards for her work.

Welty claimed to not like being labeled a regional writer, as she felt her writing was representative not of the Southern experience but of the human experience. Welty's best work did indeed rise above its setting to become universal. Nevertheless, today the fact remains that Welty is considered among the best of the Southern writers; her success in the 1940s, along with that of her Southern peers, led to Southern literature becoming institutionalized by decade's end.

Another author who first achieved success in the 1940s was Saul Bellow (1915–2005), a Jewish writer whose work tried to make sense of life in urban America, particularly in Chicago and New York. In 1944, Bellow published his first novel, *Dangling Man,* which was structured using the fictional device of journals, kept by a young man waiting to be drafted. In 1947, Bellow published *The Victim,* a book about a week in the life of Asa Leventhal, a man left alone in New York City when his wife visits a relative. Though it wasn't until the publication of *The Adventures of Augie March* (1953) that Bellow made his breakthrough, his books in the 1940s helped place him at the forefront of Jewish American writers.

Two of the more notable novels to come out of the later 1940s were *All the King's Men* (1946) and *The Naked and the Dead* (1948). Both came from equally unlikely sources: Robert Penn Warren (1905–1989), an academic also known for his being a founding editor of the *Southern Review,* which was for a time the most influential American literary quarterly; and Norman Mailer (1923–2007), a first-time novelist.

Warren was a professor at Louisiana State University, where he founded the *Southern Review.* While he published numerous poems and would eventually be recognized as a major American poet, he concentrated on his fiction in the 1940s, a decision that paid off when his novel *All the King's Men* won the Pulitzer Prize in 1946. Through the voice of narrator Jack Burden, *All the King's Men* deals with the redemption of Willie Stark, a character based on Louisiana's Huey Long, the corrupt but fascinating politician assassinated in

Norman Mailer in 1948. Photo by Carl Van Vechten from the Library of Congress Carl Van Vechten Photograph Collection. Prints & Photographs Division, Library of Congress.

1935. Norman Mailer was born in Long Branch, New Jersey, raised in Brooklyn and educated at Harvard. After college, Mailer was drafted into the army, serving in the Philippines as a rifleman during World War II. His experiences in the war inspired him to write his first novel, *The Naked and the Dead,* published in 1948. The novel is widely thought by literary critics to be among the best to have come out of World War II. The novel focuses on 13 American soldiers stationed on a Japanese-held island in the Pacific. The book describes their lives on the island and uses flashbacks to describe their past. Although Mailer continued to write fiction, he has become best known for nonfiction.

POETRY

In poetry, the generation of artists who came of age during the period between the wars continued to write. For example, Marianne Moore published *What Are Years?* in 1941; Wallace Stevens published *Parts of a World* in 1942, which included "Notes Towards a Supreme Fiction," and *Transport to Summer* in 1947; T. S. Eliot published *Four Quartets* in 1943; H. D. (Hilda Doolittle) published *The Walls Do Not Fall* in 1944; Robert Frost published *A Masque of Reason* in 1945 and *A Masque of Mercy* in 1947; Robert Penn Warren published *Selected Poems 1923–1943* in 1944; and William Carlos Williams published *Paterson: Book I* in 1946. Despite the number of established poets producing quality works, the 1940s are especially notable as an era in which a new generation of poets, including Gwendolyn Brooks, Elizabeth Bishop, Robert Lowell, and Richard Wilbur, began to move to the literary forefront. While they certainly had read, admired, and been influenced by the poets from the generation immediately preceding theirs, the poets of the 1940s are notable for reaching farther back into the American past for inspiration: to Walt Whitman, for instance. While some of the new poets echoed the modernists' despair at the dehumanizing effects of technology on human life, even more embraced Whitman's message of unity and life.

If ever a poet was a living representative of the transitional nature of literature in the 1940s, it was the African American writer Gwendolyn Brooks (1917–2000), a poet who first followed in the tradition of the Harlem Renaissance artists of the 1920s and 1930s and then later became aligned with the militant black writers who came to prominence in the 1960s. Born in Topeka, Kansas, Brooks's family soon moved to Chicago, where Brooks was schooled, eventually graduating from Wilson Junior College. Even as a child, Brooks wrote poetry, going so far as to keep poetry notebooks. She published her first collection of poetry, *A Street in Bronzeville,* in 1945. Her early poetry was deeply rooted in her Chicago experiences, detailing the minutiae of everyday black life in the inner city ("Bronzeville" was the name Chicago newspapers gave to the city's ghettoes). Combining traditional lyric forms, alliterative, heavily rhymed lines, and black colloquial speech, Brooks's work depicted not only the ghetto's despair, but its joy as well.

In 1949, Brooks released her second collection of poems, *Annie Allen,* which continued her exploration of the day-to-day aspects of urban black life. It became the first book by an African American to win a Pulitzer Prize. She continued her work in the 1950s in collections such as *Bronzeville Boys and Girls* (1956), but in the late 1960s she underwent a transformation after meeting and working with younger black poets. She decided that she should write for specifically black audiences and dropped her New York publisher in favor of African American-owned presses. She became a leading black feminist as her work grew more explicitly political and less formally structured. Gwendolyn Brooks's constantly evolving poetry is unique in its having bridged differing eras in such a way as to have been equally important to both.

Robert Lowell (1917–1977) was raised in New England, perhaps the most history-steeped region in the nation, but he spent seemingly his whole career trying to revise his own and America's past. After studying at Harvard for two years in the 1930s, Lowell broke with family tradition and moved to Ohio to attend Kenyon College to study with the poet and critic John Crowe Ransom. His poetry was in some ways confessional and his politics, considering the time period, radically liberal.

Lowell vocally opposed U.S. policies during World War II. Although he did try to enlist in the navy, he refused to be drafted into the army and spoke out against the Allies' use of saturation bombing and their insistence on unconditional surrender, eventually declaring himself a conscientious objector; in the end, he spent a year in jail for his beliefs. His first major book of poetry, *Lord Weary's Castle* (1946), elucidates what Lowell saw as the differences between what America was and what it had become, which in his view was a corrupt, materialistic nation. Throughout his career and within his work Lowell revisited America's history as well as his own, constantly and obsessively revising his poems and themes.

MAGAZINES

The magazine market thrived in the 1940s, buoyed by a national wave of reading. Many of the national periodicals born in the late 1800s and

Books

Books

NEW MAGAZINES

Gourmet, 1941

Seventeen, 1944

Ebony, 1945

Highlights for Children, 1946

Road & Track, 1947

Modern Bride, 1949

Motor Trend, 1949

WORDS AND PHRASES

beanie

bonkers

Cold War

crud

geronimo! (as an interjection)

gizmo

gobbledygook

gung ho

hep

hipster

hokey

hubba-hubba (interjection to indicate an attractive member of the opposite sex)

itty-bitty

natch

nightclubbing

perfecto

pin-up girl

sad sack

smackeroo (for money)

snafu

super-duper

sweet talk

vibe

whammy

zillion

early 1900s continued to draw millions of readers, including *Ladies Home Journal* and the *Saturday Evening Post.* The formula for a successful title seemed firmly in place—a mix of articles geared toward families, advertising, and the lure of high profile writers who churned out essays and short stories.

By 1946, *Reader's Digest* (founded in 1922) stood as the nation's most popular magazine, with a circulation of nine million. The success of *Time* magazine, established in 1923 by Henry Luce and Britton Hadden, led to others attempting to imitate the general interest format, including *Newsweek* (1933) and *U.S. News & World Report* (1948). Though the nation increasingly looked to radio and television for news throughout the decade, magazines were still an important information source. For example, John Hersey's 1946 reporting on Hiroshima for the *New Yorker* was named the best piece of American journalism in the twentieth century by the New York University Department of Journalism in 1999.

African American entrepreneurs applied the formula in developing magazines specifically targeted at black audiences. In 1942, John H. Johnson created *Negro Digest,* which used the template established by mass media titles. His success enabled him to found other magazines, including *Ebony* (1945). Originally aimed at male readers, *Ebony* gained its footing and increased popularity when it expanded to include content directed at women.

NEWSPAPERS

Journalists struggled with the balance between partisan reporting and objectivity for as long as newspapers had been produced. As the twentieth century unfolded, a focus on fact-based reporting gave way to an interpretive mode, which featured the reporter as a witness/observer who explained events and issues as they unfolded. The trauma of World War I added to this transformation of American journalism. Context became a central tenet of reporting.

As journalists struggled to figure out the best way to reach audiences, the world grew in complexity. The nation needed its reporters to also serve as analysts, providing context for stories that they did not comprehend or understand.

This kind of newsgathering helped newspapers achieve record circulation figures in the 1940s, as Americans turned to them for the latest news on efforts in World War II.

While the advent of radio in the 1930s weakened the appeal of newspapers, it did not lessen the role of journalism. The challenge for newspapers beginning in the 1940s, however, was that people were increasingly drawn away from print to radio and then, eventually, television. Citizens were hungry for content, but they turned away from newspapers in greater numbers as the decade progressed. Total weekday circulation figures increased from 41.1 million in 1940 to 53.8 million in 1950, while Sunday circulation jumped from 32.4 million to 46.6 million in the same span, but sales per household actually fell. Newspaper circulation rose with the population, but that did not translate into newspaper readership increasing as a whole.

COMICS

Gaining in popularity over the course of the twentieth century, comic books took off in the 1940s. In the previous decade, resourceful entrepreneurs realized that giving away comic books as premiums enticed consumers to purchase products. Large companies such as Procter & Gamble, Kinney Shoes, and others who produced kid-friendly merchandise gave away large runs of comics, usually from 100,000 to 250,000 copies. Some even approached 1 million.

Most of the original comic books simply reprinted characters from newspaper strips, such as *The Lone Ranger* and *Buck Rogers*. The success of these efforts gave a new generation of writers and editors the freedom to create new characters and features. Superheroes became more prevalent in the 1940s, partially in response to the early hero stories and the creation of Superman in 1938. Outside forces also helped comics gain a footing, including the rise of pulp magazines, film, and five-cent and dime novels. Radio programs aired programs directed at children. From 4:30 in the afternoon through 6:00 P.M., stations ran serials in 15-minute segments for children, sponsored by corporations that sold kids' products.

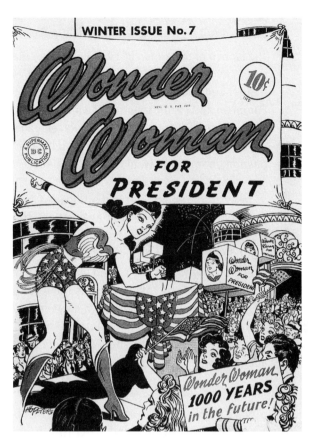

A Wonder Woman cover promoting "Wonder Woman for President—Wonder Woman 1000 years in the future!" H. G. Peters, 1943. Prints & Photographs Division, Library of Congress.

The comic book explosion represented by the introduction of Superman led the entire industry to new heights. In 1942, *Business Week* estimated that comics drew revenues of $15 million annually. Batman debuted in 1939, allowing the company DC Comics to cash in on another superhero. Fawcett Publications introduced Captain Marvel in 1940, shouting "SHAZAM" and turning the mild-mannered Billy Batson into "the World's Mightiest Mortal." Within several years, Captain Marvel outsold Superman. Only a DC Comics lawsuit for copyright infringement against Fawcett could stop Captain Marvel. After fighting the lawsuit throughout the 1940s and early 1950s, Fawcett stopped publishing the comic. *Wonder Woman,* a DC comic book also beginning publication in the 1940s, was unusual for promoting a female superhero.

DARNA: FILIPINA SUPERHERO

The launch of Superman in 1938 led to the creation of a swarm of comic-book superhero variants: Captain Marvel, Batman, Green Lantern, Wonder Woman, and more. World War II brought the superhero to a wider audience as American soldiers carried these cheap, portable, diverting adventure tales into the European and Pacific theaters of war.

One eager new reader was Mars Ravelo, a Filipino artist. Inspired by Superman and Captain Marvel, Ravelo created "Darna," a Filipina heroine with otherworldly powers who became an enduring national phenomenon. Darna would star in six decades' worth of comics, a dozen feature films, several television series, and even a ballet.

In 1947, the Philippines had just gained independence from the United States after decades of American colonial dominance. The new nation, still struggling to recover from the war's devastation, was also grasping to establish its own cultural identity. Ravelo's superheroine (originally named "Varga") defended the weak and the dispossessed with her powers of flight, super-strength, super-speed, and indestructibility. Dressed in a red bikini with matching boots, her long black hair streaming from beneath a wing-adorned red cap, Darna was the forceful and compassionate defender of the weak, a role that Ravelo wished for his country as a player on the world stage. Her human alter-ego, a young girl named Narda, was as meek and powerless as Ravelo felt the nation was at the time, and she always remained a humble rural girl, loyal to her Pinoy roots and true to her peace-loving values. Ravelo and Darna's later adaptors were careful to emphasize the qualities that tied the character to local culture and mythology.

The Nazi peril overseas and American anxiety about entering the war led to comic book heroes taking up the fight. Captain America debuted in 1941. Creators Joe Simon and Jack Kirby claimed that they created the character because the era called for a super patriot. His costume featured red stripes and a large white star across his chest, a virtual embodiment of the American flag. Others attempted the same, with one company even turning Uncle Sam into a superhero, complete with chiseled abs and bulging biceps. Shield, Minute-Man, USA, Major Victory, Daredevil, The Eagle, and other comic book heroes rose to fight Hitler during the war.

The sales figures in the 1940s were unprecedented. In 1944, for example, DC Comics published 19 titles accounting for combined sales exceeding 8.5 million copies. Fawcett reported sales of 4.5 million a year later for its eight comic books. *Captain Marvel* alone brought in $936,000 a year, or $78,000 an issue.

Entertainment

The performing arts in the 1940s were profoundly affected by the war, and the shifts only accelerated in postwar years. In addition to the continuing popularity of various dances, such as the swing dance and the Rhumba, modern dance was becoming more popular. Radio dominated American life during the decade, but by decade's end, its supremacy was being challenged by an upstart medium that would become the most culturally pervasive phenomenon of the twentieth century: television. What's more, the Hollywood film industry continued to control not just America's movie screens, but the world's as well. By the end of the decade the structure of the Hollywood studio system, some 40 years in the making, was beginning to crumble.

DANCE

Social or pleasure dancing was very popular throughout the 1940s. In the 1930s, swing dancing rose in popularity as the big bands became more and more influenced by swing jazz. Swing dancing, which included couple dances such as Jive, Jitterbug, Lindy Hop, Push, Whip, Shag, East Coast Swing, West Coast Swing, remained popular throughout the 1940s.

Especially popular in the 1940s were the Jitterbug, square dancing, and Latin dances such the Rhumba, Conga, and Samba. The popularity of the Rhumba was spurred by the Latin-inflected music of Xavier Cugat and his orchestra and the 1935 movie *Rhumba*, which starred George Raft as a dancer who wins the heart of an heiress with his dancing.

The 1940s would prove to be important transitional years with regard to the directions of ballet and other forms of dance. In 1940, Richard Pleasant and Lucia Chase founded a new dance company, the Ballet Theatre, which would later be renamed the American Ballet Theatre. Previously, American ballet companies had been heavily influenced by the traditions of European ballet, presenting classic works featuring Russian dancers or dancers with Russian pseudonyms. Conversely, the Ballet Theatre focused on American themes (although it did feature classical ballets), and its non-Russian dancers declined adopting Russian names. The company's repertoire was among the most varied in the world, and its tours packed houses across the nation. Anton Dolin, Antony Tudor, and Eugene Loring were its principal choreographers, but other troupe members contributed as well. Two of the most successful choreographers to do so were Agnes de Mille (1905–1993) and Jerome Robbins (1918–1998). De Mille was a dancer who performed around the world until 1940, when she began creating ballets based on American themes. Her first, *Rodeo* (1942, music by Aaron Copland), was adapted by the company, and its success led to ballets such as *Fall River Legend* (1948). In 1943 she created and choreographed the dance sequences for the Broadway musical *Oklahoma!* This play was the first to actually integrate dancing into the plot resulting in dance playing a much larger role in musical plays and films.

Also emerging from the Ballet Theatre was Jerome Robbins, whose first ballet, *Fancy Free* (1944, score by Leonard Bernstein), was a smash hit. They adapted it for the Broadway stage as *On the Town*. Still later, the ballet was adapted for the movies by the legendary directing team of Gene Kelly and Stanley Donen; *On the Town* (1949), featuring Kelly, Frank Sinatra, and Ann Miller, is one of the all-time great Hollywood musicals. After leaving the Ballet Theatre in 1948, Robbins was involved with the New York City Ballet for most of the years between 1948 and 1990. Robbins also created for Broadway; he was the director and choreographer of some of the most financially successful and best-loved musicals ever, including *The King and I* (1951), *West Side Story* (1957), and *Fiddler on the Roof* (1964). Following de Mille's lead, Robbins's plays typically featured a seamless blend of acting, singing, and dancing.

Also rising to national import in the 1940s was George Balanchine (1904–1983), born Georgi Melitonovitch Balanchivadze in Saint Petersburg, Russia. In 1924, Balanchine fled to Paris, where he became the leading choreographer of Sergei Diaghilev's ballet company. After immigrating to America in 1933, Balanchine helped to found the School of American Ballet. In 1948, the school's dance troupe became the New York City Ballet (NYCB), which remains one of America's leading ballet companies. As the artistic director of the NYCB, Balanchine was one of the most important choreographers of the twentieth century, noted for his creativity and willingness to experiment.

By the start of the 1940s, modern dance, which was more free-flowing, interpretive, and abstract than ballet was, gained widespread critical acceptance. Among the most notable practitioners was Martha Graham (1894–1991), who produced some of her most important work in the 1940s,

with *Appalachian Spring* (1944) the centerpiece. She was a pioneer and leading practitioner of modern dance, a movement in which dancers used the exterior physical motions to convey their interior emotional landscape. As not all emotions were "pretty," Graham sometimes surprised her audiences with abrupt moves and unconventional poses. In the 1940s she turned to women—such as Emily Dickinson, the Brontës, and various women from Greek mythology—for inspiration in her dances, trying to interpret women's feelings through motion.

Like her counterparts in the ballet of the 1940s, Graham also produced a great number of works that featured American themes. While her dances were sometimes tragic, she also produced works of great joy; *Appalachian Spring* (music by Aaron Copland) was just such a work. *Appalachian Spring*, which opened at the Library of Congress in Washington, D.C., to rave reviews, centers on two young newlyweds living on the wide Pennsylvania frontier, thus alluding to the power of landscape and place in the American imagination. Graham's performance in the piece is legendary and Copland's score won the Pulitzer Prize. Graham's overall influence on postwar American dance cannot be overstated; she is considered the mother of modern dance.

DRAMA

The 1940s marked the beginning of what has been called Broadway's golden age, fueled in large part by the rise of Method acting, the plays of Arthur Miller and Tennessee Williams, and the glory years of Broadway musicals. And while World War II affected nearly every aspect of American life, the American theatre was one of the few areas in which the war did not exert a huge impact.

No discussion of drama in the 1940s, especially concerning Miller and Williams, would be complete without mention of method acting and the Actors Studio. For years stage actors had utilized exterior actions to portray interior emotions. But beginning in the early 1900s, world-renowned Russian theatre director Konstantin Stanislavski began teaching his actors to adhere to what he called "the Method," a Freudian-influenced style of acting. Stanislavski rejected the traditional acting style, instead encouraging his actors to try to literally become the characters they were playing. Through "emotional recall" actors found, in their own pasts, experiences similar to those of the characters they were playing, thus enabling them to play their roles as realistically as possible. Also important in the method was locating a script's subtext, the emotional internal story that occurs between the lines of dialogue. As a result, dialogue sometimes became secondary to performance, and method actors were occasionally criticized for mumbling rather than enunciating their lines.

The Actors Studio, which schooled actors in method acting, was founded in New York City in 1947. Some of the most important figures in American theatre (and cinema) of the late 1940s and the 1950s, including Elia Kazan, Marlon Brando, Karl Malden, Rod Steiger, and Montgomery Clift, were members. Kazan, an ardent proponent of the method, was perhaps the most influential stage director of the 1940s and 1950s. Beginning in 1942, when he directed Thornton Wilder's *The Skin of Our Teeth,* Kazan had a 20-year run of both theatre and film success, earning him a reputation as a "two-coast genius." In addition to winning the 1948 Oscar for Best Director for *Gentleman's Agreement,* Kazan directed the original Broadway runs of both Tennessee Williams's *A Streetcar Named Desire* (1947) and Arthur Miller's *Death of a Salesman* (1949), two of the best and most famous postwar American plays. In 1954, Kazan left the Actors Studio to further concentrate on film work and writing.

Arthur Miller (1915–2005), whose *Death of a Salesman* is perhaps the best-known postwar American play, was born in Manhattan, the son of German-Jewish American parents. After graduating from high school, Miller worked for a few years at an auto parts store to earn tuition money for college, before matriculating as a journalism major at the University of Michigan. At Michigan, Miller became aware of Marxism and began to write plays. After graduating he went to work writing radio plays for the Federal Theater Project. Although Miller's best-known works were in the immediate postwar period, it's important to remember that his artistic sensibilities, like those of Tennessee Williams, were shaped by the

Depression years of the 1930s. Both wrote plays whose characters face loss of dignity in a world that is no longer secure.

In 1944, Arthur Miller made his Broadway debut with *The Man Who Had All the Luck,* a critical and financial failure. Undeterred, Miller pressed on, writing *All My Sons,* which premiered in 1947. The play, set during World War II, centers on a son's resistance to his father's insistence on running his business as though the war isn't happening, selling faulty airplane cylinder heads without consideration for the pilots who would die because of them. The play did well, but Miller's next play, *Death of a Salesman,* would be his most notable achievement.

Produced in 1949, *Death of a Salesman* was an immediate smash, critically lauded and a huge earner at the box office. The theme at the heart of the play is the failure of the American Dream as defined by the rags-to-riches myth of Horatio Alger. Willy Loman, the salesman of the title, is an American everyman, selling his wares to support his family. But after many years of trying, Loman ultimately falls short, getting fired after failing repeatedly to meet his sales quotas. As the American postwar economy was just beginning to boom, fueling an unprecedented level of consumerist materialism, Loman's story was particularly relevant. What happens to those who buy into the Dream and then can't achieve its essential promise? Is their failure the fault of the Dream, which promises what for some will be unattainable, or the dreamers who stake their measure of success on a myth? Miller's masterpiece deals with these questions, drawing attention not to the great American successes, but to the uncounted millions who fall between the cracks even after doing everything the Dream says is necessary to succeed. After the success of *Death of a Salesman,* Miller would continue writing plays (including 1953's *The Crucible*), essays, and screenplays. He would achieve fame not only as an author but as a personality, especially on account of his being convicted of contempt of Congress in 1957 for refusing to name suspected communists (a conviction overturned by the Supreme Court a year later) and his short-lived but highly publicized marriage to screen legend Marilyn Monroe.

Entertainment

Tennessee Williams (1911–1983), a Southerner whose work forever changed the American theatre, also came into fame in the 1940s. Williams was born Thomas Lanier Williams in Columbus, Mississippi. Williams enrolled in college at the University of Missouri, where he studied for two years before dropping out. He worked for a time in a shoe factory, writing all the while. It was while working at the shoe factory that he had his first nervous breakdown. After his recovery, he went back to school, eventually graduating at the age of 27. Williams subsequently moved to New Orleans to concentrate on his writing. Upon arrival he changed his name to "Tennessee" (in later life he gave so many reasons why he changed it that it's hard to know for sure) and actively embraced his homosexuality. After some modest successes, Williams had his breakthrough in 1945 with *The Glass Menagerie,* which he called a "memory play," since it was told in hindsight. *Menagerie* is a loosely autobiographical play about Amanda Wingfield, her crippled daughter Laura, her writer-son Tom (upon whose memories the

tale is based), and a gentleman caller. The play was among his best and its financial success ensured him the opportunity to pursue his craft full time.

Williams went to Mexico to write his next play, which he planned to call *The Poker Night.* Williams envisioned a play revolving around a series of poker games that would feature an attractive working-class young man named Stanley Kowalski, modeled after the real-life Stanley Kowalski, Williams's co-worker and friend during his job at the shoe factory. At the same time, Williams was working on a character named Blanche DuBois, whom he envisioned as a younger version of Amanda Wingfield. Williams quickly realized the play was far more about Blanche than Stanley, and this realization produced *A Streetcar Named Desire,* for which Williams won his first Pulitzer Prize in 1947.

Set in New Orleans, *Streetcar* is the story of Blanche DuBois, a faded Southern belle who hangs on to a long-gone past that can never be recovered. After a series of difficulties, Blanche goes to New Orleans to live with her sister Stella and Stella's husband, Stanley Kowalski. Kowalski is everything Blanche, who envisions herself a member of the Southern aristocracy, despises: a brawling, Polish laborer who drinks beer, plays poker, and bowls. (It was his electrifying performance as Stanley that thrust Marlon Brando into the national spotlight.) When the tension between the two comes to a violent head, the results are catastrophic for Blanche. Williams's use of violence and frank depictions of sexuality in many forms revolutionized the American theatre and enabled the playwrights who followed him to tackle their subjects with previously unheard-of levels of realism. Indeed, the subtext in Williams's work was especially rich and has long resulted in Method actors relishing playing his characters.

After *Streetcar,* Williams continued to compose plays, including *The Rose Tattoo* (1950) and *Cat on a Hot Tin Roof* (1955), for which he won his second Pulitzer Prize. At the forefront of all Williams's plays was human loneliness and the search for happiness in its wake. While the circumstances of his characters' lives may have been extreme, there was nevertheless a sense of the universal in their experiences. And in the loneliest

Arthur Miller, circa 1940s. Courtesy of Photofest.

and most desperately searching of his characters, *Streetcar*'s Blanche DuBois, Williams created what is by far the best-known female character in American drama. In fact, it can be argued that after Vivien Leigh's Scarlet O'Hara (*Gone with the Wind,* 1939), Blanche DuBois, also played by Leigh, is the most recognizable female character in American film. (The film version of *Streetcar,* which came out in 1951, was directed by Kazan and starred Brando as Stanley opposite Leigh. Jessica Tandy, who played Blanche on the stage, was passed over because she was thought to lack Leigh's screen presence.)

Broadway musicals also flourished in the 1940s, although many of them are not well-known today. Much of this had to do with the fact that the heyday of the Broadway musical coincided with the heyday of the Hollywood musical. While many

A scene from the original Broadway production of Tennessee Williams's play *A Streetcar Named Desire,* 1947. The cast included Marlon Brando as Stanley Kowalski, Jessica Tandy as Blanche, and Kim Hunter as Stella. Courtesy of Photofest.

dramas were adapted from the stage to the screen during this time, just as many couldn't make the transition because of what studios rightly assumed would be problems with the censors. Throughout the 1940s and into the 1950s and beyond, Hollywood would adapt successful plays—including plays such as *Oklahoma, On the Town, Carousel, Annie Get Your Gun, Brigadoon,* and *South Pacific*—for the silver screen.

MUSICAL THEATER

The 1920s represented the first golden age of Broadway theatre, with dozens of shows opening at live theaters on a monthly basis. Producer Florenz Ziegfeld was one of the brightest figures in the genre, and his musical productions catapulted many of his stars to superstar status. Though the great depression contributed to reduced audiences for stage productions, some directors and writers produced works that were highly experimental and innovative. George and Ira Gershwin used musical theater as a vehicle for their songs which, after more than 70 years, still maintain their popular appeal. It was the 1943 production of *Oklahoma!* by the legendary composer/producer team of Richard Rogers and Oscar Hammerstein II that initiated a new age in musical theatre. The Broadway version ran continuously for years, making over 2,000 performances and inspiring a new generation of musicals. *Oklahoma!* achieved a more cohesive combination of story and music than any previous production, and other producers soon began imitating the formula. In addition, the transition to film promised record audiences, and musical films like *West Side Story* (1961) and *Guys and Dolls* (1955) were blockbuster hits, drawing thousands of viewers. Though interest declined during the 1960s, the genre endured and the rock musicals of the 1970s like *Hair* (1979) and *Grease* (1978) eventually gave way to modern musicals like *Moulin Rouge* (2001). While some trends eventually disappeared into obscurity, the musical film has maintained its appeal as both a unique and a highly adaptable form of entertainment, and continues to play an active role in American entertainment.

HOW OTHERS SEE US

American Musicals in London

The landmark Broadway musical *Oklahoma!* opened in London's West End in 1947, four years into the show's record-breaking American run. It proved to be just as much of a smash with British audiences, packing houses for 1,555 performances and whetting theater-goers' appetites for more American "book musicals," like *Annie Get Your Gun* (1946), *South Pacific* (1949), and *Call Me Madam* (1950).

Many English theater critics were not quite so welcoming toward these imported productions, however. The book musicals combined dramatic themes with musical numbers that were naturalistically integrated into the story. This was a major departure from European theater tradition, which reserved music and dance for light, artificial entertainments and kept dramas strictly music-free. Gaudy song-intrusions were frowned upon by England's theater purists.

Yet, as the brash young British critic Kenneth Tynan explained it in 1952, musical dramas (as well as dramatic musicals) might almost be expected from Americans, for whom "life appears almost as a department of choreography," and whose movements "are conducted to a filtered murmur of orchestral accompaniment." To Tynan, the sense of joyous abandon that pervaded the American productions authentically rooted them in their place of origin—making them more "realistic" than any staid drama and more alive than the fantasy musicals so prevalent on the English stage.

NOTABLE THEATER

Arsenic and Old Lace, 1941 (1,444 perfs.)

Angel Street, 1941 (1,295 perfs.)

Oklahoma!, 1943 (2,212 perfs.)

The Voice of the Turtle, 1943 (1,557 perfs.)

Harvey, 1944 (1,775 perfs.)

Carousel, 1945 (890 perfs.)

Annie Get Your Gun, 1946 (1,147 perfs.)

Born Yesterday, 1946 (1,642 perfs.)

A Streetcar Named Desire, 1947 (855 perfs.)

Mister Roberts, 1948 (1,157 perfs.)

Kiss Me, Kate, 1948 (1,077 perfs.)

Death of a Salesman, 1949 (742 perfs.)

South Pacific, 1949 (1,925 perfs.)

RADIO

Radio's apex was during the 1940s, when Americans relied on it for their entertainment as well as their information about World War II. Its advertising structure, which TV would initially copy, was typically single advertisers sponsoring whole shows. Furthermore, radio had established its programming: music, news, and entertainment shows. The fact that its infrastructure was firmly established, primarily by NBC and CBS and their many affiliates, resulted in local programming often being overshadowed by nationally syndicated shows. Americans listened to the radio for news and for entertainment from across the nation.

While radio was popular prior to the 1930s, the Great Depression ushered in its golden age. Programmers created new shows in genres such as detective mysteries, westerns, soap operas, dramas, comedies, and variety shows. Most shows were serialized so fans could follow the weekly adventures of their favorite characters on a long-term basis. For example, *The Lone Ranger* was on the air for 22 years and *The Jack Benny Program* enjoyed a remarkable 26-year run. By the 1940s, American radio shows were communally shared at the same time each week by millions of people.

Also contributing to radio's popularity was the widespread use of stars. In the 1930s, radio had been populated by many recognizable vaudevillians, who were now being displaced by the rise of radio. While vaudevillians, including the

Marx Brothers, Burns and Allen, Jack Benny, Fred Allen, and Paul Robeson, were quick to join radio's ranks, Hollywood movie stars were reluctant because they believed it would lessen their cinematic appeal. Nevertheless, radio ran movie reviews, and syndicated gossip columnists such as Louella Parsons and Walter Winchell often focused on Hollywood figures. Hollywood eventually realized that more exposure for its stars would result in increased revenues at the box office.

By the early 1940s, Hollywood actors, including luminaries such as Humphrey Bogart, Katharine Hepburn, Jimmy Stewart, James Cagney, and Clark Gable, routinely participated in radio re-enactments of their films. Eventually, this crossover appeal began to work both ways, with actors such as Richard Widmark, Agnes Moorehead, Art Carney, and Don Ameche, who got their starts in radio, crossing over to movies. As the lines between the two mediums slowly blurred, America became more infatuated with its stars.

During the 1940s, virtually all radio shows seemed dominated by the war. For example, the

sole purpose of shows such as *Millions for Defense* and *Treasury Star Parade* was the selling of government war bonds. Other official messages, ranging from the urgings to plant victory

Jack Benny, an exceedingly popular radio comedian in the 1930s and 1940s. Courtesy of Photofest.

RADIO DEBUTS OF THE 1940s

The Abbott and Costello Show (1940): comedy-variety program starring the comedic duo already famous for their "Who's On First?" routine.

The Great Gildersleeve (1941): situation comedy, one of the first spin-offs in broadcasting history, about Throckmorton P. Gildersleeve (a recurring character on the popular *Fibber McGee and Molly*) and his efforts to parent his orphaned niece and nephew.

The Life of Riley (1941): situation comedy focused on a blue-collar family's misadventures, remembered for its catchphrase: "What a revoltin' development!"

The Frank Sinatra Show (1943): musical variety broadcast, later known as *Songs by Sinatra,* featuring the popular crooner.

The Adventures of Ozzie and Harriet (1944): family situation comedy starring Ozzie and Harriet Nelson and, eventually, their two real-life sons.

The Roy Rogers Show (1944): dramatic sketches and music with a western theme, starring movie cowboy Roy Rogers.

Queen for a Day (1945): audience-participation show in which women told their hard-luck stories, with the one judged most worthy crowned "Queen for a Day" and awarded prizes.

The Betty Crocker Magazine of the Air (1947): food and cooking show that offered recipes, household tips, and fashion hints for homemakers.

You Bet Your Life (1947): absurdist quiz show hosted by big-screen funnyman Groucho Marx.

Our Miss Brooks (1948): situation comedy starring Eve Arden as a wisecracking high school English teacher.

Entertainment

gardens to reminders of the importance of keeping secrets and not spreading rumors, were also regularly broadcast over the airwaves. Likewise, radio shows incorporated war themes into their scripts. It became commonplace for characters in virtually every genre to discuss the importance of volunteering to help the cause in whatever way possible. Furthermore, America's enemies were frequently depicted on radio as purely evil in order to raise passions against them on the home front. As J. Fred MacDonald notes, a particularly interesting example of the integration of war themes in radio programming could be found in shows aimed at children:

[T]hroughout the war juvenile listeners were implored on these shows to fight the enemy by collecting scrap metal, used fats, tin, rubber, and newspapers; and by buying War Bonds, writing to servicemen once a month, and planting Victory gardens. Never had a war been so directly taken to American youngsters; never had a war been as total as radio made it. One of the most compelling examples of this attitude is found in the five-point pledge to fight waste that juvenile listeners to *Dick Tracy* swore in 1943:

I Pledge

1 to save water, gas, and electricity
2 to save fuel oil and coal
3 to save my clothes
4 to save Mom's furniture
5 to save my playthings

Compliance not only gave a child inner satisfaction, but by notifying the network of his pledge, a child had his or name announced on a Victory Honor Roll which—the program announcer assured listeners—was sure to be read by General Dwight D. Eisenhower when he received it at Allied Headquarters in North Africa.[1]

In addition to radio being America's dominant wartime entertainment medium, the rise of the broadcast journalist—who reported on breaking world events live instead of merely reading pre-written text—in the 1930s had unforeseen benefits to the American public in the 1940s, when news from around the world became more relevant to

Americans' daily lives. During World War II radio broadcasts originating from various war zones were routinely broadcast during prime-time listening hours. These live broadcasts of important social and political events played an integral role in America's predominant national attitude of unity as it entered World War II. Illustrative of radio's importance as America moved toward entering the war was September 3, 1939, which J. Fred MacDonald calls "the biggest news day in the history of radio": in a mere 18-hour span, listeners heard live the British and French declarations of war against Germany, King George VI and Prime Minister Neville Chamberlain address the British people, speeches by President Roosevelt and Canadian Prime Minister Mackenzie King, and reports concerning the torpedoing of a transatlantic liner.[2] Whereas most Americans had been largely uninformed when the United States entered World War I, because of radio and its broadcast journalists Americans were aware of the events that led up to the United States entering World War II.

Perhaps nowhere is the power of radio's influence over its listeners in the late 1930s and 1940s more evident than in the field of politics. While politicians the world over utilized the medium's power, in America it was President Franklin D. Roosevelt who utilized it best. Beginning in 1933, Roosevelt's live *Fireside Chats* kept the country informed. His famous quotes such as "the only thing we have to fear is fear itself" (from his first inauguration) and "a day that will live in infamy" (from his speech to Congress after Pearl Harbor) were broadcast live, making an immediate impression on millions of Americans.

Roosevelt's masterful use of radio as a means to both soothe the public's fears and sell his party's ideas was the first instance of an American president using mass communications technology. Other politicians, particularly Republicans, who vehemently disliked Roosevelt's social policies, began using radio to convey opposing political messages, but they were too late; Roosevelt, with his regular broadcast schedule, soothing tone, and proclivity for positive spin no matter what the situation, had already established himself as the undisputed political master of the medium.

After the war, radio shows were forced to return to the music, news, and escapist entertainment formats that had been so successful in the prewar years. However, in some cases social commentary appeared where it had previously been absent. Comedians such as Fred Allen and Henry Morgan regularly satirized American politics and society, while reality-based shows such as *Dragnet, Treasury Agent,* and *The Big Story* gave radio a more realistic edge than it had in the prewar years. Also enjoying newfound popularity were radio documentaries, featuring stories on everything from the Cold War to alcoholism, and talking head discussion shows such as *Meet the Press* and *Capitol Cloakroom.* Kids' shows also reflected a new social awareness, as evidenced by Superman's frequently fighting bigotry and intolerance and the appearance of a new crop of shows featuring ethnically diverse heroes such as the Cisco Kid, the Indian Brave, and the Latino Avenger. Also enjoying a brief renaissance in the late 1940s were quiz shows such as *Truth or Consequences* and *Stop the Music!* Despite these minor exceptions, radio still largely followed the structure it had established before the war. Soldiers returning home wanted change, but radio was slow to respond. Accordingly, listening levels began to drop after the war just as television was beginning to crop up in urban markets across America.[3]

TELEVISION

At the 1939 New York World's Fair the theme was simply, "The Future." At the Radio Corporation of America (RCA) Pavilion, President David Sarnoff, was on hand to unveil his company's electronic television, which he believed would someday have a place in every American home. He also announced that the National Broadcasting Company (NBC), at that time owned by RCA, would begin airing regularly scheduled broadcasting for two hours a night. It was monopolistic vertical integration at its finest: RCA made radios and televisions and NBC, its subsidiary, produced the programming. Having introduced the first modern radio station in 1926 and the first television station in 1940, Sarnoff has been called the father of American broadcasting. Sarnoff's confidence belied the fact that there were only about 4,000 televisions in homes in New York City, that the medium was far from perfect, that there was no standard for broadcast format, distribution, or funding, and that the country was on the precipice of war. All of these factors would contribute to TV's failure to catch on until the late 1940s. Even though television didn't take off until the 1950s, much of the groundwork that contributed to its ascendancy took place in this decade.

NOTABLE TELEVISION

Kukla, Fran, and Ollie (1947–1957)

Puppet Playhouse (The Howdy Doody Show) (1947–1960)

Break the Bank (1948–1957)

Candid Microphone (later renamed *Candid Camera*) 1948–1950 (and later versions)

Texaco Star Theater (The Milton Berle Show) (1948–1956)

The Toast of the Town (The Ed Sullivan Show) (1948–1971)

The Lone Ranger (1949–1957)

Twenty Questions (1949)

In addition to questions over bandwidth, there was fighting over what the standard number of lines of resolution should be. As was its practice, the Federal Communications Commission refused to grant authorization for commercial broadcasting until there was industry unanimity on broadcast standards. In 1940, the National Television System Committee (NTSC) was organized, made up of industry representatives. Their task was to come up with industry standards for all areas of broadcasting, including transmitter power, transmitter characteristics, and picture resolution. Furthermore, while the Columbia Broadcasting System (CBS) had a mechanical method of color broadcasting, for which it lobbied hard, the rest of the industry had invested heavily in hardware and infrastructure for electronic, black-and-white monochrome transmission. In early 1941, the industry settled its differences and agreed on monochromatic black-and-white television broadcast. The NTSC presented its findings to the FCC, which on April 30, 1941, approved the NTSC's proposals and authorized full commercial television to begin broadcasting on July 1, 1941.[4] Unfortunately, the industry's infighting cost it six years. Had it begun broadcasting in 1939, it's possible the industry would have grown during the war years. But in April 1942, all new radio and television production was banned so that communications technicians could contribute to the war effort. As radio already had its infrastructure in place, it remained America's dominant information, communication, and entertainment medium throughout the war. But in 1947, with America at peace and on the cusp of an unprecedented economic boom, TV began its long-anticipated rise, rapidly becoming America's dominant medium.

Also established in the 1940s was the distribution system that has come to be known as the network system. There were primarily three networks, NBC, CBS, and the American Broadcast System (ABC). The network system consisted of a parent company that funded and produced programs which it then licensed to local affiliated stations. As NBC and CBS were both established in radio long before the advent of TV, they had a distribution network advantage over ABC, which didn't come into being until 1943. NBC initially had two networks, the red and the blue. However, the FCC felt NBC was a monopoly and in 1943 ordered NBC to divest itself of one of its television networks. The less successful blue network was sold off to Lifesavers candy manufacturer Edward J. Noble for $8 million, who promptly changed its name to ABC.

In television's early years, there was also a fourth network, Allen B. DuMont's DuMont Network. In fact, aside from NBC, DuMont was the only network to regularly run programming during the war. Unfortunately, the postwar rush for television licenses caused the FCC to panic, instituting a ban on new TV station licenses in 1948. As DuMont had no radio base, the freeze crippled its growth. When the ban was lifted in 1952, the FCC decided that there could be no more than three stations in a market. Since ABC, NBC, and CBS already had networks of affiliates, the new stations enlisted with them rather than DuMont. Because they reached more people, advertisers flocked to the other three networks. By 1955, DuMont was forced to give up.

In the early 1940s, many entertainers considered television to be more of a novelty than a legitimate entertainment form. This belief was reinforced when those outside the industry saw that those who did work in TV—most of whom came from radio and vaudeville—were treated by management as secondary to the medium. Accordingly, while the bulk of early television entertainers worked for Sarnoff's NBC, he didn't treat them particularly well. Instead, he focused his energy on further developing the technology and business interests of RCA and NBC. Conversely, CBS's William S. Paley, Sarnoff's arch enemy, was not particularly interested in the technological side of the business. Instead, he loved the arts and had a knack for handling the big and often delicate egos of entertainers. While Sarnoff concentrated on his business, Paley concentrated on Sarnoff's talent pool, such as Jack Benny, Amos 'n Andy, Burns and Allen, Red Skelton, Edgar Bergen and Charlie McCarthy, and Frank Sinatra. By the late 1940s, as a result of Paley's machinations, CBS had assumed its mantel as "the Tiffany of broadcasting" and would dominate the ratings for the next 25 years.

Two of the first two big TV series that started in the 1940s were NBC's *The Howdy Doody Show*, originally called *Puppet Playhouse*, and *Texaco Star Theater*, hosted by Milton Berle, whose popularity led to his being dubbed "Mr. Television." For those Americans who had televisions in the late 1940s, Tuesdays meant Tuesday night with "Uncle Miltie." Much of the early programming, *The Jack Benny Show, The Lone Ranger*, and *The Life of Riley*, for example, came from successful radio shows that made the jump to TV, but TV would soon develop its own stars. By the end of the 1940s, TV's formats, such as soap operas, half-hour sitcoms, hour dramas, and games shows, were firmly established.

Prior to TV's assuming its still-familiar format, educators and reformers had high hopes for television, thinking it had the potential to be a revolutionary educational tool. However, since its introduction into American society, TV had proven itself capable of mesmerizing its audience, providing advertisers with an unprecedented means of effectively selling products. Most Americans, then, weren't interested in educational programming. If people didn't watch, advertisers didn't pay for airtime to sell their products, and there was no TV. Television executives, many of whom came from radio, followed the radio proven model: Single advertisers paid for whole shows, the most common of which were half-hour genre and variety shows. Advertising with short spots for single products, wouldn't become the norm until the early 1950s.

After World War II, television began a meteoric rise that wouldn't stop until it became the Western world's dominant medium. In 1946, only 7,000 TVs were sold, each costing over $500 apiece. In 1947, the World Series, a classic seven-game affair between the then Brooklyn Dodgers and the New York Yankees, was broadcast on television for the first time, in large part because Gillette paid $50,000 for the sponsorship rights.[5] In addition to featuring one of the more notable World Series in history, the telecast used several different cameras. All over the country people packed barrooms and storefront windows to watch the games. Also in 1947, Earle Muntz, a Los Angeles car salesman, grew interested in TVs. By taking apart RCA, DuMont, and Philco TV sets, mixing and matching parts from each of the makers, and then putting them back together, Muntz figured out how to make the cheapest possible TV set. The Muntz TV sold for $170 at $10 per inch—Muntz was the first to measure TVs corner-to-corner rather than by width.[6] The next year the number of televisions sold rose to 172,000. In 1950, more than five million sets were sold.

Early Television Shows

In 1947, when commercial television officially came into being, there were only 16 stations nationwide. By 1950 there would be 107.[7] Of all the early shows, among the most successful, influential, and rabidly watched were *The Howdy Doody Show* and *Milton Berle's Texaco Star Theater*.

The Howdy Doody Show debuted on NBC on December 27, 1947, and would run until September 24, 1960. Set in the fictional Doodyville, the show featured a colorful cast of characters led by Buffalo Bob Smith, a pioneer-clad man who took his name from his resemblance to Buffalo Bill. The cast also included the mute Clarabell the Clown (played by Bob Keeshan, who would go on to become Captain Kangaroo), Chief Thunderthud, Tim Tremble (Don Knotts, who played versions of the same character after that), and Phineas T. Bluster, who hated it when other people had fun. The show was well received, especially by parents who quickly realized that if they put their kids down in front of the TV while the show was on, they'd remain relatively quiet with their eyes glued to the screen.

The star of the show was Howdy Doody, a freckled boy puppet (voiced by Smith) with eyes that could roll, a flannel shirt, blue jeans, and a cowboy hat. Kids loved the irascible Howdy, and the show's catchphrase, "It's Howdy Doody Time!", is still part of the American lexicon. Perhaps the show's most important contribution to TV was its licensing Howdy for a fee. As Howdymania swept the country in 1948, NBC came up with the idea to give away free Howdy Doody buttons. Smith announced the promotion on-air and NBC had 5,000 buttons made to meet the anticipated demand. They received 100,000 requests for buttons. NBC informed sponsors of the furor and within a few months they sold advertising spots for the next year, including sponsorship by Colgate, M&M's, Wonder Bread, and Ovaltine. Doody himself was everywhere: dolls, wallpaper, sleeping bags, watches, and any number of toys. Even in its infancy, television's advertising potential was recognized en masse by Madison Avenue advertising execs.

Milton Berle's Texaco Star Theater debuted on NBC on June 8, 1948. Berle had been a vaudeville performer and had been trying unsuccessfully for years to break into radio. When Berle's show debuted, TV had no pattern on which to base a show, so everything Berle did seemed new, even if much of it had its roots in vaudeville stages. His show was a loose collection of jokes, improv, and sketch comedy bolstered by a group of regular characters. Berle became known as "Mr. Television" and is often credited with selling more TVs than anyone in history. Indeed, his popularity was unprecedented and has since been unequaled; it's estimated that as much as 80 percent of the people who owned TVs would watch his show each Tuesday night. Berle became the highest-paid entertainer in the world, and restaurants across the country changed their closed day from Monday to Tuesday so as not to compete with "Uncle Miltie." Berle even had success with Milton Berle Makeup Kits, a product inspired by his show. For $3.98 people could get a kit that had a duplicate of Berle's trademark red wig, whiskers, a mustache, different noses, false teeth, and an eye patch.

MOVIES

In the late 1930s and early 1940s, American cinema was in a state of flux; numerous problems faced the industry, including cries for censorship and a variety of legal actions designed to break up the studios' stranglehold on worldwide distribution. However, America's entering the war in 1941 delayed the changes coming to Hollywood, at least for a few years.

Perhaps the most important issue in Hollywood in the prewar years was the Justice Department's 1938 antitrust suit against the studio system, which had a monopoly over filmmaking, distribution, and exhibition in America and, to some extent, abroad. In the early years of American cinema, dozens of film companies struggled for a market share. After a series of bankruptcies and consolidations, five main studios emerged: Paramount, Warner Brothers, 20th Century Fox, Metro Goldwyn Mayer (MGM), and Radio Keith Orpheum (RKO). The companies worked to consolidate vertically, with each eventually controlling its own production facilities, distribution networks, and exhibition outlets. In their 1940s heyday, the five majors made the majority of all American films and owned 50 percent of America's theatre capacity. Their monopoly did not go unchallenged. It appeared as though a government antitrust suit against the studios would break up their monopoly; however, on October 29, 1940, a settlement was reached and a consent decree signed, placing limited restrictions on the industry. Although the Justice Department was not satisfied with the decree and was initially set to go further, America soon entered the war and the government needed Hollywood's help to produce various kinds of public service films, mili-

tary training films, documentaries and the like; thus were the studios allowed to operate largely unimpeded until after the war.

In 1940–1941, Hollywood continued the creative transformation it had begun in the late 1930s. Individual studios were still associated with genre films featuring name stars and churned out by contract directors: Warner Brothers made crime films, MGM made musicals, Universal made horror films, and so on. But the studio system was beginning to undergo changes; an emerging group of producer-directors were beginning to be identified for their own styles, which resulted in their becoming a marketable commodity. For example, *Mr. Deeds Goes to Town* (1936) and *You Can't Take It with You* (1938) weren't sold to the public as star-driven screwball comedies so much as "Frank Capra Films." Likewise, directors such as Preston Sturges and John Ford became well known for their skills and began to enjoy greater creative autonomy in the filmmaking process. Hollywood still relied heavily on house style and star-driven genre pictures, but the success of these early "auteurs" foreshadowed the drastic changes facing the Hollywood studios in the postwar years.

Perhaps no film or filmmaker was as illustrative of 1940s producer-directors' long-term effect on Hollywood as Orson Welles and his 1941 film *Citizen Kane,* which was a relative flop upon its release but has since been acknowledged as among the most influential films ever. After getting his start in the New York theatre and achieving widespread fame as the creative force behind the Mercury Theatre (whose 1938 Halloween night radio adaptation of H. G. Wells's *The War of the Worlds* caused nationwide panic among listeners who thought the newscast-style show they were hearing was real), Welles arrived in Hollywood in 1938 with no filmmaking experience. Despite his inexperience, his reputation earned him a contract with RKO, which allowed him unprecedented creative control.

After initially trying to adapt Joseph Conrad's *Heart of Darkness,* Welles contracted screenwriter Herman J. Mankiewicz to write a script for a biopic of newspaper magnate William Randolph Hearst, as famous for his wealth as for the power his newspapers allowed him to wield. Welles

DEPICTION OF THE ENEMY DURING WORLD WAR II: JAPANESE

During World War II, the U.S. government not only fought Japanese soldiers in the Pacific arena, but also initiated a war of ideas at home. The War Department enlisted the help of writers, artists, and film producers to create a staggering variety of propaganda. Tempered by prevailing prejudices and common misconceptions about Japanese culture, propaganda posters often showed Japanese people as subhuman and savage. Frequently, Japanese were shown with ape-like faces, jaundiced skin, and front teeth protruding over their lower lip. Pamphlets and propaganda literature sometimes described the Japanese as "monkey men" or "savages" whose culture had failed to evolve.

In 1945, director Frank Capra contributed to the propaganda campaign with the short film *Know Your Enemy: Japan.* Capra's film portrayed the Japanese as a dangerous enemy with an insatiable desire for global domination. Behind images of Japanese soldiers in training, the narrative describes the Japanese people as brainwashed to follow orders from a young age. Though Capra's film occasionally expressed appreciation for the efficiency of Japanese culture, prejudice and racism colored much of the narrative, describing the Japanese, in one instance, as racially homogenous with each individual seeming as alike as "photographic prints off the same negative."

made extensive changes to Mankiewicz's script before beginning production. Welles then enlisted the help of cinematographer Gregg Toland, who had been experimenting with different camera techniques while shooting for John Ford. *Citizen Kane* starts with a mock newsreel, *News on the March,* which chronicles the recently deceased Charles Foster Kane's (played by Welles) life, ending with his last word, "Rosebud." The remainder of the film involves a series of flashbacks framed under the guise of a reporter asking Kane's former friends and family if they know what "Rosebud" means. The film's structure was new to the movies; it had multiple narratives, a technique in which individual characters recounted different versions of similar events, revolutionized the way cinematic stories could be told.

Released in 1941, Welles's masterpiece was well received critically but established studio directors bristled at the success of the "boy genius" and his open disdain for the conventions of Hollywood filmmaking. While *Kane* was nominated for nine Oscars, John Ford's *How Green Was My Valley* won the major awards. Welles never again approached the creative innovation of *Citizen Kane* (though *The Magnificent Ambersons* [1942] and *Touch of Evil* [1958] were masterpieces in their own right), but he did have the last laugh: *Citizen Kane* is widely regarded as the most influential film ever made.

When the war started, American filmmaking experienced a decided shift in content, from goal-oriented individuals and love stories to individuals yielding to the collective good (of nation, combat unit, etc.). Likely the film that started it all was Michael Curtiz's *Casablanca* (1942). In it Rick Blaine (Humphrey Bogart) is the expatriate American owner of Rick's Café Américain, a man whose mantra is "I stick my neck out for nobody" (echoing the sentiments of American isolationists). Over the course of the film, however, he learns the importance of working with others and of personal sacrifice for the greater good of humanity.

Hollywood studios were happy to work with the government to promote the war effort; their output was monitored, but their business methods weren't. Although Hollywood willingly complied with the government's request that they make propagandistic feature films, as well as newsreels, documentaries, and informational films, they were still asked to submit their products to the government's Office of War Information (OWI) for review. In the 1930s the studios had created the Production Code Administration (PCA) to review films' content as a means of avoiding government-legislated controls. President Roosevelt's June 1942 executive order creating the OWI resulted in films having to go through not one but *two* review processes before being approved for release. The formulas for virtually all film genres, from musicals to westerns to animated shorts, changed to positively reflect America's involvement in the war both abroad and at home,

Still considered one of the best film dramas ever made, *Casablanca* (1942) was directed by Michael Curtiz and starred Humphrey Bogart and Ingrid Bergman. Courtesy of Photofest.

resulting in many seemingly disparate films, falling under the general rubric of "war films."

Two genres specific to the wartime atmosphere were the World War II combat film and the woman's picture (also known as "weepies"). They enjoyed great success during the war years. These two types of movies targeted different audiences, but together they captured most of the viewing audience. The appeal of the combat film was obvious; Americans could watch reenactments of famous battles in which "our boys" performed heroically in their quest to help save the world. While these films were usually based on real events, some depictions were more fictionalized than others; virtually all of them were given a pro-American/Allies spin. Nearly all of the combat films used the wartime formula of a group of men working together as one to meet a common goal from which all would benefit. However, as the war dragged on, people, especially returning soldiers, grew disgruntled with the romanticization of the war in the early World War II combat films. Accordingly, later films were more realistic

and some even focused on individuals in turmoil instead of the group. Among the more notable of the many combat films were *Bataan* (1943), *Destination Tokyo* (1943), *Guadalcanal Diary* (1944), *Sahara* (1944), *A Walk in the Sun* (1945), and *The Story of G. I. Joe* (1945).

The need for films targeted at women was made evident in the early years of the war when a sizable demographic of the movie-going audience, young men, were leaving to fight in the war. In addition, for the first time women were entering the workforce en masse, thus earning their own money to spend. Hollywood quickly realized that if it targeted films specifically at women it could reach a large and heretofore untapped market. The studios made films that were both amenable to PCA and OWI censors and appealing to women by creating a series of home front dramas, which chronicled the lives of women doing their part for the war effort at home. While these films were generally saccharine, several, such as *Tender Comrade* (1943) and *Since You Went Away* (1944) were huge box office successes.

TOP ACTORS

Bud Abbott, 1895–1974, and Lou Costello, 1906–1959

Gene Autry, 1907–1998

Lauren Bacall, 1924–

Ingrid Bergman, 1915–1982

Humphrey Bogart, 1899–1957

Gary Cooper, 1901–1961

Joan Crawford, 1908–1977

Bing Crosby, 1903–1977

Bette Davis, 1908–1989

Henry Fonda, 1905–1982

Clark Gable, 1901–1960

Judy Garland, 1922–1969

Betty Grable, 1916–1973

Cary Grant, 1904–1986

Katharine Hepburn, 1907–2003

Bob Hope, 1903–2003

Laurence Olivier, 1907–1989

Gregory Peck, 1916–2003

Mickey Rooney, 1920–

Rosalind Russell, 1911–1976

James Stewart, 1908–1997

Spencer Tracy, 1900–1967

Lana Turner, 1921–1995

John Wayne, 1907–1979

ACADEMY AWARD WINNERS

Year of release, not year of award.

1940 Picture: *Rebecca*

Director: John Ford, *The Grapes of Wrath*
Actor: James Stewart, *The Philadelphia Story*
Actress: Ginger Rogers, *Kitty Foyle*

1941 Picture: *How Green Was My Valley*

Director: John Ford, *How Green Was My Valley*
Actor: Gary Cooper, *Sergeant York*
Actress: Joan Fontaine, *Suspicion*

1942 Picture: *Mrs. Miniver*

Director: William Wyler, *Mrs. Miniver*
Actor: James Cagney, *Yankee Doodle Dandy*
Actress: Greer Garson, *Mrs. Miniver*

1943 Picture: *Casablanca*

Director: Michael Curtiz, *Casablanca*
Actor: Paul Lukas, *Watch on the Rhine*
Actress: Jennifer Jones, *The Song of Bernadette*

1944 Picture: *Going My Way*

Director: Leo McCarey, *Going My Way*
Actor: Bing Crosby, *Going My Way*
Actress: Ingrid Bergman, *Gaslight*

1945 Picture: *The Lost Weekend*

Director: Billy Wilder, *The Lost Weekend*
Actor: Ray Milland, *The Lost Weekend*
Actress: Joan Crawford, *Mildred Pierce*

1946 Picture: *The Best Years of Our Lives*

Director: William Wyler, *The Best Years of Our Lives*
Actor: Fredric March, *The Best Years of Our Lives*
Actress: Olivia de Havilland, *To Each His Own*

1947 Picture: *Gentleman's Agreement*

Director: Elia Kazan, *Gentleman's Agreement*
Actor: Ronald Colman, *A Double Life*
Actress: Loretta Young, *The Farmer's Daughter*

1948 Picture: *Hamlet*

Director: John Huston, *The Treasure of the Sierra Madre*
Actor: Laurence Olivier, *Hamlet*
Actress: Jane Wyman, *Johnny Belinda*

1949 Picture: *All the King's Men*

Director: Joseph L. Mankiewicz, *A Letter to Three Wives*
Actor: Broderick Crawford, *All the King's Men*
Actress: Olivia de Havilland, *The Heiress*

NOTABLE MOVIES

Excluding Best Picture winners.

Fantasia (1940)*

The Grapes of Wrath (1940)

The Great Dictator (1940)

The Philadelphia Story (1940)

Pinocchio (1940)*

Citizen Kane (1941)

The Maltese Falcon (1941)

Bambi (1942)*

Yankee Doodle Dandy (1942)

Double Indemnity (1944)

Gaslight (1944)

Meet Me in St. Louis (1944)

National Velvet (1944)

Thirty Seconds Over Tokyo (1944)

Mildred Pierce (1945)

Spellbound (1945)

The Big Sleep (1946)

It's a Wonderful Life (1946)

Notorious (1946)

Miracle on 34th Street (1947)

The Road to Rio (1947)

The Treasure of the Sierra Madre (1948)

The Third Man (1949)

*Denotes animated feature.

Released during the war in 1944, *Meet Me in St. Louis,* starring Judy Garland, was a romantic and charming musical, set during the 1904 World's Fair in St. Louis. The movie is still popular with audiences 60 years later. Prints & Photographs Division, Library of Congress.

By 1945–1946, only 2 of the 36 top-grossing films were war-related, as opposed to 13 of 24 in 1942–1943. Americans were growing tired of the inundation with all things war-related.[8] Nevertheless, at the end of the war, American cinema was booming. America's was the only major national cinema still intact; American G.I.'s returned home with money burning holes in their pockets, and the economy was entering what would be the largest sustained period of growth and prosperity in American history to that time. Indeed, in 1946 American cinema enjoyed its greatest finan-cial year to date, with an astounding 100 million people per week—nearly two-thirds of America's population—going to the movies. Yet despite all the reasons for optimism, dark days were on the horizon.

Immediately after the war's conclusion, Hollywood was hit with two major blows: an eight-month studio union strike and the Justice Department's renewal of its antitrust suit against the studios. The union strike came at a time when domestic inflation was skyrocketing and the British, Hollywood's primary overseas market, had just levied a 75 percent tax on all foreign film profits. Furthermore, wartime price controls ended, which resulted in the price of film stock jumping dramatically. By the time the strike ended, the studios' overhead had risen dramatically. Compounding the situation was the Supreme Court's 1948 resolution of the Justice Department's antitrust suit, which was known as the "Paramount decree" (Paramount having been the most sought-after target); as a result of the Court ruling in favor of the Justice Department, Paramount Pictures was ordered to divest itself of its theatres by December 31, 1948, thus destroying the studio's vertically integrated business model and effectively marking the beginning of the end of the studio system in Hollywood.

The studios quickly cut back, limiting their output and reducing their production budgets by as much as half. Large-scale costume dramas, big-budget musicals, and sprawling epics quickly ceased being made at their prewar levels. Adding insult to injury was the fact that the formulas upon which Hollywood had relied on for years were, in the aftermath of 1946, not doing the business they once did.

In an effort to meet the changing persona and attitudes of its immediate postwar audience, Hollywood sought to make more realistic, socially relevant films. Traditional genres such as westerns underwent makeovers, emerging as more adult fare in such films as *Duel in the Sun* (1946) and *Red River* (1948). These "adult" westerns concentrated on the psychological and moral conflicts of the hero and his relationship to society. New types of films also began to be made. Of these new variations of films, perhaps film noir and social problem or "message" pictures were the most notable to emerge in the postwar 1940s.

In 1940, John Ford made one of the best message pictures ever, his adaptation of John Steinbeck's novel *The Grapes of Wrath*. However, America shortly entered the war, which brought production of films highlighting problems in American society to a grinding halt. But after the war, dissatisfaction with what some saw as the failed promise of an American dream led to the vogue of social problem pictures. Although problem pictures dealt with important issues such as racism and addiction, they frequently did so in a Hollywood manner, that is, societal error was recognized and dealt with in such a way that the protagonist lived happily ever after. Films such as *The Lost Weekend* (1945), a film about an alcoholic on a bender; *Gentleman's Agreement* (1947), a movie about unspoken but institutionalized anti-Semitism; and *Pinky* (1949), the tale of a black girl light enough to pass as white, all won critical accolades and enjoyed public success.

Dissatisfaction with American life also fueled the rise of film noir; but whereas problem pictures addressed social problems head on, the film noir was much more cynical and desperate (film noir literally means "black film"). Film noir was not so much a genre as a type of film; for example, crime films, police procedurals, and detective pictures could all be film noirs. Noir films, many of which were based on the hard-boiled fiction of writers like James M. Cain, Raymond Chandler, and Dashiell Hammett, had a particular feel to them that resulted in a stylized visual aesthetic combined with a nihilistic worldview reflective of America's postwar pessimism. They highlighted the dark underbelly of American society. Their sharp-tongued characters, often anti-heroes, lived on the fringes of society either by choice, circumstance, or both. They were normally set in contemporary urban settings, often started in medias res (in the middle of the action), and featured a voice-over that gave background but rarely gave away plot. Cinematically, they were shot in black and white to create shadows and weird angles to illustrate a world out of kilter. The darkest noirs focused on themes of obsession and alienation. Perhaps the one unifying theme pervasive in film noir was the idea that all of us, given the right circumstances and opportunities, are capable of terrible deeds. These films negated the human spirit. The best noirs from the 1940s and early 1950s, films such as *Double Indemnity* (1944), *Murder, My Sweet* (1945), *The Big Sleep* (1946), *The Postman Always Rings Twice* (1946), and *Sunset Boulevard* (1950), rank not only as among the best films of the 1940s, but among the finest American films ever made.

While in many ways the late 1940s were an incredibly fecund period in American cinema, the new developments happened against the backdrop of House Un-American Activities Committee (HUAC) hearings investigating possible Communist influences in Hollywood. The careers of a wide variety of Hollywood players were destroyed by people who fingered others to avoid persecution themselves. Even though a few of those accused had dabbled in Communist politics, the fact was that there was ultimately no conspiracy to infiltrate Hollywood with red propaganda. Lives were thus ruined by hearsay.

HUAC continued to have hearings on and off until the early 1950s, and Hollywood filmmaking took a decidedly conservative turn. By the end of the 1940s, the problem pictures and noirs that had proliferated just a short time earlier were being made with less and less frequency.

Fashion

of the 1940s

The greatest impact on American fashion in the early 1940s came from the U.S. government, which enacted various rationing measures that greatly curtailed stylistic innovation during the war, even while wartime rationing was much more severe in European countries. On March 8, 1942, the U.S. Government War Production Board enacted Regulation L-85, which regulated all aspects of clothing and also inhibited the use of natural fibers. Wool became scarce, silk hard to get and expensive, and rubber was unavailable for civilian use. The lack of traditional materials led to increased research toward the production of synthetics, which, with the exception of rayon, didn't really help civilians because they were diverted to military use.

Clothes were made simpler, from a shortening of sleeves and hemlines, to a reduction of the number of pockets and buttons, all to conserve fabric and other materials. For example, skirt hems couldn't be more than two inches, and there couldn't be ruffles. Skirts became somewhat boxy and hemlines rose to the knee. Belts couldn't be more than two inches wide, suit jackets were limited to no more than 25 inches in length, and pants couldn't be more than 19 inches in circumference at the hem (narrow for the time). Furthermore, clothes had to be bought and paid for with rationed coupons. For example, in 1941 a man's overcoat went for 16 coupons, a pair of pants went for 8, and shoes cost 7.[1] Despite the restrictions, American designers proved to be highly adept at working with what they had and getting around restrictions in a variety of ways.

WOMEN'S FASHIONS

Most people responded to rationing with a combination of creativity and innovation that permanently changed American fashion. One reaction was to make one's own clothes, which was becoming easier thanks to the newly created electric sewing machines, which could crank out 3,000 stitches per minute. Regulation L-85 cut civilians' supplies of wool almost in half to outfit the American military.[2] To get around the scarcity of wool, suits were made from gabardine, and women refashioned men's suits, which were often made of wool, into clothes they could wear. McCall's made patterns for transforming men's suits into ladies' suits. Ready-to-wear dressmakers soon followed, putting out "man-tailored" women's suits with narrow skirts and wide shoulders. Also contributing to the boxy look were women's blouses, with bigger, more squared shoulder pads, a style that has become forever associated with the 1940s.

Widespread acceptance of women in pants came about very quickly as women regularly started wearing slacks, or even coveralls, to work. The look was not just fashion but necessity, especially for the millions of women working in heavy industry and embodied by the image of "Rosie the Riveter." (See Advertising of the 1940s.)

While women's clothes were often fashioned after men's styles, there was still the desire for more traditionally feminine clothes. For those who had the opportunity and could afford to go out in the evening, long dresses were still the norm. Evening dresses were often adorned with sequins, which were not rationed and offered a simple way to sparkle.[3] For daytime color, women increasingly turned to dresses imported from Mexico, which were cheap, simple, and very colorful. American designers quickly incorporated Mexican and other colorful ethnic styles into their lines. Colorful plaids and Tartans were also

From the "Fashion Academy Awards," in 1941, the "Best Dressed Woman in Business" was Vivien Kellems, from the Cable-Grip manufacturer, 1941. Kellems wears the square-shouldered tailored suit typical of the era. Prints & Photographs Division, Library of Congress.

FASHION TRENDS OF THE 1940s

War rationing led to simple, functional clothing. After the war, clothes used more fabric, and were more colorful and casual.

Women: Slim skirts just below the knee; suits, shorts and trousers acceptable; clean lines; hair was longer; pageboys were popular early in the decade; more swept up, then loose waves after the war; nylons were hugely popular; Christian Dior introduced what became the "New Look" in 1947—more feminine with a focus on curves, no shoulder pads, and cinched at the waist.

Men: Zoot suits for some; military uniforms and suits for others.

Teenage girls: Ankle socks and circle-cut skirts.

immensely popular. Rayon—synthetic and not rationed—was the most common material used in dresses. Sweaters, especially cardigans, enjoyed tremendous popularity in the early 1940s, in part because of Jane Russell and Lana Turner. The well-endowed Russell had appeared in *The Outlaw* (1946) in a Howard Hughes-designed bra that greatly—and for the time quite scandalously—lifted her bosom, and Turner favored tight sweaters that emphasized her curves; the two became known as "Sweater Girls," as did the women who emulated their sweater-clad look.

Women's Accessories

Hats in all styles and shapes, from pillbox hats to turbans, were popular in the 1940s. Rationing led to experimenting with hat decorations. A woman could radically change the look of a hat with a ribbon, a veil, or feathers. Women's hair underneath their hats was typically shoulder length or slightly longer and curled or rolled. Although Lauren Bacall popularized the long bob, Rita Hayworth was known for her long, wavy, flaming red hair. The most famous hair of the 1940s arguably belonged to Veronica Lake. Lake became popular not so much for her acting as for her hairstyle, which inspired a craze in the 1940s. In a 1941 film entitled *I Wanted Wings,* Lake sported a hairstyle that would inspire a fad that lasted until the late 1940s, at which time Lake's career began to wane. Her

Veronica Lake is shown when she was the "peek-a-boo look" movie star in the 1940s. Courtesy of Photofest.

signature hairstyle was a long page boy, in which the hair fell over one side of Lake's face, usually causing one of her eyes to be covered. After the war, women's hairstyles shortened somewhat.

Because steel and leather (traditional materials in shoes) were both rationed, soles were commonly made of cork or early plastics. Many shoes, especially the popular "wedgies," were big and more unwieldy than by today's standards. Leather gloves gave way to cotton as the rationing of leather kept it from being used for gloves. Women soon discovered that cotton gloves, because they could be had in virtually any color, made accessorizing much easier.

Women's undergarments underwent a fair amount of change in the 1940s. Slips and panties began to be tighter and more form fitting. Bras changed dramatically. The strapless bra evolved into the "merry widow" style, thus giving women much more support when wearing strapless and/ or backless dresses. For women with larger busts, the first wired full-figured bras were produced, and by the late 1940s the first bullet bras—which

were cut to lift and shape breasts to make them look pointy—began to appear. While underwear had traditionally been made of silk, lack of supplies and exorbitant costs during the war led to its being made out of rayon, acetate, or cotton instead. Lastly, underwear began to be more decorative; previously plain garments started to feature laces and trims.

Men's Fashions

In general, the outbreak of World War II caused a pause in innovation in men's fashions. For the elite, this put an end to the practice of wearing different clothes at different times of the day. Much of this had to do with fabric shortages and the fact that many men enlisted in the military. In the past, military uniforms had differed according to the rank of the wearer. But in World War II the military made its uniforms more similar, regardless of rank of person wearing the uniform. Part of this was due to fabric shortages, but it was also prudent because enemies were less likely to shoot officers if they couldn't tell who was who based on the appearance of the uniforms.

The end of the war brought about a minor revolution in men's fashion: men were tired of uniforms and wanted to wear their own things. Suits began to feature long coats and full-cut slacks in part as a reaction to rationing: Long, full-cut clothing symbolized success. Suits could be bought in a spectrum of garish colors. By 1949, *Esquire* had begun to promote these louder, more loosely fitting clothes as part of the new "bold look." Also, wildly patterned and hand-painted ties became all the rage, featuring anything from rodeos and plants to pin-up girls and skyscrapers. Most shocking to those used to the previously staid and dignified look of the well-dressed American man was the rise of the casual shirt. Hawaiian shirts, featuring loud, highly colorful prints and specifically designed *not* to be tucked in, had earlier made their way to the beaches of California and Florida, but in the immediate postwar years they began to catch on nationwide. Men began to walk around without jackets and untucked shirttails. This casual look, dubbed by some as "the new sportswear," caught the eyes of European designers, who for the first time began looking to

Fashion

America for inspiration for their sportswear lines. The main men's hairstyles were either crew cuts or longish on top and neatly shorn on the sides. Men frequently wore wide-brimmed hats.

Many men also adapted military garb into their peacetime wardrobes. Ray Ban's Aviator glasses, chinos, T-shirts, trench coats, pea coats, and bomber jackets all made the jump to everyday life. In particular, Humphrey Bogart became associated with the trench coat, which he wore in a number of films, none more famously than *Casablanca* (1942). Bogart was Hollywood's leading symbol of masculine cool and his being identified with trench coats went a long way toward popularizing them. The trench coat has since become a standard item in any well-dressed man's wardrobe.[4]

Teen Fashion and the Bobby Soxers

Fashion

During the war American fashion for teenagers was subdued, in large part because of the rationing of various materials. Girls wore plain sweaters and skirts and loafers and socks, with the occasional scarf for flourish, while boys wore cuffed pants, shirts with open necks, and jackets with broad lapels. Like their adult counterparts, girls' hair was either medium or shoulder length, while boys' hair was often long on top and cropped close on the sides or in a crew cut. However, just as the end of the war and rationing changed fashion for adults, so did it change for youths, especially teenage girls. While boys continued to wear slacks and open-collared shirts, they increasingly began wearing blue jeans and white T-shirts, which had originated in the navy. For girls, the end of the war meant greater accessibility to different styles made of a wider variety of fabrics. However, in conjunction with the rise of the American ready-to-wear look that came into prominence during the war, when American women had no access to what was happening in the Paris fashion houses, teenage girls dressed increasingly comfortably, a style that came to be defined as the "American Look."

Instead of elegant evening wear and chic suits and dresses, American girls wore casual clothes: sweaters, plaid skirts with pleats, and tailored jackets, and for really casual occasions, jeans rolled up to the knees. As *Life* magazine saw it in 1945, the American Look included a slim waist, long legs, and a friendly smile revealing well-cared-for white teeth. The American girl was healthy and well-nourished; she bathed often, her nails were well manicured, her posture was excellent. She had a natural poise and enthusiasm that did not require or enjoy constricting artificial clothes. She enjoyed athletics more than evenings at expensive restaurants. Above all, she was young, white, and upper middle class.

In addition to the advent of the American Look, in the late 1940s a subculture called "bobby soxers," made up primarily of 15-to-18-year-old girls, arose in America. The bobby soxers got their name from the bobby socks that they normally wore with loafers or saddle shoes. The bobby soxers were generally thought to represent youthful exuberance, as evidenced in the 1947 film *The Bachelor and the Bobby Soxer,* in which a teenage Shirley Temple falls hard for the much older Cary Grant, who ends up with the more age-appropriate Myrna Loy, Temple's older sister in the film. Despite being considered wholesome, bobby soxers nevertheless enjoyed a certain notoriety in the popular imagination, partly as a result of the incidents that occurred at a series of Frank Sinatra concerts in New York in October 1944. The girls' over-the-top, carnal reaction to Sinatra, which included responses ranging from fainting and crying to ripping his clothes off his body and trying to sneak into his bedroom, was considered dangerous, an omen of the loosening morality of this younger generation.

AMERICAN-MADE READY-TO-WEAR

Prior to the war, Europe, specifically France, led the way in international "couture" fashion, which signified high style, upscale, and very expensive clothes. American magazines such as *Vogue* and *Harper's Bazaar* fastidiously chronicled French high fashion for American sophisticates. Information about fashion wasn't easily accessible during the war, resulting in the end of France's dominance of American high fashion. At first the glossy fashion magazines speculated about the death of high fashion, but they soon realized that fashion was not only surviving, but thriving in the United States. New York became the new international fashion center.

For years American fashions had been predominantly based on Parisian fashion trends, but the war forced American designers to create clothes on their own. What immediately separated their work from the French was the stress on functional practicality over romantic frivolity. In addition, the sheer variety of clothes available in American shops was astounding to Europeans; in London a woman would be lucky to find 10 different sizes, while in America many stores carried more than 30.

For the first time in the nation's history, American designers were beginning to be known by name. The efforts of New York-based publicist Eleanor Lambert and others, including fashion writers Lois Long of the *New Yorker* and Virginia Pope of the *New York Times* and fashion editors of *Vogue, Harper's Bazaar,* and *Life,* helped ensure the acceptance of American designers by both the fashion world elite and the general public.

American designers came from a variety of places and backgrounds, but one of the most interesting places from which they came was Hollywood. Restrictions imposed by Regulation L-85 resulted in Hollywood moving away from opulent costume dramas to more realistic costumes, thus making film more true to life. Hollywood designers set an example for the mainstream, making do with having to modify preexisting costumes.[5] Some costume designers left Hollywood and started their own collections, including Adrian (born Adrian Adolph Greenberg), Howard Greer, and Irene (born Irene Lentz).

A number of stateside couturiers enjoyed tremendous success in the 1940s, including Norman Norell, Pauline Trigére, Mainbocher, Ceil Chapman, and Hattie Carnegie. But the most influential American designer during the 1940s was ready-to-wear designer Claire McCardell. McCardell trained at New York's prestigious Parsons School of Design and worked under Richard Turk at Townley Frocks and then for Hattie Carnegie, before returning to Townley Frocks in 1940 to design under her own name. McCardell had radically new ideas about clothes, particularly sportswear. Clothes had traditionally been sold as complete ensembles, thus assuring easy shopping

Carmen Miranda in full "Tutti Frutti" style, ca. 1940. Courtesy of Photofest.

and coordinated outfits. But McCardell designed separate items of clothing—"separates"—that could be mixed and matched however a consumer chose. Initially, stores thought separates were hard to display and sell, but McCardell's idea proved so popular that it wasn't a problem.

McCardell's more notable contribution was making clothes for the average woman, not the wealthy. She felt it essential that her clothes be affordable, practical, and feminine. For example, she designed evening clothes that came with matching aprons, thus acknowledging the reality that most women did their own cooking. McCardell also

Fashion

CARMEN MIRANDA AND HER TUTTI-FRUTTI WAYS

Among the number of Hollywood actors who influenced American fashion in the 1940s was Carmen Miranda (1909–1955). Born Maria do Carmo Miranda da Cunha, she became best known for the fruit she wore on her head and elsewhere on her body. The Brazilian bombshell started as a singer and appeared in a number of Brazilian movies before getting her break in America, a stint at New York City's Waldorf-Astoria Hotel. Shortly thereafter, she appeared in a series of musical films, including *Down Argentine Way* (1940), *That Night in Rio* (1941), and *Weekend in Havana* (1941). In each of these films she wore plastic fruit, especially on her head: bananas, raspberries, cherries, and strawberries. Miranda had a reputation as an exotic, sexy, sultry Latina, and her garb inspired a craze that became known as "tutti-frutti." This fad consisted of artificial fruit, some pieces worn as earrings, bracelets or hats and other pieces used in home décor. Tutti-frutti was a fad until well after World War II, and Carmen Miranda herself remained a much-loved entertainer until her death, which occurred the morning after she performed on the *Jimmy Durante Show* on TV in 1955.

For more information see Andrew Marum and Frank Parise, *Follies and Foibles: A View of 20th Century Fads* (New York: Facts on File, 1984), 70–72.

took rationing in stride, seeing it as an impetus for innovation. When zippers were rationed she began using brass tabs and hooks instead. In response to restrictions on wool and silk, she began to incorporate denim, cotton, and jersey into her designs. While she never made tight, form-fitting clothes, her designs predated Christian Dior's "New Look" in that the shoulders of her clothes were soft and rounded. Her clothes also broke with the norm in that she left metal fastenings exposed and highlighted her trademark double seaming with contrasting colored thread. McCardell's most successful design was her "popover" dress, which came out in 1942. *Harper's Bazaar* had requested an all-purpose housework outfit. McCardell responded with the popover, made of topstitched denim and featuring a wraparound

front and an attached oven mitt. In 1942 the dress retailed for $6.95 and sold in the tens of thousands.[6] Ultimately, Claire McCardell's functional, comfortable, and well-made clothes proved to be influential in the 1940s rise of uniquely American style clothing.

CHRISTIAN DIOR'S NEW LOOK

By 1947, France had recovered enough from the war to respond to the upstart fashions of America. In February, Christian Dior, who had gotten his start selling fashion sketches to newspapers, came out with his first collection, which he called the "Corolle line." Whereas American fashions were all lines and angles, Dior's new designs featured curves, and lots of them. Dior's designs featured elastic corsets worn over a shaping girdle to cinch waists, push-up bras, and various forms of padding around the hips. Shoulder pads went by the wayside as shoulders in clothes sloped. Hemlines, which because of rationing had hovered around the knee, dropped to the mid-calf or even to the ankles. Dior's Corelle line was so revolutionary, and in many quarters so desired, that it was quickly dubbed the New Look, the name by which it is still known.

For many women, Dior's ultra-feminine, luxurious look was a welcome change from the severe fashions of the war years. However, women had grown accustomed to showing their legs, and many of them didn't want to cover them up. Furthermore, for a country just coming out of several years of fabric rationing, the New Look seemed needlessly wasteful. Many women protested, but the uproar was short lived. Women were more than ready for a different look, and Dior's New Look was embraced in the late 1940s and into the 1950s. Dior's New Look is widely considered the most influential fashion collection ever created, and Dior constantly continued to modify the look, issuing new lines every year until his death in 1957.

By the end of the decade, American fashion magazines, in large part because of the rise of Dior's New Look, had returned to covering French and other European couturiers at length. While France regained its place as the seat of international fashion, the war years gave Americans and the rest

A fashion model wears a New Look dress introduced in Paris by Christian Dior in 1947. AP Photo.

of the world the chance to see that American designers could innovate and create in their own right. After the war, stateside glossies covered Europe, but they *also* covered American styles and designers, as did European magazines. Most important was the fact that the line between ready-to-wear clothes a person could buy off the rack (or from a catalogue) at Sears and the clothes of the couturiers began to blur somewhat. Clothes made by Americans for Americans could be well made, mass produced, *and* stylish.

ZOOT SUITS AND THE ZOOT SUIT RIOTS

While most people adhered to certain styles that made them part of the mainstream, there were people participating in subcultures beyond the norm. One of the ways these subcultures were recognized was by their dress. For example, in the late 1940s a group that would later become known as "Beatniks" came into being. Influenced by jazz, existentialism, and avant-garde ideas, the Beatniks wore workmen's clothes, berets, and

goatees and tried to live an intellectual existence. Their forerunners (and to some extent their main influence and inspiration) were the hipsters, the largely African American innovators of bebop jazz. (See Music of the 1940s.)

But the most visible and controversial subculture of the 1940s was the "zoot suits." The origin of the word "zoot" as applied to suits is unknown, although it's thought to have come out of the urban culture associated with the clubs of New York City's Harlem in the mid-1930s. The zoot suit's jacket was long and single-breasted, with extra-wide shoulders and lapels and numerous buttons on the sleeve. This exaggerated jacket was worn over loose, pleated, and high-waisted trousers that tapered to the ankle. A watch on a chain worn hanging from the jacket and a wide-brimmed hat completed the outfit. The brightly colored, easily identifiable zoot suits were favored by some jazz musicians (including Dizzy Gillespie and Louis Armstrong), urban African Americans (primarily in New York City), and Los Angeles's primarily Mexican/Latino population. To some extent, general men's fashions of the late 1940s owed something to the zoot suit in that men's suit jackets became more roomy and their pants more high-waisted. Unfortunately, the zoot suit, seemingly innocuous, led directly to the Zoot Suit Riots in June 1943.

Critics found the zoot suits' ostentatious use of fabric as a deliberate disregarding of wartime fabric rationing and identified their wearers as draft dodgers. The fact that their wearers were mostly young African and Mexican American men, groups traditionally subjected to ethnic stereotyping, only exacerbated matters. Many people concluded that all "zoot suiters" were criminals and draft dodgers. At the same time, zoot suiters came to see their clothes as a social statement pertaining to their ethnicity and defiance of white authority. In California, nationalism ran high, and the ethnic communities must have felt under siege. In March and April 1942, the majority of the Japanese (nationals) and Japanese American population on the West Coast was rounded up and put in internment camps. In Los Angeles, with Japanese people removed, the Mexican American population repeatedly found itself featured in an unflattering light in local newspapers. The press, much of which centered on a "Mexican crime wave," was so negative and the white public's demand for action so high that a special grand jury was appointed to investigate the "problem."

On August 1, 1942, a zoot suiter named Henry Leyvas and some of his friends got into an altercation with another group of Latinos. The next morning a man named José Diaz was found bleeding on a nearby road. He died from his wounds, but an autopsy revealed that he was drunk at the time. A medical examiner posited that his injuries were consistent with being hit by a car. Despite this, Henry Leyvas and 24 other members of his gang were arrested and charged with José Diaz's murder. The public outcry against zoot suiters led Los Angeles police to respond. On the nights of August 10 and 11, they arrested some 600 individuals (all of whom had Spanish surnames) on charges ranging from suspicion of robbery to assault. The ensuing trial of Leyvas and his fellow detainees lasted five racially charged months. Finally, on January 15, 1943, Leyvas and eight other men were found guilty of second-degree murder. Each received a sentence of five years to life and was sent to California's infamous San Quentin prison.[7]

The Zoot Suit Riots occurred during this contentious, racially charged time. On June 3, 1943, a group of sailors on shore leave claimed they had been attacked by a group of Mexicans. In response, an estimated 200 sailors descended on Los Angeles's Mexican American community, picking out zoot suiters, beating and stripping them of their clothes. This went on for five nights, with each night bringing out more sailors and eventually soldiers who joined the fray. The police arrested primarily Latinos, and in the press the military men were said to be stemming the tide of a "Mexican crime wave." Finally, at midnight on June 7, the military command, fearing a mutiny, took the action the police wouldn't: they declared the city of Los Angeles off limits to military personnel. Some Mexican Americans faced charges, but no military man was ever convicted of anything. While there was a limited amount of protest, for the most part the silence surrounding the incident sent a deafening message to California's Mexican American community. Some historians refer to the incident as the "Sailor Riots,"

which they say is a more accurate description than "Zoot Suit Riots." Nevertheless, the zoot suit will undeservedly be linked forever in history to this ugly event.

NYLON: THE KING OF SYNTHETIC FABRICS

Although synthetic fibers had been around for a long time, it wasn't until the war and forced rationing that the importance of synthetics began to be realized. With Regulation L-85 prohibiting the use of natural fibers, synthetic fibers became essential, especially in the making of women's clothes, which were widely manufactured with rayon.

Though nylon hosiery was announced in 1938, it didn't become available to the public until May 15, 1940, a day designated by marketers as "N" (for nylon) Day. DuPont had whetted the public's appetite over the months preceding "N" Day with an advertising blitz that culminated the night before, when DuPont bought a segment on the national radio show *Cavalcade of America*. In a rigged set-up, DuPont selected a "typical" housewife to ask Dr. G. P. Hoff, Director of Research for DuPont's Nylon Division, a series of questions about the magic of nylon. Predictably, Dr. Hoff had dazzling things to say about nylon. The next morning, thousands of women nationwide started lining up hours before stores opened to get their hands on a pair of nylons. Even though customers were limited to one pair each, many women had their kids and husbands or boyfriends stand in line to buy additional pairs for them. The nation's 750,000-pair supply sold out on the first day.[8]

Initially, nylons were priced the same as silk stockings, but by 1942 things had swung heavily in favor of nylons, when they sold for anywhere from $1.25 to as much as $2.50 a pair, while silk languished at around $1.00. The success of nylons had great psychological ramifications concerning the nation's psyche. Prior to the arrival of nylon, people had been wary of synthetics, but nylon changed all that. In large part because DuPont ingeniously marketed nylon as a kind of magical product, people accepted it, and it quickly began to be used for other items, including lingerie and men's socks and ties. Women's hosiery has since become known as "nylons," stockings made from nylon fibers woven together to provide an extremely lightweight, elastic, comparatively durable and shape-forming fit.

Unfortunately for the general public, nylon was such a useful product that the War Production Board designated nylon as a product that they would take over for the military's use during the war. Beginning on February 11, 1942, all of DuPont's nylon went to the U.S. Military. The material proved useful for all purposes and was used for parachutes (which had previously used silk), tire casings, shoelaces, ropes, and even bomber noses. Women patriotically parted with their nylons, 4,000 pairs of which were needed to make two bomber tires. In 1943 alone, women turned in 7,443,160 pairs of nylon and silk stockings.[9] Betty Grable, the possessor of the most famous pair of legs in America (due to the popularity of her famous pin-up), sold a single pair of her stockings at a war bond auction for $40,000!

During the war, nylons became, for those more worried about appearances than supporting the war effort, a black market commodity, selling for as much as $12 a pair. Most women did without, although all kinds of things were tried to make naked legs look as though they were encased in nylon. Women tried various dyes to color their legs and even resorted to drawing lines up the backs of their legs to make it look as if seams were there. When Japan surrendered on August 22, 1945, DuPont immediately announced that nylons would be available to the public again in September. But DuPont had technical difficulties and had also greatly underestimated public demand for its product that when the time came it didn't even come close to meeting the demand. A crush of customers appeared at department stores nationwide every day, resulting in what was dubbed "nylon riots." They lasted for at least a year.[10] In the years after the war, nylon's use expanded to include the whole gamut of clothes and even things like curtains, carpets, and upholstery. Additionally, the number of synthetic fibers quickly multiplied with the creation of fibers such as orlon, lycra, metallic, modacrylic, and olefin. Though none of these created a stir, Americans readily accepted new synthetic fibers since nylon had already paved the way. There's no doubt synthetic fibers would have eventually become a part of everyday life, but it's unlikely that its acceptance would have happened so completely and so quickly had the war not intervened in the early years of its production.

Fashion

Food

of the 1940s

As with most other areas of American culture in the 1940s, American eating habits were greatly affected by World War II. Prior to the war, malnutrition was a major concern in America, with various reports estimating that as many as one-third of all Americans were underfed and undernourished. The advent of war effectively ended the Depression as employment rates skyrocketed. But American eating habits and customs, long tied to regional and ethnic roots, became irrevocably affected by the changes brought by war.

The war changed America demographically. Southern blacks and farmers were suffering as a result of the Depression and the end of the South's long dependence on an agricultural economy based on small individual farms. As displaced rural Americans flooded into urban areas to take jobs in the seemingly endless number of industries supporting the war effort, farming (food especially) was overtaken by massive agribusinesses. As a result, when the war ended, few farmers and farm hands returned to farming. In addition, the geographical shifts of millions of Americans during the war moved the country toward a more homogeneous diet.

RECOMMENDED DAILY ALLOWANCES

By 1940 scientists had identified and characterized many of the essential nutrients people needed to live healthily. These efforts lay the groundwork for President Roosevelt's establishment of the Food and Nutrition Board (FNB) of the National Research Council (NRC) in 1940. In order to combat malnutrition, the president requested that the FNB devise a set of dietary standards that Americans could use as a guideline for health.

In 1943 the Board came out with a set of Recommended Daily Allowances (RDAs) that reflected scientific discoveries up to that time. The recommendations advised levels for human intake of various vitamins and minerals necessary to sustain health and vitality. They were broken down into what were called the seven basic groups: green and yellow vegetables; citrus fruits, tomatoes, and raw cabbage; potatoes, other vegetables, and noncitrus fruits; milk and milk products; meat, poultry, fish, eggs, dried legumes; bread, flour, cereals; and butter and fortified margarine.[1]

During the war, RDAs began to be listed on the labels of products so consumers could keep track of their daily intakes of various nutrients. Several products underwent changes because of the RDAs. For instance, bread became "enriched," with added calcium, iron, niacin, riboflavin, and thiamin. Likewise, margarine became enriched with vitamin A and milk with vitamin D. RDAs are still in effect in America and are periodically revised.

Despite the efforts of various government agencies, postwar studies revealed that many school-aged children were still undernourished. In 1946 the School Lunch Act was passed and programs were greatly expanded to accommodate the establishment of guidelines for school lunches to adhere to RDAs. In the 1940s, most people weren't concerned about the nutritional value of school lunches; they were just happy their kids were getting a chance to eat what they assumed were healthy meals; there were few, if any, concerns about caloric intake, fat or cholesterol.

The RDAs publicized during the war made people more aware of what and how much they ate, but there were unforeseen repercussions. Many Americans decided that if the recommended daily allowance was a good thing, then exceeding it would be even better. While this was true concerning fruits and vegetables, it became quite problematic when one thought of fats and cheeses. The percentage of calories made up of saturated fats began rising in the 1940s and has been climbing ever since.

WARTIME FOOD RATIONING

When America entered World War II in 1941, it was thought that the civilian population would have to willingly participate in food rationing in order for there to be enough food for soldiers at home and abroad. In January 1942, the government instituted mandatory rationing of anything deemed "essential" to the war effort, including food. Just as in World War I, sugar, fats, meats, and canned vegetables and fruits were rationed. Mottoes for the rationing effort in World War II included "Vitamins Will Win the War" and "Vitamins for Victory," fueled in part by numerous studies that deemed more than one-third of Americans as malnourished. Likewise, out of the first million draftees, 40 percent were rejected for service on medical grounds, many of which could be directly traced to insufficient nutrition.[2] To combat the problem, the rationing effort would not only encourage moderation in the consumption of certain foods and products, but also make Americans more aware of the necessity of consuming proper amounts of vitamins and minerals to ensure mental and physical health.

There was some controversy as to whether or not Americans were even undernourished, however. The relatively high standards of the seven basic food groups may have been a stretch for most people. The "allowances" part of the RDAs connoted a *maximum* allowable intake of something. If people routinely failed to meet the maximum allowances in any one of the seven categories, then they were deemed malnourished, even though they may have been getting enough of a particular category. The numbers of people malnourished in America were likely greatly exaggerated as a result of initially unrealistic RDAs.[3] Nevertheless, scientists fought to defend their findings, despite the fact that there weren't widespread, noticeably visible manifestations of malnutrition in most of American society.

The supposed existence of malnutrition was used as a means of championing the adding of certain vitamins and minerals to Americans' food, which ultimately resulted in things like thiamin being added to bread and vitamin D to milk. Furthermore, advertisers were brought on board by the government to encourage Americans to eat certain foods. But, rather than promoting the general nutrition requirements, the big food producers emphasized the importance of eating their products over others. The idea of the seven basic food groups was essentially avoided because if companies acknowledged their existence they indirectly promoted the consumption of products of other companies.

Also, rationing was not as happily participated in as is often thought in contemporary America. Many Americans *did* willingly and fully participate in the effort, but others turned to the country's thriving black market—dubbed "Mr. Black"—for goods and services. In other countries, particularly in European countries under siege, rationing was a more obvious and immediate necessity that often ended up bringing out the best in the human spirit. For example, the British rallied together and made do, sharing as best they could what comparatively meager food stocks they had. That era of sharing and unity is still widely thought of in Britain as one of its best moments.[4] Conversely, in America, where the threat of attack wasn't a reality in citizens' everyday lives, some were resentful that their food and countless other items were rationed.

Food

RATIONING POINTS AND STAMPS

As food rationing escalated in the early years of the war, it became increasingly complicated. Initially, people were given food stamps with which to purchase a certain allocation of a particular product. While the system worked moderately well, it was messy. Nationwide, grocers had to process 14 billion points a month, which meant that they physically handled 3.5 billion stamps on a monthly basis. By 1943 food had been divided into two categories: canned goods and fresh food. Stamps were given point values and were also color-coded, with red stamps usable for canned goods and blue stamps usable for fresh food. The more in demand a product was, the more points it cost.

Item	Weight	Point Value
Porterhouse Steak	1 lb.	12
Hamburger	1 lb.	7
Lamb Chops	1 lb.	9
Ham	1 lb.	7
Butter	1 lb.	16
Margarine	1 lb.	4
Canned Sardines	1 lb.	12
Canned Milk	1 lb.	1
American Cheddar Cheese	1 lb.	8
Dried Beef Slices	1 lb.	16
Peaches	16 oz. can	18
Carrots	16 oz. can	6
Pineapple Juice	46 oz. can	22
Baby Food	4.5 oz. jar	1
Frozen Fruit Juices	6 oz. can	1
Tomato Catsup	14 oz. bottle	15

Source: Time-Life Books, eds., *1940–1950,* vol. 5, *This Fabulous Century* (New York: Time-Life Books, 1969), 166.

Often, rationing unintentionally led to rushes on products, leading to shortages caused by people panicking. Examples of this occurred with products such as coffee, and even more so, meat.

Prior to 1943 meat wasn't rationed. Instead, a voluntary "Share the Meat" campaign was launched by the government. It was a failure: consumers stockpiled meats in freezers and a real shortage soon came into being. Consequently, when the new rationing standards came into effect in 1943, meat was added to the list.[5] Americans panicked and stockpiled meat even more. A black market flourished and legitimate sellers of meat had problems getting supplies, even though the average American still consumed the same two and a half pounds of meat per week. This was due in part to the exemption from ration stamps enjoyed by restaurants and workplace cafeterias and the fact that poultry products weren't subject to strict rationing. While the rest of the Western world, especially occupied Europe and Russia, legitimately suffered from a scarcity of *any* meat, let alone decent meat, Americans continued to eat quality meat.[6]

Just as the American public's diet suffered comparatively little, so, too, did America's armed services. By virtually any standard, the American military during World War II was the best-fed wartime army in history to that point. The populaces of other countries were amazed at how much food Americans had at their disposal, as were enemies who overran their positions or were taken prisoner. At the time, some suggested that the occurrence of food shortages was due perhaps to the relative luxury to which America's military was treated when it came to food. Indeed, the average American soldier typically consumed upwards of 5,000 calories a day, an astonishing number.[7] But when the war finally ended, Americans insisted that rationing end as well, which led to the elimination of the Lend-Lease program (see Overview of the 1940s) in spite of war-ravaged Europe's suffering and need for help.

VICTORY GARDENS

One positive result of food rationing was the reinstitution of wartime victory gardens, which had first appeared in World War I. To make up for lack of fresh vegetables, in December 1941, Claude R. Wickard, secretary of agriculture, encouraged people to plant their own gardens, which were known as "victory gardens."[8] Even though fresh vegetables weren't rationed, for whatever reason, the growing of victory gardens was probably the most successful home front program during the war. People planted gardens everywhere—in backyards, vacant lots, and local parks. Americans were also encouraged to do their own preserving, which was almost as impressively successful as the campaign to plant victory gardens. At the height of the war, 75 percent of American families produced a phenomenal average of 165 jars of preserves a year.[9] As a result, when Americans were asked what they missed most during wartime, they didn't cite fruits or vegetables; instead, they often cited butter, meat, and sugar. Still, because of meat rationing and the popularity of victory gardens, during the war the consumption of eggs, milk products, and fresh fruits and vegetables rose precipitously. In 1945, Americans' per capita intake of vegetables hit its all-time high.[10]

PROCESSED FOODS

Americans may have had more money to spend on food, but they were working long hours and had far less time to cook. Instead, Americans went out to eat much more than they had in the past, but on occasions when they chose to stay home, they increasingly turned to eating processed, prepackaged foods. These were foods sold by the same giant American food companies commissioned by the government to devise quick and easy food for soldiers to eat. As a result of efforts to process food for distribution to soldiers oversees and on the frontlines, more and more food underwent some degree of processing prior to consumption. Unprecedented levels of research and production led to massive innovation in food processing. For instance, in 1941 M&M's Plain Chocolate Candies debuted in six colors: brown, green, orange, red, yellow, and violet; that year also, Cheerios cereal was first sold. In 1942, La Choy introduced canned Chinese food. In 1946, Minute Maid came out with frozen orange juice concentrate and Maxwell House with instant coffee, alongside Ragú spaghetti sauce and French's instant mashed potatoes. In 1948, the processed food trend continued when Cheetos, Nestlé's Quik, and V8 Juice all emerged in the marketplace. By 1949, both General Mills and Pillsbury had started selling instant cake mixes. Ice cream, cheese and yogurt consumption rose as their production became large scale.[11] By the end of the decade, frozen and canned foods were being consumed in ever-increasing amounts,

often at the cost of the fresh food and vegetable intake that had been at an all-time high during the war years.

FROZEN FOOD

Frozen foods existed before the 1940s, but they weren't particularly popular because while most Americans had iceboxes, they didn't keep frozen foods cold enough, causing them to turn soggy and mushy. The war changed the role of frozen foods in American life. First, refrigerators improved in the early 1940s, and more and more families, enjoying the wartime boom, could afford to buy them. Second, rationing played a role in the rise of frozen foods. Because the metal used to make cans was rationed, canned foods became scarcer. Consequently, more Americans began freezing their own food, growing more accustomed to frozen edibles in the process. Frozen food manufacturers talked the government into declaring frozen food products essential to the war effort. Lastly, with a quarter of American housewives working for the war effort, the convenience of frozen foods, especially frozen dinners, was welcome. By the end of the war, Americans were accustomed to frozen foods.

MODERNIZED KITCHENS

An increase in the number of supermarkets and labor-saving devices invented for the kitchen dramatically reduced the time cooks had to spend shopping and in the kitchen. By 1940, spacious countertop kitchens began to be standard in homes, which meant that all parts of food preparation could be done on the same continuous surface. Electric blenders, carving knives, and mixers began to be much more common, as did electric can openers, coffee grinders, and garbage disposals. KitchenAid introduced dishwashers in 1949. Most people had electric refrigerators, which meant food could be stored longer. Tupperware was introduced in 1946, and Reynolds Wrap aluminum foil followed the next year. Stores themselves were also becoming less individualized. For example, in the 1940s, markets began selling both mass-produced, precut and prepackaged meats wrapped in cellophane and bread mass-produced

FOOD HIGHLIGHTS OF THE 1940s

1941 In Anaheim, California, Carl Karcher and his wife borrow $311 to buy a hot dog cart and take in $14.75 on their first day in the fast-food business. Within five years, Karcher further trades on Los Angeles's booming car culture when he opens Carl's Drive-In Barbecue and starts selling hamburgers. (At the time of Karcher's death in 2008, more than 3,000 Carl's Jr. restaurants and associated food establishments are operating in 43 states and 14 countries.)

1941 M&M'S Chocolate Candies are introduced and soon become a favorite among American G.I.'s.

1941 General Mills launches Cheerioats cold cereal, which four years later is renamed Cheerios.

1942 Daniel Carasso, who in 1919 founded a yogurt company called *Danone* ("Little Daniel," in honor of his son) in Spain, founds America's first yogurt company. He changes the name from Danone to Dannon, to make it friendlier to American ears.

1942 Lay's Potato Chips are first sold under that name. (Before that, beginning in 1932, H. W. Lay had sold them under the Barrett Food Products brand.)

1945 A patent is filed for the process of cooking food with microwaves.

1949 The first Pillsbury Bakeoff, called the "Grand National Recipe and Baking Contest," is staged at the Waldorf Astoria Hotel in New York City. Theodora Smafield beats out 99 other finalists with her innovative "No Knead Water-Rising Twists" and pockets the $50,000 first prize. The contest becomes an annual event that continues to this day.

by corporate bakeries. Instead of going to the bakery, the butcher and the market, shoppers could just go to the new "super" markets to get everything they needed. By the end of the 1940s, however, the kitchen began to be usurped in overall usage by the family room, which routinely housed the TV.

FAST FOOD

Perhaps the single most far-reaching development in food in the 1940s was the advent of the American fast-food industry. In the early days, fast-food restaurants were welcomed exactly for what "fast food" implied: places where people could get a meal cheaply and quickly. In 1940, two now-ubiquitous fast-food chains, Dairy Queen and McDonald's, opened their doors for the first time.

Dairy Queen

In the late 1930s, the Homemade Ice Cream Company of Green River, Illinois, began to make changes to its product that would help change the food industry dramatically. The father-and-son owners, J. F. and H. A. McCullough, made traditional ice cream that had a finished temperature of around 5 degrees, which made it hard. However, the men discovered that they liked the ice cream "soft," that is, just out of the mixer but prior to being frozen. The McCulloughs began to explore ways to sell this ice cream, served at about 20 degrees. The problem, they soon discovered, was finding a machine from which to dispense the ice cream because normally ice cream was kept in freezers. They came across a hamburger stand owner in Hammond, Indiana, named Harry M. Oltz, who had a machine that they thought could work. The McCulloughs obtained the rights to the machine and its use in Wisconsin, Illinois, and all states west of the Mississippi. Oltz received a percentage of the profits from ice cream sales, as well as rights in the rest of the states. The men settled on "Dairy Queen" as a name for the restaurant.[12]

The first Dairy Queen was opened in Joliet, Illinois, in 1940 by the McCulloughs' business partner, Sherb Noble, who owned a number of ice cream stores. A year later, the McCulloughs opened their own store in Moline, Illinois.[13] While other stores soon began to open, it was the look of the Moline store, specifically the ice-cream-cone-shaped sign mounted above it, that became the visual prototype for Dairy Queens in the years to come. In the late 1940s, the McCulloughs, clueless about the gold mine they were sitting on, became weary of the restaurant industry and decided to sell out. A salesman named Harry Axene, who in his travels had seen Dairy Queens popping up all over the Midwest, bought out the McCulloughs. Axene brought with him a better understanding of business and immediately began to actively franchise Dairy Queens, selling regional licenses ranging in size from single towns to whole states.[14] The number of Dairy Queens soared from 17 locations in 1947 to over 800 in 1950, and eventually to some 2,100 in 1952.[15] Soft-serve ice cream became a national favorite, and imitators sprang up all over the country. By 1956 there were approximately 12,000 soft-serve ice cream places in the United States. Virtually all of them also served burgers, but it was the soft-serve ice cream that made them unique.[16]

McDonald's

By the 1930s the automobile had become a permanent fixture everywhere in the American landscape, perhaps nowhere more than in southern California. To meet the needs of hungry drivers, a new phenomenon evolved: drive-in restaurants. Cars could pull into a roadside restaurant where they'd be met by a carhop—typically a short-skirt-clad young woman—who would take their orders and money and bring them their food. Eventually, carhops gave way first to two-way radio receivers through which customers could place orders and then to drive-through windows, which featured a single two-way radio and a window at which customers pay and pick up their orders. In 1940, brothers Richard and Maurice "Mac" McDonald opened the first McDonald's, a drive-in in San Bernardino, California. Business was slow at first, but by the mid-1940s the restaurant had caught on.[17]

Even so, they soon determined that the drive-in business wasn't being run efficiently. In 1948 they eliminated carhops and installed a drive-through. This had the twofold result of eliminating the carhops and their wages, in addition to the teenage crowd—often unjustly associated with criminality in the 1940s and 1950s—which came to the restaurant for the carhops as much as the food. In fact, in the late 1940s and early 1950s the McDonald brothers refused to hire women, whom they thought would attract teenage boys.[18] Eliminating carhops was only the beginning. While other restaurants sought to diversify their offerings, the McDonald brothers rigidly stuck to a simple menu: burgers, drinks, and fries. They

Customers line up outside the first McDonald's hamburger stand in San Bernadino, California, 1948. AP Photo.

Food

did for restaurant food production what Henry Ford did for the automobile; they introduced mass production to fast food. They got rid of anything that had to be eaten with a knife, fork, or a spoon. They introduced paper plates, cups, and bags. Burgers came with ketchup, onions, pickles, and mustard—and that's it. No substitutions. And, most important of all, they divided up the labor into simple singular tasks, just like the assembly lines traditionally associated with industry. They called their creation the "Speedee Service System." Afterward, their meals were cheap and fast and whole families could afford to go out to dinner.[19] Their business model caught the eye of other restaurant owners and by 1952 the pair owned eight McDonald's, all in California.

Changing Tastes in American Food

It was thought that because of the great number of Americans who spent time abroad and enjoyed foreign food during the war years, after the war American tastes would diversify. While many

HOW OTHERS SEE US

Brazil: Life during Wartime

The upheaval and displacement caused by World War II had curious ripple effects in far-flung corners of the world. Brazil was far from the immediate horrors of the fighting in Europe and the Pacific, but the war still had an impact on its people and culture.

Brazil's strategic geography, long and lightly defended coastline, and substantial German population made it an area of concern for American war planners who feared that northeastern Brazil would be a prime spot for a future Nazi invasion. When German U-boats began prowling the Atlantic, threatening Brazilian ports and shipping, the government of Brazil allowed several battalions of American troops to be stationed around the country. The soldiers helped to train Brazil's own forces and manned defensive garrisons.

As a creole society, Brazil was historically very accepting of outside influences and new ideas. States like Rio Grande do Norte in northeastern Brazil were especially prone to wartime "Americanization." Wherever the American troops were stationed, news accounts reported that hamburger stands had popped up, and Brazilians in the surrounding areas began to favor local variations of the jitterbug over their own dance style, the samba. Many young women struck up relationships with the newcomers, so much so that English-language classes boomed. (Since women far outnumbered men in this part of the country, this caused less tension than might have been supposed.) Some Brazilians even began to drink their coffee American-style, with cream and sugar—a significant change in this proud coffee-producing culture, where tiny cups of strong espresso had been the norm. While a Nazi invasion never happened in Brazil, an American one—cultural, at least—did.

Food

Americans were abroad during the war, the places in which they were stationed were often ravaged and its peoples were starving; because of this, most Americans ate the food provided to them by their employer (i.e., the military), so little diversification within the American diet occurred. Still, over the course of the decade, there was a change in attitude toward eating among those with the leisure and income to pursue culinary experimentation. *Gourmet* magazine, founded in 1941 by publisher Earl MacAusland, cultivated the idea of food as not just a necessity, but also an art, something that could and should be a sensually pleasurable experience.[20] In 1940, James Beard's first cookbook, *Hors d'Oeuvres and Canapés,* was published. It was the first book devoted entirely to cocktail food.[21] Beard, who eventually became known as the "Father of American Cooking," published a variety of books, and in 1946 he hosted the first American cooking show—*I Love to Eat,* which appeared on WNBC-TV.[22] Also in 1946, America's first bona fide cooking school opened

in New Haven, Connecticut. It would later change its name to the Culinary Institute of America and move to Hyde Park, New York, where it became America's preeminent cooking school.[23] By 1949, when Beard became the restaurant critic for *Gourmet,* there existed what could be called a gourmet movement in America, although it wouldn't take full root until the 1950s.

While regional diets persisted—such as Tex-Mex in the Southwest, Asian-influenced seafood and vegetable dishes in the Northwest, and Italian food in New York City—it was in the 1940s that the American diet moved toward a shared center. There were a variety of reasons for this, including the rise of canned foods, the revolutionary introduction of prepackaged and frozen foods, and perhaps most importantly, the eating habits of millions of Americans who served in the military. Despite their exposure to foods in foreign countries, they grew accustomed to the army's "square meals" of Midwestern, All-American cooking: roast beef, potatoes, and peas and carrots.

Music

of the 1940s

As the 1940s began, people were still dancing to the enormously popular sounds of the swing bands, including Benny Goodman, Duke Ellington, Glenn Miller's orchestras, and many other famous performers. But when America entered the war things began to change; wartime travel restrictions made it tough for big groups to travel freely. Furthermore, it became more difficult to make enough money to pay a dozen or more members. The popularity of the big bands began to slowly wane. In their place came the singers, many of whom had earlier been singers with big bands. Over the course of the decade, swing played by giant bands slowly evolved into bop jazz and cool jazz, often played by smaller combos. Country music broke big nationally, and the blues began to come into its own.

YOUR HIT PARADE

On April 20, 1935, the radio program *Your Hit Parade* debuted on CBS radio. The Saturday night show was sponsored by Lucky Strike cigarettes and would run nearly continuously for 24 years, the last ten being on TV, from 1950–1959. The show played in reverse order the top songs of the week, basing the order on a combination of airplay, record and sheet music sales, and jukebox traffic. How exactly the songs were chosen

remains somewhat of a mystery. Price, Waterhouse, and Company tallied the selections and each Friday would deliver, via a Brinks armored truck, the list of that week's selections to the show's producers. While the choices were typically fairly obvious, the goal was to build hype and suspense around the songs of a given week. People across the nation tuned in on Saturday nights to find out what songs would top that week's charts. Over the years, the show featured from 7 to 15 songs, although 10 was the standard. The top three songs would each be introduced by a drum roll and a sonorous introduction by the announcer, with the final song being introduced as the "top song in the country, number 1 on your Lucky Strike hit parade." The show enjoyed huge popularity, especially in the 1940s, during which it served as a barometer for American tastes.

TECHNOLOGY AND BUSINESS

In the 1940s technology would change the nature of how music was recorded and how Americans bought and listened to records. Records prior to 1948 were 78 rpm's, which meant that a record had to turn 78 times a minute on a turntable to sound right. Hence, records required fairly big grooves, and this, in turn, meant that very few songs could fit on a single album. On June 21, 1948,

CBS unveiled the 33⅓ rpm microgroove record, which allowed 23 minutes of music to be recorded on one side. The tighter grooves also made the record (typically a 10- or 12-inch platter) more physically durable and less likely to break; even better, the tighter-grooved records sounded superior to their predecessors. To hear them people simply had to buy a cheap adapter and fit it onto the existing turntables of their record players. The move to 33⅓ rpm brought into being the idea of a "record" as a single disc on which an artist could record a series of songs as a movement rather than just single tunes. Likewise, many classical music pieces could fit in their entirety on a single record, as could the music from Broadway shows. For example, whereas before the original cast recording of *Oklahoma!* required six 10-inch 78 rpm records, it now fit on a single 33⅓. A further innovation was the 45 rpm seven-inch disc, on which approximately four minutes of music could fit on each side, an "A" side and a "B" side.[1]

Previously, records were much larger, but the switch to microgroove recordings meant that people could store more music in far less space. The comparative convenience of the newer records, in combination with the rise in "disposable" income in the middle class of the postwar era resulted in a marked rise in record sales. In 1946, twice as many records were sold as in 1945. For the rest of the decade, Americans bought approximately 10 million records a month.

In 1945, *Billboard*, a record industry trade journal, began publishing its "Honor Roll of Hits." As record sales began to move to new heights, record sales began to acquire much greater importance in the gauging of a song's success. Prior to the mid-1940s, songs were usually introduced via Broadway or the movies, and they would then be put out on a record. But after the war, and especially once records moved to 33⅓ rpms, songs more frequently became popular via records. This shift was reflected in the nature of songs on *Your Hit Parade* from 1945 to 1949, many of which climbed their way to the top via records rather than from stage or screen. Perhaps the most famous of them all, Gene Autry's 1949 version of "Rudolph the Red-Nosed Reindeer" (Johnny Marks). Autry's "Rudolph" alone would go on

Music

WAR SONGS POPULAR DURING WORLD WAR II

"I'll Be Back in a Year Little Darling" (Red Foley, among other performers)—1940

"The Boogie Woogie Bugle Boy of Company B" (The Andrews Sisters)—1941

"The White Cliffs of Dover" (Vera Lynn, among other performers)—1941

"Remember Pearl Harbor!" (various performers)—1941

"Praise the Lord and Pass the Ammunition" (Kay Kyser and his orchestra)—1942

"Blitzkreig Baby" (Lisa Stansfield)—1942

"This is the Army Mr. Jones" (Bing Crosby)—1942

"Coming in on a Wing and a Prayer" (various performers)—1943

"No Love, No Nothin' (Until My Baby Comes Home)" (Rosemary Clooney among other performers)—1944

"It's Been a Long, Long Time" (Kitty Kallen with Harry James Orchestra)—1945

"Waitin' for the Train to Come In (Waitin' for My man to Come Home) (Peggy Lee)—1945

HIT SONGS OF THE 1940s

Songs and performers.

"In The Mood" (Glenn Miller)—1940

"Green Eyes" (Jimmy Dorsey Orchestra)—1941

"White Christmas" (Bing Crosby)—1942

"Paper Doll" (The Mills Brothers)—1943

"Don't Fence Me In" (Bing Crosby and the Andrews Sisters)—1944

"Sentimental Journey" (Les Brown and the Band of Renown with Doris Day)—1945

"Nancy (With the Laughing Face)" (Frank Sinatra)—1946

"Near You" (Francis Craig)—1947

"Buttons & Bows" (Dinah Shore)—1948

"Lovesick Blues" (Hank Williams)—1949

"Rudolph the Red-Nosed Reindeer" (Gene Autry)—1949

to sell over 6 million copies, while cumulatively all versions of the song have sold mo than 110 million worldwide, second only to Irving Berlin's "White Christmas."[2]

POPULAR SONGS AND SONGWRITERS

The war heavily affected the music of the 1940s. Literally conceived on the day Pearl Harbor was bombed in 1941, "We Did It Before" (Charles Tobias and Cliff Friend) was the first original American World War II song. Only two days after Pearl Harbor, Tobias's brother-in-law, Eddie Cantor, incorporated the song into *Banjo Eyes* (1941), a Broadway musical in which he was starring. Another song written just after the attack on Pearl Harbor was "Remember Pearl Harbor" (Don Reid and Sammy Kaye), which became a hit when it was recorded a few months later by Sammy Kaye's orchestra.[3]

The first hit to actually be inspired by American participation in World War II was "Praise the Lord and Pass the Ammunition" by Frank Loesser (1910–1969). Loesser had tried and failed to write for Tin Pan Alley (an area around 28th Street in New York City where the American music publishing industry was centered) and Broadway, though he had moderate success writing music for the movies. Loesser heard of a remark supposedly made by Navy Chaplain William Maguire during an attack—"Praise the Lord and Pass the Ammunition"—which inspired him to write his song, which he published in 1942. Ultimately, several artists would record versions of the song, and it would sell millions of copies in the early 1940s. At the height of its popularity, the song was played so often that the Office of War Information (OWI) requested that radio stations refrain from playing it more than once every four hours. Loesser became a Private First Class in Special Services, for which he wrote shows for American soldiers worldwide; he wrote many more songs of note, including, "What Do You Do in the Infantry" and "Rodger Young." After the war, Loesser returned to Hollywood, where he became a highly successful lyricist.[4]

Prior to the war, Irving Berlin (1888–1989) had already established himself through his work writing for Broadway and Hollywood as one of America's foremost lyricists. Indeed, two songs he wrote prior to Pearl Harbor, "God Bless America" and "Any Bonds Today," would both become unofficial American anthems during the war. Furthermore, Berlin donated all the profits from these songs, as well as a number of others, to various war charities. But perhaps Berlin's greatest contribution to the war effort was *This Is the Army*, an all-soldier show he wrote and produced in 1942. He wanted to cast the show with actual soldiers, an idea army officials didn't like. However, he eventually convinced them that it would be a good idea; they agreed so long as the soldiers involved were first and foremost soldiers—rehearsals would have to happen after the soldiers finished their daily military duties. The show featured a cast of approximately 300 people, including Berlin himself. The show opened on Broadway on July 4, 1942, and was an immediate smash hit. It played on Broadway for 12 weeks before touring the nation and then played for soldiers throughout Europe

Irving Berlin, 1948. Prints & Photographs Division, Library of Congress.

Music

and Asia. Warner Brothers even made it into a film. Cumulatively, the show made more than $10 million for the Army Relief Fund and earned Berlin the Medal of Merit, presented by General George C. Marshall himself.

The most commercially successful song of Berlin's entire illustrious career, "White Christmas," was penned in 1942 for the film *Holiday Inn* and therein sung by Bing Crosby. It struck a chord with Americans fighting abroad, in whom it stirred a sense of nostalgia for home and family. In its first year alone, the song was recorded by several different artists, most notably Bing Crosby and Frank Sinatra, and sold several million records. The song would quickly become the most popular song in the history of *Your Hit Parade* to that time, appearing on the show 18 consecutive weeks, 10 of them in first place.[5] In addition to selling over 25 million copies in over 30 languages abroad, the song's North American record sales would ultimately exceed 110 million, with Crosby's version alone selling over 25 million copies, making it the biggest-selling single in music history.

Another highly popular song during the war was Sammy Cahn's and Jule Styne's "I'll Walk Alone." The song debuted in the film *Follow the Boys* (1944), in which Dinah Shore sang it. Her rendition was nominated for an Academy Award and sold over a million copies for Columbia Records. Likewise, Frank Sinatra soon recorded his own version of the tune for Capitol, and it sold over a million copies as well.[6] Cahn's and Styne's first success was actually their first song, "I've Heard that Song Before," which debuted in the film *Youth in Parade* (1942), in which it was sung by Frank Sinatra. It was nominated for an Academy Award and went on to be a million-selling record by Harry James and his orchestra.

IRVING BERLIN (1888–1989)

In Irving Berlin, America has one of the more quintessential and peculiarly *American* stories of the century. The son of Russian immigrants who escaped persecution for being Jewish, Israel Baline grew up on the lower east side of New York City. Like many immigrants the Baline family was poor, and Israel grew up a rascal, running with a gang and making money for his family by singing with another, older singing beggar. After showing promise, Israel got a gig as a singing waiter at Pelham's Restaurant, where he serenaded diners with popular songs of the early 1900s. After a rival restaurant's pianist published a song with success, Baline and Pelham's piano player came up with a song of their own, the pianist providing the music and Baline the lyrics. The song became popular and by a supposed misprint of the publisher, Israel Baline's name became Irving Berlin. Berlin went on to write American anthems such as "There's No Business Like Show Business," "White Christmas," and "God Bless America." Berlin never learned to play the piano very well and had help from other musicians, who were often not credited. Nonetheless, he is considered one of the greatest American songwriters, and a year before he died at the age of 101 in 1989, an all-star celebration of his works was held at Carnegie Hall.

Richard Rodgers and Oscar Hammerstein II

Before the advent of the 33 1/3 rpm record, movies and stage musicals were leading ways to introduce songs to the American public. The musical comedy, with its roots in the vaudeville tradition, had long had a place on Broadway, but Broadway musicals increasingly moved toward integrated narratives, in which the music, dancing, and story were all of a piece. It was in the evolving musical play genre that Richard Rodgers (1902–1979) and Oscar Hammerstein II (1895–1960) had their most stunning achievement, *Oklahoma!*, the play widely considered to have brought the musical into the modern era. (See Entertainment of the 1940s.)

Though they had never worked together for Broadway, composer Rodgers and lyricist Hammerstein had only written a few songs together for an amateur production. Finally, in 1943 the Theatre Guild suggested that Hammerstein collaborate with Rodgers on an adaptation of a play by Lynn Riggs called *Green Grow the Lilacs*. Rodgers agreed and thus began one of the most fruitful collaborations in the history of musical theatre. The play initially generated little enthusiasm from both financial backers and preview audiences, and the duo revised it, adding more humor and changing the name to *Oklahoma!* The show then ran briefly in Boston, where reviewers praised the play. By the time it opened on Broadway on March 31, 1943, the show had gathered critical momentum and quickly received overwhelming audience response. In 1944, Rodgers and Hammerstein were awarded a Pulitzer Prize. The show would run on Broadway for nearly six years, during which it grossed $7 million, the highest box office earnings to that time. The traveling show toured America for 10 years, appearing in more than 250 cities. *Oklahoma!* also played in cities all over the world, grossing over $40 million worldwide. The *Oklahoma!* record, which marked the first time a play's score was recorded in its entirety by its original cast, sold more than a million records, while copies of sheet music also topped out over a million. Many of the songs from the play have become American classics, including "Oklahoma!", "Oh, What a Beautiful Morning," and "People Will Say We're in Love," which was featured on *Your Hit Parade* for 30 weeks.[7]

After *Oklahoma!*, Rodgers and Hammerstein went to Hollywood, where they wrote the score (the only one on which they ever collaborated for the screen) for the popular *State Fair* (1945). Again, the duo struck gold. Their song "It Might As Well Be Spring" won the Academy Award for best song. The two then returned to Broadway with their next musical, *Carousel* (1945), which was also a big hit. In November 1945, *Your Hit Parade* played "If I Loved You" from *Carousel*, and "It Might as Well Be Spring" and "That's for Me" from *State Fair*, thus making Rodgers and Hammerstein the first composer and lyricist to have three songs on the show on the same night. After *Carousel*, the team went on to write seven more musicals together, including *South Pacific* (1949), *The King and I* (1951), and *The Sound of Music* (1959).

Another hit musical of the 1940s that marked the arrival of a major talent to Broadway was Leonard Bernstein's *On the Town* (1944). But Bernstein (1918–1990) was not just a composer.

After graduating from Harvard and studying conducting under Serge Koussevitzky and Fritz Reiner, Bernstein landed a job as an assistant conductor of the New York Philharmonic. In August 1943, conductor Bruno Walter fell ill the day of a concert that was to be broadcast nationally. Bernstein stepped in and performed magnificently, thus igniting his career. In 1944, Bernstein composed the *Jeremiah Symphony*, a serious work that placed him at the forefront of young American composers. He followed with *Fancy Free* (choreographed by Jerome Robbins), a ballet about three young soldiers on leave prowling for women. While the ballet was considered important, it didn't have the same cultural impact as a hit play. All the same, lyricists Betty Comden and Adolph Green thought it could be translated into a play. Bernstein loved the idea, and together they transformed the ballet into *On the Town*, a smash hit musical comedy in 1943. This, in turn, was made into the 1949 MGM movie of the same name, starring Frank Sinatra and Gene Kelly. For the remainder of his life, Bernstein was incredibly prolific—he wrote operas, he wrote symphonies, he wrote for movies (such as the score for *On the Waterfront* [1954]), he wrote more plays (most notably *West Side Story* in 1957), he served as the musical director of the New York Philharmonic (the first American to do so) for over a decade, and he became an author as well as a mainstay on television.

TEEN-IDOL CROONERS

Prior to the 1940s, the most popular kind of music in America was big band, or swing music. However, during the war years the bands slowly began to fall out of favor, in part because of war-era travel restrictions that hurt their ability to tour (essential to the success of a big band), and in part because of a series of musicians' strikes that led record companies to turn toward singers instead of bands to make records. In the 1940s, the previously monumental popularity of the big bands would be challenged by singers, many of whom had previously been vocalists for big bands, including Peggy Lee, Ella Fitzgerald, Sarah Vaughan, Rosemary Clooney, Doris Day, and Dinah Shore. But of all the singers of the 1940s, it was Frank

Sinatra who arguably had the greatest and most lasting impact on popular culture.

Frank Sinatra

Francis Albert Sinatra (1915–1998) was born in Hoboken, New Jersey. He had no formal training in music, but he knew he wanted to be a singer, especially after March 1932, when he saw his idol Bing Crosby sing live at the Jersey City Loews Theatre. Sinatra cut a few records during the 1930s, but he went unnoticed nationally. However, bandleader Tommy Dorsey heard Sinatra's version of "All or Nothing At All," and he signed Sinatra. Sinatra quickly learned to emulate the sounds of the band's music with his voice. He also began to learn how to phrase lyrics in his own inimitable way, which would ultimately become his vocal trademark and earn the nickname, "The Voice."

In 1940, Sinatra had his first best-selling record, "I'll Never Smile Again" (Ruth Lowe), which was followed by a number of other hits. In early 1942, in an annual national poll conducted by the magazine *Down Beat,* Sinatra was declared the top vocalist of 1941, beating out his boyhood idol Crosby, who had held the spot the previous four years.[8] Sinatra was convinced that he would be better off as a solo artist and eventually gained Dorsey's consent to go out on his own.

Sinatra soon had a devoted following, mostly made up of young women who screamed, swooned, cried, and fainted during his shows. Perhaps the most famous, or infamous, of Sinatra performances of the 1940s was a brief stint at New York's Paramount Theatre in October 1944. Though the theatre only had 3,400 seats, more than 10,000 people lined up at the box office and an estimated 20,000 more hung out in the streets surrounding the theatre. When the box office opened, a minor riot ensued, with windows being broken, people being trampled (though no one was seriously hurt), and young women fainting in the streets. The foot traffic forced the closure of Times Square and hundreds of New York police were brought in to restore order. Inside, young women went crazy every time Sinatra appeared on stage, some throwing their bras and panties at him, others crying, and many simply fainting at the sight of him. Afterwards, as he tried to make his way from the theatre, Sinatra's clothes were torn to shreds by souvenir seekers. Sinatra's songs appeared on *Your Hit Parade* throughout the decade; he had his own radio shows, and he also enjoyed success in numerous movies. After a brief lapse of fame in the early 1950s, Sinatra regained his touch with a non-singing, Academy Award-winning turn as Maggio in *From Here to Eternity* (1954). After that, Sinatra's star never waned. The unprecedented, overtly sexual teen idolatry Sinatra inspired in the 1940s anticipated the fervor that surrounded future performers, from Elvis and the Beatles to N'Sync and the Backstreet Boys.

Perry Como

Another former band singer who first made it big in the 1940s was Perry Como (1912–2001). Como was born Pierino Como in Canonsburg, Pennsylvania. Beginning at the age of 12, Como was a barber. By the time he finished high school at the age of 16, Como had procured his own shop. Como toured with Freddie Carlone's band from 1934 to 1937, at which time he signed with Ted Weems's band, with whom he sang for years. In 1943, Weems got drafted and the band broke up. Como returned to Pennsylvania, intending to reopen his barbershop. Instead, he landed a gig on the local CBS station, which led to performances in various New York nightclubs, including the Copacabana. His success brought him to the attention of Victor Records, which signed him to a contract. He released a number of modest hits, until 1946, when he exploded nationwide with "If I Loved You," a Rogers and Hammerstein number from *Carousel* and "Till the End of Time" (Buddy Kaye and Ted Mossman). The two songs sold phenomenally well; in fact, they made Como the first singer to ever sell 2 million copies of simultaneously released songs. Como went on to record many more hits, including "A Hubba-Hubba-Hubba" (Harold Adamson and Jimmy McHugh) which he sang in the 1945 film *Doll Face*. In all, Como had eight songs in the 1940s that sold over a million copies each, making him one of the most popular singers of the era.[9]

Bing Crosby

Songs from the movies often became big hits in the 1940s, but no other movie star of the era had as much crossover success as Bing Crosby (1903–1977), who by 1940 was already arguably the most popular singer in America; his popularity stemmed in large part from the songs he sang in his movies, most of which were musicals and romantic comedies. Crosby was born Harry Lillis Crosby in Tacoma, Washington. He had a relaxed, easygoing way about him in his acting and his singing, which was dubbed "crooning." In 1940, Crosby, along with Bob Hope and Dorothy Lamour, starred in the musical road film *The Road to Singapore.* This was the first of seven highly successful "Road to…" pictures. In addition to introducing his signature song, "White Christmas," in the 1942 film *Holiday Inn,* Crosby sang the Oscar-nominated "Ac-cent-tchu-ate the Positive [*sic*]" (Johnny Mercer and Harold Arlen) in *Here Come the Waves* (1944). Crosby also won an Academy Award for his role as a singing priest in *Going My Way* (1944); in this film he sang

Bing Crosby. Prints & Photographs Division, Library of Congress.

"Swinging on a Star," which that year won the Academy Award for best song. Overall, Crosby had 16 records in the 1940s that sold more than a million copies each.

Nat King Cole

In terms of popularity, Nat King Cole (1919–1965) would ultimately be on par with Sinatra and Crosby, though his success was based almost entirely on recordings. The son of a minister, he was born Nathaniel Adams Cole in Montgomery, Alabama. From an early age he played in a variety of different groups. In the late 1930s, he worked as a small-time nightclub pianist until a manager of a club encouraged him to form his own group, which he did, calling it the King Cole Trio. The Trio was strictly instrumental, but legend has it that one night an audience member begged him to sing "Sweet Loraine" (Mitchell Parish and Cliff Burwell). The audience loved it, and Cole then began singing on occasion. Capitol Records signed the Trio, and in 1944 they recorded their first best-selling record, "Straighten Up and Fly Right" (Irving Mills and Cole). The group followed this with "The Christmas Song" (Mel Torme and Robert Wells) in 1946, shortly after which Cole went solo. His first solo smash was "Mona Lisa" (Jay Livingston and Ray Evans) in 1949, which sold 3 million records.[10] Cole's singing made him arguably the best-known and most financially successful African American singer of the 1940s. He would go on to sell in excess of 50 million records in his lifetime.

POPULAR MUSICAL STYLES

Blues

The migration of southern African Americans to northern cities during the war years changed the course of the blues. Different forms of the blues had been popular in America since the early 1900s. In the late 1930s and early 1940s the influence of blues music was present in boogie-woogie and, most obviously, in the music of the swing bands. In the late 1940s in urban areas across America, these transplanted musicians developed a new variance of blues with roots in regional blues and gospel music that would come to be known as rhythm and blues (R&B).

Unlike traditional blues, which was played acoustically, rhythm and blues often used electrically amplified instruments. The introduction of the electric guitar by blues musicians such as T-Bone Walker and Muddy Waters brought new energy to the form and increased its commercial appeal. This new electric blues was at first primarily popular with African American audiences, but the music was just too different, too new, and too amazing to be segmented for long. Furthermore, because blues musicians were playing in urban centers, their music was eminently more accessible than it had previously been. Soon, white kids began to be increasingly attracted to the appealing carnality of rhythm and blues, especially in the early 1950s, with artists such as Muddy Waters, Howlin' Wolf, and John Lee Hooker. The electric blues of the late 1940s and early 1950s was a primary influence of the rock and roll revolution taken to the white mainstream in the 1950s by Elvis Presley.

Classical

In the 1940s, American classical music for the most part suffered the same fate as classical music all over the world. Because of the war European and, to a lesser extent, American composers were unable to compose as prolifically as they previously had. Furthermore, many Americans felt unpatriotic listening to music by Germans and Italians.[11] Still Leonard Bernstein's *Jeremiah Symphony* (1944) was well received and put him at the forefront of young American composers. In addition to other American composers such as Aaron Copland and John Cage, European composers such as Béla Bartók, Arnold Schoenburg, and Igor Stravinsky moved to the United States, where their works were performed throughout the 1940s. By the end of the 1940s, more Americans than ever were being exposed to classical music through radio, television, and national tours by orchestras such as the New York Philharmonic and the San Francisco Symphony. Perhaps the most famous radio (and later TV) show featuring classical music was NBC's *National Broadcasting Company Symphony Orchestra,* which the

company formed especially for Italian émigré Arturo Toscanini, who directed the orchestra's broadcast performances from 1937 to 1954.

Country

Different forms of country music had enjoyed varying degrees of popularity for many years leading up to World War II. For example, Milton Brown and Bob Wills led popular western swing bands in the 1930s and 1940s. Bluegrass got its start in the early 1940s with the music of Bill Monroe and his group the Blue Grass Boys. In the movies, singing cowboys such as Roy Rogers and Gene Autry were on-screen figures who also had successful off-screen recording careers.

The demographic shift in the white rural south as southern farmers packed up their belongings and either joined the military or moved to urban areas to work in the factories led to country music's popularity growing beyond its traditional southern boundaries. People who had no connection to the lifestyle depicted in country and western music nevertheless were enthralled with what for them was a new sound.

During the early 1940s, Roy Acuff (1903–1992) moved to capitalize on the commercial possibilities. Acuff, a singer and a fiddler, was born in Maynardville, Tennessee. In the 1930s, he cut some now classic songs (such as "The Wabash Cannonball" in 1936) with his band, the Smoky Mountain Boys. Then, in 1938 he joined the *Grand Ole Opry* radio show that originated from the Grand Ole Opry in Nashville, Tennessee. The *Grand Ole Opry,* broadcast by WSM in Nashville, had been a show since 1925. The station, though not national, was powerful enough that people from Florida to southern Canada could listen in. Acuff joined the show just as country music was starting to hit big nationwide. The show went national in 1939, and Acuff quickly became a staple, becoming the *Grand Ole Opry*'s most popular performer in the 1940s and 1950s.

The recording capital for popular music was New York City, which didn't sit well with country musicians, who were often from the South and felt that New York producers didn't understand their musical sensibility. Roy Acuff was among the first to recognize the need for country music to have its

Music

own capital, separate in geography as well as philosophy and sound from New York. In 1943, Acuff teamed with songwriter Fred Rose to form Acuff-Rose Publishing in Nashville, just one of many companies that formed in Nashville, leading to Nashville becoming known as "Music City, U.S.A.," the international capital of country music.

Not long after Acuff formed Acuff-Rose Publishing, a new subgenre of country began to emerge: honky-tonk, which took its name from "honky-tonks," the small nightclubs in which its performers practiced their trade. Previously, country music had frequently dealt with rural American farm life. Conversely, honky-tonk songs, stronger and more amplified than their predecessors, became the lament of displaced southerners, telling sad and often brutal tales of alcoholism, broken marriages, and shattered homes.

Singer/songwriter Hiram "Hank" Williams (1923–1953) was born in Georgiana, Alabama. When he was only 8 years old, he began to teach himself to play the guitar, which he would do for the remainder of his life. At the age of 14 he formed a band, the Drifting Cowboys, which was playing on local radio shows within a year. In the 1940s, Williams landed in Nashville, where he scored a

Hank Williams, 1949. Prints & Photographs Division, Library of Congress.

contract with Acuff-Rose. Williams was the first of the honky-tonk singers to hit it big nationally, in part because of his recordings and in part because of his appearances on the *Grand Ole Opry*. With his distinctive voice and great lyrics, Williams wrote and sang songs that moved people. Many of Williams's songs became hits, either for himself, as in the case of "Long Gone Lonesome Blues," or for other performers, as when Tony Bennett sold a million records with his version of "Cold, Cold Heart."

Folk Music

The popularity of folk music, festivals, and singers continued to grow throughout the 1940s, gaining fans across the political and social spectrum. At a folk music festival in Seattle in 1941 the term "hootenanny" was coined. While it's not known for sure who coined the phrase, ads for the festival appeared in Seattle's *New Dealer* reading, "The New Dealer's Midsummer Hootenanny. You Might Even Be Surprised!" The term became identified with folk music shows at which bands and individuals performed. Throughout the decade, hootenannies were held on college campuses, in clubs frequented by intellectuals and hipsters, and at labor functions nationwide. Pete Seeger (1919–) was one of the most influential folk singers who first rose to fame in the 1940s. Seeger was born in New York City to a family of musicians. In 1935 he was taken to a folk music festival in Asheville, North Carolina, an experience that would change the course of his life. He entered Harvard in 1936 but dropped out in 1938 to live the life of a musical vagabond, traveling the country by hitchhiking or hopping rail cars, learning folk tunes, and playing in migrant camps and other places. In 1940, Seeger and Woody Guthrie formed the group the Almanac Singers, and then toured the country singing socially conscious songs. After serving in the military from 1942 to 1945, during which he entertained American troops at home and abroad, Seeger returned to civilian life, helping to form and direct People's Song, Inc., a union of songwriters and a clearing house for folk music.[12]

Seeger would go on to have his greatest popular fame in the 1950s as the leader of the folk band, The Weavers. He gained notoriety as an unabashed member of the left-wing movement, which resulted in his being called to testify before the House Un-American Activities Committee in 1955. He courageously refused to tell the committee about any communist connections any of his friends and associates may have had, which led to his being indicted on 10 counts of contempt of Congress. The charges were later dismissed.

Jazz: From Swing to Bop

The era leading up to the 1940s was characterized by the popularity of the big bands, whose

HOW OTHERS SEE US

Django Reinhardt, Europe's Jazz Giant

Jazz came to Europe with the American doughboys of World War I, and the music—particularly in its syncopated, New Orleans-based form—was tremendously popular throughout the Continent and in Britain. It took nearly two decades, however, for a truly original European jazz artist to emerge.

Guitarist Django Reinhardt (1910–1953) married the music of his Romani heritage to the rhythms of American hot jazz to create a new form known today as Gypsy jazz or *jazz manouche*. Born in Belgium into a nomadic community, Reinhardt grew up near Paris playing violin, banjo, and guitar. At the age of 24, he formed a jazz group called the Quintette du Hot Club de France. The ensemble included no drums; the syncopated beat was supplied by a stand-up bass and two rhythm guitars, strummed with a percussive technique, while the lead melody lines came from Reinhardt's guitar and the violin of Stéphane Grappelli. Their fluid improvisations, as well as Reinhardt's use of diminished and augmented chords, created a sensational and distinctly European sound.

One of the best-known jazz guitarists of all time, Reinhardt went on to play and record with such legendary American artists as Louis Armstrong, Duke Ellington, and Coleman Hawkins. His influence extended into the rock era, having essentially invented the concepts of rhythm and lead guitar.

music was also known as jazz. But as the bands began to be replaced by the singers, the popularity of jazz waned. While the major labels began shying away from jazz, small companies such as Dial, Savoy, and Bluenote still put out jazz records, and serious jazz musicians were revolutionizing the form. The most fertile ground for jazz in the 1940s was in the clubs of New York City, especially those on and around 52nd Street between Fifth and Sixth Avenues, a place known as "the street of swing."[13] Clubs such as the Famous Door, the Onyx, Three Deuces, and Kelly's Stables routinely featured future legends such as Dizzy Gillespie, Charlie Parker, Lester Young, and Miles Davis, artists whose work influenced the major jazz movement of the 1940s: bop.

Dizzy Gillespie

While many artists contributed to the idea of "bop," trumpeter Dizzy Gillespie's work was at the forefront. Gillespie (1917–1993) was born John Birks Gillespie in Cheraw, South Carolina. As a teen he first studied the trombone, before taking up the trumpet. He bounced around from band to band until 1937, at which time he got a steady gig playing with the Cab Calloway orchestra. In 1943 he joined the Earl Hines ban, where he and his bandmates—Charlie Parker on alto sax, Little Benny Harris on trumpet, and Billy Eckstine on vocals—began experimenting with the new musical ideas that would evolve into bop. In 1944, Eckstine broke from the Hines band to form his own group, bringing Gillespie and Parker as well. This group furthered the development of bop with their newly emerging style.

The name "bop" comes from the terms "bebop" and "rebop," which Gillespie would sometimes utter as the closing of a triplet: "Bu-re-bop." The phrase stuck in people's minds, and they started calling Gillespie's music rebop, which was ultimately shortened to bop.[14]

This new kind of jazz was different because it didn't always carry a sustaining melody throughout a given song. Instead, a tune would begin with a recognizable melody, then the individual band members would depart from the melody to embark on wild solo-flights of improvisation. Only at tune's end would the musicians collectively

Dizzy Gillespie, 1949. Prints & Photographs Division, Library of Congress.

sunglasses. Furthermore, jazz musicians popularized much of the slang of the 1940s, including words such as "hip," "chick," "hepcat," "smooth," "square," "groovy," and the addition of "-reeny," "-rooney," or "-o-rooney" at the end of words. Gillespie's devotees were an early incarnation of the subset that would eventually become identified in popular culture as hipsters or Beatniks. (See Fashion of the 1940s.) But of all his many followers, none would be more important in the history of jazz than Charlie "Bird" Parker, who would become one of the most influential musicians in American history.

Charlie Parker

Charlie Parker (1920–1955) was born in Kansas City, Kansas. His father had abandoned his mother, who worked as a cleaning woman to support the family. When Parker was 13, she bought him a used saxophone. He was a prodigy, learning the instrument so well and so quickly that he was playing in local bands less than two years later. In Kansas City, Parker was able to see many jazz greats, including Count Basie and Lester Young. In fact, he acquired the original long form of his nickname, "yardbird," because he would spend his nights in the yards outside clubs listening to his idols and waiting for them to come out. In 1937, Jay McShann and his orchestra swung through Kansas City. Parker was given the opportunity to join the band, and he did. His playing quickly attracted the attention of other players, who were amazed at his ability to endlessly improvise without repetition. His improvisations, which according to him resulted from his experimenting with new sounds because he was bored with stereotypical swing changes, played no small part in the development of bop. For those who understood his genius, hearing Parker play was a revelatory experience. His playing could mesmerize even other musicians.

With Gillespie, Parker also played with Earl Hines and Billy Eckstine. Like Gillespie, Parker formed his own sextet and developed a strong following in New York City. In 1946, for Dial Records, Parker recorded "Ornithology" and his famous "Yardbird Suite." Despite his instrumental prowess, his music was so different from what others were

return to the theme that had been established at the beginning. Bop songs were characterized by long, intricate phrases, unusual breaks, and complicated intervals that required exceptional technique, which was what all the innovators of bop, including Gillespie, Parker, Thelonious Monk, Bud Powell, Max Roach, and others, became revered for. Bop didn't come easily to the ear at first; it took some getting used to and required an appreciation for musicality in order to enjoy it. This resulted in its initially being unappreciated in the larger context of American popular culture. But for savvy New York City music critics and intellectuals, bop was the thing in music of the 1940s: new, complex, and invigorating.

After playing with Hines and Eckstine, Gillespie formed his own sextet, which played bop exclusively, including Gillespie's compositions, such as "Groovin' High" and "Dizzy Atmosphere." Gillespie developed a kind of cult following that adored his music and adopted his style of dress, characterized by berets, goatees, and dark playing that he had a hard time getting accepted by other musicians and many critics, some of whom questioned the validity of what he was doing. For a time his genius was forgotten by all save a few of the most avid jazz aficionados, but in the early 1970s his music began to be collected and reissued, which resulted in a "rediscovery" of his talents and his being recognized as a vital innovator of bop jazz, a quintessentially American art form.

Miles Davis

Following the bop movement was cool jazz, virtually synonymous with trumpeter Miles Davis (1926–1991), even though in his later career he moved toward fusion. Davis was born in Alton, Illinois. In 1945, he moved to New York City to study music at Juilliard. However, he spent more time playing in jazz bands, including Charlie Park-er's quintet, than he did going to school. While in New York City, he heard the pioneering work of tenor saxophonist Lester Young a well-known practitioner of the hot jazz style of the 1930s. In the early 1940s, Young's music went off in a different direction. While they still improvised in an often sophisticated fashion, their music had a more discernable beat and a dreamier, softer quality. This new, relaxed sound became known as cool jazz. Davis was influenced by Young's work, and he began to move away from bop. In fact, the rise of cool can at least in part be seen as a reaction to the freneticism of bop. In 1949 and 1950, Davis gathered a group of musicians together to record several new compositions in the cool style. The best of the recordings were later released as *The Birth of the Cool* (1957) and would prove to be hugely influential for succeeding generations of jazz musicians.

Sports

and Leisure of the 1940s

SPORTS

Major League Baseball

World War II initially threatened the prosperity of Major League Baseball, but by the end of the decade, baseball was the country's most popular sport. After the attack on Pearl Harbor, baseball commissioner Judge Kenesaw Mountain Landis wrote a letter to FDR asking for guidance as to whether or not it would be appropriate to continue playing the game. Roosevelt responded with his "Green Light" letter, in which he asserted that it would be good for the country if baseball were to keep going. Despite its continuance, baseball suffered a serious talent dearth during the war, as many of its players joined or were drafted into the armed services. Even though men over 28 were exempt from the draft, the furor over Japan's attack on Pearl Harbor led many established, over-28 stars, such as Hank Greenberg, to enlist.

For nearly four years, Major League Baseball put a comparatively inferior product on the field, comprising mostly young and underdeveloped players, players well past their prime, and "4-Fers" (those who were classified as unfit for military service). Of the major leaguers present in 1941, only 18 percent remained on their teams in the spring of 1945, during which time no team had more than four of its 1941 starters.[1]

The Negro leagues, however, enjoyed their greatest levels of popularity during World War II, with a cumulative attendance of 2 million fans.[2] After integration in 1947, the Negro leagues slowly began to die out; not long after Jackie Robinson was allowed to join the major leagues, blacks who wanted to play professional baseball began coming up through the big league clubs' traditional minor league affiliates. Women's professional baseball became popular in the 1940s with the formation of the All-American Girls Professional Baseball League. Initially featuring four teams the League featured a 108-game schedule and was immensely popular during the war. Its popularity continued after the war, peaking in 1948 when its 10 teams drew almost 1 million fans. But once major league baseball was able to put a quality product on the field again, the popularity of women's baseball declined. The All-American Girls Professional Baseball League dissolved in 1954.[3]

Another consequence of the war was the institutionalization of singing "The Star-Spangled Banner" before sporting events. In 1918 the song had been sung at the World Series, where it proved popular. The song continued to be played on opening day and during the Series, and in 1931 Congress officially made it the national anthem. During the war the song began to be played more

Jackie Robinson of the Brooklyn Dodgers, poised and ready to swing. Prints & Photographs Division, Library of Congress.

frequently at games; by the end of the war, it was played before every game.[4]

When on November 25, 1944, Commissioner Landis died, Major League Baseball's very survival fell into question in some quarters. After contentious debate, A. B. Happy Chandler was elected commissioner of baseball. Under Chandler's watch, the game rebounded beyond anyone's expectations in the years following the war. Established players returned, and some of the youngsters who played during the war blossomed, so the quality of the game on the field skyrocketed. Also, with the rise of television and the continued prevalence of radio broadcasts, the game became more popular than it had ever been.

In 1941, the New York Yankees' Joe DiMaggio (1914–1999), "The Yankee Clipper," hit in an unprecedented 56 straight games, a feat considered to be among the most unreachable and unbreakable records in sports. In fact, the closest anyone has come was Pete Rose's 44-game hitting streak in 1978. DiMaggio's streak began on May 15, 1941.

JACKIE ROBINSON (1919–1972)

Born to a family of sharecroppers living in Cairo, Georgia, Jackie Robinson emerged from relative poverty to gain national fame as the first African American to be drafted into a Major League Baseball team. The historic event occurred in the 1947 season when the Brooklyn Dodgers ended decades of segregation, known unofficially as the "color line," and initiated a new and more egalitarian age for professional sports. Robinson's contribution to the growing civil rights movement may have been muted if not for his diplomacy and talent. Robinson's performance during his debut season earned him the first ever Rookie of the Year Award, and two years later he was named Most Valuable Player by the Major League Baseball Association. Despite his skill, prejudice and racism were major obstacles, and some MLB teams refused to play the Dodgers in protest over Robinson's recruitment. Robinson also played a direct role in the development of the civil rights movement, and throughout his career he traveled the country speaking to groups of whites and blacks about segregation and racial equality. In 1962, Robinson achieved another major milestone when he became the first African American to be inducted into the Baseball Hall of Fame. Robinson died of complications from a heart condition in 1972, and that same year the Brooklyn Dodgers officially retired his uniform number, "42," in recognition of his contributions to the franchise and his historic role in professional baseball history.

As it went on, people who didn't even have an interest in baseball started paying attention. It was a nice distraction amidst the country's move toward war. On June 29, DiMaggio's Yankees played a doubleheader in Washington, D.C., against the Senators. In the first game DiMaggio hit a double to tie the major league record of 41 games, set by the Saint Louis Browns' George Sisler in 1922. In the next game DiMaggio smashed a single to surpass Sisler. On July 2, he hit a home run against the hated Red Sox, breaking the Baltimore Orioles' Wee Willie Keeler's all-time record of 44 straight

Joe DiMaggio, of the New York Yankees, about to kiss his signature baseball bat, 1941. Prints & Photographs Division, Library of Congress.

games. The streak ended on July 17 against the Cleveland Indians in Cleveland. His first three times up DiMaggio faced left-hander Al Smith. DiMaggio walked his second at bat, but in his first and third at bats DiMaggio crushed balls to third baseman Ken Keitner, who both times made great stops and throws to get the out. In his last at bat, at the top of the eighth, DiMaggio came up against reliever Jim Bagby with the bases loaded. DiMaggio grounded into an inning-ending double play, and with that the streak was over, despite his having smoked the ball twice during the game. Still, as the years go on, no one even comes close to approaching DiMaggio's record. The enormity of his accomplishment merely grows in the eyes of baseball fans everywhere.

Ted Williams

In 1942, Ted Williams (1918–2002) quietly had one of the greatest all-around seasons in baseball history. It was "quiet" because Williams played for the Boston Red Sox, a team long overshadowed by the New York Yankees, who finished the 1941

A MAN OF HIS TIME: JOE DIMAGGIO

Giuseppe Paolo (Joe) DiMaggio was born November 25, 1914, in Martinez, California. The son of immigrants, he was the eighth child of Giuseppe and Rosalie DiMaggio. He often played baseball with his brother, Dominic, who went on to play for the Boston Red Sox.

DiMaggio made his Major League Baseball debut on May 3, 1936, as a player for the New York Yankees. He then led the team to four consecutive World Championship titles. He is the only athlete in North American history to be on four World Championship teams in his first four full seasons.

During World War II, DiMaggio put his baseball career on hold, serving four years in the army, though he never saw combat. He returned from the army, and in his 13 years with the Yankees, he won nine World Championships. DiMaggio was inducted into the Baseball Hall of Fame in 1955. During baseball's centennial celebration, he was named the game's greatest living player.

He retired in 1952, and after a failed marriage he dated and married Marilyn Monroe. It was a marriage that captivated the media, called "the Marriage of the Century." Though it lasted less than a year, they remained close friends. Monroe died in 1962, and for 20 years after her death, he had a dozen roses delivered three times a week to her grave. DiMaggio never married again.

His fame after retirement led DiMaggio to be the television spokesperson for Bowery Bank of New York and Mr. Coffee coffee makers. DiMaggio was also given tribute when Paul Simon mentioned him in his song, "Mrs. Robinson," written for the movie *The Graduate* (1967).

Later in life, DiMaggio donated $4 million to help create the Joe DiMaggio Children's Hospital, which opened in 1992. He also helped to open the Conine Clubhouse, a free-of-charge home for families of sick children at the hospital.

Due to complications from lung cancer, DiMaggio died in his home in Hollywood, Florida, on March 8, 1999.

season 17 games ahead of the Red Sox. More specifically, in 1941 the Yankees won the American League pennant, finishing 17 games ahead of the Red Sox. Also, Joe DiMaggio had his 56-game hitting streak in 1941. The New York media juggernaut catapulted Joe DiMaggio's 56-game hitting streak status into near mythical standing, even before the streak was over. Conversely, Williams just played consistently great ball, out of the limelight, day in and day out. While DiMaggio's streak remains one of sports' greatest achievements, Williams had a statistically superior season, hitting .406 with 37 home runs, 120 Runs Batted In or RBIs, 135 runs, and a .735 slugging percentage to DiMaggio's .357 average, 30 home runs, 125 RBIs, 122 runs, and .643 slugging percentage. Still, the Red Sox finished far behind the Yankees, and DiMaggio won the American League MVP going away. Williams was one of the first professional athletes to enlist; he was a pilot for the U.S. Marines. He would miss three prime years during the 1940s (from 1943 to 1945) and two in the 1950s (from 1952 to 1953) to fight in the Korean conflict. Statistically, he ended up as one of the greatest hitters ever to play the game—the last man in baseball history to hit over .400. As good as he was, however, baseball historians often wonder where he would have ended up had he not missed those five years in the prime of his career. Barring injuries, it's likely his numbers would have been equal to players such as Babe Ruth, Willie Mays, Hank Aaron, and Barry Bonds. And his signature season was 1941, the year he became the last man in baseball history to hit over .400.

Professional Football

In the 1920s, it was routinely thought that college players were better than their professional counterparts. In 1934 professional football began a tradition of having all-star college seniors play the previous NFL season's champion. After tying the first game, the NFL players went 5-3-1 over the next nine years. By 1940, the professional games had a loyal following, which became even larger after the national radio broadcast of the 1940 National Football League (NFL) championship game, in which the Chicago Bears blew out the Washington Redskins 73 to 0. The introduction

WORLD SERIES

1940 Cincinnati Reds (NL), 4 games; Detroit Tigers (AL), 3 games

1941 New York Yankees (AL), 4 games; Brooklyn Dodgers (NL), 1 game

1942 St. Louis Cardinals (NL), 4 games; New York Yankees (AL), 1 game

1943 New York Yankees (AL), 4 games; St. Louis Cardinals (NL), 1 game

1944 St. Louis Cardinals (NL), 4 games; St. Louis Browns (AL) 2 games

1945 Detroit Tigers (AL), 4 games; Chicago Cubs (NL), 3 games

1946 St. Louis Cardinals (NL), 4 games; Boston Red Sox (AL), 3 games

1947 New York Yankees (AL), 4 games; Brooklyn Dodgers (NL), 3 games

1948 Cleveland Indians (AL), 4 games; Boston Braves (NL), 2 games

1949 New York Yankees (AL), 4 games; Brooklyn Dodgers (NL), 1 game

of pro football to a national audience helped launch the game toward becoming America's most popular sport (at least with regard to TV ratings). In addition, the 1940 game included Dick Plasman, who became the last player to not wear a helmet in a pro game (the NFL didn't formalize the mandatory helmet rule until 1943). Also notable in that championship game was the Chicago Bears' offense, executed just as their legendary coach, George Halas, imagined it could be. At the time, other pro teams predominantly ran the football using a version of a wing formation. Only the Chicago Bears featured the "T" formation, two running backs lined up behind the quarterback. A play almost as old as the game itself, it was originally meant to be a power running formation.

The past notwithstanding, Halas and his assistant coach Ralph Jones put a man in motion and increased the width between linemen, thus opening up the game and making it much faster and more dynamic than before. The T could be

Sports

used not only as a running formation, but as a passing formation as well, which led to stardom for quarterbacks like Washington's Sammy Baugh and Chicago's Sid Luckman. It changed the game so much that by 1950, only the Pittsburgh Steelers still used the wing formation.[5]

The transition toward unlimited substitutions, which began in 1941, dramatically changed the game. Prior to the rule change, players played both offense and defense. However, as unlimited substitutions became the norm, coaches realized that they could have specific players play in specific situations to maximize their abilities. A lack of players during the war led to the league's rosters being cut from 33 to 25, and unlimited substitutions became legal. Though the rule was temporarily abolished after the war, by the end of the decade pressure from coaches and players led to its reinstatement, and the game's players became much more specialized.[6]

In 1946 the NFL integrated, or more accurately, reintegrated. Until 1933, blacks were allowed to play pro football. However, by way of a "gentlemen's agreement," after the 1933 season blacks were no longer allowed to play.[7] A new league sprung up in 1946, the All-America Football Conference (AAFC). The AAFC paid players more, and many college players went into the AAFC instead of the NFL. In addition to driving up player salaries and competition for the best players, the AAFC teams had a handful of blacks on their rosters. In order to compete, the NFL had no choice but to let black players play. After the 1949 season, the AAFC folded and the NFL absorbed three of its franchises: the San Francisco 49ers, the Baltimore Colts, and the Cleveland Browns.[8] For many reasons, including the fact that for much of the decade the best players were in the armed services, the popularity of the NFL still lagged behind that of college football.

College Football

As its players generally did not have to serve in the armed forces until after graduation, college football continued to be immensely popular during the 1940s. Prior to 1940, the college game was much like the pro game: reliant on running and variations of the wing formation. But in 1940,

just as Halas had done to the pro game, Stanford coach Clark Shaughnessey introduced his own wide-open version of the T offense. The college game changed in accordance with the pro game, becoming much more wide open and pass-friendly. Fans loved it at both levels, and players such as the army's Felix "Doc" Blanchard, Notre Dame's John Lujack, and Southern Methodist's Doak Walker became nationally recognized gridiron heroes.

Professional Basketball

The National Basketball Association (NBA) has its roots in an amalgam of pro and semi-pro teams. In 1937, the league changed its name to the National Basketball League (NBL).[9] When the war broke out, the NBL was devastated as the bulk of its players became active in the military. During the 1942–1943 season the operator of the Toledo Jim Whites (so named because they were sponsored by the Jim White Chevrolet dealership), Sid Goldberg, solved the player shortage by signing four black players to his team. While Toledo disbanded due to financial reasons, other teams integrated as well. For whatever reason, perhaps because individual black players had occasionally played professionally in the past, or maybe because basketball was out of the national spotlight, integration in pro basketball went largely unnoticed. Still, after the 1942–1943 season African Americans would not play again in the NBL for four years, after which their presence slowly became more common and accepted. While there were problems with racism for some players, pro basketball's racial integration was the least contentious of the major sports, especially when compared to the turmoil that surrounded Jackie Robinson in baseball. In 1946, a new league sprang up, the Basketball Association of America (BAA), which consisted of 11 teams. The new league was highly successful, in no small part because its teams were located in big cities such as New York, Cleveland, Philadelphia, and Boston. In 1949 the financially overmatched remnants of the NBL merged with the BAA to form the National Basketball Association.[10] The first official NBA championship was won in the 1949–1950 season by the Minneapolis Lakers, who featured

Sports

future hall-of-famer George Mikan, the league's first seven footer.

Boxing

In the era leading up to the 1940s, boxing's popularity had declined somewhat, amidst various scandals (which have perpetually plagued the sport) and outcries against its violent nature. But in the late 1930s boxing began to experience increasing popularity as a result of the ascendancy of one man: Joe Louis, "the Brown Bomber," heavyweight champion of the world. Louis was born in Lafayette, Alabama, on May 13, 1914, the son of tenant farmers. In 1926, not long after Louis's father died, his mother moved the family to Detroit, Michigan. Louis was behind academically and put in class with younger, smaller children. In addition to this ignominy, Louis suffered from a speech impediment. He dropped out of school in the sixth grade. In 1932 he began boxing, and in 1934 he turned pro.

As Jeffery T. Sammons recounts, Louis easily beat all challengers, including former heavyweight champion Max Baer in 1935. In 1936 Louis suffered his first professional loss at the hands of the German Max Schmeling, a defeat made all the more stinging by the fact that, in addition to knowing he could have easily beaten Schmeling had he taken him more seriously and trained harder, Louis had to endure Hitler's vitriol. Hitler saw Schmeling's victory as proof of Caucasian superiority. For the rematch, Louis took no chances. He trained incessantly, and when the rematch finally came on June 22, 1938, in New York City, Louis, feeling he was not only fighting for all blacks everywhere, but for America itself, annihilated Schmeling, knocking him out at 2:04 of the first round.[11] Vindicated after defeating Schmeling, Louis went on to defend his title 15 times between 1939 and the start of World War II.

Most of these title defenses were relatively easy, all save one: his June 18, 1941, defense against Billy Conn. Even though Conn was outweighed by 30 pounds, he fought a superior fight, and by the thirteenth round it was clear that Conn was so far ahead in points that all he had to do was stay away from Louis, and he'd win the fight. But Conn was convinced he could knock out Louis, so he went after him. The two men traded blows furiously, until Louis finally got the better of Conn, knocking him out with two seconds remaining in the round and winning a classic come-from-behind victory.[12]

In February 1942, Louis enlisted in the U.S. Army. Louis was intent on avoiding special treatment, but in some ways he got it anyway. For example, he was allowed to defend his title while in the service so as long as the purses went to a wartime cause.[13] While most African Americans were treated as second-class (or worse) citizens at home, there were still a number of government advertising campaigns designed to get African Americans to fight for their country, the hypocrisy of which was noted by many, black and white alike. Nonetheless, perhaps the most successful person in encouraging black enlistment was Joe Louis, who was likely the most visible and recognizable noncommissioned officer in America, as well as the person most successful in encouraging black enlistment. He appeared in a U.S. War Department film directed by none other than Frank Capra. In the film, *The Negro Soldier* (1943), Louis appeared with a black preacher. The preacher did most of the talking, connecting Louis's earlier bout with Schmeling to the current world war, the idea being that if Joe stood up to Hitler and the Nazis, then so, too, should all African Americans. The film, which by means of omission disregarded the mistreatment and inequality of blacks in America at the time, was nevertheless successful (although some felt the film subtly endorsed the military's longstanding segregation). It was released in over 3,500 commercial theaters and was required viewing for army soldiers.[14]

After the war Louis ran into financial problems caused both by his free-spending ways and high taxes. Still, he managed to beat Billy Conn on June 19, 1946, in a long-overdue rematch, and he beat Jersey Joe Walcott twice before retiring in 1949. He came out of retirement for financial reasons several times, but he never did regain his title. In his two highest-profile fights, the first a September 27, 1950, title fight against heavyweight champ Ezzard Charles and the second his final fight, an October 26, 1951, bout against young Rocky Marciano (who would go on to be the only undefeated champion in heavyweight history), he was decisioned by Charles and knocked out by Marciano in the eighth round. Louis re-retired for good, ending his career with a 68–3 record, including 54 knockouts.

As important a boxer as Louis was (he almost single-handedly resuscitated boxing's national image), he was also important for his impact as an African American icon. Prior to World War II, Louis fought 43 men, only one of which was black.[15]

During the war he was revered by blacks and whites alike for his patriotism. In fact, though there's no way to verify it statistically, many social historians feel that Louis's high profile, while distasteful to those who deemed it hypocritical, nevertheless helped to break down color barriers in American culture. Some whites were more prone to look favorably on African Americans, and he was adored by blacks in good measure. It's hard not to notice that on the heels of Louis's prewar fights against Schmeling and his dedicated and highly visible service during World War II, the acceptance of integration in the big three American professional sports (football, baseball, and basketball) became much more prevalent.[16] Louis helped pave the way.

Hockey

Professional hockey was already an established sport at the advent of the 1940s, although it was primarily popular in the upper Midwest and Northeast. The league's structure did not change dramatically during the decade, although there was a stabilization in that the financially tenuous New York Americans disbanded before the 1942–1943 season, leaving six teams (all of which are still extant) for the remainder of the decade: the Detroit Red Wings, the Boston Bruins, the Toronto Maple Leafs, the Montreal Canadiens, the Chicago Black Hawks, and the New York Rangers. While many hockey players did join the military, it didn't affect the sport much since many of the league's players were Canadian. The league never missed a game, although during the war overtime periods were done away with so players could make increasingly tight wartime train schedules.[17] As concerns the rules, the center red line was introduced in 1943. Prior to its introduction,

players couldn't pass the puck out of their own end; they had to skate it up, which made it difficult to ever get flow, let alone shots on goal. But the new rule stated that a player could pass the puck out of his own end, so long as he didn't go over the red line. This sped the game up considerably, and a new breed of scorers took advantage of the quicker game.[18] Also introduced was the All-Star Game, which debuted in 1947.

Tennis and Golf

In the 1940s, tennis didn't have widespread popularity. It was a "tween" sport: not quite pro and not quite amateur. Amateur associations controlled the world's major tournaments, thus preventing pros from playing in them. Conversely, amateurs good enough to win the tournaments often couldn't make enough money to play tennis competitively.

During the Depression and World War II, there was little public interest in golf, even though great players such as Ben Hogan and Byron Nelson played in the 1940s. In 1944, there were only 409 golf courses in the whole country.[19]

The Olympics

The Berlin Olympics of 1936, "the Nazi Olympics," were quite controversial. Strangely, rather than sidestepping controversy in choosing the site of the next games, the International Olympic Committee (IOC) chose Japan to host the 1940 Olympics. Japan diffused the controversy by withdrawing its offer to host, choosing instead to concentrate on war. Finland offered to host the games, but the IOC, shockingly, returned them to Germany. However, Germany continued to invade other European countries, and momentum to hold the games there waned until they were cancelled entirely. There were no Olympics in 1940 and 1944. The games resumed in 1948, with London hosting the summer games and St. Moritz, Switzerland, hosting the winter games.[20]

LEISURE PASTIMES

During much of the 1940s, the consumer production of leisure items was severely limited due

Sports

to the rationing of many of the materials traditionally used to make them. Toys also had a rough go of it in the forties as materials like lead (used to make lead soldiers), tin (used to make wind-up toys), steel (used to make things like replica trucks), rubber, and zinc and cast iron (used to make cap-guns and other toys) were severely restricted, resulting in many toy companies going out of business. Those companies that didn't go out of business began making things for the war effort instead of games and toys. For example, during the war, toy maker Fisher-Price made first-aid kits, bomb crates, and ship fenders. During the war the production of bicycles, wagons, ice skates, sleds with metal blades, roller skates, and balloons was severely curbed. The few toys that were produced were made most often of either cardboard or wood. It wasn't until the late 1940s that toy makers began to make a comeback in America.

Despite the realities of a wartime existence, Americans found ways to entertain themselves.

A TOY THAT HAS LIVED ON

Naval engineer Richard James created the Slinky while conducting an experiment with tension springs in 1943. The idea struck James when the springs fell to the floor and began to "walk." He took this idea and changed it into a children's toy. A word meaning stealthy and sleek, "the Slinky" was named by James's wife, Betty.

The Slinky debuted at Gimbel's Department Store in Philadelphia, Pennsylvania, in 1945, and within 90 minutes James sold all 400 toys. Currently, more than 300 million Slinkys have been sold worldwide. The only modification to the toy has been a crimp at the ends of the wire for safety. The toy is still made at its original site in Hollidaysburg, Pennsylvania.

The Slinky became a ubiquitous feature of pop culture throughout the years. The toy has made many appearances in movies. It has been attributed to uses beyond that of a toy, with NASA using variations of it in experiments aboard the Space Shuttle. In 2001, the Slinky was named the Official State Toy of Pennsylvania. The U.S. Postal Service even introduced a commemorative Slinky stamp in 1999.

They devised cheap and easy games to play; they read, listened to the radio, played games like Monopoly and card games like Canasta; and they passionately played and followed sports. When pro sports faltered during the war, they turned to college games for pleasure. And when the war and rationing finally ended, the production of items for entertainment and the popularity of professional sports, especially baseball, skyrocketed.

PASTIMES AND FADS

Book Clubs

One way soldiers liked to pass the time was reading. In fact, they read so much that their wartime reading habits helped contribute to the book club craze, which reached its peak in the 1940s. (See Books, Newspapers, Magazines, and Comics of the 1940s.) The advent of mass-market paperbacks and the boredom of American soldiers led to the rise of book clubs. In the 1940s publishers first began to print paperback versions of books that had previously been best sellers in hardcover. The paperbacks would sell for a quarter each and book clubs would print as much as half a million copies at a time. Concurrently, soldiers stationed at home and abroad often had time to kill and began reading books that they checked out of well-stocked United Service Organizations and other military libraries. Many soldiers acquired the habit of voracious reading, a habit they continued upon their return to civilian life. The soldiers' reading habits helped spark a national craze that would peak during the 1940s, when some 50 American book clubs were in full swing, including the Nonfiction Book Club, the Negro Book Club, the Catholic Children's Book Club, and the Surprise Package Book Club.[21]

Drive-In Theaters

Another leisure activity that grew immensely in popularity in the immediate postwar era was going to the drive-in theater to watch a movie. The first drive-in was opened in Camden, New Jersey, in 1933. The theater was successful, but the drive-in really didn't take root in America until just after World War II, growing from 100 or so drive-ins prewar to more than 2,200 by

Sports

1950. Part of this had to do with the rise of car culture and the increase in vehicle ownership in America. The ease of going to the drive-in made it appealing. One could just hop in the car and go to a show, no getting dressed up, no hassle, and no major dent in the pocketbook required. The theaters were ideal for middle-income families and blue-collar workers and also proved to be popular with teens looking for a place to make out.

Lawns

Of the new pastimes to emerge after the war, perhaps none has become more visibly omnipresent than Americans' obsession with their lawns, which prior to the war wasn't as widespread in mainstream culture. In American consciousness, the lawn had come to represent the joy of suburban prosperity, as evinced by home ownership. Why lawns came into being in American suburbs is unclear, but in Levittown suburbs in particular, lawns were immediately a part of the suburban cultural landscape. Indeed, homeowners were required to keep their lawns green and trimmed. (See Architecture of the 1940s.)

Pin-Up Girls

One way the soldiers in the 1940s liked to while away their leisure time—of which they sometimes had a lot—was to look at pictures of pretty, scantily clad women. The term "pin-up girl" originated in the April 30, 1943, issue of *Yank,* an armed forces newspaper. Soldiers far from home missed women. To fill the void, soldiers posted pictures of women everywhere, from the insides of their helmets to the walls of their Quonset huts. Some women became popular strictly as pin-up girls. For example, Diana Dors gained notoriety wearing a diamond-studded mink bikini (the bikini, named after the Pacific Bikini Atoll, a nuclear test site, was designed in the 1940s by French designer Louis Reard). But by far the most famous pin-ups were Hollywood movie stars such as Lana Turner and Ava Gardner. It's been said that a photo of Rita Hayworth was attached to the nuclear bomb dropped on Hiroshima. The most popular pin-up of them all was Betty Grable in a tight, white swimsuit, looking over her shoulder with her back to the camera. For that

Betty Grable in one of her famous pinup poses, a favorite of American soldiers. Prints & Photographs Division, Library of Congress.

one shot, Grable earned over $300,000 in a single year. Popular magazines, such as *Time* and *Life,* occasionally featured pin-ups on their covers; the popularity of pin-ups, which had started

Sports

As American Marines on a landing barge approach the Japanese-held island of Tarawa, Gilbert Islands, in the Pacific, one of the Marines looks at a picture of a pin-up girl. Tarawa burns in the background, 1943. Prints & Photographs Division, Library of Congress.

with soldiers, became a national phenomenon. The magazine images most beloved by soldiers were the paintings of scantily clad women drawn by Alberto Vargas—called "Vargas Girls"—that appeared in the monthly *Esquire.* They were so provocative that in 1944 the postmaster general banned them from the mail, which ultimately led to the magazine's cancellation of the popular feature.[22]

The Shmoos Craze

The 1948 introduction of Shmoos in Al Capp's comic strip *L'il Abner* started one of the last big crazes of the 1940s. Shmoos—white blobs—were a hit in L'il Abner's world, Dogpatch, which led to a brief but intense fad in the real world. Shmoos could lay eggs and produce butter or milk on demand. If they were broiled, which they loved, they would turn into steak. When they were boiled, which they also loved, they turned into chicken. Their likenesses were emblazoned on just about anything imaginable—clocks, ashtrays, pencil sharpeners, piggy banks, socks, umbrellas, ties— and sold in department stores nationwide. In 1948, Capp even had a nonfiction best seller, *The Life and Times of the Shmoo.* By 1950, Shmoo products had grossed an astounding $25 million. However, Capp was upset with the effect their popularity had on the narrative direction of his strip, so he introduced a storyline to kill them off. Dogpatch's resident tycoon, J. Roaringham Fatback, saw the Shmoos as a threat to his fortune and had them all killed by a Shmooicide squad. With their apparent extinction from Dogpatch, the Shmoo craze ended. Though the characters reappeared later in the 1950s, the excitement about them did not.[23]

Travel

of the 1940s

For most of the 1930s, many people couldn't afford to go on vacation. Then, once the wartime economy began to take off in the early 1940s, people had the disposable income needed to travel, but wartime rationing led to roads remaining unimproved and consumer automobile and tire production coming to a standstill. For most of the 1940s, then, people traveled for their jobs, not for leisure. Despite this, many events during the 1940s affected the ways people traveled in the postwar era.

THE AMERICAN AUTOMOBILE INDUSTRY

In 1940, companies faced with increasing shortages went to great lengths to ensure that what they were able to make went to paying civilian customers. In May 1940, America's industrial mobilization effort was put under the control of an advisory committee called the Council of National Defense (CND), which was headed by William S. Knudsen, president of General Motors (GM). At the CND's inception, Knudsen had no power to dictate what companies could do; he could only try to persuade them to participate. As a result, automobile companies continued to make cars for consumers. But when on February 22, 1942, the government decreed the cessation of the production of consumer automobiles, the industry had

no choice but to bear down and join the mobilization effort. The automobile industry, with its massive factories, proven mode of mass production, and huge standing work force, was the industry best suited to carry the bulk of the load. Indeed, the industry, led by General Motors, proved to be remarkably successful at producing a huge variety of products for the Allied effort.

General Motors had been filling military contracts since the early 1930s, and by the time the war broke out, GM had already assumed $5 billion worth of Allied contracts. For example, GM produced 854,000 trucks for the military during World War II for only a 10 percent profit margin, half of its peacetime profit margin. Nevertheless, the task of converting to wartime production was a monumental one, made even more difficult by the fact that two-thirds of what it was producing (i.e., 75 mm explosive shells) had nothing to do with cars. GM's patriotism paid off; $911 million was spent for equipment and new facilities, of which $809 million came from the public coffer. In addition to netting a cool $673 million in after-tax profits, GM's production capacity had increased 50 percent by the conclusion of the war. Cumulatively, GM's expansion for the war effort was second only to that of DuPont.[1]

By the time the war ended, the American automobile industry, led by the big three of GM,

Ford, and Chrysler, had produced at least 75 essential items for the effort, including 27,000 aircraft, 170,000 boat engines, and 5,947,000 guns.[2] Chrysler became the world's leading manufacturer of tanks.

Also, in response to a U.S. Army-sponsored competition, Willys Overland developed a car called the GPV, short for "General Purpose Vehicle." The name was quickly shortened to "jeep." These cars became the most essential vehicle in the Allied forces' military transport. Afterwards, surplus jeeps were sold to civilians, many of whom were returning soldiers. Jeeps quickly became popular and were the forerunners for the all-wheel-drive sport utility vehicle.

The automobile industry was instrumental in winning the war for the Allies, and not only because of the cars it produced. The industry applied its mass production techniques to other goods other than automobiles with astonishing results. For example, the industry made 100 percent of

the nation's armored cars, 85 percent of army helmets, and 87 percent of aircraft bombs.

As soon as the war ended, the clamor for new cars began. On the day Japan surrendered Americans joyously littered the streets with their gasoline ration books. Gas rationing ended the next day. People were ready to travel, and they wanted to do so in new cars, not their jalopies with rebuilt engines and re-treaded tires.

Astonishingly, in 1945, only 700 cars were made for consumer sale. Factories had to retool its factories for car production. Likewise, there were still severe supply shortages, and the government didn't lift restrictions until 1946 and price controls until 1947.[3] By the time shortages subsided and restrictions were lifted, the industry was ready to meet the demand of an unprecedented sellers' market. Prices for cars in the late 1940s were double that of 10 years earlier. But people could afford to buy them, and buy them they did. By 1949 industry output had risen to five million;

A beautiful new 1946 Cadillac model 62. Prints & Photographs Division, Library of Congress.

in 1950 it had skyrocketed to eight million.[4] By 1950, the average American automobile cost $1,800 and typically featured an eight-cylinder, 100-horsepower engine. Radios and air conditioners were options, but few people bought cars without them. Manual gearshifts were standard, but most models offered an automatic version.[5]

The biggest technological innovation in cars in the immediate postwar era was the 1947 "Kettering engine." This V-8, overhead-valve engine wasn't so much a new invention as it was a combination of two much older designs, the V-8 and overhead valves. By combining the two, the new engine could produce much more power than its predecessors, starting what would become the horsepower wars of the 1950s and early 1960s. The 1949 Cadillac had featured a V-8 engine with 160 horsepower. Its popularity led to other carmakers trying to emulate it, and in the succeeding years cars quickly grew bigger, faster, and much more powerful.

WARTIME RATIONING

While the automobile industry's output doubled during the war, the cars produced were for the government and the military. Japan's invasion of the Dutch Indies and Malaya cut off almost the entire natural supply of rubber, resulting in the severe rationing of tires. In fact, the 35 million tires on civilian vehicles were considered the nation's greatest rubber reserve, so people were asked to turn their tires in. Similarly, gas and other petroleum went to the military first. A nationwide 35 mph speed limit was imposed for the duration of the war.[6] Accordingly, by 1944 only 213 billion miles of domestic car travel occurred, down from 334 billion in 1941. Likewise, government highway expenditures, which had peaked at $2.659 million in 1938, had by 1944 dropped to $1.649 million.[7]

Innumerable cars had been nursed through the Depression; people just couldn't afford to buy new cars. Ironically, just as people began to be able to afford a new car, they stopped being made, and people were again forced to further elongate the lives of their cars, many of which had been built in the 1920s. Indeed, as the military was being provided with an impressive brand new fleet of autos, the domestic fleet was literally falling apart. Despite this, the civilian fleet remained essential to the war effort: industrial workers had to get to work in order for things to get made. As a Detroit billboard read, "There's a Ford in your future, but the Ford from your past is the Ford you've got now, so you'd better make it last."[8] To ensure that there was enough gas, the allotment for leisure travel was restricted to a mere two gallons a week, and car pools were encouraged. One famous government poster of the time warned people that, "When you ride alone, you ride with Hitler!" While there was some abuse of the ration system, including a black market for gasoline ration books, the system worked well enough to keep essential traffic on the road and moving during the war.

NATIONAL PARKS

The family camping trips to national parks that were popular in the years prior to the war declined so drastically during the war that the parks may as well have been closed to public use; even though they remained open, most people couldn't get to them. The National Park Service (NPS) road-building projects that had been buoyed by Depression-era work projects peaked in 1940 when the NPS budget was $21 million. That year 17 million people visited the various national parks. One year later, the budget was chopped to $5 million, barely enough to run the parks, let alone build new roads. Once the war ended, people headed for the parks. A then record 22 million people visited national parks in 1946. The parks did have importance during the war. For example, in July 1940, the future of the Civilian Conservation Corps (CCC) was uncertain. CCC Director James McEntee redirected the program to train young men specifically for the military work that most assumed would needed shortly. CCC camps had been used by the Army Reserve as a field training ground for its leaders and for future military recruits, who learned a variety of skills, ranging from first aid and safety to heavy machinery operation. The government saw the possibilities and mobilized the CCC to train young men in land clearing, road building, and the construction of sewer systems. Although the CCC program was

Travel

dismantled in 1941, 12,000 CCC-trained recruits had been directly assigned to a variety of military installations, where they proved invaluable in the construction of infrastructure.[9]

Adequate space to house the millions of new war workers was at a premium throughout the war. The Washington Monument and Potomac Park grounds were used to erect temporary office buildings in Washington, D.C. The big park hotels at places like Yosemite were used to house troops undergoing rehabilitation. Mount McKinley was used to test equipment under cold weather conditions; Joshua Tree National Monument was used for training in desert conditions; and Mount Rainier was used for mountain warfare training.

By 1942, recreational planning nationwide had ground to a halt. Landscape architects and other park employees were moved into defense occupations, where they had a great impact, especially in the design of military installations. Park designers' skills in planning buildings that blended into the surrounding natural landscapes proved useful in camouflage. This new field of design emerged because of advancements in airplanes and optics, which made it easier to target specific buildings from the air.[10]

Public Transportation

By the early 1940s, the American railroads had fallen behind cars and planes in the American landscape. However, the war bought the railroads some time. America wasn't yet linked coast-to-coast by roads, but it was linked by rail. When Ralph Budd, president of the Burlington Northern Railroad, asked FDR to let the railroads privately mobilize for the war effort, FDR agreed and put Budd in charge. The railroad companies had too many cars and too little business, but the war changed all that as rails were used to move soldiers and supplies all across the nation. Trains would move 97 percent of wartime passengers and 90 percent of its freight.[11] The railroads used the wartime boom to pay off debts and streamline their business, but when the war ended, so, too, did the railroad's prosperity. The automobile and the airplane quickly ascended to take the train's place.

Because of the various ship blockades abroad, international boat travel ground to a halt, and most domestic ships that weren't ferry traffic were used to move freight. After the war, ships would still be used for freight, but planes ultimately became the preferred mode of travel. U.S. public transportation systems thrived during the war; people walked and formed car pools. Bus and trolley use was at full capacity throughout the war. Similarly, rail cars, which were ostensibly only for those with essential need, were jammed full over the course of the war. With gasoline rationing, comparatively poor roadways, and cars that were falling apart, Americans had little choice but to turn to public modes of transportation. However, as soon as the war was over, Americans began to rely on automobiles more than any other form of transportation.

THE AIRPLANE INDUSTRY

Initially, airplane manufacturers were uncertain that the production line process that proved so useful for cars would work with planes, which were much more intricate in their design. Furthermore, they feared that the wartime entry of carmakers into what had previously always been a feast-or-famine industry would hurt their chances of postwar success. They preferred that automobile manufacturers remain subcontractors only. Fortunately for the aeronautics industry, its fears would be unfounded: Production lines proved remarkably adaptable to airplane manufacture, and after the war, car manufacturers had their hands full just making cars.

Two important innovations in the aeronautical industry during World War II were helicopter technology and jet engines. The U.S. military wanted an aircraft that could move quickly but could also hover in place. The helicopter, the development of which was spurred by America's entry into the war, proved to be just such an aircraft. In 1942, the United States was the first country to use helicopters in its armed services. The helicopter quickly became a standard military item for every country that could afford to maintain a fleet. Likewise, the necessities of war stimulated aeronautical companies to develop stronger, faster, and more reliable jet engines. The research and development of the jet engine during the war years led to its quickly becoming the standard for both fighter and passenger planes.[12]

The airline industry exploded during the war. In 1939, the value of the industry's output was $225 million; by 1944 it had risen to $16 billion. Before the war, the industry had been largely confined to the coasts, but demand led it to expand production facilities to places such as Ohio, Texas, and Kansas. Furthermore, the industry experienced few material shortages, as rationing ensured all available supplies were funneled directly to the manufacturers of wartime industrial equipment.

There was tremendous optimism about financial opportunities that would come with a commercial fleet, but the industry first endured a postwar employment contraction. In 1946, industry employment had shrunk to 192,000, down from the wartime of 2,080,000. But by 1948, air travel was becoming more common and more affordable, and the industry took off. Domestic service was largely carried out by reconfigured military transports, but the rising demand for air travel led to the development of new designs. Manufacturers were soon swamped with orders from domestic as well as international companies, many of whose own industries had been destroyed during the war.[13]

While the reality of plane travel didn't become de rigueur during the 1940s, the *idea* of plane travel, widely celebrated by optimistic scientists, futurists, and industry heads, captivated the American imagination. During the war years, popular magazines, newspapers, and government publications all speculated on the kinds of "air-cars" people would be flying after the war. More often than not, experts pointed to the helicopter as the most likely consumer vehicle, as evidenced

Passengers boarding a Trans World Airline Constellation, 1946. Prints & Photographs Division, Library of Congress.

Travel

by the popular 1943 Airways for Peace exhibit at New York City's Museum of Modern Art. The exhibit featured a Sikorsky Helicopter Company film that showed a man taking off in a helicopter from a New York City rooftop, apparently on his way to work. Shortly afterwards, he returns, hovering just off the ground as his wife hands him his forgotten lunch.[14] Such images made an indelible mark in the American imagination. Some educators at Columbia University and the University of Nebraska were so confident that the personal airplane would soon dominate American life, they created an *Air-Age Education* series of some 20 textbooks, aimed at preparing students for life in the coming global air age.[15]

In 1945 the *Saturday Evening Post* ran a poll that showed that 32 percent of American adults wanted to own their own plane after the war and that 7 percent felt they would definitely buy one. Many prognosticators thought the aeronautics industry would experience a consumer boom similar to that which the automobile had experienced earlier in the century.[16] Americans felt they would be entitled to the spoils of victory at war's end. They wanted their own homes and televisions, all-electric kitchens, new cars, and an airplane as well. All their other wants were attainable, so why not think a plane would be as well? In 1946, Americans did order 33,254 planes, five times more than they had ever before ordered in a single year. But in the next two years sales fell off by half, and then by half again.[17] Economic hard times were not responsible; in fact, virtually every other sector of the economy that was predicted to take off—from housing and hosiery to cars and electronic-age kitchen appliances—did so. For most people, especially those living in highly congested urban or suburban areas, owning a plane was just too expensive, impractical, and inconvenient. But despite the fact that plane ownership for the masses never took place, the dream of personal aircraft did make Americans more comfortable with the idea of flying, which prior to the war had widely been thought of as unnecessarily dangerous.

ROADWAYS

In October 1940, the Pennsylvania Turnpike, America's first superhighway, opened. It was an engineering marvel. A 160-mile, 4-lane, concrete-paved highway stretching from Harrisburg on the western side of the state to Pittsburgh in the east, it cut 5 hours off the trip's previous distance.[18] Furthermore, the wide, smooth lanes of the turnpike proved to be much safer than the earlier smaller, rougher roads. The tolls collected provided funds to maintain the original turnpike and build new roads. The Pennsylvania Turnpike was considered to be just the start of what surely would come: an interstate highway system that linked the nation from coast to coast. Other states, including Maine, New Hampshire, and Connecticut, announced plans to build their own turnpikes, but roadway funding dried up as the nation turned its attention to mobilizing for war.

In 1938, prewar highway expenditures peaked at $2.65 million, whereas in 1944 they bottomed out at $1.36 million. Some roads were built during the war, most notably Michigan's Willow Run and Davison expressways—which provided employees easy access to plants in and around Detroit—but for the most part road building stopped during the war. However, things were forever changed as a result of what Jane Holtz Kay calls "The Asphalt Exodus," which refers to the profound spatial shift that began in American culture in the postwar years. During the war, the U.S. government felt that to discourage German bomb attacks it was necessary to spread out wartime industries. So, in addition to pumping money into older manufacturing centers on the East Coast (New York, Boston, Philadelphia, etc.), the government awarded contracts to the Pacific Coast, the South, and the Southwest. Prior to the war, America's urban areas were beginning to shrink, but the war effort resulted in 4 million workers moving to the cities to work, thus stabilizing the population of older cities and skyrocketing the populations of comparatively smaller cities like Los Angeles (which gained 500,000 new residents) and Portland, Oregon (which experienced a 150% growth).[19] The war helped stem the exodus from America's big cities, but the conclusion of the war saw a radical reversion of the trend.

The end of the war signaled the start of an unparalleled era of consumerism. Americans felt they had done without for long enough; the war was over, and they felt entitled to what they wanted.

Travel

They wanted space, and they couldn't get it in the cities. They moved out to the suburbs, and they bought cars to ferry them back and forth from their urban jobs to their comparatively rural homes. The car became king, as evidenced by the fact that in 1948 Los Angeles voters turned down a public transit system, and Pittsburgh, Baltimore, and Detroit opened their first city parking garages.[20]

In 1944, anxious to address the obvious coming needs for peacetime drivers, Congress passed the Federal Highway Act, which was meant to create an interlinking National System of Interstate Highways that ran through cities. The program was underfunded, but its purpose was not forgotten.[21] In the ensuing years, as the suburbs sprang up, a clamor rose for something to be done about the "unsightly" and ill-equipped slums that characterized parts of larger American cities. In response, Congress passed the Housing Act of 1949, which was designed to fix big-city housing difficulties by instituting a poorly defined policy of urban renewal. Rather than renewing urban housing areas, the law often had the opposite effect. Money was provided to tear down slums, but not to build public housing in their place. Money was doled out to business owners and builders, but not to the working poor who

were living in the buildings that were torn down. What the Housing Act did, more than anything, was displace the poor and clear space for freeways. Prior to the late 1940s, freeways went around rather than through cities. Astute businessmen quickly realized the likely boon if roads were built *through* cities, thus allowing easy access for their desired customers: the newly affluent denizens of the suburbs springing up around every major city in America. The "urban renewal" Housing Act of 1949 ultimately had the unintended consequence of bringing about the goals of the 1944 Federal Highway Act. For poorer city dwellers, the policy was disastrous. Innumerable fraying but functional neighborhoods, many of them historic, were demolished in the late 1940s and early 1950s, displacing millions of people, some two-thirds of whom were ethnic minorities. The most notorious example of such a highway is New York City's Cross Bronx Expressway, which cut through 113 city streets and 159 buildings and turned out at least 5,000 people.

The turnpikes planned by several eastern states in the early 1940s were finished in the late 1940s, and several more, including connecting turnpikes from Pennsylvania to Ohio and Ohio to Indiana, were built.

Travel

Visual Arts

of the 1940s

American painting in the years leading up to the 1940s was primarily dominated by traditional realistic pictorial representations, although there were a small of number of Surrealist American artists. However, American artists didn't have access to the European paintings whose influence would lead to a Modernist revolutioon in American art. In the early 1940s, Modernists would come to America, bringing with them a new mode of thinking and working that would heavily shape American artists. And while the war wasn't fought on American soil, radio, newsreels, and especially newspapers and magazines featuring photographs by photojournalists, brought World War II home. As a result, American visual arts underwent a radical transformation in the 1940s.

PAINTING

By 1940, Surrealism—using unusual juxtapositions and fantastical images to express thoughts from the subconscious—had made its way to American shores. Under oppression from the totalitarianism of the Nazis' brutal regime, European artists immigrated to New York, where they continued to work in the Surrealistic mode. They socialized with their American counterparts, such as Robert Motherwell and Jackson Pollock, and it wasn't long before American artists began to experiment with Surrealism. Further exposing Americans to European Modernism were major shows at New York City's Museum of Modern Art (MoMA) in 1941 featuring Surrealist masters Salvador Dalí and Joan Miró. The unprecedented American presence of European art and artists unquestionably played a major role in American artists' embrace of a new vision, but perhaps the single most important contributing factor was World War II itself. Just as World War I resulted in the rise of Modernism, so World War II led to new modes of artistic expression. Surrealism was a reaction to the war's destruction of civilization.

By 1941, Surrealism was widely adopted by American artists. This early stage was characterized by artists who were what painter Mark Rothko called "Mythmakers," those who, in addition to European art, turned to ancient myths, Native American art, and South American art for inspiration. The Mythmakers' turn to non-European art forms for influence signaled the coming revolution in American art, in which American artists would ultimately reject European art in favor of the pursuit of their own style. Their labors would result in a new school of art: Abstract Expressionism, the first inherently American style to acquire international renown.

Abstract Expressionism, while ultimately practiced by artists the world over, was initially a New York movement, with the artists who contributed to its formation being called the "New York school." Their ranks include some of the most important American artists of the twentieth century, including Willem de Kooning, Arshile Gorky, Jackson Pollock, Mark Rothko, Robert Motherwell, Ad Reinhardt, and Clyfford Still. While the New York school has been lumped together as working in Abstract Expressionism, the term doesn't do justice to the diversity of styles of the artists. The work of the artists of the New York school changed the international perception of American art; by the mid-1950s the hub of international art had widely been recognized as having shifted from Paris to New York City, where it has remained ever since.

The New York school of abstract expressionists were arguably the most influential and revolutionary American painters of the twentieth century; however, as is often the case in art, the importance of their work was not widely understood or recognized at the time. In fact, art historians and critics have long disagreed on the defining characteristics of the form. It's generally agreed that after World War II, it could be loosely categorized as containing two primary modes of expression: chromatic abstraction and gestural abstraction. Chromatic abstraction, also known as "field painting," focused primarily on singular images of fields of color and was championed by Rothko, Reinhardt, and others. Rather than embracing the dreamy intricacy of Surrealism, they boiled their work down to more simple abstractions, often containing just a few colors. Conversely, gestural abstraction, or "action painting," was interested in the physical gestures of the painter. The gesturalists worked on a huge scale, loading their brushes with paint and using their whole bodies in the application of the paint to the canvas. What evolved from this approach was a highly personal and painterly "signature" indicative of a certain artist. De Kooning and Pollock were the most influential of the gestural abstractionists.

Mark Rothko and Willem de Kooning

Mark Rothko's (1903–1970) work has proved to be the most influential among field paintings. Born in Russia, his family immigrated to America in 1913, settling in Portland, Oregon. Rothko received a scholarship to study at Yale, but he dropped out before completing his degree. After a stint at the Art Students League in New York, he became an art teacher. His work in the 1930s concentrated primarily on figure scenes.[1] In the early 1940s, influenced by the European Surrealists, his work began to take on a more mythical tone. In 1945, he debuted at the Art of This Century Gallery in New York City; by the late 1940s his work had evolved into the field paintings with which he's become most identifiable. He worked on a large scale, creating hazy, rectangular fields of color.

Willem de Kooning (1904–1997) was born in Rotterdam, the Netherlands. He illegally immigrated to America in 1926. In the late 1930s, after a period designing murals for the Federal Art Project, he began a series of paintings depicting women. His work in the early 1940s was primarily in figure studies, but by the late 1940s de Kooning embarked on the paintings that would make his reputation: a series of black-and-white abstractions in oil and enamel.[2] After his success as an abstract expressionist, de Kooning never quit innovating and pushing himself as an artist. Although it was his black-and-white abstractions, such as *Excavations* (1950), that initially made him famous, he continued to be an influential draftsman and painter.

Jackson Pollock

Jackson Pollock (1912–1956) is considered the most influential American artist of the twentieth century, helping break the ground for artists such as Andy Warhol. Born in Cody, Wyoming, Pollock moved from place to place in the American West during his youth. By 1930, he'd found his way to New York, where he studied under Thomas Hart Benton at the Art Students League. Pollock spent the late 1930s working assorted jobs in various studios and for Federal Art Relief plans.[3]

By the early 1940s, Pollock was beginning to produce increasingly abstracted works in a vein similar to that of the other Mythmakers. He enjoyed minor success until 1945, when Pollock and his wife, artist Lee Krasner, moved to a small farmhouse in Springs, Long Island. Here, Pollock developed his revolutionary technique, his so-called drip paintings, which he produced in a short but remarkably fecund period lasting from 1947 to 1950. It is for these "drip" works, such as *Cathedral* (1947) and *Number I* (1948), that Pollock is best known. Indeed, they are most responsible for his artistic influence. Pollock wanted to move beyond traditional painting, which he felt was restricted by the necessity of the brush as the primary painterly tool. To circumvent this, Pollock placed his canvases on the floor to make it easier for him to apply paint in whatever way struck his fancy. He would fling, throw, pour, and, most famously, drip paint on his canvases, which he believed brought him in greater touch with his mind as a painter.

After his drip period, Pollock did produce a few more important works, but for the most part his artistic creativity ceased to have its innovative edge, due in large part to his deepening alcoholism and the accompanying mental instability. After his death, Pollock quickly became the most well-known and infamous American artist of the twentieth century. He was even featured on a U.S. postage stamp in 1999.

Jackson Pollock, in front of one of his paintings. Prints & Photographs Division, Library of Congress.

Norman Rockwell

Because of the war and its immediate aftermath, even less attention than normal was paid to visual artists. However, there is one artist whose work was widely known and loved by millions: Norman Rockwell.

Norman Rockwell (1894–1978) studied at the New York School of Art and then the National Academy of Design. He became the art director of the Boy Scouts of America's magazine, *Boys' Life,* while still in his teens. He was also a successful freelancer, placing his work in numerous national magazines. In 1916, at age 22, he landed his first of 322 paintings on the cover of the *Saturday Evening Post.* While he painted until his death in 1978, Rockwell's most productive period is generally considered to have been in the 1930s and 1940s, during which time his numerous *Saturday Evening Post* covers pictured scenes of idyllic small-town American life. These images were particularly cherished by an American audience that in the 1940s craved a return to normalcy. Perhaps the best example of Rockwell's popularity can be found in his *Four Freedoms* paintings of 1943. On January 6, 1941, President Roosevelt delivered a speech to Congress in which he stressed four essential freedoms—of speech, of worship, from want, and from fear—as a way to articulate to Americans what the fighting in World War II was for. After hearing the president's speech, Rockwell was inspired to create paintings interpreting each of them in scenes from everyday American life: *Freedom of Speech, Freedom of Worship, Freedom from Want,* and *Freedom from Fear.* Rockwell approached the government about painting this series, but the government wasn't interested. Rockwell painted them anyway, and they appeared in four consecutive issues of the *Saturday Evening Post.* The first, *Freedom of Speech,* shows a young man standing up and speaking at a public gathering; the second, *Freedom of Worship,* depicts in close-up people praying, presumably at a church; the next, *Freedom from Want,* shows a woman serving a magnificent turkey dinner to her family; the last, *Freedom from Fear,* shows a mother and father tucking their children into bed at night. These paintings immediately struck a chord with Americans, and the paintings were

Hasten the homecoming–Buy Victory Bonds. Norman Rockwell. Prints & Photographs Division, Library of Congress.

soon featured in a nationwide traveling exhibition sponsored by the *Saturday Evening Post* and the U.S. Treasury Department. The Office of War Information used the images on posters that were emblazoned on the bottom with the line "BUY WAR BONDS." The posters, along with the traveling exhibition, helped to sell enough war bonds to raise more than $130 million for the war effort.

In addition to his *Four Freedoms* paintings, Rockwell created a hugely important fictional character: Willie Gillis, a jug-eared G. I. featured on the cover of the *Saturday Evening Post* 11 times. Gillis was based on Rockwell's Vermont neighbor, a young man named Bob Buck, who posed for Rockwell before going off to war. Gillis was an everyman who represented for people their absent brother or son. In his last *Post* cover on May 26, 1945, Gillis, like Buck himself, returned home safe.

While Rockwell's work for the *Saturday Evening Post* brought him public adulation, it didn't win him critical success. Rockwell referred to himself as an illustrator, yet he still wanted to be taken seriously as an artist. Having his work appear in a popular medium such as the *Saturday Evening Post* instead of on gallery walls hurt his credibility among "serious" critics and artists. Interestingly, the most popular artist of his day wasn't taken seriously by the arbiters of high culture in his time, while those who went largely unrecognized by the public were eventually lionized in both the critical and popular press.

PHOTOGRAPHY

Prior to the 1940s, photography was considered by many people to be a second-class art. In the 1940s, however, the ascent of photography as a major art form began with the publication of the *Bulletin of the Museum of Modern Art* (vol. 2, no. 8, 1940/1941); the entire issue was devoted to promoting the museum's newly established photography department, which curated shows dedicated to the medium. In addition, several journals, such as *Popular Photography,* played an instrumental role in the popularization of the form.

In the prewar years, documentary and pictorialism continued to be the dominant genres practiced by photographers. Much of the work of its most visible practitioners still dealt with the Depression years, although there were the beginnings of a move away from documenting social ills toward a celebration of America's strengths. Where the advent of war brought immediate and widespread change was in the use of photography, like radio and films, as a means of chronicling the war at home and abroad. After the war, photography became far more dissonant and fractured as photographers diverged in a variety of directions, especially in terms of experimentation with and manipulation of their images.

A number of important photographers were working in the early 1940s, including Dorothea Lange, Gordon Parks, John Vachon, Marion Post Wolcott, and others. They made a reputation for themselves working as documentarists for the Farm Security Administration and the Works Progress Administration. Others, such as Ansel

Adams, Paul Strand, and Imogen Cunningham, were also practicing forms of documentary. However, of those whose work would help to characterize the early 1940s, it's particularly important to understand the contributions of Arthur "Weegee" Fellig (1899–1968) and Walker Evans (1903–1975).

A certain branch of documentation that came to the fore in the 1940s was urban documentation. At the forefront of this movement was the Photo League, a New York-based group that organized lectures and ran a small photography school. In the 1940s, Weegee was invited at various times to lecture and exhibit at the Photo League.

Following a 12-year stint as a darkroom man for Acme Newspictures, Weegee became a freelance photographer, quickly establishing a reputation as a man with a fierce nose for news; in fact, he earned his nickname (derived from the Ouija board) because he always seemed to be first on the scene where news happened. In reality, he was diligent and hardworking; he worked nights, monitoring the Teletype for breaking news reports. He also kept shortwave radios tuned to the police band in his car and apartment. As with all his work, his initial show at the Photo League, Murder is My Business, documented the crimes and weird happenings that occurred seemingly nonstop in New York City. While he was a documentarist, he didn't necessarily follow the standard direct approach to shooting a subject. Instead, his technique was characterized more by his personal visions than by a commitment to a formal methodology. He recorded urban life as a "grand carnival of human comedy." In 1943 he staged his first exhibition at MoMA, and by decade's end his fame was secured by the publication of two books, *Naked City* (1945) and *Weegee's People* (1946).

Walker Evans was a photographer closely affiliated with the Farm Security Administration and the Resettlement Administration. He is best known for his Depression-era pictures of the poverty and desperation of life in the rural American South. Many of these pictures appear in *American Photographs* (1938), the catalogue of his 1938 one-man show at the Museum of Modern Art. In the summer of 1936, on a commission from *Fortune* magazine, he lived in rural Alabama, documenting the tragedy occurring in rural America by taking pictures chronicling the lives of three sharecropping families. The writer James Agee, who had accompanied Evans in Alabama, wrote text to accompany the photos. *Fortune* magazine ultimately rejected their project. However, Evans persisted and Agee polished his text, and the two compiled a series of 31 of these images in a book entitled *Let Us Now Praise Famous Men.* The book was unable to secure a publisher, until 1941, when it was finally taken up by Houghton Mifflin. It received little attention despite the fact that it contained extraordinary photographs and vivid text to illustrate the desperation of the tenant families' lives. Ultimately, as Evans and Agee's fame grew, the book was resurrected to its rightful place among the pantheon of photographic masterpieces. Ironically, Evans's fame led him to a 20-year stint as a photographer for *Fortune* magazine, and he is widely recognized as among the most important and influential American photographers ever. (See Visual Arts of the 1930s for Walker Evans photographs.)

Photojournalism

If any one kind of photography can be said to characterize the 1940s, it is photojournalism, a style whose rise is inextricably linked to the war and the public's yearning for visually supported reporting from the various fronts. TV was in its infancy, so people turned to illustrated newspapers and weeklies for visuals of current events.

Of the many weeklies that flourished during the war years, perhaps none were more central to America's conception of the war than *Look* and *Life.* Both featured reporting on current events. Photographers such as Cecil Beaton and Margaret Bourke-White would snap their pictures and turn over their negatives to the editorial staff, who would choose images to support the text. The effect of visually supported current-event stories about the war was incredibly powerful and went a long way in shaping the public's sentiments toward the war.

In earlier years, the military had been opposed to civilian photographers on the battlefield, censoring images of American dead (showing foreign dead was okay). In September 1943, the War Department lifted that policy, arguing that

Americans needed to "understand the ferocity of the struggle and the sacrifices being made on its behalf." The American military granted photographers unprecedented access to the battlefronts, resulting in the September 20, 1943, issue of *Life* featuring a full-page picture of three dead Americans killed during the storming of Buna Beach in New Guinea.[4] Still, while photographers took pictures that showed the negative side of life for American civilians and soldiers, including photos of exhausted, dead, and dying soldiers and of Japanese people living in California's internment camps, many of the stories had a cheerleading quality to them.

The culmination of wartime photojournalism was the shocking series of photographs of the German concentration camps and other wartime horrors (including the smoldering bodies of political prisoners burned alive by retreating German soldiers) taken by Margaret Bourke-White, George Rodgers, Johnny Florea, and William Vandivert. These were published as "Atrocities" in a six-page spread in the May 7, 1945, issue of *Life*. For the public, these photos served as an explanation of and justification for American involvement in World War II.[5] In 1947, Edward Steichen, the former director of photography for the U.S. Navy, was appointed director of the Department of Photography at MoMA; he immediately began incorporating images from World War II photojournalism into shows at the museum. By decade's end, wartime photojournalism had been fully accepted as a powerful and important means of American artistic expression.

After the war, as did many other areas of American life, photography began to change rapidly. Among the most revolutionary developments was the increasing use of color in images. "Art" photography had always been in black and white. Nonetheless, in the late 1940s, some photographers began to experiment with color, even though the process was still expensive and comparatively unreliable. At the same time, color photography really took hold in the commercial realm. Glossy popular magazines, especially fashion magazines, quickly capitalized on the medium to make their pages more vivid. Color photographs were frequently used to support feature articles and were also widely adopted in magazine advertisements, where they proved to be very effective.

After the war, some photographers, led by Harry Callahan, Aaron Siskind, and Minor White, embraced the "new vision," which was photography's equivalent of Postmodernism. European émigrés came to America in droves during the late 1930s and 1940s, bringing with them the notion of conceptualizing photography through a "new vision," that is, rather than taking pictures and letting the images speak for themselves, photographers began to experiment with light and composition and to manipulate images for effect. This was highly controversial since it went completely against the grain of the American documentary style.

ENDNOTES FOR THE 1940s

OVERVIEW OF THE 1940s

1. Michael C. C. Adams, *The Best War Ever: America and World War II* (Baltimore: Johns Hopkins University Press, 1994), xiii.
2. Sean Dennis Cashman, *America, Roosevelt, and World War II* (New York: New York University Press, 1989), 13–14.
3. Cashman, *America, Roosevelt, and World War II,* 56.
4. Ross Gregory, *America 1941: A Nation at a Crossroads* (New York: The Free Press, 1989), 3.
5. Cashman, *America, Roosevelt, and World War II,* 61–62.
6. Melvyn Dubofsky, Athan Theoharis, and Daniel M. Smith, *The United States in the Twentieth Century* (Englewood Cliffs, NJ: Prentice-Hall, 1978), 320.
7. Godfrey Hodgson, *America in Our Time: From World War II to Nixon, What Happened and Why* (New York: Vintage Books, 1976), 20.
8. Dubofsky, Theoharis, and Smith, *The United States in the Twentieth Century,* 311.
9. Hodgson, *America in Our Time,* 18–20.
10. Katherine A. S. Sibley, *The Cold War* (Westport, CT: Greenwood Press, 1998), 3.
11. Allan M. Winkler, *Home Front U.S.A.: America during World War II* (Arlington Heights, IL: Harlan Davidson, 1986), 67.
12. Adams, *The Best War Ever,* 119.
13. Dubofsky, Theoharis, and Smith, *The United States in the Twentieth Century,* 322.
14. Winkler, *Home Front U.S.A.,* 64.
15. Dubofsky, Theoharis, and Smith, *The United States in the Twentieth Century,* 324.
16. Winkler, *Home Front U.S.A.,* 60.
17. Winkler, *Home Front U.S.A.,* 71.

Arts

18. "Ansel Adams Manzanar Photo Collection." Library of Congress Prints and Photographs Online Catalog. http://lcweb2.loc.gov/pp/manzhtml/manzabt.html.

19. Winkler, *Home Front U.S.A.,* 72–73.

20. Dubofsky, Theoharis, and Smith, *The United States in the Twentieth Century,* 323.

21. Winkler, *Home Front U.S.A.,* 50.

22. Winkler, *Home Front U.S.A.,* 51.

23. Winkler, *Home Front U.S.A.,* 55.

24. Dubofsky, Theoharis, and Smith, *The United States in the Twentieth Century,* 323.

25. Winkler, *Home Front U.S.A.,* 33.

26. Lois Gordon and Alan Gordon, *American Chronicle: Seven Decades in American Life, 1920–1989* (New York: Crown Publishers, 1987, 1990), 190, 284.

27. Eugenia Kaledin, *Daily Life in the United States, 1940–1950: Two Worlds* (Westport, CT: Greenwood Press, 2000), 66.

28. James R. Petersen, *The Century of Sex: Playboy's History of the Sexual Revolution: 1900–1999* (New York: Grove Press, 1999), 186.

29. Kaledin, *Daily Life in the United States, 1940–1950,* 70.

30. Kaledin, *Daily Life in the United States, 1940–1950,* 70.

31. Dubofsky, Theoharis, and Smith, *The United States in the Twentieth Century,* 318–19.

32. Michael J. Hogan, "Blueprint for Recovery." In *The Marshall Plan: Rebuilding Europe.* Posted May 2007. USINFO.State.Gov. http://usinfo.state.gov/products/pubs/marshallplan/hogan.htm.

33. Hodgson, *America in Our Time: From World War II to Nixon,* 19–20.

ADVERTISING OF THE 1940s

1. Roland Marchand, *Creating the Corporate Soul: The Rise of Public Relations and Corporate Imagery in American Big Business* (Berkeley: University of California Press, 1998), 320–21.

2. John Klotzbach, *A Sentimental Journey: America in the 1940s* (Pleasantville, NY: The Reader's Digest Association, 1998), 91.

3. Roland Marchand, *Creating the Corporate Soul: The Rise of Public Relations and Corporate Imagery in American Big Business* (Berkeley: University of California Press, 1998), 324–29.

4. James B. Twitchell, *20 Ads That Shook the World: The Century's Most Groundbreaking Advertising and How It Changed Us All* (New York: Crown Publishers, 2000), 85.

5. Twitchell, *20 Ads That Shook the World,* 87.

6. Twitchell, *20 Ads That Shook the World,* 92–93.

7. Twitchell, *20 Ads That Shook the World,* 95–98.

8. Richard S. Tedlow, *New and Improved: The Story of Mass Marketing in America* (New York: Basic Books, 1990), 64.

9. Thomas Doherty, *Projections of War: Hollywood, American Culture, and World War II* (New York: Columbia University Press, 1993), 9.

10. Doherty, *Projections of War,* 68.

11. Doherty, *Projections of War,* 67–68.

12. Gordon and Gordon, *American Chronicle,* 204, 213.

13. Nicholas Stein, "CHIQUITA. Yes, We Have No Profits. The Rise and Fall of Chiquita Banana: How a Great American Brand Lost Its Way," *Fortune,* November 14, 2001. http://www.fortune.com/fortune/articles/0,15114,367968,00.html.

14. "Television History: The First 75 Years," February 4, 2003. http://www.tvhistory.tv/1948%20TV%20Advertising.htm.

15. "Television History: The First 75 Years."

ARCHITECTURE OF THE 1940s

1. Dell Upton, *Architecture in the United States* (New York: Oxford University Press, 1998), 122.

2. Upton, *Architecture in the United States,* 122.

3. Upton, *Architecture in the United States,* 122–23.

4. Upton, *Architecture in the United States,* 234–36.

5. Upton, *Architecture in the United States,* 155.

6. Robin Markowitz, "Levittown," in *The St. James Encyclopedia of Popular Culture,* vol. 3, ed. Sara Pendergast and Tom Pendergast (Detroit: St. James Press, 2000), 147–49.

7. Markowitz, "Levittown," 147.

8. Markowitz, "Levittown," 148.

9. Markowitz, "Levittown," 148.

10. Markowitz, "Levittown," 148.

11. Upton, *Architecture in the United States,* 229–30.

12. Upton, *Architecture in the United States,* 141–42.

13. John C. Poppeliers, S. Allen Chambers Jr., and Nancy B. Schwartz, *What Style Is It? A Guide to American Architecture* (Washington, DC: The Preservation Press, 1983), 92.

14. William Jordy, *The Impact of European Modernism in the Mid-Twentieth Century* (New York: Oxford University Press, 1972), 225.

15. Carter Wiseman, *Shaping a Nation: Twentieth-Century American Architecture and Its Makers* (New York: W. W. Norton & Company, 1998), 175–76.

16. The U.S. Department of Defense, January 18, 2003. http://www.defenselink.mil/pubs/pentagon/about.html.

17. The U.S. Department of Defense.

BOOKS, NEWSPAPERS, MAGAZINES, AND COMICS OF THE 1940s

1. Charles Panati, *Panati's Parade of Fads, Follies, and Manias: The Origins of Our Most Cherished Obsessions* (New York: HarperPerennial, 1991), 231–32.

2. Lois Gordon and Alan Gordon, *American Chronicle: Seven Decades in American Life, 1920–1989* (New York: Crown Publishers, 1987, 1990), 220.

3. James R. Petersen, *The Century of Sex. Playboy's History of the Sexual Revolution: 1900–1999* (New York: Grove Press, 1999), 196–98.

ENTERTAINMENT OF THE 1940s

1. J. Fred MacDonald, *Don't Touch that Dial: Radio Programming in American Life, 1920–1960* (Chicago: Nelson-Hall, 1979), 69.
2. MacDonald, *Don't Touch that Dial,* 69.
3. MacDonald, *Don't Touch that Dial,* 78–80.
4. Joseph H. Udelson, *The Great Television Race: A History of the American Television Industry 1925–1941* (University: University of Alabama Press, 1982), 156–58.
5. Michael Ritchie, *Please Stand By: A Prehistory of Television* (Woodstock, NY: The Overlook Press, 1994), 141.
6. Ritchie, *Please Stand By,* 201.
7. Les Brown, "The American Networks," in *Television: An International History,* ed. Anthony Smith (Oxford: Oxford University Press, 1998), 149.
8. David A. Cook, *A History of Narrative Film* (New York: W. W. Norton, 1996), 444.

FASHION OF THE 1940s

1. Maria Constantino, *Men's Fashion in the Twentieth Century: From Frockcoats to Intelligent Fibres* (New York: Costume and Fashion Press, 1997), 65.
2. Constantino, *Men's Fashion in the Twentieth Century,* 68.
3. Kristina Harris, *Vintage Fashions for Women: 1920s–1940s* (Atglen, PA: Schiffer Publishing, 1996), 138.
4. Constantino, *Men's Fashion in the Twentieth Century,* 71–72.
5. Caroline Rennolds Milbank, *New York Fashion: The Evolution of American Style* (New York: Harry N. Abrams, 1989), 134.
6. Milbank, *New York Fashion,* 158–59.
7. Harris, *Vintage Fashions for Women,* 138.
8. Susannah Handley, *Nylon: The Story of a Fashion Revolution: A Celebration of Design from Art Silk to Nylon and Thinking Fibres* (Baltimore: Johns Hopkins University Press, 1999), 45–46.
9. Handley, *Nylon,* 48.
10. Handley, *Nylon,* 48–49.

FOOD OF THE 1940s

1. Elaine McIntosh, *American Food Habits in Historical Perspective* (Westport, CT: Praeger, 1995), 121.
2. Harvey Levenstein, *Paradox of Plenty: A Social History of Eating in Modern America* (New York: Oxford University Press, 1993), 64–65.
3. Levenstein, *Paradox of Plenty,* 65.
4. Levenstein, *Paradox of Plenty,* 81.
5. Levenstein, *Paradox of Plenty,* 83.
6. Levenstein, *Paradox of Plenty,* 83–84.
7. Levenstein, *Paradox of Plenty,* 93.
8. Time-Life Books, eds., *1940–1950,* Vol. V of *This Fabulous Century* (New York: Time-Life Books, 1969), 158.
9. Levenstein, *Paradox of Plenty,* 84.
10. Levenstein, *Paradox of Plenty,* 88.
11. Richard J. Hooker, *Food and Drink in America: A History* (Indianapolis: Bobbs-Merrill, 1981), 335.
12. John A. Jakle and Keith A. Sculle, *Fast Food: Roadside Restaurants in the Automobile Age* (Baltimore: Johns Hopkins University Press, 1999), 186.
13. Jakle and Sculle, *Fast Food,* 186.
14. Jakle and Sculle, *Fast Food,* 186–87.
15. Jakle and Sculle, *Fast Food,* 187.
16. Jakle and Sculle, *Fast Food,* 191.
17. Jakle and Sculle, *Fast Food,* 144.
18. Jakle and Sculle, *Fast Food,* 144.
19. Eric Schlosser, *Fast Food Nation: Eating Ourselves to Death: The Dark Side of the All-American Meal* (New York: Houghton Mifflin Co., 2000), 119–20.
20. Jean Anderson, *The American Century Cook-book* (New York: Clarkson Potter, 1997), 235
21. Anderson, *The American Century Cook-book,* 225.
22. Anderson, *The American Century Cook-book,* 247.
23. Anderson, *The American Century Cook-book,* 247.

MUSIC OF THE 1940s

1. David Ewen, *All the Years of American Popular Music* (Englewood Cliffs, NJ: Prentice-Hall, 1977), 456.
2. Ewen, *All the Years of American Popular Music,* 457.
3. Ewen, *All the Years of American Popular Music,* 427.
4. Ewen, *All the Years of American Popular Music,* 429.
5. Ewen, *All the Years of American Popular Music,* 430.
6. Ewen, *All the Years of American Popular Music,* 431.
7. Ewen, *All the Years of American Popular Music,* 444.
8. Ewen, *All the Years of American Popular Music,* 464.
9. Ewen, *All the Years of American Popular Music,* 460–61.
10. Ewen, *All the Years of American Popular Music,* 461–62.
11. Kyle Gann, *American Music in the Twentieth Century* (New York: Schirmer Books, 1997), 76.
12. Ewen, *All the Years of American Popular Music,* 483.
13. Ewen, *All the Years of American Popular Music,* 473.
14. Ewen, *All the Years of American Popular Music,* 474.

SPORTS AND LEISURE OF THE 1940s

1. William Marshall, *Baseball's Pivotal Era: 1945–1951* (Lexington: University Press of Kentucky, 1999), 6–7.
2. Benjamin G. Rader, *Baseball: A History of America's Game* (Urbana: University of Illinois Press, 2002), 159.
3. Rader, *Baseball,* 173–74.
4. Rader, *Baseball,* 172.
5. Robert W. Peterson, *Pigskin: The Early Years of Pro Football* (New York: Oxford University Press, 1997), 132–34.

6. Peterson, *Pigskin,* 137–43.

7. Peterson, *Pigskin,* 169.

8. Peterson, *Pigskin,* 165.

9. Robert W. Peterson, *Cages to Jumpshots: Pro Basketball's Early Years* (Lincoln: University of Nebraska Press, 2002), 124.

10. Peterson, *Cages to Jumpshots,* 166.

11. Jeffery T. Sammons, *Beyond the Ring: The Role of Boxing in American Society* (Urbana: University of Illinois Press, 1988), 108–17.

12. "Joe Louis Biography," Biography.com. http://search.biography.com/print_record.pl?id=17130 (January 5, 2003).

13. Jeffery T. Sammons, *Beyond the Ring: The Role of Boxing in American Society* (Urbana: University of Illinois Press, 1988), 124.

14. Sammons, *Beyond the Ring,* 126–27.

15. "Joe Louis Biography," http://www.biography.com/search/article.do?id=9386989.

16. "Joe Louis Biography," http://www.biography.com/search/article.do?id=9386989.

17. Zander Hollander and Hal Bock, eds., *The Complete Encyclopedia of Ice Hockey: The Heroes, Teams, Great Moments and Records of the National Hockey League* (Englewood Cliffs, NJ: Prentice Hall, 1970), 62–65.

18. Hollander and Bock, *The Complete Encyclopedia of Ice Hockey,* 73.

19. Lois Gordon and Alan Gordon, *American Chronicle: Seven Decades in American Life, 1920–1989* (New York: Crown Publishers, 1987, 1990), 230.

20. Allen Guttmann, *The Olympics: A History of the Modern Games* (Urbana: University of Illinois Press, 2002), 73–75.

21. Charles Panati, *Panati's Parade of Fads, Follies, and Manias: The Origins of Our Most Cherished Obsessions* (New York: HarperPerennial, 1991), 231–32.

22. Panati, *Panati's Parade of Fads, Follies, and Manias,* 204–5.

23. Andrew Marum and Frank Parise, *Follies and Foibles: A View of 20th Century Fads* (New York: Facts on File, 1984), 78.

TRAVEL OF THE 1940s

1. James J. Flink, *The Automobile Age* (Cambridge, MA: The MIT Press, 1975), 275–76.

2. Flink, *The Automobile Age,* 276.

3. Rae, *The American Automobile,* 161.

4. Rae, *The American Automobile,* 176.

5. Rae, *The American Automobile,* 176.

6. Rae, *The American Automobile,* 153–54.

7. Flink, *The Car Culture,* 189.

8. Stephen B. Goddard, *Getting There: The Epic Struggle between Road and Rail in the American Century* (New York: Basic Books, 1994), 167.

9. Linda Flint McClelland, *Building the National Parks: Historical Landscape Design and Construction* (Baltimore: Johns Hopkins University Press, 1998), 457–58.

10. McClelland, *Building the National Parks,* 458–59.

11. Goddard, *Getting There,* 167.

12. Donald M. Pattillo, *Pushing the Envelope: The American Aircraft Industry* (Ann Arbor: University of Michigan Press, 1998), 141–144.

13. Patillo, *Pushing the Envelope,* 154–56.

14. Joseph J. Corn, *The Winged Gospel* (New York: Oxford University Press, 1983), 107–8.

15. Corn, *The Winged Gospel,* 125–29.

16. Corn, *The Winged Gospel,* 108.

17. Corn, *The Winged Gospel,* 109–10.

18. Tom Lewis, *Divided Highways: Building the Interstate Highways, Transforming American Life* (New York: Viking Press, 1997), 48.

19. Jane Holtz Kay, *Asphalt Nation: How the Automobile Took Over America, and How We Can Take It Back* (New York: Crown Publishers, 1997), 223–24.

20. Kay, *Asphalt Nation,* 225.

21. Kay, *Asphalt Nation,* 225.

VISUAL ARTS OF THE 1940s

1. David Anfam, "Biographies of the Artists," in *American Art in the 20th Century: 1913–1993,* ed. Christos M. Joachimides and Norman Rosenthal (New York: Prestel, 1993), 468.

2. Anfam, "Biographies of the Artists," 444–45.

3. Anfam, "Biographies of the Artists," 464.

4. Keith F. Davis, *An American Century of Photography: From Dry-Plate to Digital* (Kansas City: Hallmark Cards, 1999), 256.

5. Davis, *An American Century of Photography,* 256–57.

1950s

Timeline

of Popular Culture Events, 1950s

1950

June 25: North Korea launches a surprise attack on South Korea, precipitating the Korean War and U.S. involvement.

At the opening of the decade, U.S. population stands at 150 million. Life expectancy measures almost 66 years for men and 71 years for women.

The average worker makes about $3,100 per year; a new national minimum wage of $0.75 per hour goes into effect in January.

Illiteracy reaches a new low in 1950: 3.2 percent.

In January, President Truman orders the United States to move ahead on developing a hydrogen bomb, after Russia successfully tests an atomic bomb in August 1949. In February, Wisconsin Senator Joseph McCarthy claims Communists have infiltrated every level of government, especially the State Department.

Sixty million Americans go to the movies each week.

All About Eve, a trenchant, sophisticated movie, proves a surprise hit and garners many awards. Two young actors make their film debuts: Marlon Brando in *The Men,* a war drama, and Marilyn Monroe in *The Asphalt Jungle,* a crime picture.

The Colgate Comedy Hour, Your Show of Shows, and *The Steve Allen Show* all premiere on network television, and Bob Hope makes the jump from radio to television, one of the first major radio comedians to do so. Soon after, most other radio stars follow suit.

In a clever marketing move, Earl Tupper decides to sell his plastic kitchen containers directly to consumers by way of "Tupperware Parties."

DuPont introduces Orlon, a new miracle fiber, and Xerox produces its first copying machine.

1951

March: Julius and Ethel Rosenberg are convicted of spying; they are executed in June 1953.

June: CBS presents the first commercial color telecast.

November: the New Jersey Turnpike opens, one of the first postwar superhighways.

The Twenty-second Amendment to the Constitution is passed in February, limiting presidents to two terms.

The number of American soldiers in Korea swells to 250,000, but in April, President Truman relieves General Douglas MacArthur of his Korean command after the general urges the invasion of China. MacArthur retires, and a parade honoring him in New York City draws over three million spectators. He then addresses Congress, and his mention that "old soldiers never die, they just fade away" results in a half-dozen hit records, along with much associated memorabilia.

The nickel telephone call becomes history when most pay phones charge a dime.

Remington Rand begins to manufacture the UNIVAC I, the first commercial business computer.

Health officials recommend the fluoridation of public drinking water as a means of reducing tooth decay.

Edward R. Murrow's *See It Now* premieres on TV, as does a new comedy series titled *I Love Lucy.*

The comedy team of Dean Martin and Jerry Lewis becomes a box office favorite.

Singers like Tony Bennett, Rosemary Clooney, Nat "King" Cole, Perry Como, Bing Crosby, Doris Day, and Frank Sinatra dominate record sales, effectively ending the reign of the big bands.

DuPont introduces Dacron, another new artificial fiber.

1952

April: An atomic test explosion in Nevada is broadcast live.

September: Richard Nixon, the candidate for vice president, delivers his famous "Checkers" speech. A record 58 million viewers tune in.

November: The Atomic Energy Commission announces the successful detonation of the first H-bomb at Eniwetok Atoll in the Pacific.

Prices climb, and the nation enters into a prolonged period of inflation.

The U.S. Postal Service discontinues the penny postcard; the new rate doubles to two cents.

General Dwight D. Eisenhower is elected president in November, ending the Democrats' monopoly on the office since 1932. Eisenhower promptly travels to Korea, fulfilling a campaign promise.

During the secure Eisenhower years, the average age for both marriages and divorces falls.

The conservative "man in the gray flannel suit" comes to epitomize both the fashions and lifestyles of the era.

Jonas Salk begins testing his experimental vaccine to ward off the ravages of polio; in the meantime, the disease strikes over 50,000 people, mainly children.

Fiberglass is introduced.

Dick Clark's *American Bandstand* debuts in January on Philadelphia television (it will become an ABC network offering in 1956). *Dragnet* premieres on TV after a successful radio run, and comedians Jackie Gleason and Ernie Kovacs introduce new shows.

RCA introduces tiny transistors that can replace bulky vacuum tubes; soon thereafter, the Sony Corporation brings out the first transistorized radios.

The Quiet Man, a movie starring John Wayne and Maureen O'Hara, reaffirms the popularity of both actors.

On college campuses across the nation, the first "panty raids" occur.

1953

June: A Korean armistice is declared for July, effectively ending the war. Peace negotiations will, however, drag on for years.

August: Russia announces that it also possesses the H-bomb.

September: Earl Warren takes the reins as Chief Justice of the Supreme Court.

Senator McCarthy's investigations into Communist influence in government capture the attention of many people.

An unknown guerilla leader named Fidel Castro launches an attack against the Cuban government on July 26th. It fails, and he goes to prison.

In a bow to the new medium's success, the Academy Awards presentation is televised for the first time, with Bob Hope serving as host.

Over 300 television stations schedule regular broadcasting, triple the number from 1950.

CinemaScope, a projection technique employing a wider screen and stereophonic sound, is introduced; *The Robe,* a religious epic starring Richard Burton, becomes the first offering using the new system.

Big, string-filled orchestras have a momentary burst of popularity among music fans. Percy Faith, Hugo Winterhalter, Frank Chacksfield, and Mantovani are among the leaders.

IBM introduces its first computer, the Model 701.

1954

January: Secretary of State John Foster Dulles unveils the defense policy of "massive retaliation."

January: The Navy commissions the U.S.S. *Nautilus,* the first nuclear-powered submarine.

March: The United States explodes the largest thermonuclear blast ever in an experiment at Bikini Atoll.

June 14: The phrase "under God" gets added to the Pledge of Allegiance.

July: Reflecting a renewed interest in jazz, the Newport Jazz Festival debuts.

December: The U.S. Senate censures Senator McCarthy.

The Supreme Court rules in May that "separate but equal" schools (those that separate students by race) are inherently unequal, one of the first major legal attacks against segregation.

In a move to stave off bankruptcy, Studebaker and Packard, two old U.S. auto manufacturers, merge in June.

That same month, Elvis Presley's first commercial recordings are released by Sun Records.

"Serious pictures," like *On the Waterfront, Rear Window, The Country Girl,* and *A Star is Born* dominate the movies as producers search for films that will lure audiences away from television.

1955

April: After extensive testing, officials declare the Salk vaccine against polio safe and effective, and inoculations of millions of children follow.

May: The Supreme Court rules that school segregation must end "within a reasonable time."

July: The first Disneyland opens in Anaheim, California.

August: The minimum wage rises from $0.75 to $1.00.

September: Actor James Dean dies in an auto accident. A cult almost immediately forms around his memory.

With the recession of 1953 clearly over, Americans purchase almost eight million automobiles.

"The Pill," an oral contraceptive for women in capsule form, is introduced. More effective than previous birth-control devices, it will help change sexual behavior throughout the country.

"Smog," a combination of smoke and fog, enters the language as a means of describing polluted air. The condition becomes particularly noticeable in Los Angeles, where the exhausts from large numbers of vehicles mix with damp air and cause a thick haze over the city.

Rock 'n' roll begins to attract a mass audience. The August release and success of Chuck Berry's "Maybelline" draws attention, and RCA Victor purchases Elvis Presley's contract with Sun Records.

1956

April: Grace Kelly, a popular movie actress, marries Prince Rainier of Monaco.

May: As a test, the United States drops the first airborne hydrogen bomb.

June: Congress passes the Federal-Aid Highway Act; it will lead to the Interstate Highway System.

July: The *Andrea Doria* sinks after colliding with the *Stockholm* off the Massachusetts coast; 60 people drown, but over 1,600 are saved.

November: Voters overwhelmingly reelect Eisenhower despite his lingering health problems.

November: The Supreme Court again attacks racial segregation, this time by ruling racially separated seating on public transportation illegal. In the meantime, rioting and protests accompany attempts at school desegregation in the South.

Freed from prison, Fidel Castro retreats to a mountain stronghold and in December again attacks the Cuban government.

Billed as a "hillbilly singer," Elvis Presley makes his TV debut on a show called *Stage Door.* Noting the publicity the vocalist's appearance inspires, Ed Sullivan books him for his *Toast of the Town.* In the meantime, Presley's "Heartbreak Hotel" proves a tremendous hit.

Country singer Johnny Cash crosses over to the pop charts with "I Walk the Line" in October. The lines dividing popular music genres continue to blur.

Disposable diapers are invented.

1957

September: The Atomic Energy Commission begins underground testing of nuclear weapons at its Nevada test site.

September: *West Side Story* opens on Broadway.

October: Russia launches an experimental unmanned spacecraft called *Sputnik*. Two months later, the Russians launch a second craft, this time with a dog aboard. The space race officially begins, with the United States far behind.

Following a dramatic showdown in September, President Eisenhower dispatches U.S. troops to Little Rock, Arkansas, after the state defies the courts, using National Guard troops to block the entry of black students into a previously all-white high school.

The Ford Motor Company introduces the much-heralded Edsel.

The Bridge on the River Kwai breaks box office records.

Popular music follows several avenues: traditional (Debbie Reynolds, Johnny Mathis), rock 'n' roll (Elvis Presley, Bill Haley and His Comets), country (Elvis Presley, the Everly Brothers), rhythm and blues (The Platters, Sam Cooke), and mixtures of all of the above.

1958

January: The United States finally launches its first satellite, *Explorer I*, but the Russians put a much larger *Sputnik III* into orbit. In July, the National Aeronautics and Space Administration is formed to coordinate U.S. space ventures.

March: Elvis Presley enters the U.S. Army.

April: A young American pianist named Van Cliburn wins the International Tchaikovsky Competition held in Moscow, becoming a star overnight.

August: First-class postage goes up a penny to four cents, and airmail follows suit, six cents to seven cents.

October: The Boeing 707 jetliner begins regular New York–Paris flights.

Unemployment creeps up to an uncomfortable seven percent as the nation enters another recession.

In order to avoid integration, Arkansas's governor closes the Little Rock schools in September and classes are held on television.

Angelo Giuseppe Roncalli becomes Pope John XXIII.

A love triangle involving singer Eddie Fisher and two women, his wife Debbie Reynolds and "homewrecker" Elizabeth Taylor, titillates the public for months and results in the divorce of Reynolds and Fisher.

Groups like Danny and the Juniors ("At the Hop"), the McGuire Sisters ("Sugartime"), the Silhouettes ("Get a Job"), and the Champs ("Tequila") begin to hold sway over individual vocalists.

"Beatnik" enters the language; it refers to people who do not conform to perceived proper behaviors. The "-nik" suffix comes from the publicity surrounding Russian successes with space satellites called "Sputniks."

1959

January: Fidel Castro overthrows the Cuban government after a lengthy revolution; his new government gains prompt recognition by the United States. Castro pays a friendly visit to the United States in April.

January: Virginia begins "massive resistance" to integration.

November: Congressional investigations into television quiz show scandals commence.

November: Ford Motor Company ceases producing the Edsel, the costliest failure in automobile history.

At the close of the decade, U.S. population stands at 179 million, an increase from 1950 of over 18 percent, the most rapid growth since 1900.

The average worker earns almost $5,000 a year, a 61 percent increase over 1950 figures.

Alaska officially gains statehood on January 3; on August 23, Hawaii becomes the 50th state.

"We will bury you," says Russian Premier Nikita Khrushchev, but he also makes a historic visit to the United States as relations warm, to a degree.

The rush to build home bomb shelters accelerates.

The United States makes a big move in the space race with the selection of the Mercury Seven, the first American astronauts: Scott Carpenter, Gordon Cooper, John Glenn, Virgil Grissom, Alan Shepard, Walter Schirra, and Donald Slayton.

Overview

of the 1950s

At the opening of the decade, the United States found itself in the enviable position of being far and away the most powerful nation on earth. Its industrial base, undamaged and immeasurably strengthened by World War II, manufactured over half of all the world's products, along with producing raw materials like steel and oil in prodigious quantities.

America itself proved the biggest single consumer of this outpouring. Denied many goods during the austere war years, citizens rushed to buy everything that appeared on the new peacetime market. This orgy of self-indulgence created a level of prosperity unseen since the heady days just before the stock market crash of 1929, resulting in a period of unparalleled growth and economic expansion that lasted through the decade.

THE ECONOMY

Between 1950 and 1960, the gross national product (GNP) escalated from $285 billion to $500 billion, a remarkable increase by any measure. Although worker productivity increased greatly, much of this growth stemmed from the changing demographics of the nation: in 1950, the U.S. census counted 150 million Americans, a figure that leaped to 179 million by 1960. More people meant more of everything: jobs, workers, goods, services—all the ingredients for a boom economy.[1]

Median family income almost doubled: between 1950 and 1960, it went from $3,083 per year to $5,976 per year. Even factoring in inflation, real wages increased 30 percent, so that food, clothing, and shelter no longer took away so much of each paycheck. New cars (instead of used models), televisions, high-fidelity units, improved telephones, alcoholic beverages, and endless entertainment saw sharply rising sales.[2]

Nevertheless, pockets of poverty persisted in postwar America. Many black Americans still toiled in underpaid, low-status jobs and lived in substandard housing. Neither did a majority of farmers and factory workers immediately share the fruits of rising prosperity. Single women, already laboring in low-paying positions, continued to lag behind their male counterparts.

CREDIT CARDS

The formation in 1950 of the Diner's Club and its issuance of a wallet-sized credit card to members led eventually to a fundamental change in American buying habits in the later 1950s and 1960s. At first, the rather exclusive Diner's Club limited its use to restaurants in the New York City area, but the idea caught on and rapidly expanded. In 1958, American Express started issuing cards of its own, and a year later Bank of America brought out its first BankAmericard (which later became Visa). This new approach to credit represented a financial, technological, and sociological breakthrough. It meant that those extending credit were guaranteed payment and that individuals no longer had to rely on cash or checks to make purchases.

The credit card revolution also reflected a profound transformation in attitudes about debt. Prior to World War II, most families owed as little as possible because they were imbued with an ethic that frowned on any indebtedness, plus most merchants demanded full payment for goods. Following the war, the rules changed as businesses exhibited a willingness to extend credit to their newly affluent customers.[3]

With credit so readily available, private debt increased sharply, going from $73 billion in 1950 to $196 billion in 1960.[4]

FAMILY LIFE

The family itself changed significantly during this period. Instead of Mom, Dad, and the usual two children, more and more couples opted for three or four children, making the 1950s one of the most youthful decades on record. By 1958, almost a third of all Americans were 15 years old or younger. "Baby boom" evolved as the term used to describe the skyrocketing numbers of children. This astonishing rise proved an economic bonanza for retailers, but schools and recreational facilities found themselves stretched to their limits.[5]

In *I Love Lucy*, a popular TV situation comedy, the husband-and-wife team of Desi and Lucy Ricardo find that Lucy is expecting. In those more innocent days of TV, network censors considered the word "pregnant" taboo, although they embraced the concept of approaching motherhood. In reality, Lucille Ball, the star of the show, had become pregnant, and so her condition was written into the series. It proved a wise move; the birth of little Ricky in early 1953 (filming took place in November 1952) was one of the most watched events in the history of American television. In a similar way, shows like *Father Knows Best, The Adventures of Ozzie and Harriet, Leave It to Beaver, Make Room for Daddy,* and *The Donna Reed Show* espoused strong family values. They painted a picture of the decade that might have been unrealistic and rose-colored, but one that has persisted as a nostalgic perception of the 1950s. (See Entertainment of the 1950s.) In the 1954 Easter issue of *McCall's* magazine, the term "togetherness" gained some media legitimacy. It meant the family worked as a unit, that Mom and Dad and the kids undertook joint activities. Everyone could work on such activities as a "paint-by-numbers" kit in the family room, an area reserved in the modern suburban home for just such activities.

Organized religion also celebrated this emphasis on the insular family. A popular slogan of the time touted "the family that prays together stays together." And so it seemed: Americans attended church in record numbers. About half the citizenry claimed church membership or affiliation in 1950; by 1960, the number had climbed to 69 percent, an all-time high to this day. During his tenure, President Dwight Eisenhower was even baptized in the White House. The new Revised Standard Version (RSV) of the Bible spent an unprecedented three years on the best-seller lists. In 1954, the words "under God" were added to the Pledge of Allegiance, and "In God We Trust" became a part of the country's coinage the following year. With the government proclaiming a Christian heritage, various evangelists found themselves drawing record crowds into churches and other venues. Chief among them was Billy Graham and his evangelistic "crusades," but Bishop Fulton Sheen, Norman Vincent Peale, and Oral Roberts also attracted large audiences.

CIVIL RIGHTS

For much of the decade, white Americans remained blissfully ignorant about racism. The fact that their beloved suburbs were often almost one hundred percent white—likewise their schools and country clubs, especially on network television and in the movies—did not seem a concern to them,. If the era also continued to see lynchings in the South, a complacent majority avoided the injustice.

Not until 1954 did civil rights develop into a widespread issue. In the landmark case *Brown v. the Board of Education,* the Supreme Court ruled against the Topeka (Kansas) Board of Education, saying that racially segregated schools and facilities were not necessarily equal, a decision that awoke the nation from its long slumber through justice for all citizens. Then, in 1955, a tired Rosa Parks refused to give up her bus seat to a white man, and the nation again had to look at the artificial separation of people by race. When bus boycotts followed, accompanied by the elevation of Dr. Martin Luther King Jr., into the national spotlight, more Americans began to realize that racial segregation could not remain a part of the fabric of American life.

In 1957, Arkansas Governor Orval Faubus refused to protect black students attempting to integrate Little Rock High School, compelling President Eisenhower to call in federal troops. By this time, the television cameras had already arrived on the scene, and the national nightly news detailed the unfolding stories of rage and repression. The civil rights movement had shifted into high gear, and American mass media had become an unblinking witness. Dr. King emerged as a spokesman for expanding civil rights and thereby became the conscience of the country. By the end of the decade, the nation found itself poised, reluctantly or not, to enter into one of the greatest social changes of the century.[6]

Mrs. Nettie Hunt, sitting on steps of Supreme Court, holding newspaper, explaining to her daughter, Nickie, the meaning of the Supreme Court's decision banning school segregation, 1954. Prints & Photographs Division, Library of Congress.

WOMEN'S ROLES

Throughout the fifties, popular media portrayed American women as possibly the best-dressed housekeepers ever seen. In television sitcoms and countless advertisements, women donned elegant dresses, high heels, and jewelry (the pearl necklace seemed almost de rigueur), and they smiled as they dusted and vacuumed. Three leading TV examples were Donna Reed as "Donna Stone" in *The Donna Reed Show,* Jane Wyatt as "Margaret Anderson" in *Father Knows Best,* and Barbara Billingsley as "June Cleaver" in *Leave It to Beaver.* In the ads, some even wore crowns—women as queens of domesticity. It mattered little that many American women chose employment and careers over homemaking.

Widely accepted in the popular mind, this comforting and stereotypical picture was challenged in real life as the fifties progressed. Large-circulation magazines countered with articles that extolled the extra earning power of a second income. Doubtless many women felt torn by such mixed messages, and statistics suggest that increasing numbers of them chose a paying job over being a full-time housewife.

Woman holding coffee pot, serving a group of nicely dressed women neighbors seated in lawn chairs, Park Forest, Illinois, 1954. Prints & Photographs Division, Library of Congress.

The number of working women swelled with the onset of World War II and defense jobs. At the end of the war in 1945, women were urged to vacate their occupations so returning servicemen could have them. Some did, but many younger women simultaneously joined the workforce, so that by 1950, 18 million held jobs, a significantly higher number than that in World War II. Those numbers continued to increase; by 1960, over 23 million American women, or 36 percent of all women, had jobs outside the home—a figure

HOW OTHERS SEE US

Japanese Brides Go to School

For the 18,000 Japanese women who married American servicemen in the years after World War II, their husbands' homeland was largely a mystery. Hollywood had given them glimpses of what everyday life in the United States was like, and the military base's PX (post exchange, or store for those living on the base) exposed them to American products. But this was hardly sufficient preparation for those who were readying themselves to move to America when their spouses' tours of duty ended.

To address this problem, in 1951, the American Red Cross set up special "brides' schools" on U.S. Army, Navy, and Air Force bases throughout occupied Japan. The five-week series of classes, run by volunteer military wives, was a crash course in American homemaking and womanhood, circa 1950: they covered a range of subjects from pie-baking to girdle-wearing to entertaining neighbors to dealing with new in-laws. Along with classroom instruction, the students got to spend twelve hours in the on-base home of one of the instructors. For most, it was their first encounter with such American appliances as refrigerators, toasters, stoves, and mixers. It was also a chance to add to their repertoire of American-style cooking. As one of the students put it, "My husband was getting tired of ham and eggs"—the only non-Japanese meal most brides could cook before brides' school. Eager to join him as a full-fledged American, she was only too happy to learn how to prepare a roast and mix a cake.

that includes 33 percent of all married women, though most of these would have been married women without children. Although they faced limited employment opportunities, many women nevertheless worked and did not spend the day at home, despite what the television, the movies, and advertising had one believe.[7]

With growing numbers of women entering the workplace, contradictions proliferated. Only about one-third of the women who entered college during the decade actually graduated. Further, fewer women went on to graduate or professional schools than was the case in the 1920s and 1930s; the 1950s female college student was more likely to marry, start a family, and put an end to her educational aspirations. As a result, American women were conspicuously absent from high-level jobs. They instead settled for the traditional employment outlets: secretarial, clerical, nursing, teaching, assembly lines, and domestic service. Just over 10 percent of working women entered a profession, and a minuscule 6 percent had management positions.[8]

NUCLEAR ANXIETY

In August 1949, the Union of Soviet Socialist Republics (USSR) exploded its first atomic bomb. This blast would cast a pall over the ensuing decade. A fear of nuclear annihilation, an underlying anxiety that ran counter to the rampant consumerism that many equate with the 1950s, became a part of the American scene.

President Truman announced in January 1950 that the United States would continue to develop a hydrogen bomb, a much more destructive version of the atomic. Shortly thereafter, the Russians commenced working on such a weapon. And so, by 1953, both nations possessed H-bombs, and the threat of total war and mutual annihilation loomed ever larger.

By mid-decade, ominous reports of huge Russian intercontinental missiles circulated. When the USSR launched *Sputnik* in October 1957, it shook the United States out of any technological complacency. No one had expected the Soviets to be the first into space; it served as a disquieting moment for any lingering notions of inherent American superiority. Part of the American

response to *Sputnik* involved spending vast sums of government money to catch up. In the spring of 1958, a reluctant President Eisenhower asked Congress to create the National Aeronautics and Space Administration (NASA), and a new component to the ongoing arms race—the space race—was officially on.

Instead of having their fears alleviated by these moves, Americans found their anxieties compounded by other steps taken by the government. Officials put into place a civil defense system that included aircraft spotters and buildings designated as fallout shelters for protection from deadly radiation. Bright yellow-and-black triangular signs were attached to the entrances

FALLOUT SHELTERS

The celebration that followed the Allied victory in World War II was tempered by the fear of nuclear war. Governments responded to threat by creating "fallout shelters," subterranean rooms built to withstand radioactive fallout and intended to house government leaders in the event of a nuclear attack. Private citizens followed the government's example and began constructing their own backyard and basement fallout shelters, thereby initiating one of the most unique architectural trends in American history. Recognizing the potential of the new market, companies soon began producing pre-fabricated fallout shelters for sale, often through mail order catalogues. While many shelters were utilitarian in design, with concrete walls and space only for essential items, others were luxuriously appointed with pool tables and wine cellars. Numerous articles were published in newspapers and magazines explaining the utility of fallout shelters and how to build and maintain one. Other companies entered the market by producing peripheral equipment, such as radiation detectors to help determine when radiation levels had reduced significantly to return to the surface. By the end of the 1960s, fear of nuclear conflict began to decline and the fad was gradually abandoned. Though the fad was motivated as much by fear as by fashion, the fallout shelter craze remains a prime example of the opportunistic nature of the American consumer market.

of stout public buildings, with the instructions to "take shelter in the event of an attack." Even the public schools had their "Duck and Cover" drills. At the news of approaching planes, students were instructed to duck under whatever was close by (such as their desk) and cover their heads with their arms for additional protection. A generation of fifties students practiced the exercise—an exercise in futility had there been an actual attack.

The government also printed many pamphlets and posters that purported to show how to survive a nuclear explosion. They encouraged building backyard bomb shelters but suggested that a reinforced basement room, suitably stocked with emergency items, would also suffice.

In a series of movies that ranged from the trite *Invasion, U.S.A.* (1952), to the modest *Magnetic Monster* (1953), to the terrifying *Them!* (1954), Hollywood played on fears of mutations, atomic war, domestic spying, and Communist infiltration. (See Entertainment of the 1950s.)

THE KOREAN WAR

On June 25, 1950, North Korean forces attacked South Korea, prompting an immediate military response from both the United Nations and the United States. Many U.N. member states shipped troops to the distant peninsula, all under a unified command. By far the largest contingent came from the United States. In 1953, the parties agreed to an armistice, and peace negotiations dragged on for years thereafter. This war boasted neither victors nor losers, an unsettling fact for Americans used to winning all their encounters with foreign adversaries. During the decade, over 1.8 million U.S. troops served in Korea, with more than 33,600 losing their lives in combat and some 103,000 sustaining wounds.[9]

American popular culture hesitated to deal with the conflict, especially given its murky political overtones. Nuclear annihilation was one thing, but an unpopular, misunderstood war in a distant land was another. As a result, the Korean conflict has come down to the present as America's "forgotten war," and it remains relatively unknown to most citizens, despite its bloody toll. (See Books, Newspapers, Magazines, and Comics of the 1950s and Entertainment of the 1950s.)

MCCARTHYISM

For many TV fans, the various Congressional hearings that marked the decade served as some of the most engrossing series on the air. They had all the elements of good popular culture: drama, heroes and villains, sensationalism, and even a few surprises. Most prominent were the McCarthy hearings into Communist infiltration in the national government. In February 1950, Joseph McCarthy, the junior senator from Wisconsin, loudly proclaimed that he had evidence that 205 active Communist agents had been employed at the State Department. Leading the Senate Investigations Subcommittee, McCarthy launched a campaign based on fears, innuendo, and smears to track down Communists in government. An outright witch-hunt, the subcommittee often used guilt by accusation to besmirch its victims. By 1957, some six million individuals had been investigated by various related agencies and committees because of alleged sympathies to the Communist cause. Out of those, only a small handful were ever convicted.

McCarthy offered no hard evidence for his ceaseless claims, but many people nevertheless took them at face value. Reelected in 1952, McCarthy began a full-scale assault on anyone he deemed subversive. Finally, in March 1954, the esteemed Columbia Broadcasting System (CBS) newsman Edward R. Murrow aired a special program on his television series, *See It Now*. He titled the special "A Report on Senator Joseph P. McCarthy," and he and producer Fred R. Friendly did the show at their own expense. CBS and its sponsors took a hands-off attitude toward the production, and the CBS "eye" logo was not to be seen. Despite its lack of network and commercial support, the presentation gave viewers a rare picture of the senator, most of it in his own words, and most of them damning. His crude, intimidating attacks on individuals and institutions smacked of a tyrant, a browbeater, a thug.

McCarthy implied that Murrow himself was a Communist sympathizer. Undeterred, McCarthy included the U.S. Army Signal Corps as one of his targets. During the televised hearings with the Army shortly after his exchanges with Murrow, McCarthy's charges went unsubstantiated.

Senator Joseph McCarthy appearing before a group of newsmen on December 3, 1953, in Washington, D.C., saying that it is "ridiculous and untrue" that he has challenged President Eisenhower's leadership. Courtesy of Photofest.

The country soon tired of his demagoguery; his influence waned, and the investigations drew to a close.

In 1956, the Senate took away his chairmanship of the investigative committee. The Senate eventually censured him and any remaining influence ended. Joseph McCarthy died in 1957; that same year, the Supreme Court began to restore rights taken away from Americans by the "Red Scare" brought about by his hearings, and the term "McCarthyism" has come to mean unfair, unsupported attacks on individuals by governmental groups, especially Congressional committees.[10]

FEARS ABOUT COMMUNISM

With a distant war in Korea being waged against Communist adversaries, and McCarthy's claims of Communist infiltration at all levels of government, a climate of fear and suspicion descended on the nation. In 1950, an organization called AWARE began publishing a newsletter titled *Red Channels;* it purported to identify 151 individuals from the performing arts that the organization found "subversive." No one—neither networks, studios or sponsors—offered to stand up and challenge these vicious attacks, and innocent people found themselves "blacklisted," unable to work in radio, film, or television. For many, the stigma of the blacklist lingered until well into the 1960s, and the damage proved permanent.[11]

This divisive atmosphere struck Hollywood particularly hard. The House Un-American Activities Committee (HUAC), an investigative arm of Congress, seized on the issue of dangerous influences corrupting the nation. Hearings were held, and many Hollywood personalities were summoned to testify. Actors, producers, directors, and writers faced a dilemma: whether or not to inform on their colleagues about possible Communist ties.

The social unrest of the Depression and the country's alliance with Russia during World War II had caused some members of the film community to take an interest in the Communist Party. For most, any real party connections proved slight, often the result of youthful curiosity in years past. The committee felt otherwise, however, and pursued a selected group of writers and producers with relentless tenacity. Ten individuals, the so-called Hollywood Ten, were cited for contempt of Congress in 1947 and blacklisted, an action that put their careers in tatters. Of course, Russia and China had been American allies in World War II, but now, in an ironic twist, the two countries were demonized as America's implacable enemies. Those persons with past or present associations with either country found themselves branded as traitors.

A sensitive film that addressed the issue of informing was director Elia Kazan's *On the Waterfront* (1954). Marlon Brando burnished his acting reputation in this movie, portraying a young boxer who must deal with conflicting loyalties. Kazan had been deeply involved in the hearings and did indeed offer evidence that proved detrimental to some of his colleagues. His film indirectly commented on the whole process and its impact on belief systems.

Don Siegel's *Invasion of the Body Snatchers* (1956), a disturbing film from the blacklisting period, worked on a different level from *On the Waterfront*. In the movie mysterious pods from outer space descend on a community, ingeniously taking over the physical appearance of its inhabitants. Who can be trusted? Who can be believed? Who is what he or she appears to be? The script played off of McCarthy-era fears and the "Red Scare" they precipitated.

For example, in 1953, the popular syndicated columnist Walter Winchell asserted that none other than Lucille Ball, star of *I Love Lucy* and one of the most popular women in America, had been a Communist. This occurred during the McCarthy hearings, when such claims could sink a career. In a moving denial, her husband Desi Arnaz addressed the charge publicly—on television, just before the beginning of one of the *I Love Lucy* shows. In response, the audience gave him a standing ovation, and the matter disappeared. More often, the taint of Communism proved fatal, true or untrue. Had Ball's show not been the most popular one on television, it seems doubtful she would have received any support.

THE EISENHOWER YEARS AND THE RISE OF TELEVISION

Dwight D. Eisenhower (1890–1969) was a seasoned military leader elected to the presidency in 1952, and his conservative, patriarchal approach to a dangerous world reassured nervous citizens. His golf game, his weekend painting, and even his health problems elicited more popular attention than did his abilities as a leader. For most Americans, he presented an image of calm authority. The decade marked, in fact, the increasing use of public relations and advertising techniques in the political arena. That Eisenhower could project such a picture of fatherly confidence overshadowed the difficulties he had articulating issues, and Americans voted their preference for imagery over content in both the 1952 and 1956 presidential elections.

The importance of strong media ties could be seen in the Republican and Democratic national conventions held in July 1952. The first such political conventions to be televised, delegates were aware of cameras and microphones everywhere, and their presence had a clear effect. Little deal making could take place outside the range of the omnipresent cameras, a decided change from the smoke-filled rooms of the past. As Republican enthusiasm for Eisenhower grew, the unblinking gaze of the national media helped him win on the first ballot. On the Democratic side, it took three ballots to nominate Adlai Stevenson, even though the party did not wish to appear divided to a national television audience.

In the midst of the 1952 campaign, Eisenhower's running mate, California Senator Richard M. Nixon, was accused of improperly using funds and accepting gifts. Alarmists urged Eisenhower to drop Nixon from the ticket. In response, Nixon turned to television and delivered his famous "Checkers" speech, a moment in television history that illustrated the enormous power the medium could wield. An estimated audience of 58 million heard and saw his denials. "Checkers" was a cute cocker spaniel, a gift Nixon challenged anyone to take from his daughters. His somewhat melodramatic defense played well; audiences viewed the charges against him as ham-handed attempts by overzealous Democrats to discredit him. In short, popular imagery overrode any reasoned investigation. Eisenhower retained Nixon in his campaign, and the two savored a strong victory.[12]

THE CULTURAL FERMENT OF THE 1950s

For many American intellectuals, the specter of an undifferentiated mass culture that could lead public opinion seemed far more frightening than any Russian warhead. They saw the nation falling into a kind of mindless conformity, accepting without question the nightly offerings of network television, along with Top 40 radio programming and big box office movies. Those elements, coupled with the paternalistic philosophy of the Eisenhower administration, created undercurrents of dissent and revolt that simmered throughout the decade.

Jack Kerouac set out to rewrite the American novel, Jackson Pollock challenged his fellow artists with abstract "drip paintings," and the suspect insolence of Elvis Presley and James Dean bothered many. Marlon Brando sweated and grunted to

***TIME* MAN OF THE YEAR**

1950 "G.I. Joe" (the average American solider)

1951 Mohammed Mossadegh (prime minister of Iran)

1952 Queen Elizabeth II (queen of the United Kingdom)

1953 Konrad Adenauer (West German chancellor)

1954 John Foster Dulles (secretary of state)

1955 Harlow H. Curtice (president of General Motors)

1956 The Hungarian Freedom Fighter

1957 Nikita Khrushchev (Soviet leader)

1958 Charles de Gaulle (president of France)

1959 Dwight D. Eisenhower (34th president of the United States)

heroes still adhered to a manly code of behavior, Norman Rockwell's *Saturday Evening Post* covers continued to captivate millions, Gary Cooper represented all that was good in the western myth, Perry Como crooned in a reassuring baritone, and good old traditional Dixieland Jazz enjoyed something of a revival. Depending on one's focus during the fifties, the decade could seem complacent and conformist, or it could be filled with threatening change and shrill individuals who turned their backs on anything held dear by generations of Americans.

For the average American, however, the intellectual debates of the era occurred offstage, unseen and unheard. With the reality of the Cold War intruding into daily lives, the thought of a cultural consensus sounded reassuring, not threatening. Rock 'n' roll seemed far more challenging to worried parents than discussions of cultural hegemony. Added to this were the changes brought about by civil rights legislation, by school integration, and by a sense of rebellion on the part of youth across the nation. Nothing was as it used to be.[13]

the delight of adolescents everywhere, and Charlie Parker and Dizzy Gillespie took jazz places it had never been before. True, Ernest Hemingway's

Advertising

of the 1950s

In days past, except for the occasional traveling salesman or print enticements found in newspapers and magazines, the home served as a sanctuary from merchants and their wares. With the advent of commercial radio in the thirties and forties, the haven of home had been breached. The rise of television in the late 1940s presented a potent new venue. It did not take long for TV to surpass both magazines and radio in advertising volume and profits, although, in an era of consumption, the public needed little urging to go out and buy goods and services.

PRINT ADVERTISING AND PACKAGING

During the 1950s, improved reproduction technologies allowed print to continue as a major advertising medium in newspapers and magazines, despite the fierce competition of radio and television. (See Books, Newspapers, Magazines, and Comics of the 1950s.) Print advertising allowed the reader the luxury of reading and rereading text that carried both informational and emotive content, while radio and TV spots were limited to fleeting, one-time responses. It did not take long for advertisers to exploit these inherent differences. An automobile advertisement in a magazine, for example, might have mentioned exact horsepower and engine specifications; the same vehicle in a TV spot would have given images of speed and power instead, with little accompanying information. Similarly, food promotions in print, while they could give an attractive picture of the item, would have told the reader about nutrition and might even have included a recipe. That same food, on television, would have been presented in such a way as to make the viewer salivate, but the likelihood of detailed information was slim.[1]

The fifties witnessed extraordinary growth among those manufacturers responsible for all the bottles, aerosols, bubble-packs, cartons, and boxes: by 1959, packaging stood alongside print advertising as a significant industry in its own right. Food featured sealed plastic bags and pressurized cans, with eye-catching slogans like "quick 'n' easy," "heat 'n' serve," "bound to please," and "ready in no time." Hand lotion flowed from dispensers with pumps, thumb tacks were displayed in fancy packages, drugs arrived in brightly labeled plastic vials, and underwear came wrapped in cellophane packs of three.

Because many items exhibited little outward difference, it became imperative that the ads promoting the product on the package persuade the customer that the item was "more convenient," "easier to use," "stronger," "neater," "cleaner," "fresher," or possessed any number of other improvements on the norm. Even standard sizes went through semantic shifts, with "large" becoming "economy size" and "small" evolving into "personal size."

Self-service increasingly emerged as the way consumers purchased goods in stores; the once knowledgeable and friendly grocery clerk or shop owner ready to help the shopper was replaced by employees not necessarily trained to assist customers. Consumers therefore relied on advertising for both information and the stimulus to buy; packaging at times assumed greater significance than the item itself.

RADIO ADVERTISING

As an advertising medium, radio underwent a significant decline during the fifties; it fell from 9 percent of all ad dollars in 1952 to stabilize at approximately 6 percent in 1959. Television emerged as the big winner, rising from 6 percent of all ad dollars in 1952 to 13 percent in 1960.[2]

Short, catchy jingles, long a staple of radio commercials, continued as a primary means of capturing listeners' attention, albeit sometimes on a background, or subliminal, level. Ad agencies occasionally used the same jingle on both TV and radio, such as those used by Pepsi-Cola and Coca-Cola. Familiarity became the key, and media repetition achieved it. The heady days of radio's advertising dominance essentially came to an end in the 1950s, but the medium remained an important carrier of commercial messages.[3]

EARLY TELEVISION ADVERTISING

Advertisers came warily to television in the early fifties. The charges for sponsoring a show seemed astronomical compared to radio, as much as 10 times higher. The production costs for TV commercials greatly exceeded those charged in radio or print media; moreover, advertisers and their agencies had to produce a visual TV ad.

In the early days of TV, sponsors and their ad agencies took the primary responsibility for the packaging of shows. That power led to abuses, especially in the area of censorship. A car manufacturer might have objected to a competitor's vehicles being shown, or a cigarette company might have rejected the sight of anyone smoking pipes

or cigars. The situation changed toward the end of the decade, sparked by the quiz show scandals of 1958–1959, when the networks took over more of the decision making. The creation and production of new series fell more and more to packagers that had no connection to sponsors or networks. Ultimately, ad agencies found themselves reduced to buying time and had little control over content. (See Entertainment of the 1950s.)

The commercials themselves reflected the growth of television. The early 1950s witnessed a variety of cartoons and animations as producers capitalized on TV's ability to show movement. Ajax Cleanser had its "pixies," little creatures that demonstrated the product's effectiveness, and Autolite featured endless rows of marching sparkplugs, thanks to stop-action filming techniques. Later, Speedy Alka-Seltzer, a friendly little character, showed how the product would make a person feel better, and the Jolly Green Giant's "Ho, ho, ho" echoed throughout homes everywhere. Charlie the Tuna epitomized the cool hipster, right down to his beret, Mr. Clean's muscled strength could overcome the worst spills and stains, and the Pillsbury Doughboy personified cuteness.

Live action figured prominently in the formative years of TV commercials. The Men from Texaco introduced Milton Berle, the star of *Texaco Star Theater* (1948–1953), one of television's first real hits. In 1951, the famous Budweiser Clydesdales came to television. Although they had represented the brewery since the nineteenth century, they proved an instant hit and have been appearing in Budweiser commercials ever since. Unfortunately, few of these early commercials survived to the present day. No one saw any reason to preserve them, so aside from some snowy kinescopes, a visual record of an important part of popular culture will always remain incomplete.[4]

GROWTH IN TELEVISION ADVERTISING

By mid-decade, Americans mastered, via television, a new language of consumerism. The incessant growth brought certain costs. Most television commercials in the early 1950s ran for a full minute, sometimes more, allowing mini-stories to be told, ideas worked out, humor developed, a wealth of details included. But production costs and ad time on television did not come cheap; by the end of the 1950s, producers spent, on average, anywhere from $10,000 to $20,000 for a one-minute ad. In contrast, a minute of content for an entertainment show cost around $2,000. As a result, television ads shrank to 30 seconds of airtime.[5]

Annual U.S. spending for advertising rose from $5.7 billion in 1950 to almost $12 billion at decade's end. Newspapers and television together consumed almost two-thirds of the advertising dollar; the remainder was divided among magazines, radio, direct mail, outdoor, and other miscellaneous outlets. Television managed only a paltry $41 million in ad revenues in 1950. By 1952, it swelled to $336 million and began to close in on

radio's ad income ($473 million). Furthermore, TV reached a truly national market in its advertising, whereas both radio and newspapers served more local clients. At mid-decade, television became the leading carrier for national advertising; by 1959, a single national TV spot could penetrate 90 percent of American homes something no other medium could accomplish. Ad revenues had surged to over $1.5 billion, second only to newspaper advertising.[6] Automobiles counted among the most heavily promoted products during the 1950s; out of the top ten TV advertisers, nine manufactured motor vehicles. General Motors reigned as the single biggest advertiser in the United States, although giant Procter & Gamble's products did place second in overall

Betty Furness displaying a refrigerator. In the 1950s, especially earlier in the decade, commercials were often broadcast live. Courtesy of Photofest.

expenditures. Individually, however, Procter & Gamble's ads for Camay, Crisco, Prell, Tide, and other brands did not equal the amounts spent on Chevrolets, Oldsmobiles, and Buicks.[7] (See Travel of the 1950s.)

American television exploited the renown and talents of major show business personalities: Eddie Fisher sipped Coca-Cola; Henry Fonda touted beer; Frank Sinatra crooned about shampoo; Jack Benny plugged just about anything; and Lucille Ball and Desi Arnaz, TV's most popular couple, smoked Philip Morris cigarettes on camera. Even acclaimed film director Alfred Hitchcock, the sardonic host of *Alfred Hitchcock Presents* (1955–1965), entered into the commercial side of television production. He made deprecating remarks about Bristol-Myers, his longtime sponsor, and viewers loved it—as did Bristol-Myers—because his put-downs of the company's ads made them memorable. The seemingly daring jabs amused his audiences, and no one informed them that they had all been carefully scripted; in the meantime, the sponsor happily watched sales increase. The endless endorsements of celebrities like these created a strong link between consumerism and entertainment, and celebrities emerged as effective salespeople.

While celebrities promoted products on television in the 1950s, unknowns became celebrities as a result of their work in commercials. Betty Furness, an actress appearing on television in the late 1940s, became an extremely popular spokeswoman for Westinghouse appliances throughout the 1950s and also hosted talk shows on television and on radio as well as appearing on programs. She was a smart, authoritative, and attractive woman, in an era where women in commercials were too often merely attractive mannikins.

MEDIA AND THE MESSAGE

Regardless of the medium carrying the message, American advertising during the 1950s presented endless images of the good life. An ad for floor wax might be staged in a kitchen that most consumers only dreamed of; but the imagery came across clearly: use this product and your kitchen will resemble the one in the ad. Fantasy, social values, and the hard sell came together

unlike in any previous era. Borrowing a device long employed by car manufacturers and the fashion industry, promoters of a wide range of consumer goods began to espouse planned obsolescence in their ads. The product might not really need replacement, but the new model had to be an improvement over the old version. Watch makers recommended having a "wardrobe" of timepieces, one for every occasion. Appliance manufacturers began to make their previously all-white washers and dryers in a rainbow of fashionable colors—they might not wash or dry any better, but they fit better into the modern home than plain old white.

With incomes rising and the economy booming, "No money down, attractive terms!" seemed a reasonable way to accumulate goods. Ads promoted trading old furniture for new, along with carpeting, appliances, and a host of other products. "Why be tied down to old, out-of-style furniture [or anything else]?" the argument went. "Trade-in now and get the latest styles."

QUESTIONING THE MESSAGE

A downside to the decade-long buying spree of the fifties involved customer dissatisfaction with many of the products bought. In their rush to keep store inventories up, manufacturers sometimes skimped on the quality of the merchandise. New homeowners had to contend with leaks and faulty wiring as construction crews rushed to finish tract houses. Relentless consumer demand caused most manufacturers and distributors to deem such complaints as minor annoyances. Unfortunately, the broad questions of quality and assurance went largely unaddressed during the 1950s as developers and contractors tried even harder to sell more goods, shoddy or not.

Author Vance Packard released *The Hidden Persuaders* in 1957. This best-selling book claimed that all manner of colors, shapes, concealed symbols, and other devious devices in advertising manipulated the consumer. Packard's work served as a damning indictment of advertising, and led to calls for investigations into industry methodologies. The thought that advertising might affect people on a subliminal level stimulated considerable public debate.[8]

ADVERTISING SLOGANS OF THE 1950s

"Takes a licking and keeps on ticking," Timex watches, 1952*

"You're in good hands with Allstate," Allstate, 1951

"Tastes good like a cigarette should," Winston cigarettes, 1954*

"Aren't you glad you use Dial? Don't you wish everybody did?" Dial soap, 1953

"Does she...or doesn't she?" Clairol hair coloring, 1956*

"The man in the Hathaway shirt," Hathaway shirts, 1951*

"Look, Mom! No cavities!" Crest toothpaste, 1958*

"See the U.S.A. in your Chevrolet," Chevrolet, 1951*

"They're gr-r-reat!" Kellogg's Frosted Flakes*

"Think Small," Volkswagen, 1959*

"The Marlboro Man," Marlboro, 1955*

"Sometimes you feel like a nut, sometimes you don't," Mounds and Almond Joy candy bars, 1953*

"Melts in your mouth, not in your hand," M&Ms, 1954*

"A little dab'll do ya," Brylcreem, 1950s*

"Silly Rabbit, Trix are for kids," Trix cereal, 1959

"Leave the driving to us," Greyhound Lines, Inc., 1957*

"Double your pleasure, double your fun," Wrigley's Doublemint Gum, 1959

*Among *Advertising Age's* "The Advertising Century: Top 100 Advertising Campaigns," http://adage.com/century/campaigns.html.

Packard's claims were not really new—other books and articles had come to the same conclusions—but *The Hidden Persuaders* struck a responsive chord. Despite their ferocious consumerism, a majority of Americans tended to distrust the very ads that urged them to buy, buy, buy. But little, beyond debate that revealed some popular misgivings about the advertiser's trade, came from the book's revelations. One title in particular summed up the popular image of the advertising executive: Sloan Wilson's *The Man in the Gray Flannel Suit* (1955). Although the hero of this best-selling novel actually worked in public relations, its title contributed a phrase to the American lexicon. It also furthered the popular apprehension that advertising and public relations, or "Madison Avenue," the New York street commonly associated with many such agencies, were inherently manipulative and dishonest.

ADVERTISING AND WOMEN

Throughout the twentieth century, most shopping and spending—upwards of 80 or 90 percent by most estimates—was done by women. Thus, many ads of the 1950s targeted women. Most advertising agencies consisted of men, however, a discrepancy that led to ad copy written by males but meant for women. American advertising exhibited rampant stereotyping and gender bias throughout the decade, and the idea that a woman should live for her husband and family became a dominant image. It all fit in with the outward conservatism and conformity that characterized the period.[9] By emphasizing the image of women as housekeepers, ads depicted women as virtual servants, serving meals, doing dishes, cleaning, dusting, and vacuuming. Some humorously asked, "Who does all this work?" and then answered the question with a picture of an attractive, well-dressed, aproned, high-heeled woman of indeterminate age. The woman of the 1950s, at least in much American advertising, functioned as little more than stylish help.

But domestic help with a difference: her portrayal also included decision making. Not only did the American woman shop in 1950s advertising, but she also decided what would be purchased. Big-ticket items, like appliances, television sets, and even automobiles, were displayed with a fashionable woman choosing this or that model. Males may have been present, but they functioned as background filler, not as major players. Manufacturers and their advertising agencies eagerly bought into the concept of the woman as primary selector and arbiter of family wants and needs.

From a typical print ad of the 1950s for Formica, a well-dressed woman arranges a vase of flowers in her spotless kitchen, because all of her housework has been finished, "thanks to the easily wipeable Formica surfaces." Getty Images.

General Mills's maternal trademark, Betty Crocker, also underwent a facelift in the 1950s. It did not mark the first or last time, but marketing experts at the food company wanted to express a warmer, less professional look than the one then gracing boxes of their cake mix. They felt that their corporate logo should suggest everyone's image of "mother," but a more stylish one, a helpful, loving person who could dispense advice without intimidating.

The new Betty Crocker had a touch of gray at the temples, a broader smile, and she seemed happy. In response to changing media demands, Betty Crocker also took on television. *The Betty Crocker Television Show* ran 1950–1951, and *The Betty Crocker Star Matinee* came along in 1952. Impersonated by actress Adelaide Hawley, millions of viewers accepted her as "real," a situation that reflected the power of repeated advertising.

Mom, portrayed in advertisements such as those with Betty Crocker, was in charge and decisive and presided over a happy home. She did not go to an office. She went shopping—to buy more goods. In truth, by 1957, women comprised a third of the workforce, so the happy housewife with endless time to shop existed as a part of popular mythology. The push for ease and efficiency led to many advertising campaigns in the 1950s, both print and broadcast, that involved more than just items for the kitchen. Automatic transmissions in cars, wrinkle-free clothing, easy-to-use wallpapers, and quick-drying paints were counted among the many products aimed at the busy woman.

CHILDREN AND ADVERTISING

Next to women (and often posed with them), children occupied an important niche in 1950s advertising. The ages of consumers made little difference, and children were seen as especially vulnerable to persuasive messages. For example, Ovaltine, the venerable chocolate drink, targeted the youthful viewers of its popular television series, *Captain Midnight* (1954–1956), a show that had previously run as a popular serial on radio (1939–1949). The use of premiums to lure larger audiences dated back to early broadcasting, and Ovaltine chose to carry on the tradition. TV viewers, just like the generation of avid radio listeners before them, could obtain decoder rings that deciphered secret messages, badges, identity cards, and official membership certificates by purchasing jars of Ovaltine and saving the labels that served as cash toward these gifts. Only a handful of other sponsors followed suit, however, and the practice declined during the decade. (See Entertainment of the 1950s.)

Advertising aimed at children also freely used cartoon figures, such as Kellogg's Tony the Tiger for Frosted Flakes in 1955, and Snap! Crackle! Pop! for Rice Krispies. These were but the first of a vast menagerie of animated characters that would entice children on television screens and packages for decades to come.

The usual products, such as baby food, candy, bath powders, soaps, toys, and games, consistently employed children as the focus of their advertising.

The helpless, or hapless, father-male lurked in the background. He beamed proudly, but his role remained clearly a secondary one. Less likely products—automobiles, tires, television sets, appliances, furniture—also showed children to broaden their appeal, especially to women. Stereotyping, however, continued to plague such advertising. Little boys were depicted roughhousing, playing sports, or working with tools, whereas little girls served tea from miniature pots, pretended to clean house, or played nurse. Ads with adolescents continued in this mode. The idea of gender-appropriate behaviors, so ingrained in the American psyche, saw little change during the 1950s.[10]

MEN AND ADVERTISING

Despite the emphases placed on women in advertising, men appeared in many ads of the 1950s, and more often than not they did manly things. They raced cars, slugged baseballs, hunted, or built something, usually in the company of other men. Although women portrayed in American advertising excelled as housekeepers, shoppers, or consumers, they somehow seemed at a loss when it came to comprehending how complex things worked. It still took male expertise—traditional male authority—to conquer the inner workings of mechanical devices or to explain complex topics, like current events and finances.

For example, popular newscaster John Cameron Swayze, in a long-running series of ads commencing in 1952, touted the indestructibility of Timex watches ("it takes a licking and keeps on ticking"), insinuating it took more than style to market a wristwatch. Actor Ed Reimers for many years told people that they were in the "good hands" of Allstate insurance, his rich baritone voice assuring viewers that a man understands a whole life policy. In these instances, the actors carried on the theme of the square-jawed, decisive, and self-sufficient male.

Women, if present at all in this kind of ad, usually looked on, but they seldom participated. On the other hand, when 1950s advertising dealt with domestic themes and deigned to include men, the situation reversed: it was the man who became the nonparticipant. He loafed on a chaise lounge while his wife gardened; he was ensconced

An advertisement illustrated with a family playing musical instruments. Everybody, even the baby in the high chair, has a bottle of 7-Up soda, 1950. Prints & Photographs Division, Library of Congress.

in an easy chair while household activities occurred around him. For whatever reasons, advertisers seemed reluctant to portray men as assisting in the duties of the home, although occasionally an ad would portray mom, dad, and the kids enjoying a product together.

MINORITIES AND ADVERTISING

One area of ad stereotyping that changed in the fifties involved the depiction of African Americans. With blacks breaking previously inviolate color lines in sports and entertainment, and with civil rights beginning to inch forward, people found the old derogatory images—the shuffling, cartoonish figures of the recent past—offensive. Words like "Sambo," "Uncle," and "pickaninny," along with demeaning uses of dialect, gradually disappeared from ad copy of the 1950s, although companies continued to wrestle with how best to portray

CIGARETTE ADVERTISING

Surveys in the postwar era showed just how widespread smoking had become. Almost half of all Americans—60 percent males, 30 percent women—smoked at least a pack of cigarettes a day. In 1954, however, the American Medical Association (AMA) issued a study based on the smoking habits of 188,000 men. In it, the AMA established a link between smoking and the incidence of cancer. The gist of this report ran in the high-circulation *Reader's Digest,* forcing an immediate response from the tobacco industry. In full-page newspaper ads, spokesmen denied any correspondences between smoking and cancer.

In 1954, Winston Cigarettes appeared, backed by the slogan "tastes good, like a cigarette should." Much to R. J. Reynolds's delight, the grammar upset some purists (the "like" should be "as," they claimed), and Winston emerged as a major brand in a crowded field, soon occupying the top spot among filter brands.

Another classic ad campaign that occurred at this time involved the Marlboro Man. Marlboro cigarettes had originally appeared in 1924, marketed as a cigarette appropriate for sophisticated women. The brand never did particularly well, and so Phillip Morris, the maker of Marlboros, decided to redo its faltering product in 1954.

In 1955, the revamped Marlboros came out; advertisements pushed them as "masculine," a smoke for "rugged men" with "man-sized flavor," and packaged in a sturdy "flip-top box" that would not cave in and could be opened with one hand. Thanks to a massive saturation campaign, the Marlboro Man—a tall, lean westerner in leather and denim—soon evolved into a national icon. Immediately identifiable, his smoking was associated with manly pursuits, and Marlboros rose to become one of the most popular cigarette brands in the United States.

minority groups. Most major advertisers chose not to depict African Americans or any minority ethnic groups at all. As a result, a significant portion of the population received no acknowledgment, rendering them all but invisible. When blacks did receive some recognition, it occurred too often around products with racial associations, such as hair straighteners and bleaching creams, items that appeared primarily in limited (i.e., nonwhite) markets.

TOOTHPASTE ADVERTISING

Some of the most hotly fought ad campaigns of the fifties involved toothpastes. At the beginning of the 1950s, Colgate-Palmolive's toothpaste led the way with the jingle: "It cleans your breath while it cleans your teeth." For most of the decade, Colgate outsold all others.

HUMOR IN ADVERTISING

Some advertising in the 1950s, especially that aimed at the newly affluent middle class, used deadpan humor. Because readers could linger over them, such ads more often appeared in magazines. Television exposure was deemed too brief for appropriate understanding, although that attitude softened as the decade progressed and viewers became more media-literate. For example, in 1956 the first Clairol advertisements appeared, created by the advertising agency of Foote, Cone and Belding, and sporting the now-famous line, "Does she…or doesn't she?" Despite the clever innuendo, the question referred to the use of hair coloring, and "only her hairdresser knows for sure." Not only was the copy unique, so, too, was the subject: in the 1950s fewer than 10 percent of women would admit to coloring their hair. Both the ads and the product were runaway successes, and Clairol would dominate the field until almost the end of the century.

The Volkswagen "Think Small" ad campaign of 1959, created by the Doyle, Dane, Bernbach advertising agency, showed a black-and-white picture of the Volkswagen Beetle and was distinctive in its honesty and wry humor, unusual for the period, and for the type of ad copy usually run for automobiles. Instead of equating their car with masculine prestige, or family use, the ad suggested the Beetle's unique and unusual qualities.

For their part, Procter & Gamble brought out Crest toothpaste in 1955. Searching for a gimmick to attract the public, Procter & Gamble discovered "Fluoristan." In the early fifties, the government included sodium fluoride in most municipal drinking water. Fluoride had been demonstrated an effective dental decay preventative. The compound reduced the number of cavities among Americans with fluoride-treated water by 50 percent. Wisely sensing the public goodwill toward fluoride, Procter & Gamble in 1956 began marketing Crest as containing stannous fluoride or Fluoristan, as they christened it.

Fluoristan was coupled with a memorable phrase "Look, Mom! No cavities!" in 1958. Crest took off in sales. Numerous photographers, along with the immensely popular illustrator Norman Rockwell, created a series of television, magazine and newspaper ads of delighted kids proclaiming their absence of cavities. The Food and Drug Administration (FDA) soon gave the toothpaste its seal of approval, but because millions had already been buying Crest for years, the FDA's blessing only heightened its success.[11]

TRADING STAMPS

In 1951, a Denver grocery store began offering S&H Green Stamps. Trading stamps had first appeared at the end of the nineteenth century as a means to promote sales among participating merchants. They flourished during the Depression years, but their use fell off during World War II. The idea came around again in the 1950s and found shoppers eager to collect them. The early success of S&H Green Stamps spurred the giant Kroger supermarket chain to join with six other firms to introduce their own Top Value Stamps in 1955.

By the end of the decade, more than 80 percent of all American families were collecting trading stamps, receiving one stamp for every ten cents spent. Redemption centers sprouted like weeds, and every enterprise, from gas stations to department stores, offered them. The three-inch-by-five-inch book of stamps became a ubiquitous part of American shopping. As a rule, it took 1,200 stamps to fill one book, or $120 in purchases. The cash value of a filled book was about $3, so people had to redeem a lot of books for even small items.

Items that stamp collectors could "redeem" with the stamp books included small appliances, such as toasters, electric frying pans, and hairdryers, but also baby cribs, baseball mitts, and many other items. Some 250 to 500 different stamp companies operated during the 1950s, generating over half a billion dollars in revenue.[12]

PUBLIC RELATIONS

A close relative of advertising, public relations enjoyed phenomenal growth during the 1950s. By promoting corporate and organization identity instead of products or services, the image of the parent company became as important as the product. This led to a new term: "image advertising." Many manufacturers wanted to stress the company itself, especially those that made numerous products.

The DuPont Corporation, a giant chemical conglomerate, sponsored both *The DuPont Theater* (1956–1957) and *The DuPont Show of the Month* (1957–1961) on television. In carefully nuanced messages instead of traditional commercials, DuPont spokesmen talked of corporate responsibilities, commitment to excellence, and the role of a large company in serving its employees and families. General Electric, in like manner, spent millions on *The General Electric Theater* (1953–1962) extolling its many roles within the community, not the least of which was that of a major defense contractor dedicated to the security of the nation. Incidentally, GE featured Ronald Reagan as the genial host of the series, a position that catapulted him to political fame. AT&T, General Motors, U.S. Steel, Standard Oil, Ford Motor Company, and numerous other large industrial leaders took similar approaches, intent on getting out a message that cast a positive light on their activities.

POLITICS, PUBLIC RELATIONS, AND ADVERTISING

Politics is an area that blurs the lines between advertising, public relations, and popular culture. The 1952 presidential campaign, pitting Republican Dwight Eisenhower against Democrat Adlai Stevenson, marked the first large-scale use of both print and broadcast appeals for candidates and parties. This innovation became especially apparent in Eisenhower's quest for the presidency. General Eisenhower had, in 1948, authored a best-selling book titled *Crusade in Europe*. Written prior to his candidacy, the book chronicled the Allies' victory in World War II and his role as Supreme Commander, and its popular success brought him further public acclaim.

Eisenhower's run for the presidency employed the resources of Batten, Barton, Durstine, and Osborne (or BBD&O), a large New York advertising firm. Immediately capitalizing on the popularity of the general and his book, his candidacy would be called a "great crusade," and BBD&O began to focus on images instead of issues. Eisenhower—or "Ike," as millions fondly remembered him from his days during the war—was presented as a trusted soldier, one whose fatherly wisdom could simplify complex issues, but not too fatherly: the image-makers wanted Eisenhower to also be personable and appear in full command of his powers. In his TV spots, he read from large cue cards, so he would not have to wear glasses and appear elderly, and the familiar "We Like Ike" became the cheer of his supporters.

Stevenson, on the other hand, attempted to discuss the problems of the day, saying there were no easy choices, no pat explanations, in the Cold War era. But he came across as too smart, too distant. He lacked the folksy touch BBD&O worked relentlessly to associate with Ike. One commentator dredged up an old term used to denigrate an overly learned person: "egghead." It stuck, and Stevenson could never shake the image of an intellectual out of touch with the people.[13]

Eisenhower won in a landside. The campaign illustrated to all the power of image-based advertising, especially in politics and on television. The candidates spent tens of millions of dollars getting their messages out, far more than in any previous presidential race. Henceforth, American election campaigns and American politics would never be the same.

Architecture

of the 1950s

After 16 years of depression (1929–1945), recession, and war, Americans stood poised to embark on the biggest building and buying binge the world had ever seen. The return of millions of veterans, stoked by pent-up demand and available money, set the stage. As industry turned back to civilian needs, builders and developers could barely meet the demand for new housing. The result was the mass production of standardized middle-class dwellings in huge suburban tracts. The ubiquitous ranch house emerged as a popular icon of the 1950s, while commercial architecture and innovative design frequently took a back seat in this rush to build.

COMMERCIAL ARCHITECTURE

For most Americans, any growth in commercial architecture during the 1950s seemed incidental to their primary interest: acquiring a home of their own. Nevertheless, the decade-long construction boom consisted of more than just personal residences; the skylines of most cities also underwent change.

Elite architects like Philip Johnson, Eero Saarinen, Edward Durrell Stone, Frank Lloyd Wright, and the firm of Skidmore, Owings & Merrill (featuring Gordon Bunshaft, in particular) busily signed contracts and watched their works

rise across America. For the fifties, among commercial structures large and small, the glass box emerged as the dominant form.

The glass-fronted office or shop became commonplace, a direct outgrowth of the International Style, but the majority lacked any particular distinction. Extruded aluminum framing, maybe an inset panel or two of colored anodized aluminum, along with glass and anonymous detailing characterized these diluted interpretations of the style. But it served as a cheap, fast way to create commercial spaces, and people liked the openness it gave the businesses enclosed within. Supermarkets, banks, insurance firms, loan agencies, car dealerships, gas stations, department stores, and myriad other commercial establishments quickly adapted to this kind of modernism.

THE SHOPPING CENTER AND THE SHOPPING MALL

Voracious demand and extra dollars in the postwar years signaled that consumers wanted quantity, variety, and convenience. Also, the continuing move to the suburbs by so many middle-class families meant they lived a distance from urban downtowns, the traditional location for shopping. Out of all this emerged big urban and suburban shopping centers consisting of vast paved parking lots with numerous structurally related shops and stores clustered in the middle. Later came more sophisticated shopping malls, an architectural original that clustered stores around a central hub and often featured a climate-controlled environment.

Throughout the 1950s, outlying rural property that bordered cities could still be found in most places at reasonable prices. These open tracts offered endless free parking, and the space to build huge stores and an array of specialty shops. The thirties and forties had seen the rise of the strip shopping center, usually a small parking area and a long row of businesses that abutted a street or highway. The new shopping centers and malls of the fifties, however, took that simple concept much further, with many more establishments including large "anchor tenants," such as department stores and supermarkets. Fancy restaurants—as opposed to fast food—were located inside them also. Many included movie theaters, and some offered multiple screens toward the end of the decade. The space allotted for parking grew geometrically, often covering acres of flattened land, further proof of how the automobile had restructured American society.

Victor Gruen, an architect and designer, pioneered the development of the modern day mall. Outside Minneapolis, Minnesota, he created Southdale, a commercial center that was an immediate success when it opened in 1956. Gruen enclosed the entire development under a single roof, giving shoppers constant air-conditioned or heated comfort. In addition, he made it a place for socializing and entertainment by including a large food court. Its widespread acceptance led other communities to demand malls of their own.[1]

ROADSIDE ARCHITECTURE AND THE HIGHWAY

New high-speed, multilane highways increasingly defined American life. People zoomed past commercial establishments and seldom slowed down. Easy access became paramount, and a sophisticated system of signs and symbols guided drivers in their quest for goods and services.

The superhighways linking the nation also brought with them innovative designs for roadside services. The earlier structures shaped like giant pigs, ducks, coffeepots, and flying fish had begun to disappear. Their replacements reflected postwar aspirations to be modern. Some employed unusual and bizarre shapes and colors, along with plastics, stainless steel, fiberglass, neon tubing, and anything else their developers thought would be eye-catching. Triangles instead of rectangles, boomerangs instead of triangles, abstractions instead of boomerangs—everything had to be scaled to the moving automobile.

After the 1956 launch of the Russian space vehicle *Sputnik I,* shapes that suggested the space race became immensely popular. Rocket-like imagery, along with hints of satellites, planets, suns, stars, and constellations appeared with great profusion. Atomic designs followed close behind—atoms, complete with rotating neutrons and protons, sparkled above even the most mundane of enterprises.

Collectively, this constituted an architecture of wonder, almost anti-gravitational in its effects, and brought about by advances in building technology. Plastics led the way; their malleability, the ease with which they could be molded into infinite shapes, lent them to creative design. Nowhere was freeform architecture better displayed than on the trendsetting West Coast, especially in drive-in restaurants and diners.

THE SIGN AS SYMBOL

In another bow to the highway, commercial signs grew to monumental size in order to be seen from greater distances while traveling at high speeds. In fact, architects conceived of the entire structure as an integrated sign—from the orange roofs on a Howard Johnson's to the golden arches of a McDonald's. Broad expanses of glass allowed a view into the interior and all that transpired there, a kind of billboard to advertise function. This openness suggests a democratization of architecture and a reproach to elitism. Transparent walls mediated between the exterior and the interior, while private space and public space blended into one.

An example of the iconic role signs played can be found in the familiar green and yellow roadside emblem that announced a Holiday Inn during the fifties. Founded in 1954 and still new to many people, the chain's towering sign featured an exploding star, a huge boomerang arrow, the words "Holiday Inn" in a distinctive script, and a large marquee that advertised coming events, meal specials, perhaps a birthday or anniversary, and ongoing activities within. Its sheer size demanded recognition, and the sign itself became an icon, a visual magnet promising food, shelter, and economy.

Holiday Inns of America, the corporate owners of the chain, recognized the value of their sign and registered it as an official trademark. Although its design and dimensions have changed over the years, the sign is never sold; franchise holders lease it, allowing it to remain the property of the corporation.[2]

Another illustration of the iconic sign would be the famous golden arches of McDonald's hamburger stands. In reality they do not mean or represent anything; they exist simply as shapes—parabolas, to be exact. But they have become associated with the company, with fast food, and have assumed a symbolic meaning of their own. First introduced in 1953 at a new McDonald's in Phoenix, Arizona, the golden arches immediately garnered attention. The growing restaurant chain saw to it that they were replicated in all subsequent stands. With time, the arches have diminished in size, but they continue to symbolize the company and have become the corporate logo. (See Food of the 1950s.)

RESIDENTIAL BUILDING

The triumph of the suburbs and the building of thousands upon thousands of new homes overshadowed all other architectural endeavors. Virtually everything that occurred in American residential architecture and design in the immediate postwar years came to fruition in the 1950s. New technologies allowed architects freedom to create new spaces in house interiors, stronger building materials promised greater durability and weather resistance, and the quest for economical housing meant these advances would be employed on a vast scale.

"Houses of the Future" became a minor fad during the postwar years. Usually sponsored by suppliers and trade groups, these for-display-only homes were shown across the country and drew large crowds. They tended toward the avant-garde in their design, but they incorporated such prefabricated details as plywood for walls, laminated roofs, metal trusses and wall framing, pre-assembled windows, gypsum-board ceilings, and a host of other innovative structural details. The large picture windows and open interior areas would come to characterize many ranch houses in the ballooning suburbs. Most potential buyers wanted something that, on the exterior at least, looked traditional and resembled the other houses in the neighborhood. Many building advances may have been incorporated into these new homes, but they were not obvious to passersby.

Despite the reluctance of homebuyers to move into anything futuristic in the least, architects continued to display their modernistic concepts. Perhaps the most famous of these varied designs was the all-metal Lustron House. Manufactured between 1948 and 1950, this functional dwelling featured a steel frame with porcelain-enameled steel panels available in six colors. The Lustron House cost roughly $7,000 at the time, a very reasonable price, and about 2,500 were built, some of which remain in use.

Other conceptual homes of the era included the Look House (1948), sponsored by the popular *Look* magazine. *House & Garden* erected the House of Ideas in 1952, and in the following year *Life* magazine underwrote the Trade Secrets House. *Arts and Architecture,* another influential magazine, organized the Case Study House Program; it commissioned architects to design and build modern dwellings that featured the latest in construction details and furnishings. Monsanto's experimental House of the Future (1954), a cruciform-shaped structure constructed of molded plastic, fiberglass, and concrete, became a permanent exhibition at Disneyland in 1957. Major manufacturers furnished the dwelling with futuristic furniture and appliances. The curious gawked at it, but they went home and built brick-and-wood ranch houses with early American detailing. Probably the most significant result that came from these varied designs was an increased utilization of prefabricated components.[3]

RANCH HOUSES AND SPLIT-LEVELS

A postwar power grid that took transmission lines into the open countryside surrounding

Monsanto's "House of the Future" in the Tomorrowland section of Disneyland Park, Anaheim, California, 1957. Prints & Photographs Division, Library of Congress.

built-up areas, coupled with a growing highway system, made the relentless growth of suburbs possible. Because most adults had access to automobiles, the distance between urban and rural space ceased being an important consideration. Sprawling subdivisions soon sprang up around the perimeters of cities and towns, occupying areas once thought of as "too far away" from city life.

The home design most favored by developers, realtors, and buyers alike has come to be called the ranch house. In the years surrounding World War II, early examples of the style had begun to appear in the San Francisco Bay area, giving rise to the name "California Ranch." In reality, however, many elements contained in the design could be traced to the long, low residences, or Prairie style homes, that Frank Lloyd Wright and his followers pioneered in the early part of the twentieth century. Whether original or derivative, the fifties ranch was basically a one-story rectangle, with the long side facing the street. Employing simple

frame construction methods, ranch houses could be easily and economically assembled on site. As a rule, a carport (an open, roofed garage) served to shelter the family car.

A large inefficient picture window on the street side let in heat during the summer and cold during the winter, but because homebuyers wanted it, it became a basic part of the house. As a result, the sales of air conditioners and bigger heating systems surged. In a neighborhood of ranch homes, everyone looked out at one another, and everyone could likewise look in. At the same time, it existed as a sealed environment; ranches did not extend a greeting to those on the street. They had a front entry, but no front porches. Activities were oriented to the backyard for privacy, with a tiny patio behind the house for outdoor family entertaining and dining.

To the millions who bought them during the 1950s, the ranch house symbolized an informal lifestyle. The term "cookout" entered the national vocabulary at this time, and almost overnight, a cheap, portable charcoal grill became a necessity. The ubiquitous kettle version made its first appearance in 1952, and the aroma of steaks being grilled on the patio became commonplace. It all fit an image of familial togetherness that seldom tolerated significant differences.

Most ranch houses possessed less square footage than the designs they replaced, the four-squares, bungalows, and revivals of the 1920s and 1930s. But they gave the illusion of being spacious and open, and housewives did not have to repeatedly climb stairs to a second floor. Developers marketed them as efficient, pleasant, and casual—attributes homebuyers wanted in the 1950s.

Old favorites like Cape Cods and Colonial Revivals were still built during the decade, but the ranch house and its variants emerged as the overwhelming favorite for the new American suburb. Inexpensive plans abounded: *Better Homes and Gardens* and *House & Garden* both published them. In glowing articles, they espoused the advantages of leisurely living and offered economical blueprints. Its low cost and simplicity made the ranch the ideal starter home, and the prosperity of the fifties allowed more and more Americans to become first-time homeowners.

By the mid-fifties, a popular variation on the style emerged. Considered a "split-level" house, the design typically allowed for a central entrance and a landing at mid-level; one section of the house stood two stories in height, consisting of private bath and bedroom areas on the upper floor and informal areas like the family room on the lowest level. The middle or ground-level section consisted of one story and tended to be more formal, with the living room, dining room and kitchen. The lower level contained a family room and garage or carport. Split-levels provided designated living (public) and sleeping (private) areas and became a favorite in the late 1950s. While managing to retain the simplicity of the ranch style, they accommodated more rooms and increased overall floor space than did ranch houses, yet both could be erected on cramped suburban lots, especially sloped ones.

HOUSE TRAILERS AND MOBILE HOMES

In the immediate postwar years, about eight percent of the population lived in house trailers, a carryover from emergency wartime housing. During the 1950s, trailers grew into "mobile homes"; they went from 8 feet to 10 feet in width, and could hardly be called mobile. The travails of living in this kind of structure were depicted in *The Long, Long Trailer,* a 1954 movie comedy starring Lucille Ball and Desi Arnaz. Riding a crest of popularity because of their hit television series, *I Love Lucy* (1951–1957), the couple tackled any and all stereotypes about trailer living in the film.

Trailer parks, later renamed "Mobile Home Parks" in an attempt to impart a sense of greater permanence, became a part of the American landscape. In terms of modern housing, trailers and mobile homes exemplified true factory prefabrication.[4]

HOUSING GROWTH

In 1945, at the conclusion of the war, about 40 percent of Americans owned homes. Over 50 percent of the new homes sold during most of the decade received financing through Veterans Administration or Federal Housing Administration mortgages. With these incentives, builders erected almost 15 million homes, a new national record. By 1960, 60 percent of Americans owned their own homes. Most middle-class people saw real salary gains and increased buying power during the decade, but not black citizens; their median incomes lingered at about 40 percent of what white people earned. As whites fled to the welcoming suburbs, blacks found themselves confined to the cities, making do with older, often inferior housing. Some developments even had "whites only" clauses built into their contracts, and not until later would these restrictions be dropped. Playwright Lorraine Hansberry captured this dilemma in *A Raisin in the Sun* (1959). An American classic, the play (also a movie in 1961) treated realistically the inequalities that remained manifest in this otherwise prosperous decade.

LEVITTOWN

Across the country, new suburban towns rose seemingly overnight. Communities like Lakewood (outside Los Angeles), Park Forest (outside Chicago), Lexington (outside Boston), and a number of other huge subdivisions built thousands of homes in the early fifties. But the largest, the most ambitious of all, was Levittown. For many, the name has become synonymous with American suburbia.

In reality, three separate Levittowns exist in the United States. The name acknowledges William J. Levitt, a builder who pioneered the mass production of interchangeable parts for home construction. Levitt and many of his fellow builders gained practice during World War II assembling tracts of temporary housing for defense workers and military families. Preassembled components were trucked directly to sites, where cheap, unskilled workers could put them together. By employing techniques he learned during the war, Levitt reduced the need for expensive skilled labor to about a quarter of the tasks. The construction process, refined and simplified, ranged from painting (each color a separate step) to tile laying. At its peak, a new home went up in Levittown every 15 minutes.[5] In 1947, the first Levittown appeared just below Hicksville, Long Island, on what were once potato fields; it consisted of over 17,000 homes, almost all of them built in a similar one-and-a-half-story Cape Cod style. They provided 800 square feet of living space on a small (60 feet by 100 feet), barren lot. By using a traditional Cape Cod design as his first model, Levitt unwittingly encouraged both the early American and do-it-yourself crazes that swept the suburbs in the 1950s. Although the typical dwelling had no spare space for a home workshop, enterprising woodworkers found a niche in the unfinished attic or in a corner for projects. Despite the initial success with Cape Cods, the public's desire for ranch houses predicated Levitt's second phase. In then rural Bucks County, Pennsylvania, just north of Philadelphia, he created the next Levittown in 1951. As he had done on Long Island, Levitt built some 17,000 ranches, along with schools, parks, and stores. The third and final Levittown, situated just across the Delaware River in Willingboro, New Jersey, also consisted of ranch style homes, about 11,000 of them; construction began in 1958.

Those Cape Cods shared almost identical floor plans, as did the ranches; it kept costs down. The exteriors varied only by degree: a few minor changes in detailing and some choices in colors. As the first Levitt version of the American suburban Dream House took shape in the late forties, it provided buyers a kitchen, bath, living room, and two bedrooms. Upstairs, an unfinished attic space could be converted to additional bedrooms. In an admission of television's growing influence, these early Cape Cods included a built-in 12½-inch TV set and a washing machine already hooked to water lines. Building the TV into a wall and connecting the washer to plumbing made them parts of the house, not separate purchases by the buyer, and qualified them to be part of the mortgage. Major kitchen appliances, like a refrigerator and a stove, also were included in the original purchase price of $7,000–$8,000.[6] Levitt's choice of a ranch style for his subsequent developments reflected changing consumer needs. Slightly more spacious than the earlier Cape Cods, it cost about $9,000. These homes boasted three bedrooms, a necessity for the bigger families most suburbanites desired. Family rooms, spacious areas that allowed for everyone to come together, became a demand item. Likewise, utility rooms designed to hold an automatic washer and a dryer reflected the buying power and consumerist bent of 1950s families. The once ubiquitous backyard clothesline became a relic of the past, as did the old wringer washing machine.

Certainly, conformity characterized the new postwar American suburb. The original Levittown stipulated that homeowners keep their tiny lots tidy and well mowed. And mow they did; in the 1950s the powered rotary mower replaced the old-fashioned hand-powered reel mower. For some, the lawn became an end in itself, a celebration of the final taming of nature. In order for no backyard to detract from its neighbors, laundry could only be done on certain days in certain neighborhoods, and it was to be dried on identical metal racks, not hung from clotheslines. The rules forbade fences, so yards flowed into one another, contributing to the overall anonymity of the development. And to complete the bland neighborhoods, racist covenants for Levittown excluded African Americans, Puerto Ricans, and other ethic minorities from buying homes. If a Levittown homeowner tried to sell a house to someone from a minority group, the seller could be sued by the neighbors.

HOME FALLOUT SHELTERS

As fears about nuclear war increased during the 1950s, many families decided to construct fallout shelters either in their basements or backyards. Such a move supposedly gave protection from nuclear explosions and radioactive fallout to any users. These shelters ranged from elaborate multiroom underground facilities well stocked with food and water to simple cave-like excavations designed to protect a family at the time of the initial blast. Whatever shape the shelter took, the idea gave people pause. Leading popular magazines like *Life* ran articles complete with detailed plans to accommodate this interest, and the government obligingly provided pamphlets with titles such as *You Can Survive, The Family Fallout Shelter,* and *Atomic Attack.*[7]

DESIGN

Designers

A number of designers established names for themselves in the fifties. People like Harry Bertoia (wire furniture), Charles and Ray Eames (laminated plywood and molded plastic "Eames chairs"), George Nelson (storage systems and platform benches), Eero Saarinen (molded fiberglass "Tulip chairs"), and Russel Wright (plastic

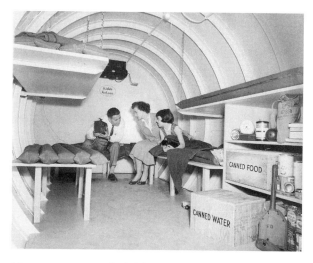

Man, woman, and child seated in "Kidde Kokoon," an underground bomb shelter, 1955. Prints & Photographs Division, Library of Congress.

and ceramic dinnerware, including the popular "American Modern" line) became known to the public. Advertising promoted their names along with their designs, and it was chic to buy a product designed by someone famous and respected.

ICONIC ACCESSORIES OF THE 1950s HOME AND OFFICE

The hooded, freestanding fireplace, ideally suited for family rooms, made its first appearance in 1953, and it immediately caught on. "Atomic clocks" also sold well throughout the decade. They featured round faces representing the nucleus of an atom and radiating numbers on spokes that symbolized the rotating particles. Pole lamps relied on a spring-loaded pole that created a snug fit between floor and ceiling. Adjustable reflectors up and down the length of the pole directed light as needed. For the open spaces of a modern house, these fixtures could be placed almost anywhere.

The classic rotary desk telephone was commercially introduced in the early fifties. Because AT&T and Bell Laboratories then held a monopoly on all telephones in use, virtually every American home had at least one of these black plastic instruments. Almost indestructible, there existed no other piece of technology better known to the general public, and its sleek, contemporary lines resonated with the times.

Similarly, the Rolodex rotary card file was introduced in 1958. Completely manual—flip the cards until the desired information comes up—they could be updated or edited easily. Its polished metal and plastic holder seemed to symbolize the modern office. Although the Rolodex predated the personal computer, it remains a valuable tool that employs minimal technology.

The gaudy 1950s jukeboxes, particularly in the models created by Paul Fuller for the Wurlitzer Company, sum up much of the decade's design trends. Brightly lit, with cascading and blinking colors, lots of shiny surfaces, and angles that suggest Detroit cars of the era more than anything else, their flashiness epitomized the era.

Kitchens and Appliances

The immensely popular ranch houses of the 1950s gave considerable attention to kitchens, especially the appliances that would be found there. As a result, this once neglected room emerged as an important display area for modern design. Because most ranches put a premium on available space, the kitchen became home to built-in cabinets and appliances. This emphasis signified a blend of the technologically new and the traditional. Cabinets faced in early American knotty pine with wrought-iron hardware would share space with an advanced, all-electric range.

Much commercial design of the 1950s carried over the Streamline Moderne characteristics developed during the late 1930s and 1940s, but designers found themselves pressed to create a distinctive 1950s look in small appliances and dinnerware. They responded with plain, unadorned pieces, especially in the case of casual china. Featuring hourglass and tulip shapes in cups and pitchers, they gave saucers and plates sharp, dynamic lines instead of the curves and rounded edges that so characterized streamlining. Accessories that dispensed with ornamentation quickly became the favorites of consumers. Flatware likewise was redesigned, often becoming sculptural in its lines, with stainless steel emerging as a new favorite at the expense of traditional silver. Even prosaic pots and pans enjoyed a facelift, displaying crisper lines and more ergonomically shaped handles.

Polyethylene, a durable but flexible plastic and one of the technological advances of the postwar era, was used to make everything from refrigerator containers to garbage cans. It would not crack or break, resisted cold, and could be cheaply mass produced in a rainbow of colors. Brands like Tupperware and Rubbermaid attracted millions of shoppers, and Tupperware parties in private homes proved a novel and effective way to merchandise their modern-looking polyethylene containers.[8] (See Food of the 1950s.)

Melamine, another sturdy plastic, gained renown as a revolutionary new product for dinnerware in 1952. Virtually unbreakable and available in white and pastels, it complemented the appliances and furnishings found in the modern kitchen. Even the lowly sink received a new look. The basin could be had in stainless steel and plumbing manufacturers offered faucets that mixed hot and cold water from a single, moveable spigot.[9]

Modern kitchens received an unanticipated emphasis from television. Cooking shows, cheap and easy to produce in the early days of TV, usually featured a lineup of shiny new appliances loaned by willing merchants. A spacious work island might constitute the entire set. In addition, the major networks often employed kitchens as props in their situation comedies. Many of these series, such as *The Donna Reed Show* (1958–1966), *Father Knows Best* (1954–1962), *Leave It to Beaver* (1957–1963), and *Ozzie and Harriet* (1952–1966) set numerous scenes in sparkling, well-equipped kitchens.

Books

Newspapers, Magazines, and Comics of the 1950s

At the forefront of the decade were two of American's greatest writers, William Faulkner and Ernest Hemingway. Faulkner won the Nobel Prize in literature in 1950, followed four years later by Hemingway. This international recognition briefly boosted their appeal and made them the subjects of considerable popular attention.

By and large, Faulkner and Hemingway were supplanted by the usual run of best sellers and assorted ephemeral titles that sold in astronomical numbers and then disappeared. Mysteries, lurid novels, social studies, along with self-help and how-to books galore, dominated the trade lists.

BOOKS

Paperbacks

Paperback books rose to dominance in popular publishing, accounting for over one-third of all the books sold in the United States. Pocket Books, founded in 1939, had by 1950 become the leading publisher of the less expensive paperbound titles, and they continued to maintain a $0.25 cover price.[1]

The success of Pocket Books led to an expansion of publishing imprints. Cardinal Editions, a subsidiary of Pocket Books, came along in 1951. In 1954, the Pocket Library was created, consisting of reprints of earlier Pocket Books and Cardinal Editions titles, but at higher prices. At the end of the decade, the Pocket Library evolved into the Washington Square Press but continued to offer reprints.

Other publishers, envious of the paperback empire Pocket Books had created, launched their own series. Avon Books debuted in 1941, and throughout the forties and fifties its garish covers, most featuring semi-clothed women, rivaled anything the cheap pulp magazines displayed on newsstands. By 1951, Avon released a dozen new titles a month.

Still more paperback firms, some new and some boasting fresh imprints from established houses, appeared during the fifties. Familiar names like Ballantine (1952), Beacon Books (1954), Berkley Books (1955), and Monarch (1958) commenced publishing. The dominance of the expensive hardcover book had ended, and popular mass-market writers found expanded outlets for their work.

The racy covers on many 1950s Popular Library titles, led to the formation of a Congressional committee in 1952. The committee recommended that the postmaster general ban any books with covers deemed pornographic from interstate or international shipment, a move that gave the U.S. Post Office censorship powers. The paperback publishers themselves responded by toning down their covers.

NOTABLE BOOKS

Pippi Longstocking, Astrid Lindgren (U.S. edition, 1950)

The Martian Chronicles, Ray Bradbury (1950)

The Caine Mutiny, Herman Wouk (1951)

Catcher in the Rye, J. D. Salinger (1951)

From Here to Eternity, James Jones (1951)

Charlotte's Web, E. B. White (1952)

Invisible Man, Ralph Ellison (1952)

East of Eden, John Steinbeck (1952)

The Power of Positive Thinking, Norman Vincent Peale (1952)

The Old Man and the Sea, Ernest Hemingway (1952)

Fahrenheit 451, Ray Bradbury (1953)

Casino Royale, Ian Fleming (U.S. edition, 1954)

The Blackboard Jungle, Evan Hunter (1954)

Lord of the Flies, William Golding (1954)

Peyton Place, Grace Metalious (1956)

The Cat in the Hat and *How the Grinch Stole Christmas,* Dr. Seuss (1957)

On the Road, Jack Kerouac (1957)

Dr. Zhivago, Boris Pasternak (U.S. edition, 1958)

Lolita, Vladimir Nabokov (1958)

By the beginning of the 1950s, paperbacks constituted a thriving part of the publishing industry. Some of the larger houses even released original titles, not just reprints of hardcover books. Many mystery novels made their debuts in paperback because most people bought the cheaper paper editions anyway. Publishers expanded this practice to include such popular genres as westerns, science fiction, thrillers, fantasy and horror, romances, and much in sports and humor.

In 1950, the ABC television network aired *The Adventures of Ellery Queen,* a series based on a fictional detective whose adventures were popular novels during the 1930s and 1940s. It ran for two unspectacular years, but NBC brought the private eye back for the 1958–1959 season. In like manner, novels began to feature Perry Mason, outwardly a lawyer but in actuality a sleuth who had enjoyed considerable acclaim in the preceding two decades. Capitalizing on this popularity, CBS Radio ran *Perry Mason* from 1943 to 1955, but Mason's greatest fame came in 1957 when the network moved the series to television, creating one of the most successful shows in TV history. It would run until 1966. Naturally, the publishers of both Ellery Queen and Perry Mason promptly issued fresh paperbound editions of their adventures, introducing a new generation of readers to the popular mystery series.[2]

Best Sellers

Despite the inroads made by the ubiquitous paperback, most best-seller lists continued to spotlight hardback titles. Simplistic religious literature boomed as people sought an easy spiritual security. Norman Vincent Peale, the popular pastor at New York's Marble Collegiate Church, wrote *The Power of Positive Thinking* (1952), a consistent best seller for several years. The book argues that material wealth and an optimistic outlook go hand in hand. Although it did not originate with Peale's work, the motto "the family that prays together stays together" gained widespread credence during the 1950s, and its message found support in *The Power of Positive Thinking.* His success assured, Peale also published *Guideposts* magazine and wrote a weekly column for *Look* magazine.

The long-awaited Revised Standard Version, or RSV, of the Bible came out in 1952. The work of 32 biblical scholars over 15 years, the book was applauded by most people everywhere as a needed update to the King James Version. During 1952 and 1953, it overwhelmed fiction and nonfiction titles, with over three million copies sold. By 1954, the RSV still led all nonfiction with close to another million copies purchased.[3]

The evangelist Billy Graham (1918–) emerged as a multimedia phenomenon in the 1950s. He joined the ranks of religious writers with *America's Hour of Decision* in 1951. He followed it with *Peace with God* in 1953 and *The Secret of Happiness* two years later. In 1956, Graham began a newspaper column, "My Answer," that quickly received nationwide syndication. He participated in two periodicals, *Christianity Today* and *Decision Magazine*. In 1950, he incorporated his work, creating the Billy Graham Evangelistic Association, which produced films and radio and television broadcasts. In the summer of 1957, Graham led one of the largest religious crusades New York City had ever seen, drawing nearly two million people to Madison Square Garden. He also became a personal friend and confidant to President Eisenhower, a role he would consistently play with succeeding presidents.[4]

This religious/spiritual enthusiasm—some likened it to a new awakening—carried over into film, radio, and television. Monsignor Fulton J. Sheen (1895–1979) gained fame by virtue of his long-running NBC radio show, *The Catholic Hour* (1930–1961). In 1953, the network broadened his radio program to include television. The televised *Catholic Hour* evolved into *Life is Worth Living* (1953–1955) and then into *Mission to the World* (1955–1957). The television exposure, along with his good looks, low-key delivery, and common sense values, made Sheen a show business celebrity. Prime-time scheduling put the bishop up against comedian Milton Berle, and although he could never topple the popular Berle, he did well, and the two referred to one another humorously. (See Entertainment of the 1950s.)

American author J. D. Salinger is seen in this undated photo. AP Photo.

J. D. Salinger

Just as the movies had their teen stars in the fifties, so did the publishing world. Holden Caulfield, the lonely hero—or antihero, as contemporary critics delighted in calling him—of J. D. Salinger's *The Catcher in the Rye* (1951) captivated audiences everywhere, and came to epitomize contemporary youth. The novel attracted a large public and soon appeared on required reading lists in innumerable high schools and colleges. Holden's distrust of adults and simultaneous yearning for the security and stability of family served as a good metaphor for the decade. While the novel drew praise from the start, there was an equal amount of criticism, with some calling for the book to be banned, censored, or restricted on account of its adult themes. Seen as an important spark in the so-called teenage revolution of the late 1950s, Salinger won critical and popular

praise for his simple, honest dialogue and unusual narrative style.[5]

Ernest Hemingway

Established writers like William Faulkner (*The Mansion,* 1959) and John Steinbeck (*East of Eden,* 1952) continued to produce significant works, but only Ernest Hemingway (1899–1961) succeeded in reaching a truly large audience. *Life* magazine published his *Old Man and the Sea* (1952) in its entirety, so certain were the editors that millions would be attracted to this brief, allegorical work. On September 1, 1952, one week before the book's publication, the magazine printed five million copies, a record number. The editors had guessed correctly; *Life* sold out and the book shot straight onto best-seller lists everywhere. The Book-of-the-Month Club featured it, and Hemingway enjoyed the largest single audience he would ever have. In 1958, Hollywood released a film based on the novel, with Spencer Tracy taking the lead role.

Mickey Spillane

American readers might profess admiration for the likes of Hemingway, Faulkner, and Steinbeck, but when they bought books en masse, their purchases suggested that their tastes were oriented toward authors writing in a more violent and graphic style. In sheer sales, no one could top Mickey Spillane (1918–2006), the creator of detective Mike Hammer. Hammer, a private eye only outwardly cut from the mold established by Raymond Chandler, Dashiell Hammett, and other hard-boiled writers of the thirties and forties, was crude and brutal, but neither he nor his creator seemed to care. In addition, Hammer functioned as a strong anti-Communist, rampant homophobe, and, some would add, misogynist. In Hammer's primitive code, sexual deviance led to moral weakness, and that made a person a target of Communist infiltrators ready to pounce on any human frailty.

The first of the Hammer stories, *I, the Jury*, came out in 1947 and took off like a rocket. By 1952, Spillane's titles—such as *My Gun is Quick* (1950), *Vengeance is Mine* (1950), *One Lonely Night* (1951), *The Big Kill* (1951), and *Kiss Me Deadly* (1952)—accounted for one-quarter of all paperback books sold in the United States. Hollywood quickly rushed out dark, moody versions of *I, the Jury* (1953; remade in 1982), *Kiss Me Deadly* (1955), and *My Gun is Quick* (1957).[6]

Television jumped on the Spillane bandwagon in 1958 with a syndicated series titled *Mickey Spillane's Mike Hammer*. Starring Darren McGavin as the tough investigator, it ran for 78 half-hour episodes.

Grace Metalious

Another prominent writer of the period was Grace Metalious (1924–1964). Her claim to fame rests with one blockbuster novel, *Peyton Place* (1956). The book introduced readers to a complex, interrelated cast of characters that moved from one steamy episode to another. Since its release in 1956, the novel has established itself as one of the all-time American best sellers, with over 12 million copies sold.

Originally written to challenge every sexual taboo in America, in its final form *Peyton Place* was somewhat toned down. But even with editing, *Peyton Place* managed to include adultery, incest, illegitimacy, and graphic sexual descriptions, making it a "must read" for millions.

Thanks to its notoriety and huge sales, *Peyton Place* appeared on the big screen in 1957. Metalious, not happy with what editors had done to her work in both novelistic and cinematic terms, nonetheless wrote a sequel, *Return to Peyton Place* (1959). Panned by critics, the book sold well on the strength of the original and likewise became a movie in 1960.[7] (See Entertainment of the 1950s.)

Vladimir Nabokov

With the publication of the Mike Hammer thrillers and *Peyton Place*, in addition to several other controversial novels, America's sexual innocence drew to a close. The release of *Lolita* by Vladimir Nabokov (1899–1977) in 1955 hastened that closure. First published by the Paris-based Olympia Press, the book finally found an American house willing to carry it in 1958. Never officially banned in the United States in either its European or American editions, the novel stunned critics, drove would-be censors wild, sold millions of copies, and dominated best-seller lists soon after its release. The story involves the adventures, both comic and sexual, of a 12-year-old girl and her ardent middle-aged suitor, Humbert Humbert. Nabokov contributed two new words to the language: "Lolita" and "nymphet." Both refer to underage girls who are sexually wise beyond their years. The author until this time had been noted mainly for dense, academic novels that had little to do with eroticism, so *Lolita* came as a surprise and had the book world talking for years after its publication.

The Beat Generation and Jack Kerouac

The work of the so-called Beat Generation in literature favored an improvisational approach, and its supporters claimed that true spontaneity in the arts outweighed a text in which the author carefully positioned every word. In their eyes, emotion (or the expression thereof) supplanted traditional craft, an attitude that put them in

"HURRICANE LOLITA"

Vladimir Nabokov (1899–1977) taught at Cornell University from 1948 to 1959. Nabokov's controversial book *Lolita* is about an older European, Humbert Humbert, who comes to America and has an affinity for young girls. He encounters 12-year-old Dolores Haze (Lolita) and marries her mother so he can be near her daughter. Following the journey of Humbert, the book is full of satire and sexual innuendos and brought the new words "Lolita" and "nymphet" into American language. Four publishing companies rejected *Lolita* before Olympia Press in Paris published it in 1955.

Initially, Nabokov wanted to use a pen name as he was afraid he would be fired from Cornell because of the roundly denounced subject of pedophilia. *Lolita* took America by storm and was soon referred to as "Hurricane Lolita." Although never banned from the United States, Nabokov's book was banned from individual schools and many public libraries.

The effect *Lolita* had on American culture is profound. The tone of the story is celebratory, glorifying the United States in the fifties. The use of language in Lolita is stunning; the Russian-born Nabokov once remarked that he was in love with the English language. With the publication of *Lolita,* a more sexually adventurous publishing culture ensued. The word "Lolita" is now associated with a very seductive and attractive young girl. Two movies of the same name were released, the first in 1962, directed by Stanley Kubrick, and the second in 1997, directed by Adrian Lyne. Both films faced harsh criticism and many American film companies refused to distribute them. Kubrick's 1962 cinematic adaptation was meticulously censored in Hollywood, much like critics wanted to do with Nabokov's novel.

league with many of the abstract expressionists then active in painting. (See Art of the 1950s.)

Like their counterparts in the other arts, the Beat writers rejected much of modern mass culture, claiming that it was sterile and lacking in any substance. Their work first manifested itself on the West Coast, particularly in the coffeehouses and bistros of San Francisco. "Beat" quickly entered the language, denoting novelists, poets, and other creative types of the 1950s who rebelled against the status quo.

After the successful launch of the Russian *Sputnik* spacecraft in 1957, the suffix "–nik" took on a certain cachet and was added to the word "beat." The resultant "beatnik" veered away from the original; it carried negative connotations, implying a person loafed, possessed a beard (but seldom long hair), wore scruffy clothes and sandals, and displayed numerous bad habits. Poet and publisher Lawrence Ferlinghetti ran the City Lights Bookstore in San Francisco, and there many of the more famous Beat writers and poets congregated. Novelists William S. Burroughs (*The Naked Lunch,* 1959) and Jack Kerouac (*On the Road,* 1957), alongside poet Allen Ginsberg (*Howl,* 1956), emerged as prominent members.[8]

Kerouac (1922–1969) in particular came to symbolize this free-spirited movement. He called his technique of unpunctuated, stream-of-consciousness prose "sketching," a nod to its similarities with the ongoing art scene. In 1957 *On the Road,* his best-known novel, appeared. Written in the early 1950s in a seemingly spontaneous, nonstop, impulsive style, it attracted a wide range of readers. *On the Road* was followed in 1958 by *The Subterraneans* and *The Dharma Bums,* but their success relied in large part on the reputation earned by *On the Road.*

Poetry

A few established poets like Robert Frost and Carl Sandburg could still attract a handful of readers, but serious poetry held little popular appeal in the 1950s. Robert Lowell, perhaps the best of a new, postwar generation of poets, enjoyed the praises of critics, but that kind of recognition failed to generate any wave of public acclaim or sales.

One exception was Allen Ginsberg's long, rambling poem *Howl.* Published in 1956 by City Lights Press and initially released in San Francisco, the local police deemed it obscene and seized all copies, giving the work more publicity than it might otherwise have received. A trial ensued, and both

Allen Ginsberg, left, and William S. Burroughs chat in their later years. AP Photo.

Lawrence Ferlinghetti (the publisher) and his store manager (who sold a copy to a law officer) were cleared. Meanwhile, *Howl* reaped huge sales and became the top-selling book of poetry in the United States in the 1950s.

Nonfiction

Nonfiction titles purporting to analyze the social changes taking place in contemporary America found large, receptive readerships. David Riesman's *The Lonely Crowd* (1953; with contributions from Nathan Glazer and Reuel Denney) stood as a trailblazing sociological study that suggested Americans could lose their individuality in a quest for "togetherness," a favorite term of the time. The book maintained that Americans, more and more subjugated to the will of a faceless majority, lived anonymous, undirected lives, and that newfound prosperity—signified by the acquisition of material goods—deadened any responses to this situation.

Author William Whyte examined the question of an oppressive work environment in his best seller, *The Organization Man* (1956). Whyte argued that American businesses forced their employees into a kind of unthinking conformity; the title became a phrase to describe almost anyone working in a white-collar job. Whyte's thesis said that Americans, particularly American men, had lost touch with the spirit of individualism and self-reliance. Instead, the modern corporation imposed a self-serving philosophy of cooperation and loyalty to the company, and their millions of "organization men" wallowed in a kind of sameness and conformism.

Tied to all the foregoing was a concern about growing materialism. In a pair of studies, Vance Packard attacked the rampant consumerism of the 1950s. *The Hidden Persuaders* came out in 1957. Using many examples, he attempted to show how manipulative advertising had convinced Americans to purchase goods based on psychological needs instead of the more historic ones of scarcity and insufficiency. (See Advertising of the 1950s.)

On an altogether different plane, Alfred Kinsey's much-awaited *Sexual Behavior in the Human Female* made big publishing news upon its release in 1953. A companion to his controversial *Sexual Behavior in the Human Male* (1948), readers found much to discuss in the two volumes. His findings indicated that Americans, especially American women, were not quite as proper as they seemed. From outrage to enthusiastic support, the book remained on the best-seller lists for much of the year. For an essentially dry academic treatise on behavior, its popular success came as a surprise.

The Great Books Program

The middle class has traditionally viewed self-education in a positive light, picturing it as an old, desirable American trait. In 1947 Robert Maynard Hutchins, president of the University of Chicago, initiated with others what they published as *The Great Books of the Western World,* or the Great Books program. Owing as much to marketing as to education, the program caught the public interest and in 1952 became available as a 54-volume set. Sold under the auspices of the Encyclopedia Britannica publishing group, *Great Books* promised a library of works deemed basic to what a well-read person should know. Included in the undertaking were over 500 works by writers ranging from Aristotle to Virginia Woolf. A clever two-volume *Syntopticon* served as a guidebook, or outline, to the thousands of pages of text.

The series enjoyed a modest success, at least in sales, during the 1950s. The nicely bound volumes had color-coded spines (e.g., red for philosophy and religion) and the publishers marketed them as a handsome addition to any home library. Purchasers were encouraged to meet informally with other buyers to have group discussions, or "great conversations," as Hutchins put it.[9]

Dr. Spock

If some aspired to greater knowledge, others merely wanted advice on raising children and healthy diets. Pediatrician Benjamin Spock (1903–1998) published his first edition of *The Common Sense Book of Baby and Child Care* in 1946, and the postwar baby boom caused it to become a perennial best seller, especially in the 1950s. The book served as a bible for millions of young mothers; on only 13 pages of the over 300-page book does Dr. Spock specifically address fathers and fatherhood. Generally speaking, Spock recommended flexibility and restraint when dealing with infants and children, in contrast to the sterner messages of earlier advice manuals. *The Common Sense Book of Baby and Child Care* became one of the most popular books in the annals of American publishing.[10]

MAGAZINES

In 1950, magazines remained a leading mass medium in terms of advertising revenue. Television, however, whittled away at this figure, just as it would do with all print media. Adding to their woes, paper and printing costs rose sharply, and postage rates for magazines jumped a whopping 30 percent in 1959. As a result of all these economic pressures, many old, established titles would disappear during the decade.

With the realization that advertisers wanted magazines that reflected specific readerships, a flood of new titles came out during the 1950s. Most were specialty, or niche, magazines, periodicals that catered to specific interest groups instead of a vague general populace. Finding a

blend of materials that would appeal to both the specialist and to the generalist became the challenge for editors.

Playboy

One of the most important new magazines of the era was *Playboy*. The first issue appeared in October 1953. Almost single-handedly the creation of Hugh Hefner (1926–), *Playboy* attempted to be both spicy and sophisticated. Operating on a shoestring budget, Hefner published the first issue without a date or number because he was not sure it would go beyond one issue. He need not have worried. Overnight, *Playboy* captured an audience of college males and young men. Of course, the fact that the first Playmate centerfold featured Marilyn Monroe unclothed did not hurt sales. One of Hollywood's top stars by 1953, Monroe had posed for the shot before her rise to fame in the movies; Hefner had obtained the picture through a photo agency.

Espousing a philosophy of sexual freedom and materialism, the magazine managed to hire

Books

Publisher Hugh Hefner looks over proof sheets for *Playboy,* in Chicago, 1961. AP Photo.

the best authors for both fiction and nonfiction articles. Hefner wrote lengthy editorials justifying the lifestyles portrayed within the periodical's pages. Advertisers, sensing something new and lucrative, flocked to *Playboy,* making it one of the most profitable magazines of all time.

From its inauspicious beginnings, Hefner and his staff expanded from a tiny Chicago office to the Playboy Mansion, a splendid old house where intellect and ribaldry, jazz and parties, could intermix and become models for readers of how the sophisticated male spends his time. Circulating a profitable one million copies a month by the close of the decade, *Playboy* dominated an important niche market for advertisers: young males with money to spend and tastes honed by the advice provided in their favorite new magazine.[11]

TV Guide

The 1953 debut of *TV Guide* proved as culturally important as the introduction of *Playboy.* The brainchild of publisher Walter Annenberg, the new magazine found its inspiration in the success of a local publication in Philadelphia that provided complete listings of local television programming. He discovered other cities had similar periodicals, including one in New York that called itself *TV Guide.* Annenberg bought out several of these magazines, including the New York edition, so he could have the rights to the name.

Annenberg's staff prepared articles and features for the magazine, along with the all-important network schedules; regional editions of *TV Guide* then added local programming to the listings. The first issue hit newsstands in April 1953, just after actress Lucille Ball delivered her real-life baby. The event had been cleverly worked into her TV comedy series, *I Love Lucy.* In an ingenious marketing move, *TV Guide* capitalized on the enormous public interest about the birth by putting Ball's new son, Desi Jr., on the magazine's first cover.

Millions of people either subscribed or picked up a copy of the magazine at supermarkets and drug stores. Except for the veteran *Reader's Digest, TV Guide* soon enjoyed the highest circulation of any magazine in the country, selling about six-and-a-half million copies a week in 1959.[12]

Sports Illustrated

Sports Illustrated, a product of Henry Luce's *Time-Life* empire, made its debut in August 1954. The publication reached an audience in excess of 600,000 its first year. *Sports Illustrated* aimed its content at the mainstream sports fan, substituting great photography for endless statistics and offering probing articles on events influencing sports, such as illegal gambling.

Fan Magazines

As they had done throughout the 1930s and 1940s, Hollywood fan magazines continued to flourish into the fifties. A mix of fact and innuendo, they directed their content primarily at women of all ages eager to read about the makeup secrets and love lives of their favorite stars. *Photoplay,* the acknowledged leader among the dozens of such periodicals available at newsstands, boasted a monthly circulation in excess of one million readers.

As the decade progressed, the fan magazines turned increasingly sensational, a desperate attempt to hang onto readers, but one doomed to failure. The magical glitter that once characterized Hollywood had begun to wear off by the late fifties, and tawdriness could not replace it.

Science Fiction Magazines

With the onset of the Atomic Age, there existed fears of what the future might hold. Publishers capitalized on this anxiety with endless tales of radioactive monsters, mutations, and nuclear devastation. By 1953, some 35 different science fiction magazines could be found on newsstands. Little more than updated versions of the old sex-violence-horror pulp magazines of the 1920s and 1930s, and printed on cheap paper and adorned with garish covers, they nonetheless did well, attracting a wide readership.

Many of the stories from these magazines, collected and reprinted in equally cheap paperback anthologies, led to original, novel-length works, prompting a small boom in science fiction. Of course, success in one medium leads to imitation in another, and so Hollywood produced

NEW MAGAZINES

Golf Digest (1950)

Prevention (1950)

Jet (1951)

The Family Handyman (1951)

Mad (1952)

Playboy (1953)

TV Guide (1953)

Sports Illustrated (1954)

Bon Appétit (1956)

Car and Driver (1956)

GQ (1957)

Golf Magazine (1959)

innumerable sci-fi movies; network radio had series like *Dimension X* (1950–1951) and *X-Minus One* (1955–1958); and television began the first of its many ventures into the realm with early shows like *Out There* (1951–1952) and *Tales of Tomorrow* (1951–1953).

Other Specialty Magazines

Since teenagers had become an important, affluent component of American society in their own right, a host of journals catered to them. Possibly the best known was *Seventeen;* its first issue appeared in 1944, but the magazine did not hit its stride until the 1950s, when it emerged as almost essential reading for young girls in junior and senior high schools. With the ages at which women married declining sharply during the late 1940s and early 1950s, savvy marketers began to use the pages of magazines like *Seventeen* to advertise not just teen fashions, but household items such as furniture and appliances. Competitors like *Young Miss* (1955; later re-titled *YM Magazine*) followed *Seventeen*'s lead; the potential of the youth market was not to be ignored.

Males, young and old, could read *Golf Digest* (1950–), or indulge their fantasies about auto racing with *Road & Track* (1947–), *Hot Rod* (1948–), *Motor Trend* (1949–), and *Car and Driver* (1956–). *American Heritage* (1949–) and *Horizon* (1958–)

appealed to anyone interested in history, and *Modern Maturity* (1958–) went out to millions of older Americans. Those needing spiritual uplift had *Guidepost* (1952–), whereas *Prevention* (1950–) focused on health care. By the end of the decade, over 8,000 periodicals were published in the United States, up from approximately 6,000 in 1950. Most of these had extremely limited circulations and readerships.[13]

Some Failures

The 1950s also witnessed the deaths of a number of venerable titles. General interest weeklies, once the mainstays of the business, led the list of the fallen. For instance, the *American Magazine,* which traced its lineage back to 1876, ceased publication in 1956; *Woman's Home Companion, Frank Leslie's Popular Monthly,* and *Liberty* also closed up shop at about the same time. They blamed their failures on a lack of advertising revenue, a most compelling reason. But other circumstances also contributed to the fall of these once thriving journals. One example illustrates the problems faced by all.

After a 61-year run, *Collier's* general interest magazine ceased publication in 1956. At the time of its demise, its circulation totaled almost four million, a healthy number of readers. No one could say with any precision exactly who read *Collier's;* marketing research that might have provided such information was then in its infancy, and a large circulation figure offered no guarantee advertisers' target audiences were included in that number.

In addition, *Collier's* operating costs, from postage to paper to staffing, continued to rise. The magazine refused to change its editorial policies, suggesting to advertisers that *Collier's* readers were older and more conservative, not the active, youthful consumers that agencies desired. Newcomers like *Playboy* and *Sports Illustrated* could claim they went primarily to young, middle-class males, and *Time* and *Newsweek* could boast of the education and business backgrounds of their constituencies, and advertisers reacted accordingly. Women's magazines already had a defined readership, although many attempted to refine that by appealing to specific groups of women. The exceptions

WORDS AND PHRASES

beatnik

bopera (a nightclub specializing in bop music)

cat (male who is both hip and cool)

chick

cool

dig (to understand)

do-it-yourself

drag strip

dragster

egghead

far out

fish stick (frozen food)

hip

hot dog (a race driver)

junk mail

litterbug

pony tail

sex kitten

skygirl (airline stewardess)

smog

smust (combination of smoke and dust)

sock hop

souped up

square (unfashionable and uncool person)

squaresville (dull)

telethon

UFO

urban legend

whomp

wumgush (nonsense)

Books

seemed to be the broad-based general magazines. Even the largest circulation magazine of them all, the *Saturday Evening Post,* would fall in 1962.

NEWSPAPERS

The American newspaper had enjoyed its greatest success and influence during the 1920s. The economic problems of the Great Depression, followed by World War II and the simultaneous rise of radio, dimmed that luster. Some smaller papers enjoyed readership gains, but most major metropolitan dailies lost circulation between 1950 and 1960.

Consolidation and Chains

The consolidation of older papers that characterized the 1940s continued on into the 1950s. The economic pressures of successfully running a daily paper took their toll, and the era of the two-or-three-newspaper city was drawing to a close; most communities found themselves with only one paper. Those papers that survived tended to be morning editions. Between 1945 and 1960, 350 daily newspapers went out of business, the majority of them evening papers. Some closed down entirely and others merged or consolidated with what was once the competition.

Many independent papers became parts of newspaper chains. Older names like Hearst and Scripps-Howard continued to own significant groups of papers, but their overall holdings dipped as newspapers merged or went out of business. Relatively new groups like Newhouse, Cox, Knight Newspapers, Ridder Publications, and Gannett acquired operations in many different locales. By the 1950s chains controlled about half of national newspaper circulation, both daily and Sunday. Competition remained strong in those remaining cities with multiple papers, and chain ownership did not appear to bring about any sameness of product nor did it silence editors and columnists, as some had feared. A chain did, however, bring financial resources not always available to independent papers.

Economic Woes

Newspapers commanded 37 percent of all U.S. ad revenues in 1950, but by 1960, the newspapers' share of the advertising pie, both local and national, shrunk to 31 percent. This marked the first downward shift in newspaper advertising since the Depression. At the same time, TV's share of the advertising pot rose from 3 percent in 1950 to about 30 percent in 1960, a tremendous increase. In addition to the loss of important advertising revenue, labor unrest brought about several devastating newspaper strikes. In 1953, a prolonged walkout over wages crippled journals in New York City. Detroit and Cleveland papers suffered strikes in 1955. After hard-fought negotiations failed, New York newspapermen again walked out in the fall of 1956. The city did without newspapers for 11 days before the two sides reached a compromise. These instances illustrate but a few of the crippling union-management clashes that swept through the country in the fifties. At the end of each big disruption, the settlement invariably hit management hard, especially in the area of circulation. During these recurring strikes, readers discovered they could do without a daily paper. When a strike was resolved, not all former readers returned; lower circulation meant lower ad rates, and that meant decreased revenue. Beleaguered owners frequently ended up raising prices, a move that drove away more readers.

Although gross revenues rose during the 1950s, expenditures climbed at an even faster rate, outweighing any increases in profits. As owners bought new technology to cut costs, workers feared for their jobs, and any savings usually disappeared in a new and bitter round of labor negotiations. As the number of personnel required to put out a modern newspaper dropped sharply, edgy labor unions exacted a stiff price in wages and benefits. Modernization and automation brought with them a host of "featherbedding" clauses in union contracts that allowed unneeded workers to stay on in obsolete jobs. In the worst cases, several papers went out of business, furthering the decline of the American newspaper.[14]

Publishers did put into play some innovative ideas during the decade, including increased use of color in the printing process. Both editorial and ad copy featured more color layouts. But this technological progress came at a considerable cost. Aging printing equipment had to be replaced, and traditional lead type became a thing of the past. The composing room evolved from a noisy redoubt of hot metal into an operation relying on fewer and fewer people. But most analysts considered it money well spent as newspapers strove to compete more effectively with other media.

Newspapers and the Cold War

The Cold War dominated the front pages. The doings of the House Un-American Activities Committee (HUAC), such as its investigations into Communist infiltration of Hollywood, received coverage. Readers no doubt thought that Reds hid under every bed during the near-hysteria of the McCarthy era.

Editorial cartoonist Herbert Block, better known as "Herblock," was among the first to challenge the stridency of the anti-Communist campaign being waged by Senator McCarthy. In stinging cartoons that commenced in 1950, Herblock created both the word and the idea of "McCarthyism"—unfounded allegations designed to create fear, a kind of bullying attitude toward opposing attitudes.

The Korean War likewise gained extensive coverage, and strict censorship hobbled efforts to report an accurate picture of the hostilities. General Douglas MacArthur, the commander of Allied forces, kept a tight lid on all news, including the threat of courts-martial for reporters who broke his rules. Thus, nothing negative, including specific words like "retreat," saw print. The public could read about the war, but what they received distorted the facts.[15]

Advice Columnists

A feature that increased greatly in popularity was advice to the lovelorn. Although such columns were not new to American newspapers, two women who happened to be twins—"Ann Landers" (Esther Friedman) and "Abigail Van Buren" (Pauline Friedman)—increased the readership of such material significantly. Both enjoyed wide syndication, although their columns remained completely independent of one another. The "Ann Landers" column led the way, first appearing in the *Chicago Sun-Times* in 1955. Her sister followed a year later with "Dear Abby" in the *San Francisco Chronicle*.

The Friedman twins were much more direct, eschewing the usually sappy messages their predecessors had followed; at times, they could even be critical of the letters they received. They provided a fresh approach to journalism aimed at the "woman's page," and readers responded positively, making the columns popular features read by women and men alike.

COMICS

By the 1950s, comic strips were a standard feature of virtually every American newspaper. Many of the old pioneers continued to appear daily on the comic pages, but a number of new artists and writers broke into this highly competitive business in the years following World War II. The decade turned out to be one of transition, as action and adventure gave way to more humor and family-oriented themes.

As a rule, the younger cartoonists preferred a simpler visual style, rejecting much of the detail that characterized so much prewar comic art.

Charles Schulz

In 1947, a struggling young cartoonist named Charles Schulz (1922–2000) finally sold his daily strip, *Li'l Folks,* to a St. Paul newspaper. Three years later, United Features Syndicate picked up a revised version of Schulz's strip. Renamed *Peanuts,* eight newspapers initially ran it. By the end of the decade, the strip, featuring a round-headed boy named Charlie Brown and his circle

Charles Schulz, seated at drawing table with a sketch of Charlie Brown, 1956. Prints & Photographs Division, Library of Congress.

of friends, appeared in over 400 dailies. Schulz recognized the money to be made in merchandising: *Peanuts* lunch pails, posters, books, and other paraphernalia proliferated, especially in the 1970s. The books alone, simple compendiums of the newspaper strips, sold in the hundreds of thousands.

Hank Ketcham

In 1951, *Dennis the Menace* by Hank Ketcham (1920–) made its debut. Like *Peanuts,* it quickly gained readers and popularity, distinguishing itself by being a single-panel cartoon. Dennis himself was an incorrigible yet loveable five-year-old who reflected the old American adage that "boys will be boys." Margaret, the primary girl appearing in the cartoon, was smart but prissy, and her presence reinforced some gender stereotypes. By the end of the decade, *Dennis* ran in more than 600 daily papers, and 7 bound collections had been issued.

Mort Walker

The Cold War raged throughout the fifties, and the Korean conflict (1950–1953) cost America thousands of lives in casualties. Young men had to register for the draft, and each month trainloads of new recruits entered basic training. Small wonder, then, that a comic strip about citizen soldiers found a receptive audience. *Beetle Bailey,* created by Mort Walker (1923–), met that need.

In the late 1940s, Walker created a strip about a hapless young collegian called "Spider." But no syndicates wanted college humor, so in 1951 the character, now named "Beetle," found himself inducted into the Army. An immediate success after the change, *Beetle Bailey* climbed to the top ranks of comics. The humorous trials of Beetle, Sergeant Snorkel, General Halftrack, and others soon had the strip syndicated in over 700 papers.

Walt Kelly

With Mickey Mouse, Bugs Bunny, and Felix the Cat attracting young readers, few papers expressed much interest in yet another talking dog, cat, or the like. Cartoonist Walt Kelly (1913–1973) managed to introduce a newspaper strip called *Pogo* in 1949. *Pogo* seems, superficially at least, to have been a continuing group of fables set in the Okeefenokee Swamp of Georgia.

Animals made up the cast: Pogo the possum, his friend Albert the alligator, Porky the porcupine, Seminole Sam the fox, and so on. Kelly endowed each character not only with personality, but also often with distinctive lettering in the speech balloons. Some even spoke in their own dialects.

Pogo tried to present a running commentary on the human condition. Greed, anger, envy, laziness—all the usual foibles had their day in poetic retellings read by young and old. Current events even received some play, most memorably a 1952 episode that involved Senator Joseph McCarthy. McCarthy—appropriately depicted as a jackal and named "Simple J. Malarkey"—received his comeuppance in Kelly's hands.

Pogo fans supported a merchandising blitz featuring their favorite swamp figures and a series of *Pogo* books became perennial best sellers. The phrase, "I Go Pogo," insinuated itself into the language after the diminutive possum ran for political office. With over 500 papers subscribing to the strip, *Pogo* stood as an unexpected success story in the rough-and-tumble world of comics.

Comic Books

In the years following World War II, a comic-book boom occurred; newsstands featured some 650 different titles, and by the early 1950s annual sales had climbed to 1 billion copies. The super-heroes of World War II (Captain America, Black-hawk, Superman, Captain Marvel, etc.) seemed dated by the end of the forties, although a few of them did fight Commies, Reds, and any other enemy sympathizers during the Korean conflict. Teenage comic characters (Buzzy, Andy Hardy, Katy Keene, Suzie, Henry Aldrich, etc.) also appeared out of step with the times, especially with rock 'n' roll entering the picture. One exception was the *Archie* comic book series, chiefly popular among preteen girls, featuring teenage characters Archie Andrews; his rich girlfriend Veronica; the girl next door, Betty; Archie's friend Reggie; and the hapless Jughead, who always got into trouble.

In keeping with the decade, all the characters were white, but they were fairly attuned to popular culture. Archie comics and spin-offs are still in publication today and have a Web site. Harmless tales of animals like Mighty Mouse, Woody Woodpecker, and Peter Rabbit, along with the whole Disney menagerie also remained steady comics sellers that underwent little change.

Throughout the late forties and early fifties, publishers, in an attempt to lure more males to their product, freely used "cheesecake," attractive women in skimpy attire. "Jungle comics," most of which starred half-dressed, statuesque women, proved especially popular in the early fifties. Sheena, Queen of the Jungle, led the pack but had competition from numerous others wearing leopard skins and little else. For their female readers, publishers borrowed from the popular confession magazines of the day and created *Secret Romances, Sweethearts, Young Love, Young Romance,* and a

Captain America (Marvel Comics). Shown center: Captain America/Steve Rogers. Courtesy of Photofest.

host of similar titles. Like radio soap operas and their pulp counterparts, these comics stressed domesticity, along with torn emotions, broken hearts, jealousy, and some heavy breathing and innuendo, but virtually no sex.

William M. Gaines

In 1947, William M. Gaines (1922–1992) inherited his father's company, Educational Comics (EC on their cover logo). The firm published children's materials, which Gaines considered hopelessly behind in the changing world of comic books. He tried westerns and science fiction and finally developed a new line of horror comics in 1950. Gaines used the old logo, although he changed the initials to mean "Entertaining Comics." Titles like *The Haunt of Fear, Shock Suspen-Stories, Tales from the Crypt,* and *The Vault of Horror* immediately found an adolescent/young adult market. Controversy dogged this new EC line, however, because the stories contained explicit drawings that critics thought exceeded all bounds of good taste.

Publishers ignored most of the criticism, and a flood of horror and fantasy comics appeared on newsstands, along with a number of violent crime comics. *Astonishing, Chamber of Chills, Crime Exposed, Crime Suspense Stories, Gangsters and Gun Molls, Terrifying Tales, Uncanny Tales, Weird Worlds,* and *Witches Tales* were among the titles of these new sensations. Sales soared and the chorus of disapproval rose in volume.

Despite threats of censorship within the industry, Gaines remained undaunted; in 1952 he launched a new comic destined to become a classic: *Mad.* A kind of combination horror comic and satirical takeoff on movies, radio, celebrities, and the like, it mixed gore with hilarious spoofs of much ongoing popular culture. His target market of primarily adolescent boys reacted positively, but his timing was poor. In 1953, Congress began an investigation into the whole comic book industry (discussed above), and distributors were wary of anything like *Mad.* As a result, Gaines altered *Mad*'s format in the summer of 1955. He eliminated color, printed on a higher quality paper, raised the price, and called the "new" *Mad* a magazine. Now newsstands could carry *Mad*

somewhere other than in the comic racks, solving the problem. In addition, the new *Mad* focused almost exclusively on satire, making it a favorite of high school and college students. From that point onward, the magazine earned a profit and stirred little controversy—except occasionally from those who served as the butts of its sometimes barbed humor.[16]

Comics and Censorship

While Gaines tinkered with *Mad,* rival publishers were stepping over most boundaries of good taste in their horror and crime comics. In 1954, psychiatrist Fredric Wertham published *Seduction of the Innocent.* Subtitled *The Influence of Comic Books on Today's Youth,* the book set off a groundswell of debate, much of it focusing on juvenile delinquency. Wertham, a prominent social critic, claimed in his book that reading comics led to antisocial behavior, although he offered no supporting research. He claimed crime and horror comics provided virtual blueprints for criminal acts. Wertham maintained that the level of sex and violence in most comics would lead young, susceptible readers to juvenile crime. A handful of carefully cropped illustrations suggested that comic books contain hidden pornographic drawings.[17] That same year, a congressional committee led by Senator Estes Kefauver began investigating the causes of juvenile delinquency and added comic books to its list of subjects. Dr. Wertham, his book already a controversial best seller, was asked by the committee to lead the attack on the industry. In the fall of 1954, 26 publishers of comic books formed the Comics Code Authority, a self-regulatory industry body. The Authority came up with "a seal of approval," an emblem that had to prominently adorn the covers of most new comic books found on newsstands in the United States. Many wholesalers refused to stock comics that lacked this seal, so the industry quickly fell into line. Gaines dropped his horror series, as did many others. The bland content of the new approved titles bore little resemblance to the freewheeling stories of just a few months earlier.

By 1955, only about 300 comic titles remained on newsstands, about half of what had been available

5 years earlier, and overall sales had fallen sharply. Despite the industry's efforts, the public no longer saw comic books as harmless entertainments. While senators and psychologists searched for hidden meanings in comic books, television—another visual medium—was busy establishing itself in American homes. It presented itself to millions of kids as an electronic successor to the comic book and did more to hasten the industry's decline than any congressional hearings or muckraking books could do.

The latter half of the 1950s, therefore, found the comic book industry treading water. Innocuous children's comics fared well, and science fiction, provided it avoided anything too frightening, had a following. Crime comics virtually disappeared from the racks, and horror and fantasy were toned down into blandness. A few superheroes—Superman, Batman, Wonder Woman—held on during these dark times, but not until the 1960s would the industry recoup and thrill a new generation of readers.[18]

Books

Entertainment

of the 1950s

The ascendancy of television as the nation's most popular medium marked the 1950s. At the beginning of the decade, 9 percent of American households possessed at least one TV; by 1959, some 86 percent owned receivers, leaving movies and radio as the big losers. By 1953, plummeting attendance had caused a quarter of the nation's movie theaters to close. Radio went from a schedule filled with variety to one essentially of popular recordings, brief hourly newscasts, and occasional sports.

MOVIES

Technical Innovation and Novelty

Weekly movie attendance had dropped from highs of over 80 million down to about 46 million patrons in 1952. In response, Hollywood began experimenting with technical gimmicks that might lure people back into theaters. After all, television, the film industry's archrival, was limited to a tiny screen and a monochromatic picture. Many large budget films already enjoyed color and high-fidelity sound; what else might the technical effects people accomplish?

One of the first attempts to get audiences back proved ill-fated: 3-D (three-dimensional). The Natural Vision Corporation manufactured film stock that held double images. Through the use of polarized lenses, those images could be reconfigured to give the illusion of depth. Amid much fanfare, millions dutifully donned ill-fitting cardboard glasses with green and red cellophane lenses to watch *Bwana Devil* (1952), the first of several mediocre 3-D offerings. It was followed by such titles as *It Came from Outer Space* (1953), *House of Wax* (1953), and *Creature from the Black Lagoon* (1954). The 3-D format might have fared better if the initial releases had been superior films, but Hollywood provided hastily made and poorly acted features.

About the same time as 3-D's introduction, another innovation came along. For many years, the projected theatrical image maintained a ratio of 1.33:1, meaning that the screen measured 1.33 times wider than its height. Over time, this ratio had become the standard and today accounts for the familiar shape of most television screens. The movie industry, desperate to compete with television, began to tinker with screen dimensions and proportions in hopes of widening the image.

In 1952, the Cinerama Corporation released *This Is Cinerama!* The film began innocuously enough: a black-and-white picture appears on a standard screen, and all seems normal, just like any other Hollywood feature. But the black-and-white becomes color, the screen swells, and suddenly the audience finds itself in the midst of a terrifying roller coaster ride as the huge screen wraps an arc of 146 degrees. The horizontal-vertical ratio had been changed to 2.55:1, with images now 2.55 times wider than they were tall. *This Is Cinerama!* enjoyed immediate popularity in the select cities where it first showed on a limited basis, and other theaters quickly lined up for wide-screen adaptations.

CinemaScope made its debut in 1953. For CinemaScope, the screen retained its traditional flatness and only one camera and one projector were involved, an innovation any theater could adapt. The first feature movie in CinemaScope, *The Robe,* came out in 1953. The wider screen, with its panoramic vistas and illusion of depth, soon became the preferred way to show big-budget pictures.

By 1955, almost all large American theaters had been equipped to show films in wide-screen versions, although the proportions were later reduced to somewhere between 2.2:1 and 1.85:1. The use of Panavision lenses provided sharp definition and an overall lack of distortion. When the studios released their wide-screen movies to television, parts of the horizontal image disappeared, because the TV screen accommodated only traditional films.

The success of wide-screen movies in the 1950s meant that audiences were less inclined to watch films of traditional width. In response, the studios released some of their vast libraries of old movies to television. Because of various union agreements, most of the pictures initially shown on TV had been made prior to 1948. Yet, with the television industry paying top dollar to get popular movies, more recent films became available after the mid-fifties. In 1955, RKO released 740 features to C&C Television Corporation for television viewing. The unions agreed to this transaction, and the following year over 2,500 more movies became available to TV. Despite their long-standing rivalry with the new medium, all the major Hollywood studios shared their troves of pictures with television by 1958.[1]

Drive-Ins

The decade also witnessed the popularization of the drive-in theater. The idea of watching

NOTABLE ACTORS

Marlon Brando, 1924–2004

Gary Cooper, 1901–1961

Bing Crosby, 1903–1977

Doris Day, 1924–

Glenn Ford, 1916–2006

Betty Grable, 1916–1973

Audrey Hepburn, 1929–1993

William Holden, 1918–1981

Bob Hope, 1903–2003

Rock Hudson, 1925–1985

Gene Kelly, 1912–1996

Grace Kelly, 1929–1982

Burt Lancaster, 1913–1994

Dean Martin, 1917–1995, and Jerry Lewis, 1926–

Marilyn Monroe, 1926–1962

James Stewart, 1908–1997

Elizabeth Taylor, 1932–

John Wayne, 1907–1979

movies in the comfort and privacy of an automobile originated in the early 1930s, but not until the 1950s did entrepreneurs push the concept. By 1956, over 7,000 drive-ins dotted the nation. Some consisted of a cleared rural field with wooden speaker posts and a crude snack bar; others boasted elaborate layouts with sculpted rows, so cars parked at the proper angle for optimum viewing, and the new snack bars often offered as much variety as a traditional restaurant. (See Travel in the 1950s.)

The Youth Market

The 1950s marked the full realization of movie marketing for the burgeoning teenage population along with the production of films starring actors who could pass for adolescents.

In 1954's *The Wild One,* Marlon Brando (1924–2004) played a lawless biker who brings his motorcycle gang to an innocent, unsuspecting town. Mumbling and clad in boots, tight jeans, and a

T-shirt, he terrorized not only the townspeople, but also much of the audience. Teenage boys, however, saw in this inarticulate hero a kind of amoral role model. Yet, in that same year, Brando won an Academy Award for Best Actor in *On the Waterfront*. His sensitive portrayal of a victimized boxer caught up in mobs and crime demonstrated he could handle almost any role.

No one typified the disaffected, aloof teen character better than James Dean (1931–1955). Although he had major roles in only three movies— *Rebel without a Cause* (1955), *East of Eden* (1955), and *Giant* (1956)—Dean came to symbolize the alienation of youth. In both his films and in his life, he represented the loner struggling against the forces of conformity. His untimely death in an automobile accident only served to elevate him to cult hero.

Young people also had their own movies. Most famously perhaps, *The Blackboard Jungle* (1955) purported to show how juvenile delinquency was rampant in American schools. Vic Morrow

The Wild One (1953). Marlon Brando as Johnny Strabler/Narrator. Courtesy of Photofest.

(1929–1982) played a sullen teen who seemed incapable of good behavior. Sidney Poitier (1927–), in his first major screen role, portrayed one of Morrow's fellow gang members. Glenn Ford, as their teacher, tries to reach the boys and break up their gang. In the background, Bill Haley and His Comets pound out "Rock Around the Clock," creating an association between rock 'n' roll and delinquency, just as people frequently connected jazz with crime.

A host of youth-and-rock films followed the success of *Blackboard Jungle*. In 1956, *Don't Knock the Rock; Rock Around the Clock; Rock, Pretty Baby;* and *Rock, Rock, Rock!* graced theater marquees. *Teenage Doll* (1957), *Go, Johnny, Go!* (1958), *High School Confidential!* (1958), and *Teenage Bad Girl* (1959) mixed delinquency with drugs, making American high schools seem like hotbeds of crime and perversion.

Film Themes

The fifties contributed numerous outstanding films on many subjects. They ranged from original dramas like *All About Eve* (1950), sophisticated comedies (*Some Like It Hot*, 1959), sweeping westerns (*Shane*, 1953), epics of war (*The Bridge on the River Kwai*, 1957), imaginative science fiction (*Destination Moon*, 1950), to the most forgettable "B" pictures imaginable (*Zombies of Moratau*, 1957). Within all this variety evolved three cinematic themes: 1) a liberal bias that argued for sensitivity and tenderness, 2) a mainstream approach that attempted no ideological stance other than entertainment, and 3) a conservative leaning that capitalized on the ongoing anti-Communist rhetoric of the period along with the idea of conforming to the perceived needs of American society. Examples of the first group might include *A Place in the Sun* (1951) or *Paths of Glory* (1957). For the mainstream category, typical choices could be *Singin' in the Rain* (1952) and *Giant* (1956). *I Was a Communist for the FBI* (1951) and *Strategic Air Command* (1955) could represent the third category. Within those broad categories, however, lay much ambiguity; in the movies of the 1950s, nothing was as simple as it seemed.

The Cold War and the Movies

Uncertainty became a recurring motif in the films of the fifties: who is good, who is evil? Who can be trusted? A kind of cinematic extension of the Cold War, the movies at times spelled out any doubts in simplistic plots, as in *Big Jim McLain* (1952). John Wayne, who starred as an agent of the House Un-American Activities Committee, had no problem second-guessing as he hunted down subversives. Made during the height of the McCarthy investigations, *Big Jim McLain*, along with a number of similar films, played on the popular fear of Communist infiltration into the fabric of American life. It took energetic lawmen to root out this menace, although

civil libertarians may have winced at some of the methods employed.

In other pictures, however, audiences were sometimes left hanging. For instance, in *Invasion of the Body Snatchers* (1956), townspeople discovered ominous pods in their idyllic community. Were these pods some alien life form, or might they really have been Communists in disguise? Ostensibly a science fiction film, *Invasion of the Body Snatchers* could easily be interpreted as an allegorical approach to spies and paranoia.

The movie *12 Angry Men* (1957) starring Henry Fonda presented a drama about a man upholding an unpopular cause and focused on a hung jury—eleven for a murder conviction, one not so sure. Despite great pressure, especially from

12 Angry Men (1957). Shown: E. G. Marshall, Henry Fonda, Lee J. Cobb, Edward Binns, George Voskovec, Jack Klugman, Joseph Sweeney. Directed by Sidney Lumet. United Artists/The Kobal Collection. Courtesy of Picturedesk.

COLD WAR MOVIES

The Cold War, which gripped American culture from the 1920s until the 1980s, exerted a major influence over all facets of American society. In the film and television industries, the Cold War had a pervasive and complex influence. In 1947, the film industry came under the scrutiny of the House Un-American Activities Committee, which interviewed hundreds of actors, directors, writers, and other film personnel for suspected links to Communist organizations. This scrutiny was in relation to films that were perceived to have a pro-Communist message and, as a result, some film companies were urged to produce films with strong anti-Communist themes. The 1948 film *The Iron Curtain* was one of the first anti-Communist films to come from a major Hollywood studio, telling the story of a defector attempting to flee to the West. Blending fantasy adventure with propaganda, Hollywood released a string of films in the 1950s with paranoid themes in which the protagonists discovered spies and/or secret Communist societies operating in their communities. Some of these films may seem comical by modern standards, with titles like *I Married A Communist*. The effect of the Cold War was present even in films that had no overt references to Communism, as in a number of westerns in which the protagonists were engaged in diplomatic struggles between ideological enemies. Until the mid-1980s, Russians and Asians were consistently cast as the villains in Hollywood adventure films, providing the substrate for the remarkably successful James Bond films and a number of other blockbusters of the 1960s, 70s, and 80s. While American culture changed during the Korean Conflict and the Vietnam War, Hollywood writers and producers used their films both in support of and in sharp criticism of the ongoing struggle against Communism. It wasn't until the late 1980s, as fear of the Russian threat and danger of nuclear war dissolved, that the Cold War's influence on Hollywood cinema began to decline.

several indignant jurors (the truly "angry" ones of the title), the holdout argues his position and gradually brings the others to his point of view. A microcosm of popular thinking during the fifties, the film did a superlative job of defending the individual's right to confront the majority, no matter how hopeless or extreme his or her position may be.

Somewhat unusual in that it was adapted from a television play, *12 Angry Men* first appeared on the CBS series *Studio One* in 1954. Reginald Rose scripted both the teleplay and the screenplay. The winner of many awards and an almost instantaneous television classic, it reversed the traditional procedure of movies being adapted to television. When it appeared on TV, the country was in the midst of the Army-McCarthy hearings, a tempestuous series of encounters between Senator Joseph McCarthy and a legal team representing the U.S. Army. During the lengthy debates, McCarthy revealed himself to be a bullying inquisitor, a man ready to destroy others in his obsessive quest for dubious information. In short, some of the more aggressive jurors and their arguments in the original *12 Angry Men* resembled Joseph McCarthy and his tactics.

Other Cold War events had their moments on film. In June 1950, North Korean troops flooded across the border into South Korea. The invasion immediately escalated into an encounter between the so-called Free World and the Communist Bloc. Hollywood likewise responded with a series of low-budget combat movies depicting Americans at war. Most of the Korean-era films were forgettable, although *Pork Chop Hill* (1959) stood as a notable exception. Directed by the esteemed Lewis Milestone and starring Gregory Peck, the picture addressed both the battle of the same name and some of its political implications.

Several films attempted to capitalize on the mistreatment of American prisoners of war during their confinement. *The Rack* (1956) gave a good psychological portrait of such a soldier after his return home. The movie also served as an effective stepping-stone in the career of Paul Newman.

Serious Films

When it came to straightforward dramatic storytelling and mass production, Hollywood in the 1950s had no equal, though French, Italian, Swedish, and Japanese directors also

ACADEMY AWARD WINNERS

Year of release, not year of award.

1950 Picture: *All About Eve*
  Director: Joseph L. Mankiewicz, *All About Eve*
  Actor: Jose Ferrer, *Cyrano de Bergerac*
  Actress: Judy Holliday, *Born Yesterday*

1951 Picture: *An American in Paris*
  Director: George Stevens, *A Place in the Sun*
  Actor: Humphrey Bogart, *The African Queen*
  Actress: Vivien Leigh, *A Streetcar Named Desire*

1952 Picture: *The Greatest Show on Earth*
  Director: John Ford, *The Quiet Man*
  Actor: Gary Cooper, *High Noon*
  Actress: Shirley Booth, *Come Back, Little Sheba*

1953 Picture: *From Here to Eternity*
  Director: Fred Zinnemann, *From Here to Eternity*
  Actor: William Holden, *Stalag 17*
  Actress: Audrey Hepburn, *Roman Holiday*

1954 Picture: *On the Waterfront*
  Director: Elia Kazan, *On the Waterfront*
  Actor: Marlon Brando, *On the Waterfront*
  Actress: Grace Kelly, *The Country Girl*

1955 Picture: *Marty*
  Director: Delbert Mann, *Marty*
  Actor: Ernest Borgnine, *Marty*
  Actress: Anna Magnani, *The Rose Tattoo*

1956 Picture: *Around the World in 80 Days*
  Director: George Stevens, *Giant*
  Actor: Yul Brynner, *The King and I*
  Actress: Ingrid Bergman, *Anastasia*

1957 Picture: *The Bridge on the River Kwai*
  Director: David Lean, *The Bridge on the River Kwai*
  Actor: Alec Guinness, *The Bridge on the River Kwai*
  Actress: Joanne Woodward, *The Three Faces of Eve*

1958 Picture: *Gigi*
  Director: Vincente Minnelli, *Gigi*
  Actor: David Niven, *Separate Tables*
  Actress: Susan Hayward, *I Want to Live*

1959 Picture: *Ben-Hur*
  Director: William Wyler, *Ben-Hur*
  Actor: Charlton Heston, *Ben-Hur*
  Actress: Simone Signoret, *Room at the Top*

produced artistic triumphs. For example, *The 400 Blows* (France, 1959), *La Strada* (Italy, 1954), *The Seventh Seal* (Sweden, 1957), and *Rashomon* (Japan, 1950) are today generally considered classics of cinema, but limited distribution and audience reluctance to watch foreign films made their popular impact almost nil during the decade. (See "Foreign Films" below.)

Hollywood's glossy, dramatic interpretation of the 1950s stressed the white, middle-class values familiar to a majority of Americans. Only a handful of films examined minority groups in a sympathetic way, and these generally did poorly at the box office.

In *Executive Suite* (1954) some of the basic tenets of fifties corporate culture received examination. Based on Cameron Hawley's best-selling 1952 novel of the same name, the movie posited the belief that, for a man, a successful career must come first—family and personal concerns of necessity were secondary. The idea of women in the upper echelons of business life remained foreign to most American filmmakers; women nurtured the bruised egos of their men when the competition got rough, but they seldom entered the fray themselves.

Author Sloan Wilson penned another popular novel of the period, *The Man in the Gray Flannel Suit* (1955). Made into a movie in 1956, its title became a metaphor for both male fashions and advertising executives. (See Advertising of the 1950s.) A slick story about the lives of New York ad men on Madison Avenue, both book and movie claimed to depict contemporary manners and mores, smoothly glossing over any difficult questions that might arise. Like *Executive Suite,* the male characters must choose between family and career. A successful job, a secure place in the system, an understanding wife—these were the goals to be attained in 1950s America.

Not every successful drama portrayed a buttoned-down, flannel-suited businessman, however. *Marty* (1955), a completely unanticipated hit, was a low-budget production that made a star of actor Ernest Borgnine and proved that occasionally audiences could be more discerning than expected. Yet another transfer from television, *Marty* first appeared on *The Goodyear Playhouse* in 1953, with Rod Steiger in the lead role. Marty worked as a butcher, not an ad man, and Paddy Chayefsky's script (he wrote both the teleplay and the screenplay) gave a moving portrayal of urban loneliness. A commercial success, *Marty* garnered four Academy Awards, including Best Picture and Best Actor.

Film Noir

Most critics agree that the period from 1940 to 1960 marks the time of the greatest film noir, or "black film," productions. Little existed in film noir that moviemakers had not attempted before, but the success with which the industry produced a long string of pictures employing certain techniques gave rise to the term. As the phrase suggests, dark, shadowy dramas distinguished the noir style, and cinematography became as important as plotting, a condition that assured black and white as the preferred colors of the medium.

No one director, cinematographer, or studio, stood out as being preeminent in the noir style. For the twenty years that mark its greatest popularity, film noir enjoyed a wide audience. A successful noir film used tried and familiar imagery. A neon sign flickering on a fog-enshrouded street, cigarette smoke backlit by lamps or headlights, the interplay of extreme light and dark, nighttime in the darkened city as a metaphor for danger. Such familiarity stood at the heart of much popular culture; the fulfillment of expectations brought people back to formulaic movies, fiction, television, and music.

Mysteries represented the best noir films of the fifties. Audiences already knew the image of the detective, cigarette dangling from his lips, trench coat pulled tight against a misty rain. Most pictures in this genre were low-budget affairs, employing actors who had not attained true star status; instead they relied on plot, dialogue, and mood. A few of the more enduring titles included *In a Lonely Place* (1950), *Night and the City* (1950), *Detective Story* (1951), *Strangers on a Train* (1951), *Sudden Fear* (1952), *The Big Heat* (1953), *Cry Vengeance* (1954), *Kiss Me Deadly* (1955), *The Killing* (1956), *The Sweet Smell of Success* (1957), and *Touch of Evil* (1958).

A number of events sealed the doom of film noir. In an attempt to lure more viewers, movie screens grew larger and color became the preferred film stock. Television, with the intimacy of the small screen and with most productions still produced in black and white, quickly claimed much of the noir territory. By the end of the decade, the style had virtually disappeared from theaters.[2]

Musicals

Metro-Goldwyn-Mayer (MGM) completely dominated the musical genre, starting with the rambunctious *Annie Get Your Gun* in 1950 and wrapping up the decade with *Gigi* in 1958. Using top talent, and matching that with quality production values, the studio produced a series of movie musicals that have come to be considered classics.[3]

Many of Hollywood's musicals have been adaptations of previous Broadway offerings. For example, *Annie Get Your Gun* had opened on Broadway in 1946; Ethel Merman, one of the great stars of the American stage, played Annie Oakley. When discussions of a movie version came up, Merman was not available and the coveted role fell to Betty Hutton, a veteran dancer and singer. It proved a wise choice, and the commercial success of the filmed *Annie Get Your Gun* (1950) emboldened Hollywood to plunge ahead with numerous other musical offerings.

Continuing the practice of borrowing from Broadway, *Gentlemen Prefer Blondes* (1953) took a 1947 play and added to the mix two potent sex symbols of the era, actresses Marilyn Monroe and Jane Russell. The growing popularity of Monroe assured a strong box office return and even spurred a lackluster sequel, *Gentlemen Marry Brunettes* (1955). In a bit of unusual casting, MGM convinced Marlon Brando to play Sky Masterson in 1955's *Guys and Dolls,* the studio's adaptation of the classic 1950 musical. With help from a strong score and excellent costars, Brando managed to carry his part. By this time, musicals were such a major constituent of film production that actors clamored for roles in them.

A big hit on Broadway in 1943, Richard Rodgers and Oscar Hammerstein's *Oklahoma!* finally made it to movie theaters in 1955. The picture's commercial success led to still more stage-to-screen conversions of older plays such as *Anything Goes* (stage, 1934; film, 1956), *Pal Joey* (stage, 1940; film, 1957), and *Carousel* (stage, 1945; film, 1956). The studios maintained a strong relationship with Broadway; although relatively few people ever saw a New York stage musical, millions watched the film version. In addition, radio and television further popularized

the music from these productions, often making the score more familiar than the play itself.[4] (See "Theater" below.)

Two the greatest musicals of the 1950s were created specifically for the screen: *An American in Paris* (1951) and *Singin' in the Rain* (1952), both from MGM and both featuring Gene Kelly, one of America's great dancers. Their popular success marked the rise of the movie musical during the decade. Given their cinematic production values—large, changing sets, varied camera angles, manipulation of time and space—they would have been difficult, if not impossible, to replicate on even the most modern stage.

By 1958, box office receipts had dwindled. As a kind of last gasp, *Gigi* (1958) established stardom for Leslie Caron, but Rodgers and Hammerstein's long-awaited *South Pacific* (1958) arrived to anemic reviews because it lacked the original Broadway cast of Mary Martin and Ezio Pinza. Because of the high production expenses of musicals, the long rise of the Hollywood musical had decidedly slowed down.

Religious Spectacles

As competition from television grew more intense, studio executives employed a device available only to film: the ability to project large-scale action and spectacle onto the screen.

Early on producers turned to the religious epic. Boasting elaborate staging, these spectacles tended to be set in the early Christian era. This made allowances for all the old, tried-and-true props of miracles in the desert, gladiators and chariots, mystics and believers, and fantastic costumes and sets. Historical and theological accuracy never seemed a concern. Among the more notable efforts were *Samson and Delilah* (1950), *Quo Vadis?* (1951), *David and Bathsheba* (1951), *The Robe* (1953), *Solomon and Sheba* (1959), and the last religious saga of the decade, *Ben-Hur* (1959).

As long as audiences did not object to the obvious tinkering with the Bible, they could sit back and enjoy Charlton Heston hurling down thunderbolts as Moses in *The Ten Commandments* (1956) or racing his chariot around the Roman Forum in *Ben-Hur* (his acting style lent itself well to such pictures). Utterly lacking in subtlety,

CECIL B. DEMILLE

Cecil B. DeMille (1881–1959) was one of the early giants of American film. Born to modest economic beginnings, DeMille was that great American trope, the man who became a legend by lifting himself up by the bootstraps. An indefatigable self-promoter, DeMille paved the way for the director as celebrity, exemplified by Woody Allen, Alfred Hitchcock, and Martin Scorsese. DeMille successfully navigated the transition from silent films to talkies and is perhaps best known for his film *The Ten Commandments,* which he directed both as a silent version in 1923 and as a full-blown, nearly four-hour extravaganza in the 1956 version with Charlton Heston as Moses. What makes DeMille so interesting is the fact that he's an example of a highly successful man affected by all the major changes of the twentieth century. For instance, he was seriously hurt by the stock market crash of 1929, emerging almost broke. Afterward, he left with his wife for Europe, hoping to drum up interest in movie deals. Unsuccessful overseas, DeMille returned to Hollywood, scored a single film deal at Paramount, turned a profit, and stayed at Paramount for the rest of his life.

the religious epics' calls to blind faith in an age of anxiety and ambiguity gave audiences a brief time-out from contemporary concerns. Unlike so many forgotten films from the era, the religious epics have developed a life of their own. At Christmas and Easter, network, cable, and satellite broadcasters run them over and over, and the ratings remain consistently high.

Science Fiction

The technological advances of the decade, coupled with fears about nuclear weapons and their aftermath, led to the production of a number of science fiction films. In many instances, the monsters and aliens that populated these films were depicted as the results of well-meaning but poorly executed experiments.

At the opening of the decade, films like *Destination Moon* (1950) and *Rocketship X-M* (1950) utilized straightforward stories of space exploration.

They reflected the growing certainty that space would be the next frontier and carried no subtext about an out-of-control technology.

The War of the Worlds (1953), a dazzling version of the classic 1898 H. G. Wells story, cautioned against an over-reliance on machines and resolved itself in an almost religious way, with the Martians being destroyed by earthly germs.

Most of the cinematic science fiction of the fifties, however, came across as dark and pessimistic. In *The Day the Earth Stood Still* (1951), a flying saucer announces the arrival of a visitor from "somewhere else," presumably a much-advanced civilization. The visitor, accompanied by an impregnable robot named Gort, warns Earth that it must stop experimenting with atomic weapons and submit to more enlightened leadership. To refuse will mean destruction.

The idea that nuclear knowledge could have threatening consequences took on urgency as the decade progressed and weaponry became more deadly. The thought of mutual assured destruction (MAD), as the policy was known, only reinforced the anxieties of the time. *The Thing* (1951) played on this fear. Scientists stationed at an Arctic outpost discover a nonhuman intruder. The monster is seen only briefly, allowing audiences to imagine what they will. As much a horror picture as an exercise in science fiction, *The Thing* also fit in nicely with the anti-Communist rhetoric of the time. The story suggested that suspicious characters lurked everywhere; one risked everything to let down his guard.

If *The Thing* stood as a cautionary tale, then *Invaders from Mars* (1953), *Creature from the Black Lagoon* (1954), *Them!* (1954), *Tarantula* (1955), *It Came from Beneath the Sea* (1955), and *It Conquered the World* (1956) showed what scientific carelessness could cause. Children saw things that their parents could not believe; mutated creatures rose up from muck or hatched from eggs; insects grew to incredible sizes, and horrible creatures invaded an unprepared Earth. The fact that Hollywood produced so many movies with similar themes suggests the remarkable popularity of these films during the 1950s.[5]

These pictures tended to be a mix of horror, bad acting, cheap special effects, and silly stories. The intended audience—usually teenagers packed into

Poster for *Earth vs. the Flying Saucers,* a 1956 movie starring Hugh Marlowe, Joan Taylor, and Donald Curtis, illustrated with flying saucers and dead Earth people and spacemen from an alien planet. Prints & Photographs Division, Library of Congress.

a car for an evening of drive-in entertainment—did not mind, and only a few of the films rose above their perceived audience. For instance, *Forbidden Planet* (1956) has come to be recognized as a minor science fiction classic. Based loosely on Shakespeare's *The Tempest,* the story involves space explorers looking for a lost colony of adventurers who end up in a brave new world on a distant planet. Robby the Robot steals the show, an obedient, good-natured mechanical servant anxious to please his human masters.

The last years of the decade saw special effects displacing plot and character. Radiation from botched experiments caused unanticipated results in *The Incredible Shrinking Man* (1957), whereas a human brain implanted into a huge robot created the opposite effect in *The Colossus of New York*

(1958). *The Deadly Mantis* (1957) delivered just what its title promised: a huge mantis released from centuries-old sleep. In *The Blob* (1958), Steve McQueen battles a Jell-O-like creature; only he and other teens can save the earth. Regardless of storyline, all these films returned to a theme of meddling with the natural order of things and its horrible results.

Westerns

Some of the best films of the fifties involved cowboys, Indians, shoot-'em-ups, and the mythic story of the West. On the other hand, many of the westerns produced during the decade survived as little more than cheap "B" movies, quickly shot on the back lots of Hollywood studios and rushed into distribution. Either way, the western occupied a significant part of the era's movie history.

The 1950s began with the "B" western already an established part of the film industry. Lesser known studios found such productions their lifeblood, shooting countless features from 60 to 90 minutes long and often inserting stock footage from previous movies to hold down costs. They relied on an array of actors, both good and bad. For example, singing cowboy Gene Autry made some 30 forgettable low-budget westerns during the decade, but diehard fans kept asking for more.

The rise of the so-called adult western on television shifted Hollywood's production of "B" westerns to the small screen. The big-budget variety continued to be made consistently throughout the 1950s. With wide screens, Technicolor, and top stars, Hollywood could still turn out a product that drew crowds at the box office and was unavailable to television.

Although a bit old for a western hero, Gary Cooper rose to the occasion in *High Noon* (1952), a classic of the genre, and it gained him an Academy Award for Best Actor. In this movie, Cooper plays a beleaguered sheriff who must stand alone and resist the simplistic thinking of the crowd. Made at a time when "going along" and the concept of the compliant "organization man" were in vogue, the picture portrayed a good character in a bad situation. In reality, many equally good people found their reputations and careers ruined by overly zealous investigative committees, and few individuals would stand with them against this kind of attack.

As a rule, the movie western looked to the good side of American myth. Occasionally, however, a movie came along that showed its dark underside. In 1956, John Wayne collaborated with director John Ford, the man with whom he had made some of his best films. The result of this collaboration was *The Searchers,* a story about the dogged search for the whereabouts and fate of Wayne's niece, played by Natalie Wood. In a complex plot that covers years, Wayne's character emerges as an Indian-hater, a man obsessed by racial fears. Both Ford in his direction and Wayne in his performance emerged as problematical figures; the Indians were treated with sensitivity,

a rarity in westerns at that time, but the hatred and the single-mindedness of the quest reflected much about American society at the time.

Because they claimed to be based on history, westerns at times supported themes that would be forbidden in other movie genres. For example, racism appeared not just in *The Searchers,* but in many 1950s westerns. White supremacy overrode everything, and Indians assumed the roles traditionally taken by blacks. Throughout the decade, Wayne burnished his image as a defender of staunch conservative values, a position that endeared him to many, but irritated others.

Women's Movies

During the 1950s, dozens of pictures seemingly played on the feelings of women. Formulaic, the movies tended to feature strong women characters that must endure an emotional roller coaster as they resolved complex relationships. The male characters, usually presented as weak or downright weepy, relied on the strengths of a caring woman. In consideration of the times, however, even the strongest women deferred to the men in the story.

Collective studio thinking about these films dictated that the audience wanted wrenching emotional drama, often at the cost of plausible stories or convincing acting. A liberal amount of sex—usually more implied than depicted—did not hurt box office receipts. A prime example was *Magnificent Obsession* (1954). The title speaks volumes: this film did not deal with a normal love affair or some distant goal; rather, it dealt with an obsession. The film focuses on a drunken playboy whose actions lead to the accidental death of a good man and loss of sight for the man's wife. After much soul-searching, he mends his ways, becomes a surgeon, and proceeds to restore the widow's sight. Melodramatic in every frame, *Obsession* typified this category of picture. It also made a star of Rock Hudson, and, as evidence of the durability of the genre, it had been filmed once before; in 1935 Robert Taylor played the same role and received the same star treatment.

Bigger at the box office than *Magnificent Obsession* was *Peyton Place* (1957). Based on the steamy, best-selling 1956 novel by Grace Metalious, the movie promised lurid sex and lots of it. It also

Entertainment

offered an all-star cast headed by Lana Turner, Arthur Kennedy, and Lloyd Nolan. The studio Twentieth Century-Fox spared no expense, either in production or marketing, riding the wave of success enjoyed by the book. It assured audiences that here, on account of the melodramatic plot, was a "three handkerchief movie," meaning emotions ran high and tears poured out, a common assumption among those producing films for women.

Peyton Place may not have satisfied everyone, but it nevertheless drew people to theaters. Peyton Place, a fictional small town in rural New Hampshire, serves as the focus of the story. The vaunted sexual revolution had not yet occurred, and traditional morality still ruled the day. Metalious's frank presentation of behaviors that exceeded most norms caused a storm of controversy—and resulted in sales and admissions that probably exceeded most early estimates. What the novel detailed in explicit detail, the movie, given Production Code restrictions, only hinted at. (See Books, Newspapers, Magazines, and Comics of the 1950s.) The sex may have been oblique, but the heavy breathing and melodramatic acting of

the cast seemed to titillate 1957 audiences, calling attention to a prurience usually repressed by American popular culture.

Come Back, Little Sheba (1952) and *The Country Girl* (1954), two acclaimed films, strove to rise above their tawdry material. Thanks to strong performances by their female leads, they succeeded. Shirley Booth (*Little Sheba*) and Grace Kelly (*Country Girl*) both won Academy Awards, lending credence to the importance Hollywood placed on this kind of feature.

Foreign Films

Toward the end of the decade, European and Japanese filmmakers had begun to distribute increasing numbers of movies in the United States. Accordingly, struggling neighborhood theaters transformed themselves into "cinemas" or "art houses." These theaters found a small but enthusiastic following for the latest imported movies. For most of the 1950s, however, the impact of foreign films remained negligible and the mass audience stayed faithful to Hollywood's offerings.

HOW OTHERS SEE US

Hooray for Bollywood

The film industry of India, affectionately known as "Bollywood," is big business, producing up to 1,000 features a year and reaching audiences throughout Southeast Asia and around the world. Bollywood films are famous for their elaborate musical numbers, complex plots, and lengthy running times.

All these traditions can be traced back to the films of director Mehboob Khan (1907–1964), who drew on the look and mood of American movies during Hollywood's Golden Age while espousing traditional Indian values. *Andaaz* (1949), regarded as the first modern film of the newly independent India, reflected the technical gloss and fashionable sets of any American drama in the service of a love-triangle storyline that reflected clashing Indian and Western mores. The design and cinematography of Khan's 1952 epic *Aan,* one of the earliest all-color Indian features, was influenced by American adventures such as *The Thief of Baghdad.* What's more, Khan's best-known film, *Mother India* (1957), recalled *Gone with the Wind* in its length and historic sweep, *Stella Dallas* in its enshrinement of maternal suffering, and the entire catalog of MGM movie musicals in its song and dance numbers.

In *Mother India,* Khan made his strongest bid at filming a global blockbuster, one that would be definitively Indian while appealing to audiences elsewhere. He visited Hollywood in 1958 to pitch the film for American distribution and to explore joint ventures with American producers. *Mother India* was released in the United States the next year (in a much-edited version called *A Handful of Grain*), and though it was not a commercial success—one American critic called the film "unorthodox" in its "howling, suffering and musical hopping," while another concluded that it would be "difficult for average movie fans to appreciate"—it did garner an Academy Award nomination for Best Foreign Language Film, the first Indian production to do so.

In 1956, *And God Created Woman,* a French film by director Roger Vadim, shocked audiences with an opening sequence that showed a supine—and unclothed—Brigitte Bardot, the "woman" of the title. The import pitted would-be censors against film-as-art supporters. The censors lost, and the movie made several million dollars in the United States. Its success encouraged quality pictures like *Wild Strawberries* (Sweden, 1957), *Throne of Blood* (Japan, 1957), *Black Orpheus* (Brazil, 1959), and *Hiroshima, Mon Amour* (France/Japan, 1959).

One foreign film from 1956 deserves mention in any discussion of popular culture: Japan's *Godzilla: King of the Monsters!* A cheaply made picture about a sleeping monster awakened by atomic blasts, it features clips of American actor Raymond Burr intercut with the Japanese story. This arbitrary intrusion proved needless, distracting, and at times hilarious; the fascination of *Godzilla* rests with the monster and its ensuing actions. A hulking beast crudely shot in miniature stop-action sequences, Godzilla wreaks havoc on every model city he attacks. Stilted, awkward, amateurish—*Godzilla* quickly rose to cult status. Since 1956, over twenty sequels have been shot, none matching the original.

Censorship

Hollywood chafed under the restrictions on language, imagery, and content imposed by the Production Code Administration, a group of industry censors that had been ruling what could and could not be seen and said in films since 1934. For example, characters could not swear, sex could only be hinted at, and nudity was banned. In order to be assured distribution, all commercial movies had to pass Code approval, thus allowing it to effectively control American movie content.

In 1953, a light comedy titled *The Moon Is Blue* defied the Production Code. Directed by the esteemed Otto Preminger and adapted from a hit Broadway play, the film employed innuendo freely, as well the forbidden words "virgin," "seduce," and "pregnant." Denied a seal of approval, United Artists released it anyway, and the subsequent publicity caused the feature to do well. Defenders of the film argued that movies have protection

under the free speech clause of the Constitution. The defense proved successful, the first of several successful challenges to the outmoded Production Code, and caused censors to loosen their grips significantly.

With its authority weakened, and with continuing assaults on its rules and worries about declining attendance at theaters, the Code underwent significant revision in 1956, allowing Hollywood to put previously forbidden subjects on the screen, something television could not also do because of its governance by the Federal Communications Commission. In short order, pregnancy, interracial marriage, miscegenation, abortion, and prostitution, could all serve as legitimate movie topics, provided directors handled them in a seemly manner.

RADIO

In the immediate postwar period (1946–1949), radio experienced extensive growth as new stations went on the air. Ninety-five percent of American households owned at least one radio in 1950, and more than half of all U.S. automobiles had radios by the early 1950s. Then, with the beginning of the new decade, listenership plummeted. Faced with the inevitability of change, radio went about reinventing itself, returning to its roots of music and news. By the close of the 1950s, virtually no original programming could be heard on network or locally independent stations; all had gone to a schedule of disc jockeys and recorded music, with a sprinkling of sports and news.

Radio's Dilemma

New stations, long postponed by the Depression and World War II, came into being at a rapid rate in the late forties and early fifties. The number of AM (amplitude modulation) stations jumped from 930 in 1945 to more than 2,300 by 1952. FM (frequency modulation) experienced even more explosive growth, jumping from just 46 stations at the end of the war to over 600 broadcasters in 1952. In addition, several hundred would-be operators, just waiting for the opportunity to go on the air, had licenses pending in 1952 with the Federal Communications Commission (FCC).[6]

RADIO DEBUTS OF THE 1950s

Big Jon and Sparkie (1950): children's show about the adventures of a "little elf from the land of make-believe."

The Bob and Ray Show (1951): national broadcasts of Bob Elliott and Ray Goulding's deadpan comic parodies of pop culture.

Silver Eagle (1951): the daring exploits of Jim West, a Canadian Mountie.

I Was a Communist for the FBI (1952): an FBI agent infiltrates a Communist Party cell in this ultra-patriotic drama aired at the height of the McCarthy era.

Space Patrol (1952): in the twenty-first century, Earth's Commander Buzz Corey leads the fight against evil interplanetary forces.

Gunsmoke (1952): U.S. Marshal Matt Dillon maintains law and order in Dodge City in this classic western starring William Conrad, which begins on TV in 1955 with James Arness as Dillon.

My Little Margie (1952): situation comedy about a New York City widower and his madcap 21-year-old daughter; its radio run coincides with a TV show featuring the same name and cast.

Hour of Decision (1953): Sunday-morning sermons with the Reverend Billy Graham.

X Minus 1 (1955): science fiction anthology series, with scripts adapted from the stories of writers such as Robert A. Heinlein, Ray Bradbury, Philip K. Dick, and Isaac Asimov.

Have Gun—Will Travel (1958): radio version of the successful TV western about the professional gunman Paladin in 1875 California.

By 1959, despite the fierce competition of television, 3,431 AM and 850 FM stations could be found across the United States. Yet, despite the growth in numbers of stations and receivers in the postwar years, significant changes occurred in ownership and programming. Only half of the nation's broadcasters continued to be associated with a network (ABC, CBS, Mutual, or Keystone), a situation that would accelerate throughout the remainder of the decade. Even with this setback, the networks scheduled more programming during the 1953–1954 season than they ever had. Their efforts, however, failed; affiliations continued to drop, and network programming dropped off sharply after 1954.[7]

Two years later the networks had ceased most original radio productions. Gone were the comedians, the mysteries, the variety revues, and all the other elaborate programming that so characterized immediate postwar American radio. Within the same period, more and more TV stations came on the air, associating with the ABC, CBS, and NBC networks. Television could claim more entertainers, more big names, and more variety, while radio helplessly watched its former stars move to the new medium. National advertisers moved their accounts to television as well.

In spite of the loss of national accounts, total radio advertising revenue actually rose in the early 1950s. The creation of new AM stations and the expansion of regional and local radio advertising helped compensate for the decline in network revenues, with precipitous losses being absorbed by the networks themselves. A national medium evolved into a localized one; by the end of the decade, two-thirds of a typical station's income came from local advertisers.

FM Broadcasting

One area of radio held out great hope for broadcasters: FM. The 1950s were expected to be FM's glory decade, with people everywhere acquiring new receivers and listening to quality high-fidelity programming. But people did not rush to buy FM radios and sponsors did not line up. Instead, people rushed to buy new televisions and sponsors lined up to buy time on television. In addition, a series of unwise decisions by the FCC during the late 1940s limited the FM spectrum available to radio broadcasters, further dampening enthusiasm for the creation of new stations.

During this time, strong AM stations frequently owned a fledgling FM operation. As a result, the programs on both AM and FM were often the same. Why buy an expensive new FM receiver, why sponsor a show, when the same programming could be heard on AM? FM stations that attempted independent programming, usually classical music, attracted small, dedicated audiences. Advertisers displayed little interest in such limited listenership and only a handful of new FM stations came on the air for most of the 1950s, including subsidized educational stations often run by colleges and universities.[8]

Stereo Broadcasting

Radio stations had been experimenting with stereo programming since 1952. Their approach usually involved broadcasting through dual channels, one on the AM frequency and the other on FM. Although this form of stereophonic transmission worked, it required separate AM and FM receivers that could be played independently of one another. A combination AM-FM receiver would not work because the two formats could not be played at the same time, plus 1950s sets had only one speaker, not the requisite two.

Because television sound is broadcast over the FM band, experimentation continued with occasional musical shows playing on one channel through a television set, while the other channel played over an AM radio. The gambit failed. The AM sound proved inferior to FM; not only that, listeners had to have a radio and TV on simultaneously. Not until the early sixties did stereophonic broadcasting through a single source become technologically feasible.

Science Fiction

Despite declining advertising revenues and disappearing audiences, a momentary bright spot for radio programmers lit up in the form of science fiction. During the 1950s, a spate of new shows attracted listeners, and they shared common themes of space exploration, invention, and fantasy. One of the first was *Dimension X,* an NBC production that premiered in 1950 and ran well into 1951. Capitalizing on the vogue for science fiction movies, the show used imaginative sound effects instead of futuristic visual sets. In 1955, NBC scheduled *X-Minus One,* a virtual twin to *Dimension X.* It ran until 1958, adding new scripts and new fans to the genre.

Both *Dimension X* and *X-Minus One* borrowed from the popular science fiction pulp magazines of the day. Authors like Ray Bradbury, Robert Bloch, Robert Sheckley, and a host of others, all veterans of the pulps, contributed to both series. Not to be outdone, CBS scheduled a series titled *Escape* (1947–1954). Focusing more on adventure stories than straight science fiction, *Escape* nonetheless enthralled listeners with tales of survival and fantasy. It, too, relied on the pulp magazines for many of its writers, finding their detailed, descriptive writing styles well suited to the aural medium of radio.

Two science fiction radio series aimed at younger audiences that had counterparts in television were *Space Patrol* (1950–1955) and *Tom Corbett, Space Cadet* (1952); both were products of ABC-Radio. ABC-TV also produced *Space Patrol* for television from 1950 to 1955. *Tom Corbett, Space Cadet* enjoyed a considerably longer and more varied life on TV. The series began in 1950 on CBS, shifted to ABC in 1951, and then went to NBC for two years. DuMont, a small TV network of the time, picked it up for the 1953 and 1954 seasons, and the show returned to NBC in 1955 where it ended that summer.

Top 40 Programming

While radio was losing all its old mainstays, a new concept in broadcasting began taking hold in the Midwest. In 1955, a station in Omaha, Nebraska, played only those songs identified in published lists as being the most popular in the country. Limited to hits listed from number 1 to number 40, the concept proved successful with youthful audiences, and while many smaller stations adopted the practice, some of the larger urban markets proved resistant. Top 40 programmers based their rationale around the perception that, it being the mid-1950s, most popular music would consist of rock 'n' roll, and station directors assumed the audience would consist primarily of teenagers.

Surveys showed that the youth market was the primary block of listeners, so the Top 40 format became irresistible to many stations. At the same time, the move to Top 40 proved the death knell for most network productions, other than news and sports. Using colorful, talkative disk jockeys, along with contests, giveaways, and other promotions, stations succeeded in attracting a large listener base and, more importantly, numerous sponsors.

In order to lessen criticism of their programming practices, many stations began to experiment with more varied formats in the late 1950s. "Oldies" (songs from the recent past), adult contemporary, religious, country and western, jazz, and middle of the road emerged as programming approaches evolving from the Top 40 concept. By the end of the decade, American AM radio had clearly decided that its future lay with recorded popular music.

TELEVISION

Regularly scheduled television broadcasts began in the United States in 1927, but few people had access to the new TV technology. In 1946, wartime restrictions were lifted and receivers could again be manufactured. Sixteen stations were on the air in 1947, a number that jumped to 107 by 1951. As ownership of television sets swelled, people became increasingly literate in the visual sense, making decisions about who and what they liked and disliked on the basis of the images projected on their TV screen.

Early Broadcasting

In the beginning, much television drama relied on traditional theatrics—actors moving about on a small stage, all within the gaze of a fixed camera. Producers gave emphasis to creativity in playwriting and performance, and the medium's debts to legitimate theater and vaudeville were many. By the early 1950s, however, television became much more cinematic and much less static a medium, looking to Hollywood for aesthetic inspiration.[9]

Postwar commercial television struggled, primarily from a lack of equipment and technical problems. Between 1948 and 1952, the Federal Communications Commission imposed a freeze on new stations as the industry sought to solve numerous shortcomings. In time, most licenses gained approval, and by the end of the fifties, well over 500 TV stations (515 commercial, 44 educational) had gone on the air.[10]

Network television, with the successes and failures of radio as models, moved quickly in the early 1950s to provide as much variety as possible. The TV menu presented to viewers every evening rivaled anything radio had provided in its best days—plus, a picture accompanied the sound.

VHF, UHF, and ETV

The FCC, in 1951, allowed many new stations to broadcast on the UHF (ultrahigh frequency) waveband, a move that opened up the potential for more than a thousand additional stations across the country. Designed to supplement the VHF (very high frequency) band where all broadcasters had previously been assigned, UHF broadcast channels 14–89. VHF carried channels 2–13 (channel 1 was reserved for emergencies and service broadcasting). The FCC stipulated that channels 14–69 could carry commercial stations, reserving 70–89 for special broadcasting. This well-meaning move attempted to open up competition to many more stations, but it overlooked the fact that most existing sets could pick up only VHF signals.[11]

To get around the inability of existing television sets to receive UHF signals, a number of devices came on the market that promised to overcome the problem. These gadgets attached to a set's existing antenna terminals and supposedly expanded its range. They provided inferior picture quality, however, and few people rushed out to buy them. Not until ten years later, in 1961, did the FCC decree that all new receivers had to have the ability to pick up UHF as well as VHF broadcasting. As a result, very few UHF stations could make a commercial go of it in the fifties, since sponsors were loath to support channels that only a few could receive.

The FCC also ruled in 1951 that some television channels had to be reserved for educational programming, or ETV (educational television). In 1953, the first ETV station began broadcasting and was soon followed by a number of others. Out of this grew National Education Television (NET), a loose grouping of stations dedicated to creating educational programs. Instructional TV frequently went on the air early in the morning (5:30–6:00 A.M.) to allow working people to take courses. By 1959, 45 NET stations had come on the air. Because most of them got assigned to the UHF band, they lacked any commercial support, and without subsidies their survival proved problematical.[12]

Television Impacts

During the transition from radio to television, roughly from 1948 to 1952, many cities had no television reception. Studies found that movie attendance dropped sharply in areas receiving a signal, while those without TV reception showed no commensurate drop. In a similar fashion, people did not go out to sporting events or restaurants as frequently when they could watch TV at home. Even libraries reported lower circulation in cities with access to television. By the mid-1950s, however, virtually the entire country could receive at least one channel, and any remaining pockets of isolation were quickly identified and efforts made to reach them. Television had become, in just a few short years, the primary carrier of both entertainment and information. In fact, by 1960, 13 percent of American households had more than one TV set, a sure sign of the medium's success.[13]

Television proved an expensive investment for consumers. In 1952, a typical black-and-white set with an 11- or 12-inch screen cost about $250, plus installation. A rooftop antenna was also a necessity in most places to get reasonable reception.

But mass production soon brought the high prices down, the screens grew larger, and the overall quality rose. By the middle of the decade, the same amount of money would buy a vastly improved 21-inch set.

In 1955, General Electric introduced the first truly portable TV set. Until then, receivers were large, bulky boxes, often handsomely constructed with wood cabinets, and they could easily weigh over a hundred pounds. The new GE model had a 14-inch screen and weighed only 26 pounds. A sturdy handle ran the length of the casing for convenient carrying. No longer disguised as part of a living room suite, the portable TV found a ready audience. By 1956, virtually every manufacturer offered portable models, and they assumed their place as "second sets." Television had gone from being a novelty to a mass medium in which second and even third sets became commonplace in American homes.

Color Television

In a race with rival NBC, CBS had come up with the technology to broadcast in color at the beginning of the decade, but the network's rush to be first overlooked major problems. Sets lacked the equipment to pick up the color signal broadcast by CBS. The first color receivers compatible with the CBS system appeared in 1953 and cost $1,000 or more. Despite their color compatibility and their ability to reproduce black-and-white signals in addition to color ones, the networks broadcast virtually nothing in color, making the purchase impractical.

At the time of these color experiments, Americans were purchasing black-and-white sets at a record pace, virtually all of them incompatible with CBS's proposed system. Rather than have so many people buy new, expensive color sets, the FCC approved rival NBC's color technology as the national standard. The NBC system, while inferior in overall quality to CBS's, was compatible with existing receivers, so viewers could watch color broadcasts in black and white. Economy won out over technology, with the result that consumers had to accept a second-rate color image while not having to purchase a second set.

By 1954, both NBC and CBS began limited color telecasting using the NBC system. ABC, short on cash and perennially in third place among the three networks, did not begin color broadcasts until 1958. The whole controversy turned into a major victory for NBC and made them the industry leader for the remainder of the decade. In 1957, NBC's famed "color peacock" was born, and its colorful tail feathers served as an icon for the network. By that time, a fairly good color set could be purchased for around $600, and the networks worked at presenting more and more of their lineup in "living color." Most shows and series remained black-and-white, but by 1957, the networks transmitted about 500 hours of color annually—still less than two hours a day. They called these color shows "specials": one- or two-hour productions independent of any ongoing series.[14]

TV Ratings

While the FCC attempted to impose order in the color debates, the Big Three networks wanted to know who watched what programs. The idea of tracking audiences and their preferences originated with radio in the 1930s. In 1950, the firm of A. C. Nielsen landed contracts with the TV networks to collect data about the viewing public. They used the Nielsen Television Index, a meter attached to a TV set that monitored when a particular channel was on and for how long. Nielsen's sample audience consisted of 1,200 families across the United States that had agreed to have the machine installed in their homes.

The meter, crude by later standards, could not prove if anyone actually watched, only that the set had been tuned to a specific channel. Nevertheless, the results impressed broadcasters, who presented this information to advertisers with authority. The network with the best ratings (i.e., the most sets tuned to that network) could therefore charge the highest fees for advertising time in that slot.

NOTABLE TELEVISION SHOWS

The Ed Sullivan Show (The Toast of the Town) (1948–1971)

Talent Scouts (with Arthur Godfrey) (1948–1958)

Texaco Star Theater (The Milton Berle Show) (1948–1956)

The Garry Moore Show (CBS, 1950–1964).

The Jack Benny Program (1950–1964; 1964–1965),

What's My Line? (1950–1967)

Dragnet (1951–1959)

I Love Lucy (1951–1957)

American Bandstand (1952–1989)

The Jackie Gleason Show (1952–1959)

Alfred Hitchcock Presents (1955–1962)

Gunsmoke (1955–1975)

The Mickey Mouse Club (1955–1959)

The $64,000 Question (1955–1958)

The Steve Allen Show (1956–1960)

Have Gun, Will Travel (1957–1963)

Leave It to Beaver (1957–1963)

Wagon Train (1957–1965)

Television Programming

American television, the most popular mass medium ever, reflected contemporary culture, but it presented a distorted picture of that culture. For most of the decade, the daily and nightly schedules called for shows about white middle-class characters, a narrow, one-dimensional picture of modern society.

Slightly more than a third of the 1950s TV schedule was devoted to the wide category of "drama." This included crime and detective shows, dramatic series, original teleplays, and westerns. Another quarter to a third of all programming presented music, comedy, and variety shows, although toward the end of the decade, that percentage dropped. Quiz shows, long a staple of the television day, occupied roughly 15 percent of the schedule. Children's programming accounted for just less than 10 percent. News and information (weather, sports, interviews, and the like) usually garnered 7 percent. Finally, about 5 percent of the TV schedule, classified as "miscellaneous," included programs like movies, specials of various kinds, and some cultural offerings.[15]

Live Broadcasting

Unlike most television today, live broadcasting characterized the pioneer period of the medium. Instead of using film or videotape, over three-quarters of all productions were broadcast directly from a studio, or "live." As a result, most of the visual record of the early formative years (1947–1951) of commercial television has been lost forever. Since few shows could afford the costs of elaborate film production, they sometimes synchronized a regular movie camera with the flickering, on-screen television image. The resulting film, called a "kinescope," served as an inferior copy of the original production. So poor was the reproduction quality that few kinescopes were made; except for some rare but grainy pieces of film, priceless performances will never again be seen.

In 1951, magnetic videotape came on the market. It proved vastly superior to kinescopes, but early videotapes hardly equaled later ones. It took several more years of constant refinement to achieve quality reproduction. As the technology improved, most production shifted over to the new format, one that allowed editing of the final image. By the end of the decade, less than 30 percent of all television remained live. Purists might argue that TV lost spontaneity with the advent of videotape, but most audiences enjoyed watching smooth, polished productions without glitches.

Packaged Television

As American television strove to find technical and aesthetic standards for itself, the networks and sponsors shared in developing and producing much prime-time programming. Although this level of control sometimes led to abuses (see Advertising of the 1950s), it also meant American television frequently displayed more diversity and variety than would later be the case. For example, *Omnibus* (CBS, 1952–1956; ABC, 1956–1957; NBC, 1957–1959) was perceived as a "highbrow" show that appealed to audiences with education and money. As long as sponsors had control of *Omnibus,* this limited, niche audience fit their marketing strategies. Consequently, *Omnibus* enjoyed a long run, even though it never achieved great ratings.

The second half of the fifties saw the networks airing almost 50 new shows each and every season. Only about 20 or so of these new entries made it to a second season; many were canceled after just a few episodes. Neither the networks nor the sponsors could turn out new material at such a rate, and so companies known as packagers stepped in. Packagers would bring an idea for a show to the network or sponsor. The packager would create a pilot, or a sample program, assembling writers, actors, and any technical facilities that might be required. The packager would next oversee the actual production of the show in question. Using this process, packagers produced almost two-thirds of network programming by the end of the decade. Sponsors and advertising agencies bought time, not the production itself, and thus had much less say about any aspect of the shows they financed.

For the packagers, syndication emerged as a profitable sideline. Once a show had run its course and no longer appeared in the regular schedules, the packager could rent it to any station for a fee. As a result, popular 1950s series like

Dragnet, Leave It to Beaver, and *I Love Lucy* could seemingly go on forever in syndication, creating handsome residual payments.

Another way to satisfy television's insatiable demand for shows involved lengthening them. The early fifties had 15-minute and half-hour productions, a carryover from radio, but 1955–1959 saw the hour show move into dominance. By the end of the decade, hour-and-a-half and two-hour productions were not unusual.

Variety and Comedy Shows

Commercial television early on established itself as a vehicle for comedy. At the beginning of the decade, NBC granted comedian Milton Berle a 30-year, multimillion-dollar contract. Already a veteran of the last days of vaudeville, Berle took to television naturally, and his *Texaco Star Theater* (1948–1956) quickly became a favorite among those with receivers.

The Texaco Star Theater reached its zenith in the early fifties, and Berle was dubbed "Mr. Television." As one of the first comedy/variety shows, *The Texaco Star Theater* established many of the standards for subsequent TV comedy. Berle's visual comedy appealed to audiences because of his lack of restraint. Pies in the face and banana peels worked well in the early days of the medium. In time, however, audiences looked for something a bit more sophisticated, and in 1956, NBC canceled both his show and his aforementioned contract.

At the same time NBC introduced *The Texaco Star Theater,* rival CBS launched a variety show called *Toast of the Town* (1948–1971). Working on an initial budget of only a few hundred dollars, the show's host, syndicated newspaper columnist Ed Sullivan (1901–1974), brought together a collection of performers that might have reminded audiences of the days when vaudeville was king. The formula worked, despite the obvious unease Sullivan exhibited under the unblinking eye of the television cameras. *Toast of the Town* (renamed *The Ed Sullivan Show* in 1955) became an early TV hit and reigned supreme among variety shows for years. Sullivan himself remained stiff and ill at ease throughout its celebrated run, perhaps a part of the show's success.

Throughout the fifties, *The Ed Sullivan Show* meant show-business variety, a traditional revue. From trained animal acts to current superstars to European opera personalities, his hour-long program featured them all. Any entertainers desiring national exposure had to, at some point in their careers, appear on the *Sullivan* show. In 1956, Elvis Presley made the first of several appearances there. The reaction was electric; Presley's on-screen gyrations triggered sensational record sales and denunciations from many a pulpit. But the reaction also demonstrated how deeply television had penetrated American lives by 1956. Sullivan may have seemed stilted and inarticulate on camera, but he was the premiere star-maker in the country.

Cavalcade of Stars (1949–1952), another entry in the catalog of TV variety shows, starred comedian Jackie Gleason. He created a number of comic characters, the best known of whom was Ralph Kramden, the main figure in a running skit within the show titled "The Honeymooners." It proved so popular that CBS lured him away from the DuMont network, and the resultant *Jackie Gleason Show* (1952–1957) is remembered today as one of the most imaginative offerings ever to appear on television.

Other comedy/variety shows worthy of note included: *Your Show of Shows* (NBC, 1950–1954), *The Colgate Comedy Hour* (NBC, 1950–1955), *The Jack Benny Program* (CBS, 1950–1964; NBC, 1964–1965), and *The Garry Moore Show* (CBS, 1950–1964). By the late 1950s, the big, multitalented variety show went into decline.

Situation Comedies, or "Sitcoms"

An outgrowth of radio comedy, the sitcom endured fewer changes than any other format in TV. As television productions grew ever more expensive, the sitcom remained the only genre that held to the familiar half-hour format.

One sitcom in particular dominated the 1950s: *I Love Lucy* (1951–1957). This all-time favorite premiered on CBS in October 1951 and became the weekly comedy show by which all others were judged. By 1952, *I Love Lucy* ranked as the most popular show on television, a position it would hold through much of its six-year run.

The series featured Lucille Ball (1911–1989), her real-life husband Desi Arnaz, and costars William Frawley and Vivian Vance. Everyone involved was very talented, but Lucy dominated the show.

Though few realized it at the time, *I Love Lucy* proved instrumental in the death of live television. Until then, most situation comedies and other TV fare were televised live, with no retakes when mistakes occurred and no editing. One of the first shows to use film, both Ball and Arnaz believed they would have greater control of the production process in that format. *I Love Lucy* had a studio audience, and no one seemed to mind that the show combined live television and traditional movie techniques. The comedy ran through the 1957 season and soon thereafter went into network and syndicated reruns, thanks to its being preserved on film. A knowledgeable businesswoman, Ball insisted on residuals—set fees for repeated airings—something few others did in those early days of television. Because *I Love Lucy* remained in constant syndication, Ball and Arnaz became wealthy in a short period of time.[16]

For many, the sanitized view of family life many 1950s sitcoms provided has evolved into a kind of collective nostalgia for a way of life (white, middle-class, suburban) that never accurately represented America. Certainly, *I Love Lucy* presented a picture of strong middle-class aspirations and familial bonds, a recurring theme

Entertainment

I Love Lucy (CBS). Shown from left: William Frawley, Vivian Vance, Lucille Ball (as Lucy Ricardo), Desi Arnaz, 1956. Courtesy of Photofest.

found in much of the television fare of the day. In the show, Lucy had little to do except concoct schemes while husband Desi held down a regular job. The humor came from the portrait of Lucy as a harebrained, forgetful, cute, but harmless wife. It was hardly a flattering picture, but the humor kept it from becoming a mean-spirited stereotype. This characterization of women received reinforcement in other sitcoms. In *The Burns and Allen Show* (CBS, 1950–1958), Gracie Allen revived a character she had successfully developed in radio comedy in the 1930s. The real-life wife of George Burns, her comedic "Gracie" was, like Lucy, a scatterbrained woman who constantly befuddled her more conventional husband. Both Lucille Ball and Gracie Allen were such brilliant comedians, however, that the artifice worked and no one took any offense.

Father Knows Best (radio: NBC, 1949–1953; television: CBS, 1954–1955; NBC, 1955–1958; CBS, 1958–1962; ABC, 1962–1963) looked to the other half of marriage in presenting a patient, wise, warmhearted, and wonderful husband-father figure in Jim Anderson, portrayed by actor Robert Young. Anderson was a man who calmly oversaw his family and provided the solid rock they all leaned on. Their home fit a suburbanized ideal, and actress Jane Wyatt as Margaret, his sweet and lovely wife, served as the antithesis of the Ball/Allen characters. Always smartly dressed, including heels and a crisp, spotless apron, she existed solely for her family, leaving wage-earning and decision-making to her spouse.

Another show that first found its niche on radio was *The Adventures of Ozzie and Harriet* (radio: CBS, 1944–1948; NBC, 1948–1949; ABC, 1949–1954; television: ABC, 1952–1966). A success on radio, it went to greater fame as the longest-running sitcom ever. Ozzie Nelson played himself in the husband-father role, and his wife Harriet (Hilliard) Nelson enacted her real-life role as spouse and mother. The couple's two sons, David and Rickie, played themselves, and audiences watched them grow. For everyone the roles remained clear: Ozzie, despite a bumble or two, remained at the head of the table, and Harriet was the immaculate wife, always at home for her men. Ozzie appeared to hold no job, and seemed to be a stay-at-home dad, dispensing paternal wisdom

and guiding his sons through childhood and adolescence.

The focus shifted to the offspring of these happy matches in the popular *Leave It to Beaver* (CBS, 1957–1958; ABC, 1958–1963). The idyllic families portrayed in these domestic comedies looked at the decade through the rosiest of glasses, and they painted a lasting picture that some nostalgia buffs persist in viewing as the correct and accurate one for the period.[17]

Music and Television

Music of all kinds provided a backdrop for most commercial TV productions. For example, Perry Como, a popular 1950s crooner, had success both with recordings and television. He headlined *The Chesterfield Supper Club* (NBC, 1948–1950; CBS, 1950–1955), a 15-minute mix of music and patter that grew into *The Perry Como Show* (NBC, 1955–1963), a big-budget, hour-long music and variety series that endeared him to millions of viewers. Similarly, singer Dinah Shore parlayed her vocal talents into the long-running *Dinah Shore Show* (NBC, 1951–1962). Her show grew into an hour-long variety package in 1957. Faithfully sponsored by Chevrolet throughout the decade, her theme song, "See the U.S.A. (in Your Chevrolet)," doubtless contributed to Chevrolet's strong sales position during those years.

A mediocre pianist with a gift for flamboyant showmanship first appeared on home screens in 1951. Born Wladziu Valentino Liberace, he became an instant hit as Liberace. By 1952 he had been picked up by NBC for a summer series, and from there he moved into syndication. Innumerable stations ran his show, and he returned to ABC for the 1958–1959 season.

Liberace's show featured a trademark candelabrum that rested atop his grand piano as he played, and he costumed himself in an ever-changing, outlandish wardrobe made from gold lamé, sequins, and anything else he thought might catch the audience's eye. His enormous success surprised everyone, but his mix of kitsch and homogenized light classics captivated viewers ready for something new and different.

Another new musical series that made no pretense of presenting "great" compositions was *The*

Lawrence Welk Show (ABC, 1955–1971). Hosted by a folksy bandleader who featured polkas, waltzes, and "champagne music" (popular favorites played in a "bubbly" manner), it found a large and appreciative audience among older Americans looking for an escape from a constant stream of Top 40 pop. At one point during the 1950s, Welk had three different shows on ABC, but they all featured his innocuous blend of musical styles. The success enjoyed by his orchestra pointed up the lack of programming for adults outside the usual 21–40 age demographic.

Television Drama

During the period 1950–1955, countless dramatic shows proliferated across the TV dial as intense, one- or two-hour live, original dramas. The stories exploited the camera's ability to create gripping characters without the benefit of sweeping scenery or special effects. During the 1950s, the networks moved many of their operations from New York City to Los Angeles. Filmed performances supplanted live ones, and the "anthology" concept of individual and original dramas came briefly into vogue. These stories bore no relation to preceding or succeeding ones and eventually were replaced by continuing series with familiar characters and settings that carried over from week to week.

Because so many anthology dramas appeared on television, their quality was uneven. For every "Our Town" (*Producer's Showcase*, 1955, with Paul Newman and Frank Sinatra), or "The Miracle Worker" (*Playhouse 90*, with Patty McCormick and Teresa Wright), plenty of utterly forgettable dramas also came on the air.

In a significant reversal of tradition, some of the best of the new television dramas later made the transition to the movie screen. Distinguished teleplays like Paddy Chayefsky's *Marty* (TV, 1953; movie, 1955), Reginald Rose's *12 Angry Men* (TV, 1954; movie, 1957; remade as television movie in 1997), Rod Serling's *Patterns* (TV, 1955; movie, 1956) and *Requiem for a Heavyweight* (TV, 1956; movie, 1962) can be counted among a number of such productions. Some critics would argue that the originals surpassed their cinematic versions.

Television Soap Operas

Recognizing both the popularity and profitability of radio "soaps," television producers early on decided to create their own serials. With the appearance of more and more TV soap operas during the afternoon hours of the broadcasting day, one of the last bastions of network radio fell into cancellation (see "Radio" this chapter).

A remarkable thing about soap operas is how many have been attempted. In 1954 alone, the networks launched thirteen new serials, and as the titles show, only three survived beyond that opening season. But the industry remained undeterred; every year new soap operas appeared, with just a few enjoying any success. Six CBS soaps stayed on the air for twenty years or more: *As the World Turns, Edge of Night, Guiding Light, Love of Life, Search for Tomorrow,* and *The Secret Storm.* Such longevity continues to be almost unheard of in the competitive world of commercial television, a world that considers most new offerings lucky to last their first season.

The afternoon soap operas tempted audiences with daily commentaries on the manners and mores of contemporary America. Working on small, confined sets, the TV cameras relied on intimate close-ups of the characters, thereby exaggerating their emotional responses to ongoing events. The plots moved at a molasses-like pace so viewers could miss an episode or two and not lose any continuity, a device taken directly from their radio counterparts. The black-and-white world of the soaps—both technically and morally speaking—reflected a period searching for some absolutes. Their stories punished adultery, seldom presented divorce as an option, condemned pregnancy outside marriage, and tended to portray all men as emotionally weak and all good women as strong and resourceful. But femmes fatal lurked everywhere, and only the most solid families could resist their temptations.

The TV networks liked the low staging costs of the serials, and their dominance of afternoon programming guaranteed high ratings, which in turn meant sponsorship never became a problem. When soap operas first made the move from radio to TV, they retained the old 15-minute length. But production pressures, along with the need to air more commercials, led most TV soaps to go to a half-hour format in the mid-1950s.[18]

Westerns

In the second half of the 1950s, westerns began to appear nightly on the nation's television sets. Long a favorite of the movies, many felt that the expansiveness of the western would not translate well to the small screen. These prognosticators, however, were proved wrong. The stampede began modestly with *Hopalong Cassidy* (NBC, 1949–1951; syndication thereafter). Shortly afterward, radio's long-running *Lone Ranger* began to share time with a television counterpart (radio, 1933–1954; ABC, 1949–1957). Traditional shoot-'em-ups like *The Roy Rogers Show* (NBC, 1951–1957), *Wild Bill Hickok* (syndicated, 1951–1958), *The Cisco Kid* (syndicated, 1950–1955), and *Death Valley Days* (syndicated, 1952–1970) also found audiences. Their success led to new series, designed more with the small screen in mind. Walt Disney's *Frontierland* (a spin-off of his own

The Lone Ranger (ABC) 1949–1957. Shown from left: Clayton Moore (as The Lone Ranger), Jay Silverheels (as Tonto). Courtesy of Photofest.

Disneyland, ABC, 1954–1961) produced a brief series on Davy Crockett during the 1954–1955 season. The success of all four episodes, usually considered more children's shows than serious western fare, gained the networks' attention.

From 1955 on, the industry produced some 50 different television western series. These new shows may not have been cinematic epics, but their tight, character-focused plotting found millions of at-home viewers. First and foremost among this genre was *Gunsmoke* (CBS, 1955–1975), a deftly plotted series that became the archetypal television western. One of the few radio successes of the 1950s, *Gunsmoke* had begun on CBS Radio (1952–1961), with gravel-voiced William Conrad playing Marshall Matt Dillon, a stern lawman ensconced in Dodge City, Kansas. James Arness played Dillon in the TV version, and his selection for the part proved perfect typecasting. Tall and rugged-looking, Arness embodied John Wayne, Gary Cooper, Henry Fonda, and a host of other actors often associated with westerns. (Wayne was actually offered the role but turned it down and suggested Arness.) Each episode involved intense character studies instead of sprawling action scenes. It befell the marshal to resolve conflicts, which meant lots of talk and limited physical activity. Occasionally, the producers incorporated stock footage of the Kansas prairies, but most of the action consisted of interior shots or exterior ones on the carefully bounded main street of the Dodge City set.

The show became a hit, displacing *I Love Lucy* and dominating the ratings throughout the late 1950s. *Gunsmoke* remained on the air until 1975, making it one of the longest-lived series of any kind in prime time.

By the 1959–1960 season, audiences could choose from 30 westerns. The stories featured strong male leads who suffered identity crises, resisted discrimination, and generally fought against dishonesty and persecution. The old standbys of rustlers, stagecoach robbers, and gold thieves—not to mention cowboys and Indians—had virtually disappeared as subjects.

The networks happily adopted the term "adult western" to identify their hot new offerings. In no time at all, their rosters had grown to include titles like those listed below in "Adult Westerns of the 1950s."

Adult Westerns of the 1950s

ABC	CBS	NBC
Cheyenne (1955–1963)	*Gunsmoke* (1955–1975)	*Bat Masterson* (1958–1961)
Colt .45 (1957–1962)	*Have Gun, Will Travel* (1957–1963)	*Bonanza* (1959–1973)
The Lawman (1958–1962)	*Rawhide* (1959–1966)	*The Californians* (1957–1959)
Maverick (1957–1962)	*Tales of the Texas Rangers* (1955–1957)	*Laramie* (1959–1963)
The Rifleman (1958–1963)		*Tales of Wells Fargo* (1957– 1962)
Sugarfoot (1957–1960)		*Wagon Train* (1957–1962; ABC, 1962–1965)

Note: Listed alphabetically by network.

The emphases placed on character and psychological motivation differentiated this new breed of western from the traditional movie version. The sweeping scenery so characteristic of a movie western was lost on the small screen. Because virtually all television production used black and white during the 1950s, directors could film in color. Indians on the warpath, cavalry charges, stampedes, isolated forts, and all the other icons associated with the genre had to be replaced with new methods of storytelling.

Taking their cue from the many dramatic shows already running on television, producers employed close-ups and many interior shots. They filmed most of the shows on studio back lots, and budget constraints meant few large-scale sets. So the television western evolved into an intimate dramatic form that owed as much to traditional theater as it did to the movies.[19]

Television Quiz Shows

Led by *The $64,000 Question* (CBS, 1955–1958) and a handful of other big-money productions, television quiz shows attracted an unusually receptive audience. *The $64,000 Question* grew out of a successful radio quiz called *Take It or Leave It* that had run on CBS from 1940 to 1947. At that time, NBC took over the show, renaming it *The $64 Question,* a reference to its top prize. Contestants started at $1 and kept doubling their money ($1-$2-$4-$8-$16-$32-$64) through a sequence of seven questions. It ran on radio until 1952 and contributed the phrase "the sixty-four dollar question" to the language.

Television producers wanted big jackpots to draw big audiences. Contestants became overnight celebrities on these extravagant shows. Columnist and psychologist Joyce Brothers won $64,000 on *The $64,000 Question* late in 1955; scholarly Columbia College professor Charles Van Doren won $129,000 on *Twenty-One* the next season. That was just the beginning. A 10-year-old, Robert Strom, amassed a record $242,600 on *The $64,000 Challenge* in 1958, but Teddy Nadler shortly surpassed him, becoming the biggest

The $64,000 Question. Prints & Photographs Division, Library of Congress.

Selected Television Quiz Shows of the 1950s

ABC	CBS	NBC
Break the Bank (1948–1949 and 1954–1956; NBC, 1949–1952; CBS, 1952–1953; NBC, 1953)	*Beat the Clock* (1950–1958; ABC, 1958–1961)	The Big Surprise (a.k.a. The $100,000 Big Surprise, 1955–1957)
Treasure Hunt (1956–1957; NBC, 1957–1959)	Dotto (CBS [daytime] and NBC [nighttime], 1958)	Break the $250,000 Bank (1956–1957)
	I've Got a Secret (1952–1967)	Masquerade Party (1952, 1957, 1958–1959, and 1960; CBS, 1953–1954; ABC, 1954–1956; CBS, 1958; CBS, 1959–1960)
	Pantomime Quiz (1949–1951, 1952–1953, 1954 and 1955–1957; NBC, 1952; DuMont, 1953–1954; ABC, 1955; ABC, 1958–1959)	The Price Is Right (1956–1963; ABC, 1963–1965; CBS, 1972–present)
	The $64,000 Challenge (1956–1958)	*Queen for a Day (1956–1960)
	*The $64,000 Question (1955–1958)	*The Quiz Kids (1949–1952; CBS, 1953–1956)
	To Tell the Truth (1956–1968)	Tic Tac Dough (1956–1959)
	*Truth or Consequences (1950–1951; NBC, 1952–1965)	Twenty-One (1956–1958)
		*Twenty Questions (1949; ABC, 1950–1951;
		DuMont, 1951–1954; ABC, 1954–1955)
		*Two for the Money (1952–1953; CBS, 1953–1957)

Note: Listed alphabetically by network. An asterisk (*) indicates the show was also broadcast in a radio version.

winner of them all, with a total of $252,000 on the same show. When a popular contestant, such as Brothers or Van Doren, seemed on the verge of winning big money, ratings ran high, often eclipsing such powerhouses as *I Love Lucy* or one of the increasingly popular adult westerns. The shows proved cheap to produce, sponsors liked their simplicity, and no one seemed to grow tired of them. Some of the better-known network quiz shows are listed in "Selected Television Quiz Shows of the 1950s."

The sky seemed the limit, but later in 1958 a grand jury investigation revealed that many contestants had been supplied hints or outright answers for shows like *Dotto, Twenty-One,* and *The $64,000 Challenge.* During congressional hearings conducted in 1958 and 1959, Van Doren, the darling of the audiences, admitted receiving assistance, and his testimony helped axe any

remaining series. Overnight, audience faith in quiz shows evaporated.

Although the boom for big-money quiz shows fizzled out, a number of more innocuous variations survived. For instance, *The G.E. College Bowl* premiered in 1959 on CBS amid all the scandal, and *What's My Line?* (CBS, 1950–1967), a long-running series, quietly endured. With no prizes, the rewards were more cerebral. The humorous patter of moderator John Charles Daly and panelists Dorothy Kilgallen, Arlene Francis, Bennett Cerf, and a weekly visiting panelist, constituted the proceedings. A devoted audience faithfully followed the witty conversation as the group attempted to identify unusual professions or trades pursued by a succession of guests.

Another unique quiz show was *You Bet Your Life* (NBC, 1950–1961), a carry-over from radio (ABC, 1947–1949; CBS, 1949–1950; NBC, 1950–1956) hosted by the irreverent comedian Groucho Marx. Moderator George Fenneman served as the perfect foil to Groucho and his barbs. Throughout both its radio and television incarnations, *You Bet Your Life* awarded modest cash prizes as contestants took their chances with Groucho and a series of easy questions.

Crime Shows

Faced with the overwhelming success of westerns and quiz shows, the old reliable crime, police, and private-eye shows virtually disappeared from the nightly schedules for much of the decade. Jack Webb's *Dragnet* (NBC, 1951–1959; movie version in 1954) and Erle Stanley Gardner's *Perry Mason* (CBS, 1957–1966) proved to be exceptions. *Dragnet,* a police procedural, was unique: it had a radio twin that debuted on NBC in 1949 and lasted until 1957. Thus, the two—radio and TV broadcasts— ran simultaneously and featured virtually the same casts. *Perry Mason* starred actor Raymond Burr as a lawyer who behaves more like a private detective. It, too, enjoyed a radio run on CBS from 1943 to 1955. No overlap existed between the two media, since actor John Larkin portrayed the radio Mason during the 1950s. A perennial favorite, *Perry Mason* remained a weekly television offering well into the 1960s, whereupon it enjoyed a second life in a long series of made-for-TV movies that lasted until 1993.

In 1958, in the midst of the quiz show debacle, ABC premiered two new crime series, *Naked City* (1958–1963) and *77 Sunset Strip* (1958–1964), moves that reinvigorated the genre. ABC introduced *The Untouchables* in 1959, a crime series that brought the life and legend of G-Man Eliot Ness to the small screen, along with the familiar voice of columnist Walter Winchell as narrator. *The Untouchables* ran until 1963, and enjoys the dubious honor of ranking among the most violent series ever made for network TV.

News

The 1950s saw news and information emerge as important components of the television broadcast day. In 1948, CBS had introduced *Douglas Edwards with the News,* a show Edwards would

anchor until 1962. The next year, NBC premiered *The Camel News Caravan,* a similar news show hosted by John Cameron Swayze. He remained in that spot until 1956, when the team of Chet Huntley and David Brinkley took over with *The Huntley-Brinkley Report,* a program that continued for the next 14 years. Both audiences and critics praised the effectiveness of the duo at the 1956 political conventions, but NBC decided to replace the rather bland Swayze. It proved a wise decision; for the remainder of the decade, *The Huntley-Brinkley Report* grew in popularity, finally overtaking perennial front-runner CBS during the 1959–1960 season.

In 1952, ABC inaugurated *All-Star News,* an hour-long evening newcscast (the CBS and NBC counterparts ran 15 minutes). ABC replaced it in early 1953 with *ABC News,* a more conventional quarter-hour offering hosted by John Daly (also the host for *What's My Line?*). These early network newscasts played like glorified radio broadcasts, and all the anchors came from radio backgrounds. At first, the newscasters read scripts directly into the camera. Very few film clips were employed—most visuals consisted of still photographs projected onto the screen.

Edward R. Murrow. Prints & Photographs Division, Library of Congress.

EDWARD R. MURROW

In the early 1950s, the most renowned news-caster on television was Edward R. Murrow on CBS. Murrow had made a name for himself in World War II with dramatic radio broadcasts from London and Europe. Upon his return to the United States, he and his CBS colleagues put together a powerful news team.

Murrow created two innovative shows, *See It Now* (CBS, 1951–1958) and *Person to Person* (CBS, 1953–1961). *See It Now* was adapted from a program he had created for CBS Radio titled *Hear It Now* (1950–1951), which he had in turn taken from a series of phonograph recordings made for Columbia Records called *I Can Hear It Now*. The success of these endeavors led to weekly television broadcasts featuring in-depth research on current events. Public affairs programs, *See It Now* focused on reporting and *Person to Person* consisted of wide-ranging interviews with people in the news. On *See It Now* in 1954, Murrow exposed Senator Joseph McCarthy as an unprincipled bully and therein brought about the downfall of the Wisconsin politician.

See It Now inspired many later investigative shows. CBS, although immensely proud of the series, also saw it as a liability. A prime-time offering, *See It Now* did not draw as many viewers as competing comedy and quiz shows. In 1955, CBS replaced its weekly broadcasts with six to eight specials a season. Finally, in 1958, CBS canceled the series outright. Embittered over what he perceived as the sacrifice of good reporting for commercial gain, Murrow himself appeared less and less on television for the remainder of the decade and left commercial TV in 1961.

A show that predated the regular network newscasts was NBC's *Meet the Press,* a lively discussion of current events that premiered in November 1947. Still going strong at this writing, *Meet the Press* ranks as the oldest news program on network television. *Meet the Press* invites top journalists and guests to discuss issues, a format that usually allows reporters to grill the guests.

In 1952, both the Republican and Democratic national conventions were televised; for the first time, Americans witnessed the whole presidential nominating process. Compared to more recent convention coverage, the 1952 events seemed awkward affairs, if for no other reason than the difficulties encountered by reporters as they lugged around bulky equipment. President Eisenhower in 1955 allowed TV cameras to tape his press conferences. Eisenhower's staff had editing privileges, but the footage presented the public with an image of its president at work. He also permitted radio microphones, along with the same editing provisos. For many Americans, the television tapes reinforced Eisenhower's persona as a paternal leader, the first inkling of TV's image-making capabilities.

As the public grew accustomed to getting news from television—instead of from newspapers, magazines, or radio—the perception of how to interpret the steady stream of information went through a significant shift. People saw TV as immediate journalism, news of and on the hour. It might not have been reflective, but it provided a stream of images that changed almost constantly.

Sports

In the early days of television, the heavy cameras and associated equipment made any kind of mobility difficult. As a result, sports telecasting consisted of those activities in which a stationary camera could be set up and easily follow the action. This helps to explain the popularity of wrestling, boxing, and even roller derby in the early 1950s. The ring and the track provided limited spaces the camera could cover without trouble. Although earlier attempts had been made to televise baseball, football, basketball, and tennis, the constant movement and the large areas required by these sports created problems for camera crews.

Television technology, however, evolved quickly in the fifties, and soon cameras became smaller and more portable. Because of the newness of TV, and the belief that it would hurt attendance, many teams resisted the medium. They had come to terms with radio, and they tended to receive substantial payments from stations for the privilege of broadcasting. It would take time before the networks worked out similar television contracts to everyone's satisfaction. But once TV gained a foothold in sports, radio's position weakened commensurately. Soon, only local radio stations carried sports, and they usually broadcast their small home teams, not the big games or professional sports events that television was taking over.

As many had feared, attendance at major sporting events took a plunge in tandem with TV's growing coverage. Many communities blacked out broadcasts of games played locally in an effort to lure people back to the stadiums and arenas. But with so much being offered on the television schedule, attendance continued its drop. During the decade, minor league baseball suffered a 60 percent decline in patrons; boxing saw an even greater loss of fans at live events.

Between 1950 and 1959, the amount of money paid for telecasting rights skyrocketed as teams and leagues demanded ever-larger payments

from the networks. At the same time, Americans demonstrated an insatiable demand for televised sports, so the networks paid the asking prices.

Children's Programming

From the beginnings of commercial television, children have been recognized as a vast potential audience. *Kukla, Fran and Ollie* (NBC, 1948–1954; ABC, 1954–1957), *The Soupy Sales Show* (ABC, 1955–1960), *Paul Winchell and Jerry Mahoney* (NBC, 1950–1956; ABC, 1957–1961), and a host of other children's shows attempted quality programming aimed at younger audiences. Sponsors loved the dedication of these youthful viewers, making most series profitable. NBC's *Howdy Doody* (1947–1960) became one of the most successful of the early children's shows. The show featured a cowboy marionette and the zany citizens of Doodyville, including Buffalo Bob and Clarabell the Clown, and captured the hearts of American youngsters. *Howdy Doody* avoided the

Captain Kangaroo. Prints & Photographs Division, Library of Congress.

satire and occasional cynicism of later children's programming, projecting instead a naïveté that charmed parents and enthralled their offspring.

In 1955, in response to the success of *Howdy Doody,* CBS launched a successful morning children's show called *Captain Kangaroo* (1955–1984). Featuring Bob Keeshan (who had formerly played Clarabell on *Howdy Doody*) as a kind and amiable man who happened to have a collection of equally gentle friends, the long-running series spoke directly to children and never patronized them. ABC, perennially in third place among the Big Three networks, signed a contract with Walt Disney Productions to present some of their family-oriented programming. This decision resulted in the evening *Disneyland* (1954–1961; title changed to *Walt Disney Presents,* 1958–1959, and then *Walt Disney's World,* 1959–1961). The deal to produce *Disneyland* included an afternoon offering titled *The Mickey Mouse Club* (1955–1959). The overwhelming popularity of these shows made ABC much more of a competitor for the remainder of the decade.

The Mickey Mouse Club proved so successful that *Howdy Doody* moved from weekday afternoons to Saturday mornings the following year. With children's TV programming commanding the late-afternoon time slot, the last of radio's old-time adventure serials finally ceased production.

The content of *The Mickey Mouse Club* consisted of items borrowed from the Disney Studio's vast vaults, such as cartoons and documentaries. The Mouseketeers, a group of child performers who sung and danced their way through each afternoon show, enchanted legions of devoted viewers. *The Mickey Mouse Club* actually carried over from similar clubs founded during the 1930s. The Mouseketeers, all wearing their little black beanies with mouse ears, chanted "M-I-C-K-E-Y M-O-U-S-E" like a ritual. Adults remained conspicuously absent from most productions, except for genial Mousketeer leader Jimmie Dodd and sidekick Roy Williams, who drew caricatures and cartoons during the show.

Experimentation

In a different realm, NBC's Sylvester "Pat" Weaver created *Today* and shared with others in the development of *The Tonight Show.* Unique for their use of short, unconnected pieces, both *Today* and *The Tonight Show* initiated a new kind of television format. *Today* made its debut in January 1952 with host Dave Garroway, a role he would retain until 1961. An early-morning mix of news, weather, features, and interviews, the network attempted to capture a new segment of the audience. *Today* got off to a shaky start, experiencing difficulties in picking up sponsors and affiliates, but growing numbers of viewers began turning on their TVs when they arose from bed. When a chimpanzee named J. Fred Muggs joined the cast in 1953, children also began to watch, and the ratings soared; the chimp remained a regular until 1957. Patching in local news and weather every half hour gave the show regional appeal, and *Today* emerged as a consistent moneymaker for NBC. It has become one of the longest-running shows in the history of television, and its popularity dealt another blow to radio, which until then felt assured of the morning audience.

The history of *The Tonight Show* is not nearly as simple as that of *Today.* NBC had experimented with late-night programming, but none of its efforts attracted big audiences. Finally, *The Tonight Show* took form as a local New York City telecast in 1953; it joined the national network in 1954 with the versatile Steve Allen as host. The 90-minute show, a kind of late-night comedy version of the early-morning *Today,* gained a significant audience almost immediately. Allen left in 1957, but comedian Ernie Kovacs took the reins of *Tonight* two evenings a week from October 1956 to January 1957. Then came *Tonight! America After Dark* from January to July 1957, a dismal failure. Finally, Allen's permanent replacement, Jack Paar, came on board that summer. Ratings soared, and Paar hosted until 1962.

THEATER

Although much theatrical activity took place on the local and regional levels throughout the 1950s, New York City's Broadway remained the home for most major productions. For most people, seeing a hit play with big-name performers meant seeing the movie adaptation. Fortunately, the film industry did just that, quickly translating Broadway's best into a string of movies.

Musicals

The biggest theatrical box office grosses came from musicals, most of which soon came out as movie versions.

Many of these musicals have become perennial favorites for local and regional theater productions, and many high school and college drama groups have attempted them as well. *Guys and Dolls, The King and I,* and *The Music Man* can claim countless amateur productions, and *My Fair Lady* and *West Side Story* have become true American classics. In addition, these musicals have crossed the line from being plays seen by an essentially white, middle-class audience living in or near New York City, to plays known by all, from rural to suburban to urban, all races, and all economic classes. They have become part of the collective culture of the nation and certainly qualify as products of popular culture.

Through extensive and well-promoted media interplay, public awareness of Broadway and its top-drawing productions achieved high visibility during the 1950s. The addition of names like

NOTABLE THEATER

Guys and Dolls, 1950 (1,200 perfs.)

The King and I, 1951 (1,246 perfs.)

The Seven Year Itch, 1952 (1,141 perfs.)

The Teahouse of August Moon, 1953 (1,027 perfs.)

The Pajama Game, 1954 (1,063 perfs.)

Cat on a Hot Tin Roof, 1955 (694 perfs.)

Damn Yankees, 1955 (1,019 perfs.)

Inherit the Wind, 1955 (806 perfs.)

My Fair Lady, 1956 (2,717 perfs.)

The Music Man, 1957 (1,375 perfs.)

West Side Story, 1957 (732 perfs.)

Gypsy, 1959 (702 perf. perfs.)

The Miracle Worker, 1959 (719 perfs.)

A Raisin in the Sun, 1959 (530 perfs.)

The Sound of Music, 1959 (1,443 perfs.)

Rodgers and Hammerstein, Cole Porter, Irving Berlin, and Lerner and Loewe assured box office success. As soon as rights could be secured, Hollywood brought out glossy film versions of musicals that had even a modicum of popularity (see "Movies" this chapter). In the meantime, record companies released original cast albums, usually with extensive liner notes. Vocalists and musical groups, especially in the realm of jazz, created interpretative albums of specific musicals, further increasing the listenership of the scores. This flurry of recording activity carried over into radio. Disc jockeys pushed individual songs, and many a composition achieved hit status, both in its original form and in its many adapted versions.

Entertainment

"Serious" Plays

Dramatic plays were also offered to playgoers during the fifties. T. S. Eliot's *The Cocktail Party* (1950) introduced British actor Alec Guinness, destined to make a popular name in films like *The Bridge on the River Kwai* (1957); unfortunately, few saw him in Eliot's play. Arthur Miller's *The Crucible* (1953), and Samuel Beckett's *Waiting for Godot* (1956) also received raves from critics but did not reach truly national audiences.

In particular, Miller's *The Crucible,* ostensibly about the Salem witch trials, concealed a thinly veiled attack on another kind of witch hunt, McCarthyism and the methods of the House Un-American Activities Committee. For its limited Broadway audience, it proved an immediate hit, but Hollywood didn't make a film version until 1996, and regional theater groups mounted few productions of the drama.

Taking a cue from its television success in 1957, Broadway staged William Gibson's powerful *The Miracle Worker* in 1959, starring Anne Bancroft and Patty Duke in the story of the life of Helen Keller. It provided vibrant theater, but only when Bancroft and Duke re-created their stage roles in a 1962 movie did the true mass audience experience this drama.

DANCE

Some elements of modern dance captured a significant audience during the 1950s. Many TV variety shows featured individual dancers or dance troupes who performed routines that could be considered more modern than traditional.

The popularity of musicals, both on stage and on film, allowed for occasional forays into modern dance. Gene Kelly, a popular star in many movie musicals, was an outstanding dancer and choreographer. His roles in the hugely successful *An American in Paris* (1951) and *Singin' in the Rain* (1952) gave him the artistic freedom to direct and star in *Invitation to the Dance* (1956). The picture did not do well at the box office, but it did provide an inventive approach to modern dance. In a technological and editing tour de force, Kelly performs with characters taken from the popular Hanna-Barbera cartoons of the period.

On a more popular front, people attempted to master the mambo, along with other Latin-influenced dances such as the rumba and the merengue. The Cuban cha-cha and the West Indian calypso also attracted dance fans and spawned a number of best-selling records. Old-fashioned

Entertainment

square dancing reappeared as the anything-early-American fad spread into leisure activities. *The Arthur Murray Party* (all networks, various dates, 1950–1960) offered more formal instruction. Hosted by Arthur and Kathryn Murray, two successful and popular dance instructors, the show consisted of a mix of teaching, exhibition, and salesmanship for their studios. Despite its blatant commercialism, the series introduced viewers to ballroom dancing, along with many new novelty steps.

More in keeping with the changing times, Dick Clark's Philadelphia-based *American Bandstand* (ABC, 1957–1987) ran on afternoon network television. Teen-oriented, the show quickly showed national audiences that young people had developed a complex body of dances to accompany rock 'n' roll. The show allowed teens—and probably a healthy number of adults—all across the country to learn the latest dance steps. (See Music of the 1950s.)

Fashion

of the 1950s

In the postwar years, via insistent marketing and advertising, manufacturers convinced consumers of the necessity of updating their wardrobes. New items constantly appeared on the racks, rendering their once stylish predecessors obsolete. In a similar manner, products ranging from automobiles to waffle irons went through model changes, making the 1950s the first true era of planned obsolescence. With more disposable income than ever before, however, Americans accepted this obvious manipulation.

SYNTHETIC FIBERS

In the 1950s, technology and creativity combined to make life easier and better. For clothing manufacturers, this meant an array of synthetic fibers that would be adaptable to any kind of apparel. Led by the giant DuPont chemical corporation ("better things for better living" read the company slogan), acrylics and polyesters came on the market, revolutionizing what people wore. Orlon, a DuPont acrylic, went into production in 1952 and emerged as the material of choice for sweaters and other casual wear; it felt soft and resisted pilling. Thanks to Dacron, DuPont's name for a polyester fiber introduced in 1953, shirts, blouses, suits, and dresses, could be tossed in the washer and hung to dry, emerging fresh and crisp in a matter of hours.

These man-made fibers made possible significant changes in fashion, and because they were synthetic, they could be mass-produced in bold, fluorescent colors, a trend that carried over into bright costume jewelry. Consumers discovered a few disadvantages with these early synthetics: if not cleaned regularly, they took on an unpleasant chemical odor. And, for some, polyesters and acrylics possessed a cheap, artificial look—too crisp, too bright—but most people shopped eagerly for "no-iron, drip-dry" clothing.

In the late 1940s, a Swiss hiker named George de Mestral became annoyed with the various burrs that clung to his clothing when he was outdoors. He noted that the burrs used an ingenious hook-and-loop locking process to catch onto clothing, and from this came Velcro. By the mid-1950s, he had a nylon locking tape in production. He chose "vel" from "velvet," and "cro" from "crochet," and a new fastener came on the market.[1]

WOMEN'S FASHION

Following trends established during the depressed thirties and wartime forties, few American women looked to Europe, much less France, for fashion inspiration. A growing number of young and energetic domestic designers provided plenty of attractive designs, most of which were

An advertisement for Orlon, made by DuPont, showing the benefits of the easy-to-care-for fabric. Courtesy of the Hagley Museum and Library.

quickly translated into inexpensive, ready-to-wear items available at the nearest dress shop or department store. These styles gained a name of their own: the "American Look."

European designers continued to have a limited impact among more wealthy clients. The French design houses, especially those of Christian Dior and Givenchy, along with the Spanish Balenciaga, exported the "New Look" in the early years of the decade. Cinched waists and billowing skirts characterized this import, and costly materials and complex construction placed the New Look out of the financial range of many women. In 1956, the "sack dress" (or chemise dress) appeared on American shores. Initially a subject of ridicule because of its basic shapelessness, women nonetheless bought the design, often in inexpensive knock-offs manufactured domestically. In the later fifties, manufacturers began labeling it a "shift," betting this term would be more acceptable and less liable to ridicule than "sack." The sack/shift/chemise continued

as a favorite for women around the nation, becoming an enduring part of American popular fashion for years.

In the early 1950s, a career woman wore tailored wool suits over silk blouses when going to work. She also donned gloves and a hat, both fashion carryovers from earlier times. To be "dressed up," no woman would think of leaving the house without the proper accessories. The pillbox hat dominated throughout the decade. Her shoes, equally dressy, often came with thin stiletto heels. In cool

A typical outfit for a well-dressed woman in the summer of 1956: a polka dot sun dress, straw hat, and heels. Prints & Photographs Division, Library of Congress.

weather, a clutch coat finished off the ensemble. The simple frocks worn by Mamie Eisenhower more accurately represented the mass market. Despite derision by many fashion commentators, the president's wife epitomized middle-class tastes and values, and her simple wardrobe illustrated the conservative fashions most women chose to wear.

Business executive or housewife, women still found themselves saddled with heavy and constricting underclothing. Bras had wires, complex stitching and padding. Virtually all women wore girdles or corsets. At the beginning of the decade, these "foundation garments" tended to be cumbersome and uncomfortable, but synthetics made possible new, streamlined girdles that allowed for tight, straight, slim skirts and slacks. Garter belts, panties, stockings, liners, slips, and possibly even a large number of petticoats, starched and stiffened, added to the burden.

Films and Fashion

Even with the triumph of the American Look, Hollywood remained infatuated with the mystique of Paris and high fashion. Such frothy movies as *Lovely to Look At* (1952), *The French Line* (1954), and *Funny Face* (1957) allowed endless displays of designer styles. For example, the high-powered casting of Audrey Hepburn and Fred Astaire in *Funny Face* caused the film to do well at the box office, not its costuming.

A contrast between the New Look and the American Look could be seen in the styles worn by actresses Audrey Hepburn (*Roman Holiday* [1953], *Sabrina* [1954], *Love in the Afternoon* [1957], etc.) and Marilyn Monroe (*Gentlemen Prefer Blondes* [1953], *The Seven Year Itch* [1955], *Some Like It Hot* [1959], etc.). The former represented innocence, while the latter exuded glamour. Hepburn was chic; Monroe was Hollywood.

On the glamour side, Monroe presented an image of sex, using her well-endowed figure—even behind costumes—as part of her movie presence. Revealing décolletage and tight outfits was her stock in trade, styles that few American women would, or could, imitate. On the innocent side, the basic black dresses and sailor tops Audrey Hepburn wore became the most copied of all Hollywood costumes during the fifties, fitting in nicely with the simplicity that characterized the American Look. Marilyn Monroe might have had her legions of fans, but the appearance most women strove for emulated Hepburn's gamine/pixie appeal.

Singer-actress Doris Day mediated between Audrey Hepburn and Marilyn Monroe. In a series of successful comedies—*Lucky Me* (1954), *Teacher's Pet* (1958), *The Tunnel of Love* (1958), *It Happened to Jane* (1959), and *Pillow Talk* (1959)—Day came to epitomize the 1950s American woman/girl. Immaculately dressed and coiffed, but in very American fashions that neither glamorized nor hinted at high styles, Day usually played an attractive young woman who, despite the best intentions, got herself into goofy or difficult situations. But she also got out of them, with her honor always intact.

Women's Hair Styles

Younger women frequently wore their hair pulled back in a manner dubbed a "ponytail." Many others, however, wore their hair cut short in a "poodle cut," the perfect clip to accompany a poodle skirt. Both the ponytail and the poodle cut emphasized a girlish appearance, but the poodle cut required bi-weekly trims and many curlers at night. In honor of Mamie Eisenhower, the president's popular wife, and her long-established style of bangs on the forehead, "Mamie Bangs" became an overnight sensation for many women.

Both Toni home permanents and Miss Clairol hair coloring came along in 1950. The famous Clairol advertising slogan, "Does she or doesn't she?" appeared in 1956. Because of their impact, beauty shops across the nation noted a fall-off in business. The enormously successful *Gentlemen Prefer Blondes* (1953) cast Marilyn Monroe (the blonde) alongside Jane Russell (the brunette), suggesting that gentlemen did indeed prefer the blonde look and resulting in 3 out of every 10 brunettes dying their hair blonde.[2] In the late 1950s, bouffant hairdos became popular. The "Bouffant Look" involved putting one's hair in elaborate curlers, or rollers, and applying generous amounts of hairspray to preserve the style. The lacquered hair stood out from the head and could be arranged in numerous styles. Bouffants, however, took patience, and they were somewhat fragile. For women with the time and inclination, however, the bouffant marked a change from all the girlish, natural styles that had flourished earlier in the 1950s.

The rise of the bouffant meant the decline of the hat. As long as a hairstyle remained uncomplicated, a hat could be worn. But the fragility of a bouffant almost always precluded a hat. Only the simplest berets and pillboxes survived, and even they often looked strange atop mounds of lacquered hair.

In the areas of hygiene and makeup, roll-on deodorants gained an immediate following in 1955; "no-smear" lipsticks also came out in 1955 and sold well. Throughout the decade, Max Factor had legions of cosmetic customers; the firm's pancake foundation emulated Hollywood, giving a woman an unblemished appearance. Eye shadow and eyeliner also became commonplace applications.

FASHION TRENDS OF THE 1950s

Clothing continued to become more casual during the fifties. Jeans became popular among men and women, and teens began wearing their own styles, rather than smaller adult clothing.

Women: Separate skirts and blouses; high-waisted slacks end above ankles; sweaters worn over pointed bras; beaded necklaces; patterned fabric; straight line dresses with a matching jacket or cardigan; shorter hair in the early fifties; by end of decade, bouffant and hair in loose waves brushed full at the sides.

Young women: Sheath dresses fitted from bust to hip; full skirts; poodle skirts with appliquéd poodle at or near hemline; sweater sets; saddle shoes; rolled up jeans or Capri pants with Dad's shirts; pony tails.

Men: Popularity of hats drops; sports jackets and sport shirts gain in popularity; crew cuts.

Young men: Duck tail or flat top haircut; Marlon Brando look: black boots and black leather motorcycle jackets; James Dean or "greaser" look: tight blue jeans and t-shirts; pack of cigarettes rolled in sleeve.

MEN'S FASHION

Traditional Attire

American men tend to be traditional in their clothing choices, and the 1950s proved no exception. The conservative, three-button suit dominated business wear. It had narrow lapels, straight legs with cuffs, and often featured shades of gray or other somber colors. Shirts generally came in white or pale blue broadcloth, either in button-down or spread-collar styles.

Narrow ties decorated with subtle patterns or stripes usually accompanied these sedate suits, although equally sober bow ties might have been worn instead.

A plain and serviceable tan or beige raincoat reinforced the uniform look that so characterized male fashion. Rain or shine, a hat completed the outfit, usually a felt fedora for most weather and maybe a Panama style when temperatures rose. Snap-brim hats (the brim was smaller and less pronounced than fedoras) were also in vogue, as were tweedy and velour hats, both variations on the snap-brim design. Regardless of what he wore, the properly dressed man in the 1950s still had to don a hat.

Men's Casual Wear

For the more casual male, Bermuda shorts gained acceptance as warm-weather alternatives to long trousers. Until 1953, such a clothing item would not have been found in a man's closet, but, for some reason, staid, conservative American males liked them. A few daring souls even showed up at the office in jacket, tie, and Bermudas, but that went too far in the minds of most men. By 1959, however, most people considered them entirely appropriate as leisurewear, just another item in any well-stocked closet.

As the decade drew to a close, more and more men's slacks, both casual and dress, lost their bagginess, and the unpleated, cuffless look dominated.

The success and acceptance of rock 'n' roll, especially as personified by Elvis Presley, helped usher in denim as an adult leisurewear fabric. Denim jeans, also called blue jeans or dungarees, had long been associated with low-paid laborers

Man wearing a single-breasted grey flannel suit and hat, popular in 1953. Prints & Photographs Division, Library of Congress.

and juvenile delinquents. Schools forbade them, commentators railed against their bad influence, and adolescents everywhere wanted them. Seen increasingly in movies and on television, jeans continued to carry their negative connotations for many, but for an equally large number they represented freedom from dress codes. By the end of the decade, the stigma attached to blue jeans was wearing off, and more and more men had taken to adding denim to their leisure wardrobe.[3]

Male Hair Styles

Throughout the decade, short hair dominated—crew cuts, flattops, butch cuts (the last thought to go with a tough-guy image), or just simple short haircuts. The crew cut required some attention; many men applied moustache wax or pomade to their hair to keep the cut erect for the day.

Sideburns were often equated with gangsters and hoodlums. But when Elvis Presley and a number of other rock 'n' roll stars sported sideburns, some men quickly adopted them. Overall, though, the hair remained short. As the decade drew to a close, more hair "on the sides and top" became fashionable, pushing aside the crew-cut look.

THE YOUTH MARKET

Unlike prior decades, young people in the fifties constituted a formidable consumer force. They had money and few qualms about spending it, making teenage and young adult fashions one of the most profitable postwar lines of attire. Styles for both children and adolescents became ever more elaborate and varied as manufacturers awoke to the potential market before them.

Instead of owning outfits that mimicked adult styles, young people in the fifties delighted in putting on clothes they could call theirs and theirs alone. For the first time, a unique, identifiable style emerged, and designers jumped at the opportunities presented by this prosperous youth culture.

Young Men's Clothing

Two primary styles evolved for young men in the fifties: the conservative or "preppy" Ivy League look, and the cool "greaser" look. Class and economic lines often determined the choice.

Those bound for college or white-collar jobs opted for the Ivy League style. For formal, dress-up wear, the suit possessed three buttons, often included a vest, and the trousers had unpleated fronts and straight legs. The shirt was an oxford button-down; the tie featured rep stripes or a muted paisley, and the shoes tended to be businesslike wing-tips. The trend as a whole aimed at a kind of elegance, from close-cropped hair to the flawlessly tied Windsor knot on a narrow tie. In fact, the young men of the fifties frequently attired themselves more carefully than did their fathers, who persisted in wearing versions of the nondescript suits of the thirties and forties.

The preppy casual look included tweedy sport coats, unpleated cotton khaki slacks, and oxford-cloth button-down shirts, usually in a solid pastel such as pink, a particular favorite. Some might have fancied a bold waistcoat or vest. These tended to be two-sided reversible garments, with a bright paisley on one side and a more conservative solid color on the other; they were worn with ties and never left open. Sweaters featured either a V-neck or crewneck. Penny loafers (so called because a shiny penny could be inserted into the space on the leather instep), carefully scuffed white bucks or "dirty bucks" (the leather came in a tan or light brown color) completed this studied casualness.[4]

Many junior and senior high school-aged males, along with those who decided against college or engaged in blue-collar trades, bowed to the imagery found in much mass media, choosing the "greaser" or "hood" look. Although it has come to be associated with working-class youth, it also signified rebellion against parental and societal restrictions imposed on youth in general. Nevertheless, fashion rebellions could only go so far. Males still wore neckties for most social affairs. The greaser look included shaped suits and sport coats that often came in charcoal gray or pastel tones and emphasized long lapels that plunged dramatically to the waist; the jacket closed with either a single or double button slightly below the belt line. Slacks, often called "rogue trousers," occasionally sported set-in side seams of contrasting colors; most featured double and triple pleats and pegged bottoms (taken in at the cuff). Highly polished shoes, preferably cordovans (an expensive leather then much in vogue), finished the outfit.

Often a billowing roll collar highlighted dress shirts, and French cuffs with huge, showy cufflinks added the finishing touch. For the truly stylish, these shirts came in bright pink or black, graced by a slender red or black necktie.

More memorable, however, was the casual dress of the hoods and greasers, a look that swept through the ranks of American adolescents. Tight blue jeans, T-shirts, leather motorcycle jackets, wide belts, boots, slicked hair often styled in a ducktail (so called for its resemblance to the tail feathers on a duck), and sideburns characterized the look. The more radical, controversial hood costume included such touches as rolling up a pack of cigarettes in the sleeve of a T-shirt and wearing chains and studs. Its most famous manifestations came in 1954's *The Wild One*, a teen-oriented movie starring Marlon Brando and in 1955's *Rebel without a Cause*, starring the soulful James Dean. The outfits worn on screen evolved into a virtual uniform for everyday wear, and critics associated such dress with juvenile delinquency and a host of other social ills.

School administrators around the country attempted to ban the hood look. Connotations

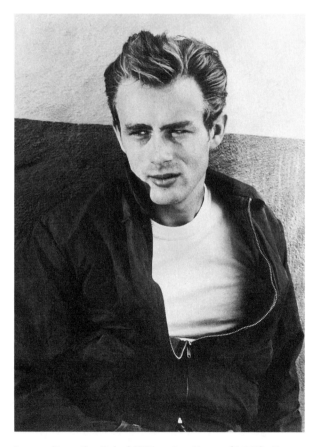

James Dean in *Rebel Without a Cause* (1955). Dean, who was killed in a car accident in September 1955, was emulated by many young people. Courtesy of Photofest.

dictated that anyone wearing this garb was a rebel and a nonconformist, and to worried parents and officials looking tough suggested juvenile delinquency.

Singers Elvis Presley and Carl Perkins both had big hits with the same song, "Blue Suede Shoes," in 1956. The result was a rush to buy suede shoes, preferably blue, of course. Rockers like Presley, Little Richard, Jerry Lee Lewis, and Chuck Berry began influencing all sorts of trademark costumes that teens everywhere admired. Adolescents might not have emulated every item of clothing a star wore, but they were aware of the connections between fashion and music, especially rock 'n' roll.

Young Women's Clothing

Trendsetting magazines like *Vogue* and *Seventeen* helped to usher in the new teenage market by running constant features that stressed youthful fashions. In this way they targeted the growing number of teens in the country. Department stores stayed close behind, setting up teenage departments to cater to the new clientele.

Just like menswear, approaches to youthful fashions differed among various groups. Turned-up jeans accompanied by a white, untucked shirt too large because it belonged to Dad or Big Brother, together formed a virtual uniform for teenaged girls outside of school. They finished off the outfit with bobby sox and loafers or saddle shoes. In all, it served as a comfortable, inexpensive, and very popular style.[5]

The preppy look of the early fifties emerged as a major style success. It featured a full skirt with a tiny waist, its fullness emphasized by the starched crinoline petticoats underneath and at times even a four-foot diameter hoop to maintain its symmetry. The poodle skirt, a flaring skirt often constructed of felt with poodle appliqués and a cinched belt, also burst onto the scene. Though it proved only a momentary variation, it won many adherents. Popular footwear included flats, ballerina shoes that resembled slippers more than anything else. Some young women wore white bucks, as did innumerable males, but most carried a chalk bag to keep theirs spotless; the "dirty buck" look existed primarily for men.

A few teenaged girls took on the trappings of a feminine greaser look. Heavy makeup, tight sweaters over an obviously padded bra, and a general air of lawlessness characterized this appearance. Male or female, the greaser look served more as a statement about rebellion than about fashion.

Both men and women wore Bermuda shorts during the 1950s, and the style had many fans. As an alternative to Bermudas, shorter shorts, or even "short shorts," gained popularity for girls. By 1957, this new article of clothing aroused hot debate among school administrators and public authorities. It centered on what constituted "too short." Adolescents loved the squabble, and a music record, *Short Shorts,* by the Royal Teens briefly made the charts in 1958. Although the debate would continue long after the fifties were over, dress codes began to appear in junior and senior high schools across the nation.

Capri pants offered another choice. Pants that reached only to midcalf, Capris came in a variety of bright colors and could be worn with virtually

Boy in Davy Crockett "coonskin" cap and jacket. Prints & Photographs Division, Library of Congress.

any top, qualities that quickly made them a hot seller. Capris were also called "pedal pushers" because they had no cuffs to catch on a chain when riding a bicycle.

Children's Styles

Durability and practicality characterized most children's clothing. Blue jeans, such the contentious item for adolescents, did not achieve widespread acceptance for kids until the 1960s. Instead, tradition ruled, and items like sun suits, jumpers, and overalls outsold anything new or controversial.

Hardly a fashion or a style, beanies mounted with plastic propellers became a fad for youngsters in 1952. Completely nonfunctional, the propeller rotated in a breeze or when the wearer walked or ran. (See Sports and Leisure of the 1950s.) With the growing popularity of westerns on television,

it came as no surprise that cowboy outfits for boys and girls enjoyed a new life. Fringed jackets, embroidered shirts, jeans, vests, Stetson hats in kids' sizes, and cowboy boots all sold well, with Hopalong Cassidy, Roy Rogers, and Dale Evans ensembles particular favorites. But in 1954 and 1955, *Disneyland* (1954–1990), a popular and long-running show, ran a five-part miniseries depicting the life and times of Davy Crockett. Each segment entertained millions of viewers and set off a merchandising craze for Crockett-inspired items. By far the most successful was the coonskin cap reputedly worn by the woodsman. By 1956, the fad had run its course, but before it was over every little boy and little girl had to have one. Also in the Disney empire was the *Mickey Mouse Club* television show, which led to children clamoring to wear Mickey Mouse Club ears, that is, black beanies with mouse ears.

Food

of the 1950s

FOOD

After the belt-tightening of the Great Depression and the rationing of the war years, Americans felt ready for good food, and the prosperity of the postwar period gave them the freedom to indulge themselves. In response, food manufacturers and distributors offered a cornucopia of new tastes, new recipes, and new ways of preparing dishes of all kinds.

The Kitchen as Cultural Symbol

The 1950s may be remembered as the decade that rediscovered the kitchen, often making it the symbolic center of the modern house. With a return to peace, millions of women had been released from wartime work in order to make room for discharged servicemen, but this created the problem of making use of time once taken by a job. Writers, columnists, and advertisers sought to glorify the role of the housewife in this new society. They assumed that women would find their primary fulfillment in being mothers, wives, cooks, and hostesses. Endless articles claimed that the work that awaited women in the home provided far more rewards than any occupation they might have previously held.

One clever way to celebrate kitchen skills involved having competitions among homemakers. Pillsbury Flour inaugurated its annual Bake-Off in 1949. Designed to promote their flour products, these well-publicized contests also allowed cooks to show off their talents—a reinforcement of the idea that a woman's place was in the kitchen, even if she spent her time there creating new cakes and muffins for competition.

Cookbooks

The leading cookbooks of the period stressed creativity and modernity, urging the contemporary homemaker to take advantage of new technologies. The competent use of rotisseries, grills, blenders, immersible electric skillets, portable mixers, chafing dishes, electric can openers, and all the other postwar appliances flooding the market signified a modern, efficient kitchen. With the right equipment, a housewife could play canasta in the morning, go shopping in the early afternoon, chauffeur the kids after school, or do a dozen other personal chores and still put an attractive, nutritious dinner on the table.

With frozen and freeze-dried foods sometimes encompassing entire dinners and canned goods of every variety available, the old image of slaving over a hot stove and laboriously preparing every dish from scratch lost validity, at least in view of a new generation of cookbooks. Even the traditional casserole was glamorized and modernized, thanks to recipes designed to take advantage of prepared ingredients and easy cooking.

Books like *Betty Crocker's Picture Cook Book* (1950; many editions), *The Complete Small Appliance Cookbook* (1953), and *The Complete Book of Outdoor Cookery* (1955), along with magazines like *American Home, Woman's Day,* and *Ladies' Home Journal,* featured shortcuts and practical hints on using the latest foodstuffs available at the local supermarket. They proved so popular that sales and circulations soared; *Betty Crocker's Picture Cook Book* alone had sold over a million copies by 1951. One best seller, 1952's *The Can-Opener Cookbook,* went through several revisions and editions during the decade, and its title spoke volumes about what modern cooks really wanted.

Incomes also rose rapidly during the 1950s, but the percentage budgeted for food rose even faster. Prepared foods, frozen dinners, snack items, and a wide range of exotic canned goods cost more than traditional groceries, but homemakers were willing to spend the additional dollars to save time.

Supermarkets

To accommodate increased spending for food—and to adapt to changing demographic patterns, especially the growth of the suburbs—new, more modern supermarkets sprang up across the land. Between 1948 and 1958, the number of supermarkets in the United States doubled to over 2,500, with most of the expansion occurring outside central cities. Affluent suburbs benefited most, because the middle-class families moving there tended to spend more on groceries.

At the beginning of the decade, American supermarkets, although in the minority among grocers, accounted for about a third of all sales. By 1959, they claimed roughly 70 percent of all sales, and yet still comprised only 11 percent of all grocery stores. At the same time, they grew in size: by the early 1950s, a typical supermarket carried about 4,000 items, or two to three times as much

as they stocked just before World War II. Their usable floor space doubled during the decade, and their hours lengthened until some in more populous areas stayed open 24 hours a day, 7 days a week.[1]

Suburban supermarkets provided vast parking lots, air conditioning while shopping, bright fluorescent lighting, and huge inventories. It all seemed a far cry from the cramped, stuffy, mom-and-pop stores most consumers remembered from their days in the city.

The modern supermarket became an icon, a showcase for the abundance of America. When England's Queen Elizabeth II visited the United States in 1957, one item on her itinerary was a stop at a typical supermarket. Soviet leader Nikita Khrushchev likewise wanted to see one during his 1959 tour. This modern day successor to the traditional grocery store had emerged as a weapon in the Cold War. To many, its vast array of goods symbolized the triumph of capitalism.

Barbeques

In 1951, Sears, Roebuck and Company offered a new item: a rectangular charcoal grill on an aluminum cart. The age of the home barbeque had arrived. A competing firm added a hood to the basic design; it protected the grill from the weather, while also reflecting heat for faster, more even cooking. By 1957, grills using gas instead of charcoal appeared, and a wondrous array of utensils, aprons, and cooking aids could be purchased. The grill moved cooking to the backyard, making this exterior space an extension of the house. But because cooking on the grass lacked sophistication and class, concrete or brick patios were designed for grilling sites. "Patio dining" and "cookouts" became stylish, and furniture makers rushed to design new lines of outdoor accessories to accommodate the fad.

Grilled food tended to be hearty fare, so the job of cooking all these steaks, sausages, and roasts fell to men, a chore they readily accepted. Males who would not be caught in a kitchen donned aprons, fireproof mitts, and chef's hats as they concocted secret sauces and marinades for their specialties. It proved a curious role reversal, but one most men enjoyed.

THE COOKOUT CRAZE

In 1950s America, one of the most popular recreational activities for middle-class Americans was the family cookout. The word "cookout" emerged between 1947 and 1949 to describe the new trend of the social barbecue, blending outdoor cooking with social networking. Evoking images of family and friends sipping cocktails around a backyard pool while hamburgers and steaks simmer over a grill, the cookout became an iconic American activity. Soon the industry expanded and, by the mid-1950s, companies were offering hundreds of products aimed at the cookout aficionado. From gourmet barbecue sauces and outdoor cocktail sets to stylish clothing for the backyard chef, the cookout developed into a nationwide craze. Cookouts were common in the films of the day, depicted as a glamorous social activity. While the trend was most common among middle-class Americans, it also infiltrated the upper echelons of society, and cookouts became popular among the celebrity set. Style and architectural magazines began emphasizing the backyard patio and poolside as important parts of the decorative environment, and companies produced a wide variety of equipment and furniture to help families set up the perfect cookout environment. While the fad eventually declined in intensity, the appeal of backyard gatherings never fully disappeared and many Americans in the twenty-first century still consider the cookout as an essential all-American pastime.

Popcorn and Other Snack Foods

Popcorn has been around for thousands of years. Native Americans reputedly ate the cooked kernels long before the arrival of Columbus, and it had been a familiar item for many years on American grocers' shelves. But the popcorn of the early 1950s also had its drawbacks: as corn loses its water content, it also loses its unique quality of expansion, or "popping." Consumers therefore expected a fair number of "duds" or "old maids," as unpopped kernels were (and still are) somewhat quaintly called. In 1952 an agronomist named Orville Redenbacher created a hybrid corn that retained moisture and thus popped more evenly. Redenbacher could not persuade any of the major popcorn labels to take on his new product, so he began marketing, under his own name, his improved version in the mid-fifties. An immediate success, it served as an ideal product for the new age of TV and snacks such as perennial favorite Chex Party Mix. Chex Mix came into being in the 1950s and was often made during the holidays. It consisted of a combination of the three cereals Wheat Chex, Rice Chex, and Corn Chex, mixed together with butter, Worcestorshire sauce, nuts, pretzels, and more and then baked. Potato chips and Fritos were also popular as party items, snacks to enjoy around the house. For special occasions, dried Lipton Onion Soup mix and sour cream became the perfect dip for chips.

Children and Sugary Cereal of the 1950s

In the late 1940s, Post Cereals introduced a product called Post Sugar Crisp, beginning a revolution in children's breakfast habits. Sugar Crisp was promoted, on the box and in advertisements, by cartoon bears named Handy, Dandy, and Candy. The use of such characters presaged nothing new—Little Orphan Annie, Buck Rogers, Donald Duck, Mickey Mouse, and many others had already promoted various foodstuffs—but the resulting onslaught of sugar-coated breakfast cereals could not have been predicted. Perhaps the wide availability of sugar, after its strict rationing during World War II, awakened a sweet tooth in the American public, and these new, candy-like concoctions helped satisfy it.

Rival manufacturers quickly climbed aboard the sugar bandwagon. Kellogg's Sugar Pops could be found on grocery shelves in 1950, followed closely by the same company's Sugar Frosted Flakes. Tony the Tiger served as the spokesman, telling kids everywhere that "they're gr-r-reat!" In case they missed any finicky children, Kellogg's continued with Sugar Smacks in 1953. By this time, the sugar content had reached 56 percent, and Cliffy the Clown smiled at youngsters from the box. Later in 1957, Smaxey the Seal was happy to invite children to eat Sugar Smacks.

Rocky and Bullwinkle, hits in a popular television cartoon series called *Rocky and His Friends* (1959–1961), touted Trix, a new General Mills cereal that boasted 46 percent sugar content. And, to be on the safe side, General Mills also had Frosty-O's, this time with the Frosty-O's Bear lending encouragement. The sugar sweepstakes intensified as the 1950s progressed, leading to such inventions as Kellogg's Cocoa Krispies and General Mills's Cocoa Puffs.

The rise in popularity of television brought out endorsements from many new TV celebrities. Hopalong Cassidy, a favorite cowboy in early television, represented Post Raisin Bran, the beloved Howdy Doody stepped in for Rice Krispies, and Tom Corbett, Space Cadet on television, promoted three Kellogg's brands: Pep, Corn Flakes, and Raisin Bran. Even Superman pushed Sugar Smacks, with Clark Kent urging the chief, Perry White, to try some in one commercial of the early 1950s.[2]

Pizza

Pizza had been introduced in America by the thousands of Italian immigrants who arrived in the late 1800s and early 1900s. However, it had yet to capture the American imagination en masse. In 1943, as Jean Anderson observes, Ric Riccardo and Ike Sewell began serving a new kind of pizza at Pizzeria Uno, their north side Chicago restaurant. They encased cheese, tomatoes, and sausage in a thick, high crust baked to golden perfection—they called their creation deep-dish pizza. People flocked to Uno's and before long other pizza makers began copying their pizza and by the end of the 1940s deep-dish pizza became nationally known as Chicago-style pizza.[3] In contrast, New York-style pizza differed in that it featured a thin crust that was only on the bottom of the pizza—it wasn't as yeasty a pie as its Chicago counterpart. But most people liked both kinds of pizza, and the dish became nationally loved. In its early incarnations, pizza was sometimes known as "tomato pie," and in the 1950s, more widely as "pizza pie." In the 1950s, pizza places began being franchised, a practice that, as evinced by the success of chains like Little Caesar's, Pizza Hut, and Domino's, continues to flourish in the twenty-first century.

Frozen Foods

Most of the problems associated with freezing foods and preserving their freshness and tastiness had been solved by the early 1950s. Thereafter, the frozen-food industry boomed, growing fourfold during the decade. Some 2,500 different frozen-food plans across the country offered home delivery of specified frozen foodstuffs. Participants checked off the desired fruits, vegetables,

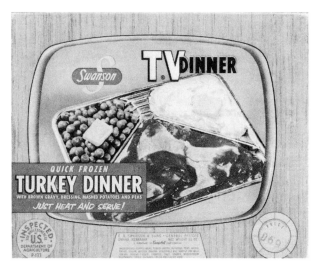

An original Swanson's TV Dinner, left. In 1954, it originally sold for 98 cents in a package with a picture of a TV set with knobs. It became the first TV dinner, which changed American culture so much that the original package is now in the Smithsonian. A more recent version is pictured to the right. AP Photo.

TV dinners, desserts, and so forth, from handy lists, called in the order, and the items would be delivered to their doorsteps.

In 1951, the Omaha-based Swanson Company began selling frozen turkey potpies nationally. They had a surplus of turkey, and took a gamble that homemakers would like the convenience of

FOOD HIGHLIGHTS OF THE 1950s

1950 High school dropout William Rosenberg opens a small doughnut and coffee shop in Quincy, Massachusetts, and calls it Dunkin' Donuts. He licenses the first of many franchises in 1955.

1950 *Betty Crocker's Picture Cook Book* (also known as "Big Red"), the first of more than 200 cookbooks written under the name of the fictional Crocker, is published.

1952 The Wiener Whistle—a bright red and yellow plastic whistle shaped like a hot dog— appears in packages of Oscar Mayer All-Meat Wieners as a promotional giveaway.

1952 Introduction of Cheez Whiz, a pasteurized processed cheese spread.

1954 Seventh-grade dropout Harlan Sanders founds Kentucky Fried Chicken.

1954 Swanson introduces Swanson TV Dinners.

1957 General Foods Corporation rolls out "a new instant breakfast drink discovery!," Tang, a powdered, orange-flavored drink mix added to water to make a beverage. In 1962, astronaut John Glenn drinks it in orbit during food experimentation, but contrary to popular belief, Tang was not invented by or for NASA. It does, however, become more popular after its link with the space program.

1957 Emerson Drug Company, maker of Bromo-Seltzer, introduces Fizzies, tablets that create an instant carbonated soda drink when dropped into water. Marketed to children as well as adults, the popular tablets are discontinued in 1969 when the cyclamates they contain are linked to certain types of cancer.

1959 Jiffy Pop, popcorn sold packaged in its own heating pan, hits the supermarkets.

a meal that required only heating before serving. The potpies did well, and in 1954 Swanson expanded their line to include a turkey dinner that came in a stamped aluminum tray divided into sections that held dressing, potatoes, and buttered peas along with the turkey. To reinforce the idea that this dinner had been designed for eating while watching television, the box it came in resembled a TV screen. The "picture" represented the meal inside, and the "knobs" allowed for product information. By the time the giant Campbell Soup Company bought Swanson in 1955, the Nebraska firm was shipping 25 million TV dinners a year.

When Swanson first started distributing its potpies and TV dinners, few dining rooms or kitchens contained television sets. The popularity of TV dinners in general prompted the design and mass production of TV trays—small, collapsible metal or plastic trays that could be set up in the living room in front of the television receiver. Consumers bought millions of them during the 1950s, which meant they ate supper while watching their favorite shows, a telling comment about both the impact of television and the growing informality that characterized the decade.[4]

Appliances and Other Kitchen Helpers

The 1950s not only witnessed a number of new foods and approaches to their preparation, but also a rapid expansion of kitchen technology. For example, Tupperware, a line of storage containers made from flexible polyethylene, took off in 1951 with the clever marketing ploy of the "Tupperware Home Party." The containers themselves, invented in 1940 by Earl S. Tupper, had been available in stores since 1945, but sales and interest lagged. In 1951, Tupper hired Brownie Wise to oversee home parties where Tupperware products would be sold directly to individuals. Wise capitalized on the idea of women working and socializing simultaneously. A uniquely direct selling system, known as the "Hostess Plan," used churches, clubs, and sororities, as well as friends and neighbors to sell to one another. Tupperware Parties became an overnight success, and soon the versatile plastic could only be obtained this way—the pastel bowls with the tight lids had been withdrawn from stores.

The Tupperware Party symbolized the suburban 1950s, and in 1954, Wise became the first woman ever to appear on the cover of *Business Week*. Tupperware, available in popular 1950s colors, affirmed the machine aesthetic, a utilitarian product that could be economically massproduced, and it caught the imagination of millions of consumers.[5] In 1952, the Dow Chemical Company introduced Saran Wrap. The first of many flexible plastic wraps, it gave an airtight seal around just about anything.

Faster cooking seemed to be on the horizon in 1954, when the Raytheon Company brought out the Radar Range, the first gasless, flameless cooking device on the market. The invention cooked foods by bombarding them with microwaves. The Radar Range's large, bulky size and high price tag made it practical only for commercial use. In the 1960s smaller, more affordable microwave ovens appeared in appliance stores, but these compact units, so new and so different, took a long time to gain public acceptance. It wasn't until the mid 1970s that households begin to buy them in significant numbers.

Refrigerators, on the other hand, had by 1950 become a standard appliance. The challenge for manufacturers involved how to render existing refrigerators obsolete in their owners' eyes. Here again the idea of planned obsolescence did not limit itself to the automotive field and yearly model changes; the enormous appliance market likewise entertained the concept. In 1951 Westinghouse introduced a line of refrigerators that automatically defrosted themselves. By 1954, General Electric advertised models available in several colors instead of just white.

Not to be outdone, Kelvinator introduced in 1955 the first side-by-side refrigerator, the "Foodarama." Instead of a freezer and a refrigerator served by a single door, their model featured a door for each function. Three years later Whirlpool extolled their first frostless model, a design so advanced that it eliminated defrosting of any kind.

An American chemist at the DuPont Company created Teflon in 1938, but not until 1948 did the company begin to employ it for industrial purposes. A French inventor perfected a way to make the plastic adhere to aluminum, and his discovery was marketed abroad as Tefal in the 1950s. Teflon-coated pans finally made their way across the Atlantic late in the decade, but the response to Tefal/Teflon remained tepid.[6]

Fast Food

As Americans moved to the suburbs, their jobs more often than not remained in the city. This trend may have added to the nation's mobility, but it also meant people traveled farther to work and spent more time on the road and less time with their families. Increased activities took young and old away from their homes, and a rush to eat began to characterize the typical suburban kitchen. No more sit-down dinners with everyone present; families ate frozen dinners and other prepared foods, often on the run or alone in front of a television set.

This speeding up of American life did not limit itself to the home; when on the road, people wanted restaurants that offered food in a hurry. In response, the restaurant industry promoted fast food, food that could be prepared and consumed, literally, in minutes.

In 1954, salesman Ray Kroc peddled a product called Malt-A-Mixer, or Multimixer, a device for making multiple milkshakes in restaurants. On a visit to the McDonald Brothers' hamburger stand in San Bernardino, California, inspiration hit: he envisioned a restaurant that massproduced not just milkshakes, but all the other items that have come to be associated with fastfood establishments. The McDonald brothers had already franchised eight of their stands; after some negotiation, Kroc acquired future franchising rights to expand the number of McDonald's stands, although the brothers retained their original operations. Following some management disagreements, Kroc purchased the entire chain from the brothers in 1961, along with their name, and proceeded to create the hamburger empire that still calls itself McDonald's. The distinctive golden arches, the company trademark, had first appeared in 1953. Six years later, Ray Kroc had some 145 McDonald's stands across the nation, with thousands more to come.[7] (See Architecture of the 1950s.)

The Development of Some Prominent Fast-Food Chains during the 1950s

Year	Establishment	Location
1950	Dunkin' Donuts	Quincy, Massachusetts
1951	Jack in the Box	San Diego, California
1952	Church's Fried Chicken	San Antonio, Texas
	Kentucky Fried Chicken	Corbin, Kentucky
1953	Sonic (Top Hat Drive-In)	Shawnee, Oklahoma
1954	Shakey's	Sacramento, California
	Burger King (InstaBurger)	Dade County, Florida
1955	McDonald's (Ray Kroc)	Des Plaines, Illinois
	Mister Donut	Revere, Massachusetts
1957	Gino's	Baltimore, Maryland
1958	Pizza Hut	Wichita, Kansas
	Burger Chef	Indianapolis, Indiana

These new fast-food chains deeply influenced American eating habits. For example, the purchases of frozen potatoes, usually in the form of french fries, soared. In a similar manner, ketchup and pickle consumption also rose dramatically. Even iced tea and soft-drink sales were affected by this phenomenon. Burger, fries, and a Coke quickly emerged as standard fare for millions of Americans (see "The Development of Some Prominent Fast-Food Chains during the 1950s").

Haute Cuisine

As food grew increasingly convenient, the inevitable cost was taste. For many, that seemed an acceptable trade-off. A minority, however, opted for flavor and a more aesthetic approach to food. With so much kitchen technology available, why be merely a cook when one could be a chef?

The reasons behind this shift in attitude evolved slowly and often had little to do with food. For example, the 1950s saw transatlantic air travel become a reality available to many people. And, with broadened horizons and exposure, more and more Americans experienced true foreign foods, not their Americanized imitations. Popular travel books and guides devoted considerable space to dining abroad, with the result that larger supermarkets and specialty stores began to stock items from distant shores.

For both the traveler and the stay-at-home, magazines like *Gourmet* (founded 1941) offered exotic recipes and advertising that tempted both eye and palate. Their circulations rose, prompting the publication of Samuel Chamberlain's *Bouquet de France* (1952) and Fernande Garvin's *The Art of French Cooking* (1958), two cookbooks that appeared on best-seller lists. At the same time, newspaper and magazine columns brought food experts like James Beard and Craig Claiborne a measure of popularity, and their appearances on television cooking shows introduced more foreign fare to millions.

DRINK

Almost 20 years had passed since the repeal of Prohibition, and the opinions of Americans toward the consumption of alcohol had mellowed. In addition, millions of people served in the armed forces during World War II, exposing them to cultures with more permissive attitudes about drinking. At home, virtually everyone consumed soft drinks, and an overwhelming majority also drank coffee or tea.

Alcoholic Beverages

During the 1950s, hard liquors—whiskey, Scotch, gin, vodka, rum, and the like—gained widespread acceptance. Consumption of liquor in general rose from 190 million gallons to 235 million gallons between 1950 and 1960. Hollywood capitalized on the implied stylishness of drinking in movies like *All About Eve* (1950), *My Man Godfrey* (1957), and *Auntie Mame* (1958). These films vividly celebrated the conviviality associated with the use of alcohol, adding to the mystique surrounding liquor, fashion, and elegance.[8]

Overall, the cocktail epitomized drinking and the 1950s. As long as they did not seem too exotic or outlandish, cocktails ruled as the drinks of choice for the middle class and above. Martinis, manhattans, gimlets, old-fashioneds—were served in restaurants, classy bars, and even in suburban homes. For example, the martini, a potent concoction made from gin and vermouth, emerged as a status drink during the decade. To many, a well-made martini represented sophistication and the pursuit

Food

of perfection. A popular assumption insinuated that those on the way up, or those who had already gotten there, drank martinis. And if media imagery had any validity, men and women in equal numbers consumed them. Cocktails, either at home or in a lounge, became an American ritual.

Throughout the decade, books, movies, recordings, and magazines regularly depicted drinking, an explicit endorsement of the practice. In *The Catcher in the Rye* (1951), J. D. Salinger's classic adolescent novel, even the youthful Holden Caulfield visits a cocktail lounge because he knows drinking signifies an important rite of passage in America. (See Books, Newspapers, Magazines, and Comics of the 1930s.)

In the film *The Big Hangover* (1950), star Van Johnson exhibited a peculiar weakness for alcohol, more an allergy than an addiction. One sip and he went out of control, which made for a silly commentary on imbibing, but the point about the dangers inherent in alcohol consumption was nonetheless driven home. "Days of Wine and Roses," presented as an episode of television's *Playhouse 90* in 1958, took a much more serious view of problem drinking. Starring Cliff Robertson and Piper Laurie, the story involves an upwardly mobile young couple who descend into alcoholism. Sophistication slides into degradation as they find themselves powerless to fight their addiction. (*Days of Wine and Roses* went on to became a successful movie in 1962, starring Jack Lemmon and Lee Remick.)

Songwriters also addressed drinking issues, often memorably. In 1943, *The Sky's the Limit*, a movie starring singer/dancer Fred Astaire. Astaire sings "One for My Baby (and One More for the Road)," a mournful lament, but the song languished until 1954, when *Young at Heart* appeared in theaters. Frank Sinatra and Doris Day shared the leads, allowing Sinatra to croon "One for My Baby" and make it his own. Recorded a number of times during the 1950s, "One for My Baby" would henceforth be associated with Sinatra, lost love, and drowning sorrow in a bottle.

A cocktail party of the 1950s, given by millionaire Robert P. McCulloch at his impressive modern house. Photo by Loomis Dean//Time Life Pictures/Getty Images.

Not every piece of music dealing with drinking during the fifties focused on the lugubrious side of alcohol. The Clovers, a popular vocal group, recorded "One Mint Julep" in 1951. Bandleader Buddy Morrow cut an up-tempo instrumental version of the song in 1952 that became an instant hit. Many other areas of popular culture, especially print advertising, endorsed drinking. (See Advertising of the 1950s.)

Other Beverages

Coca-Cola completely dominated the soft-drink industry in the early years of the decade. *Time* magazine even had the Coke logo on its cover in 1950, and the accompanying article talked of its amazing popularity around the globe. The company claimed 69 percent of the U.S. market, whereas Pepsi-Cola could only attract about 15 percent. A strong television marketing campaign by Pepsi throughout the fifties did narrow Coca-Cola's lead somewhat, however.

Coca-Cola maintained its dominance in the highly competitive industry by utilizing stylized illustrations of wholesome pretty girls enjoying a Coke. These illustrations, usually unsigned, were recognizable to millions. Always decorous, they appeared around the world as the company expanded its bottling and franchising efforts during the 1950s.[9]

The ubiquitous red and white Coca-Cola colors could be found in insulated coolers, on board airliners in special carriers, and, of course, at the fast-food shops and drive-ins springing up around the country. In 1955, amid great advertising fanfare, the company introduced a variety of larger bottles and cans. With all this marketing, and bolstered by instant recognition, familiarity, and endless celebrity endorsements, Coca-Cola must be seen as one of the most successfully advertised products of the 1950s or any other decade. The pretty model holding up a refreshing Coke emerged as an American icon: life was good, and Coke made it better.

The rise of the supermarket cut into Coca-Cola's sales. While most of the smaller, more traditional grocery stores had for years carried only Coke products, supermarkets carried all brands. They granted equal aisle space to Pepsi and others, giving shoppers more choices. In another arena, the two giants competed for exclusivity clauses in the rapidly expanding fast-food chains. For instance, McDonald's served only Coca-Cola, whereas Burger King featured Pepsi products.[10]

In the early 1950s, scientists conducted experiments to find an efficient way to bottle beverages in steel containers. The war in Korea had created some steel shortages, slowing development, but progress was made toward perfecting an economical steel container that would not impart a metallic taste to the liquid within. Around 1955, steel cans appeared on grocery shelves, often with conical tops and screw-on caps to preserve carbonation. Three years later, the Coors Brewing Company introduced an aluminum beverage container for its line of beer. These early cans required a separate opener, or "church key" as some called them; the popular pull tabs would not appear until the 1960s.

In keeping with the move toward greater speed and ease in the kitchen, a host of new powdered beverages came on the market. In 1954, Carnation Instant Nonfat Dry Milk became available. Lipton Instant Tea, mixed with boiling water, provided the 1958 consumer a quick cup of tea; the following year, a glass of juice could be made by mixing Tang's orange drink powder with cold water.

Food

Music

of the 1950s

The fifties opened with American popular music in the doldrums. The big bands had disappeared, and smaller groups and vocalists suffered hard economic times. Recording and playback technologies changed, but as far as popular selections went, disc jockeys, already a well-established radio institution by the 1950s, controlled most programming. Not until the mid-fifties would pop music again emerge as a major force in American culture, powered by rock 'n' roll and its young fans.

POPULAR HITS AND TOP 40

At the onset of the 1950s, the public annually purchased about 189 million records, a respectable figure. But as the decade progressed, the numbers rose: 277 million by 1955, and an astounding 600 million by 1960. Rock 'n' roll changed the face of American popular music; the typical record-buyers of the late 1940s and early 1950s were in their early 20s, but by the close of the decade teenagers bought 70 percent of all records.[1]

The content found in most mainstream pop songs of the early fifties was exemplified by two number one compositions: "Cry" (1951) and "How Much Is That Doggie in the Window?" (1953). Singer and teenage heartthrob Johnnie Ray recorded "Cry," a slow lament about lost love. His producers, sensing a possible hit, included on the

"B" side—or "flip side"—of the record another song about tears titled "The Little White Cloud That Cried"; it climbed to number two on the charts. Patti Page cut "How Much Is That Doggie in the Window?" two years later. Its title to the contrary, the lyrics involve a person traveling away from her sweetheart and wanting to get him a puppy as a companion and watchdog. Inserted throughout the tune are barks and "arfs."

Both songs illustrated the vapid sentimentality that characterized much popular music of the first half of the decade. Record producers envisioned a monolithic audience ready to accept their product without question. In reality, composers and musicians struggled with many new approaches to their craft, but their efforts tended not to register with a corporate mentality satisfied with the status quo.

Similarly, American radio dispensed throughout the broadcast day only the most noncontroversial music. Drama and variety shows, displaced by television, had virtually disappeared from network schedules by the end of the decade, and stations at first seemed content to play the Top 40 hits. Unscientific at best, these lists included all manner of music, from western swing to avant-garde jazz, but tended to be characterized by bland songs aimed at an unseen mass audience.

Distinctive patterns of musical transfer from one medium to another existed in the fifties. For example, the background music to the TV detective show *Peter Gunn* (1958–1961) received almost as much popular acclaim as the series itself. A swinging band led by Henry Mancini tried to capture the ambience of smoky nightclubs and lurking danger. An RCA Victor album of soundtrack songs from *Peter Gunn* sold extremely well and made Mancini an in-demand composer, arranger, and conductor.

Because millions of people attended the movies every week, often a single song from a particular film could enjoy hit status. Adding airplay could draw an audience in excess of that which saw the picture itself. In 1952, Hollywood released a western titled *High Noon*. The movie became a big hit, and a song from the soundtrack soared to the top of the charts. "Do Not Forsake Me, Oh My Darling" featured country singer Tex Ritter, and its sad, rambling story attracted listeners and sales.

CHANGING TECHNOLOGY

To facilitate locating radio stations, preset buttons for car receivers appeared on dashboards in 1952. This handy device already existed in home sets. The transistor radio, first marketed in 1954 and adapted for cars in 1956, made music more portable. Stereo recording of music commenced in 1954; by 1958, stereophonic records had become available to the public. These innovations demonstrated the importance of radios and recordings in making the hits of the day readily available to listeners.

Disc jockeys and program managers emphasized playing only the most current and popular songs, so that audiences frequently heard the same numbers over and over, even if they chose to change stations. A fast pace characterized radio programming of the day; it provided the maximum amount of music and advertising. Identifying the station became as important as its selections, because listeners tended to return to specific stations if they thought they could catch their favorite music. The DJs repeatedly proclaimed call letters and frequencies in order to get listeners to return. The Top 40 formula attracted a broad audience, and over 1,000 such stations could be heard across the country at the end of the fifties.

Record Speeds and High Fidelity

Until the end of the 1940s, the 78-rpm recording completely dominated the market. The records themselves tended to be heavy and breakable; the relatively high speed meant faster wear and increased surface noise. Most of the records measured 10 or 12 inches in diameter, which meant about three to five minutes playing time per side.

Columbia Records had, in 1947, introduced the 33⅓ rpm recording. This slower speed allowed for much longer recording and playback times, as a result, new albums contained numerous songs, or tracks. The "33" or "LP" (for long playing) enjoyed huge success, but did not replace single-play recordings.

In 1949, RCA Victor introduced its 45-rpm singles, seven-inch records (one song per side) with a large, one-and-a-half-inch center hole. Manufactured with lightweight vinyl instead of the more brittle shellac of 78s, their slower speed meant clearer, less-scratchy sound and greater durability. RCA wisely marketed a single-speed 45-rpm player early in the fifties. Compact, portable, and virtually unbreakable, it featured a fat, one-and-a-half-inch spindle that accommodated the new discs. An instant hit with teenagers everywhere, 45-rpm records and players took possession of the singles market, a fact reflected in steadily rising sales throughout the decade, accounting for 98 percent of all single sales by 1959.

With 78s, 45s, and 33s all on the market, consumer confusion resulted. The sales of 33⅓ albums soared throughout the fifties, but it would take time for record buyers to adjust to the new technologies of record reproduction for single discs. For many years, makers of record players had to make their units adjustable to three speeds (33⅓ rpm, 45 rpm, and 78 rpm) and two needles (one playback needle for the older 78s people still had in their collections and the other for the newer microgrooved 45s and 33s).[2]

SINGERS

Both male and female singers dominated the popular market during the early fifties. Among the men, the choices ran the gamut from relative old-timers like Bing Crosby ("True Love," 1956) and Frank Sinatra (*Songs for Swingin' Lovers*

Music

album, 1956) to fresh-faced newcomers like Eddie Fisher ("Oh! My Pa-Pa," 1953) and Johnny Mathis ("Wonderful! Wonderful!" 1957), to the operatic arias of tenor Mario Lanza ("Be My Love," 1951). The women more than held their own: Teresa Brewer ("Let Me Go, Lover" 1954), Doris Day ("Que Sera, Sera," 1956), Connie Francis ("Who's Sorry Now?" 1958), Peggy Lee ("Fever," 1958), Patti Page ("The Tennessee Waltz," 1950), and Jo Stafford ("Shrimp Boats," 1951) could match any of their male counterparts in the competition for hits and sales.

Vocal groups, usually trios or quartets, also had their moments on the Top 40 charts. The Four Aces recorded "Heart and Soul" in 1952, and the Hilltoppers reached hit status with "P.S., I Love You" in 1953. On the female side, the Andrews Sisters continued a long string of successes with "I Can Dream, Can't I?" in 1950 and the McGuire Sisters made the charts in 1954 with "Goodnight, Sweetheart, Goodnight."

While singers (Frank Sinatra, Bing Crosby and others) who had started singing with bands gained even greater success in solo careers, the fifties witnessed the decline of the big bands, those large aggregations that seemed so invincible during the thirties and forties. Many orchestras simply disappeared; others broke up into quintets and sextets in an attempt to remain active, and a hardy few hung on, hoping for a renaissance that never materialized.

JAZZ

Constant experimentation and exploration marked the decade. The music clearly had a popular following, but the audience divided into various and competing preferences. Labels for schools of jazz abounded, such as Dixieland, cool, bebop, funk, progressive, and West Coast. Tommy Smalls, better known as "Dr. Jive," drew impressive audiences for his radio shows. What's more, he owned a nightclub, Smalls Paradise, in Harlem that was a favorite with rhythm and blues bands. His influence was such that even Ed Sullivan, the host of television's *Toast of the Town,* had him organize a segment that showcased the talents of many black entertainers who would otherwise not get such national coverage.[3]

Some of the most innovative jazz was improvised and played during the 1950s, by such performers as Miles Davis, Bill Evans, the Modern Jazz Quartet, Art Blakey, Charlie Mingus, John Coltrane, Ornette Colman, Thelonius Monk, and more, to name only a small number of outstanding performers and composers. Yet, despite all the experimentation in jazz throughout the period, the overwhelming majority of fans preferred mainstream music with a danceable rhythm and obvious melody.

The growing audience of jazz, albeit one divided into many niches, convinced producer George Wein to stage an outdoor festival at staid Newport, Rhode Island, during the summer of 1954. He featured musicians from all schools, and it attracted a sell-out crowd. The Newport Jazz Festival went on to become an annual event.

COUNTRY AND WESTERN

Although it lived on the fringes of true popular culture throughout the 1950s, country music did find a growing audience, both rural and urban. For the most part, the larger radio stations ignored it. When it finally gained precious airtime, it usually occurred on small, low-power stations located primarily in the Southeast, Midwest, and Southwest. In the more densely populated upper half of the nation it received little exposure. But the demographics that would eventually favor country tunes were changing. During World War II, a great many rural Americans had made the move to large cities to take jobs in the burgeoning defense industries; they brought with them a rich heritage of music that most of their new urban neighbors knew little about. As the postwar years progressed, increasing numbers of independent radio stations began to play this music as part of their daily broadcasting.

Hank Williams, the first musician in this genre to reach the big time, had a string of hits that virtually defined country and western for years to come. "I'm So Lonesome I Could Cry" (1950) and "Your Cheatin' Heart" (1952), with their stories of torment and suffering, inspired the later music of a generation of performers. Williams himself died in 1953, when he was just 29, having lived the life he portrayed in his music.

Patsy Cline got her break when she appeared on the popular television series, *Arthur Godfrey's Talent Scouts* in 1957. Her theme song, "Walkin' After Midnight," soared to the top of both the country and the popular charts. Her success helped pave the way for both women and country artists in general to cross over successfully into the more lucrative field of pop music.

Two brothers, Don and Phil Everly, combined their talents and produced a string of country-tinged hits beginning with "Bye, Bye Love" and "Wake Up, Little Susie" in 1957. They followed those successes with "All I Have to Do is Dream" and "Bird Dog" in 1958. With a strong beat and

HOW OTHERS SEE US

Cowboys: The New Samurai

The postwar occupation of Japan by the United States led to cultural mixing on a grand scale, especially when the unintended consequences of the occupiers' rules and regulations came into play. When, in an effort to short circuit Japan's martial traditions, General Douglas MacArthur decreed a ban on samurai stories, Japanese publishers turned to an American-based alternative: the western. By 1953, comic books aimed at young boys included the adventures of American cowboys like Tim Holt in translation, as well as original Japanese stories with Old West themes; radio serials featured characters like the Chakkari Kid shooting out of ambushes. Young Japanese boys could be seen at play in full western regalia, complete with pint-size cowboy hats and holstered toy six-shooters.

At the same time, country and western music surged to popularity in Japan, propelled in part by the pop crossover hits that country stars like Hank Williams were enjoying on the American hit parade. Japanese musicians formed bands with names like the Chuck Wagon Boys, the Western Ramblers, the Wagonmasters, and the Straw Hat Band. These groups incorporated American instruments like the banjo alongside the traditional Japanese samisen. With musicians dressed in high-heeled cowboy boots and ten-gallon hats, they attracted American G.I.'s and Japanese music fans alike.

a nasal twang, they expanded the parameters of popular music, leading to the amalgamation of country music, rock 'n' roll, and traditional song formulas, a mix usually called "pop rock."

FOLK MUSIC

Like country and western, folk music usually dwelled at the edges of popular American music. In 1958, however, a crew-cut, buttoned-down group of young men called The Kingston Trio began to inch up the pop charts with hits like "Tom Dooley" (1958) and "M.T.A." (1959). The trio resurrected old American melodies, as well as wrote their own compositions, and they added a bit of contemporary gloss to their arrangements, making them popular with a wide range of audiences. Their "Scotch and Soda" (1958) and "Sloop John B" (1958), demonstrated that folk songs could be melodic and fun, steering clear of the political or social overtones that marked much of the music by musicians who would follow them.

ROCK 'N' ROLL

The year 1953 marked a turning point in American popular culture. A certain band broke onto the music scene with a raucous number called "Crazy Man Crazy." They followed it with their hit version of "Shake, Rattle, and Roll" in 1954; this tune had originated with Big Joe Turner, an African American bluesman little known to white audiences at the time. The hit, the one millions of young people bought and knew, was performed by Bill Haley and His Comets. Their arrangement, along with the earlier "Crazy Man Crazy," electrified record buyers, most of whom had never heard music quite like this. The group added to their success with "Rock Around the Clock" (1954), another up-tempo number that helped make "rock" a part of the national lexicon. "Rock Around the Clock" also played on the soundtrack of *Blackboard Jungle,* a violent 1955 film about juvenile delinquency that equated rock music with antisocial behavior. (See Entertainment of the 1950s.)

Sensing a groundswell of youthful approval, Cleveland disc jockey Alan Freed decided to push rock 'n' roll on his popular radio series, *The*

Music

HOW OTHERS SEE US

One, Two, Three O'Clock...

The first international rock 'n' roll hit was "Rock Around The Clock" by Bill Haley and His Comets, a Philadelphia-based country/blues band. The song was recorded and released in the United States in 1954, but it didn't make an immediate impact until it was chosen for use in a certain movie's soundtrack.

That movie was *Blackboard Jungle,* a story of disaffected inner-city teens and the teacher who reached out to them. Released in the spring of 1955 and starring Sidney Poitier and Glenn Ford, *Jungle* was a huge success with young audiences in the United States and around the world, and they took to the theme song as well. The driving beat of "Rock Around The Clock" caught their attention as it played behind the opening credits, and soon there were reports of teens dancing in the aisles of theaters as the movie began. Sometimes these impromptu dance parties morphed into violence and vandalism, it was said. That spring, "Rock Around The Clock" became the first rock single to hit number one on the American pop charts; in November, it went to number one in Great Britain; the song sold 100,000 copies in Australia shortly thereafter, breaking sales records.

By 1957, when Haley and his band became the first rock act to tour in Europe, young people in most of the continental capitals—including London, Stockholm, Berlin, and Vienna—were "jumping" to "this latest jazz development," as press reports described the new musical trend. (Parisians, it was said, remained immune to the driving beats.) And while some adults decried rock-loving teens as hooligans, barbarians, or worse, others shrugged off the fad as being "no worse than the Blackbottom and Charleston of yesteryear."

Moon Dog Show. His growing audience enjoyed it, and the ratings shot up. In fact, Freed would later claim that he created the term "rock 'n' roll," although many would say the phrase had long existed among veteran rhythm and blues players as a euphemism for sex. Freed emerged as a leading dance and record promoter as well as a powerful disc jockey. He moved in 1956 to New York City's WINS, where he inaugurated a late-night show that introduced still more listeners to rhythm and blues and rock 'n' roll. The program gained immediate success, and the rock format quickly became established on both national and local radio.[4] Parents, school administrators, zealous ministers and priests, and general upholders of civic virtue combined to attack rock 'n' roll in the waning years of the decade. Overall, the critics had little impact on the music, on sales, or on American teenagers. Rock 'n' roll continued to be the biggest-selling format in American pop.

As for the music itself, nothing terribly original distinguished the work of Bill Haley and his group; black bands had been playing similar music since the 1940s, but the white audience knew little about them. Radio stations, most of which were white-owned, had been effectively segregating music for years. "Race records," recordings aimed at a predominately black clientele, differentiated between white and black bands. Because of such practices, rhythm and blues, which characterized much of this music, went unheard and unappreciated by the majority of listeners.

By the later 1950s, the hybridization of rhythm and blues and rock 'n' roll led to hits like "Blueberry Hill" (Fats Domino, 1956), "Searchin'" (the Coasters, 1957), "Chantilly Lace" (the Big Bopper, 1958), and "Kansas City" (Wilbert Harrison, 1959). Significantly, most of these artists were black, and their success portended a major racial breakthrough in popular American music. Although most black musicians continued to labor in the shadow of their white counterparts, many black artists finally blossomed into recognizable stars in their own right. The era of white performers dominating the popular charts drew to a close. Chuck Berry (1926–), had some fame in the 1950s for such lasting hits as "Maybellene" (1955), "Roll Over Beethoven" (1956), "Sweet Little Sixteen" (1958), and "Johnny B. Goode" (1958), but it was not until decades later that his

Chuck Berry, 1959. Prints & Photographs Division, Library of Congress.

contributions received the credit they deserved, with some ranking "Johnny B. Goode" as the best rock and roll song ever composed and performed, and Berry as the father of rock 'n' roll.

In light of this change, some white rock 'n' rollers attempted to incorporate a more authentic rhythm and blues element into their music. For example, in 1957 Jerry Lee Lewis struck a responsive chord with youthful audiences with his "Whole Lotta Shakin' Goin' On" and quickly followed that with "Great Balls of Fire." Together, his two records sold millions of copies. For many white artists, an easy approach to audience acceptance involved performing covers of songs popularized by black performers. For example, Ricky Nelson's "I'm Walkin'" (1957) grew out of the original by Fats Domino (also 1957); the McGuire Sisters' "Sincerely" (1955) came from an original by the Moonglows (1954); and the aforementioned "Shake, Rattle and Roll" (1954)

by Bill Haley and His Comets was first recorded by Joe Turner, also in 1954. The numbers of such covers precludes any definitive listing, but it was obvious that the practice was widespread. The use of white artists to cover black performers represented a continuing fear among record producers: somehow black artists could not attract a large (i.e., profitable) white audience. They would be proved wrong, but it took much of the decade to convince them. In fact, one of the singular accomplishments of 1950s music involved the eventual success of integrating black performers into the previously all-white mainstream. In many ways, this blending of musicians and compositions served as a preview of the civil rights triumphs of the late fifties and early sixties. Popular American music moved far ahead of social change, and it helped open many doors previously closed to minority artists.

Teenagers deserved much of the credit for the integration of black and white musical forms. In their record purchases, concert attendance, and other measurable preferences, they displayed a remarkable lack of bias when it came to music—especially rock 'n' roll.[5]

Teenage slang, always a sure means of separating teens from adults unsure of the nuances of new meanings for old words, took on distinct black overtones. The jargon spoken by musicians, especially black jazz musicians—words like "cool," "hip," "crazy," and so forth—was quickly picked up by teens everywhere.

As is the way with adolescents, the more adults condemned rock 'n' roll, the more teens gravitated toward it. Record sales soared, concerts featuring any bands even vaguely connected to this new music sold out, and the movie industry geared up to make a glut of films featuring rock artists. A heady time for all, and no one personified the era better than a young man from Tupelo, Mississippi.

ELVIS PRESLEY

The career of Elvis Presley (1935–1977) began quietly. In 1953, he made a private recording of a song called "My Happiness." In 1954, he cut a series of tracks for tiny Sun Records in Memphis, Tennessee. His version of "That's All Right,

Mama" caught the ears of those whom he had previously failed to impress, especially Sam Phillips, the owner of the label.

Phillips had created Sun Records in 1952. He championed many of the best black blues artists of the day, since the segregated nature of the music business prevented them from getting contracts with the major recording companies. He looked for white singers who could approximate what black vocalists had been doing for years because he wanted to introduce the larger white audience to real rhythm and blues. His solution brought forth a hybrid music called "rockabilly."

Rockabilly blended white country ("hillbilly") music with black rhythm and blues. A dominant rhythm section, coupled with an uninhibited vocalist, created a mix that possessed a lively beat and urged listeners onto the dance floor. Phillips helped foster the early careers of Johnny Cash, Jerry Lee Lewis, Roy Orbison, Carl Perkins, and, of course, Elvis Presley. Unfortunately for Phillips, the success of these new artists meant they soon

Elvis Presley. Prints & Photographs Division, Library of Congress.

left Sun Records and headed for greener, more profitable pastures. He would never be a wealthy part of the rise of rock 'n' roll, but Sam Phillips would always be an integral part.

For Elvis Presley, the early Sun recordings led to a spot on the stage of the Grand Ole Opry radio broadcast in 1954. The positive response to that event led to regular appearances on the *Louisiana Hayride Show.* His star rapidly rising, Presley's career was taken over by "Colonel" Tom Parker, an astute manager if ever there was one. In fact, Parker deprived Sam Philips of his star singer. In November 1955, Parker engineered an RCA Victor recording contract for Presley that would result in an unprecedented string of hits in 1956: "Heartbreak Hotel" (the single sold eight million copies in six months), "Blue Suede Shoes" (Presley's version far outsold Carl Perkins's 1955 Sun recording), "Hound Dog" (first recorded by Big Mama Thornton in 1952), "I Want You, I Need You, I Love You," and "Love Me Tender," making him the hottest new star in popular music.

His RCA Victor album was called, simply, *Elvis Presley* (1956), and it broke all existing sales records. From January 1956 until his induction into the army in March 1958, Elvis Presley had 14 consecutive million-selling singles, an amazing achievement. The king of crossover, most of Presley's hits could be simultaneously assigned to the mainstream, country, rhythm and blues, and rock 'n' roll charts. His appeal was so great that virtually no other entertainer could match him on individual hits. A second RCA Victor album, *Elvis* (1957), likewise soared to the top.[6]

In 1956, Parker successfully negotiated a movie contract for Presley. His first release was to be called *The Reno Brothers,* but the inclusion of the ballad "Love Me Tender" convinced the producers to capitalize on Presley's soaring popularity as a singer. The movie was re-titled *Love Me Tender,* and it cashed in at the box office. Its success led to *Loving You* and *Jailhouse Rock* in 1957, both also titled after songs included in the films. A fourth film, *King Creole,* came out in 1958.

Presley's television appearances on *The Ed Sullivan Show* have become the stuff of legend. Parker worked long and hard to get Presley on the top-ranked variety show in the fall of 1956. He had already appeared on several other programs by that time, but Sullivan ruled the ratings, and Parker knew that a few minutes on his show would introduce Presley to his largest audience ever. Time proved him right; over three-quarters of the American viewing audience tuned in to see him. An instant hit, he appeared three times. The gyrations of "Elvis the Pelvis" had upset enough viewers that CBS took no chances: by his third visit, cameramen had been instructed to shoot him from the waist up. But even the upper half of Presley attracted viewers, and the show drew a record audience.[7]

Elvis Presley projected a controversial image that troubled many Americans. From his rocker black slacks and pink jackets to his superstar satins and gold lamés, Presley delighted in costume. And it went beyond mere attire; his sideburns and brilliantined hair bothered some, and others decried his dancing as lascivious and degrading. But no one denied that his success, along with the acceptance of rock 'n' roll into American culture, announced the arrival of a new, probably unbridgeable, generation gap, along with a revolution in sexual mores. Although Presley would continue to be a superstar until his death in 1977, for the second half of the 1950s his name was synonymous with rock 'n' roll and the discovery of a new musical form.

Riding the crest of unparalleled success, Presley entered the army in March 1958. The greasy

hair came off, and he disappeared into active duty. Upon his return from service in 1960, Presley would immediately reclaim his spot as one of America's top entertainers.

PAT BOONE

Despite the huge success of Elvis Presley, other singers managed to hold their own during the later fifties. Singer Harry Belafonte had back-to-back hits with "Jamaica Farewell" in 1956 and the "Banana Boat Song" ("Day-O!") in 1957; their success spurred a brief public clamor for calypso music. Nat "King" Cole ("Ballerina," 1957), Perry Como ("Dream Along with Me," 1956), Johnny Mathis ("Chances Are," 1957), and Andy Williams ("Canadian Sunset," 1956) epitomized the clean-cut vocalist performing syrupy ballads that offended and threatened no one.

A young vocalist named Pat Boone (1934–) was about the only male singer to challenge Presley with any regularity in the popularity sweepstakes. In 1957, he struck double gold with "Love Letters in the Sand" and "April Love." American teens were torn: the slow, sincere lyrics enunciated by Boone, or the suggestive, dangerous course plotted by Presley ("All Shook Up" and "Jailhouse Rock"). In typical adolescent fashion, Boone and Presley alternated with their respective hits.

Determined to win a broad audience, Boone turned to covers of black hits. In 1955, Fats Domino, a reasonably successful black singer, had recorded "Ain't That a Shame." Boone cut a much less "soulful" version of the song that same year, and it promptly reached number one. Little Richard, a colorful rhythm and blues performer, enjoyed a big hit with "Tutti Frutti" in early 1956. But Boone scored an even bigger hit on the same song; in fact, his 1956 cover of "Tutti Frutti" outsold Little Richard's original. Boone could take raunchy rhythm and blues songs, sanitize them, and have pop hits. Later in 1956, he again took a Little Richard number, this time "Long Tall Sally," and made it acceptable to parents and—more importantly—radio play. For many record executives, Pat Boone singing Little Richard's songs just seemed safer and more proper than hearing Little Richard performing them himself.[8]

Music

HIT SONGS OF THE 1950s

Songs and performers.

"The Tennessee Waltz" (Patti Page)—1950

"Unforgettable" (Nat King Cole)—1951

"You Belong to Me" (Jo Stafford)—1952

"Your Cheatin' Heart" (Hank Williams)—1953

"Sh-Boom" (The Crew-Cuts)—1954

"Rock Around The Clock" (Bill Haley and His Comets)—1955

"Maybellene" (Chuck Berry)—1955

"All Shook Up" (Elvis Presley)—1957

"At the Hop" (Danny and the Juniors)—1958

"It's Only Make Believe" (Conway Twitty)—1958

TELEVISION AND POPULAR MUSIC

Two shows that chronicled the changes in American music were *Your Hit Parade* (NBC, 1950–1958; CBS, 1958–1959) and *American Bandstand* (local, 1952–1957; ABC, 1957–1987; syndicated, 1987–1989). Both attracted primarily adolescents and young adults.

An outgrowth of the enormously popular radio show (NBC, 1935–1937; CBS, 1936–1947; NBC, 1947–1953) of the same name, *Your Hit Parade* premiered on television in July 1950, and soon outshone its radio counterpart. It would flourish for much of the decade, but rock 'n' roll finally did it in at the end of the 1959 season.

What *Your Hit Parade* had accomplished so successfully was to chart the sales and appeal of a weekly list of the 10 top-rated popular songs. Starting at the bottom, the singers and orchestra worked their way up to number one, breathlessly announcing the title with just enough time to perform it. This approach generated audience suspense, and people enjoyed second-guessing the cast, trying to guess which title would hold the coveted position for that particular week.

Radio stations became specialized in the later years of the decade with jazz, classical, country, Top 40, rock, and a number of other varieties playing to niche audiences, and the show's choice of a number one hit no longer necessarily represented everyone's favorite.[9]

In the meantime, Dick Clark's *American Bandstand* made its national network debut in 1957. Prior to that, it had been a local show in Philadelphia, premiering in 1952 with film clips of older pop stars performing their hits. *American Bandstand,* from its inception, reflected an effort by one local television station—Philadelphia's WFIL-TV—to save some money and fill some otherwise empty hours. The networks provided soap operas in the early afternoon, but programming remained the locals' responsibility heading toward dinner time. Records and a disc jockey came cheap; because the shows were frequently simulcast on both radio and TV, a station could stand to make a modest profit in both mediums.

The early *American Bandstand* featured no dancing teenagers, that is, until low ratings drove the producers to innovate. They invited the audience to perform on camera and rate records for "danceability," while live singers lip-synched popular tunes. It looked amateurish and technical problems frequently arose, but viewers loved it. The best move, however, came with the introduction of a new host, Dick Clark (1929–), in July 1956. In no time, Clark emerged as the youthful voice of rock 'n' roll, first in Philadelphia and then across the country after ABC added the show to its late afternoon lineup. Always spiffy in jacket and tie, and blessed with boyish good looks, he reassured nervous parents of young viewers everywhere; he would go on to host *American Bandstand* until 1989.

In 1956, *American Bandstand* did not hesitate to televise blacks and whites together on the dance floor, a picture of diversity noticeably lacking on most home screens. ABC and the sponsors

American Bandstand, with the clean-cut host, Dick Clark, in coat and tie. Prints & Photographs Division, Library of Congress.

expressed nervousness about this breach of unspoken racial rules, but the mostly adolescent audience appeared oblivious. Clark nevertheless had to be insistent about racial mixing from the outset, it being a time when TV still depicted blacks in stereotypical roles or not at all. He also made white America much more aware of black music and its composers and performers. By not backing down to network censors and commercial worries, he helped make rock 'n' roll a dominant musical form, and opened the audience's eyes to social change.[10]

CLASSICAL MUSIC

Classical music enjoyed modest popular success in the 1950s. The improved aural quality of FM enhanced orchestral compositions, and the development of the long-playing phonograph record in 1947 allowed these stations to play selections in their entirety. Unlike AM radio, the inherent limitations of a 3-minute song followed by a 60-second commercial did not drive FM programming. Fortunately, a number of FM stations enjoyed subsidies underwritten by universities and other groups, since a common perception existed among most radio producers that classical music could not draw large audiences. Since AM broadcasters relied on commercial support and usually lived on tight budgets, those lucky FM stations provided outlets for alternative musical programming.

Despite limited broadcasting, serious music, in reality, had a sizable listenership, something borne out by steady record sales throughout the decade. It might not have been popular culture on the scale of rock 'n' roll, but a handful of American composers like Samuel Barber, Aaron Copland, Howard Hanson, William Schuman, and Virgil Thompson found modest success both on FM radio and through recordings.

A young composer and conductor named Leonard Bernstein (1918–1990) emerged as a primary spokesman for classical music to millions of Americans. His compositions, ranging from film scores (*On the Waterfront*, 1954) to operas (*Trouble in Tahiti*, 1952) to blockbuster Broadway plays (*Wonderful Town*, 1953; *West Side Story*,

1957), along with his leadership of the New York Philharmonic, made him a man about music, and his face became familiar to many. Using the medium of television, he undertook to discuss music with shows such as *What is Jazz?* (1956), and introduced young people to the modern symphony orchestra. Bernstein's engaging mannerisms and openness to all musical forms helped the cause of serious music.

Just as Bernstein's star was rising, another major voice in American classical music allowed his to set. Arturo Toscanini, the tempestuous but popular conductor of the NBC Symphony Orchestra, retired in 1954 at the age of 87. For most Americans, Toscanini personified serious music; his recordings on the RCA Red Seal label outsold virtually all other classical offerings, and his weekly radio broadcasts went out to 200 NBC affiliates during the early 1950s. His farewell performance in 1954 drew a huge radio audience and resulted in a standing ovation from those in attendance. Radio would never again have a personality to match Toscanini's, and classical music virtually disappeared from the AM dial.[11]

On Christmas Eve 1951, Gian-Carlo Menotti, a young American composer, premiered an opera destined to become a seasonal classic: *Amahl and the Night Visitors*. Commissioned by NBC television, it proved melodious and accessible. Although Americans generally looked askance at anything vaguely operatic, *Amahl and the Night Visitors* quickly became established as a Christmas favorite and was performed live around the country.

Another event that kept some attention focused on the classical side of music involved cultural exchanges conducted between the United States and Russia. Despite the saber rattling of the Cold War, many in government strongly encouraged continued dialog by exchanging artists. This meant that American orchestras and performers would periodically visit the Soviet Union, and vice versa. Most of the time, though, the performers being exchanged were symphony orchestras, string quartets, and individual classical soloists; only on occasion did jazz musicians or popular performers receive State Department invitations.

Music

Major groups like Bernstein's New York Philharmonic or the Philadelphia Orchestra would find themselves en route to Moscow, and their Russian counterparts would wing their way to New York City. It seemed a good way to establish and strengthen cultural ties between the two superpowers, and it also served as a kind of cultural blackmail: when a diplomatic breakdown occurred, artists would be forbidden to travel from one country to another. After the diplomats resolved their issues, the exchanges resumed.

Sports

and Leisure of the 1950s

SPORTS

Overall, the health of Americans had never been better than in the 1950s. By late in the decade, the increased use of antibiotics lessened the seriousness of many illnesses. For example, the Salk and Sabin vaccines diminished polio's damaging effects markedly. Still, doctors observed that American youth seldom did as well as their European counterparts in various tests of physical fitness and concluded that American kids were out of shape. These findings came to a head with the creation of the President's Council on Youth Fitness in 1957. This group helped spur the development of Little League teams and other kinds of organized sports.

In the realm of professional athletics, the American and National Leagues in 1950 agreed to allow the World Series to be televised. NBC, the network making the request, in turn paid the leagues $6 million for the privilege, thereby ushering in the era of big money, sports and television. At the same time, the 1950s witnessed the beginning of the end of racial segregation in most professional sports.

Baseball

In 1951, Willie Mays made his debut with the New York Giants, as did Mickey Mantle with the New York Yankees. Joe DiMaggio also retired, but the Yankee dynasty continued: from 1949 to 1953, the team won an unrivaled five straight World Series. In 1954, the Cleveland Indians made the record books by winning 111 games during the season; then, in an irony of ironies, they lost the series with four straight losses to the New York Giants.

During the 1956 World Series between the New York Yankees and Brooklyn Dodgers, Yankee Don Larsen pitched a perfect game (no hits, no runs), the first time this extraordinary event had occurred in World Series play, and only the second time in organized baseball since 1922.

The advent of cross-country air travel, especially by jet in the later 1950s, made truly national teams in any sport a reality. Improved transportation signaled the movement of teams westward, something that commenced in 1953 when the Boston Braves shifted to Milwaukee and continued in 1955 with the Philadelphia Athletics going to Kansas City. The St. Louis Browns, however, defied the trend and headed east to become the Baltimore Orioles in 1956. At the conclusion of the 1957 season, New York lost two of its three legendary franchises: "Dem Bums," the Brooklyn Dodgers, moved to Los Angeles, and the New York Giants transferred to San Francisco.

Despite the shifting allegiances of teams, baseball maintained its hold as the national pastime of millions of fans. And supporting a trend apparent

A happy President Eisenhower getting ready to throw out the first baseball to inaugurate the new season in 1956. Standing to the left is Washington Senators manager Charley Dressen and to the right is Yankees manager Casey Stengel. Prints & Photographs Division, Library of Congress.

since the 1930s, Hollywood continued to produce films about the game. *The Jackie Robinson Story* (1950) found Robinson playing himself in a movie about his making history as the first black player in the major leagues.

Basketball

For the most part, basketball remained essentially regional in its appeal. In 1950, a number of leading college teams, including the University of Kentucky, Bradley University, and New York University, received stiff penalties for violating recruiting rules. The scandal dampened public enthusiasm for the sport and led to a Hollywood film entitled *The Basketball Fix* (1951). In an effort to speed up play, the relatively new National Basketball Association (formed 1950) adopted the 24-second shot clock in 1954. This rule stipulated that a team in possession of the ball must shoot within 24 seconds, thus cutting down on stalling and boring low-score games.

An illustration that shows the popularity of watching sports on television in the 1950s, especially baseball. Here, people outdoors are drinking beer and eating hot dogs while watching a World Series game on television. Illustration, Prints & Photographs Division, Library of Congress.

WORLD SERIES

1950 New York Yankees (AL), 4 games; Philadelphia Phillies (NL), 0 games

1951 New York Yankees (AL), 4 games; New York Giants (NL), 2 games

1952 New York Yankees (AL), 4 games; Brooklyn Dodgers (NL), 3 games

1953 New York Yankees (AL), 4 games; Brooklyn Dodgers (NL), 2 games

1954 New York Giants (NL), 4 games; Cleveland Indians (AL), 0 games

1955 Brooklyn Dodgers (NL), 4 games; New York Yankees (AL), 3 games

1956 New York Yankees (AL), 4 games; Brooklyn Dodgers (NL), 3 games

1957 Milwaukee Braves (NL), 4 games; New York Yankees (AL), 3 games

1958 New York Yankees (AL), 4 games; Milwaukee Braves (NL), 3 games

1959 Los Angeles Dodgers (NL), 4 games; Chicago White Sox (AL), 2 games

On a more popular level, the court and ball-handling wizardry of the all-black Harlem Globetrotters inspired two films, *The Harlem Globetrotters* (1951) and *Go, Man, Go!* (1954). Both relied on the comedy routines the famous team had made their own, giving audiences unfamiliar with the story of the Globetrotters a chance to see them in action. At a time when black actors had few chances in mainstream films, these two pictures did well at the box office.

Bowling

By 1950, bowling found itself the country's leading participation sport. It had moved from seedy alleys with human pinsetters, usually boys, to bright, modern establishments that featured fully automatic machines. As the decade wore on, it continued its growth, with leagues of every description forming across the nation.

Boxing

In a nationally televised bout, Jersey Joe Walcott became the oldest heavyweight champion in history by defeating Ezzard Charles in 1951. Thirty-seven at the time, he enjoyed a short-lived reign. In September 1952, Rocky Marciano, having brutally beaten an aging Joe Louis in 1951, knocked out Walcott and gained the heavyweight title. The victory marked Marciano's forty-third straight win with no losses. He held the championship for the next four years, finally retiring undefeated (49–0) in 1956, the first heavyweight champion to do so.

Although boxing fans traditionally paid the most attention to the heavyweight division, in the fifties the middleweights also captured headlines. Sugar Ray Robinson, a graceful and colorful fighter, won the crown in 1951. He proceeded to win and lose the title four times during the decade. But his presence, along with a number of other talented fighters in that class—Rocky Graziano, Jake LaMotta, Gene Fullmer, and Carmen Basilio—made the middleweights considerably more interesting and popular than the heavyweights.

The Joe Louis Story came out in 1953; it featured Coley Wallace as the most popular heavyweight

Sports

champion ever. The film did a modest job of re-counting Louis's trials in private life and his glory in the ring. A more ambitious picture was *Somebody Up There Likes Me* (1956). Paul Newman played middleweight Rocky Graziano, portraying him as a complex, thoughtful person, instead of just a slugger. The film explored Graziano's Italian American roots, and a fine supporting cast raised the picture above the general run of boxing epics.

The Gillette Safety Razor Company, on its *Gillette Cavalcade of Sports* (1948–1960), spurred popular interest in boxing with televised bouts on Friday nights. The long-lived series had such a level of success that occasionally additional sponsored matches were telecast on weeknights. For a time, boxing occupied an important niche in prime-time television.

Football

During the 1950s, professional football surpassed college games in popularity for the first time ever. In December 1958, the Baltimore Colts defeated the New York Giants, 23 to 17 in overtime, to win the National Football League crown in a nationally televised game. With the popular quarterback Johnny Unitas leading the Colts, this game is thought by many to be among the greatest football contests ever. The ratings success of the broadcast did not go unnoticed, and professional football became a regular part of television sports coverage. People everywhere could follow their favorite teams, and individual players emerged as stars in the growing professional leagues. Because football consists of a period of planning followed by a burst of energy within a small, prescribed place, it proved a format ideally suited to television with its alternating schedule of shows and commercials.

In 1957, rookie Jim Brown of the Cleveland Browns began a systematic attack on the football record book, rushing for over 900 yards in his first season. The following year he almost doubled that figure, and continued to rush over 1,000 yards annually well into the 1960s. As a final note, Vince Lombardi, destined to become a football legend in his own time, took over the coaching responsibilities for the Green Bay Packers in 1959.

Golf

The fifties have been called the Ben Hogan era. His attention and devotion to golf brought legions of admirers to the sport. But it took a personable young player named Arnold Palmer to transform golf into the popular game it has become. Palmer led the Professional Golfers Association (PGA) in winnings during 1958; he collected over $42,000 for the year, a new high, and his easygoing manner made him the darling of fans and helped golf take its place as a major sport on television.

Tennis

Despite little public interest through much of the 1950s, tennis nonetheless enjoyed a few moments of popular acclaim. In 1953, American Maureen Connolly captured the women's "Grand Slam" by winning the Australian, French, English, and U.S. singles titles. In 1957, New Yorker Althea Gibson won both the Wimbledon Women's Singles and the U.S. National, the first black to win those crowns. Newspapers, however, devoted more space to Gussie Moran during the early 1950s. She shocked staid galleries by wearing an outfit that included lace panties. For women's sports attire, a new level of casualness had announced itself.

Horse Racing

In 1953, Native Dancer piqued public consciousness by winning the Preakness and the Belmont. Although "the Gray Ghost," as he was nicknamed, failed to win the Kentucky Derby and thus the Triple Crown, he endeared himself to millions. The photogenic horse played with kittens in his stall and seldom paid much attention to his jockeys. He won 21 of his 22 total starts. *TV Guide* magazine claimed he ranked next to Ed Sullivan as a television attraction, and fans plucked at his mane and tail to get some "souvenirs" whenever they had the opportunity.[1]

Track

As a rule, track generates little popular attention, but the early fifties witnessed unprecedented interest in the sport. Milers from many nations were inching up on a mark once considered impossible to achieve: the sub-four-minute mile. Finally, in May 1954, Englishman Roger Bannister ran a 3:58.8 mile, the first to crack the four-minute barrier. With the feat finally accomplished, the under-four-minute mile became almost commonplace. Attention shifted from when to who would be the first American to do it. At last, Don Bowden salvaged some national honor with a 3:58.7 mile in the summer of 1957. No other American would repeat that feat during the 1950s.

Swimming

In a series of movies that revolved around her prowess as a swimmer, Esther Williams emerged as one of only a handful of noted swimmers during the decade. In her films, which relied on spectacle more than on plot, Williams dived, water-skied, and splashed her way to stardom. Her pictures included *Pagan Love Song* (1950), *Skirts Ahoy!* (1952), *Million Dollar Mermaid* (1952), *Dangerous When Wet* (1953), *Easy to Love* (1953), and *Jupiter's Darling* (1955).

As innumerable families moved to the growing suburbs, the home swimming pool became a popular status symbol. From just a few thousand installations in the late 1940s, well over 100,000 pools were gracing suburban homes by the end of the decade. Sometimes they served as well-used recreational accessories; for many, however, the swimming pool functioned as another emblem of material success. Regardless of purpose, the boom in home swimming pools can be traced directly to the 1950s.[2]

The Olympics

American Bob Mathias, just 17 and fresh out of high school, won the decathlon gold medal in the 1948 Summer Olympics in London. In 1952, the games moved to Helsinki, Finland, where Mathias repeated his feat, and the press promptly declared him "the World's Greatest Athlete," an unofficial title. Out of his success came a movie, *The Bob Mathias Story* (1954), starring the medal-winner himself in the title role. The film helped stir interest in the postwar Olympics and doubtless spurred a few young men to practice harder for the 1956 Melbourne games.

What captured the most public attention in Helsinki, however, involved the political overtones of the event. The Cold War was being fought on Finnish playing fields. The Communist bloc nations insisted on totaling points and accumulating medals, thrusting aside individual competition as unimportant. Most press coverage of the events focused on how many medals Russia or the United States would gain by winning the competition. It brought an unfortunate politicizing to the games, something that has carried forward ever since.

FADS

With the war behind them and industry back on a peacetime schedule, Americans relaxed, comfortable in their new prosperity and ready for novelties. The fads that characterized the fifties may seem silly to later generations, but they lacked the desperation and underlying anxieties of the outlandish stunts and daredevil antics that had marked the thirties and forties. The fifties, by and large, represented youthful high spirits.

College Pranks

Colleges across the nation weathered several fads that gained considerable press attention. First and foremost were the panty raids, a spring ritual in which male students "raided" the co-eds' dorms, expecting—and receiving—undergarments tossed from the windows as their trophies. The raids first emerged as a campus rage in 1952, and remained popular for the rest of the decade.

In the late fifties, instead of cramming for exams, students crammed into anything small, from telephone booths to Volkswagen Beetles. The idea involved getting as many people as possible jammed into an allotted space. The unofficial record for people in a phone booth claimed that 24 students had successfully wedged themselves into the tiny space.[3]

Flying Saucers and UFOs

People spotted UFOs (unidentified flying objects) everywhere throughout the decade. The trend began in 1947, when a pilot reported objects that resembled saucers flying outside his plane. From there, the sightings multiplied. Between 1950 and 1959, citizens filed a yearly average of 650 reports. The U.S. Air Force spent over $500,000 investigating reports, although it never could definitively identify an extraterrestrial object. In a lengthy document issued in 1955, the government denied that flying saucers or other UFOs had ever violated U.S. airspace. Instead, authorities tried to explain them away as weather balloons and other scientific materials that happened to be seen by an anxious public.

The lack of proof served as little deterrent to the film industry. A spate of movies sharing the common thread of extraterrestrial visitors ensued, including *The Flying Saucer* (1950), *The Day the Earth Stood Still* (1951), *The Thing* (1951), *It Came from Outer Space* (1953), and *The War of the Worlds.* By the end of the decade, however, the UFO fad had exhausted itself.

Hula Hoops and Frisbees

The hula hoop and the Frisbee were introduced to an unsuspecting American public in 1957. Both products of the Wham-O Manufacturing Company, they proved runaway best sellers for kids of all ages. For a time, nothing came close to the hula hoop in sales; one cost only $1.98, and dealers could not keep them in stock. An Australian invention, hula hoops (bamboo rings, in this case) caught the eye of Wham-O, and the firm

Sports

At the height of the hula hoop craze, various techniques are demonstrated in Los Angeles on August 20, 1958, as children ranging from age 2 to 16 competed for prizes on Art Linkletter's *House Party* television show. Groups including the Girl Scouts, Brownies, Blue Birds, and Campfire Girls were represented. AP Photo.

fashioned their own models out of lightweight polyethylene plastic so they would float.

The Frisbee, on the other hand, did not enjoy as sensational a beginning as the hula hoop. It received its unusual name, so the story goes, from the Frisbee Baking Company of Bridgeport, Connecticut. Customers would sometimes keep the aluminum pie plates from the bakery, tossing them in the air for fun. Walter Morrison, a California carpenter, refined the pie plate concept into the plastic disc so familiar today. Wham-O bought out Morrison and attempted to market his disc as a "Pluto Platter," but the public persisted in calling it a Frisbee. After a year or so, Wham-O trademarked the word "Frisbee" in 1959, and the name has stuck.[4]

GAMES

As in all periods of American life, people enjoyed games. Indoor, outdoor, athletic or intellectual, for young or for old, new introduction or old favorite, games constituted an important part of the nation's leisure activities. A card game that found favor everywhere, canasta traced its roots to rummy, another popular game. The name means "basket," and refers to the tray full of discards that players vie to win. Canasta landed on American shores in 1949, an import from Uruguay, and gained legions of fans almost immediately. In 1950, Oswald Jacoby, a respected expert on many card games, published *How to Win at Canasta,* and it quickly climbed the best-seller lists. Enthusiastic players formed clubs, and canasta quickly surpassed bridge as the nation's favorite card game.

Canasta's dominance began to falter around 1952. The public was ready for something new, and a word game that had been developed in the 1930s waited in the wings. That game, of course, was Scrabble. It had never really caught the public fancy. The creation of Alfred M. Butts, Scrabble struggled from the time of its invention, until word of mouth and determined marketing finally got people excited about it 20 years later. In its early years, Butts called his invention "Lexico"; in 1938 he christened it "Criss-Cross."

In 1947, with no interest and no sales, Butts went into partnership with friend James Brunot, who renamed the game "Scrabble" in hopes of generating public curiosity. The word means to scratch or to scrape soil. In the game, players "scratch up" small wooden tiles with letters on them in hopes of creating combinations that form words. In 1952, for no apparent reason, the game suddenly took off. The two men could not keep up with demand, and Selchow & Righter, a large game manufacturer, took over, a move that paved the way for mass production. By the mid-fifties, millions of Scrabble games sold each year, with no end in sight.[5]

TOYS

A buying binge in the prosperous 1950s soon replaced the austerity of World War II. Toys of every description flooded a market grown accustomed to inferior cardboard and poorly cut wood imitations of the metal and cast toys of the past. Metal, rubber, and plastics, all materials in short supply during the war, became the materials of choice for the postwar market.

Toys and Television

The first toy ever heavily advertised on TV, Mr. Potato Head achieved runaway success in 1952. Made by Hasbro, Mr. Potato Head initially used a real potato (supplied by the consumer) for the head. Hasbro provided the eyes, mouths, ears, and other facial adornments. In 1953, Mr. Potato Head wed Mrs. Potato Head in a widely promoted ceremony. Offspring, or "small fries," soon followed. In 1964, the growing family became all plastic and no longer involved real potatoes.

The saturation advertising that Hasbro employed on television for all its products, especially on Saturday mornings when kids watched cartoons, brought about the toy's popularity. Their huge sales volume soon convinced other toy manufacturers to imitate this new promotional approach, making television the primary ad outlet for children's items.

Another illustration of the power of television in influencing buying patterns can be found in *Beany and Cecil* (1950–1955), a low-budget, syndicated children's show. Its stories revolved around the adventures of two hand puppets, one of whom, Beany, at times wore a beanie festooned with a plastic propeller on the crown. The show's youthful audience seemed quite taken with this unique headgear, and its popularity soon achieved fad proportions.

Toy manufacturers began to produce them, and cereal giant Kellogg's offered propeller beanies to those who sent in a certain number of box tops. Soon, the caps could be seen everywhere, particularly in schoolyards atop the heads of proud boys. By the end of the 1950s, the craze had run its course, *Beany and Cecil* was canceled, and kids had turned to other interests. In 1962, the show was resurrected in an animated format.

Captain Video, a long-running (1949–1957) TV science fiction series, along with *Tom Corbett, Space Cadet* (1950–1955), inspired many toy manufacturers to work out licensing agreements with the two shows so they could capitalize on their popularity among children. Rings, flashlights, ray guns, rockets, and space vehicles of all kinds counted among the items released.

Hopalong Cassidy and Davy Crockett, however, proved more popular than Captain Video and Space Cadet. Introduced on the big screen in 1934, Hopalong (actor William L. Boyd), his white horse Topper, and crew moved to NBC-TV in 1949. At first, the network merely recycled the 65 old films, but in 1951 they began producing the actual television series, creating an additional 52 episodes. *Hopalong Cassidy* emerged as a marketing bonanza: a radio show, a syndicated comic strip, and merchandise galore. Hopalong Cassidy cowboy outfits become the rage for little boys, complete with six-guns, holsters, and spurs. Other toys, towels, raincoats, pajamas, rugs, bedspreads, candy, and miscellaneous items appeared bearing Hoppy's name. The pioneering television show carried on until 1954.[6]

At the end of 1954, *Disneyland,* Walt Disney's own show on ABC television, began a five-part series to tell stories about frontiersman Davy Crockett. Overnight, this character from the nation's past surpassed even Hopalong Cassidy. The episodes made a star of Fess Parker, and immediately captured the imaginations of young viewers everywhere. The show's theme, "The Ballad of Davy Crockett," was released as a single record and sold in the millions. Countless books recounting the hero's adventures enjoyed similar sales. Virtually anything that could be stenciled with the name "Davy Crockett" found a market, from toys to camping gear. In all, the Disney studios marketed over 3,000 items. Today, most people who lived during the 1950s recall the Davy Crockett hat, a replica of a coonskin cap, complete with a dangling tail. The hat used both real and imitation raccoon fur, and for a brief period any Crockett gear leaped to the top of children's wish lists. (See Fashion of the 1950s.)

In 1955, Hollywood rushed out *Davy Crockett, King of the Wild Frontier* and followed that with *Davy Crockett and the River Pirates* (1956). In reality, these movies consisted of the television episodes strung together into feature-length productions. By the end of 1955, *Disneyland* had moved on to other things and Davy Crockett disappeared from the lineup.[7]

TOYS OF THE DECADE

Numerous toys introduced during the 1940s didn't take off in popularity until the 1950s. Die-cast scale models of cars, trucks, and other wheeled vehicles, manufactured under the name of Matchbox Toys, first appeared in 1947, but sales did not soar into the millions until the 1950s.

The Slinky, in reality a 1945 toy, also took off in popularity during the next decade. The embodiment of simplicity, a Slinky consists of a flexible coil, or spring, that has provided endless entertainment for generations of kids and their parents.

Another surprise, Silly Putty was first developed in 1945 by the General Electric Company in the course of a search for synthetic rubber. No one quite knew what to do with it until a marketing expert sensed its potential as a toy. Tens of millions of egg-shaped containers of the putty sold between its introduction in 1949 and the end of the 1950s. After its initial appearance, however, Silly Putty came under criticism because of its tendency to stick to clothing and hair. Engineers revamped the formula so the silicone would no longer adhere to almost anything.

Powered Toys

Japanese imports began to appear with battery-powered motors during the early fifties. American

Sports

manufacturers, unable to compete with low Asian prices, began marketing their own imported lines, complete with motors and batteries. It marked a profound change for domestic companies that had once felt secure against foreign competition.[8] When Russia launched its *Sputnik* satellite in 1957, the toy industry responded with innumerable space-oriented offerings. Japanese manufacturers took the lead in futuristic toys. Robots, adapted from such hit movies as *The Day the Earth Stood Still* (1951) and *Forbidden Planet* (1956), proved especially popular. Robby, the clever robot in *Forbidden Planet,* emerged as something of an icon in the toy industry. Indeed, all manner of mechanical figures that could walk, move their limbs, and imitate other human behaviors fascinated children.

Barbie

Although her real impacts would not be felt until later decades, it is worth mentioning Barbie in the context of the fifties. This famous doll made her first appearance in toy stores at the beginning of March 1959, wearing distinctly fifties-style elegant and sophisticated clothing. The creation of Ruth Handler, one of the founders of Mattel Toys, Barbie became a favorite doll almost immediately.

HOBBIES

In a culture that valued work and productivity, the concept of spending time in worthwhile pursuits was strongly encouraged. A hobby was supposed to be a pleasurable activity, not the whiling away of precious time.

Do-It-Yourself

From a home-built fallout shelter in the backyard to a pine umbrella stand for the front hallway, do-it-yourself supported projects of every kind. So widespread was the idea of creating, building, modernizing, repairing, and sprucing up things around the home without professional help that *Time* magazine devoted its August 1954 cover story to the popularity of "doing it yourself."

Almost overnight, home workshops from simple to sophisticated became commonplace. The home itself emerged as a primary hobby—its proper

More and more people in the 1950s decided to do home repairs and remodeling without professional assistance, but as this picture shows (admittedly contrived), do-it-yourself work was never as easy as it was portrayed by those promoting it. Prints & Photographs Division, Library of Congress.

upkeep and improvements occupied many a do-it-yourselfer's time. The sales of multipurpose power tools and simple power devices, like table saws, jigsaws, lathes, and drills enjoyed surging popularity, along with quality hand tools.[9] Lumberyards and home supply stores flourished, urging on the public with attractive displays of plywood, free how-to brochures and plans, in addition to much in-store advice. Advertising emphasized father-son bonding, but seldom did mothers or daughters appear, at least in the idealized workshop. Despite the gender bias found in most depictions of woodworking and carpentry, home improvement and the do-it-yourself craze ultimately transcended gender barriers when it came to projects outside the confines of the home shop.

To assist families, the home improvement industry brought out such laborsaving innovations as pre-pasted wallpaper and complete paper hanging kits. Paint rollers, patented back in 1869, did not come into widespread use until the early 1950s. Latex paint was introduced in 1949; its easy soap-and-water cleanup made it an instant hit with do-it-yourselfers. By mid-decade, most paint stores featured color-mixing machines.

Such traditional women's magazines as *American Home, Better Homes and Gardens, House & Garden, House and Home, House Beautiful, McCall's,* and *Woman's Home Companion* devoted considerable space to do-it-yourself projects of every kind. Now a woodworker could craft a frame to hold the paint-by-number canvas someone had patiently labored over for many hours. In fact, frame kits that would accommodate specific canvases could be purchased, and a home magazine might provide helpful hints about correctly hanging pictures on a living room wall. (See Art of the 1950s.)

Not just women's magazines supported the popularity of the do-it-yourself concept, however. *Popular Mechanics, Popular Science Monthly,* and *Mechanix Illustrated* moved from their traditional articles about science and mechanics to an increasing emphasis on how-to pieces. In no time, they watched their circulations rise. For example, 1951 saw the launch of a magazine called *The Family Handyman.* Within a few issues, it attracted over 200,000 readers. *The Better Homes and Gardens Handyman's Book,* first published also in 1951, quickly soared to number five on some nonfiction lists for the year.

Model Making

Model airplanes of every description came in easy-to-assemble formats. At first, old firms like Cleveland and Strombecker dominated the field, with kits made from wood, usually balsa, an extremely lightweight variety. A single-edge razor blade, glue, a handful of tissue paper, and patience allowed both kids and adults to construct aircraft, some of which actually flew with rubber bands or small gasoline motors. As the 1950s progressed, the introduction of effective glues usable on plastic permitted firms like Monogram and Revell to create hundreds of intricately detailed car, train, ship, and airplane models from all eras. Modelers forgot the traditional balsa and tissue models in the rush to assemble the precision replicas that flooded the market in the later fifties.

If planes and ships held no appeal, one could always turn to model railroading. By the early 1950s, more than 1,000 model railroad clubs existed in the United States. Just like model airplanes, people viewed it as a male pastime, with women and their daughters permitted only on "visiting days." The clubs existed more as fraternities, meant for male bonding.

Crafts

Women were not forgotten in the hobby boom. The makers of paint-by-number kits, buoyed by high sales, introduced other craft supplies that they marketed directly to women. (See Visual Arts of the 1950s for more information on paint-by-number kits.) Toleware, an old art involving lacquered or enameled metalware usually with an applied design, became a big seller. The hobbyist applied premixed paints directly to prepared metal plates, waste cans, clasp purses, and many other items to complete the design. A kind of elaborate version of paint-by-numbers, the toleware packages proved a popular hit.[10]

Mosaic sets, in which colored stones supplied in the kit were arranged according to a carefully rendered drawing, likewise flourished. This kind of do-it-yourself artistry constituted only a small part of a much larger 1950s phenomenon. The proliferation of kits of all kinds gave a little boost to those who might have been intimidated by a blank canvas or a metal plate with no design. In addition, the decade saw would-be artisans flock to woodworking classes, stained glass lessons, ceramics courses, and a host of other hands-on experiences.

Travel

of the 1950s

Henry Ford may have introduced the mass production of motorized vehicles with his Model T Ford in 1908, but the car as a major component of popular culture did not become a reality until the 1950s. The Great Depression of the 1930s and the scarcities imposed by the war had combined to create a population anxious to purchase automobiles in record numbers. Everyone waited for Detroit to retool, to move from defense production back to consumer goods.

DRIVING AND AMERICAN LIFE

The prosperity of the 1950s created a boom for automakers the likes of which had never before been seen. By 1955, the number of cars on the road doubled from 1945. A big, powerful, showroom-new American automobile symbolized success; throughout the decade, dealers sold over seven million cars and trucks each year. By 1958, about 70 percent of all American families owned an automobile. Most people bought new models, and three-quarters or more of them had radios. The end of the fifties saw some 50 million cars on America's roads, or one automobile for every 3.58 persons.[1]

The move of the middle class to the suburbs was coupled with a desire for new cars. Almost overnight a new category of worker emerged: the automobile commuter. Around large cities like Boston, New York, and Chicago, commuting by railroad had long been in place, fostering the image of employees patiently awaiting a train to take them to their jobs.

In much of the country, however, the thought of being far from one's job still struck many as a novel idea. Even with rapid suburban growth, there were few attempts to connect outlying areas to passenger rail lines or bus systems. By mid-decade, mass transit no longer held a high place in anyone's list of priorities. This abandonment of commercial transportation left employees with only one choice: driving to work.

But if Dad took the family car to his job, what would Mom do about grocery shopping, schools, and clubs? The answer lay in the rise of the two-car family. Supermarkets located in a shopping center often miles from one's home displaced the corner grocery store. As school districts consolidated, the neighborhood school became a fond memory. Access to an automobile was deemed a necessity, and over 10 percent of all families possessed more than one car by the end of the decade. Parking emerged as an urban problem that grew out of suburban living. Each morning, millions of commuters descended on American cities, parked their cars, put in an eight-hour day, and then returned to the suburbs. Cities contemplated building huge parking lots, and yet their downtown businesses saw little commerce. Shoppers flocked to the new, outlying malls springing up almost as fast as the housing developments they were built to serve. The 1950s marked the Age of the Automobile and all its concurrent problems.

Superhighways

By 1950, most roads in the United States proved woefully inadequate to handle all the new cars. The picturesque parkways of the 1930s, designed for recreational driving, no longer met transportation needs. But the freeways and expressways dedicated to speed moved millions quickly and efficiently. The prosperity of the 1950s allowed such construction to begin in earnest.

In the late thirties and early forties, the Bureau of Public Roads had come up with ambitious plans for an interregional highway system. The war put these plans on hold. After the war, the 1950 opening of an eastern extension of the Pennsylvania Turnpike, "America's Dream Road," along with a western addition in 1951, marked the beginning of a momentous chapter in the modernization of American roads.

In 1950, construction commenced on the New Jersey Turnpike, a multilane toll road that owns the dubious honor of being the most heavily traveled highway in America; the final link opened in 1952. In order to save money, engineers on the project paid little heed to aesthetics, saying such efforts were superfluous and distracting. Turnpike driving, in New Jersey or anywhere else, involves anonymous rest stops, service areas, and sustained high-speed driving.[2]

Other states likewise constructed new highways, multilane expressways that enjoyed limited access and permitted no intersecting streets, no railroad crossings, and no stoplights.

Financed largely by the states themselves and through the imposition of tolls, all this ambitious building slowed precipitously in 1956, when the federal government unveiled its own plans for highways.[3]

The Interstate Highway System

In 1954, the Federal-Aid Highway Act laid the groundwork for a massive system of modern roads but set aside insufficient monies. In 1956, the Interstate Highway Act provided $25 billion for construction fees, 90 percent of which would be provided by federal funding, the money coming from gasoline and road use taxes. This gargantuan plan mandated the development of some 41,000 miles of new highways. The project got underway and soon moved into high gear. Interchanges on the growing interstates emerged as new economic centers, with motels, gas stations, and restaurants appearing almost overnight. Many communities reinvented themselves by creating vast malls and industrial parks outside the traditional city center. If people flocked to the suburbs, why not provide urban amenities and jobs there also? Businesses of all kinds began to move some or all of their operations to these new towns that grew on the fringes of older population centers. In the 1950s, however, the vast majority of traditional jobs remained in the cities. The advent of the interstates constituted a demographic shift of almost unimaginable proportions, and much of it occurred in the latter part of the decade.

Automobiles of the 1950s

With postwar prosperity and unprecedented demand for new automobiles, unfamiliar names like Muntz and Crosley briefly made their appearance, but few actually sold. Most smaller companies failed during the fifties, a decade of consolidation that saw the Big Three—General Motors, Ford, and Chrysler—tighten their grip on the American consumer.

Throughout the 1950s, GM claimed 40 percent or more of the total market. Ford had about a quarter of the pie, followed by Chrysler, with approximately 15 percent. Smaller, independent domestic companies, along with a slow but rising tide of imports, divided up the remainder. There were slim pickings for the competition; in 1955, 1956, and 1959, the Big Three's combined market share averaged 94 percent.[4]

Industry Innovations

The 1950s remain one of the most remarkable periods in American motoring history. Those 10 years saw the introduction of the hardtop, a pillar-less four-door automobile that blended a sedan with a convertible. The hardtop quickly

The price tag makes the picture perfect !

The lowest-priced convertible of the low-price three offers many years-ahead Thunderbird features

There's nothing newer in the world—**FORD**

Full page advertisement for Ford automobiles, showing a 1958 Ford Fairlane 500 convertible and man, woman, and two children on beach, 1958. Prints & Photographs Division, Library of Congress.

became the most popular body style of the era; it brought the outdoors into the car's interior. Its design complemented similar attempts in home construction, where carports, patios, and glass sliding doors, blurred the boundaries between the house and the yard. At the onset of the 1950s, most American cars had six-cylinder motors, but through clever marketing, the public became convinced that bigger engines would provide greater acceleration, speed, and torque for the larger cars pouring out of Detroit. By the end of the decade, more than 80 percent of new American cars had eight-cylinder motors, V-8s as they were commonly called. See "American-Made Automobiles, 1950–1959" for a list of models of American cars available for the decade.

In 1953, General Motors introduced the Chevrolet Corvette, a fiberglass-bodied sports car designed to compete with the influx of foreign sports cars then entering the market in significant numbers. The Corvette cost approximately $3,200—

expensive then—but modest sales encouraged the company to promote the car. Two years later, Ford introduced its Thunderbird, another two-seat sports car created to share in that growing market. The T-Bird became an immediate favorite with the public and sales quickly surpassed those of the Corvette. Ford in 1958 changed its Thunderbird into a four-seat model, and any aura of a true sports car disappeared. General Motors, on the other hand, continued with its line of two-seat Corvettes, giving them a virtual monopoly for American-made sports cars.[5]

Hot on the heels of Thunderbird's success, Ford introduced the Edsel in 1957 amid great fanfare. It entered salesrooms as the first completely new American brand in years. With a price in excess of $5,000, the Edsel was aimed at the upscale buyer. But the Edsel's design turned off potential purchasers. Sluggish sales finally forced the automaker to drop the Edsel in the fall of 1959. This ill-fated attempt to bring out a new car cost Ford $250 million, making it the costliest automotive failure in history and causing the term "Edsel" to be synonymous with any great business disaster.

Foreign Competition

Detroit ignored foreign imports, calling them "cheap" and "crowded." U.S. automakers assumed Americans would naturally "buy American," and at first they seemed correct in their dismissal of foreign competition. A trickle of imports in the early 1950s hardly warranted concern, but by 1957, foreign manufacturers had captured 10 percent of the market. At this same time, another warning sounded for Detroit because, for the first time ever, the United States imported more automobiles than it exported.

To illustrate: Volkswagen sold only 330 of its Beetles in 1950. By 1955, the trickle had grown to a stream, after about 30,000 of the ungainly "Bugs" were imported. At the close of the decade, the company sold over 150,000 Volkswagen sedans, and potential buyers had to get on a waiting list. In addition, Volkswagen's German manufacturer also marketed the Volkswagen camper van, or Westphalia, one of the few mass-produced vehicles designed for touring and camping at the time. The Westphalia proved an immediate success, capitalizing on a wave of auto tourism that flourished

Travel

American-Made Automobiles, 1950–1959

Popular Name	Parent Company	Production Years
Buick—also called Century, LeSabre, Riviera, Roadmaster, Skylark, Special, others	General Motors	Buicks were manufactured throughout the decade.
Cadillac—also called Coupe de Ville, Eldorado, Fleetwood, others	General Motors	Cadillacs were manufactured throughout the decade.
Checker—also called Specials, Superbas	Checker Motors	Designed and built as taxis, Checkers first became available to the public in 1959.
Chevrolet—also called Bel Air, Delray, Impala, Nomad, Styleline, others; in addition, Chevrolet marketed a sports car called a Corvette	General Motors	Chevrolets were manufactured throughout the decade; the Corvette sports car was introduced in 1953.
Chrysler—also called New Yorker, Newport, 300, Town and Country, Windsor, others	Chrysler Corporation	Chryslers were manufactured throughout the decade.
Continental—also called Mark II, Mark III, Mark IV	Ford Motor Company	Continentals were manufactured 1956–1958; afterward, they were marketed as Lincoln Continentals.
Crosley—also called Hotshots, Super Sports	Crosley Appliances	A midget car, Crosley ceased production in 1952.
DeSoto—also called Adventurer, Custom, Firedome, Fireflite, Firesweep, others	Chrysler Corporation	DeSotos were manufactured throughout the decade.
Dodge—also called Coronet, Royal Lancer, Sierra, Wayfarer, others	Chrysler Corporation	Dodges were manufactured throughout the decade.
Edsel—also called Citation, Corsair, Ranger	Ford Motor Company	The Edsel was introduced in 1958; production ceased in 1960.
Ford—also called Country Squire, Crestliner, Fairlane, Galaxie, Skyliner, Tudor, Victoria, others; in addition, Ford marketed a sports car called a Thunderbird	Ford Motor Company	Fords were manufactured throughout the decade; the Thunderbird sports car was introduced in 1955.
Frazer—also called Manhattan, Standard	Kaiser-Frazer Corporation	The Frazer was in production only from 1946 to 1951.
Henry J—also called Corsair, Vagabond; another version, called the Allstate, was marketed through Sears, Roebuck	Kaiser-Frazer Corporation	One of the first compact cars, the Henry J was in production from 1951 to 1954; the Allstate was sold from 1952 to 1953.
Hudson—also called Italia, Hornet, Super Jet, Wasp, others	Hudson Motors (merged into American Motors Corporation in 1954)	Hudson ceased production in 1957.
Imperial—also called Crown Southampton, Custom, Newport253	Chrysler Corporation	A luxury Chrysler, Imperials gained autonomy in 1955 and remained so for the decade.
Kaiser—also called Dragon, Manhattan, Special, Traveler; in addition, Kaiser marketed a sports car called a Darrin	Kaiser-Frazer Corporation	The Kaiser was in production only from 1949 to 1955; the Darrin sports car was marketed only in 1954.

American-Made Automobiles, 1950–1959 (*continued*)

Popular Name	Parent Company	Production Years
Lincoln—also called Capri, Cosmopolitan, Premiere, Continental Mark IV	Ford Motor Company	Lincolns were manufactured throughout the decade; in 1959, the formerly autonomous Continentals took on the Lincoln name.
Mercury—also called Medalist, Montclair, Monterey, Park Lane, Turnpike Cruiser, others	Ford Motor Company	Mercurys were manufactured throughout the decade.
Muntz—also called Jet	Muntz Motors	Muntzes were manufactured from 1950 to 1954.
Nash—also called Airflyte, Ambassador, Metropolitan, Rambler, Statesman; in addition, Nash marketed a sports car called a Nash-Healey	Nash-Kelvinator (merged into American Motors Corporation in 1954)	Nashes were manufactured until 1957; the Rambler brand became autonomous in 1955; the Nash-Healey sports car was marketed from 1951 to 1955.
Oldsmobile—also called Dynamic 88, Fiesta, Futuramic, Golden Rocket, Holiday, Starfire, Super 88, others	General Motors	Oldsmobiles were manufactured throughout the decade.
Packard—also called Clipper, Custom Eight, The Four Hundred, Mayfair, Pacific, 250, others	Packard Motors (merged into Studebaker-Packard in 1954)	Packards remained in production until 1958.
Plymouth—also called Belvedere, Cranbrook, Fury, Savoy, Special, Suburban, others	Chrysler Corporation	Plymouths were manufactured throughout the decade.
Pontiac—also called Bonneville, Catalina, Chieftain, Safari, Star Chief, Streamliner, others	General Motors	Pontiacs were manufactured throughout the decade.
Studebaker—also called Commander, Champion, Conestoga, Golden Hawk, Hawk, Lark, President, Scotsman, Sky Hawk, Starliner, others	Studebaker Corporation (merged into Studebaker-Packard in 1954)	Studebakers were manufactured throughout the decade.
Willys—also called Aero-Ace, Aero-Eagle, Aero-Wing, Bermuda, Jeep, Jeepster, others	Willys-Overland (merged with Kaiser-Frazer in 1954 to form Kaiser-Willys Sales Corporation)	Willys cars were manufactured until 1955; the Jeep (considered a truck, not a car) continued production throughout the decade.

Much of the information for this table was adapted from Consumer Guide, eds., *Automobiles of the '50s* (Lincolnwood, IL: Publications International, 1999), 4–96.

throughout the 1950s. With nothing comparable on the market, Volkswagen enjoyed a monopoly.

Volkswagen reinforced its already significant foothold among U.S. consumers by capitalizing on a humorous, self-effacing ad campaign crafted by the American firm of Doyle, Dane, Bernbach, Inc. The campaign commenced in the fall of 1959.

The ads, appearing in various print media, consisted of a succession of single black-and-white photographs that included a Beetle but seldom under glamorous circumstances, and some pithy copy touting the reliability or uniqueness of the car. They resonated with people, both for their deadpan humor and their honesty, and served as a welcome break from the monotony of most automobile advertising. As the 1950s came to an end, Volkswagen, already the front-runner among imports, seemed poised to become a major competitor in the American automobile market.[6] Detroit made no effort to design and manufacture compact U.S. models until late in the decade. Finally, in 1959, Ford introduced its Falcon, Chevrolet followed suit with its Corvair, and Plymouth promoted its Valiant. Meanwhile, many other American-made cars only grew larger and more gadget-laden. Chrome bullets poked out from complex chrome grilles, salesmen touted electric door locks and powered mirrors, and air-conditioning became more commonplace.

Automotive Design

Until the 1950s, most American automobiles possessed a utilitarian look. With the postwar era, however, style overtook safety and practicality. Influenced by Hollywood, fashion, science fiction, technology, military aircraft, and unfettered imaginations, Detroit took off on a design flight unlike anything encountered before.

Breathless advertising promoted cars that suggested streamlined rockets and swept wing jets. Names like (Buick) LeSabre; (Ford) Thunderbird and Galaxie; (Hudson) Jet and Super Jet; and (Oldsmobile) Rocket 88 and 98 spoke of aerodynamics and speed. In addition, the dashboard and its instrumentation often resembled something found in an aircraft cockpit, further reinforcement of the car-plane symbolism. By the mid-1950s, the analogies between automobiles and airplanes became impossible to ignore.

During this period of excess, automotive designers discovered the fin. A completely nonfunctional appendage that grew out of the rear fender, it became the symbol of the 1950s American automobile. With each yearly model change, fins grew larger and more prominent. By the middle of the decade, they soared into the air; they lengthened the body, and everybody wanted them. As quickly as fins had emerged as a style statement, the desire evaporated with the close of the decade. But the extra long 1959 Cadillac Coupe de Ville will always be remembered for resembling nothing less than a jet aircraft poised for takeoff.

HARLEY J. EARL

Harley J. Earl (1893–1969) helped popularize the concept of annual design during his tenure at General Motors. Starting with a team of 50 people, the group eventually swelled to over 1,000 by the 1950s. Earl brought styling on a grand scale to automobile manufacturing. He pushed for planned obsolescence in design and stated that he wanted cars that looked longer and lower.

Earl consciously employed symbolism in auto design. In addition to tail fins, he pioneered the wrap-around windshield and the free use of sculptural chrome. Earl liked the look of a World War II fighter plane called the P-38 but better known as the Lockheed Lightning. He admired its streamlining, particularly its unusual twin tail booms. Hints of this crept into the 1948 Cadillac, in the form of slightly exaggerated rear taillights. In the 1950s, manufacturers other than General Motors also raised and flared the rear fenders of their products. Thanks to Earl, the race for bigger, more flamboyant, more outlandish fins was on.

Movies, Music, and Automobiles

The presence of automobiles in virtually every contemporary movie objectified the concept that the car represented American culture. In many ways, the movies of the 1950s also served as dramatic commercials for the auto industry, showcasing the necessity of individual transportation in contemporary America.

Although few commercial movies dealt with cars, per se, a handful did focus on aspects of motoring. Films that dealt with the hot-rodding fad of the 1950s included *Hot Rod Girl* (1956), *Hot Rod Gang* (1958), and *Joy Ride* (1958).

In 1951, Jackie Brenston and the Kings of Rhythm scored a minor musical hit, "Rocket 88," a song that celebrated Oldsmobile's latest model, as well as the pleasures of "cruisin'" around town in a new car. Brenston's success inspired other car-and-music numbers like "V-Ford Blues" (1951), "Cadillac Daddy" (1952), "Drivin' Slow" (1952), and "Maybelline" (1955). Some groups, like the Cadillacs and the El Dorados, even took popular automobile names as their own.

Vehicles for Travel

Immediately following World War II, Americans took to the road in record numbers. For many, a converted bus served as their mobile vacation residence. Though a bus conversion required time and handyman skills, the do-it-yourself craze of the era facilitated such endeavors. Entrepreneurs, eager to accommodate this small but growing market, came out with all sorts of gadgets, from small, portable stoves and refrigerators to nylon window screens and mesh patios. Elaborately furnished vehicles were often the result of this. Several small firms launched the limited production of prefabricated motor homes. For example, Nash, an old-line automobile company, advertised reclining seats that converted to full-size beds in its sedans.

Detroit's postwar station wagon reflected the need for more than mere transportation. Throughout the 1950s, station wagons grew in size, and dealers promoted their dual use as transportation and vacation vehicles that allowed for sleeping in the large cargo areas. The concept caught on, and sales soared, with one out of every eight American cars a station wagon in 1956. Americans appreciated the utility of hauling groceries and kids during the week, attractive all-steel bodies, and the ability to pack the family's gear and still have room left for crowded sleeping on vacation trips.[7]

THE GROWTH OF TOURISM

From 1951 onward, either in her 15-minute music show on television, *The Dinah Shore Show* (1951–1957), or her hour-long variety offering, *The Dinah Shore Chevy Show* (1957–1962), singer Dinah Shore invited her viewers to "See the U.S.A. in your Chevrolet." This advertising theme song crept into the popular mind.

Auto travel doubled in the United States between 1950 and 1960. Recreational travel led the way, and Americans equipped themselves for travel as never before. Leisure clothing, luggage, convenience foods, camping and boating supplies, sporting goods, and souvenirs enjoyed rapid increases in sales.

For the first time, most American employers offered workers with at least one year of service paid vacations, a situation that led to longer, more frequent trips. The number of paid holidays also increased during the 1950s, and the baby boom of the immediate postwar years created a new, young population of families eager to travel. For many, particularly those with children in school, summer meant one thing: a journey by automobile. Over 80 percent of such travel was undertaken by car, compared to 13 percent by train, and the miniscule remainder by air or ship. On average, these auto trips ran from one to two weeks on the road, with stopovers at motels, hotels, and the homes of friends or relatives. Some camping also took place, but on a limited scale. Almost half of all families engaged in vacation touring during the 1950s, and their journeys tended to be about 600 miles in length. Education and economic status played a role in travel. Those in the middle class possessing high school and college degrees proved more prone to travel; the greater a family's affluence, the farther they chose to go.[8]

Most American tourists during the 1950s traveled to locations within the continental United States; any border crossing usually meant Canada. In addition, more than half those Americans traveling by car tended to return to the same place annually.

Many tourists chose to journey to one or more of the many national parks and monuments. The National Park Service found itself coping with thousands of additional visitors each year, a job made difficult by antiquated and inadequate facilities. Tourism at parks and monuments increased from 19 million visitors in 1950 to over 38 million in 1959. Most of these tourists arrived by automobile, requiring additional parking and lodging. As road building kicked into high gear across the United States, more and more tourist facilities were erected alongside the new highways. Motels, restaurants, service stations, and assorted attractions rose at an accelerated pace, making travel easier than it had ever been.

MOTELS, HOTELS, AND DRIVE-IN BUSINESSES

To accommodate this horde of motorists, American lodging underwent significant changes. The venerable motor hotel, or "motel," evolved from pedestrian clusters of little buildings, or cabins, to

Travel

elaborate architectural designs that called themselves "motor inns." In addition, the field proved ripe for quality lodging, a concept that brought in corporate financing. Chains like Best Western, Howard Johnson's, Ramada, and Travelodge soon dominated the market, and the small, independent motel owner faced overwhelming competition.

Kemmons Wilson, a Tennessee architect and builder, led the motel charge. He opened the first Holiday Inn in Memphis in 1954. It had 120 rooms, far more than other motels of the day. In addition, the venture offered air-conditioning, in-room telephones, free ice, and other features new to the industry. Holiday Inn become an immediate, popular success, and Wilson continued building; by the end of the decade more than 200

Holiday Inns graced the American landscape. About 30,000 motels had been scattered around the United States in 1950, by 1960 that figure had mushroomed to 60,000 and showed no signs of slowing.[9]

The 1950s also witnessed the growth of the drive-in, from theaters to markets to restaurants to banks. Many businesses rebuilt existing structures to accommodate automobiles. Once stodgy banks now welcomed customers with drive-up windows. Numerous restaurant and fast-food chains evolved by catering to vehicular traffic, not walk-ins. The movie business, buffeted by the competition of television during the 1950s, enjoyed a brief rejuvenation with the meteoric rise in popularity of the drive-in theater. (See Entertainment of the 1950s.)

Drive-in theater sign advertising *River of No Return,* 1954. Prints & Photographs Division, Library of Congress.

DRIVE-IN THEATER

The first drive-in theater was built in New Jersey, when Richard Milton Hollingshead Jr., heir to a thriving Camden, New Jersey, chemical business, decided to combine his two loves—cars and movies—to create an innovative theater experience. Hollingshead's theater opened in June 1933 to a sold-out crowd and was filled to capacity for weeks. Imitators soon opened similar theaters in Pennsylvania and Massachusetts, and the idea caught on across the country, with drive-ins opening in California by the end of the decade. Part of the drive-in's appeal was that parents could bring their children along, pack a picnic, and avoid babysitting costs. In some states, professional babysitters actually gathered to protest drive-in theaters for taking their business. Some drive-ins provided playgrounds for the kids and even supervised activity rooms.

It wasn't long before young couples began using drive-ins as a place to engage in nuzzling and occasionally more explicit behavior, but the better outdoor theaters hired an attendant to walk among the parked vehicles, making sure—with a sharp tap on a steamy window—that couples did not "go too far." Nonetheless, unease about the theaters led to a state of moral outrage among some who felt that drive-ins were responsible for encouraging lewd behavior among America's youth. The popularity of drive-ins peaked in the 1950s, coinciding with the height of "car culture," in which buying, fixing, and driving cars were the most popular pastimes in the country. The popularity of the drive-in declined during the 1960s, and by the 1980s there were only a few drive-in theaters left across the country. The rise of environmentalism dealt another blow to the popularity of car-centric activities like drive-in theaters, but a few have remained in the twenty-first century.

AMUSEMENT PARKS

As millions of people embarked on vacations, entrepreneurs everywhere attempted to entice them with endless attractions. The 1950s saw a long line of seedy parks and zoos, tourist traps, and outright frauds—all of it advertised with endless cheap signs that dotted the highways. Walt Disney's concept of family entertainment brought about a marked change in roadside attractions.

In 1954, the Walt Disney Company began construction of a large recreational facility in Anaheim, California. It opened as Disneyland in July 1955. Taking its name and much of its funding from the popular ABC television series, the park was profitable within months of its opening. By the end of 1957, Disneyland had recorded its ten-millionth visitor. Instead of the traditional roller coasters and Ferris wheels that typified most parks, Disneyland used American history, the company's own cartoon characters, and other innovative approaches to differentiate it from the competition. Walt Disney himself meticulously oversaw each and every step in the development of the park. It began immediately to be a popular family vacation destination to those who lived in California and its popularity spread to families

Walt Disney sits on a rock in front of the Sleeping Beauty Castle in the Fantasyland section of Disneyland on opening day of the amusement theme park in Anaheim, California, on July 17, 1955. AP Photo.

Children enjoying the cup and saucer ride in Disneyland during its opening days in Anaheim, California, July 19, 1955. AP Photo.

living elsewhere in the United States, who often combined a road trip across country to get to Disneyland.

MINIATURE GOLF

A brief fad during the Depression years, Americans rediscovered miniature golf during the booming 1950s. Instead of being located in towns and cities, however, the new courses tended to be situated along commercial strips in suburban areas.

Often, these reincarnations of older, simpler courses now served as lures to get motorists to pull off the busy highway. Many miniature golf operations followed in the path of the originals—home-built affairs with crude hazards and rough detailing. But when coupled with motels, drive-in theaters, or as part of large suburban shopping centers, they displayed a growing sophistication in design, with more polished layouts featuring fancy, carpeted "fairways," more complex hazards, and fluorescent lighting for night play. By the end of the decade, miniature golf (called in some areas "goofy golf" or "goony golf") had been reestablished as a favorite roadside pastime.[10]

RAIL TRAVEL

The decline of American rail service continued into the 1950s. Total track mileage fell below what had existed at the turn of the century as rail companies slashed service and facilities. In 1950, railroads still transported over three-quarters of distant passenger traffic. But by 1960 the airlines had captured almost two-thirds of this traffic;

Travel

the railroads had only about 39 percent. Clearly, Americans preferred the speed and convenience of air travel to the slower trains.[11]

Fighting back, railroad lines experimented with "Vistadome" observation cars and "slumber coaches" in the mid-1950s as a way of luring passengers, but the innovations had only limited success. Many lines spent large sums of money on passenger amenities, but the costs always exceeded any gains in revenue.

The speed of jet planes, the convenience of automobiles, and the difficulty of getting trains to specific destinations all contributed to the railroads' decline. American railroads also faced the onerous problems of obsolete equipment and the tremendous expense of modernizing. Rather than upgrade their stock, they attempted to divest themselves of passenger service, arguing it cost too much to maintain. After considerable indecision, Congress and the Interstate Commerce Commission began to allow many lines to discontinue passenger service. As a result, by late in the decade, only about half of the available tracks carried passengers, and in many small and medium-sized cities, passenger trains existed only as a memory.

If the railroads saw any future at all in passenger service, it existed with commuters situated around the nation's larger cities. The challenge of transporting millions of commuters from home to work and back again might have been a bonanza for the railroads in those areas, but it seldom happened.

AIR TRAVEL

Prosperity meant that Americans strove to enlarge their travel horizons. With only a couple of weeks at their disposal, they wanted to reach their destinations quickly, and that translated into air travel—the speedier the better.

Commercial airlines competed fiercely with each other to offer faster, longer flights. In 1953, TWA became the first airline to provide nonstop service between New York and California. In 1957, Pan American Airways offered nonstop flights over the profitable North Atlantic route,

flying passengers from New York to London. Rival lines quickly caught up, and no one airline held an advantage for more than a few months.

In October 1958, BOAC (British Overseas Airways Corporation) led the transition into jet travel by unveiling the de Havilland Comet passenger jet. It flew nonstop between London and New York in just over six hours, or about half the flight time of propeller-driven craft. That same month, Douglas and Boeing, the two largest U.S. airplane manufacturers, began marketing their own models, especially Boeing's 707, destined to become one of the most successful and popular jets of all time. Soon domestic carriers offered jets to several overseas cities.[12]

As airplanes accommodated more and more passengers, the airlines began offering different grades of seating. They modeled this move on what railroads had long practiced: coach and first class. First class provided the traveler a slightly larger seat and more amenities, but coach offered a lower fare. Between 1950 and 1960, passenger boardings more than doubled to almost 40 million, mainly at the expense of the beleaguered railroads. In 1955, for the first time, the number of air passengers surpassed those riding trains.[13]

This rise in air traffic brought a rush to build or modernize facilities to keep up with demand. The government reacted to the growth of air travel by creating the Federal Aviation Administration (FAA) in 1958; it oversaw air safety.

SHIP TRAVEL

On its maiden voyage in July 1952, the S.S. *United States,* a brand-new American luxury liner, established a transatlantic speed record of 3 days, 10 hours, 40 minutes from the United States to England, a mark that remains unbroken. On the westward return, the *United States* took only 3 days, 12 hours, 12 minutes. As fate would have it, these accomplishments coincided with the rapid growth of North Atlantic air travel, where the same crossing took only a matter of hours. The *United States* would be decommissioned in 1969, and the era of the great ocean liners would draw to a close.

Travel

Visual Arts

of the 1950s

In the postwar era, it seemed that many artists turned their backs on realism and representation, believing that a fevered improvisation held more significance than a carefully rendered study. Some critics assured audiences that true art expressed raw emotion and that traditional painting had become hopelessly passé. Most American museums, conservative by nature, nonetheless relied on more traditional art to attract patrons.

PAINTING

Popularizing Art

By the early 1950s, more Americans attended college than ever before; as a result, a rise in demand for art took place. In galleries and "art shoppes" across the country, the sales of original paintings increased markedly, and department stores and other nontraditional shopping outlets saw a soaring demand for prints and lithographs. Museums large and small experienced growth, and exhibitions of every kind welcomed patrons eager for "culture."

With the exception of a few larger cities, most museums focused on well-known artists or classic periods in art, like the Renaissance or the "Old Masters" of the eighteenth and nineteenth centuries. Exhibitions displayed little contemporary work because curators feared public rejection or

lack of funding. Even in the late fifties, the greater part of major shows continued to revolve around traditional, representational art.

Established realistic artists like Edward Hopper (1982–1967), Georgia O'Keeffe (1887–1986), Ben Shahn (1898–1969), and Charles Sheeler (1883–1965), continued to produce work of considerable merit. A younger painter, Andrew Wyeth (1917–) increased his already significant audience throughout the decade. His meticulously detailed watercolors made him one of the most popular painters of the period.

Commercial television, rapidly becoming the most popular carrier of mass culture, occasionally attempted to add some luster to its usual lineup of sitcoms, detective shows, dramas, and sports by sponsoring a program dedicated to the so-called high arts—classical music, ballet, serious drama, painting, sculpture, and others. Because television is a visual medium, painting was the obvious choice for such prestige-minded presentations. Shows like *Omnibus* (1952–1959), *Camera 3* (1956–1979), and *Person to Person* (1953–1960) provided periodic outlets for discussions of contemporary painting, a subject not much broached in mass media.

Such productions, however, usually simplified artistic expression, a patronizing approach that attempted to both demystify art and make it understandable to the public. This came about because of the networks' ambivalence about anything modern or different. Outside of New York City, those artists working in the most modern, or avant-garde, styles could seldom gain an audience, whereas tried-and-true realists like Norman Rockwell and Grandma Moses were trotted before the cameras and received enthusiastic acclaim. In some popular magazines, a few of the more experimental painters might find their work discussed or reproduced, but often with a sardonic tone.

Norman Rockwell

As in previous decades prolific artist and illustrator Norman Rockwell (1894–1978) continued to serve as the epitome of a good, hardworking painter. A superb technician and stylist, Rockwell's talents also embraced a storyteller's vivid imagination. His greatest successes might be the covers of the *Saturday Evening Post.* Rockwell painted 322 cover illustrations for the popular magazine, beginning in 1916 when he was only 22 and ending in 1963. The *Post* boasted high circulation. Four million people, on average, saw each cover, allowing him the largest audience ever enjoyed by an artist.[1] Rockwell chose to focus on the passing American scene, with a penchant for folksy settings cast in a warm, sentimental glow. Viewers could identify with a Rockwell narrative and make sense of the story. With this approach, which capitalized on his technical skills, he set the standards for American illustration from the 1920s through the 1950s.

Norman Rockwell's artwork has been a lasting art, successfully blurring the line between high and low culture by focusing on popular culture. His work appeals to a large, diverse mass of people, and his public acceptance has ensconced him as the most beloved—and possibly the most influential—American artist of all time.

Grandma Moses

Anna Mary Robertson Moses (1860–1961), better known to the public as "Grandma Moses," came to widespread attention during the 1940s. A self-taught primitive painter, already in her eighties, she at first employed common house paint, cheap brushes, and worked on any flat surfaces she could find. Gradually, however, she refined her techniques and began to employ artists' oils. Moses possessed a keen business sense; in her own, plainspoken way, she understood audiences and promotion.[2]

She painted her recollections of rural America of the late nineteenth and early twentieth centuries. The details of farming—tiny cows and pigs, immaculate little houses, barns, and lots of people going about their everyday chores—filled her compositions. Her vision and technique may have been naïve, and she consistently portrayed an America that never truly existed but that could be reconstructed in the collective memory. It struck a responsive chord with urbanized and suburbanized viewers, and soon sophisticated metropolitan galleries clamored for her paintings.

By the 1950s, people everywhere recognized the work of Grandma Moses. For audiences put off by abstraction and other modern movements, she served as the perfect antidote. Her intricately detailed pictures of a bucolic past held great appeal in an age threatened with nuclear annihilation. In

Grandma Moses in rocking chair. Courtesy of Picture-desk.

addition, her simple compositions told would-be artists that they, too, could paint. It all tied in nicely with the do-it-yourself craze that swept the country during the decade. President Harry Truman, more of an amateur piano player than painter, publicly lauded Moses, and at the same time denigrated "modern art."

Grandma Moses's created an estimated 1,500 paintings between 1938 and 1961. Her work could be found reproduced on ceramics, tea towels, greeting cards, and a host of other products, and she served as the subject of a TV documentary in 1955. Moses died in 1961 at 101 years of age, having remained an active artist until a few months before her death.

Abstract Expressionism

In retrospect, Abstract Expressionism can be seen as one of the defining movements in modern art. Sometimes referred to as the "New York school," it signaled the shift of contemporary art from Paris to New York City. Unlike most movements in so-called high, or elite, culture, Abstract Expressionism received considerable press coverage, but this emotional, expressionistic approach to painting had little public appreciation during the 1950s.

Paintings featuring jagged slashes of color and energetic brushstrokes with no identifiable images characterized the style, one that was personal in emotion, but monumental and public in scale. Over time, Abstract Expressionism affected every aspect of visual art, from advertising to fashion to traditional painting, but by itself the movement could hardly be considered a significant part of popular culture. Ripples from Abstract Expressionism permeated the nation's visual sensibility, so that wallpaper, fabrics, costume jewelry, graphics, illustration, and iconography reflected it in a variety of ways.

Artist Jackson Pollock (1912–1956), thanks to his colorful personality and unique method of dribbling and splattering paints directly onto a canvas, became the subject of much of the attention focused on this new generation of artists. Dubbed "Jack the Dripper" in mass magazines, he seemed to symbolize the creative genius as only slightly removed from madness. For most Americans, however, it was all undecipherable squiggles and blotches of paint, devoid of meaning—an unpopular art worth neither time nor attention. Even with the flurry of media interest, the general public remained unaware of these changes in the art world.[3] (See also Visual Arts of the 1940s for more information on Pollock.)

Paint-by-Number

In a decade marked by interest in hobbies and "do-it-yourself," a growing number of would-be artists tried painting. Palmer Paint Company, a Detroit-based firm hit upon the clever idea of do-it-yourself paintings that could be undertaken by anyone. Out of this came "Paint-by-Number." Palmer introduced its new product in 1951, and used the trade name Craft Master. Although they did not invent the concept—several other firms had similar products on the market by the late 1940s—the Palmer kits caught the public fancy. A boxed paint-by-number kit included up to 90 tiny capsules of premixed oil paint, two brushes, and a carefully printed canvas that showed a composition broken down into its constituent parts. Prices ranged from $1.00 for a 12-color kit to $8.95 for a panoramic, 90-color Super Craft Master. The canvases looked like nothing more than tracings of original works. Minuscule outlined and numbered units separated details into light and dark, providing most of the colors and shadings found in the original. By matching the numbers to those on each vial of paint, and then applying the paint to the predetermined areas, a semblance of the original work would begin to emerge.[4]

Abhorred by critics and loved by the public, paint-by-number proved dull, tedious work, and it allowed for little or no improvisation. But the completed painting could usually be identified as a reasonable copy of the original—or so thought millions of would-be Rockwells and Rembrandts bent over their canvases, carefully applying paint as instructed. A popular response to the incomprehensibility of much modern art, the paint-by-number subjects provided traditional, recognizable realism, and proud artists who had labored over the numbered diagrams could claim the finished product was an original of sorts. Paint-by-number kits were frequently worked on by children, who either enjoyed their results or quickly grew bored with filling in all the areas, although there were various kits especially for children, with horses and dogs as favorite subjects.

Craft Master saw demand for its products peak in 1954, with over 12 million units sold. By the mid-fifties more than 35 firms competed for would-be painters. For many, the fad represented a cheapening of traditional art, an unwonted intrusion by amateurs into the sacrosanct world of high art; for those eagerly purchasing the latest Craft Master kit, however, it gave them an outlet for creative urges once hidden because of lack of education, training, or even skill.

SCULPTURE

Among the handful of sculptors to achieve some renown during the 1950s, Alexander Calder (1898–1976) is best remembered for his "mobiles"—large, hanging arrangements of abstract organic shapes that turned and shimmered with the slightest breeze. They appeared to defy gravity floating above the spectator's head, and their bright colors caught the eye. People enjoyed looking at them, and their modern, nonrepresentational appearance did not detract from this

The Tree (1966) by Alexander Calder is an example of the stabiles he made in the 1950s and 1960s. This one, installed at the Missouri Botanical Garden, St. Louis, has been popular with the public. Prints & Photographs Division, Library of Congress.

pleasure. Calder mobiles graced several new buildings, bringing about an unconscious acceptance of more abstract sculpture. He also constructed a number of "stabiles"—large, motionless metal pieces that resembled his mobiles, but remained stationary on the ground. Calder fortunately won numerous commissions for his modernistic constructions, and the public tended to respond favorably to his work.[5]

PHOTOGRAPHY

Amateur Photography

By the 1950s, Americans everywhere were familiar with documentary photography. Every week, a new copy of *Life* or *Look* magazine arrived in their mailboxes, each filled with photographs chronicling events throughout the world. More importantly, such periodicals gave the public images of how the nation lived—what it consumed, what it liked and disliked, and what it found important. These magazines presented, in visual form, essays about American culture aimed at a vast audience. In addition, book-length collections of photographs, ranging from the hardships of the Great Depression to the horrors of World War II and the Korean War, graced people's coffee tables, and inexpensive cameras and film had long since made amateur photography accessible to all.

Home photography boomed in the 1950s. In the years following World War II, the giant Eastman-Kodak Corporation virtually monopolized the sales of small cameras and projectors. The mass importation of competitive German and Japanese cameras did not kick into high gear until the later 1950s and early 1960s. As a result, Kodak Brownies and Hawkeyes dominated the market for small, inexpensive cameras. In addition, the Brownie 8mm movie camera, introduced in 1951, allowed anyone to shoot home movies inexpensively.

About the only area of amateur photography not under Kodak's thumb involved instant pictures. In 1947, the first Polaroid instant cameras went on sale. The early models carried hefty price tags and proved sophisticated devices. Gradually prices came down, along with the cameras' complexity; by 1954, a Polaroid "Highlander" could be bought for $60, and consumers found it simple to use. Instant photography remained a niche market, though a popular one, and Polaroid's camera had no competition throughout the decade.

The Family of Man

In 1955, New York's Museum of Modern Art mounted a huge photography show titled The Family of Man. Organized by the respected photographer Edward Steichen (1879–1972), the exhibit consisted of over 500 images that attempted to show, as its title stated, the connectedness—the family—that is mankind. The museum displayed the work of 273 photographers from 68 different countries, the final choices culled from an initial, wide-ranging survey of over 6 million pictures. The majority came from the voluminous files of *Life* magazine, and staffers reduced the millions to the 503 photographs in the exhibition. Steichen and his colleagues chose well; the show's success immediately dispelled any worries about its appeal: no grouping of black-and-white photographs, before or since, has ever attracted such a large audience.[6]

It has been estimated that by the end of the twentieth century well over 9 million people had seen The Family of Man, either by attending the exhibition or by purchasing the best-selling book of the same name that reproduced the photographs. The book, however, cannot be equated with the show. The exhibition, laid out thematically and sequentially, moved viewers from room to room. The photographs themselves varied greatly in size and presentation. The book, on the other hand, existed as a record of the photographs and reproduced them in roughly the same size on its pages, outside the context of the exhibition.

Many critics attacked the show as playing on cheap emotion, that it came across too sentimentally and lacked intellectual rigor, yet therein rested its appeal. Steichen and his colleagues correctly assumed that people would react emotionally, not intellectually, to the imagery. Their theme built on the concept of the family overcoming the perils of the modern, industrialized world,

making the exhibition particularly appropriate for the family-centered fifties. The hundreds of photographs linked common events—birth, eating, sleeping, love, death—into universal experiences; they did not fall into the category of "art photographs" designed for the enjoyment of the connoisseur. In the United States, The Family of Man attracted a primarily middle-class audience. It displayed the American ideal of the pursuit of happiness through clear images. So well did it reflect then current national values that the U.S. Information Agency took the show on a 7-year worldwide tour, visiting over 60 countries.

ENDNOTES FOR THE 1950s

OVERVIEW OF THE 1950s

1. See Clifford Edward Clark Jr., *The American Home: 1800–1960* (Chapel Hill: University of North Carolina Press, 1986), 206; and Richard Layman, ed., *American Decades: 1950–1959* (Detroit, MI: Gale Research, 1994), 85.

2. J. Ronald Oakley, *God's Country: America in the Fifties* (New York: Dembner Books, 1986), 228.

3. Oakley, *God's Country*, 231.

4. James S. Olson, *Historical Dictionary of the 1950s* (Westport, CT: Greenwood Press, 2000), 66–67.

5. Theodore Caplow, Louis Hicks, and Ben J. Wattenberg, *The First Measured Century: An Illustrated Guide to Trends in America, 1900–2000* (Washington, DC: The AEI Press, 2001), 68–69, 78–79, 84–85.

6. An overview of the civil rights crisis can be found in James T. Patterson, *Grand Expectations: The United States, 1945–1974* (New York: Oxford University Press, 1996), 375–406.

7. Oakley, *God's Country*, 298–99.

8. Eugenia Kaledin, *Daily Life in the United States, 1940–1959: Shifting Worlds* (Westport, CT: Greenwood Press, 2000), 91–115.

9. TIME-LIFE Editors, *The American Dream: The 50s* (Alexandria, VA: Time-Life Books, 1998), 82–85.

10. For more on the McCarthy era, see Patterson, *Grand Expectations*, 165–205.

11. Douglas T. Miller and Marion Nowak, *The Fifties: The Way We Really Were* (Garden City, NY: Doubleday, 1960), 314–21.

12. See Oakley, *God's Country*, 136–37, and Layman, *American Decades*, 195–210

13. A discussion of the culture debates can be found in Dwight Macdonald, *Against the American Grain* (New York: Vintage Books, 1965), especially the lead article, "Masscult and Midcult," 1–75.

ADVERTISING OF THE 1950s

1. A collection of reprints of 1950s advertisements can be found in Jim Heimann, ed., *50s: All-American Ads* (New York: Taschen, 2001).
2. Donald C. Godfrey and Frederic A. Leigh, eds., *Historical Dictionary of American Radio* (Westport, CT: Greenwood Press, 1998), 4–9.
3. An anthology of old radio commercials can be found on Golden Age Radio, *101 Old Radio Commercials* (Plymouth, MN: Metacom, n.d.), compact disc.
4. Two Internet sources for old television commercials are The Internet Archive (http://www.archive.org/movies/movies.php) and USA TV ADS (http://www.usatvads.com).
5. Paul Rutherford, *The New Icons?: The Art of Television Advertising* (Toronto, Canada: University of Toronto Press, 1994), 10–14.
6. Lawrence R. Samuel, *Brought to You By: Postwar Television Advertising and the American Dream* (Austin: University of Texas Press, 2001), 46–50, 122–28.
7. Stephen Fox, *The Mirror Makers: A History of American Advertising and Its Creators* (New York: William Morrow, 1984), 172–73.
8. Joseph L. Seldin, *The Golden Fleece: Selling the Good Life to Americans* (New York: Macmillan, 1963), 227–54.
9. Daniel Delis Hill, *Advertising to the American Woman, 1900–1999* (Columbus: Ohio State University Press, 2002), vii–xi.
10. Jim Hall, *Mighty Minutes: An Illustrated History of Television's Best Commer-cials* (New York: Harmony Books, 1984), 193–211.
11. Mary Cross, ed., *A Century of American Icons: 100 Products and Slogans from the 20th-Century Consumer Culture* (Westport, CT: Greenwood Press, 2002), 116–17.
12. Gerry Schremp, *Kitchen Culture: Fifty Years of Food Fads* (New York: Pharos Books, 1991), 55–56.
13. Oakley, *God's Country*, 131–37.

ARCHITECTURE OF THE 1950s

1. Christopher Finch, *Highways to Heaven: The AUTO Biography of America* (New York: HarperCollins, 1992), 225–47.
2. John A. Jakle, Keith A. Sculle, and Jefferson S. Rogers, *The Motel in America* (Baltimore, MD: The Johns Hopkins University Press, 1996), 262–85.
3. Both Arthur J. Pulos, *The American Design Adventure, 1940–1975* (Cambridge, MA: MIT Press, 1988), 50–107, and Lester Walker, *American Shelter* (Woodstock, NY: The Overlook Press, 1996), 238–53, 258–63, are useful sources on innovative architecture of the 1950s, including prefabricated dwellings.
4. The trailer phenomenon is covered in Allan D. Wallis, *Wheel Estate: The Rise and Decline of Mobile Homes* (New York: Oxford University Press, 1991) and Andrew Hurley, *Diners, Bowling Alleys, and Trailer Parks: Chasing the American Dream in Postwar Consumer Culture* (New York: Basic Books, 2001), 195–272.
5. Kenneth T. Jackson, *The Crabgrass Frontier: The Suburbanization of America* (New York: Oxford University Press, 1985), 234–45.
6. Gwendolyn Wright, *Building the Dream: A Social History of Housing in America* (New York: Pantheon Books, 1981), 240–61.
7. Elaine Tyler May, *Homeward Bound: American Families in the Cold War Era* (New York: Basic Books, 1988), 103–13, and Willard Bascom, "Scientific Blueprint for Atomic Survival," *Life* 42, no. 11 (March 15, 1957): 146–62.
8. Alison J. Clarke, *Tupperware: The Promise of Plastic in 1950s America* (Washington, DC: Smithsonian Institution Press, 1999), covers the Tupperware phenomenon.
9. An overview of changing domestic design can be found in Arthur J. Pulos, *The American Design Adventure, 1940–1975* (Cambridge, MA: MIT Press, 1988), 110–61.

BOOKS, NEWSPAPERS, MAGAZINES, AND COMICS OF THE 1950s

1. An overview of the paperback revolution can be found in Richard Lupoff, *The Great American Paperback: An Illustrated Tribute to Legends of the Book* (Portland, OR: Collectors Press, 2001).
2. Another source of information on paperbacks is Piet Schreuders, *Paperbacks, U.S.A.: A Graphic History, 1939–1959* (San Diego: Blue Dolphin Enterprises, 1981).
3. James S. Olson, *Historical Dictionary of the 1950s* (Westport, CT: Greenwood Press, 2000), 245.
4. For a biography of Graham, see William Martin, *A Prophet with Honor: The Billy Graham Story* (New York: William Morrow, 1991).
5. For an introduction to writers of the period, including Salinger, see Jonathan Baumbach, *The Landscape of Nightmare: Studies in the Contemporary American Novel* (New York: New York University Press, 1965).
6. Richard Layman, ed., *American Decades: 1950–1959* (Detroit, MI: Gale Research, 1994), 46.
7. Emily Toth, *Inside Peyton Place: The Life of Grace Metalious* (New York: Doubleday, 1981).
8. Holly George-Warren's collection, *The "Rolling Stone" Book of the Beats: The Beat Generation and American Culture* (New York: Hyperion, 1999), provides a starting point for studying these writers.
9. For more on the Great Books Program, visit The Great Books Foundation Web site, http://www.greatbooks.org/about/index.shtml.
10. See Lynn Z. Bloom, *Doctor Spock: Biography of a Conservative Radical* (Indianapolis: Bobbs-Merrill, 1972), and Jessica Weiss, *To Have and to Hold: Marriage, the*

Baby Boom & Social Change (Chicago: University of Chicago Press, 2000), 92.

11. Theodore Peterson, in his *Magazines in the Twentieth Century* (Urbana: University of Illinois Press, 1964), provides sketches of the periodicals discussed in this section.

12. Jay S. Harris, ed., *"TV Guide": The First 25 Years* (New York: Simon & Schuster, 1978).

13. Most of the failures and successes among magazines of the 1950s are listed in Amy Janello and Brennon Jones, *The American Magazine* (New York: Harry N. Abrams, 1991).

14. A standard history of newspapers is Frank Luther Mott, *American Journalism, A History: 1690–1960,* 3rd ed. (New York: Macmillan, 1962), 803–57.

15. Louis Solomon, *America Goes to Press: The Story of Newspapers from Colonial Times to the Present* (New York: Crowell-Collier Press, 1970), 104–23.

16. For more on Gaines and his connections to the comic-book industry, see Frank Jacobs, *The Mad World of William M. Gaines* (Secaucus, NJ: Lyle Stuart, 1972).

17. William W. Savage Jr., *Comic Books and America, 1945–1954* (Norman: University of Oklahoma Press, 1990), 95–103.

18. Bradford W. Wright, *Comic Book Nation: The Transformation of Youth Culture in America* (Baltimore, MD: The Johns Hopkins University Press, 2001), 154–225.

ENTERTAINMENT OF THE 1950s

1. Kenneth Hey, "Car and Films in American Culture, 1929–1959" in *The Automobile and American Culture,* ed. David L. Lewis and Laurence Goldstein (Ann Arbor: University of Michigan Press, 1983), 193–205.

2. John Douglas Eames, in *The MGM Story: The Complete History of Fifty Roaring Years* (New York: Crown, 1975), 232–97, covers the giant studio during the 1950s.

3. An overview of the stage and film is Amy Henderson and Dwight Blocker Bowers, *Red, Hot & Blue: A Smithsonian Salute to the American Musical* (Washington, DC: Smithsonian Institution Press, 1996).

4. MGM/UA has released three videos (VHS format) that cover movie musicals. They are *That's Entertainment!*, dir. Jack Haley Jr. (1974), *That's Entertain-ment! Part II,* dir. Gene Kelly (1976), and *That's Dancing!,* dir. Jack Haley Jr. (1985).

5. John Baxter, *Science Fiction in the Cinema* (New York: A.S. Barnes, 1970), 102–69.

6. Christopher Sterling and John M. Kittross provide a history of postwar American radio in *Stay Tuned: A Concise History of American Broadcasting* (Belmont, CA: Wadsworth Publishing, 1990), 246–315.

7. Frank Luther Mott, *American Journalism, A History: 1690–1960,* 3rd ed. (New York: Macmillan, 1962), 822–28.

8. Sterling and Kittross, *Stay Tuned,* 253–55, 277–90.

9. A discussion of the aesthetics of television can be found in Karal Ann Marling's *As Seen on TV: The Visual Culture*

of Everyday Life in the 1950s (Cambridge, MA: Harvard University Press, 1994), 165–201.

10. As was the case with radio (above), Sterling and Kittross's *Stay Tuned,* 290–300 is also a good source on television history.

11. Sterling and Kittross, *Stay Tuned,* 324–28.

12. Erik Barnouw, *Tube of Plenty: The Evolution of American Television* (New York: Oxford University Press, 1982), 140–48.

13. Lawrence W. Lichty and Malachi C. Topping, *American Broadcasting: A Source Book on the History of Radio and Television* (New York: Hastings House, 1975), 522.

14. Irving Settel and William Laas, *A Pictorial History of Television* (New York: Grosset & Dunlap, 1969), 59–60.

15. A number of statistical and chronological studies of TV programming can be found in most libraries. One is Alex McNeil's *Total Television: The Comprehensive Guide to Programming from 1948 to the Present,* 4th ed. (New York: Penguin Books, 1996).

16. A good source on *I Love Lucy* and other popular sitcoms is Gerard Jones, *Honey, I'm Home. Sitcoms: Selling the American Dream* (New York: Grove Weidenfeld, 1992), 3–133.

17. Lynn Spigel, in *Make Room for TV: Television and the Family Ideal in Postwar America* (Chicago: University of Chicago Press, 1992), discusses the domestic sitcom at length.

18. For more on this television genre, see Muriel G. Cantor and Suzanne Pingree, *The Soap Opera* (Beverly Hills, CA: Sage Publications, 1983), 47–95.

19. For more on this television genre, see J. Fred MacDonald, *Who Shot the Sheriff? The Rise and Fall of the Television Western* (New York: Praeger, 1987).

FASHION OF THE 1950s

1. Lynn Schnurnberger, *Let There Be Clothes: 40,000 Years of Fashion* (New York: Workman Publishing, 1991), 373.

2. Kate Mulvey and Melissa Richards, *Decades of Beauty: The Changing Image of Women, 1890s–1990s* (New York: Checkmark Books, 1998), 127–29.

3. Frank W. Hoffmann and William G. Bailey, *Fashion & Merchandising Fads* (New York: The Haworth Press, 1994), 35.

4. Jane Dorner, *Fashion in the Forties and Fifties* (New Rochelle, NY: Arlington House, 1975), 79–101.

5. Ernestine Carter, *The Changing World of Fashion: 1900 to the Present* (New York: G.P. Putnam's Sons, 1977), 71.

FOOD OF THE 1950s

1. Rom J. Markin, *The Supermarket: An Analysis of Growth, Development, and Change* (Pullman: Washington State University Press, 1963), 1–3, 43–52.

2. See a commercial featuring Clark Kent, Perry White, and Jimmy Olson all eating up some Sugar Smacks. YouTube, http://www.youtube.com/watch?v=GZGcSna6NnU.

3. Jean Anderson, *The American Century Cook-book* (New York: Clarkson Potter, 1997), 243.

4. Kenneth Morris, Marc Robinson, and Richard Kroll, eds., *American Dreams: One-Hundred Years of Business Ideas and Innovation from "The Wall Street Journal"* (New York: Light Bulb Press, 1990), 136.

5. Alison J. Clarke, *Tupperware: The Promise of Plastic in 1950s America* (Washington, DC: Smithsonian Institution Press, 1999), 34–128.

6. Charles Panati, *Extraordinary Origins of Everyday Things* (New York: Harper & Row, 1987), 105–7.

7. The story of Ray Kroc and McDonald's can be found in John F. Love, *McDonald's: Behind the Arches* (New York: Bantam Books, 1986).

8. Two books about American drinking habits are Barnaby Conrad, III, *The Martini: An Illustrated History of an American Classic* (San Francisco: Chronicle Books, 1995), and Joseph Lanza, *The Cocktail: The Influence of Spirits on the American Psyche* (New York: St. Martin's Press, 1995).

9. Chris H. Beyer, *Coca-Cola Girls: An Advertising Art History* (Portland, OR: Collectors Press, 2000), 216–69.

10. Mark Pendergrast, *For God, Country and Coca-Cola* (New York: Charles Scribner's Sons, 1993), 237–76, has much on the "cola wars."

MUSIC OF THE 1950s

1. J. Ronald Oakley, *God's Country: America in the Fifties* (New York: Dembner Books, 1986), 280.

2. Russell Sanjek, *Pennies from Heaven: The American Popular Music Business in the Twentieth Century* (New York: Da Capo Press, 1988), 333–66.

3. Wes Smith, *Pied Pipers of Rock 'n' Roll: Radio Deejays of the 50s and 60s* (Marietta, GA: Longstreet Press, 1989), 160ff.

4. Another study of the American disc jockey is Arnold Passman, *The Deejays* (New York: Macmillan, 1971).

5. Richard Welch, "The Making of the American Dream: Rock 'n' Roll and Social Change," *History Today* 40 (February 1990): 32–39.

6. Among the many biographies is Peter Guralnick, *Last Train to Memphis: The Rise of Elvis Presley* (Boston: Little, Brown, 1994).

7. A good study of the Presley phenomenon is Greil Marcus, *Mystery Train: Images of America in Rock 'n' Roll Music* (New York: E.P. Dutton, 1975).

8. See Arnold Shaw, *The Rockin' 50s* (New York: Hawthorn Books, 1974), 122–29, and Joe Smith, *Off the Record: An Oral History of Popular Music* (New York: Warner Books, 1988), 109–10.

9. For the radio version, see John Dunning, *On the Air: The Encyclopedia of Old-Time Radio* (New York: Oxford University Press, 1998), 738–40; for television, see Alex McNeil, *Total Television: The Comprehensive Guide to Programming from 1948 to the Present,* 4th ed. (New York: Penguin Books, 1996), 936.

10. For more on American Bandstand, visit The Museum of Broadcast Communications Web site, http://www.museum.tv/archives/etv/A/htmlA/americanband/americanband.htm.

11. Dunning, *On the Air,* 177–78.

SPORTS AND LEISURE OF THE 1950s

1. More on Native Dancer can be found online, including at the Unofficial Thoroughbred Hall of Fame, http://www.spiletta.com/UTHOF/nativedancer.html.

2. Joseph L. Seldin, *The Golden Fleece: Selling the Good Life to Americans* (New York: Macmillan, 1963), 54.

3. For information on pranks, as well as other fads, see Charles Panati, *Panati's Parade of Fads, Follies, and Manias* (New York: HarperCollins, 1991), 266–68.

4. Charles Panati, *Extraordinary Origins of Everyday Things* (New York: Harper & Row, 1987), 372–73.

5. For information on Scrabble and other games, see Andrew Marum and Frank Parise, *Follies and Foibles: A View of 20th Century Fads* (New York: Facts on File, 1984), 82, 86.

6. Panati, *Panati's Parade of Fads, Follies, and Manias,* 251–52.

7. Paul Sann, *Fads, Follies and Delusions of the American People* (New York: Crown Publishers, 1967), 27–30.

8. For a good overview of powered toys, see Richard O'Brien, *The Story of American Toys: From the Puritans to the Present* (New York: Abbeville Press, 1990), 164–85.

9. For a discussion of this phenomenon, see Carolyn M. Goldstein, *Do It Your-self: Home Improvement in 20th-Century America* (New York: Princeton Architectural Press, 1998).

10. Both William L. Bird Jr., *Paint by Number: The How-To Craze that Swept the Nation* (Princeton, NJ: Princeton Architectural Press, 2001); and Dan Robbins, *Whatever Happened to Paint by Numbers? A Humorous Personal Account* (Delavan, WI: Possum Hill Press, 1998) cover this phenomenon.

TRAVEL OF THE 1950s

1. Joseph L. Seldin, *The Golden Fleece: Selling the Good Life to Americans* (New York: Macmillan, 1963), 48–49.

2. Information on the New Jersey Turnpike and other 1950s highways can be found in Angus Kress Gillespie and Michael Aaron Rockland, *Looking for America on the New Jersey Turnpike* (New Brunswick, NJ: Rutgers University Press, 1989).

3. John B. Rae, *The Road and the Car in American Life* (Cambridge, MA: MIT Press, 1971), 170–94.

4. The business side of the industry is discussed in James M. Rubenstein, *Making and Selling Cars: Innovation and Change in the U.S. Automotive Industry* (Baltimore, MD: The Johns Hopkins University Press, 2001), 185–215.

5. Automobile Quarterly Editors, *Corvette! Thirty Years of Great Advertising* (Princeton, NJ: Princeton Publishing, 1983), 6–57.

6. The Volkswagen story is detailed in Frank Rowsome Jr., *Think Small: The Story of Those Volkswagen Ads* (Brattleboro, VT: Stephen Greene Press, 1970).

7. A good study of these vehicles is Roger B. White, *Home on the Road: The Motor Home in America* (Washington, DC: Smithsonian Institution Press, 2000), 83–162.

8. John A. Jakle, *The Tourist: Travel in Twentieth-Century North America* (Lincoln: University of Nebraska Press, 1985), 185–89.

9. Wilson's account is given in Kemmons Wilson, *The Holiday Inn Story* (New York: The Newcomen Society, 1968).

10. Chester H. Liebs, *Main Street to Miracle Mile: American Roadside Architecture* (Baltimore, MD: The Johns Hopkins University Press, 1985), 136–51.

11. Oakley, *God's Country*, 396.

12. American Heritage Editors, *The "American Heritage" History of Flight* (New York: Simon & Schuster, 1962), 375.

13. Richard Layman, ed., *American Decades: 1950–1959* (Detroit, MI: Gale Research, 1994), 87.

VISUAL ARTS OF THE 1950s

1. More on Rockwell's work can be found in Thomas S. Buechner, *Norman Rockwell: Artist and Illustrator* (New York: Harry N. Abrams, 1970), and Maureen Hart Hennessey and Anne Knutson, *Norman Rockwell: Pictures for the American People* (New York: Harry N. Abrams, 1999).

2. Two good studies of Grandma Moses are Jane Kallir's *Grandma Moses: The Artist Behind the Myth* (New York: Clarkson N. Potter, 1982) and in Karal Ann Marling's *As Seen on TV: The Visual Culture of Everyday Life in the 1950s* (Cambridge, MA: Harvard University Press, 1994), 75–80.

3. Irving Sandler, *The New York School: The Painters and Sculptors of the Fifties* (New York: Harper & Row [Icon], 1978), 1–28.

4. Two histories of this phenomenon are William L. Bird Jr., *Paint by Number: The How-To Craze That Swept the Nation* (Princeton, NJ: Princeton Architectural Press, 2001); and Dan Robbins, *Whatever Happened to Paint by Numbers? A Humorous Personal Account* (Delavan, WI: Possum Hill Press, 1998).

5. For more on Calder, see Joan M. Marter, *Alexander Calder* (New York: Cambridge University Press, 1991).

6. An overview of the show can be found in Eric J. Sandeen, *Picturing an Exhibition: "The Family of Man" and 1950s America* (Albuquerque: University of New Mexico Press, 1995).

Resource Guide

PRINTED SOURCES

Adams, Michael C. C. *The Best War Ever: America and World War II.* Baltimore: Johns Hopkins University Press, 1994.

Adler, Thomas P. *American Drama 1940–1960: A Critical History.* New York: Twayne Publishers, 1994.

Agee, James, and Walker Evans. *Let Us Now Praise Famous Men.* Boston: Houghton Mifflin, 1941.

Allen, Douglas, and Douglas Allen Jr. *N. C. Wyeth: The Collected Paintings, Illustrations and Murals.* New York: Crown Publishers, 1972.

Allen, Frederick Lewis. *The Big Change.* New York: Bantam Books, 1952.

———. *Only Yesterday.* New York: Harper & Row, 1931.

———. *Since Yesterday.* New York: Bantam Books, 1940.

Ambrose, Stephen E. *Eisenhower: The President.* New York: Simon & Schuster, 1984.

Appelbaum, Stanley. *The New York World's Fair, 1939/1940.* New York: Dover Publications, 1977.

Austin, Joe, and Michael Nevin Willard, eds. *Generations of Youth: Youth Cultures and History in Twentieth-Century America.* New York: New York University Press, 1998.

Balio, Tino. *Grand Design: Hollywood as a Modern Business Enterprise, 1930–1939.* New York: Scribner's, 1993.

Barfield, Ray. *Listening to Radio, 1920–1950.* Westport, CT: Praeger, 1996.

Barnouw, Erik. *A History of Broadcasting in the United States.* Vol. 1, *A Tower in Babel.* New York: Oxford University Press, 1966.

Belasco, Warren James. *Americans on the Road: From Autocamp to Motel, 1910–1945.* Cambridge, MA: MIT Press, 1979.

Best, Gary Dean. *The Nickel and Dime Decade: American Popular Culture During the 1930s.* Westport, CT: Praeger, 1993.

Biskind, Peter. *Seeing is Believing: How Hollywood Taught Us to Stop Worrying and Love the Fifties.* New York: Pantheon Books, 1983.

Bourke-White, Margaret, and Eskine Caldwell. *You Have Seen Their Faces.* New York: Modern Age Books, 1937.

Boyer, Paul. *By the Bomb's Early Light: American Thought and Culture at the Dawn of the Atomic Age.* New York: Pantheon Books, 1985.

Brendon, Piers. *The Dark Valley: A Panorama of the 1930s.* New York: Alfred A. Knopf, 2000.

Brenner, Joel Glenn. *The Emperors of Chocolate: Inside the Secret World of Hershey and Mars.* New York: Random House, 1999.

Brunas, Michael, John Brunas, and Tom Weaver. *Universal Horrors: The Studio's Classic Films, 1931–1946.* Jefferson, NC: McFarland, 1990.

Buechner, Thomas S. *Norman Rockwell: Artist and Illustrator.* New York: Harry N. Abrams, 1970.

Buxton, Frank, and Bill Owen. *The Big Broadcast: 1920–1950.* New York: The Viking Press, 1972.

Casey, Steven. *Cautious Crusade: Franklin D. Roosevelt, American Public Opinion, and the War Against Nazi Germany.* New York: Oxford University Press, 2001.

Cashman, Sean Dennis. *America, Roosevelt, and World War II.* New York: New York University Press, 1989.

Cohn, Jan. *Creating America: George Horace Lorimer and the* Saturday Evening Post. Pittsburgh: University of Pittsburgh Press, 1989.

Coontz, Stephanie. *The Way We Never Were: American Families and the Nostalgia Trap.* New York: Basic Books, 1992.

Corn, Joseph J. *The Winged Gospel: America's Romance with Aviation, 1900–1950.* New York: Oxford University Press, 1983.

Crafton, Donald. *The Talkies: American Cinema's Transition to Sound, 1926–1931.* New York: Scribner's, 1997.

Diggins, John Patrick. *The Proud Decades.* New York: W. W. Norton, 1988.

Doherty, Thomas. *Projections of War: Hollywood, American Culture, and World War II.* New York: Columbia University Press, 1993.

Elder, Glen H. Jr. *Children of the Great Depression.* Chicago: University of Chicago Press, 1974.

Ely, Melvin Patrick. *The Adventures of Amos 'n' Andy: A Social History of an American Phenomenon.* New York: The Free Press, 1991.

Erenberg, Lewis A. *Swingin' the Dream: Big Band Jazz and the Rebirth of American Culture.* Chicago: University of Chicago Press, 1998.

Ewen, Stuart. *Captains of Consciousness: Advertising and the Social Roots of the Consumer Culture.* New York: McGraw-Hill, 1976.

Ewen, Stuart, and Elizabeth Ewen. *Channels of Desire: Mass Images and the Shaping of American Consciousness.* New York: McGraw-Hill, 1982.

Finch, Christopher. *The Art of Walt Disney: From Mickey Mouse to the Magic Kingdoms.* New York: Harry N. Abrams, 1975.

———. *Norman Rockwell's America.* New York: Harry N. Abrams, 1975.

Flink, James J. *The Car Culture.* Cambridge, MA: MIT Press, 1975.

Fox, Stephen. *The Mirror Makers: A History of American Advertising and Its Creators.* New York: William Morrow, 1984.

Galbraith, John Kenneth. *The Affluent Society.* Boston: Houghton-Mifflin, 1958.

Garraty, John A. *The Great Depression.* New York: Harcourt Brace Jovanovich, 1986.

Gelernter, David. *1939: The Lost World of the Fair.* New York: Avon Books, 1995.

Goulart, Ron. *The Adventurous Decade: Comic Strips in the Thirties.* New Rochelle, NY: Arlington House, 1975.

Green, Harvey. *The Uncertainty of Everyday Life: 1915–1945.* New York: HarperCollins, 1992.

Greene, Suzanne Ellery. *Books for Pleasure: Popular Fiction, 1914–1945.* Bowling Green, OH: Popular Press, 1974.

Grier, Katherine C. *Culture and Comfort: Parlor Making and Middle-Class Identity, 1850–1930.* Washington, D.C.: Smithsonian Institution Press, 1988.

Halberstam, David. *The Fifties.* New York: Villard Books, 1993.

Harrison, Helen A. *Dawn of a New Day: The New York World's Fair, 1939/40.* New York: New York University Press, 1980.

Hearn, Charles R. *The American Dream and the Great Depression.* Westport, CT: Greenwood Press, 1977.

Heide, Robert, and John Gilman. *Dime-Store Dream Parade: Popular Culture, 1925–1955.* New York: E. P. Dutton, 1979.

Heidenry, John. *Theirs Was the Kingdom: Lila and DeWitt Wallace and the Story of the Reader's Digest.* New York: W. W. Norton, 1993.

Hilmes, Michele. *Radio Voices: American Broadcasting, 1922–1952.* Minneapolis: University of Minnesota Press, 1997.

Jackson, Kenneth T. *The Crabgrass Frontier: The Suburbanization of America.* New York: Oxford University Press, 1985.

Jakle, John A., and Keith A. Sculle. *The Gas Station in America.* Baltimore: Johns Hopkins University Press, 1994.

Jakle, John A., Keith A. Sculle, and Jefferson S. Rogers. *The Motel in America.* Baltimore: Johns Hopkins University Press, 1996.

Johnson, J. Stewart. *American Modern, 1925–1940: Design for a New Age.* New York: Harry N. Abrams, 2000.

Jones, Edgar R. *Those Were the Good Old Days: A Happy Look at American Advertising, 1880–1930.* New York: Simon and Schuster, 1959.

Jones, Max, and John Chilton. *Louis: The Louis Armstrong Story.* Boston: Little, Brown, 1971.

Kennedy, David M. *Freedom from Fear: The American People in Depression and War, 1929–1945.* New York: Oxford University Press, 1999.

Kern-Foxworth, Marilyn. *Aunt Jemima, Uncle Ben, and Rastus: Blacks in Advertising, Yesterday, Today, and Tomorrow.* Westport, CT: Greenwood Press, 1994.

Kisseloff, Jeff. *The Box: An Oral History of Television, 1920–1961.* New York: Viking Press, 1985.

Lears, Jackson. *Fables of Abundance: A Cultural History of Advertising in America.* New York: Basic Books, 1994.

Madden, David, ed. *Proletarian Writers of the Thirties.* Carbondale: Southern Illinois University Press, 1968.

Manchester, William. *The Glory and the Dream: A Narrative History of America, 1932–1972.* 2 vols. Boston: Little, Brown, 1974.

Mangione, Jerre. *The Dream and the Deal: The Federal Writers' Project, 1935–1943.* Boston: Little, Brown, 1972.

Marchand, Roland. *Advertising the American Dream: Making Way for Modernity, 1920–1940.* Los Angeles: University of California Press, 1985.

Marshall, William. *Baseball's Pivotal Era: 1945–1951.* Lexington: University Press of Kentucky, 1999.

May, Elaine Tyler. *Homeward Bound: American Families in the Cold War Era.* New York: Basic Books, 1988.

McElvaine, Robert S. *Down and Out in the Great Depression: Letters from the "Forgotten Man."* Chapel Hill: University of North Carolina Press, 1983.

———. *The Great Depression: America, 1929–1941.* New York: Times Books, 1961.

Offner, Arnold. *Another Such Victory: President Truman and the Cold War, 1945–1953.* Stanford: Stanford University Press, 2002.

Patterson, James T. *Grand Expectations: The United States, 1945–1974.* New York: Oxford University Press, 1996.

Pendergast, Tom. *Creating the Modern Man: American Magazines and Consumer Culture, 1900–1950.* Columbia: University of Missouri Press, 2000.

Savage, William W. Jr. *Comic Books and America, 1945–1954.* Norman: University of Oklahoma Press, 1990.

Schudson, Michael. *Advertising, the Uneasy Persuasion: Its Dubious Impact on American Society.* New York: Basic Books, 1984.

Seymour, Harold. *Baseball: The Golden Age.* New York: Oxford University Press, 1971.

Shannon, David A. *Between the Wars: America, 1919–1941.* Boston: Houghton Mifflin, 1979.

———, ed. *The Great Depression.* Englewood Cliffs, NJ: Prentice-Hall, 1960.

Smulyan, Susan. *Selling Radio: The Commercialization of American Broadcasting, 1920–1934.* Washington, D.C.: Smithsonian Institution Press, 1994.

Stilgoe, John R. *Borderland: Origins of the American Suburb, 1820–1939.* New Haven, CT: Yale University Press, 1988.

Stowe, David W. *Swing Changes: Big-Band Jazz in New Deal America.* Cambridge, MA: Harvard University Press, 1994.

Strasser, Susan. *Never Done: A History of American Housework.* New York: Pantheon Books, 1982.

———. *Satisfaction Guaranteed: The Making of the American Mass Market.* Washington, D.C.: Smithsonian Institution Press, 1989.

Swados, Harvey, ed. *The American Writer and the Great Depression.* Indianapolis, IN: Bobbs-Merrill, 1966.

Swanberg, W. A. *Citizen Hearst: A Biography of William Randolph Hearst.* New York: Scribner's, 1961.

———. *Luce and His Empire.* New York: Scribner's, 1972.

Wainwright, Loudon. *The Great American Magazine: An Inside History of* Life. New York: Alfred A. Knopf, 1986.

Wald, Carol. *Myth America: Picturing American Women, 1865–1945.* New York: Pantheon Books, 1975.

Waldau, Roy S. *Vintage Years of the Theatre Guild, 1928–1939.* Cleveland, OH: Press of Case Western Reserve University, 1972.

Wallechinsky, David. *The People's Almanac Presents the Twentieth Century: The Definitive Compendium of Astonishing Events, Amazing People, and Strange-but-True Facts.* Boston: Little, Brown, 1995.

Wallis, Michael. *Route 66: The Mother Road.* New York: St. Martin's Press, 1990.

Walton, Thomas. "The Sky Was No Limit." *Portfolio* 1 (April/May 1979): 82–89.

Ward, Geoffrey C., and Ken Burns. *Jazz: A History of America's Music.* New York: Alfred A. Knopf, 2000.

Ware, Susan. *Holding Their Own: American Women in the 1930s.* Boston: Twayne, 1982.

Washburne, Carolyn Kott. *America in the Twentieth Century: 1930–1939.* New York: Marshall Cavendish, 1995.

Watkins, Julius Lewis. *The 100 Greatest Advertisements: Who Wrote Them and What They Did.* New York: Dover Publications, 1959.

Watkins, T. H. *The Great Depression: America in the 1930s.* Boston: Little, Brown, 1993.

———. *The Hungry Years: America in an Age of Crisis, 1929–1939.* New York: Henry Holt, 1999.

Watters, Pat. *Coca-Cola: An Illustrated History.* Garden City, NY: Doubleday, 1978.

Waugh, Coulton. *The Comics.* New York: Luna Press, 1947.

Wecter, Dixon. *The Age of the Great Depression, 1929–1941.* Chicago: Quadrangle Books, 1948.

Weibel, Kathryn. *Mirror Mirror: Images of Women Reflected in Popular Culture.* Garden City, NY: Anchor Books, 1977.

Weisberger, Bernard A., ed. *The WPA Guide to America.* New York: Pantheon Books, 1985.

West, Elliott. *Growing Up in Twentieth-Century America: A History and Reference Guide.* Westport, CT: Greenwood Press, 1996.

West, Nancy Martha. *Kodak and the Lens of Nostalgia.* Charlottesville: University Press of Virginia, 2000.

White, David Manning, and Robert H. Abel, eds. *The Funnies: An American Idiom.* New York: The Free Press, 1963.

White, G. Edward. *Creating the National Pastime: Baseball Transforms Itself, 1903–1955.* Princeton, NJ: Princeton University Press, 1996.

White, John H. Jr. *The American Railroad Passenger Car.* Baltimore: Johns Hopkins University Press, 1978.

Whyte, William H., Jr. *The Organization Man.* New York: Doubleday Anchor Books, 1956.

Wigmore, Deedee. *American Scene Painting and Sculpture: Dominant Style of the 1930's and 1940's.* New York: D. Wigmore Fine Art, 1988.

Wilder, Alec. *American Popular Song: The Great Innovators, 1900–1950.* New York: Oxford University Press, 1972.

Williams, Martin T. *The Jazz Tradition.* New York: Oxford University Press, 1983.

Wilson, Elizabeth. *Adorned in Dreams: Fashion and Modernity.* Berkeley: University of California Press, 1985.

Wilson, Richard Guy, Dianne H. Pilgrim, and Dickran Tashjian. *The Machine Age in America: 1918–1941.* New York: Harry N. Abrams, 1986.

Wilson, Sloan. *The Man in the Gray Flannel Suit.* New York: Pocket Books, 1955.

Winkler, Allan M. *Home Front U.S.A.: America during World War II.* Arlington Heights, IL: Harlan Davidson, 1986.

Wood, James Playsted. *Magazines in the United States.* New York: Ronald Press, 1956.

———. *The Story of Advertising.* New York: Ronald Press, 1958.

Young, Dean, and Rick Marschall. *Blondie & Dagwood's America.* New York: Harper & Row, 1981.

MUSEUMS, ORGANIZATIONS, SPECIAL COLLECTIONS, AND USEFUL WEB SITES

Bradley, Becky. "American Cultural History, 1950–1959." Lone Star College-Kingwood Library Web site. http://kclibrary.lonestar.edu/decade50.html.

> One in a series of Web sites dedicated to examining American cultural history in the twentieth century, Bradley provides an overview of the decades and extensive links to additional resources.

Dwight D. Eisenhower Presidential Library & Museum. 200 Southeast Fourth Street, Abilene, KS 67410, http://www.eisenhower.archives.gov/.

> One of 12 Presidential Libraries administered by the National Archives and Records Administration, the library is a national repository for the preservation of historical papers, audiovisual materials, and artifacts relating to Dwight D. Eisenhower. The library's holdings exceed 26 million pages, over 300,000 photographs, and 66,000 museum artifacts. The Eisenhower Presidential Library & Museum makes these records accessible through research, museum exhibits, public programs, and educational outreach.

Franklin D. Roosevelt Presidential Library. 4079 Albany Post Road, Hyde Park, NY 12538, http://www.fdrlibrary.marist.edu/index.html.

> The Franklin D. Roosevelt Library was built under President Roosevelt's direction between 1939 and 1940 on 16 acres of land in Hyde Park, New York, donated by Roosevelt and his mother, Sara Delano Roosevelt. The library resulted from his decision that a separate facility was needed to house the vast quantity of historical papers, books, and memorabilia accumulated during his lifetime of public service. The accompanying Web site offers further information about research, education opportunities, and exhibits at the museum. Of particular interest are the thousands of online, copyright-free photographs available for download, featuring pictures of Franklin and Eleanor Roosevelt, the Great Depression, the New Deal, and World War II.

Goodwin, Susan. "American Cultural History: The Twentieth Century, 1940–1949." Lone Star College-Kingwood Library Web site. http://kclibrary.lonestar.edu/decade40.html.

One in a series of Web sites dedicated to examining American cultural history in the twentieth century, Goodwin provides an overview of the decades and extensive links to additional resources.

The Harry S. Truman Library & Museum. 500 W. US Hwy. 24, Independence MO 64050, http://www.trumanlibrary.org

The Truman Library is one of 12 presidential libraries administered by the National Archives and Records Administration. It is supported, in part, by the Harry S. Truman Library Institute, the not-for-profit partner of the Truman Library. The Institute seeks to promote, through educational and community programs, a greater appreciation and understanding of American politics, history and culture, the process of governance, and the importance of public service, as exemplified by Harry S. Truman.

Library of Congress. "Great Depression and World War II, 1929–1945." American Memory Web site. http://lcweb2.loc.gov/ammem/ndlpedu/features/timeline/depwwii/depwar.html.

Developed to help teachers and students use the vast online collections of the Library of Congress, the Web site offers many primary sources from the Great Depression and World War II eras. The time period is broken into topical subpages that provide greater detail on specific topics.

Nelson, Cary. "The Great Depression." Modern American Poetry Web site. http://www.english.uiuc.edu/maps/depression/depression.htm.

The site features additional information that grew out of Nelson's editing the *Anthology of Modern American Poetry* for Oxford University Press. Realizing that the book could not be comprehensive, Nelson and a team of scholars filled the Web site with additional information about American poets. The Great Depression portion of the site offers a superb overview of the economic downturn and its global consequences, with colorful maps that provide greater insight into the challenges of the worldwide depression. Some 11 poets from the era are featured, with biographical information, reviews, and examples of their writing.

Sutton, Bettye. "American Cultural History, 1930–1939." Lone Star College-Kingwood Library Web site. http://kclibrary.lonestar.edu/decade30.html.

One in a series of Web sites dedicated to examining American cultural history in the twentieth century, Sutton provides an overview of the decades and extensive links to additional resources.

VIDEOS/FILMS

Band of Brothers. Produced by Steven Spielberg, Tom Hanks, Preston Smith, Erik Jendresen, and Stephen Ambrose. 705 minutes. Distributed by Home Box Office, 2002. 6 DVDs.

An original HBO miniseries that aired in 2001, *Band of Brothers* tells the story of Easy Company, 506th Regiment of the 101st Airborne Division, U.S. Army, an elite rifle company that parachuted into France early on D-Day morning. The troops fought in the Battle of the Bulge, captured Hitler's Eagle's Nest at Berchtesgaden, and suffered heavy casualties.

Coming Apart: Nothing to Fear. (Century: Events that Shaped the World, Vol. 9). Produced by Carrie Cook. 43 minutes. Distributed by ABC Video, 2006, [1999]. DVD.

In the early 1930s, unemployment, widespread hunger, and a mood of fearful pessimism and simmering unrest were Herbert Hoover's legacy. This documentary highlights the early days of Franklin D. Roosevelt's presidency, when he battled to transform the New Deal from a campaign slogan to nothing short of a social revolution—while staving off attacks by those who viewed him as a potential dictator and his reforms as a threatening turn to the left.

FDR. Written and produced by David Grubin. 270 minutes. Distributed by PBS, 1994. Videocassette.

> Franklin Delano Roosevelt led America through the two greatest crises of the twentieth century: the Great Depression and World War II. The documentary focuses on FDR's early years and political successes through his presidency and death.

FDR: A Presidency Revealed. Edited by Bob Kanner, Eric Dennis, and Mindy Gregg. 300 minutes. Distributed by New Video, 2005. DVD.

> A comprehensive original program from the History Channel, featuring exclusive interviews, rare audio recordings, newly-unearthed home movies, and diary entries, that reveals a never-before-seen side of FDR's presidency.

Jazz. Produced by Ken Burns, Lynn Novick. 1095 minutes on 10 Discs. PBS Home Video. 2000. DVD.

> Originally aired on PBS, this 10-disc package of the history of jazz in the United States features the 10 episodes of the show. Discs four through eight cover 1930–1955.

The Manchurian Candidate. Produced by George Axelrod and John Frankenheimer. 129 minutes. Distributed by MGM Home Entertainment, 2004. DVD. Originally released as a motion picture in 1962.

> A U.S. Army platoon, captured in the Korean conflict, is whisked to Manchuria for three days of experimental drug-and-hypnosis-induced conditioning that transforms them into human time bombs. Returning to America as war heroes, one of them is used by his mother to promote the political career of her Joseph McCarthy-like husband.

Sands of Iwo Jima. Produced by Merian C. Cooper. 109 minutes. Distributed by Artisan Home Entertainment, 2000. DVD. A motion picture starring John Wayne originally released in 1949.

> Stryker (Wayne), a hard-nosed Marine sergeant prepares a company of recruits for combat in World War II's Pacific Theater. Their training is soon put to the test in a battle against the Japanese on Iwo Jima. The famous flag-raising on Mt. Suribachi is depicted near the film's conclusion.

Saving Private Ryan. Produced by Steven Spielberg, Ian Bryce, Mark Gordon, and Gary Levinsohn. 169 minutes. Distributed by DreamWorks Home Entertainment, 1999. DVD.

> Captain John Miller (Tom Hanks) must take his men behind enemy lines to find Private Ryan (Matt Damon), whose three brothers have been killed in combat. Faced with impossible odds, the men question their orders. Why are eight men risking their lives to save just one? Surrounded by the brutal realities of war, each man searches for individual answers and the strength to triumph over an uncertain future with honor, decency, and courage.

Surviving the Dust Bowl. Written and produced by Chana Gazit. 60 minutes. Distributed by WGBH Educational Foundation, 1998. DVD.

> The documentary presents the story of thousands of settlers, who, lured by the promise of rich, plentiful soil, traveled to the Southern Plains, taking with them farming techniques that worked well in the North and East. They plowed millions of acres of grassland, only to have the rains stop in the summer of 1931. The catastrophic eight-year drought that followed led observers to rename the region "The Dust Bowl."

Index

About the Editor and Contributors

SET EDITOR

Bob Batchelor teaches in the School of Mass Communications at the University of South Florida. A noted expert on American popular culture, Bob is the author of: *The 1900s* (Greenwood, 2002); coauthor of *Kotex, Kleenex, and Huggies: Kimberly-Clark and the Consumer Revolution in American Business* (2004); editor of *Basketball in America: From the Playgrounds to Jordan's Game and Beyond* (2005); editor of *Literary Cash: Unauthorized Writings Inspired by the Legendary Johnny Cash* (2006); and coauthor of *The 1980s* (Greenwood, 2007). He serves on the editorial board of *The Journal of Popular Culture*. Visit him on the Internet at his blog (pr-bridge.com) or homepage (www.bob batchelor.com).

CONSULTING EDITOR

Ray B. Browne is a Distinguished University Professor in Popular Culture, Emeritus, at Bowling Green State University. He cofounded the Popular Culture Association (1970) and the American Culture Association (1975) and served as Secretary-Treasurer of both until 2002. In 1967 he began publishing the *Journal of Popular Culture,* and in 1975 the *Journal of American Culture.* He edited both until 2002. He has written or edited more than 70 books and written numerous articles on all fields in literature and popular culture. He currently serves as Book Review Editor of the *Journal of American Culture.*

CONTRIBUTORS

David Blanke, author of *The 1910s* (Greenwood, 2002), is currently Associate Professor of History at Texas A&M University, Corpus Christi. He is the author of *Hell on Wheels: The Promise and Peril of America's Car Culture, 1900–1940* (2007) and *Sowing the American Dream: How Consumer Culture Took Root in the Rural Midwest* (2000).

Kathleen Drowne, coauthor of *The 1920s* (Greenwood, 2004), is Assistant Professor of English at the University of Missouri, Rolla.

Patrick Huber, coauthor of *The 1920s* (Greenwood, 2004), is Assistant Professor of History at the University of Missouri, Rolla.

Marc Oxoby, PhD, teaches English and Humanities classes for the English Department at the University of Nevada, Reno. He has worked as a disc jockey and as the editor of the small-press literary journal *CRiME CLUb.* A regular contributor to the scholarly journal *Film and History* and *The Journal of Popular Culture,* he has also written for several other periodicals as well as for *The St. James Encyclopedia of Popular Culture, The International Dictionary of Films and Filmmakers,* and *New Paths to Raymond Carver.*

Edward J. Rielly, Professor of English at St. Joseph's College in Maine, has taught on Western film and the history of the west for many years. He is author of several nonfiction books, including *F. Scott Fitzgerald: A Biography* (Greenwood 2005) and *The 1960s* (Greenwood, 2003). He has also published 10 books of poetry.

Kelly Boyer Sagert, is a freelance writer who has published biographical material with Gale, Scribner, Oxford, and Harvard University, focusing on athletes and historical figures. She is the author of *Joe Jackson: A Biography* (Greenwood, 2004), *The 1970s* (Greenwood, 2007), and the *Encyclopedia of Extreme Sports* (Greenwood, 2008).

Robert Sickels, author of *The 1940s* (Greenwood Press, 2004), is Assistant Professor at Whitman College, Walla Walla, Washington.

Scott F. Stoddart, coauthor of *The 1980s* (Greenwood, 2006), is the Dean of Academic Affairs at Manhattanville College, New York, where he currently teaches courses in cinema and musical theatre history.

Nancy K. Young, is a researcher and independent scholar. She retired in 2005 after 26 years of a career in management consulting. With her husband, William H. Young, she has cowritten three recent Greenwood titles, *The 1930s* (2002), *The 1950s* (2004), and *Music of the Great Depression* (2005).

William H. Young, author of *The 1930s* (Greenwood, 2002) and coauthor of *The 1950s* (Greenwood, 2004), is a freelance writer and independent scholar. He retired in 2000 after 36 years of teaching American Studies and popular culture at Lynchburg College in Lynchburg, Virginia. Young has published books and articles on various aspects of popular culture, including three Greenwood volumes cowritten with his wife, Nancy K. Young.

ADDITIONAL CONTRIBUTORS

Cindy Williams, independent scholar.

Mary Kay Linge, independent scholar.

Martha Whitt, independent scholar.

Micah L. Issitt, independent scholar.

Josef Benson, University of South Florida.

Ken Zachmann, independent scholar.